MENTAL AND SCHOLASTIC TESTS

BY

SIR CYRIL BURT

M.A., D.SC. (OXON), HON. LL.D. (ABERDEEN)

Professor of Psychology, University of London
Formerly Psychologist, Education Officer's Department, London County Council

With a Preface by

SIR ROBERT BLAIR LL.D.

Formerly Education Officer, London County Council

SECOND EDITION

NEW YORK   TORONTO
STAPLES PRESS LIMITED
CAVENDISH PLACE, LONDON, W1

First Issued	*December,* 1921
Second Impression	*September,* 1922
Third Impression	*November,* 1927
Fourth Impression	*January,* 1933
Fifth Impression	*February,* 1939
Second Edition	*October,* 1947

Made and Printed in England by
STAPLES PRESS LIMITED
at their Gt. Titchfield Street, London establishment.

PREFACE TO THE SECOND EDITION

Several impressions of this book have been published since it first appeared as a London County Council Report. In issuing this further edition the present publishers have been good enough to allow me to make certain additions and revisions, so far as is possible under the present conditions of printing. But the Report itself is primarily an account of the actual surveys and of the construction of a definite set of scales. Hence there is comparatively little in its substance that calls for change or emendation.

After so long an interval a word or two is perhaps needed as to the origin of the inquiries here described. The appointment in 1913 of a Psychologist to work in the Education Department of the London County Council was the first of its kind ; and the duties had therefore largely to be defined by the psychologist himself in the light of his own growing experience. My formal instructions were to " assist teachers by developing means both for the examination or ascertainment, and for the education or training, of various types of children needing special provision or attention." This referred primarily to the study of sub-normal pupils (the mentally deficient, the dull and backward, the delinquent, and the nervous), but was also intended to cover the super-normal (i.e., children suitable for transfer to secondary schools, trade schools, art schools, central schools, and the like, on the ground of higher or specialized ability) and particularly the junior county scholarship examination. In the case of both subnormal and super-normal the problem was envisaged as one of detection and training rather than of diagnosis and treatment : that is, it was expressly considered to be a task for an educational psychologist rather than for a school medical officer or psychiatrist. That view, indeed, was shared in those days by the majority of medical officers themselves, who were still a little sceptical about the feasibility of introducing what would nowadays be called child guidance. The social aspects of the work proved to be of great importance ; the medical aspect, though not to be neglected, of less significance. For inquiries in these directions the Council's psychologist was able to rely on the generous aid of the school doctors and social workers (care committee visitors) as well as on that of teachers and voluntary assistants. His office thus developed into the earliest official child guidance centre in this country ; and a special tribute of thanks is due to the Education Officer, Sir Robert Blair, and to the Chief Inspector, Dr. C. W. Kimmins, for their early and effective support of such a scheme.

In addition to the examination of individual cases referred for special guidance, it was agreed that, if the test-methods proved reliable, systematic surveys should be carried out from time to time, not only to determine the number of children needing special provision, but also to ascertain any alterations in the general level of the pupils' intelligence and educational attainments. For this there were two main motives. Like many writers at that date I believed that, owing to recent changes in the birth-rate, the mentally defective and the mentally retarded were multiplying far more rapidly than the normal or supernormal; while other critics, particularly employers, had complained that, owing (it was supposed) to the introduction of less formal methods of instruction, attainments in the fundamental subjects of the curriculum, especially in reading, spelling and arithmetic, had been steadily declining. Today these problems are no less urgent.

The general programme of research was divided into several sections or stages. It was decided to deal first with what may be loosely called the intellectual classification of school children, and to start on the problem of detection and selection. The study of moral, disciplinary, and temperamental difficulties—in other words, of the delinquent and the neurotic—came later. The work embodied in the present report was therefore concerned mainly with the construction and standardization of tests for assessing pupils who were either subnormal or supernormal in intellectual abilities and attainments.

The fact that the book, as its title implies, is confined almost exclusively to the subject of testing may have lent some colour to the common notion that the functions of the educational psychologist are restricted primarily to the development and application of mental and scholastic tests. More than once I have been taken to task for " assuming that the entire personality of the child could be studied by quantitative methods alone." That this is far from my true attitude should have been plain from many statements scattered throughout the present volume. Indeed, in the hope of forestalling any such misconception, I declared, as emphatically as I could at the very outset, a warning against any such inference. In the final sentences of the *Introductory Note*, I " insisted upon one fundamental truth," namely, that " tests infinitely more scientific than those set out below can still be but the beginning, never the end of the examination of the child." The need to take into account physical, temperamental, and social factors, and to observe each child's personality as a whole, had also been fully stressed in my Report on " Provision for Backward Children" (reprinted as *Development Memorandum, No. 1*, P. S. King, 1920, later expanded into the volume on *The Backward Child*). In practical psychology, observation is no less important than testing ; and this principle holds good for the teacher quite as much as for the psychologist. In nearly every case the observational judgments of the pupils' own teachers provided the original basis of comparison by means of which our tests were first validated ; and I have constantly urged how essential it is for every teacher to keep systematic records of their day to day impressions of each pupil's abilities, character, and general progress (cf. below, pp. 296f.). Psychology is the science of the whole mind, not of its cognitive aspects only ; and I may repeat that in my view, as in the view of those who made the appointment, the function of the school psychologist is to deal with every aspect of the child's personality and with all forms of training, moral and emotional as well as intellectual.

In spite of the many years that have passed, most of the tests here described are still being used more or less in their original form. The test-materials have been reprinted in a small *Handbook*; and some are available in separate sheets. But those who employ them will frequently require to refer to the fuller instructions or explanations given in the first and third sections of this book. This is true even of the Binet-Simon scale: for all the more modern versions still retain a large proportion of the original test-questions; and some of the most recent revisions have incorporated many of the recommendations put forward in this volume. Nor is there as yet any other publication which attempts a detailed description of how these tests may best be presented to the British child.

The theoretical section of the book seeks to evaluate the merits and limitations of the tests in the light of an experimental and statistical analysis, and to explain at length how the standardization was carried out and the chief conclusions reached. Later surveys have indicated that, even if some change may have since occurred in the average intelligence and attainments of the London school population, this would be too slight to make any serious difference in the general standards here given. Nevertheless, now that conditions are reverting to normal, it is to be hoped that new surveys on a similar scale will be undertaken, and more careful comparisons made. For such purposes the methods here described and the material included will still prove helpful.

Many of the devices which were first used for problems in educational psychology have lately found a fresh application in other branches of practical psychology, particularly those that have been developed during the war. During investigations on personnel selection in the armed forces and more recently in selecting applicants for the Civil Service or for industry, the difficulties and questions that were met with in the earlier fields of work with children have reappeared in the attempts to test and assess the abilities of adults. Hence some account of the way such problems were originally envisaged and attacked may still be of value. A number of the technical procedures that have since become commonplaces in psychological investigations were then used almost for the first time. Item-analysis, tetrachoric coefficients, the correlation of persons, the assessment of factor-measurements by simple averaging, the method of scaling tests from percentage scores, the use of representative sampling, the application of partial regression equations—these were essentially new; indeed, corrections for selection and partial regressions were sufficiently novel in psychological work to provoke considerable controversy at the time. These and other procedures adopted or devised will be found fully illustrated in the pages that follow. I have made no attempt to summarize the later contributions to these topics: they will, of course, now be found in almost any textbook dealing with the subject: for example, in J. P. Guilford, *Psychometric Methods* (1936), W. S. Monroe and M. D. Engelhart, *The Scientific*

Study of Educational Problems (1936), or A. L. Edwards, *Statistical Methods for Students of Psychology and Education* (1946).

It should, however, be remembered that in its origin the present Report had an immediate purpose to fulfil. It was based on selected Memoranda, which had been submitted to the Education Officer during the years 1918, 1919, and 1920, and formed a sequel to the previous series, published in 1917 under the title *The Distribution and Relations of Educational Abilities*. The primary aim of this earlier series was to convince the Education Officer and his fellow-officials of the value of the new methods ; and in that publication a bald and scientific style was therefore preserved. In deciding to issue the papers in this later volume the officials in their turn desired to convince others, and to appeal primarily to the teachers, school medical officers, and lay members of the education committee and council of that day. Accordingly, when preparing the memoranda for a wider circulation, I was asked to attempt " a more colourful and persuasive presentation." This is my excuse for the somewhat florid and rhetorical style, which now must seem, not only out of place, but out of date. The rigorous pruning that I should have preferred to make is unfortunately not practicable under present conditions of printing.

For much the same reason, many of the formulae adopted and the modes of analysis introduced were described very briefly, without incorporating the fuller mathematical discussions advanced to defend them in the previous reports on which the book was based ; and later issues gave little more than summaries or references. Those reports are now for the most part unobtainable or out of print. And I have frequently been urged to bring all the relevant matter together in a single publication. Accordingly, I have taken this opportunity to print or reprint discussions and proofs from the earlier papers, with minor revisions where necessary. For permission to include extracts from official or semi-official memoranda, I am indebted to the Council and its officers ; and I am especially grateful to Miss Beasley for help in selecting relevant portions and rearranging them for incorporation here. I have further to thank the Staples Press, Limited, and particularly their Publishing Assistant, Miss Esther Thomas, for the help and courtesy they have shown in seeing the new edition through the press.

Above all, I should like to record the deep indebtedness of all educational psychologists to the Council itself for its generosity in publishing at its own expense the results of these numerous researches, and that at a time when mental testing and educational psychology were a novel, and, in the view of many, a transient, development, and when the printing of test-materials and long tables of results would have been far too costly for an author to undertake in his private capacity. In this country psychological and educational journals have always depended for financial support on lay subscribers who are easily repelled by formulae and figures ; and consequently their editors have rightly been chary of publishing articles of a statistical or technical nature. As a result, the tables of frequency-distributions and of percentages for various age-groups to be found in this volume are still almost the only examples available for those who wish to re-examine such data from various points of view. From time to time they have been used by American writers like Courtis and Thurstone for illustrating and testing formulae for growth-curves, and more recently by students and research-workers who wished to try out fresh modes of analysis. If I may judge from the many requests I have received, they are still in demand for such purposes, as well as for the purpose of comparison in subsequent surveys.

But my own chief debt of gratitude is due to the numerous teachers, care committee workers, medical officers, and research students, who combined to make these early investigations possible. Indeed, with their generous aid, so much material was collected during my service for the London County Council that, in spite of the further reports and papers since published, much of the extensive data is yet awaiting full analysis. I trust that in the near future teachers and psychologists will be able to cooperate once again in a renewed attack on the numerous problems that are of perennial interest to them both, and that a comparative study of the earlier and the later results may prove both practicable and profitable.

C. B.

University College, London.
December, 1946.

CONTENTS.

———

	PAGE
PREFACE TO THE SECOND EDITION BY THE AUTHOR ..	iii
PREFACE BY SIR ROBERT BLAIR, LL.D.	xix
INTRODUCTORY NOTE BY THE AUTHOR	xx

MEMORANDUM I.—The Binet-Simon Scale : Practical Use of the Method.

1.	The General Nature of the Binet-Simon Tests	1
2.	General Directions for the Use of the Scale	9
3.	Special Directions for the Individual Tests	24
4.	Other Versions	68

Appendices to Memorandum I	75–140

MEMORANDUM II.—The Binet-Simon Scale : Theoretical Validity of the Results

1.	The General Scope of the Investigation	141
2.	The Order of Difficulty of the Tests : and their Allocation to Appropriate Ages	143
3.	The Distribution of Intelligence	159
4.	The Mental Ratio	163
5.	The Line of Demarcation between Normals and Defectives	175
6.	The Relations between Mental Ability and Educational Attainments	187
7.	The Application of the Tests to Juvenile Delinquents ..	196
8.	The Influence of Sex and Social Status	202
9.	The Diagnostic Value of the Tests	211
10.	Summary and Conclusion	219

PAGE

APPENDICES TO MEMORANDUM II 222–284

MEMORANDUM III.—TESTS OF EDUCATIONAL ATTAINMENTS.

1. Need and Uses of Scholastic Tests 285

2. Practical Suggestions for the Use of the Scales 288

3. Instructions for the Several Tests—

    i. Tests of Reading 297

    ii. Tests of Spelling 315

    iii. Tests of Arithmetic 323

    iv. Tests of Writing 335

    v. Tests of Drawing 345

    vi. Tests of Handwork 356

    vii. Tests of Composition 358

4. Extreme Range of Individual Variation 360

5. Relative Backwardness of Defectives in the Various Subjects 363

6. Conclusion 366

APPENDICES TO MEMORANDUM III 367–460

INDEX OF SUBJECTS 461

INDEX OF NAMES 466

TABLES.

TABLE		PAGE
I.	Computation of Marks	13
II.	Key for Converting Test-Scores into Mental Ages	*facing* 19
III.	Number of Children Passing the Several Tests. Ordinary Elementary Schools	144-5
IV.	Ditto. Special (M.D.) Schools	147
V.	Correlations between the Orders of Difficulty found by Various Investigators	149
VI.	Larger Changes in Age-Assignments	153
VII.	Conversion of Mental Ages based upon Binet's Original Scales	154
VIII.	Differences in Order of Difficulty for Normals and Defectives	155
IX.	Averages and Variability at Each Age for Children of Ordinary and Special (M.D.) Schools	157
X.	Distribution of Intelligence. Ordinary Elementary Schools	160-1
XI.	Ditto. Special (M.D.) Schools	162
XII.	Ditto. Percentiles for Each Age-group	163
XIII.	Mental Ratios obtained from the Same Children during Five Successive Years	164
XIV.	Annual Change in Mental Age and Mental Ratio in the same Children. Grouped according to Age ..	167
XV.	Ditto. Grouped according to Mental Ratio	168
XVI.	Ditto. Grouped according to both Age and Ratio ..	169
XVII.	Distribution of Intelligence with Standard Deviation as Unit	173
XVIII.	Line of Demarcation between Normals and Defectives	181
XIX.	Correspondence between Mental and Educational Ratios	189
XX.	Observed and Partial Correlations between Age, Intelligence, School Attainments, and the Results of the Binet-Simon Tests	194
XXI.	Observed and Partial Correlations between the Binet-Simon Tests and Attainments in the Several School Subjects	196
XXII.	Juvenile Delinquents. Distribution of General Intelligence at Each Age	197

TABLE		PAGE
XXIII.	Juvenile Delinquents. Distribution of Educational Attainments at Each Age	198
XXIV.	Ditto. Distribution of General Intelligence and Educational Attainments Irrespective of Age	198
XXV.	Differences Due to Social Status	203
XXVI.	Home Conditions of Children attending Schools of Poorest, Median, and Best Social Status	203
XXVII.	Differences Due to Sex	205
XXVIII.	Differences in Order of Difficulty for Children differing in Social Status or in Sex	206
XXIX.	Association between Performances in Tests and Differences in Sex and Social Status	209
XXX.	Correlations between Tests and Teachers' Estimates ..	212
XXXI.	Coefficients of Colligation (ω) between Success in Tests and Intelligence as Estimated by Teacher	217
XXXII.	Assignments for the Several Tests according to Different Investigators	224-7
XXXIII.	Fourfold Table to Illustrate the Conception of Association	229
XXXIV.	Norms for Supplementary Tests.. .. .. ..234, 250
XXXV.	Correlations for Supplementary Tests	277
XXXVI.	Arithmetic (Four Fundamental Rules) : Percentage of Error	330
XXXVII.	Incidence of Left-Handedness among Normals and Defectives	339
XXXVIII.	Relative Attainments of Children of Special (M.D.) Schools in Test of the Chief Subjects of the School Curriculum	365
XXXIX.	Graded Reading Test (Accuracy)	427
XL.	Ungraded Reading Test : Two- and Three-letter Monosyllables (Accuracy)	427
XLI.	Ungraded Reading Test : Two- and Three-letter Monosyllables (Speed)	428
XLII.	Reading (Comprehension) : Directions Test (Individual Examination)	428
XLIII.	Reading (Continuous Test) : Speed	429
XLIV.	Reading (Continuous Test) : Accuracy	429
XLV.	Reading (Continuous Test) : Comprehension ..	430
XLVI.	Spelling	430
XLVII.	Dictation	431
XLVIII.	Arithmetic (Oral Test)	431
XLIX.	Arithmetic (Written Test) : Mechanical	432

TABLE		PAGE
L.	Arithmetic (Written Test) : Problems	432
LI.	Arithmetic (Four Fundamental Rules) : (i) Addition	433
LII.	Arithmetic (Four Fundamental Rules) : (ii) Subtraction	433
LIII.	Arithmetic (Four Fundamental Rules) : (iii) Multiplication	434
LIV.	Arithmetic (Four Fundamental Rules) : (iv) Division	434
LV.	Writing (Speed)	435
LVI.	Writing (Quality)	435
LVII.	Drawing (Quality)	436
LVIII.	Handwork (Speed)	436
LIX.	Handwork (Quality)	437
LX.	Composition (Speed)	437
LXI.	Composition (Quality)	438
LXII.	Composition (Length of Sentences)	438
LXIII.	Calculation of Difficulty of a Test in terms of Mental Age	442
LXIV.	Probit Method of Calculating Test Difficulty	448
LXV.	Analysing Marks in Scholarship Examination	450

SCHEDULES.

SCHEDULE   PAGE

I.   Sample Record-Card for the Binet-Simon Tests (with Original Age-Assignments) 5

II. Sample Record-Form for the Binet-Simon Tests (with Revised Age-Assignments) .. .. .. *facing* 19

III. Classification of Spelling Errors (A) 319

IV. Classification of Spelling Errors (B) 321

V. Analysis of Quality of Handwriting 338

FIGURES.

FIGURE		PAGE
1.	Test 13. Copying a Square. Evaluation of Results. Binet's Examples	31
2.	Test 13. Copying a Square. Order and Direction in which the Lines are drawn	33
3.	Test 22. Copying a Diamond. Evaluation of Results. Binet's Examples	37
4.	Test 22. Copying a Diamond. Order and Direction in which the Lines are drawn	38
5.	Test 26. Divided Card. Position of Intact and Divided Cards as shown to the Child	41
6.	Test 48. Memory Drawing. Evaluation of Results :	
	(a) Children's Reproductions of the "Truncated Pyramid" ..	54
	(b) Children's Reproductions of the "Greek Key Pattern" ..	55
7.	Test 61. Folded Paper :	
	(a) as shown	65
	(b) as reproduced	65
8.	Test 63. Reversed Triangle :	
	(a) as shown	69
	(b) as drawn	69
9.	Tests 6, 29, and 56. Describing Pictures :	
	(a) Ages III., VI., and XII. (i)	81
	(b) do. do. (ii)	83
	(c) do. do. (iii)	85
10.	Test 10, Age IV. Comparing Lines	87
11. (a)	Test 11. Age IV. Comparing Faces (i)	89
(b)	do. do. do. (ii)	91
(c)	do. do. do. (iii)	93
12.	Test 13. Age V. Copying Square	95
13.	Test 17. Age V. Four Colours	97
14.	Test 22. Age VI. Copying Diamond	99
15.	Test 23. Age VI. Transcription	101
16. (a)	Test 32. Age VII. Missing Features (i)	103
(b)	do. do. do. (ii)	105
(c)	do. do. do. (iii)	107
(d)	do. do. do. (iv)	109
17.	Tests 36 and 44. Ages VIII. and IX. Reading and Reproduction	111

FIGURE								PAGE

18.   Test 48.   Age X.   Memory Drawing   113

19.   Test 55.   Age XII.   Rearranging Mixed Sentences (i) ..   115
    do.   do.   do.   do.   (ii) ..   115
    do.   do.   do.   do.   (iii) ..   115

20.   (a) Test 57.   Age XIII.   Suggestion   117
    (b)   do.   do.   do.   119
    (c)   do.   do.   do.   121
    (d)   do.   do.   do.   123
    (e)   do.   do.   do.   125
    (f)   do.   do.   do.   127

21.   Diagrammatic Representation of the Test Series as a Linear
    Scale   151

22.   Distribution according to Mental Age of Children of Ordi-
    nary Elementary and Special (M.D.) Schools at Each
    Chronological Year   ..   ..   facing 159

23.   Overlapping of Consecutive Age-groups   171

24.   Distribution according to General Intelligence of Children
    of Ordinary Elementary and Special (M.D.) Schools facing 174

25.   Distribution of Juvenile Delinquents according to General
    Intelligence and Educational Attainments   199

26.   Average Number of Tests passed at Each Age by Children
    of Ordinary Elementary and Special (M.D.) Schools
    and of Superior and Poorer Social Status   ..   facing 203

27.   Abac to determine from Two Given Percentages the Corre-
    sponding Coefficient of Association   231

28-38.   Porteus Mazes :
    28.   Age III.   258
    29.   Age IV.   259
    30.   Age V.   260
    31.   Age VI.   261
    32.   Age VII.   262
    33.   Age VIII.   263
    34.   Age IX.   264
    35.   Age X.   265
    36.   Age XI.   266
    37.   Age XII.   267
    38.   Age XIV.   268

39.   Examples of Mirror-Script and Inverted Writing   341-3
40.   Examples of Choreic Handwriting   344
41.   Drawing. Drawing by Backward Girl. To illustrate "Mixed
    Profile "   351
42.   Drawing. Median Sample for Defectives. Aged 10   ..   352
43-52.   Handwriting.   Median Specimens for Each Age :
    43.   Age 5   399
    44.   Age 6   400-1
    45.   Age 7   402
    46.   Age 8   403
    47.   Age 9   404

FIGURE   PAGE

48.   Age 10   405
49.   Age 11   406
50.   Age 12   407
51.   Age 13   408
52.   Age 14   409

53-64.   Drawing.   Median Specimens for Each Age :

53.   Age 3   411
54.   Age 4   412
55.   Age 5   413
56.   Age 6   414
57.   Age 7   415
58.   Age 8   416
59.   Age 9   417
60.   Age 10   418
61.   Age 11   419
62.   Age 12   420
63.   Age 13   421
64.   Age 14   422

PREFACE BY SIR ROBERT BLAIR, LL.D.,
Education Officer, London County Council.

The present volume consists of three memoranda prepared by Mr. Burt. The first memorandum deals with the practical use of the psychological scales for testing the intelligence of children ; the second discusses the theoretical validity of the results obtained ; and the third gives in considerable detail suitable tests of various educational attainments.

Mr. Burt criticises the suggestions of American experts such as Yerkes, Goddard, and Terman for the improvement of the Binet-Simon scale : and summarises in the light of his own investigations the type of tests for intelligence most suitable for London children at different ages. He finds that children of the ordinary elementary schools in London are in intelligence slightly above the level of other children of similar social status tested elsewhere with similar scales : that delinquents differ from normals rather by backwardness and instability than by mental deficiency in the narrower sense : and that the defectives of the London special schools differ from normals far less in lack of intelligence than in lack of school ability : and concludes that " when the dull and backward are recognised as requiring definite educational provision a larger proportion of the special school cases will doubtless be accommodated in the special classes in the ordinary school, rather than associated with those whose future lies for ever in an institution."

There is a great and growing demand for reliable mental tests. Mr. Burt, who is undoubtedly one of the greatest living authorities on these tests, has dealt with the present position in a scholarly and very interesting manner. The memoranda contain the results of much valuable research, and will be of the greatest value to London teachers, especially in connection with the discovery of special ability, the promotion of children, and the institution, where necessary, of backward classes. They will also appeal strongly to a larger public outside the London area.

Mr. Burt's results provide, as it were, a first rough sketch of the intellectual and educational progress of the average London child throughout the years of elementary school life. Teachers, both in London and elsewhere, should find it an interesting problem, and a matter for scientific research upon their own initiative, to check the norms here tentatively suggested, alike in general ability and in the special subjects of the ordinary curriculum, for children of different ages, of different sex, and of different social types : and to compare with these norms the standard of attainment actually existing among their own pupils and in their own schools.

R. BLAIR.

L.C.C. Education Offices,
Victoria Embankment, W.C. 2.
July, 1921.

xix

INTRODUCTORY NOTE.

The object of the following work is to present a provisional set of practical scales for measuring intellectual ability and educational attainments. They are designed for the use of teachers and of all who may wish to examine children in ordinary and special elementary schools. Tests with the necessary test-materials, standards by which to compare the results, instructions for administering the former and cautions for applying the latter, are given and discussed in detail.

Intellectual ability is considered primarily in its broadest form, that commonly described as general intelligence ; and is treated as measurable by the most popular tests, those devised by Dr. Simon and the late Professor Binet. Supplementary tests for measuring intelligence and some suggestions for measuring specific abilities are appended ; but it is with the Binet-Simon scale that the earlier half of the book has in the main to do. The first memorandum deals with its practical use ; the second with its theoretical validity. In my endeavour to standardise the practical instructions I have received inestimable help both from Dr. Simon, the only surviving author of the scale, and from nearly every English psychologist who has hitherto had occasion to use it. In my endeavour to standardise the theoretical criteria, I have been concerned chiefly with the diagnosis of mental deficiency — the purpose for which the scale has been most widely employed. In this part of the work I have occasionally admitted, what elsewhere I have sought so far as possible to exclude, discussions of a more abstract and technical tone. It is my belief that all who adopt, and may perhaps refine, the methods of psychology, should, whether their interest be purely practical or partly theoretical, know something of the scientific foundations upon which those methods must be built.

The third memorandum deals with the measurement of educational attainments. In it I have limited myself to tests of the chief branches of the elementary school curriculum—reading, spelling, arithmetic, composition, and the simpler manual subjects. As before, I have had predominantly in mind the discrimination of ordinary and special school cases. The tests themselves, together with practical instructions for applying and evaluating the tests, are again given at length ; but I have not thought it necessary to enlarge once more upon their theoretical basis.

Here I desire to express, however inadequately, my gratitude to all—whether psychologists, medical officers, teachers, or children —who have assisted in the preparation of these scales. To the technical skill and ready assistance of Mr. A. W. Phillips, who has supervised the printing of these pages, the volume in its final form owes a particularly heavy debt. To my father, Dr. C. Barrow Burt, who has corrected the proof-sheets and compiled the index, my obligations are too deep for formal acknowledgment. Most of all my gratefulness is due to Dr. C. W. Kimmins, late Chief Inspector to the London County Council, for his kindly sympathy and continuous encouragement during the past eight years. I may add that I shall always welcome data, criticisms, and suggestions of whatever kind, from those who may trouble to test the scales and to communicate the fruit of their experience.

This, too, is perhaps the place to insist upon one fundamental truth. Tests, infinitely more scientific than those set out below, can still be but the beginning, never the end, of the examination of the child. To take a young mind as it is, and delicately one by one to sound its notes and stops, to detect the smaller discords and appreciate the subtler harmonies, is more of an art than a science. The scientist may standardise the method ; to apply that method and to appraise the results, demands the tact, the experience, the imaginative insight of the teacher born and trained.

CYRIL BURT.

20 December, 1920.

Mental and Scholastic Tests.

Memorandum I.

THE BINET-SIMON SCALE : PRACTICAL USE OF THE METHOD.

1.—*THE GENERAL NATURE OF THE BINET-SIMON TESTS.*

Discrepancies between Ability and Attainment.

A simple method for testing the abilities of children has become in educational administration an urgent practical need. No appeal is more often addressed to the psychologist than the demand for a mental footrule. Teachers, inspectors, school medical officers, care committee visitors, the officers of juvenile criminal courts, all have long felt the want for some such instrument ; many have endeavoured to devise their own. For school know-ledge, it is true, teachers should be able to invent appropriate tests. Every term—indeed every day—they are examining the educational gains of their pupils. But something more is needed. Attainment is a poor measure of capacity, and ignorance no proof of defect. Merely from school work, neither normal ability nor abnormal, neither high ability nor low, can con-clusively be inferred.

To argue that wherever attainments are meagre, ability must also be low, will always be precarious. Poor health, poor homes, irregular attendance, lack of interest, want of will—these are far commoner as causes of in-ability to spell or calculate than are inherent weakness of intellect and genuine defect of mind. Certainly, the dull are usually backward ; but the backward are not necessarily dull.

Nor does a high measure of ability always confer a high standard of school work. Popular criticisms of contemporary education are replete with instances of undetected genius, of school incompetents who succeed in after life, dull boys who make brilliant men. Newton and Barrow, Goldsmith and Sheridan, Watt and Stephenson, Wellington and Clive—the careers of these, and of many a celebrity still living, alike attest that a dunce at lessons may prove a prodigy in disguise. Yet the customary inference is not the true corollary. It is not so much our methods of instruction that are at fault as our methods of diagnosis. It is not for failing to adapt itself to these excep-tional personalities, but for failing to discover these exceptional personalities, that the school lies open to criticism.

More than once a striking incongruity between ability and achievement was encountered or suspected by the Chief Examiner and myself when reporting upon the efficiency of the scholarship system set up by the London County Council, and when interviewing, orally and individually, possible scholarship candidates in typical London schools. On the whole, it must be owned, with questions framed by experts deftly and discreetly, with answers marked by experts according to an appropriate statistical scheme, the scholarship examination proves unexpectedly successful in selecting, by means of a brief, wholesale, written test, from some thirty thousand children annually, the ablest one or two per cent. But it may be surmised that the efficiency of the papers set becomes greater in proportion as their resemblance to a routine examination on school attainments becomes more and more remote ; and, for the rest, into secondary schools, constituted as they are at present, the cleverest genius, destitute of a certain minimum of academic knowledge, could hardly be admitted. Occasionally, it is true, an able child is found whose gifts have a technical bias, rather than an academic; and whose intelligence, therefore, may be grossly underrated in school, unless it is judged by tests of manual construction rather than of scholastic knowledge. But too often it is through the neglect to discover three or four years ago the richness of his real capacity that the poverty of a child's attainments is observable to-day. A test of intelligence, applied at the age of seven or eight, would avert much unmerited failure at the age of ten or eleven. Among the brightest children in our schools not a few miss scholarships because at an earlier age their ignorance of scholastic rudiments has relegated them to a class below their actual merits. They have remained, like sundials in the shade, with their available powers unused, because their presence has been left unilluminated.[1]

Even with average children, the amount and accuracy of their present knowledge forms but a rough, uncertain index of their power to acquire more knowledge. No matter how homogeneous a class may be at the beginning of a term, by the end of it a few will have forged far ahead of the majority and others lag behind. It is what a child *can* learn, not what he *has* learnt, that should count. The golden maxim should be this : promote by attainment rather than by age, and by ability rather than by attainment. In too many schools the order of precedence is inverted. First consideration is always to be accorded to the child's innate intelligence.

Hence, in all questions of school organisation, in all questions of class promotion, but above everything, where subnormal or supernormal pupils are concerned, *the teacher, besides examining the child's acquired school knowledge, should also possess some means of gauging his inborn mental capacity.*

The Practical Value of Intelligence Tests.

The children for which such tests are pre-eminently needed are those who are definitely above or definitely below the average. And among these it is not for the extreme types merely that the want of a test is most imperative—for the rarer cases of mental defect on the one hand, or of scholarship ability on the other. *Rather it is upon the large mass of moderate ability and of moderate disability that notice should more frequently be focussed*— upon the backward pupils of the ordinary school, and upon the future candidates for the central school. For them the means of early discrimination might well be improved. For them, too, even such special accommodation

---

[1] There is a growing tendency in more advanced areas to retain children in the infants' department until a later age than has hitherto been usual. There is also a tendency in the more advanced infants' departments to postpone to a later age the formal scholastic work. A senior department receiving a child at the age of eight has but two years to thrust him forward to the level of standard VI. by the time he sits for the Junior County Scholarship Examination. Too often children promoted from the infants' departments under such conditions are examined with formal tests of elementary scholastic work, and judged by the standard of attainment traditional in the senior school. As a consequence, even the brightest may appear educationally backward, and for the next eighteen months be destined to slow instead of rapid promotion. An intelligence test, such as that described below, if employed instead of, or in addition to, the formal tests of reading and number, would enable the cleverest infants both to be transferred at an earlier age from the infants' department to the senior, and, within the senior, to be promoted more speedily through the lower classes of the school.

as is available might profitably be enlarged. A closer search must yield a larger number.

It is, then, among such cases, that the tests will most widely be employed. The defective may be discovered by the medical officer ; the scholarship winner may be discovered by the scholarship examination ; but the detection of intermediate degrees of mental ability or weakness must rest primarily, if not solely, with the teacher. To the teacher, therefore, some handy method of estimating intelligence from the earliest ages of school life should be, for this purpose, a welcome, practical boon.

For assessing mental ability apart from school attainments the simplest and most celebrated tests in existence are those popularly associated with the joint names of Binet and Simon. They are not, as we shall find, the most accurate. But a technique thoroughly scientific could not possibly be employed by the schoolmaster without special laboratory experience. And all that he needs is a practical guide with whose authority he is already familiar.

To measure ability with exactitude is a difficult, technical feat. Indeed, tne general employment of tests among teachers some psychologists would wholly deprecate. But, provided it is explicitly realised that to the diagnosis of a teacher untrained in psychological method no final validity can attach, little harm and much good will ensue. To make psychological examinations, to pronounce judgments upon children's mentality, is part of a teacher's professional duty. A test of intelligence will confer no new functions : it can only tender additional aid. With a simple scientific invention a layman may accomplish much that before was possible to none but the expert. But the use of such a device must always be mechanical, and its scope confined and limited. Put into a child's hand a pair of compasses, and he will draw circles Giotto might envy. Yet no one unpractised in draughtsmanship, armed merely with this instrument, would expect forthwith to delineate the complete and faithful portrait of a man.

Construction of the Binet-Simon Scale.

The Binet-Simon scale consists of about sixty graded tests for measuring the intelligence of school children. The tests were originally devised by two Parisian psychologists, Alfred Binet and Theodore Simon, to assist administrative authorities in examining school children suspected of mental deficiency and recommended for transfer from the ordinary school to special classes. More particularly the inventors had in mind the French Commission nominated, in 1904, a few months before the publication of their first proposals, by the Minister of Public Instruction, to enquire into the training of defectives. The scale has since been widely used in many different countries, most of all in the United States. It is explicitly recommended for use in doubtful cases of suspected deficiency by the Chief Medical Officer of the Board of Education in his Annual Report ; and a summary of the entire scale is there published.[1]

The construction of the scale can be best understood by reference to the copy of the record-card appended on page 5. Binet's final version, published in his sole name, and known as the 1911 scale, contained fifty-four tests. In theory, as indicated by the schedule, five tests were assigned to each age from three years to adult life. Actually, however, the years XI., XIII., and XIV., and, apparently by oversight, one test for age IV., were omitted.

---

[1] See *Annual Report for* 1912 (Appendix E., " Schedule of Medical Examination of Children for Mental Defect," pp. 373–375).

Intelligence was to be measured in terms of *Mental Age*. An average child aged 7, for example, should pass all the tests up to and including those assigned to age VII.,[1] but should fail in every test for a later age. Similarly, for the other years. A child, therefore, whose mental ability was unknown, was to be given first the tests allotted to his own age ; if he passed these, he was regarded as normal ; if he failed, he was given the easier tests assigned to lower ages. A child who could pass tests up to and including those for age VI. only, was marked with a mental age of VI., regardless of his true age by the almanac. If his calendar age was seven, he would be recorded as backward or " retarded " by one year, his so-called mental age being subtracted from his real or chronological age. A retardation of two years in children under nine, and of three years in children over nine, was held indicative of mental deficiency.

In practice a child seldom breaks down abruptly at the end of one of the test-groups. Accordingly, with a child who passes stray tests from several ages Binet suggested that to the highest age for which all the tests are passed without exception the examiner should add one-fifth of a year for every additional test thus sporadically passed. Clearly, were the scale complete, comprising five tests for every year from age one onwards, we should but need to add up the number of tests passed and then divide by five in order to obtain the mental measurement directly in terms of mental years.

Tests of Specific Capacities.

The tests seem originally to have been chosen to yield information about specific capacities as well as about intelligence as a whole.[2] The plan which I have used in the record card facilitates such an analysis. The arrangement is based upon a broad classification of the tests according to their special nature. In the first column are inserted the computation and money tests ; in the second the drawing tests ; in the third the tests of weight-discrimination and of memory for numbers ; those of line-discrimination, of memory for sentences, of reasoning (definition, differences, etc.) in the fourth ; the observation tests (pictures) in the fifth ; and the literary tests (reading, writing, dictation) to the right of the double line. With a child, therefore, who succeeds in such practical tests as drawing and counting money, but fails, as so many merely backward children do, principally in memory and literary tests, the unevenness of attainment may be instantly revealed by a single glance at his record.[3]

To discover that a child is backward is of value. To measure exactly how much he is backward is of greater value. But to analyse precisely where and for what reason he is backward constitutes a problem of the highest practical importance. And, this being so, it is unfortunate that the serial gradation of the same test was not adopted systematically for every specific function, and carried without a break through every mental age.

---

[1] In accordance with the usual convention mental ages are printed in Roman numerals, and chronological ages in Arabic.

[2] Binet, in his earlier articles, speaks of intelligence as composed of " faculties "—attention, memory, sensorial intelligence, comparison, abstraction, and so forth. (Compare, *e.g.*, *The Intelligence of the Feeble-minded*, p. 133.) But later this assumption retreats into the background. Dr. Simon doubts, he tells me, whether light can be thrown upon special capacities by means of the tests. Cf. below, pp. 314-315, and Appendix IV, pp. 135-9.

[3] This record card, based as it is upon the age-assignments of the earlier French versions, is not recommended for use in an unmodified form. It formed the starting-point of our investigations ; and is printed here solely to illustrate the construction of the scale.

SCHEDULE 1.

Sample Record Card. Tests of the Binet-Simon Scale, arranged according to the Original Age-assignments.

Name...
School..
Address.......................................

Born..
Examined ....

Age 12
Standard..........

		1911 SERIES.				1908 SERIES.		
AGE III.	Surname.	Pointing.	2 Numbers.	6 Syllables.	Picture (E).			
IV.	Sex.	Naming.	3 Numbers.	2 Lines.				
V.	4 Pennies.	Square.	2 Weights.	10 Syllables.	Divided Card.			
VI.	13 Pennies.	Diamond.	Comparing Faces.	Definition (U).	Morning & Afternoon	Age.	16 Syllables.	
VII.	3 Pence & 3 Ha'pence.	4 Colours.	Right & Left.	Triple Order.	Picture (D).	Copying Script.	Fingers.	4 Coins.
VIII.	Missing Features.	Date.	5 Numbers.	Differences (C).	Count 20 to 1.	Reading (2 Facts).	Dictation.	
IX.	9 Coins.	Change.	Months.	Definition (C).	Easy Questions.	Reading (6 Facts).	Days of Week.	
X.	Sentence-Building (2).	Memory Drawing.	5 Weights.	Absurdities.	Difficult Questions			
XII.	Sentence-Building (1).	Suggestion.	00 Words in 3 mins.	Definition (A).	Mixed Sentences.			
XV.	Problems.	3 Rhymes.	7 Numbers.	26 Syllables.	Picture (I).			
ADULT.	Folded Paper.	Re-statement.	Difference (P, K).	Differences (A).	Reversed Triangle.			

Mental Age.............. Retardation............ Ratio............

Need for an English Standardisation of the Tests.

The success of a scale so constructed turns upon two preliminary conditions : the exact standardisation of the procedure, and the exact standardisation of the results. By the Binet-Simon tests as hitherto used in this country neither of these twin requirements is adequately fulfilled.

In England, indeed, a standardisation of the procedure has scarcely been attempted. Special adaptations have been constructed for Italy, for Germany, for Russia, for Sweden, for Turkey, and for Japan. And, in America, guides, manuals, and nutshell syllabi have appeared almost beyond count. But no textbook has been published specifically for British use.[1] English investigators are forced to improvise each his own adaptation, from the French or from the American, or in the light of the difficulties and mis-constructions he himself encounters in testing his examinees. The inevitable consequence is a diversity in method which would entirely stultify Binet's age-assignments, even were those age-assignments directly applicable to English children.

Those conversant with but one version of the tests barely appreciate what a playground the scale has proved for variation in technique. For practically every test there are almost as many procedures as investigators. Illustrations of the more salient divergences may perhaps be cited ; they will serve to demonstrate the pitfalls that beset the translator, and to impress the examiner with the paramount importance of strict uniformity in method.

The most flagrant variations arise from the attempt to substitute for French coins their English equivalents. Take, for example, Test 43. Here Binet required the child to name the nine commonest coins. In the English currency these are ¼d., ½d., 1d., 6d., 1s., 2s., 2s. 6d., 10s., and £1. To begin with, the florin and the half-crown occasion, by their similarity, a confusion which is not presented by any of the French coins : and uniformity becomes still more elusive with the introduction of Treasury notes of varying designs. Further, instead of the farthing, two investigators—McIntyre and Rogers—employ a five-shilling piece ; and another—Moore—adds a threepenny piece. Test 40 repeats all these perplexities, and adds one or two of its own. Here the French child is provided with the common coins, and is asked to return change for four *sous* out of a *franc*. What is the English equivalent ? Moore requires change for twopence out of a shilling ; McIntyre and Rogers change for fourpence out of a florin—a much harder feat. In Test 32 the latter ask the children to add two halfpennies and two sixpences instead of the usual three halfpennies and three pennies ; others adopt an American form of the test, and require the child to add the amount in stamps. Nor are the coinage tests by any means the sole source of variation. The whole process of turning French instructions into English idiom is prolific in

---

[1] Miss Johnston, one of the first to employ the Binet tests, published an early description in the *Training College Record* (November, 1910. Cf. *J. Exp. Ped.*, March and November, 1911). But it is brief ; and now I understand, difficult to procure. Mr. Winch's description (*Child Study*, Vol. VI., Nos. 7 and following), which has appeared since my standardisation was commenced, has the rare merit of being written by one who knows from experience how to give directions to children ; but it does not always supply the express formulæ to be recited by the examiner ; and at times departs considerably from Binet's own instructions His earlier schedule (*Mental Tests for Backward and Defective Children*, published by Ralph, Holland and Co. 35 and 36 Temple Chambers, E.C.) is in the former particular quite explicit. It is, indeed, more nearly " fool-proof " than any of the other versions. But it deviates quite as definitely from Binet. His articles do not carry the tests beyond infants' schools ; and his schedule only carries them as far as tests for age VIII. For the purpose of securing the most significant answers his departures, in my view, are usually better than the originals. He has, for example, boldly and excellently redrawn both the " pretty " and " ugly " faces and the faces with missing features. But the new drawings yield results which, though less equivocal in them-selves, are yet hardly comparable with other investigations His age-assignments, as well as those of Miss Johnston, will be found in an Appendix (p. 224) ; and the more important of his modifications in notes to my own instructions (pp. 24-68).

alternatives of unequal difficulty.[1] Notably the versions of the sentences to be memorised differ enormously ; and in rendering the instructions to be recited to the candidate it is almost impossible to preserve the nuances of the original. Finally, the time-limits prescribed by the French authors are rigidly observed here, entirely ignored there, and superseded elsewhere by personal innovations. Plainly, therefore, there is an urgent case for standardising a uniform procedure.

Nor is the standardisation of the results in any way more exact. As yet no one in this country has compiled a trustworthy series of age-norms. The special function of the tests is to facilitate the diagnosis of mental deficiency. This was their original purpose ; and this will be the ground of their increasing use. The norms, therefore, would require for their establishment the application of the same procedure to large samples, not only of normal, but also of defective school children, with a view to averaging the mental ages for each. No such comparative enquiry has hitherto been made.

Imperfect though the Binet scale may be, yet, until schools, courts, and prisons are equipped with psychological experts, its vogue will continue, and its popularity advance at a constantly accelerated rate. Those, therefore, who use the tests should use them in the least defective form. They should not be left to extemporise, in the intervals of routine duties, their own methods and their own criteria, or else be constrained to adopt uncritically norms of performances which may be accurate perhaps in Paris or California, but are unquestionably fallacious for England. They should be supplied with a standardised procedure and with standardised norms—a procedure which has been experimentally adjusted to English idioms and to English customs, norms which have been statistically deduced from extensive trials with English children, trained in English homes and taught in English schools.

The Present Version.

The version that follows is based upon a careful translation of the relevant parts in the original articles of Binet and Simon. To translate a set of instructions and problems first standardised upon foreign children is from its very nature a task fraught with difficulties. Wherever there seemed a choice of adequate renderings, I have been guided always by the canon, as comprehensive as it is concise, which Dr. Simon has in his letters on the matter repeatedly urged : " *Le bonne traduction est elle qui d'après l'experience laisse l'épreuve à l'âge auquel elle est placée.*" Dr. Simon has himself done me the honour and kindness of examining my penultimate version, and has not only replied in detail to numerous specific questions, but fully annotated the suggestions with which he found himself in disagreement. In the very few instances where I have not accepted the change he would propose, I have given both my reasons and his criticisms. Properly to express my gratitude for his trouble and generosity is more than I find it possible to do.

During the last eight years typewritten copies of the translated instructions have been in circulation and in use among a small but increasing band of teachers and experimenters. These investigators have from time to time communicated valuable improvements in the phrasing of the formulæ or in the explanation of the procedure. Amended versions have since been submitted to all the English psychologists who have carried out researches by means of the scale, and to Dr. Simon himself. Shortly before his death in 1911,

---

[1] Miss Town's authorised translation for American examiners of the practical instructions given in the *Bulletin de la Société libre pour l'Étude Psychologique de l'Enfant,* actually gives, for many of the questions, one rendering in the text and a different one in the summary in the Appendix.

M. Binet also wrote expressing his interest in our efforts. The final version, given in the following pages, owes much to the criticisms and suggestions so magnanimously bestowed.[1]

Of the various recensions published by Binet, that known as the 1908 scale is still by several investigators preferred to his last, that of 1911. The 1908 scale contained fifty-nine tests. The number of tests assigned to each age varied from four to eight. Of these, fifty were retained in the later series ; nine were omitted, chiefly on the ground of their scholastic nature. Four new tests in the new version brought its total up to fifty-four—five for each of eleven ages with the exception of age four, which has four.

Many examiners, especially those who started their records with the earlier scale, have found the omissions and insertions of the 1911 version both inconvenient and unnecessary. In order, therefore, that any person adopting the present version may render his results comparable with those secured by either the 1908 or the 1911 scale, every test in the two scales has been incorporated. Further, the set of memory tests has been completed by the addition of " 4 numbers " and " 6 numbers "—the latter already added by Goddard, Bobertag, and Terman, and both already used by many investigators to provide progressive practice with equal increments of difficulty. The entire version described below thus embraces sixty-five tests.

In their application to the English child the tests are found to require much reassortment both in the order of difficulty and in the age-assignments, as laid down originally by Binet and Simon. Order and assignment have, in consequence, been radically reinvestigated ; and the tests are now arranged in a revised seriation and classified anew for age. The changes are of first importance. With Binet's original age-assignments, many older London children, who are undoubtedly normal, appear defective ; and many younger children, who are undoubtedly defective, prove hard to convict of deficiency.

The modifications introduced into the procedure are almost entirely confined to such as are inevitably involved in translating the tests from French into English, and in transferring the scale and its materials from one country to another. That the tests, as is claimed of certain wines, have been improved in their quality by the passage of the Channel is more than I venture to pretend ; but at least it has not, I trust, been injured. In a few places an attempt has been made to rectify what seemed an obvious slip, or to make clear what seemed an unintentional obscurity. But, where any definite departure from the original has been made, the changes or insertions are, in the detailed description that follows, placed within brackets. In every case the alterations are slight ; and in every case they are introduced merely to carry out more completely the spirit of the original.

That I have adopted principles so tame and conservative does not imply that I think or have found the plan of the original version faultless. On the contrary, I am of opinion that, for exact and scientific purposes, an entirely new scale, or rather a new series of scales, must be constructed, built up afresh from the very foundation ; to tamper or tinker with the old will not be sufficient. So ambitious a reconstruction, however, is not my present aim.

(1) I have to acknowledge my grateful indebtedness, not only to Dr. Simon, but to the following who also read and criticised the typescript of my earlier versions : Miss M. Bridle, Mr. B. Dumville, Professor J. A. Green. Miss K. Johnston. Dr. E. O. Lewis, Dr. J. L. McIntyre. Mr. R. C. Moore, Professor Agnes Rogers, Miss N. G. Taylor, and Mr. W. H. Winch, and the numerous teachers both at London and Liverpool who have assisted in the whole enquiry. Mlle. Erna Reiss, member of the " Société pour l'Étude Psychologique de l'Enfant," who has attended Dr. Simon's classes, has kindly acted as intermediary. between Dr. Simon and myself.

It is an undertaking that would demand not a single research, but a lifetime of researches. And, before the novelty could be accepted, an impartial criticism of the scales to be displaced should first be issued, based upon a fair and extended trial of those scales in their original authentic form—in a form where the results shall be comparable with both those of the first authors and those of subsequent investigators, and not in a modified and doctored version, half old, half new.

For these reasons it has seemed desirable to follow as narrowly as possible the descriptions given by Binet and Simon themselves. The scope of comparison thus available will be far wider than if any later revision—the "Vineland," the "Stanford," the "Point-Scale," or some new personal adaptation suited to London children and to the adapter's favourite theories —had been chosen as the foundation of the work. Accordingly, whether as merit or demerit, it may, I think, fairly be claimed that the following version adheres more closely to the original procedure of the French authors than any of the published revisions.

2.—GENERAL DIRECTIONS FOR THE USE OF THE SCALE.

Order of Giving the Tests.

The tests are set out below in an inverse order of difficulty ; that is to say, a test that, on an average, is passed by a larger percentage of children in the ordinary elementary schools of London is placed earlier in the list than one passed by a smaller percentage. In theory, the examiner follows this programme, the principle being to work from the easier to the harder tests, until the child can do no more. But to ply a child of medium age and ability with either the easiest or the hardest of the set would be superfluous. Hence in practice Binet has advised examiners *to begin with tests suited to the child's true age : to work backward, if necessary, until he succeeds with at least five consecutive tests, and then to work forward, until he fails with at least a further consecutive five.* The order of difficulty, however, varies profoundly from one school to another. In particular, certain tests, such as picture (interpretation), suggestion (lines), and most of the tests with coins, prove disproportionately simple for defectives. Accordingly, to avoid missing any problem that a child may possibly perform, it is advisable *to conduct the child over an extensive range of tests.* To every child should be given, if time permits, tests for at least four consecutive age-groups. The examination will thus last, not twenty minutes, as stated by Binet and Simon, but between thirty and forty minutes. With children under seven, half an hour is the longest period for which the examination should be protracted without a break. When, therefore, the child has to be put through the numerous tests assigned below to ages V. and VI., and, generally, upon the first sign of flagging or fatigue, the sitting should be adjourned, and only resumed after a few minutes' intermission spent by the child, if possible, moving in the open air.

With a defective, to commence, as above advised, upon tests appropriate to his actual age, would mean working backward from harder to easier. This is against the general rule. But the order of increasing difficulty should not be followed slavishly. I would suggest that the ensuing considerations should govern the sequence of presentation :—

(1) The initial tests should act as shock-absorbers ; their purpose is to allay the nervousness and engage the interest of the child, and at the same time enable the examiner to obtain a broad preliminary estimate of the child's general level, with an eye to concentrating

later upon more crucial tests, that is, upon such, and such alone, as may seem not too far above or below his capacity to be worth the toil of applying. With this object the *picture test* is commonly selected as the first. Pictures, it is said, touch instantly upon a responsive chord in the most lethargic child ; and, according to the Binet-Simon scale, the replies will indicate one of at least three alternative levels—age III., VI., or XII. For London children mentally between V. and IX. years I find *naming coins* even more successful. The sight of a penny will, as a rule, fetch a sparkle to the eye and a word to the lips, when pictures richer in colour and action than the Binet-Simon series have left the child listless and mute. Some children are a little apprehensive of unusual allurements proffered by a stranger ; their suspicions may be disarmed by opening with more business-like questions as to *name* and *age* for the younger children, or with familiar school tests, such as *reading*, or *reciting the weekdays* or *the months*, for the older.

(2) As soon as the child has become habituated to the examiner's voice, the successive *memory tests* (*syllables and numbers*) may be applied. The method demands that every child should start from the shortest series, and gradually pass to the harder, thus obtaining a regular amount of practice. The two memory-tests consequently provide in a brief space of time a broad range of exercises over which the child's ability may be judged.

(3) As soon as the examiner has a rough notion of the ages between which the child must be tested more particularly, he should proceed to the *easier and shorter of the crucial tests* thus indicated. Anything likely to discourage or fatigue the child should not be given too early in the sitting.

(4) *Tests requiring alertness or effort,* however, should not be postponed to the very end. The oral problem-tests—definitions, absurdities, easy and hard questions, sentence-building, rhymes—should, therefore, be put when the child has warmed up to the process—having overcome his initial shyness, not yet jaded or bored, pleased perhaps by his success over the simpler tests, not yet disheartened by his failure in the harder.

(5) Being of a routine nature, the *scholastic tests*—reading, weekdays. months—may, if not already given, follow those tests that exact deeper thought and impose a harder strain.

(6) The *tests requiring apparatus,* or demanding movement on the part of the child—drawing, writing, weights, triple errand, divided card—may be reserved for the close of the sitting. They furnish a relief from the tedium of incessant question and answer ; and may at times be of service earlier in the sitting if the child shows signs of breaking down through emotion or fatigue. It is, indeed, Dr. Simon's habitual practice to intersperse such tests throughout the examination, and so continually to refresh the child by as much change and variety as possible. But, as a rule, the disturbance of papers, chairs, and tables makes it convenient to hold back these tests until the very last.

(7) Apart, however, from these special considerations, the general principle is to *work from the easier test to the harder.* And, before the child is dismissed, the examiner should glance through his records to see that, in disarranging the order of difficulty to suit the varying mood of his examinee, no test, whose issue is doubtful, has been left a blank.

Records.

For recording the results three methods are in general use, based respectively on what may be termed the schedule-system, the card-system, and the register-system :—

(1) The method favoured apparently by most American investigators requires a separate ·schedule for each child. These schedules usually consist of a folded quarto or foolscap sheet similar to that reproduced on pages 19–23. Upon each is printed, in summary form, the questions to be asked, and the time to be allowed. Blank spaces are left in which the child's replies may be entered in full. To the novice some such plan is helpful for practice. But, once the details of the instructions have been learnt by the examiner, such full directions for giving the tests (only a few of which are, of course, required for any given child) become, when printed afresh upon every record, wasteful, cumbersome, and confusing.

(2) If the records of each child are to be kept separately, a card, such as that depicted on page 5, is by far the most convenient.[1] On the front of the card, in the small compartments, some symbol indicating failure or success can be entered by the examiner ; and, if necessary, a figure or two can be affixed, touching the general nature of the response—the number of seconds consumed, the proportion of answers correct—or some initial letter added indicating the general attitude of the child—his timidity (T), hesitation (H), fatigue (F), excessive willingness or over-anxiety (W +), lack of willingness or negativism (W — or N), lack of attention or of interest (A — or I —). Upon the back of the card the drawings and the writing can be executed by the child himself, and replies of special interest or comments upon special points appended by the examiner. The record can then be filed for reference in a card-index drawer.

(3) If during the same enquiry a large number of children are to be tested, by far the most economical system is that modelled on the plan of the ordinary mark- or attendance-register. In a square-ruled note-book the names or numbers of the tests are entered in order along the margin at the top, and the names and ages of the children tested down the margin at the left. If several pages are needed, the inner leaves may be cut back an inch or two at the top to save re-writing the test-headings afresh on each opening. There is thus a horizontal row of squares for every child, and a vertical column for every test. For each child's success in each of the tests the symbol " 1 " may be entered ; and for each failure the symbol "0." To cross-cast the marks for the tests, or to total those for the children, is then an easy matter. From time to time, as Binet has himself observed, the most experienced of examiners may entertain a doubt whether he should mark a given answer as a failure or as a success ; in this emergency " $\frac{1}{2}$ " may be recorded ; " $\frac{3}{4}$ " may be employed when the child appears to have succeeded in principle, although his performance does not conform strictly to prescription ; and " $\frac{1}{4}$ " for the inverse case. Resort to such fractions should be an exception. To give the child a measure of

---

[1] Unless Binet's own arrangement, as there given, is specially preferred, the titles should be rearranged according to the order of difficulty and age-assignments shown in the schedule on pages 19–23.

C

credit for a partial or reasonable answer is not their purpose. Such a method of partial credits, although in the view of many revisers a desirable reform,[1] would conduce to higher total scores, and so subvert the accepted scheme of standardisation. Fractions represent a shortcoming in the examiner, not in the child.

Binet's own records were based upon a "register" plan. But, as he rightly urges, the list of marks or symbols should be supplemented by a verbatim statement of the child's replies, conscientiously recorded with the fulness and precision of a Boswell. For this he recommends a second note-book, and the assistance of a clerk or secretary, who may, he says, be "a child of thirteen or fourteen, provided he is intelligent and his recording receives a little supervision."

Apart from the bare fact of failure or success, the most important points to record are these : (1) the commission of absurdities, either (a) in statement, or (b) in procedure ; and (2) mechanical automatism in the replies. Under these heads and sub-heads the following are the commoner types of error. (1a) In memory for syllables, in sentence building and in mixed sentences—making up sentences that have no sense. In the picture test—lengthy disconnected catalogues of objects that are not visible. In date, coins, and reading—inventing impossible dates, non-existent coins, or statements not read. (1b) In five weights—arranging the boxes neatly in rows or piles without any attempt to weigh them. In change—picking up any coins that lie to hand, without any attempt to observe their amount. (2) In memory for numbers, or counting backwards—gliding into a recitation of the numbers in their natural order. In definition and differences (concrete) —repeating the words to be defined or contrasted ("a table is a table," " glass is glass, and wood isn't ").

Such peculiarities are often far more conclusive of deficiency than a mere backwardness in mental age. Indeed, it would be well to adopt Binet's further suggestion ; and note in the mark-register (e.g., by underlining the 0 or 1) tests in which the child's responses are unusually absurd or exceptionally good.

Wherever time permits, however, the child's replies should be taken down sentence by sentence and word for word—always for the picture, definition, questions, and differences tests ; often for the absurdities and problems tests ; and as far as possible for the free association test (sixty words in three minutes). To a second person the nature of the replies actually uttered is likely to carry far more conviction than a bare series of marks, which can only indicate whether in the private opinion of the examiner those replies were successful or not. For some tests—for example, definition (class) and memory drawing—the standard of success is extremely arbitrary, and bound to waver from one investigator to another. In such tests, too, even one and the same examiner may wish, particularly in the early stages of his work, to revise his criterion of failure or success. Only when detailed records have been preserved can this be effected.

For brief accounts a second note-book is inconvenient and unnecessary. The mark-register will serve. Its openings may be devoted to quantitative marks and to verbal notes alternately. And then, if every other leaf is cut down at the outer margin as well as at the top, the notes can be written on the second opening in a line with the child's name, which will itself be entered on the margin of the first. Thus, whether symbolic or verbal, all the records relating to the same child will be found together.

---

[1] Yerkes' Point-scale is a notable instance of this modification. (See below, p. 72).

Computation of Marks.

The child's intelligence is to be measured by the total number of tests which, actually or by implication, he has successfully performed. Start, therefore, with the serial number of the test immediately before his first failure, and count on one for every subsequent success. Thus, the number of tests scored in the following record (Table I) would be 36 + 4 = 40.

TABLE I.—COMPUTATION OF MARKS.

No. of test	1 to 30	31	32	33	34	35	36	37	38	39
Score (Passed or Failed)..	not given		P	P	P	P	P	F	P	P

No. of test	40	41	42	43	44	45	46	47	48	49	50 to 65
Score (Passed or Failed)..	F	P	F	P	F	F	F	F	F	not	given

Reference to the age-assignments will show that the first thirty-five tests are passed, on an average, by a child of 7·0. The child in question has passed five tests beyond this number—forty in all ; whether they are in fact the first forty consecutively, is not material. Six tests beyond that number would have given him an extra year. He may therefore be credited with a mental age of 7⅖ years.

The key facing page 19 enables the examiner to convert, by merely reading off the figures in the body or the margins of the chart, a given number of tests actually scored into an equivalent mental age, or to estimate from a given age the equivalent number of tests that should presumably be scored.

The approximate mental ages that would have been assigned by Binet according to either the 1908 or the 1911 scale are shown in Table VII (p. 154). To obtain this Binet age more precisely in fractions (used by Binet himself only in the 1911 scale), the tests would need to be re-entered according to the order shown on the record card above (page 5) ; and the fifths of a year added to the highest age for which the child passes every test. This procedure, of course, will be adopted only by those who for some special purpose wish to compare their results with those of investigators following Binet's original versions. A failure in an earlier age was disregarded by this method, if the child completely recovered in a following year. Such recoveries are not common ; and the table annexed will, as a rule, be sufficiently accurate.

Instead of mental age or retardation, many later investigators have preferred to measure ability in terms of a *Mental Ratio*. The mental ratio is found by dividing the mental age by the chronological age.[1] Thus, a child aged eight, with a mental age of VI., has a mental ratio of $\frac{6}{8}$, or 75 per cent. It has been claimed that during school life the ratio remains approximately constant. From this it would ensue that we have a means of predicting at an early age the mental level which a child will reach in any subsequent year of life.

The scale has been used to measure the intelligence, not only of subnormal, but also of supernormal children. A child aged eight with a mental age of IX. is said to be advanced by one year. His mental ratio would be 112 per cent. Genius has been assigned a mental ratio of 200 per cent. or over. Apparently this was the mental ratio of Sir Francis Galton ; for his early correspondence and attainments show that at the age of four to five his ability was equal to that of an average child of from eight to ten— that is, twice his actual age. In elementary schools ratios over 150 are hardly ever to be met. And, on the whole, with brighter children in older

---

[1] See below, p. 163.

years—for example, in examining candidates for Junior County Scholarships or Central Schools—the Binet-Simon scale gives unsafe estimates. Reasoning tests, such as those described in an appendix[1] to these memoranda, have furnished results that are far more secure.

Norms for London Children.

In Table IX (p. 157) of the following memorandum will be found the average number of tests passed at each age by children of London schools, both ordinary elementary and special (M.D.). Here, as elsewhere, the ages indicate age last birthday : 9 — refers to children between 9 years 0 months and 10 years 0 months, and therefore on an average 9·5 years. In Table XVIII (p. 169) the ages and scores headed " borderline " give the limits suggested as demarcating the normal from the deficient. It should be observed that a slight deviation either above or below such a limit is not sufficient to prove either normality or deficiency. Nor, indeed, should a diagnosis of mental deficiency ever be made except by a properly qualified expert who will, of course, always explore other fields of information besides those afforded by pure psychological tests.[2]

Local Revision of Norms.

I have argued above that the method of applying the tests should follow with the utmost rigour that recommended by Binet and Simon. But a narrow rule of strict conformity, although imperative in the standardisation of the procedure, seems inexpedient in the standardisation of the results. In the results, however, comparability with Binet will still be attained only so long as they are expressed either in terms of the number of tests passed, or else in terms of mental ages derived according to Binet's own formula as enunciated on a previous page. If the mental age or ratio is computed according to the new scheme—a scheme necessitated by the progress of normal London school children and by the organisation of the London special schools—then immediate comparability ceases. Tables are given which enable either form of computation to be used.

For new districts new standards will probably have to be found. Thus, if tests are used in rural districts, the age-assignments would require to be lowered considerably.

Those who seek to procure fresh norms for other areas will save time and labour, if they adopt the recognised device of sampling ; to taste the quality of a wine and its vintage it is unnecessary to drain the whole cask. For rough purposes the following procedure is recommended as rapid but tolerably exact. Suppose it is desired to establish a norm for ordinary children aged ten. To test every child is not essential. Were the whole group ranked in order of ability, then the middle child in the list (the " median ") would represent by his intelligence the average of his group, quite as adequately as the arithmetic mean computed in the usual way. In a well-organised school the children near the centre for ability should be found in the class or standard corresponding to the age in question. To determine this standard, subtract six from the age. For age ten, the typical representatives should thus be located in standard IV. In a class of fifty there may be twenty of that age. But here again none but the middle children need be tested. To discover them, do not, as is commonly done, ask the class teacher to pick out average pupils. Almost invariably you will be given children above the arithmetic

---

(1) See p. 249.

(2) I have given a list, and discussed the value, of these supplementary sources of evidence in *Studies in Mental Inefficiency.* I. 4., p. 77. " The Definition and Diagnosis of Mental Deficiency."

mean. Let the teacher eliminate, one by one, the six best, and then the six poorest. The remaining six or eight, when tested, will yield an average almost identical with that obtained from working child by child through the whole age-group. If possible, several schools should be thus examined, as results fluctuate surprisingly from one school to another. Failing that, select a school which is approximately median, both as regards the teaching efficiency of the staff and as regards the social and cultural status of the pupils' homes ; and by the same abbreviated plan proceed to ascertain the norm required.

The General Conduct of the Examination.

Most of the following cautions were enunciated, and reiterated, by Binet himself. They appear obvious. Yet the experience of those who have supervised the Binet-testing carried out by students and field-workers is unanimous in stressing their need.

Whenever it is proposed to use the tests for an examination by the Binet-Simon method, the examiner should *adhere with meticulous exactitude to the procedure described for every test.* In no way should he alter the wording of the instructions to be repeated to the child. The formulæ may seem as arbitrary as the rules and rigmaroles of heraldry : but conventions are inevitable for uniformity ; and without uniformity comparison becomes invalid. The novice is apt to presume that the test involves doing the task as he himself would understand it from the directions, and is accordingly beguiled into improvising supplementary aids and explanations. Binet makes it clear that, in his method, this is erroneous ; he points out, for example, that Test 10 does not depend on estimating the child's power to discriminate lengths ; often it turns simply on his power to grasp that the phrase " point to the longer " implies comparison. Similarly, if the directions require the examiner to say, " Make a sentence with these three words," and if, fearing that the child may not understand the word " sentence," the examiner explains, " Tell me something, and use these three words when you say it," then he altogether dislocates the age-assignment of the test. Thus the test consists not so much in the way the child carries out certain operations, but in the way he responds to certain standardised formulae. The scale, in effect, is virtually a graded " instructions test."

Observe studiously the number of errors that may be countenanced ; and, in following the time-limits, be punctilious, yet not pedantic. From visitors who have watched the actual procedure of Binet or of Simon, I gather that these authors did not intend the time-limits always and everywhere to be blindly enforced.[1] Some latitude is on occasion sanctioned. This, I apprehend, should vary with the test. In Test 51 (sixty words) three minutes should be allotted punctually to the second. In Tests 49 and 50 (difficult questions and absurdities) the grace of a few additional seconds may at times be accorded. On the whole, I would suggest abiding tenaciously by the prescribed limit in the more mechanical tests, but, in the tests that demand more reflection, granting to the steady, cautious child a reasonable margin.

During a test neither teach nor criticise. These are the two lapses to which, by sheer force of professional habit, the teacher most inclines. Criticism diminishes candour and destroys self-confidence. Instruction transforms the examinee's entire attitude toward the remainder of the tests ; and, by prolonging the interview, exhausts his attention and depletes his interest, before the test-series is concluded. Accordingly, so long as the

---

[1] Dr. Simon's own reply on this point is : "Les temps indiqués ne sont que des guides."

child is doing his best, greet every response as if entirely satisfactory. Give no hint before he answers ; no clue as to his correctness when he has replied.

Be shy of the presumption that, because a child fails in the examination room, he will fail equally in duties out of school. Many a child, most of all the child from a poor home, leads a life as duplex as that of Jekyll and Hyde, just as he speaks two dialects, and obeys a double code of morals : in the street he plays the precocious urchin ; in the school he is put down as mentally deficient. Conversely, beware of inferring that, because a child knows a particular fact, or can do a particular duty outside the examination room, he should, therefore, succeed when the same task is set him as an oral test. Teachers, as a rule, are acutely disappointed in their children's performances at the Binet tests, and are eager to have the question rephrased or the time-limit extended. Fortunately, with most children, intellectual capacity is less affected by the artificiality of the conditions than are mood and disposition. Nevertheless, nearly every child loses much of his natural spontaneity ; and that his method produces this effect, Binet frankly avowed. "The examination," he says, "makes them in a certain way seem less intelligent than they are ; this is the general rule." He does not, however, formulate the exception. Certain temperaments are braced and stimulated by the unusual situation. The plausible, sociable, excitable girl will often by her specious chatter appear brighter than she really is, particularly if her age entails a selection of tests that are predominantly linguistic. For such deviations allowance should be made after, not before, the mental age has been obtained by the usual method.

"Every psychological test," it has been said, "is inevitably a test of intelligence." Too often it is forgotten that every test of intelligence is also a test of emotion. *A neglect of the emotional aspect of an examination of intelligence may send many a normal child to the special school as mentally deficient.* No matter how scrupulously uniform the procedure, how sympathetic the examiner's tone, the child's excitability will introduce disturbances in unknown quantity. To appeal constantly to the invigorating emotions—to pleasure, curiosity, pride, self-display, sociability, confidence ; and to banish utterly the depressing emotions—anxiety, fear, grief, disgust, shyness, self-suppression, sense of failure, these are the soundest rules. It is the business of the examiner to keep the subject in that state of exhilaration which enables him always to do his best. The child should quit the room ardent for still more tests, and displaying to his fellow-candidates a countenance which inspires them with an equal avidity to essay their own powers.

Avoid all pomp and circumstance. By a tactful use of the customary civilities—a compliment, a handshake, or a smile—court and keep that atmosphere of intimacy which psychological testing presupposes. It was said of Mirabeau that, alike in private intercourse and on public occasions, he possessed *le don terrible de familiarité.* This "formidable gift" is one which the psychologist must possess and cultivate until it is formidable no longer. The test-room manner should be as proverbial for its tone of sympathy as the "bedside manner" for its urbanity and ease. With younger or low-grade children the tests should be conducted rather in the spirit of a game. With older children a friendly question about their evening hobbies or their pets at home, an admiring comment on some badge or ornament with which they have bedecked themselves for the solemn occasion, may instantly win their confidence. A child that remains stubbornly mute, or timidly monosyllabic, while standing stiffly to attention in the examination chamber, will often burst into speech if taken for the shortest walk in the open air.[1] In

---

[1] Terman also finds that with a strange child, "it is advantageous to go out of doors with him for a little walk around the University buildings."

any event, do not begin the tests proper until the child is at his ease, and *rapport* is established. Rather. defer the tests.

Almost invariably, following Binet, the published instructions insist that the examiner should, where possible, be alone with the child. By their presence, it is true, teachers and relatives often render the child more hesitant and self-conscious ; sometimes, too, they are unable to resist a word of help, rebuke, correction, or extenuation. Yet many a child becomes even more timid when closeted alone with a stranger ; and nearly always the teacher, from his previous knowledge, can cast a helpful gleam of light upon obscurities in the child's responses and behaviour. A girl, particularly a subnormal girl, should not, as a rule, be tested by a male examiner, except in the presence of a third person. The chaperon may conveniently be an intelligent elder girl from the same school, who may also perform the offices of a monitor, to usher in each examinee promptly, or even, as suggested by Binet, those of a secretary, to take down the replies in writing.[1] But, be they who they may, all spectators should keep unobtrusively in the background, and observe strict silence while the examinee remains in the room.

With laudable anxiety, not only to catch the child's replies, but also to observe his attitude and procedure, the examiner is at first apt to discompose the child by fixing his eyes vigilantly upon him. Against such a habit Binet inserts an express caution. Towards the end of the sitting, when the child is busied with reading or writing, the examiner may venture to scrutinise him thoroughly. But at the start his glances should seem casual and uncritical.

When a child does not answer immediately, the usual practice of Binet-testers is to wait five or ten seconds ; then repeat the question kindly ; then wait about half a minute patiently—punctuating the interval with tactful exclamations of encouragement[2] ; and so pass to the next question. With many borderline children, however, taciturnity and hesitation spring from a species of examination-paralysis, in its nature emotional rather than intellectual. In such cases, to evoke an answer, every possible resource, save a threat, a reprimand, a demonstration of the method or an explanation of the formulæ, should be exploited. Where failures are due to external interruptions or to initial embarrassment, revert to the same test later.

Periods of silence may grow as disconcerting as a running fire of interrogation or perpetual censure and correction. Constantly, therefore, in a quiet tone, exhort a shy child with words which will stimulate, without helping him. It is a safe and sensible maxim never to touch the child. Yet there are exceptional moments when a friendly grasp of the shoulder, arm, or hand, as if to draw a reserved child nearer, or to turn a bashful child full face, may prove an effective stimulus, when all verbal incitement fails. As a rule, adapt your manner freely to each new personality ; but never adapt the questions. Throughout the sitting keep the child's mind brisk and busy. Never leave him waiting or watching while you write your notes or prepare your apparatus.

Candidates about to be examined should not be left loitering outside

---

[1] An adult assistant, familiar with the examiner's methods and acquirements, and able to take full notes in shorthand, is, of course, eminently preferable to a child. And I may here express my indebtedness to Miss V. G. Pelling and Miss P. C. Woursell, who, throughout the latter part of my investigations, rendered invaluable services both as recorders and in numerous other ways.

[2] Dr. Simon's note on this paragraph deserves to be quoted : " Nous encourageons, il me semble, plus que vous ne semble le faire. . . . ' Voyons.—Eh bien, mon bonhomme ?—Allons !—Ça vient ?' Nous taperions sur l'épaule du sujet ou secouerions sa main.—le tout avec douceur, affectueusement, sans brusquerie ; dans le ton général que vous indiquez, en effet, mais plus vivant—en rapport, je pense, avec notre tempérament."

the room in unemployed suspense. It is better for them to be summoned directly from the classroom. If, to save time, one child is left waiting while another is tested, he should be given a book or a toy with which to amuse himself. After the sitting is over he should return straight to his class-room, warned, if necessary, not to chatter about the tests. The fact is, how-ever, that very little aid can be gained from gossip. Nor is one child, as a rule, desirous of helping another to do better than himself. A brief appeal to his sense of fair play is usually sufficient. A further precaution lies in testing the less intelligent children first. However willing, the dull can tender little assistance to the bright.

Modified and Unmodified Procedure.

In testing a particular individual it will often chance that the examiner, who has rigidly and faithfully pursued the original instructions, fails to satisfy himself that the child's ostensible performances represent his genuine powers. In justice to the child it is then hard to withstand a temptation to amplify the test a little, and fit the method to his individual needs. Is there not, it may be asked, a danger in a pharisaical conformity, no less than in a free and tolerant elasticity ? Has it not always been the wisdom of England, in compiling rubrics and liturgies as well scientific as ecclesiastic, " to keep the mean between the two extremes, of too much stiffness in refusing, and of too much easiness in admitting, variations from things established by authority ? "

To overcome these difficulties, and to meet these special cases, I suggest the following principles. Distinguish scrupulously between an unmodified and a modified procedure ; and admit the latter only so far as it will not invalidate the former. Do not confuse the responses wrung from the child by further elaborations of the method with those that might be obtained by a nice adherence to the original prescriptions. First, give the test as directed below, neglecting for the moment *addenda* in brackets ; and record the child's reaction : as a rule, these directions, which are Binet's own, provide the minimum of instruction, time, and trials, which may be regarded as adequate for the normal child. After the child has enjoyed a fair chance to respond to the strict and stereotyped procedure, then, if he still fails, or if his response has been ambiguous, proceed with any modifications that may suggest themselves as appropriate. As far as possible, choose additional formulæ and additional material from those already used by other investi-gators. These are indicated in the notes appended to the translated instructions. The child may now be helped more freely—perhaps a demon-stration given, or the answer to a first example illustratively educed. The scores respectively obtained " without assistance " and " with assistance " should be kept distinct, and denominated as such. On the former alone should the mental age be based. To prevent such aid affecting subsequent tests, either by instruction or by fatigue, it is often wiser to return to the tests needing the supplementary procedure at the end of the sitting or on another day. Routine examiners, whose time unfortunately is too short to secure scores comparable with those of other investigators, and whose duty is primarily to determine the level of the individual children, must almost inevitably work out for themselves an abbreviated set of tests and a modified scheme of procedure suited more particularly to the specialities of their cases. In such an event they will beware of quoting the mental ages as if they had been reached by the full scale and the rigid method. They will themselves be all too keenly conscious of the fallibility of a diagnosis obtained in one short interview lasting but ten or fifteen minutes.

TABLE II.

KEY FOR CONVERTING TEST-SCORES INTO MENTAL AGES.

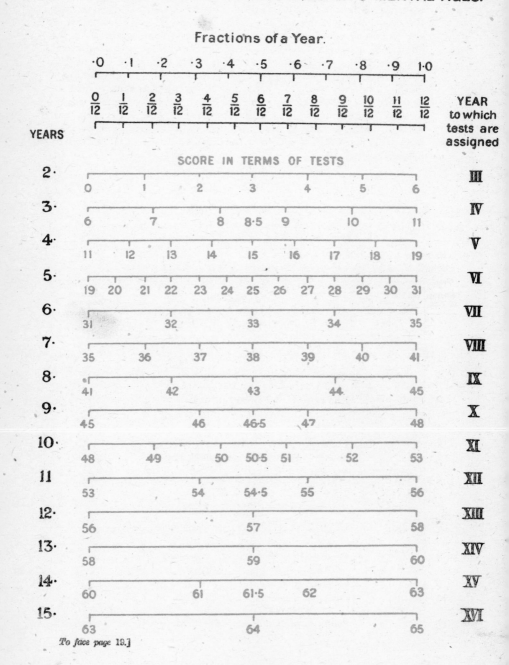

Fractions of a Year.

| ·0 | ·1 | ·2 | ·3 | ·4 | ·5 | ·6 | ·7 | ·8 | ·9 | 1·0 |

| $\frac{0}{12}$ | $\frac{1}{12}$ | $\frac{2}{12}$ | $\frac{3}{12}$ | $\frac{4}{12}$ | $\frac{5}{12}$ | $\frac{6}{12}$ | $\frac{7}{12}$ | $\frac{8}{12}$ | $\frac{9}{12}$ | $\frac{10}{12}$ | $\frac{11}{12}$ | $\frac{12}{12}$ |

YEARS — YEAR to which tests are assigned

SCORE IN TERMS OF TESTS

YEARS	SCORE	YEAR assigned
2·	0 1 2 3 4 5 6	III
3·	6 7 8 8·5 9 10 11	IV
4·	11 12 13 14 15 16 17 18 19	V
5·	19 20 21 22 23 24 25 26 27 28 29 30 31	VI
6·	31 32 33 34 35	VII
7·	35 36 37 38 39 40 41	VIII
8·	41 42 43 44 45	IX
9·	45 46 46·5 47 48	X
10·	48 49 50 50·5 51 52 53	XI
11·	53 54 54·5 55 56	XII
12·	56 57 58	XIII
13·	58 59 60	XIV
14·	60 61 61·5 62 63	XV
15·	63 64 65	XVI

To face page 19.]

These concessions, then, must be made in practical work. But in scientific enquiry and for comparable research it is wiser to forgo them. Here, of the two avoidable extremes, it is better to side with the rabbis of precision than to consort with the apostles of laxity.

Explanatory Note to Table II.—To find a child's mental age, look among the red figures in the body of the table for the total number of tests passed (both actually and by implication); say, 40. The figure on the same horizontal line in the left-hand margin gives the year (7· . . .), and the black figure immediately above in the top margin gives the additional fraction of a year (. . . ·8), corresponding to the test-score. The mental age, therefore, for a child who has passed 40 tests is 7·8.

Conversely, to find the number of tests a child should pass at a given calendar age, say $11\frac{4}{12}$, look first down the left-hand margin for the year, and then along the lower row of fractions in the upper margin for the months. Imaginary straight lines drawn horizontally and vertically from the two numbers will intersect in the body of the table near a red figure which will show the number of tests that should be passed, namely 54.

SCHEDULE II.
Sample Record Form.

(List of Binet-Simon Tests in average order of difficulty with revised age-assignments.)

Name of Child . . . . Age . . . . . . Born . . . .
School . . . . Standard . . . . Date of Test . . . .

Number of Test.	Border-line.	Scale.	Tests.	Success of Response.
			AGE III.	
			(Children aged 2 to 3 should do half the following tests.)	
1			Points to nose . . . ., eyes . . . ., mouth	
2			Repeats 2 numbers (1 trial correct out of 3) : 3 7 . . . ., 6 4 . . . ., 7 2	
3	$3\frac{1}{2}$		Knows sex. Boy or girl (if boy) . . . . Girl or boy (if girl)	
4			Gives name . . . ., and surname	
5			Names knife . . . ., key . . . ., penny	
6			Pictures. Enumerates items in 2 out of 3 : (i) . . . . (ii) . . . . (iii)	
			AGE IV.	
			(Children aged 3 to 4, or in grade 0, should do half the following tests.)	
7	$4\frac{1}{2}$		Repeats 6 syllables : **"I am cold and hungry"**	
8			Repeats 3 numbers (1 trial correct out of 3) : 9 1 4 . . . ., 2 8 6 . . . ., 5 3 9	
9			Counts 4 pennies	
10	$5\frac{1}{2}$		Points to longer of 2 lines (5 and 6 cm.) ; all trials correct	
11			Points to prettier faces. (All 3 pairs correct.) 1st . . . ., 2nd . . . ., 3rd . . . . pair.	

Number of Test.	Border-line.	Scale.	Tests.	Success of Response.
			AGE V.	
			(Children aged 4 to 5, or in grade i., should do half the following tests.)	
12			Performs triple order : (i) Key on table...., (ii) shuts door...., (iii) brings book....	
13			Copies square recognisably....	
14			Repeats 10 syllables : "**His name is Jack ; he's such a naughty dog.**"....	
15		'08	Gives age....	
16	6½		Distinguishes morning and afternoon (if morning)....; *vice versa* if afternoon....	
17			Names 4 colours (in about 6 secs. : no error or second trial) : B...., Y...., G...., R....	
18		neither	Repeats 4 numbers (1 trial correct out of 3) : 3 6 8 1...., 5 7 4 9...., 8 5 2 6....	
19			Compares 2 weights (all trials correct except first random) : (i) 3 and 12 g.... (ii) 6 and 15 g.... (iii) 3 and 12 g....	
			Procedure :............................	
			AGE VI.	
			(Children aged 5 to 6, or in grade ii., should do half the following tests.)	
20		'08	Knows (without counting) number of fingers on right hand...., left hand...., both	
21			Counts 13 pennies....	
22			Copies diamond recognisably....	
23	7½	'08	Copies from script (legibly, but errors allowed): "**See little Paul**"....	
24		'08	Names days of week without error in 10 secs. M...., T...., W...., Th....., F...., S...., Su....	
25		'08	Names without error 4 coins : 1s....., 1d....., 6d....., ½d.....	
26			Reconstructs divided oblong card (in about ½ min.) Procedure :..................	
27			Defines by use (3 out of 5) : (i) **horse**...., (ii) **chair**...., (iii) **mother**...., (iv) **table**...., (v) **fork**....	
28			Repeats 5 numbers (1 trial correct out of 3) : 5 2 9 4 7...., 6 3 8 5 2...., 9 7 3 1 8....	
29			Pictures. Describes items in 2 out of 3 : (i)...., (ii)...., (iii)....	
30		'08	Repeats 16 syllables : "**We are going for a walk ; will you give me that pretty bonnet ?**"	
31	8½		Shows right hand....; left ear....	

Number of Test.	Border-line.	Scale.	Tests.	Success of Response.
			AGE VII.	
			(Children aged 6 to 7, or in grade iii., should do half the following tests.)	
32			Recognises missing features (3 out of 4): (i) mouth...., (ii) eye...., (iii) nose...., (iv) arms....	
33			Adds without error 3 pennies and 3 half-pennies (in 15 secs.)....	
34	9½		States differences between concrete objects (2 pairs out of 3 in 2 mins.): (i) **fly—butter-fly**...., (ii) **wood—glass**...., (iii) **paper—cardboard**....	
35		'08	Writes from dictation (legibly, but errors allowed): "**The pretty little girls.**"....	
			AGE VIII.	
			(Children aged 7 to 8, or in standard I., should do half the following tests.)	
36		'08	Reads, without assistance, passage prescribed; and recalls 2 items out of 20 ....items.	
37	10½		Answers easy questions (2 out of 3): **What would you do,**—(i) **if missed train**...., (ii) **if broke something**...., (iii) **if struck accidentally**....	
38			Counts backwards from 20 to 1 (in about 30 secs., with only 1 error)....	
39			Gives full date. Day of week...., day of month (3 days error allowed)...., month ...., year....	
40			Gives change for 2d. out of 1s. (coins to necessitate silver). Money given: ....pennies, ...halfpennies, ...sixpence, ...other coins.	
41	11½	neither	Repeats 6 numbers (1 trial correct out of 3): 2 5 0 3 6 4...., · 8 5 3 9 1 6...., 4 7 1 5 8 2....	
			AGE IX.	
			(Children aged 8 to 9, or in standard II., should do half the following tests.)	
42			Names the months of the year (in 15 secs., with only 1 error): J...., F...., M...., A...., M...., J...., Jy...., A...., S...., O...., N...., D...	
43			Names 9 coins (in 40 secs., two trials if necessary): ½d....., 2s....., 10s....., 6d....., ¼d...., 2s. 6d...., 1d....., 1s...., £1....	
44	12½	'08	Reads, without assistance, passage prescribed; and recalls 6 items out of 20. ....items.	
45			Defines in terms superior to use (3 out of 5): (i) **horse**...., (ii) **chair**...., (iii) **mother**, ..., (iv) **table**...., (v) **fork**....	

Number of Test	Border-line.	Scale.	Tests.	Success of Response.
			AGE X.	
			(Children aged 9 to 10, or in standard III., should do half the following tests.)	
46	13½		Arranges 5 weights in order (2 out of 3 trials correct, the whole in 3 mins.) : (i)...., (ii)...., (iii).... Procedure :	
47			Builds 2 sentences with 3 words in 1 min. : "**London, money, river.**" Number of sentences given...., viz. "................"	
48		'11	Draws 2 designs shown simultaneously for 10 secs. (1½ correct) : (i) ...., (ii)	
			AGE XI.	
			(Children aged 10 to 11, or in standard IV., should do half the following tests.)	
49	14½		Explains absurdities (3 out of 5 in 2 mins.) : (i) **Cyclist killed ; may not get better**.... (ii) **Three brothers,—Jack, Tom, and self** .... (iii) **Railway accident ; not serious ; 47 killed** .... (iv) **Girl cut in 18 pieces ; killed herself** .... (v) **Shall not kill myself on Friday because unlucky**	
50			Answers difficult questions (3 out of 5 in 20 secs. each) : (i) **What to do, if late going to school** .... (ii) **What to do, if asked about boy, not known** .... (iii) **Why forgive unkindness if done when angry ?** .... (iv) **Why judge a person by what he does, not by what he says ?** .... (v) **What to do before undertaking something important**	
51	15½		Gives 60 words in 3 mins. Chief topics : .... / .... / .... / .... / .... / .... / Total	
52			Repeats 7 numbers (1 trial correct out of 3) : 9 6 8 4 7 5 1 ...., 4 8 2 0 3 6 5 ...., 5 9 2 8 1 3 6	
53			Builds 1 sentence with 3 words in 1 min. : "**London, money, river.**" No. of sentences given...., viz. "................"	
			AGE XII.	
			(Children aged 11 to 12, or in standard V., should do half the following tests.)	
54			Gives 3 rhymes (like Jill, hill, etc., in 1 min.) to "**obey**" : (i)...., (ii)...., (iii)....	
55			Rearranges mixed sentences (2 out of 3 in 1 min. each) : (i)...., (ii)...., (iii)....	
56			Pictures. Interpretation (infers situation ; or suggests emotion, in 2 out of 3) : (i)...., (ii)...., (iii)....	

Number of Test.	Border-line.	Scale.	Tests.	Success of Response.
			AGE XIII.	
			(Children aged 12 to 13, or in standard VI., should do half the following tests.)	
57		'11	Resists suggestion of lines (2 out of 3 equal pairs). Pairs : (iv)...., (v)...., (vi).... .... correct judgments.	
58			Solves 2 circumstantial problems : (i) Dead body...., (ii) man dying....	
			AGE XIV.	
			(Children aged 13 to 14, or in standard VII., should do half the following tests.)	
59			Repeats 26 syllables : "The other morning I saw in the street a tiny yellow dog. Little Maurice has spoilt his new apron."	
60			Defines abstract terms : (i) Kindness........ (ii) Justice........ (iii) Charity........	
			AGE XV.	
			(Children aged 14 to 15, or in standard ex-VII., should do half the following tests.)	
61			Draws the folded and cut paper : .... holes.	
62			Gives difference between abstract terms (2 out of 3) : (i) idleness—laziness,.... (ii) poverty—misery,.... (iii) evolution—revolution,....	
63			Draws the reversed triangle (C at B ; and AC along AB) : (i) ACB a right angle .... (ii) AC shorter than AB .... (iii) CB shortest	
			AGE XVI	
			(Children aged 15 to 16 should do at least one of the two following tests.)	
64		'11	Re-states Hervieu's Reflection on Life : It is neither good nor bad, but mediocre ; for .... It is not so good as we wish,.... It is better than others wish for us	
65		'11	Gives 3 differences between a President and a King : (i) Not hereditary...., (ii) not life-long...., (iii) powers more limited :...	

Total number of tests passed (actually or implicitly). ————————

Mental Age (M). (To be obtained by means of Table II.) ....

Physical Age (A)..

Retardation or Advancement (A $\sim$ M). ....

Mental Ratio $\left(\dfrac{M}{A}\right)$ ....

Explanatory Note.—The ages in the second column (headed "borderline") are set against figures in the preceding column, which indicate the number of tests that should, theoretically, be passed at each year specified before a child can be rated as normal. Thus, at age 10½, a child who answers more than thirty-seven tests is (so far as can be judged by the Binet-Simon scale) unfit for a special (M.D.) school The examiner will abstain from inferring that the test thus numbered must necessarily be crucial for that age[1]; and, generally, from using this theoretical indication in any rigid or mechanical fashion.

The figures in the column headed "scale" indicate, for tests omitted in either the 1908 or the 1911 version, which scale included them. "Neither" indicates that the test specified was omitted in both.

3. SPECIAL DIRECTIONS FOR THE INDIVIDUAL TESTS.[1]
The Use of the Directions.

The following pages contain detailed directions for carrying out each of the tests in the Binet-Simon Scale.

For clearness and for convenience of arrangement, details regarding materials required, instructions to be given, evaluations to be made, have been sorted severally under their appropriate heads. All general discussion upon the psychological nature or purpose of each test has been omitted. And, for rapid reference, the instructions to be recited to the child, and the leading conditions in evaluating the child's replies (relating principally to trials, errors, and time allowed), are printed in heavy type.

Any addition to, or departure from, the original French instructions,[2] which may change the difficulty of the test, is inserted in square brackets. The annotations also include a brief notice of the more important modifications suggested in previous revisions. The allusions to Yerkes and to Terman refer to the new versions, known respectively as the "Point-Scale Method" and the "Stanford Revision and Extension." These versions digress very considerably from the Binet-Simon arrangement, not only in procedure, but also in the selection of tests. A brief description of them is, therefore, appended to this section. The allusions to other investigators refer to recensions published in their name. For strict comparability, either with the results of Binet and Simon, or with those of the present investigation, such recommendations should be ignored. They will, however, be found suggestive in elaborating a modified procedure, as already described.

AGE III.
1.—Understanding Simple Commands.

Procedure. **"Show me,"**[3] [" put your finger on,"[4] " point to "]....

    (i)...."**your nose**"....
    (ii)...."**your eyes**"....
    (iii)...."**your mouth.**"

Each request (repeated several times, if necessary) should be given and answered separately.

---

(1) For crucial tests, see below, p. 181.

(2) For brevity and distinction I refer to the original French instructions by the title of "Binet," although the article most frequently cited was written and signed by both Binet and Simon; and my references to "Dr. Simon" allude to notes privately communicated to me by Dr. Simon in commenting upon my version.

(3) I prefer the interrogative to the imperative ("will you show me?"—or even "can you . . .?" though this may evoke nothing but a nod or a head-shake). With the interrogative it is easier to convey an impression of gentleness: the imperative is somewhat stern. Further, in the interrogative the auxiliary

Evaluation. **All three injunctions** should be correctly performed : but **abundant repetition** and free encouragement may first be used.[5] (Opening the mouth, winking the eyes, etc., may be accepted.)

[Terman adds (iv) "hair"; requires three out of four to be correct; but allows using a doll, and the questions : "Is this its (*or* your) nose ? . . . Then where is its (*or* your) nose ? "]

2.—Repeating Numbers.

Procedure. **"I am going to say some numbers. [Listen : and] say them after me."**

	(For use only after failure in first set.)		
(i) "5"	"8"	"9"	
(ii) "37"	"64"	"72"	(Age III.)
(iii) "914"	"286"	"539"	(Age IV.)
(iv) "3681"	"5749"	"8526"	(Age V.)
(v) "52947"	"63852"	"97318"	(Age VI.)
(vi) "250364"	"853916"	"471582"	(Age VIII.)
(vii) "9684751"	"4820365"	"5928136"	(Age XI.)[6]

The rate should be **two per second** : utterance should be **without rhythm, emphasis, or inflection.** Do not tell the child if he is wrong.[7] Do not repeat the same series. Merely give him another chance with another series. Failure owing to interruption does not count. [While uttering the numbers or syllables, hold up the hand or finger to prevent the child starting to reply, before the entire phrase or list has been completed. Drop the hand as a signal to child that you have finished and he is to begin.]

Evaluation. **One correct repetition** out of **three trials** counts as success. Note, therefore, the longest number the child can repeat. The age at which series of different lengths can be repeated is given in the last column above.

The repetition of figures in their natural order, *e.g.*, 9 6 4 5 6 7 8, should be noticed as an instance of automatism. The "perseveration" of correct numbers, given in the wrong order, is also of interest, though rarer.

3.—Naming Own Sex.

Procedure. **"Are you a little boy or a little girl ? "** (for a boy). **"Are you a little girl or a little boy ? "** (for a girl).

The words "girl" and "boy" should be clearly and equally emphasised.

If the child says "yes" or "no," or merely echoes part of the phrase, repeat the question in the same form. [Dr. Simon does not, with some

---

words serve to rouse the child's attention and accommodate his ear to the stranger's voice, before the really important words are uttered. In deference, however, to the representations of Mr. Dumville and others, and to Binet's own language, I have finally adopted, both here and elsewhere, the imperative. In a vote taken among some 300 teachers the majority (64 per cent.) favoured the imperative; the minority were chiefly mistresses in infants' schools. According to Dr. Simon, the examiner should never use the prhase "Will you . . . ? " But I am told that the French equivalent for this interrogatory form would appear somewhat strained and circumlocutory when used with very young children.

(4) Dr. Simon considers "Put your finger on " to be too definite and exact. It is, however, used by Binet (*Development of Intelligence*, p. 185).

(5) Dr. Simon would not encourage the child too freely; but he would also not insist too precisely that each of the three injunctions should be successfully performed.

(6) Repeating eight numbers appears harder than the hardest of the tests assigned to age XVI below. Terman would assign it to the level of " Superior Adults."

(7) There is, as Dr. Simon observes, no harm in saying : " That was nearly right," or " Try again ; listen carefully "——phrases which imply that a mistake has been made. It is not the information, but the discouragement that the examiner should guard against.

D

translators, allow the examiner to ask the two questions separately : " Are you a little girl ? " " Are you a little boy ? " Even then, it would be well to revert to the original form, to detect happy guesses.]

4.—Giving Surname.

Procedure. " **What is your name ?** " If the child merely gives his Christian name, ask, " **And what else ?** " . . . . [Tommy] what ? . . . . [" What is your mother's (daddy's) name ? " (Melville.) " What do they call your mother ? . . . . Mrs. . . . . what ? " (Dumville—much easier form).]

Evaluation. If child gives the surname he has sometimes been known by —*e.g.*, stepfather's, or mother's (when illegitimate)—record it as correct.

5.—Naming Simple Objects.

Materials. (i) A **penny**, (ii) a closed pocket **knife**, and (iii) a common kind of **key**.

Procedure. " **What is that ?** " [or, " What is this called ? "], showing each object successively.

Evaluation. **All three** must be named, but slight errors, such as " money," " pennies," " halfpenny " for " a penny " are allowable.

The average order of ease is—penny, key, knife ; a pocket-knife, particularly closed, is not familiar to poorer children at this age. A table-knife (used by Winch) would be much easier. [Terman adds (iv) a watch, (v) a lead pencil ; and requires three correct responses out of five.]

[Suggestibility may often be evoked by first asking the child to point to certain objects named, and then giving names of objects that are not in front of him, or inventing meaningless names. The same procedure may be adopted with the following test.]

6.—Describing Pictures.

Materials. Binet's three pictures—chosen as containing people, and suggesting a story, and having a certain standardised difficulty. (See Figures 9 (*a*), (*b*), and (*c*), pp. 81–5, Appendix II.)

There can, I think, be little doubt that pictures better printed, larger, coloured (as Saffiotti's), representing actions in progress (as Bobertag's), showing children[1] (as both Bobertag's and Saffiotti's), would be much more appropriate than Binet's original engravings. Many investigators use pictures of their own. But the above alone have been standardized ; and, as Dr. Simon adds, *tout est là !*

Procedure. " **Look at this picture and tell me all about it.** " Binet's instructions are : " What is this " ; and, if the child says, " a picture," " Tell me what you see there." It seems better, however, to avoid leading phrases like " What can you see in it ? " (which suggests enumeration), and " What are they doing ? " (which suggests interpretation). Repeat instructions **once** for each picture, if there is no answer. [Words of praise or encouragement alone may be added : " Isn't it a pretty picture ? . . . . Do you like it ? " Or even, " That's right," if the child is on the point of saying something, but is withheld by shyness.]

Evaluation of Replies. Record the type of response given to the first

---

(1) Binet originally introduced picture-tests to determine the interests and temperamental characteristics of children as well as their mental level. Pictures containing children are helpful because the child tested then more readily identifies himself with the principal figure.

picture. If doubtful, use the second and third, and record the type of response most frequently given, *i.e.*, employed for **two pictures out of three.** Binet distinguishes three types of response corresponding to three stages of development.

A. *Enumeration* (E). (Age III.)

Replies giving a mere list of persons, objects, or details.

E.g., (i) " A man, boy."
    (ii) " There's an old man and a lady," etc.
    (iii) " I can see a room with a chair, a table, and a looking-glass and there's a man and a sofa."

Two items at least should be enumerated. If the child only gives one, do not ask, " Anything else ? " but proceed to another picture. [Terman requires three items in at least one picture out of three, given without urging.]

One may also distinguish and note : (i) enumeration of people only ; (ii) enumeration also of objects—not common until age four.

For Enumeration the average order of ease with the three pictures appears to be (i) man and woman, (ii) man and boy, (iii) convict.

B. *Description* (D). (Age VI.)

Phrases indicating actions or characteristics. *E.g.*,

    (i) " They're pulling a cart."
    (ii) " A man and a woman sitting on a seat." " An old man asleep."
    (iii) " A man standing on a bed and trying to look out of the window." " A man looking at himself in the glass."

For Description, the average order of ease is, in my results : (i) convict, (ii) man and woman, (iii) man and boy. This, however, is probably dependent on the order in which they are given. A child, having given enumerations for the first or first and second, may feel impelled to do more for the later picture. Intrinsically the man and boy would seem easiest for description.

C. *Interpretation* (I). (Age XII.)

Replies going beyond what is actually visible in the picture, and mentioning the situation or emotion it suggests. *E.g.*,

    (i) " They're moving." " They've a heavy load." " They can't pay their rent." " A rag-picker."
    (ii) " Miserable." " Poor." " Have no home." " The man is saying his prayers." " His daughter " (or " wife ") " is sitting beside him." " A man in trouble."
    (iii) " A prisoner." " He wants to get out." " He's trying to see what's in the yard." " He's lonely " or " thinking." " A man on board ship."

For Interpretation, the average order of ease appears to be : (i) man and woman, (ii) convict, (iii) man and boy. The first lends itself to sentimental comments. With the second *what* the man sees is usually what the child imagines *he* would see (*e.g.*, his own back yard). By encouraging the children to talk about the pictures considerable insight may be obtained into the child's inner life, especially with the neurotic (cf. below, p. 362).

AGE IV.

7.—Repeating Syllables.

Procedure. "**Listen**" ["Listen again," if this is not the first memory test] "**and say this after me.**" The phrases should be pronounced **deliberately and with expression.** Begin with (iii); but if the child remains silent the examiner may give him first a shorter sentence (i or ii), and then, apparently, try (iii) again.

The sentences to which no age is assigned should be given to provide a little incidental practice. [For the shorter sentences, a more suitable form is, "Can you say 'father'?" "Now say...." etc.]

(i)	(2 syllables)	"**Father.**"
(ii)	(4 syllables)	"**My hat and shoes.**"
(iii)	(6 syllables)	"**I am cold and hungry.**" (Age IV.)
(iv)	(8 syllables)	"**Here is the cloth ; my hands are clean.**"
(v)	(0 syllables)	"**His name is Jack ; he's such a naughty dog.**" (Age V.)
(vi)	(12 syllables)	"**It is raining outside ; and Tom is working hard.**"
(vii)	(14 syllables)	"**We were having a jolly game ; I caught a little mouse.**"
(viii)	(16 syllables)	"**We are going for a walk ; will you give me that pretty bonnet ?**" (Age VI.)
(ix)	(18 syllables)	"**Mabel has just torn her frock ; I have given twopence to that poor beggar.**"
(x)	(20 syllables)	"**We should never be cruel to birds. It is night ; and we are all going to bed.**"
(xi)	(26 syllables)	"**The other morning I saw in the street a tiny yellow dog ; little Maurice has spoilt his new apron.**" (Age XIV.)

Evaluation. Allow **no error** at all, except mispronunciations due to speech defects. [Binet's sentences appear to have been deliberately composed of two clauses.[1] This seems unfortunate, as even an intelligent child may accidentally forget one. In translating them I have endeavoured to keep the general sense of the original, while making the phraseology more natural for a child than a literal rendering would be. Winch (like Terman and others) uses a single connected sentence ; but (in a letter to me) agrees that a disconnected sentence is necessary for strict comparability. Winch requires two correct, Terman one, out of three sentences of the same length.]

8.—Repeating Numbers.

Procedure. "**Listen : and say these numbers after me.**"
(For use only after failure in first set.)
"**9 1 4**" | "**2 8 6**" "**5 3 9**"

Evaluation. **One correct repetition** out of **three trials** counts as success. (See p. 25. Test 2.)

---

[1] Dr. Simon thinks that the recurrent disjunction is "ni voulu, ni essentiel." He adds, however, that in preliminary trials of a chance assortment those sentences were probably found to present least difficulty to the child's comprehension which happened to consist of two separate clauses. But it is the disjunction of sense rather than of syntax that confuses the bright child's memory.

9.—Counting Pennies.

A. 4 *Pennies.* (Age IV.)

Materials. 4 pennies placed, not in a row,[1] but haphazard, though without touching each other.

Procedure. **" Do you see these pennies ? Count them, and tell me how many there are."**

If the child at first answers at random, add : **" Count them aloud,"** or **" Count them with your finger."** [" Point to (touch) each penny as you count it " Dr. Simon considers too specific. It might be of interest to see if the child who has failed with the bare command can do the test when shown how ; *e.g.,* as Terman recommends : " Count like this : one, two—" touching the first two with the finger as each is counted. But do not use an answer thus elicited for strict comparisons.]

Evaluation. **Two attempts** may apparently be allowed ; since, according to Binet, the first random answer, if wrong, does not count as a failure. Binet and Terman insist that the child shall **point accurately,** and not merely give the right number at the end.

Note if the child can count verbally by giving the numbers mechanically in correct sequence, without being able to count practically, *i.e.,* to apply the numbers correctly to successive objects.

B. 13 *Pennies.* (Age VI.) *Procedure,* etc., as before.

10.—Comparing Two Lines.

Materials. Two parallel horizontal lines, 5 cm. and 6 cm. (2 in. and 2⅖ in.) respectively, previously drawn in ink on a card or paper, the longer 3 cm. (about 1¼ in.) below the shorter, with its centre under that of the other. (See Figure 10, p. 87, Appendix II.) (Dr. Lewis suggests to me from his experience that for a genuine test two or three sticks evoke better replies.)

Procedure. **" Do you see these lines ? Which is the longer ? "** [" Put your finger on the longest (biggest) one."—Terman.][2]

Evaluation. **No hesitation** is allowed.

[Some investigators allow the examiner to repeat the instruction. English children will often respond more readily to the injunction : " Put your finger on the long one." But Binet insists that the child shall not only perceive the difference, but also understand, without any further help, that the phrase " the longer " implies making a comparison. Miss Johnston, however, tells me Binet allowed her to use the positive form " long." Personally, I find it rare for a child to respond to the latter and not to the former. If there is the least likelihood that the child is guessing, turn the card round and repeat. All responses must apparently be correct. Terman requires three correct responses out of three, or five out of six.]

---

[1] Binet's direction is translated " side by side " (*loc. cit.,* p. 200) ; but Dr. Simon says definitely " not in a row." [I place the four coins at the four corners of a diamond, and the thirteen coins with five along each of the two axes of a diamond and three along each of the four sides, always disturbing a little the regularity both of my movements and of the rows, so as to suggest no definite method to the child.]

[2] Mr. Dumville suggests to me the following formulæ for Tests 10, 11, 19 : " One of these lines (boxes, faces) is longer (heavier, prettier). Which is it ? (Find out which box it is.)" This avoids many difficulties, but appears to lighten the difficulty of the test. I find " tell me which . . ." more provocative than " show me which . . .", or simply, " which . . ." ; but Dr. Simon expressly prefers the two last ; and rejects such a phrase as " the long one."

11.—Comparing Faces.

Materials. Binet's six faces, shown two only at a time. (See Figure 11 (*a*), (*b*), and (*c*), pp. 89–93, Appendix II.)

Procedure. "**Which is the prettier of these two faces?**"[1] [If "prettier" seems not to be understood, "prettiest," or "which do you like the best of these two ladies," or "which is the nice one," may evoke correct answers. But these last two should not be counted for purposes of strict comparison. Some "like" the ugly ones best, because they are funny.]

I. using Binet's original plates, which show all three pairs on one page, it is better to cover the lower while dealing with the first or second.

Evaluation. **All three comparisons** must be correctly made on the **first attempt. Repeat the questions once, if silence makes it necessary.**

[Not a few intelligent children, with some accuracy, tell the examiner that Binet's pictures are "all ugly." In such a case, ask "which is the least ugly?" Winch's pictures show clearer differences, but make the test easier.]

AGE V.

12.—Performing a Triple Order.

Materials. Key and book, appropriately placed. Arrange the room while the child is carrying out one of the drawing or writing tests, or better before the interview begins ; unless compelled, the examiner should not allow himself or the child to be distracted from the text.

Procedure. "**Do you see this key? Go and put it on the table. Then shut the door. And after that, bring me the book that is on the chair near the door. Do you understand? First, put the key on the table ; then shut the door ; then bring me the book.**" [Note repetition of instructions. Do not let the child commence until this is completed. Detain him by the arm rather than risk breaking your injunction to say, "Stop, I haven't finished yet." Point to the objects as you mention them.]

Evaluation. **All three** commissions must be performed spontaneously **without any further instructions** or hint. [If the child hesitates for long, he may be urged by saying, "Well, and what now?" "What have you forgotten?" But no success evoked by such prompting should be assigned to his credit. Accept variations in the order ; but note them as of possible diagnostic significance. Terman insists on the order being correct. Binet says "put the key on the chair." Hence, correct order would mean coming back to the chair. But I understand this additional complication was not intentional.]

13.—Drawing a Square from Copy.

Materials. A square, each side measuring about 3 to 4 cm. (1½ inches), drawn beforehand in ink, preferably on a card. (See Figure 12, p. 95, Appendix II.) Plain paper. Pen and ink [deliberately advised by Binet, making the task more difficult. Most American adapters and most English teachers prefer pencil].

Procedure. "**I want you to copy this for me**" (pointing to square). "**Draw it here**" (handing pen and paper). [If encouragement is needed : "What do you think this shape (picture) is? See if you can make one like it." Do not use the word "square" yourself. Allow left-handed children to use the left hand, if they prefer ; but note the fact.]

---

[1] See footnote to preceding test.

FIGURE 1

Test 13. Copying a Square.

Evaluation of Results. Binet's Examples of Satisfactory and Unsatisfactory Reproductions.

Satisfactory.

Unsatisfactory.

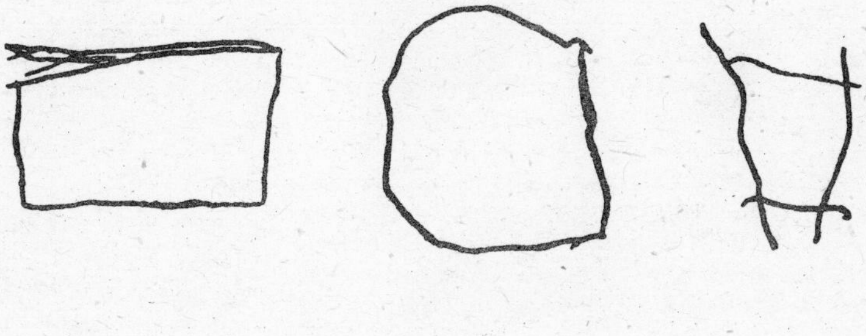

Evaluation. (See Figure 1.) The drawing passes if it can be **recognised as an attempt at a square**. It should have the four sides fairly distinct, the four angles roughly right angles, and should be more like a square than a decided oblong, *i.e.*, an oblong equivalent in shape to two juxtaposed squares. If one side is twice the other, if the lines cross considerably at the corners or bend round without any angles, then the drawing fails. The size (usually reduced) does not matter. Permit **only one attempt**. [The test should take about one minute (Bobertag). Goddard apparently allows the child as many attempts as he wishes. I should only allow a second attempt if the child started afresh spontaneously before completing the first.]

[Terman requires three attempts with pencil, and one out of three correct : and thus can note improvement or fatigue of attention, and auto-criticism as shown by the child's own selection of a best attempt.]

Note how far the defects of the attempt are due to difficulties with the instrument (nib, penholder, ink, etc.) rather than with the figure to be drawn.

Note the child's power of self-criticism (" Have you copied it correctly ? " " What is wrong ? "). Excessive satisfaction with an unsuccessful reproduction is significant.

Observe whether the child looks at the copy only before he commences, or also after he has finished to compare it with his product, or repeatedly during the process of drawing. Observe also if he turns the paper round for each successive line.

In a detailed investigation, mark on the child's copy, by the method shown in Figure 2 : (i) the order, (ii) the direction of the lines, as they are drawn. According to age, teaching, and manual ability, children vary greatly in their procedure. The following features appear to characterise the better drawings and to indicate higher manual skill : (i) starting from the top left-hand corner rather than from any other corner (the latter, however, is rare) (Figure 2, *a*, *b*, and *c*) ; (ii) drawing both horizontals from left to right and both verticals from above downwards (Figure 2, *a* and *b*) ; and, as a consequence, (iii) commencing three or four lines discontinuously (*i.e.*, starting from a point other than where the last line left off) (Figure 2, *b*) rather than continuously with the last (Figure 2, *c* and *d*) ; (iv) drawing all four lines continuously (Figure 2, *c* and *d*) rather than drawing the first pair continuously and then starting a second continuous pair discontinuously with the first pair (Figure 2, *a*) ; (v) in continuous drawing, drawing in clockwise direction (starting with top horizontal) (Figure 2, *c*) rather than counter-clockwise (starting with left-hand vertical) (Figure 2, *d*) ; (vi) where all lines or pairs of lines are drawn discontinuously, starting with the (left-hand) vertical (Figure 2, *b*) rather than with the (top) horizontal (Figure 2, *a*) (the former, however, appears late and may be due to teaching) ; in (v) and (vi) the differences are perhaps significant only in younger children : in either case the later method—though still characteristic of backward individuals is commoner than the former among older children. Very rarely does a child start by drawing two opposite and parallel lines.

14.—Repeating Syllables.

(10 syllables) **" His name is Jack ; he's such a naughty dog."** (For *Procedure* and *Evaluation*, see p. 28, Test 7, No. v.)

FIGURE 2.

Test 13. Copying a Square.

Order and Direction in which the Lines are Drawn.

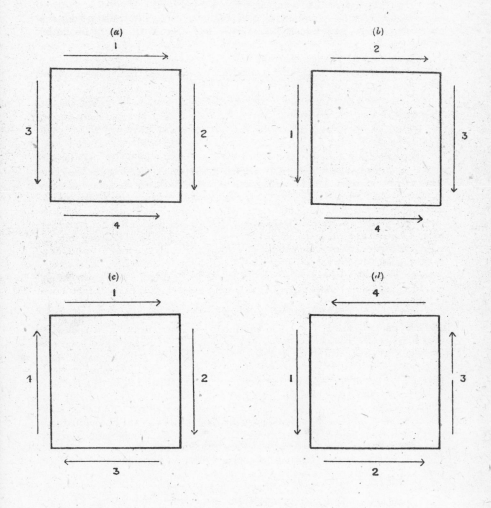

15.—Giving Age.

Procedure. " **How old are you ?** "

Evaluation. Child should give his age last birthday in years. [However certain the child appears, always, if possible, verify the response.]

Note : children very often say " seven " when they mean " getting on for seven." Hence, if the first answer seems wrong, ask specifically : " How old were you last birthday ? " Parents occasionally give an infant entering school and a child about to leave school an age above the true one ; and dull children (except when about to leave) an age below the real one. The child's answer should be accepted if it corresponds with what it has commonly or recently been told. In such cases do not insist too rigidly that the child shall give an age identical with the age given by the birth certificate or register. [Note extenuating circumstances—*e.g.*, life in orphanage or neglected home where the child may have never heard his age, or celebrated his birthday.]

16.—Distinguishing Morning and Afternoon.

Procedure. " **Is it morning or afternoon now ?** " (in the morning) ; or, " **Is it afternoon or morning now ?** " (in the afternoon).

Evaluation. **Repeat** the question, if there is any possibility of the child having merely echoed one of the words thoughtlessly. [The questions : " Have you had your dinner yet ? " " What will it be after tea ? " . . . " just after you have had breakfast to-morrow morning ? " elicit answers of interest for comparison with the above.]

17.—Naming Four Primary Colours.

Materials. Four oblong pieces of paper, 2×6 cm. ($\frac{4}{5} \times 1\frac{2}{5}$ in.), coloured bright (" saturated ") red, yellow, blue, and green, and gummed beneath one another on a card. (See Figure 13, p. 97, Appendix II.)

Procedure. " **What colour is this ?** " pointing to each in turn.

Evaluation. **No error and no second attempts** are allowed. The test should take about **6 secs**. But the time-limit does not appear to be strictly enforced. (" Scarlet " or " pink " is accepted for the red. If colour-blindness is suspected, test the child by requiring it to match shades of wool.)

The order of difficulty appears to be : (i) Red, (ii) Green, (iii) Blue, (iv) Yellow (undoubtedly hardest).

18.—Repeating Numbers.

Procedure. " **Listen, and say these numbers after me.** "

(For use only after failure in first set.)

" **3 6 8 1** " | " **5 7 4 9** "   " **8 5 2 6** "

Evaluation. **One correct repetition** out of **three trials** counts as success. (See p. 25, Test 2.)

[The repetition of four numbers is included by Binet in neither the 1908 nor the 1911 scale. Most investigators have used it for practice ; and it is embodied in the versions of Yerkes and Terman.]

19.—Comparing Two Weights.

Materials. Four small similar boxes (about $1 \cdot 5 \times 2 \cdot 5 \times 3 \cdot 5$ cm.) ($\frac{3}{5} \times 1 \times 1\frac{2}{5}$ inches) weighing 3, 12, 6, and 15 grams.

Procedure. " **You see these boxes** " (showing first the pair weighing 3 and 12 grams placed 5 or 6 cm. apart). " **Which is the heavier ?** " [or " heaviest "].[1]

If the child merely points, add without any gesture : " **Take them in your hands and weigh them.**" [A shy child may be encouraged by first asking : "How can you find out ?" English children respond better to the instruction "Lift them" or "Feel them, and give me the heavy one." But do not use this modification if strict comparability is required. Kuhlman and the Stanford Revision allow a demonstration : Binet and Yerkes, for the test proper, prohibit it. In any case, do not put them in his hands. If he merely lifts one, or both together, do not correct him. If the child fails completely to understand, it is then interesting to put them successively into his hand, and ask "Which is the heavier ?" But his response in this case does not count. If there is any suspicion that the first success may have been due to chance, repeat the experiment with another pair (6 and 15 grams) ; and then with the first pair again. It would probably be advisable to make three trials in every case, although Binet does not enjoin this.]

Evaluation. **All three trials** (except the first random guess) must apparently be correct ; if in any doubt, continue the repetitions. [Terman accepts two out of three.]

Note if the child fails to weigh them in his hand, until so instructed, or if he merely arranges them in a pile or a row.

Note the child's procedure : mere inspection, shaking, listening, simultaneous lifting, successive lifting, same hand, different hands, use of fingers, palm, back of hand, single movement, repeated movement up and down, repeated trials, etc. The child's spontaneous procedure is so distinctive that the help suggested above should not be given too readily.

AGE VI.

20.—Giving Number of Fingers.

Procedure. " **How many fingers have you on your right hand ?** " . . . " **And how many on your left hand ?** " . . . " **How many does that make on both hands together ?** " If the child attempts to count, prevent him, saying : " No, don't count."

Evaluation. The replies must be made **without stopping to count ;** and **all three questions**[2] must be correctly answered. " Four . . . Four . . . Eight "—apparently exclusive of thumbs—may be accepted.

Note automatisms, or sequence of numbers, *e.g.,* " Five . . . Five . . . Five," or " Five . . . Five . . . Six."

21.—Counting Thirteen Pennies.

Materials. 13 pennies placed haphazard. [See footnote ([1]) p. 29.]

Procedure and *Evaluation.* (See Test 9 B., p. 29.)

([1]) See footnote to Test 10. Binet's formula is : " Tell me which is . . ." (*loc. cit.,* p. 196). Dr. Simon thinks " Give me . . ." is perhaps preferable."

([2]) So Binet states quite explicitly. Dr. Simon, however, says : " Cette décomposition simplifie l'épreuve. Il faut demander doublée : (How many fingers have you on both your hands together ?)."

22.—Drawing Diamond from Copy.

Materials. A diamond or rhombus, about 7 cm. (2¾ inches) high, and 4 cm. (1½ inches) across, with sides 4 cm. long, drawn as before on a card. (See Figure 14, p. 99, Appendix II.) Paper, pen, and ink.

Procedure. ["**Now I want you to**[1]] **copy this for me**" (pointing to diamond). "**Draw it here**" (handing pen and paper).

Evaluation. (See Figure 3 for Binet's samples.) The drawing passes **if it can be recognised** as a diamond. Binet requires at least one pair of opposite angles to be fairly equal, at least one pair of adjacent sides to be fairly equal, and the vertical diameter to be longer. Absolute parallelism of the opposite sides is not insisted upon. The pass-standard is thus considerably below what an uninstructed teacher would be apt to accept as a satisfactory reproduction.

Points analogous to those specified above (p. 32) as worthy of notice in the case of the square may be noted in the case of the diamond. The following features are common in the successful drawings, but their diagnostic significance is small, as they are frequently found also in the unsuccessful drawings : (i) Drawing the upper left-hand line first, as Figure 4 (*a*) and (*b*) (other methods are rare) ; (ii) starting from the top corner rather than from left-hand corner as Figure 4 (*b*) ; (iii) drawing every line downward, as Figure 4 (*b*) ; (iv) completely or incompletely discontinuous drawing, rather than completely continuous drawing (as Figure 4 (*a*) : comparatively rare) ; (v) incompletely continuous drawing, proceeding clockwise, as Figure 4 (*a*) (especially if starting from the left-hand corner) rather than counter-clockwise ; (vi) drawing the side pairs continuously (the second pair commenced discontinuously), as Figure 4 (*b*), rather than the top two continuously and the bottom two continuously ; (vii) drawing all lines discontinuously rather than drawing only one pair continuously (when only one **pair is so drawn**, it is usually the right-hand pair, drawn last) ; (viii) of those that are drawn upward, the top-left is the commonest, as Figure 4 (*a*) ; the bottom right the next commonest ; such movements are facilitated by twisting the paper a little clockwise. As a rule, one of the other lines is drawn upwards only when it is the last line in continuous drawing.

23.—Transcription.

Materials. "**See little Paul**" written, with the two capitals as indicated, in a bold, copy-book handwriting on a card or sheet of paper. (See Figure 15, p. 101, Appendix II.) Paper, pen and ink.

Procedure. "**Will you copy that for me ?**" [Allow left-handed children to use the left hand, if they prefer ; but note the fact.]

Evaluation. The test is passed, if the copy is **sufficiently legible to be read** by a person who did not know what was to be written.

Teachers should note that, despite appearances, it is a test neither of calligraphy nor of orthography.

24.—Naming Days of the Week.

Procedure. "**[Can you tell me] what are the days of the week ?**"

Evaluation. The days must be named in order, **without error** or hesitation, **in 10 secs.** Some children, beginning at "Monday," fail at first by

---

[1] It is usually convenient to ask for the copy of the diamond immediately after the square has been drawn ; and some such little circumlocution makes the transition from test to test a little less austere. Dr. Simon, however, writes : "Draw this here, please—ne suffit-il pas ? " And many teachers, as noted above, prefer throughout the brief curt command.

FIGURE 3.

Test 22. Copying a Diamond.

Binet's Examples of Satisfactory and Unsatisfactory Reproductions.

Satisfactory.

  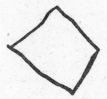

Unsatisfactory.

FIGURE 4.

Test 22. Copying a Diamond.

Order and Direction in which the Lines are Drawn.[1]

(*a*). Scheme to illustrate the commonest type and method among the younger or duller children.

(*b*). Commonest method among the older or brighter children.

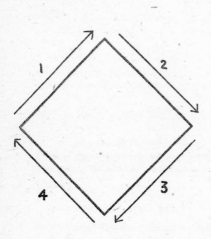

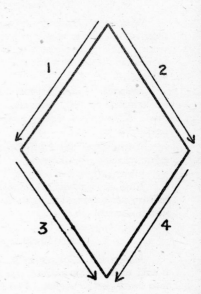

---

[1] My results differ somewhat from those of Mr. Winch's (*Child Study*, VII. No. 6, p. 103, where also Figs. 1 and 2 are, apparently by a printer's error, identical). But Mr. Winch's copy appears to have been a square, not, as Binet's, a rhombus. In figure (*a*) above it will be noted that the method tends to result in a rough square, and, since the vertical diameter is not longer than the horizontal, fails.

forgetting " Sunday " at the end ; [allow correction, if 10 secs. has not expired]. Backward children often succeed eventually with encouragement, but not within the time-limit. Such successes should not count as satisfactory.

The order for ease of remembrance, judged by average infrequency of omission, appears to be approximately : (i) Monday, (ii) Tuesday, (iii) Saturday, (iv) Wednesday, (v) Sunday, (vi) Friday, (vii) Thursday (by far the most frequently omitted).

[Terman asks also " What day comes before . . . Tuesday ? " etc., and requires two such questions to be correctly answered. A common and yet more useful type of question is : " What is the day after to-morrow ? " " What was the day before yesterday ? " But application is always harder than mechanical repetition.]

Note especially what may be termed circular automatism (recommencing, when the series has been completely enumerated).

25.—Naming the Four Commonest Coins.

Materials. Four common coins, ½d., 6d., 1d., 1s.,[1] placed heads uppermost in this order in a row upon the table. The coins should be but little worn ; the copper pieces should not be new. [It will generally be convenient to combine Test 43 with the present test by using all the nine commoner coins.]

Procedure. Ask " What is this ? " pointing to each of the coins in succession. Neither examiner nor child should handle them or turn them over. (If the child replies " money," ask : " Yes ; but what do we call this particular piece ? ")

Evaluation. All four should be named correctly to pass Test 25. No error whatever is allowed.

[Terman requires only three out of four to be correctly named.]

Note any special circumstance (*a*) facilitating or (*b*) impeding a satisfactory performance in this and other money tests, *e.g.*, (*a*) selling papers, (*b*) institution life.

26.—Reconstructing Divided Oblong Card.

Materials. Two cards the size of a lady's visiting card (about 6 cm. × 9 cm., or 2¼ × 3½ inches), one intact, the other divided along one diagonal into two equal triangles. Place the triangles so that the longest sides (hypotenuses) are at right angles,[2] but do not face towards each other.[3] (See Figure 5.)

[Before cutting the card, black one side. This does not appear to alter the difficulty of the test ; but prevents turning over.[4]]

Procedure. " One of my cards has been cut in two ; can you put the pieces together again to make a whole one like this ? " (pointing to the intact one).

---

[1] The highest of the coins mentioned by Binet is the 5-franc piece, not the 1 franc ; but with English children the 5-shilling piece would hardly be included among " les 4 pièces de monnaie usuelles." Dr. Simon would agree with the substitution of the shilling, if experience showed that it kept the test nearer to the original age-assignment, as, of course, it does.

[2] Binet and Simon (tr. Town). *Method of Measuring Development of Intelligence*, p. 25 (1911 scale).

[3] Binet and Simon (tr. Kite). *Development of Intelligence*, p. 199 (1908 scale). The latter instruction rules out Melville's position ; the former rules out Terman's (which is easier) and Safflotti's and. Winch's (first) position (both of which are harder and necessitate turning over).

[4] In Dr. Simon's procedure I understand that there is an actual difference of tint on the two sides, one being a deeper grey.

If the child merely looks at the cards without touching them, say : " Move them about and see if you can fit them together " ; and, if necessary, place one in his hand.

See that the child does not turn one triangle over. If the child makes a wrong combination and appeals for judgment, give no opinion. Remain silent ; or say merely, " What do *you* think ? " [Drummond and Melville allow the irregular shape obtained by putting diagonals together, with one card turned over. This is surely, in Dr. Simon's phrase, *trops indulgents*.]

Evaluation. [Allow ½ min., Bobertag.] A child sometimes sits contemplating a wrong combination ; and it is difficult to know whether this represents his final attempt. In this case do not judge it too hastily, but ask : " Is that right ? "[1]

[Terman requires two successes out of three trials—somewhat conventionally defined.] **Note the child's procedure,** which is usually far more significant than the mere fact of failure or success, *e.g.*, a single combination alone attempted, the same combination repeated, systematic investigation of many combinations, uncritical acceptance of impossible combinations, superposition or juxtaposition of intact card.

27.—Defining Concrete Terms.

Procedure. " What is . . ."

(i) . . . " a horse ? "
(ii) . . . " a chair ? "
(iii) . . . " a mother ? " [McIntyre and Rogers, " school " ; Bobertag " soldier "].
(iv) . . . " a table ? " [Bobertag, " doll " ; Yerkes, " baby "].
(v) . . . " a fork ? " [Yerkes, " spoon "].

[For age V. Terman substitutes " doll " for " mother " and adds (vi) " pencil " ; and for age VIII. uses (i) balloon, (ii) tiger, (iii) football, (iv) soldier, or, if any is unfamiliar, automobile, battleship, potato, store. A word used with success by many school medical officers in England is " kitten " or " cat."]

Binet's order is (i) fork, (ii) table, (iii) chair, (iv) horse, (v) mother. But " fork " is a most difficult word to begin with ; and it is better to place " chair " before " table," else the child may think first of the multiplication table.[2] [If a child uses " thing " or " something " for " horse " or " chair," then, " mother," or perhaps " horse " (if not already given), should follow, otherwise even a bright child having given " thing " for " chair," " table," and " fork " without correction, is apt from sheer inertia to offer " thing " as the genus of " horse."] The best order, therefore, appears to be as above. But even so, a bright boy may reply for both " chair " and " horse " with the automatism " it has got legs." If so, proceed at once to " fork ".

The instructions may be repeated ; but use no other form of words. [A child is often at first silent in this test. Urge him by saying : " You have seen a horse, haven't you ? " " You know what a chair is ? " (Beware of saying " What is a chair like ? " or " for ? " " What does a horse do ? ") Give the child a minute to reply.—Melville.]

---

[1] Or better, says Dr. Simon : " ' Ça y est ? ' avec le sens de : ' avez-vous fini ? ' " But " Have you finished ? " or its equivalents in English often provokes a hesitant child to say " Yes " impulsively, just as perhaps " Is that right ? " conveys the opposite suggestion.

[2] Dr. Simon agrees : " L'ordre que nous indiquions n'avait rien d'impératif. L'ordre proposé est en effet meilleur."

FIGURE 5.

Test 26. Divided Card.

Position of Intact and Divided Cards as shown to the child.[1]

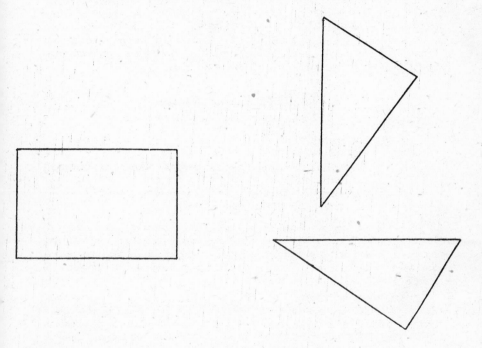

---

[1] This arrangement appears to be that adopted by Dr. Simon. But before one of our number attended his classes, we interpreted Binet's description to mean (as Mr. Winch also interpreted it) that "the two hypotenuses (the edges to be joined) should be far away from each other as possible" (*Child Study*, Vol. VII, No. 3, p. 42), though still remaining (contrary to Mr. Winch's interpretation) at right angles. This resulted in an arrangement which would be given by interchanging the top or bottom triangles as above shown. The inclusion of these earlier results may possibly have made the test appear a little harder than it should, although I can find no clear evidence of this.

E

Evaluation of Replies. The character of **three replies out of five** determines the value of the test.

The following are the commoner types of definition. Note "U" or "C," according as child defines (A) in terms of Use, or (B) in terms superior to Use, *e.g.*, in terms of Class.

A. **Use** includes either (1) Action, *i.e.*, Functional Use ; or (2) Purpose, *i.e.*, Use for Us, and denotes a mental level of age VI., *e.g.* :—

> (*a*) "it runs, draws a cart" (= A. 1) ; "it is to pull our things along" (= A. 2).
> (*b*) "she minds the babies."
> (*c*) "*something* to have your dinner on" ; "where the plates are put" ; "something you eat with" (relative pronoun omitted).
> (*d*) "*what* you eat *with*" ; "you have it *for* a meal."

The order of difficulty for Use (treating terms superior to use as including knowledge of Use) is : (i) chair, (ii) table, (iii) horse, (iv) mother, (v) fork.

B. Terms **superior to Use** include either (1) Class or Genus (with or without "Differentia"), or (2) Description (including colour, shape, size, structure, substance, etc.) ; and are taken to denote a mental level of age X., *e.g.* :—

> (*a*) "an animal."
> (*b*) "*a thing to* sit on" ; "*something that* you pick up your food with." ("Thing" and "something," however, are not accepted for "horse" or "mother.")
> (*c*) "a lady" ("a woman" is less common among poor children ; "a parent" at this age rarer still).
> (*d*) "*one who* cooks our dinners."
> (*e*) "got four legs" ; "it's silver."
> (*f*) "a piece of wood" ; "part of the furniture."
> (*g*) "an *instrument* to eat with" ; "an *article* to sit on."

The order of difficulty for Class (or other terms superior to use) is : (i) horse, (ii) table, (iii) mother, (iv) chair, (v) fork.

The variations in the age-assignments of definition superior to use depend largely on the inclusion of such replies as B (*b*), (*d*), (*e*), and (*f*), under A rather than under B.

It will be seen that the distinction between A (*c*) and B (*b*) is somewhat arbitrary ; but it seems to correspond with the spirit of Binet's examples, and with a genuine difference in mental level.[1] Saffiotti appears to exclude description from definition "superior to use" ; and many older defectives below the level of age X. are prone to describe.

Yerkes omits "mother" ; and gives 1 point for definition by use and 2 for definition superior to use.

[Many classifications of children's definitions have been attempted. For example, McIntyre and Rogers discriminate the following types : (1) Purely Functional ; (2) Prelogical Classification, with Function ; (3) Pure Description ; (4) Prelogical Classification, with Description ; (5) (Pure) Classification, Logical, but with no Specification ; (6) Logical Definition (Logical Class, specified by adding Description and Functions). No simple division precisely corresponds with a difference of intellect. Logical relevance and complexity are perhaps most significant.]

---

[1] Dr. Simon also accepts it.

Emotional attitudes are often conspicuous in this test—older children are sometimes amused, sometimes confused, by being asked so simple a question as "What is a chair ? "; while "What is a mother ?" often arouses emotional embarrassment.

28.—Repeating Numbers.

Procedure. " Listen, and say these numbers after me."

(For use only after failure in first set.)

" 5 2 9 4 7 " | " 6 3 8 5 2 " " 9 7 3 1 8 "

Evaluation. One correct repetition out of three trials counts as success. (See p. 25, Test 2.)

29.—Describing Pictures : Mere Description (D.)

Procedure. (See p. 27, Test 6 B.)

Evaluation. The child should use phrases indicating actions and characteristics. *E.g.,*

(i) " They're pulling a cart."

(ii) " A man and a woman sitting on a seat." " An old man asleep."

(iii) " A man standing on a bed and trying to look out of the window." " A man looking at himself in the glass."

30.—Repeating Syllables.

(16 syllables) " We are going for a walk ; will you give me that pretty bonnet ? "

Procedure and *Evaluation.* (See p. 28, Test 7, viii.)

31.—Distinguishing Right and Left.

Procedure. (1) " Show me your right hand " . . . (2) " Show me your left ear."

Evaluation. The child must perform both correctly without any kind of help. Hesitation and self-correction (without any hint) are allowed ; if by a slip the child shows his left hand or right ear, the experimenter waits a moment for a spontaneous correction, which is allowed to pass, but his manner of waiting should not suggest that the first action was wrong. If the correction is itself incorrect, the child fails.

[Terman adds : (3) " Show me your right eye " ; and requires three correct answers out of three, or five out of six. Dr. Lewis suggests left leg.]

Note uncertainty or confusion, as distinct from ignorance ; and any cue or clue (hand used for writing, hand marked by scar, etc.). If the child fails in right and left, can it distinguish up and down, a distinction that is usually far easier ?

Note left-handed children, who sometimes are confused by hearing other children told that their right hand is the one they write with.

AGE VII.

32.—Recognising Missing Features.

Materials. Binet's four pictures of faces without mouth, nose, eye, and of a body without arms. See Figure 16, (*a*), (*b*), (*c*), and (*d*), pp. 103-9, Appendix II. (in the view of Bobertag and others the eyebrow should be erased in the third picture). [Saffiotti adds a table with one of the distant legs omitted.]

Procedure.[1] " **Look at this** [man's] **face.** [Can you] **tell me what has been left out ?** " And, for the others : " **What has been left out here ?** " [or " **in this drawing ?** "]. [The American translation—" lacking " or " missing "—is often unintelligible to English children. Begin with the face without the mouth ; proceed with eye, nose, leaving arms until last.]

If the child says " her body," the examiner may reply : " No, in the *face* " (emphasising the last word) ; [or, " Oh, I was only trying to draw her face. What must I put in to finish the drawing of her face ? " . . . " What have I forgotten in drawing her face ? " or pass to the figure without arms, and then return to the faces. Similarly, an additional attempt is suggested if the child (with some accuracy) observes : " She's got no teeth," " He's bald."] Otherwise **no second attempts** should be allowed with the same picture.

[Terman begins : " There is something wrong with this face. It is not all there," etc. ; and allows help with the first picture—" See, the eye is gone "—if necessary. Melville repeats " What else ? " until the child finds the correct reply, giving him five chances in all.

Answers thus obtained, however, should not be counted for strict comparability. Dr. Simon expressly states that, having already drawn attention to the part intended to be depicted by the word " face," which may be repeated and emphasised, the examiner should receive the reiterated reply " body and arms " as a failure.[2]]

Evaluation. **Three correct answers** with the four pictures are required. [For the last picture " hand(s) " or " finger(s) " may be taken as correct (Melville). The whole should be done in 20 to 25 secs. (Bobertag).]

The average order of difficulty is : (i) arms, (ii) mouth, (iii) eye, (iv) nose. But to commence with missing arms would suggest body and arms for the rest.

Note references to what a profile drawing cannot show : " her other ear," etc.

33.—Adding Three Pennies and Three Halfpennies.

Materials. Three pennies and three halfpennies, set out separately, but not in a row, nor all the pennies entirely apart from all the halfpennies. [Since an entirely haphazard order, such as Binet and Simon imply, may occasionally favour some children *e.g.*, when two halfpennies fall side by side, I arrange the coins alternately and place them at the six corners of an imaginary hexagon.]

[As they have neither half-cent nor two-cent pieces, American investigators, copying Goddard, are forced to use stamps. Some examiners, even in this country, follow them. But, to English children, as to French, the stamp is far less familiar than the corresponding coin.]

Procedure. " **Count this money for me ; and tell me how much there is altogether.** "

[Winch asks : " Suppose we had all halfpennies, how many would there be ? " This elicits the same number as the French ; but is undoubtedly harder ; and, therefore, seems less strictly analogous. To use shillings and

---

(1) The wording in instruction for this test has proved unusually difficult to standardise. Dr. Simon's comments on the present form are " ' Man's (face) ' et ' can you tell ' semblent inutile ? ' Left out ' parait trop précise ; toute fois c'est peu de chose ' ; et ' I was only trying . . .' semble excessif." Simply to repeat " . . . in this *face* " is his suggestion.

(2) I fear, however that I have on this last point been a little less rigid than Dr. Simon would have wished. Hence, the present grading of the test may perhaps represent it as a little easier, than it actually should be.

florins would serve the same end better, if the child knew the florin was equivalent to two shillings.]

Evaluation. **No error** and **no repetition** of the instructions is allowed. [Melville allows telling the child to " point to each and say how much it is altogether." This, however, usually evokes the answer " six."] The test should be done in 8 to 10 secs. Binet adds : " It is useless to wait **15 seconds.**"

Note the child's method of " counting " (ask, if necessary, " How do you get that answer ? ") Does he, for example, begin with pennies or half-pennies, counting by pennies or by halfpennies either adding by twos for the pennies, or merely counting twice to each one, or simply counting the six coins ?

Note outdoor activities bearing on this test (selling papers, " running errands," etc.).

34.—Stating Differences between Concrete Objects.

Procedure. **" You know what a butterfly is, don't you ?** . . . **And you know what a fly is ?** . . . **They are not the same, are they ?** . . . **In what way are they not the same ? "** [**" What is the difference between a fly and a butterfly ? "** If the child hesitates, add : " They are different, are they not ? Well, do you think you can tell me what the difference is ? "] [1]

Most investigators translate Binet's word (" pareil ") quite literally (" alike "). The awkwardness of such a phrase, however, seems to puzzle some children ; I have not found any child troubled by the use of " same " for " similar." To ask : " How can you tell ' glass ' from ' wood ' ? " will sometimes precipitate a reply, but the answer should not count, if otherwise unobtainable. (Even if the child says he does not know the objects, ask for the differences nevertheless. Encouragement is particularly necessary in this test.)

The following words are suggested by Binet ; and the differences between them should be demanded in order :—

    (i) **fly, butterfly ;**
    (ii) **wood, glass ;**
    (iii) **paper, cardboard.**

[So much depends upon the child's familiarity with the particular objects that, for a genuine test, more objects are desirable : *e.g.*, horse, donkey ; tram, bus ; apple, orange, etc. Winch uses : (i) milk, water ; (ii) wood, iron ; (iii) cow, sheep. Terman uses' for (iii) stone, egg. Yerkes uses apple, banana for (i) ; and paper, cloth for (iii).]

Evaluation. **Two out of three** statements must be correct. Any true difference, though trivial, will pass. But if the child repeats the same difference, *e.g.*, " it is larger," it is insufficient. [Note the stereotypy, and ask : " In what other way are they not the same ? "] Often a child takes a minute for one reply ; but if he takes longer than **two minutes** for all he fails. [Allow 20 secs. each (Goddard, Whipple). But this is plainly too brief to be comparable with Binet's recommendations.] However, as Dr. Simon observes, in this test *le temps est peu important.*

[Yerkes allots two points for each reply.]

The order of difficulty is as above, except where children are unfamiliar with butterflies.

---

[1] Dr. Simon expressly does not authorise these suggestions.

35.—Writing from Dictation.

Materials. Pen, ink, paper.

Procedure. " **Will you write this down for me on this piece of paper ?** ' **The pretty little girls.** ' "

[Apparently the phrase is to be uttered as a whole, and not dictated word by word ; but it may be repeated.]

Evaluation. The **words must be separate and sufficiently legible** (and presumably the spelling sufficiently accurate) for the words to be read by a person who did not know what had been dictated.

AGE VIII.

36.—Reading and Reproduction.

Materials. A translation of Binet's passage, printed or typed in three paragraphs, with English place-names and money values substituted for the French. (See Figure 17, p. 111, Appendix II.) My translation is somewhat easier than the American versions. These often translate French words of Latin origin by English words from the same roots. The latter are far less familiar to English children than the former are to French.[1] Even with this simplification some of the words are unusually difficult for children of the age for which it was intended.

Procedure. " [**Will you**] **read this for me** [**please**] ? " **Two seconds after** the reading is finished, remove the passage, and say : " **Tell me what you have been reading about.**"

[Many investigators read the passage to the child, if he cannot read it fairly well himself. Binet, however, says : " If the child cannot read the more difficult words[2] of the test . . . interrupt the exercise and consider the test not passed."[3] Rigidly interpreted, this seems to mean that a complete failure to read, even incorrectly, more than one word results in failure. But very few children, who succeed in reading the words with absolute correctness, fail in recalling more than two facts. Hence, a little leniency in the mechanical part of the reading seems advisable, particularly in the rendering of " 150,000," " 5th," and perhaps " September." Dr. Simon agrees : *peu importe sa manière de lire.*]

Binet deliberately sets no time-limit, as speed depends upon school practice. He gives in round figures, roughly corresponding with those found in my own experiments with the translated version, the following average times for reading the French (53 words) :—

At 8 years	..	..	.. 45 secs.
At 9 years	..	..	.. 40 secs.
At 10 years	..	..	.. 30 secs.
At 11 years	..	..	.. 25 secs.

No child, he adds, can recall six items unless he can read the passage in one minute at most.

Evaluation. Each correct phrase or word as indicated below constitutes one item. Record their number, and if possible the whole reproduction *verbatim.* If a child invents statements that have not been read, these

---

[1] The words used, says Dr. Simon, should be those current in ordinary speech.

[2] *Development of Intelligence* (Miss Kite's translation), p. 212. Binet's words are "*les mots assez difficiles.*"

[3] Dr. Simon seems a little less severe. If the difficulty of the words makes the child forget the thread of the ideas, *tant pis pour lui.* But apparently if he can still reproduce the required number of items correctly, he passes. He is, however, not to be assisted in the reading.

should be noted in the detailed record. Inaccuracy in the reading itself does not count against the child.

A. *Recalls two items.* (Age VIII.)

B. *Recalls six items.* (Age IX.)

The following arrangement of the passage indicates which words or phrases count in the marking as unitary items. The total number of items is twenty.[1] Words or phrases in parenthesis are, more or less, repetitions of preceding portions ; and are, therefore, not to be counted again.

THREE | HOUSES | ON FIRE. |

LONDON, | September | 5th. |

A big | (fire) last night | burnt down *or* destroyed (three houses) | in the middle of the city. |

Seventeen families | now have no homes.| (The loss is more than) 150,000 pounds.|

A young barber|, who saved | a baby | in its cradle|, was badly | hurt | about the hands.|

37.—Answering Easy Questions.

Procedure. " **Tell me this** " :

(i) " **[Suppose you have to go somewhere by train] : what must you do if you miss the train ? "** . . .

(ii) " **What ought you to do, if you broke something that belonged to somebody else ? "**

(iii) " **If one of the other boys (girls) hit you by accident, without meaning to, what should you do then ? "** . . .

If no answer is given, repeat the question as usual, not sternly, but pleasantly prefixing : " Did you catch what I said ? " Do not vary the wording.

I have adopted the above form (" *suppose* you . . .," " *if* you . . .") for the more usual and more literal version (" *when* you . . ."), because so many children do not in the latter case grasp that the examiner is putting an imaginary case ; the French (" quand *on*," not " quand *tu* ") implies this. The phrase " when *one* . . .," used by some translators, seems quite out of the question in addressing little children.[2] The preliminary clause adopted in the first question (" suppose . . .") makes the question fairer for those who by some accident have never been in a train ; and renders certain inadmissible replies, which otherwise would in actual life be correct (*e.g.*, " take a 'bus " or " tram "), rare among intelligent children, and their conventional rejection more legitimate. On the other hand, it slightly emphasises the personal note of the English " you "; and, in making the question a trifle less general, makes it perhaps a trifle more easy.

I have rearranged the questions in order of increasing difficulty. Such rearrangements are desirable, not only upon general principles, but also to economise time ; if the child fails utterly over the first, the busy examiner will not ask the remainder. since such a child is not likely to answer both of the harder questions.

---

[1] Binet does not reckon the number of the month as a separate item. and accordingly obtains a maximum of only nineteen.

[2] " If *we* " is a fairer rendering, and more natural in the first question.

Evaluation. **Two out of three** must be answered satisfactorily.

(i) *Satisfactory Answers.*—[By convention, must always imply waiting for the next train.] *E.g.*, " Wait for another." " Take the next." [" Take a taxi."]

    Unsatisfactory Answers.—" Run after it." " Try not to miss it." " Go home again." [Terman accepts the last for isolated localities with but one or two trains a day.]

(ii) *Satisfactory Answers.*—Imply either restitution, apology, or confession. [Terman rejects confession without apology. Binet, however, expressly accepts the reply " acknowledge it."] *E.g.*, " Pay for it." " Own up." " Buy another." " Ask to be forgiven." " Say I was sorry." [" Tell mother " is acceptable only if the boy assumes the article belonged to his mother.]

    Unsatisfactory Answers.—" I should cry." " Mend it." " Hide it."

(iii) *Satisfactory Answers.*—[Imply either ignoring or excusing the act.] *E.g.*, " Do nothing." " Forgive him." " Tell him to be more careful."

    Unsatisfactory Answers.—" Tell teacher." " Hit him back."

Binet gives a much fuller list of questions in his 1905 version; and appends a more complex method of evaluation. (See 1905 scale, transl. Kite, p. 124, *et seq.*)

The average order of ease is as above, the first being, according to my figures, more suitable for age VII. [For age VIII. Terman includes nos. (ii), (iii), and no. (i) from Test 50 ; and requires two out of three to be correctly answered. No. (i) from the present test he assigns to age VI. Yerkes omits (iii) and allots 2 points to each reply.]

38.—Counting Backwards, 20—1.

Procedure. **" You can count, can't you—1, 2, 3, and so on ? Now, do you think you could count backwards ? Start at 20 and go on until you reach 1."** If the child does not understand, **" Count like this : 20, 19, 18,"** proceed no further.

[Dr. Simon asks the weaker children to count forward first. Yerkes suggests that the experimenter always count from 25 to 21, and then pause for the examinee to continue.]

Evaluation. **One uncorrected error** (either of omission or inversion) is permitted. Binet allows only **20 secs.,**[1] proceeds in the instructions only to 19, and implies counting to 0. But Dr. Simon writes definitely that the omission of zero is not an error. [Yerkes allows 30 secs. ; Terman 40 secs. ; both, with Goddard, Bobertag, and others, accept counting to 1. He gives 4 points if the child can count from 20, 3 from 15, 2 from 10, 1 from 5. Bobertag and Terman would not be " pedantic about the time-limit " in this test.] The child who thinks out the numbers by counting up from 1 each time fails.

Note especially if a child, after perhaps counting backwards for two or three numbers, loses the " guiding idea," and starts counting forward.

Note also if the child has been specifically taught this exercise in school.

39.—Giving Full Date.

Procedure. **" What is the date to-day ? "** If the word " date " is not understood, ask in detail : **" What day of the week is it to-day ? "** **" What month is it ? "** **" What number of the month ? "** **" And what year ? "**

---

(1) In practice, apparently, half a minute or more was often allowed.

[These supplementary questions make the test somewhat easier ; but, though not expressly suggested by Binet, seem to have been adopted by most examiners in actual practice.]

Evaluation. **All four items** must be correctly given ; but an **error of three days either way** is allowable for the day of the month (unless that involves an error in naming the month). [Presumably, if the child remembers mechanically that it is "the fourth month," but cannot explain that this month is April, he fails.]

Note, for this test especially, any influence of school instruction ; also clues peculiar to specific dates (*e.g.*, the child's own birthday, or some other anniversary).

The average order of ease is : (i) day of week, (ii) month, (iii) year, (iv) day of month.

[An applied problem, curiously difficult even for supernormals, is : "What is the year now ? . . . How old are you ? . . . Then, in what year were you born ?"]

40.—Giving Change.

Materials. All the commoner current coins ($\frac{1}{4}$d., $\frac{1}{2}$d., 1d., 6d., 2s., 2s. 6d., 10s. £1 and 1s., and, in addition, the three pennies and three halfpennies. The five boxes used for the weights.

The shilling is kept by the experimenter to pay for the box. The rest, with the boxes, is placed near the child. Apparently it should be **impossible to give the correct change in pennies and halfpennies alone**, *i.e.*, in copper without silver,[1] although the money actually mentioned by Binet would allow it.[2]

Procedure. **" Now, shall we play at shop for a change ? You shall be the shopkeeper. Here are some boxes for you to sell : and here is your cash. See how rich you are. Now will you sell me one of your boxes? How much are they each ? Twopence, shall we say ? Well, here is the money. Can you give me the right change, please ? "** (The experimenter holds out his hand for the money. Note, however, that he should not inform the child what coin he is offering him. The long explanation is Binet's. For rapid work it is perhaps unnecessary. But it makes a pleasant relief to a tedious series of short injunctions, such as may have been given for preceding tests.)

Evaluation. The child **must actually hand over** the right amount (sixpence and fourpence in pennies or in pennies and halfpennies) ; merely stating it correctly as "tenpence" does not count.

[Terman gives three verbal problems without coins (4 c. out of 10 c., 12 c. out of 15 c., and 4 c. out of 25 c.) ; and requires two correct answers out of three.]

Note the child's mental and practical procedure ; and out-of-school activities that may have helped him.

---

(1) Cf. Bulletin (tr. Town), *Method of Measuring Development*, p. 39, and 1908 scale (tr. Kite), *Development of Intelligence*, p. 219.

In Dr. Simon's procedure, if I am correctly informed, there is usually a *sou* missing, when the child tries to make up the money in copper only. But a rigid uniformity does not seem to have been felt so necessary with the French coins. Among the translations of this test there are countless variations in materials and instructions. (See above, p. 6.)

(2) Cf. Town, *loc. cit.*, p. 38. Kite, p. 218 : (the "sixty-five centimes" appears by oversight to include the fifteen in copper previously mentioned. "Further apart" seems a mistranslation for "de plus").

41.—Repeating Numbers.

Procedure. **" Listen, and say these numbers after me."**

(For use only after failure in first set.)

" 2 5 0 3 6 4 " | **" 8 5 3 9 1 6 "** **" 4 7 1 5 8 2 "**

Evaluation. One correct repetition out of three trials counts as success. (See p. 25, Test 2.)

[The repetition of six numbers was included by Binet in neither the 1908 nor 1911 scale. Most investigators have used it for practice ; and it is definitely embodied in the versions of Goddard, Yerkes, and Terman.]

AGE IX.

42.—Naming Months.

Procedure. **" [Can you] tell me all the months of the year ? "** [If the child is silent, Terman and Melville do *not* allow examiner to start him by saying, " January " ; and Dr. Simon is disposed to agree with them.]

Evaluation. Binet allows **15 secs.** and **one error**. [Terman requires, in addition, two out of three " check-questions," or applied problems, to be answered correctly, *e.g.*, " What month comes before April ? " . . . " before July ? " etc.]

Average order of ease is : January, February, December, March, November, April, July, May, September, June, October, August—the last five being those most often omitted.

43.—Naming Nine Common Coins.

Materials. Nine coins, all placed in a row on the table with the **heads upwards** : similar coins should not be adjacent, and the commoner coins of any one metal should not be named first.

[Order upon table : ½d., 2s., 10s., 6d., ¼d., 2s. 6d., 1d., 1s., £1.]

While current One Pound and Ten Shilling notes must be allowed.

Procedure. Ask : **" What is this ? "** pointing to each in succession. Neither examiner nor child should handle them or turn them over.

Evaluation. **All nine** should be named correctly in **40 secs.** If an error is attributable to passing confusion, Binet allows a **second trial** of the whole series after a few minutes. [An interesting variant is to ask the child to pick out certain coins by name. In cases of confusion, Melville asks certain catch-questions : " Have you ever seen a 1-dollar bill ? " (or other notes or coins which do not exist)]

Average order of ease is : 1d., ½d., ¼d., 1s., 6d., £1, 10s., 2s. 6d., 2s., 3d., 5s., 4s.). [The busy examiner will observe that failure or success depends chiefly upon the florin, and occasionally, if this is not confused with the half-crown, upon the half-sovereign. It is unwise, however, to put the florin the first of all.]

44.—Reading and Reproduction.

Recalls Six Items.

Procedure and *Evaluation.* (See p. 46, Test 36 B.)

45.—Defining Concrete Terms by Class or Description.

Procedure and *Evaluation.* (See p. 40-3, Test 27, B.)

The child's replies should be entered in full for subsequent reference in the detailed record.

AGE X.

46.—Arranging Five Weights in Order.

Materials. 5 boxes, identical in colour, shape, and size (about $1\cdot5 \times 2\cdot5 \times 3\cdot5$ cm., or $\frac{3}{5} \times 1\frac{2}{5} \times 1$ inches), and loaded with shot and cotton-wool or candle wax to weigh, without rattling, 3, 6, 9, 12, and 15 grams (approximately one, two, three, four, and five-tenths of an ounce, or, more exactly, 46, 93, 139, 185, and 231 grains). To assist checking the correctness of the arrangement, key letters, *e.g.*, B, I, N, E, T, rather than numbers or the true weights, may be written in order on the bottom of the boxes.

Procedure. **"Do you see these boxes? They all look the same. But they don't weigh the same. Some are heavy and some are light. I want you to find the heaviest and put it here. Then find the one which is a little less heavy, and place it next; then the one which is still less heavy; then the one which is lighter still; and, last, the one which is lightest[1] here."** (Point in each case to the appropriate place.) [Add, if the child fails through hesitation: "Do you understand? Here the heaviest, then the next heaviest, then a lighter one, and then a lighter one still, and the lightest of all, here—all in a row according to their weight." But do not record the result thus obtained as an unqualified success. Binet explicitly says: "Some do not understand our instruction and remain motionless. So much the worse for them."[2]]

Allow three trials, if necessary, mixing the boxes in haphazard order again before each fresh trial.

Evaluation. The arrangement must be absolutely correct in **two out of three trials;** and the whole accomplished in **three minutes.**

Of special interest and perhaps of even greater diagnostic value is the subject's **procedure.** Does he (*a*) fail to attack the test altogether, remaining motionless—piling up or playing with the boxes; (*b*) grasp the idea of series, but not series *by weight*—arranging the boxes in a row haphazard; (*c*) fail to grasp the idea of a *descending* series—picking out the lightest and heaviest, or heaviest only; (*d*) fail to find an adequate method—picking out weights by absolute impression; (*e*) pair them all systematically; (*f*) fail merely to distinguish the differences of weight—through haste or poor sensibility (for methods of discriminating weights, see above, Test 19, p. 35); (*g*) correct the arrangement of any individual weight as he goes on, or (*h*) verify the arrangement of the whole series, when he has finished? [The test seems improved if the differences in weight are more readily distinguishable, and the task thus made purely a logical rather than partly a sensory one.]

[Yerkes allows two trials; and gives 2 points if all the weights are correctly placed, and 1 if all but one are correctly placed.]

The average order of ease is: (i) 15 g., (ii) 3 g., (iii) 6 g., (iv) 12 g., (v) 9 g.[3]—the fifteen-gram weight being nearly always correctly placed, and the nine-gram most frequently wrong.

([1]) Dr. Simon writes: "Your final indication, 'lightest of all'" (my original phrase) "aids the child too much"; and suggests "here one a little less heavy, and here one a little less heavy, and so on." Binet, however, specifies the final weight by the superlative.

([2]) 1908 scale, *loc. cit.*, p. 221.

([3]) The ease of the midmost, and, next, of those adjacent to it, has been described as "probably a general psychological law common to all series." It is, of course, due simply to the fact that, for the heaviest or lightest, there is only one weight differing from it by only 3 g., while for the other three there are two; and for the midmost only are there two differing from it by only 6 g. The ease of 6 g., as contrasted with 12 g., agrees with Weber's laws: that of 15 g., as contrasted with 3 g. contradicts it, but is probably due to asking specifically for the heaviest first.

47.—Sentence Building with Three Words.

Materials. Paper, pen, ink ; and a card with " London, river, money " written on it.[1]

Procedure. **" I want you to make up a sentence for me with these three words in it—London, river, money."** Hand the card to the subject, and **repeat : " London, river, money. Write a sentence containing those three words."** [Add, if the child fails through hesitation : " Just tell me something with those three words in it." This, however, which constitutes an explanation of the word " sentence," is expressly disallowed by Binet.] Binet suggests reading the words several times ; and insists that something be written, whether it satisfies the child himself or not. Outside London it is customary to employ the name of the nearest town that is on a river ; but the change seems scarcely necessary. [Most American investigators, following Goddard, conduct this test orally. Binet's written procedure handicaps many backward children who would otherwise pass.]

[Yerkes emphasises that *one* sentence is desired. Terman explains " sentence "—" a sentence is made up of words which say something "—and uses (i) boy, ball, river ; (ii) work, money, men ; (iii) deserts, rivers, lakes ; and requires two out of three to be satisfactory.]

Evaluation. Allow **one minute** " for finding the sentence." "Three quarters of it should be written within that time " (Binet).

A. **One Idea or Sentence** indicates a mental age of XI. ; *e.g.*, " In the river at London I found some money." " In the mint which is near the river at London money is made." " The river is a source of much money to London. " A set of sentences in which the thought is well co-ordinated into a unitary story or description passes. " London is a big place. It has a river in it. And many people come there to make money." Binet cites stories of between thirty and forty words. With an intelligent child the key-words occupy leading positions in the thought, which has clearly been suggested by them.

B. **Two Distinct Ideas or Sentences** indicate a mental age of X. ; *e.g.*, " London has money and rivers." " There is a river in London ; I should like some money."

C. **Three Distinct Ideas or Sentences** constitute a failure ; *e.g.*, " London is a town ; (and) there is a big river ; (and) some people have money." [The addition of " in it " to the last two clauses would constitute a success.]

Enter " 1," " 2," or " 3 " according to the number of sentences given ; and, in the detailed record, enter the sentences written and the time taken. At least three-quarters of the test should be written in a minute.

Binet (but not Terman) expressly accepts sentences of types A and B even when absurd ; *e.g.*, " London is a city of money by the rivers." " In London there is money, which has a large river." They indicate, he observes weakness of judgment, but at the same time a mental age of X. or XI. Complete omission of one or more words fails.

Yerkes gives 4 points for one sentence, 2 for two sentences.

Note, in addition, (i) the definiteness of the statement, and (ii) the logical intimacy of the associations formed, both with one another and with the key-words—points which, according to certain investigators, are particularly significant of intelligence.[2] [Rational, rather than grammatical, coherence should have been made the basis of evaluation.]

---

(1) The last two words are not a precise translation of Binet's words—*fortune, ruisseau ;* but the words selected by some translators—" fortune." " gutter "—do not conform to Dr. Simon's criterion, which he repeats for this test ; namely, that the English words should yield, as far as is possible without altering the general nature of the test, the original age-assignments. The card, I gather, is not always used.

(2) For a detailed study of the test, see Meumann, " Über eine Neue Methode der Intelligenz-Prüfung," *Z. für Päd. Psych.*, 1912, p. 145.

Binet states that this is one of the rare cases in which a child may succeed by having heard of the test from another child. Should there be any likelihood of this, ask at the outset : " What do you think I have been asking the others to do with these words ? " and, if necessary, substitute other words.

48.—Drawing Two Designs from Memory.

Materials. Binet's two designs, drawn previously on a single card or sheet, kept out of sight until required. A pencil and plain paper. A watch showing seconds. (See Figure 18, p. 113, Appendix II.)

Procedure. " **There are two easy drawings on this card. I want you to look at them very carefully until I take them away ; and then try if you can draw them both from memory on this paper afterwards. You will only see them for a very few seconds. Now look at them *both* carefully first of all. Ready ? Now ! "** The drawings are held steadily in front of the child, the truncated pyramid on the left, for exactly **10 secs. ;** and then taken away and concealed. " **Now try and draw them for me here.**"

[The plain paper should be previously placed ready in front of the child so that he does not forget the designs while paper is found. The pencil should be held out to him with the left hand, as the drawing is turned over with the right. If the pencil is handy at the start, the child may disturb the test by mistakenly attempting to copy them in the middle of the exposure.]

Evaluation. (See Figure 6 (*a*) and (*b*).) **The whole of one** and a **half of the other** must be reproduced with fair correctness. **No second attempt** is allowed. Neatness of drawing does not count. The examiner must be careful not to interpret " fair exactness " more strictly for older than for younger children The standard accepted in the case of this test is thus far below what the uninstructed teacher would accept as a satisfactory reproduction.

Several printed versions of the tests reproduce sample drawings for guidance in evaluating the results. Binet does not. If the examiner is in doubt, he may award the child a fraction instead of either " 0 " or " 1." [Yerkes allots 2 points to each design according to their degree of merit. Melville gives sample drawings obtaining full, half, and no marks respectively. But for the Greek key pattern his second " no mark " sample appears better than his second " half mark " sample.]

I suggest the following rough rules :—

A. For the Greek Key Pattern to count as " half-correct," the drawing should show *one* only of the following errors :—

    (1) omitting or wrongly reproducing the right or left half of the drawing ; or,

    (2) omitting the three centre lines ; or,

    (3) omitting one or wrongly reproducing one or both terminal squares ; or,

    (4) substituting curves for right angles ; or,

    (5) inverting the whole figure.

Two such mistakes (*e.g.*, omitting the central pillar and twisting one " curl " outwards) constitute complete failure for the test.

B. For the Truncated Pyramid to count as " half-correct," the drawing should show four of the following errors :—

    (1) omitting or reversing the lateral decentralisation ;

    (2) substituting squares or upright oblongs for the broad oblongs ;

    (3) omitting one of the twelve lines ;

    (4) joining one of the oblique lines to the side of one of the oblongs instead of to the corner ;

    (5) doubling the relative size of the inner oblong.

Five such errors result in failure.

FIGURE 6 (*a*).

Test 48.   Memory Drawing.   Evaluation of Results.[1]

(*a*).   Children's Reproductions of the 'Frustum' or 'Truncated Pyramid.'

(i) Successful.

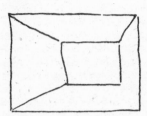

(ii) Half Correct.

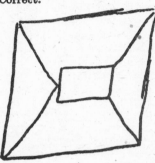

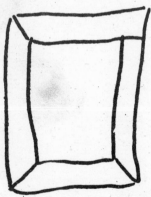

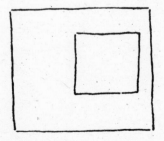

(iii) Failures.

FIGURE 6 (*b*).

Test 48. Memory Drawing. Evaluation of Results [1] (*continued*).

(*b*). Children's Reproductions of the Greek Key Pattern.

(i) Successful.

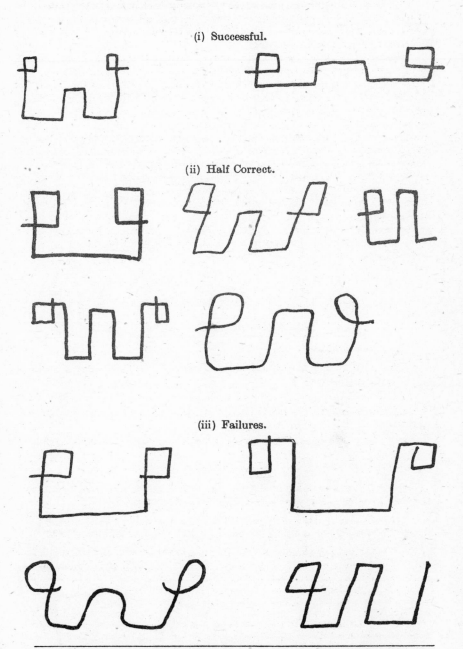

(ii) Half Correct.

(iii) Failures.

[1] The above examples are not given as typical reproductions, but rather as borderline cases, where judgment has been found difficult, to illustrate the somewhat conventional application of our arbitrary principles of evaluation. Thus the successful reproductions are mostly poor ones, and the failures good ones.

Thus, a non-truncated pyramid (with the four lines of the inner oblong omitted) passes as half correct if the oblique lines meet in a point distinctly displaced from the centre of the larger oblong; otherwise it fails.

The size of the drawings, absolute, or relative to each other, their position relative to one another, the slight vertical decentralisation of the truncated cone, and (at any rate within wide limits) the relative size of the parts of the Greek key may be disregarded.

As regards difficulty, with the copy we have used, the truncated cone is drawn successfully with far greater frequency than the Greek key pattern. A further investigation has shown that this is due to two factors. First, the figure on the left tends to attract attention first and most of all. This factor is the only one mentioned by Binet as operative. Reversing the position, however, reveals that, in addition, the truncated cone is easier intrinsically. The reversed arrangement, therefore, should, and in fact very nearly does, equalise the net difficulty of the two. To adopt this interchange would be an obvious improvement. This may be effected without redrawing the figure, by simply showing it upside-down.[1] By some curious mischance, Binet's illustration shows the truncated cone on the right[2]—the illustration being copied by Whipple,[3] Goddard,[4] and by Terman.[5] Since, however, in the text Binet expressly states : "the section of the prism is always represented to the left," there would seem to be no doubt that for strict comparability with Binet's own procedure the arrangement I have printed and have used is the correct one.

AGE XI.

49.—Explaining Absurdities.

Procedure. "Listen carefully to what I am going to say. There is something in it that is really quite silly [and impossible[6]]. See if you can tell me what is wrong."

(i) " ' One day, a man fell off his bicycle on to his head ; and was killed instantly. He was taken to the hospital ; and they fear he may never get better.'—What is there silly in that ? "

(ii) " ' I have three brothers—Jack, Tom, and myself.'—What is silly in that ? " (Female examiners must preface this with " A boy said to me " ; or else substitute " I have three sisters—Jane, Mary, and myself.")

(iii) " ' Yesterday there was a railway accident ; but it was not a serious one. Only forty-eight people were killed.'—What is silly in that ? "

(iv) " ' Once the body of a poor girl was found in a wood, cut into eighteen pieces. They say that she killed herself.'—What is silly in that ? "

(v) " ' A man once said : " If I should ever grow desperate and kill myself, I shall not choose a Friday to do it on ; for Friday is an unlucky

---

[1] Strangely enough, Healy and Fernald represent this diagram upside-down, but with the prism still to the left. See *Tests for Practical Mental Classification*, p. 25 (a monograph containing many new and suggestive tests).

[2] Cf. *Development of Intelligence* (tr. Kite), pp. 60, 282. But in the *Bulletin* it is on the right. Cf. *Method of Measuring Development of Intelligence* (tr. Town), Fig. 8.

[3] *Manual of Mental Tests*, 1st ed., p. 48. The Greek Key pattern represented on the left both in the 1905 and in the 1911 series.

[4] *Binet's Measuring Scale*, revised edition, p. 7.   [5] *Measurement of Intelligence*, p. 261.

[6] " Trop précis : ' silly ' doit suffire " (Dr. Simon).

day, and would bring me bad luck." '—[What is foolish in what the man said ?[1]]."

[Terman, following Binet a little more literally, begins : " I am going to *read* a sentence, which has something foolish in it, some nonsense " (the phrase translates " une bêtise "). But it seems hardly desirable to read one's tests, if it can be avoided.]

In accordance with general principles, I have rearranged the questions in order of increasing difficulty.

[Whipple, Yerkes, and others, rightly objecting to the gruesome character of the above, have substituted other examples.]

Evaluation. **Three absurdities** should be detected **out of five.** [Terman requires four. Wallin allows about 2 minutes only for the 3 correct answers. Terman suggests about 30 seconds for each ; but time-limits should not be rigidly pressed. If a child's first statement is not quite clear or conclusive— *e.g.,* " myself is silly " in answer to (ii)—say : " Explain what you mean." Otherwise allow no second chance.]

(i) *Satisfactory :* " He couldn't get well if he was already dead." " First you said he was dead ; and then you said he wouldn't get well again."

Unsatisfactory : " They ought to have taken him to the mortuary." " If he fell off his bicycle he wouldn't fall on his head." " Riding a bike before he could balance."

(ii) *Satisfactory :* " You have only two." " You are not your own brother." " You shouldn't count yourself."

Unsatisfactory : " You should put yourself last."

(iii) *Satisfactory :* " It must have been serious if forty-eight were killed." or " if anybody was killed." " If it wasn't serious, only one or two would have been killed." Dr. Simon agrees with Melville, and would accept : " Forty-eight isn't serious in war-time."

Unsatisfactory : " Forty-eight people couldn't be killed in a railway accident."

(iv) *Satisfactory :* " You can't cut yourself into eighteen pieces." " If she killed herself she couldn't cut herself up."

Unsatisfactory : " It is silly to kill yourself," or " to cut yourself." " Nobody could cut her into eighteen pieces." " Nobody would kill themselves," or " cut themselves."

(v) *Satisfactory :* " If he killed himself, the day wouldn't matter." " He couldn't have bad luck if he was dead."

Unsatisfactory : " He is silly to believe in bad luck." " Friday isn't unlucky." " Friday is all right because Jesus was killed on a Friday." " If he was desperate, he wouldn't wait till Friday."

The average order of ease is as above, namely : (i) cyclist ; (ii) brothers (which is often peculiarly harder for children of poor, illiterate classes) ; (iii) railway accident (which, however, seems easier for boys than for girls) ; (iv) girl's suicide ; (v) suicide on Friday (much the hardest ; more suitable for age XII.).

The emotional attitude of the child should be noted.

50.—Answering Difficult Questions.

Procedure. " [Can you] tell me this ? "

(i) " **What should you do if you found you were late on your way to school ?** "

---

[1] " Un peu plus précis que ce que nous demandons habituellement " (Dr. Simon).

F

(ii) "**If someone asked you what you thought of a boy** [or, if the examinee is a girl, **of a girl]**[1] **whom you did not know very well, what should you say ?** "

(iii) "**Suppose**[2] **a boy does something that is unkind : why do we forgive him more readily if he was angry than if he was not angry ?** "

(iv) "**Why should we judge a person by what he does and not by what he says ?** "[3]

(v) "**Suppose you were going to undertake something very important : what should you do first of all ?** "

Repeat a question **once**, if necessary, but do not vary the wording.

Evaluation. Allow **20 secs.** for reflection on **each** question. **Three out of five** must be answered satisfactorily.

(i) *Satisfactory :* " Hurry " or " Run." [" Go straight to school " may be accepted, if it appears that the child sometimes plays or carries out errands on its way.]

Unsatisfactory : By convention, anything not embodying the idea of hurrying : " Get the stick." " Leave earlier." " Get up sooner next time." " Ring the bell." " Get a note to excuse me."

(ii) *Satisfactory :* Anything that suggests the need of making an enquiry or withholding an opinion : " I couldn't say anything." " I could not tell him without finding out." " Tell him to ask somebody else." " Say what I know and no more." [" I should say ' I do not know ' " seems a satisfactory statement ; but see next paragraph.]

Unsatisfactory : Usually unintelligible : " You must make up something." " Say he's rather nice." [" Say I don't know his name " is rejected by Simon as merely repeating part of the question. *Cf.* also Binet, 1908 scale, tr. Kite, p. 226.]

(iii) *Satisfactory :* Anything suggesting that anger may constitute an excuse, however badly expressed : " Because he didn't know what he was doing." " Because he'd be sorry afterwards." " Because he lost his temper."

Unsatisfactory : Anything suggesting disapproval of anger : " He oughtn't to get angry." " Because he might hit me again."

(iv) *Satisfactory :* Anything *implying* words are more deceptive than actions, though both need not be mentioned : " You can rely on his actions, but not on what he says." " Because he might not always speak the truth." " Actions speak louder than words." " Actions speak for themselves." " He might be boasting." " When he's angry, he might say things he didn't mean."

Unsatisfactory : Usually unintelligible : " Because you can't tell." " You ought to speak the truth."

([1]) I have here rendered " une personne " " boy or girl," because otherwise I find children may give the right answer (" I couldn't say anything ") for a wrong reason—namely, because they assume at once that since he is a " person " (which to them implies an adult), they could not in any case be expected to deliver an opinion, though they might (as in no. iv) tacitly judge him.

([2]) Dr. Simon thinks that in French, at any rate, this form, literally retranslated, would decompose the sentence too much, and render it too easy. In English, however, especially in class-room English, " suppose " is practically a conditional conjunction. He adds that the equivalence of the phrases is only to be judged by their effect in practice upon the age-assignments, and certainly, thus judged, my version does not make the questions too easy. Binet, indeed, in both the 1908 and 1911 scales, placed this test at age X.

([3]) Binet uses the abstract nouns " actions " and " words "; but with this form the replies turn very largely on the child's accidental familiarity with the proverb : " Actions speak louder than words."

(v) *Satisfactory* : Anything implying preliminary preparation as to method (reflection, practice, seeking advice or help), or preliminary consideration as to expediency or possibility : " Think it over." " Ask someone about it." " Prepare for it." " Say my prayers." " Think whether I could manage it." " Ask someone to help me."

Unsatisfactory : Usually unintelligible : " Not do it." " Try to do my best." [Some say : " Wash," "tidy myself," "put on a clean collar " ; in that make it clear that you mean *doing* something important, not *going* somewhere important.]

The questions vary widely in difficulty. The easiest is answered by three times as many children at this age as is the hardest. The average order of ease is : (i) late for school (more suitable for age VII.) ; (ii) unknown boy ; (iii) actions and words ; (iv) forgiving angry blow (stated by Binet to be the hardest) ; (v) undertaking something important (in English, vague and difficult to understand, rather than hard to solve ; more suitable for age XII.).

[For age X. Terman includes only (iii), (iv), and (v) ; and requires two correct replies out of three. He assigns no. (i) to age VIII. Yerkes includes (i) and (iii) from Test 37, and (iii), (iv) from the present test ; and allows case 2 points for each satisfactory answer.]

Emotional reactions should be noted.

51.—Giving 60 Words in Three Minutes.

Procedure. " I want you to give me as many words as you possibly can in three minutes. Some children can give more than two hundred. Keep saying words like this till I stop you : ' box, coat, tree, cart,' and so on— any words you like. Are you ready ? Now start." If he breaks off, encourage him by saying : " Very good. Keep on."

Note that the statement that some can give two hundred is deliberately inserted ; also give exactly the same four examples to every child.

Evaluation. **60 words** must be given exclusive of repetitions. If the child gives sentences, start him again, saying : " You must give separate words." Observe the exact time with the second-hand of a watch. Count the words as they are given by a stroke or other mark for each. [Yerkes gives 1 point for 30 to 44 words ; 2 for 45 to 59 ; 3 for 60 to 74 ; 4 for over 75.]

It is interesting to record the changes in rate (by starting a fresh group of strokes after each half-minute), and the key-words of the child's various topics ; it is seldom possible to put down all the words. The average number of words given in the successive half-minutes by those who nearly or quite succeed in the test proved in our experiments to be as follows :—

1st	2nd	3rd	4th	5th	6th	half-minute
19·3	13·4	10·3	8·5	7·3	6·6	words

It will be noted that more than twice as many words are given in the first minute as in the last. The test consumes a disproportionate amount of time ; and, for rapid words, success or failure may often be inferred from the performance during the first minute alone. Bright children tend to maintain a more nearly uniform rate ; young or backward decline very rapidly.

The words themselves illustrate individual differences in mental content in a most striking way.[1] It is often interesting to keep this test until

---

[1] The associative reaction, both in this and other forms, has been extensively used by Freud and other psychoanalysts. An elaborate early study was made by Binet, with his two daughters as subjects See *L'Étude Experimentale de l'Intelligence*, esp. Chapters II to IV.

last, and at the close to ask the child how each word or topic came to be thought of. Among girls the introspections are highly suggestive. Even without such explanations, the examiner may note the following : a tendency to long themes, or to short themes constantly changed (a change of topic with almost every word is, as Binet notes, characteristic of young and of backward children ; they exhaust an idea in barely naming it ; on the other hand, bright children may be delayed by too persistent an adherence to the same theme, when all the commoner associations with it have been exhausted) ; the general character of the ideas—objective or subjective (ego-centric) ; the topic of the themes—objects in the room, objects seen at home, or out of doors, the child's own person, recent memories (recent lessons, stories recently read), remote memories ; the general nature, richness, and refinement of the vocabulary drawn upon—abstract words (often a sign of culture or intellect), unusual words, parts of speech other than nouns, repetitions (often suggestive of the mental stereotypy of the deficient) ; the type of connection between the words (logical association—especially association by similarity, accidental association—of time, place, etc., verbal associations—by rhyme, etc.). Occasionally, a sudden delay or other emotional reaction may suggest that the child has approached a " complex " (a system of strongly toned emotional ideas, more or less repressed).

[Since so many children tend to enumerate simply the objects that they see around them, some investigators require the child to shut his eyes (a little embarrassing to a nervous child) ; and others to repeat only names of things. Terman prefers to work in a room as bare as possible. I understand, however, that Dr. Simon does not consider such precautions important ; and the child's natural tendency is itself of interest.]

52.—Repeating Numbers.

Procedure. " Listen, and say these numbers after me."
(For use only after failure in first set.)
" **9 6 8 4 7 5 1** " | " 4 8 2 0 3 6 5 " " 5 9 2 8 1 3 6 "

Evaluation. One correct repetition out of three trials counts as success. (See p. 25, Test 2.)

53.—Sentence-Building with Three Words.

Materials. Paper, pen and ink, and a card with " London, river, money " written on it.

One Idea or Sentence.
Procedure and *Evaluation.* (See p. 52, Test 47 A.)

AGE XII.

54.—Giving Three Words to Rhyme.

Procedure. " Do you know what a rhyme is ? When two words end with the same sound, we call them rhymes. ' Jill ' rhymes with ' Hill,' because they both end in ' ill.' Do you understand ? . . . Now can you give me three words which rhyme with ' obey ' ? "

Evaluation. The child must give **three** genuine words that rhyme in **1 minute.** Binet's instructions to the child ask for " other words " or " all the words." It saves time to specify three to the child. If the child gives nothing, or has not given enough, urge him by saying : " What (else) rhymes with ' obey ' ? " Apparently " disobey " may be accepted as one of the three. Monosyllables ("play," "bay") are quite as correct as dissyllables ("to-day," "away," "hurray"). Some children lose time in searching for the latter only.[1]

[Terman, Goddard, Kuhlman require 3 words to be given for 2 out of 3 of the following: "day," "mill," "spring." With these words Terman locates the test at age IX. Others use the word "defender," and locate it at age XV. Others, again, require only two correct rhymes, or allow 1½ mins. for the three, if the two have been given in 1 min.]

55.—Rearranging Mixed Sentences.

Materials. Three cards containing three mixed sentences. (See Figure 19, pp. 115, Appendix II.)

Procedure. "**Put these words in order, and find out the sentence which they make.**" [Many children do not gather from Binet's instructions that they are to read out a sentence. But he implies that not to understand his instructions is to fail. If they fail, it is interesting to see if they would have succeeded with simpler instructions. "Here is a puzzle for you. Can you read what this card says?" (The child reads it as it stands.) "You don't understand what that means, do you? The words are all mixed up in the wrong order. Now do you think you could put them together in their proper order, and read them out so that they make sense?"]

[If the child, reminiscent of the word-building tests, inserts words, say: "No, you must not add any other words." If, however, he omits a word, do not give him a second chance with the same exercise.]

Evaluation. **Two correct** solutions must be given out of three. Only **1 minute** is allowed for **each**.

[Yerkes allots 2 points to each reply.]

Correct solutions are :—

(i) "A good dog defends his master bravely."
   "A dog defends his good master bravely."

["A master defends his good dog bravely" is, according to Binet, "poor" and apparently incorrect. Terman gives half credit to the two last.]

(ii) "I asked my (the) teacher to correct the (my) paper."
(iii) "We started for the country early this morning."
   "This morning we started for the country early."[2]

Most investigators accept a forced or rhetorical order : *e.g.*, "For the country this morning we started early."

The order of ease is as above ; the last is distinctly harder than the other two.

56.—Describing Pictures : Interpretation.

Procedure. (See p. 27, Test 6, C.)

Evaluation. The child goes beyond what is actually visible in the picture and mentions the situation or emotion it suggests.

(i) "They're moving." "They've a heavy load." "They can't pay their rent." "A rag-picker."

---

(1) Dr. Simon sanctions these suggestions, writing : "Toutes ces remarques semblent justes."

(2) The more literal renderings of the French idioms, given by other translators, are in (i) "courageously" for "bravely," and in (iii) "at an early hour" for "early this morning." This alters the difficulty of the test as compared with the French results. In a discussion on this point, Dr. Simon writes : "'Bravely' convient très bien. Je crois que votre traduction 'this early morning' (sic) est plus accessible que notre expression 'de bonne heure.' Je l'accepterais toute fois."

(ii) " Miserable," " poor," " have no home." " The man is saying his prayers." " His daughter " (or " wife ") " is sitting beside him." " A man in trouble."

(iii) " A prisoner." " He wants to get out." " He's trying to see what's in the yard." " He's lonely," or " thinking." " A man on board ship."

AGE XIII.

57.—Resisting Suggestion.[1]

Materials. A book of six leaves with two lines drawn in the same straight line on one page in each opening. (See Figure 20 (a) to (f), pp. 117–127, Appendix II.) In the first three pairs, the right hand line is always longer than the left, and each pair longer than the last ; in the next there pairs all the lines are equal. The lengths are given on page 77.

Procedure. For the first three pairs : **" Which is the longer of those two lines ? "** For the last three, without changing the tone : **" And of these ? "** the question being repeated for each pair.

Evaluation. Record whether child's judgments are right or wrong in each case ; especially with reference to the last three. The child succeeds if he judges **two out of the three equal pairs** to be equal. [In one version (*Bulletin*) the child is given ½ mark—*i.e.*, one-tenth of a year—if he judges one of the last three pairs to be equal.]

[Yerkes allots one point for each of the last three replies and accepts any resistance to suggestion, whether the child judges the line on the left to be equal or greater than that on the right.]

Note whether the child's errors seem attributable strictly to suggestion, to inattention, to impulsive heedlessness, or to a genuine judgment that the equal lines are unequal after studying them. Note also any emotional reaction.

[As an index of intelligence there is now general agreement that this test is comparatively worthless. It is one of the very few omitted by Terman from the Stanford Revision. Suggestibility is a most important characteristic for investigation in the case of backward or delinquent children. But the particular forms of suggestibility that are operative in practical or social life are not elicited by such tests as the above. A far better test is provided, when the child is describing a picture from memory (" *Aussage* " or " Testimony " test), by cross-examining him indirectly upon fictitious objects not really present in the picture (*e.g.*, in picture (i), " Was the little boy wearing a straw hat, or a cap ? ") But the acceptance of suggestion will reveal itself throughout the whole course of the examination ; and should be noted accordingly.]

58.—Solving Circumstantial Problems.

Procedure. [" **Can you guess the answer to this riddle ? "**]

(i) " **One day a woman, walking in Epping Forest, stopped still, terribly frightened. Then she hurried to the nearest police-station, and told the policeman she had just seen, hanging from[2] the branch of a tree, a—what do you think it was she saw ? "**

(ii) " **My next door neighbour has had three visitors. First, a doctor called ; then a lawyer ; and then a clergyman. What do you think has been happening there ? "**

---

[1] The age-assignment of this test is particularly difficult. See footnote (²) p. 223.
[2] " ' Hanging from,' me parait " (says Dr. Simon) " plus précis que notre simple preposition 'à.' Mais c'est peut-être inevitable."

[Terman adds a third problem ; and requires two correct out of three. There is, however, a general agreement that the above questions are ill chosen.]

Evaluation. **Both** questions must be correctly answered.

(i) *Satisfactory :* Replies must contain the idea of someone hanged. [If the child answers " a man," " a dead person," ask : " How did he get up in the tree ? "]

[A large number of children from better homes are at this age almost ignorant of such tragedies, even from gossip or reading. They reply : " It was only a bit of a sheet," or " a boy trying to frighten her." In such cases I would allow a second answer, first explaining : " No, she was not a silly woman, easily frightened " ; or " it was daytime " ; but insist on the conventional reply, before scoring the answer as correct.]

Unsatisfactory : " A bird," " someone robbing a nest," " an escaped German," " a monkey," " a serpent."

[Many investigators accept such responses as the last, if the child can explain them intelligently ; *e.g.*, " the serpent had escaped from the Zoo," or " perhaps it happened in America." The specification of a well-known neighbouring wood, which should be substituted for " Epping Forest " elsewhere than in London (Binet speaks of " the forest of Fontainebleau "), excludes many of these doubtful replies.]

(ii) *Satisfactory :* " Someone is dying." " He is very ill."

Binet accepts the latter ; but it could be inferred from the visit of the doctor and clergyman alone. Dr. Simon, however, thinks " very " implies a vague appreciation of the presence of the other visitors. [If the child replies " ill " or " very ill," I would then ask : " Why did the lawyer " (and " clergyman ") " come ? " and accept only a logical answer within the child's range of knowledge. Terman expects the child to understand that the lawyer came to " make " (read ?) the will and the clergyman to " preach the funeral." But much vaguer answers should, I think, be accepted ; *e.g.*, the lawyer came to arrange about the man's money, the clergyman to pray for him ; or both came because he wanted to confess something before he died ; but not, " the clergyman was his son " ; the lawyer " a friend of the family." As a rule, unless the child fails to reply or replies very absurdly, I would, by convention, accept " very ill " and reject " ill." Imaginative embellishments—*e.g.*, unwarranted specifications, " *his child* is dying," etc.—should be noted. Occasionally a child can ingeniously and logically justify such inferences as " a murder," " a marriage," " a baby was born " (" the lawyer was employed to get the man to marry the girl " : Terman). But, as a rule, these replies are mere invalid guesses.

Thus evaluated, the second problem proves somewhat easier, though comparatively few children in elementary schools connect lawyers specifically with wills.]

AGE XIV.

59.—Repeating Syllables.

(26 syllables)   **" The other morning I saw in the street a tiny yellow dog. Little Maurice has spoilt his new apron."**

For *Procedure* and *Evaluation* (see p. 28, Test 7, xi).

60.—Defining Abstract Terms.

Procedure. " [Can you tell me this?] What is [meant by[1]] . . . (i) kindness ? " (ii) ". . . justice ? " (iii) ". . . charity ? "

[For "kindness"—undoubtedly an unsatisfactory stimulus-word—Yerkes substitutes "obedience," and allots 2 points for each reply. Terman substitutes "pity," "revenge," and "envy" for (i), and requires 3 correct replies out of 5.]

Evaluation. **Two** must be correctly defined **out of three.**

Satisfactory definitions—

For (i), contain the double idea (or instance) of (*a*) affection, tenderness, politeness, or consideration, which is (*b*) shown to others. *E.g.*, "being polite or good to others " is correct. "Being kind," "doing something good " are inadequate ;

For (ii), contain the idea of treating people according to their merits, or of protecting the innocent and their interests, or of punishing the guilty. *E.g.* "When you punish wicked people," "playing fair " ;

For (iii), contain the two ideas of (*a*) poor or unfortunate people, and (*b*) showing kindness to them. *E.g.*, "When you give poor people some money," of "giving alms."

If a child, in his reply, uses the same word or a derivative, *e.g.*, for "kindness," "being kind to someone," ask : "Yes ; but what does *that* mean ? "

AGE XV.

61.—Drawing from Imagination the Cuts in a Folded Paper.

Materials. Two sheets of paper about 15 cm. (6 inches) square. A pencil. One sheet has been folded in four like a letter ready for an envelope, and reopened. In the middle of the edge which presents but a single fold a small triangular notch, about 1 cm. deep, is drawn.[2] (See Figure 7 (*a*).)

Procedure. " **Here is a sheet of paper that I am going to fold into four.**"[3] (The examiner refolds the paper while the child watches.) " **Suppose now I cut out a notch, just here. When the paper is unfolded again, what would it look like ? Will you show me on this piece of paper how and where it would be cut ? **" The examiner places the folded paper in front of the child with the corner showing the folds towards him, and the pencil-mark uppermost and visible. The child must not touch the paper shown to him, nor fold another sheet. [Beware of saying "draw the holes," as this of itself indicates that more than one hole is required.]

Evaluation. **Two diamond-shaped holes** should be drawn in a line with each other, one near the centre of each half of the paper. (See Figure 7 (*b*).)

[It appears indifferent whether the perforations should lie in a horizontal or in a vertical straight line, or whether the major axis of the tiny

---

(1) Dr. Simon would prefer, " What is kindness ? "

(2) Binet says *drawn :* but his illustration, unlike mine, shows it actually *cut out.*

(3) Binet's fuller description of the procedure (1905 scale, tr. Kite, p. 67) varies somewhat from the later (1908 scale, *ib.*, p. 234), which, at first sight, implies that the paper is presented already folded. But I understand a change in the method was not intended. Goddard, I am told, folds the paper in front of the child. Terman also does so, drawing the child's attention especially to each fold , and, further, actually cuts the paper, which necessitates a fresh pattern-sheet for each child. Saffiotti cuts off the folded corner also, thus producing three diamond-shaped perforations. Dr. Simon prefers that the paper should be folded and cut afresh for each child.

FIGURE 7.

Test 61. Folded Paper.

(*a*). As shown.

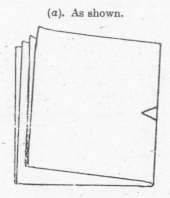

(*b*). As reproduced.

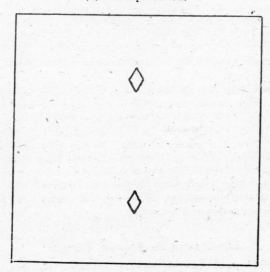

diamonds drawn should be vertical or horizontal. To justify this I would suggest that the paper should always be square, and that angle of the notch be a right angle. Terman insists on the creases being drawn ; but disregards the shape.]

Note if the child has been helped by special previous experience ; *e.g.,* a course on paper folding.

62.—Giving Differences between Abstract Terms.

Procedure. " **What is the difference between . . .**"

A.   (i) " **pleasure and happiness** " . . .
    (ii) " **poverty and misery** " . . .
    (iii) " **evolution and revolution ?** " . . .

[The words suggested by Binet (1911) are :—

B.   (i) paresse, oisiveté ;
    (ii) évènement, avénement (the latter variously rendered " advent " (Goddard) or " prevent " (Huey)) ;
    (iii) évolution, révolution ; and in 1908 scale :—

C.   (i) pauvreté, misérie, instead of paresse, oisiveté ; and, in addition to (ii) and (iii), as above—
    (iv) plaisir, bonheur ;
    (v) orgeuil, pretention.]

The additional pairs, however, are extremely difficult to translate satisfactorily. For an efficient test it would probably be better to adopt and try out fresh pairs of words altogether. "Attention" and "intention" (Saffiotti and others) give far more satisfactory results than any of the words literally translated. In discussing the selection of the three most appropriate English words, Dr. Simon wrote : " l'experience peut seule prononcer." My experience and my experiments are alike in favour of the provisional choice suggested above.

[Terman uses A (ii), (iii), and B (i) (" laziness " and " idleness ") ; adds " character " and " reputation " ; and requires three correct replies out of four.]

Evaluation. **Two out of three** must be correctly answered. Good replies should bring out an opposition or antithesis between the differentiating ideas ; *e.g.*, in (i) "happiness" should be contrasted as superior to, or more general than, "pleasure" ; in (ii) having little money should be contrasted with being in misery or pain ; in (iii) slow change should be contrasted with sudden change. But Binet allows mere differences ; *e.g.*, evolution is the movement of troops, revolution is an insurrection. [Terman, however, does not accept definition without a real contrast.]

The average order of ease is : (i) poverty and misery ; (ii) pleasure and happiness ; (iii) evolution and revolution.

63.—Drawing the Reversed Triangle.

Materials. Paper and pencil for drawing. An oblong card, about 10 × 15 cm. (4 × 6 inches), cut across the diagonal, as used for the divided card test. The card is first laid on the table before the subject with the cut edges touching.

Procedure. (See Figure 8(*a*).) " **Look carefully at the lower piece of this card. Suppose I turn it over and lay this edge** " (pointing to line A—C without moving the card) " **along this edge** " (A—B of the upper triangle) ; " **and suppose that this corner** " (C) " **is placed just at this point** " (B) ; " **what would it all look like ?** Now I am going to take the piece away " (remove the lower triangle from view). " **Imagine it placed as I told you ; and draw its shape in the proper position. Begin by drawing the shape of the top triangle.** "

Evaluation. (See Figure 8(*b*).) The essential points are : (i) A C B must be preserved as a **right angle ;** (ii) **A C must be made shorter** than A B ; [(iii) Saffiotti adds : B C must retain approximately its original length, as the shortest of the three lines].

AGE XVI.

64.—Summarising Hervieu's Reflections on Life.

Procedure. " **Attend carefully to what I am going to read to you. When I have finished I shall want you to tell me in your own words the *meaning* of what I read. Listen :**

" ' **Many opinions have been given on the value of life. Some say it is good ; others say it is bad. It would be truer to say that it is just medium. For, on the one hand, the *happiness* it brings us is never so great as *we* should like ; and, on the other hand, the *misfortunes* it brings us are never so great as our *enemies* would want us to have. It is this mid-way quality that makes life fair ; or, at least, prevents it from being altogether unfair.** '[1]

" **Now see if you can give me, in your own words, the sense of what I have just read to you.** "

[There are so many different ways of emphasising the words in the long, penultimate sentence—each impressing the child's intelligence and memory in a different way—that I have ventured for uniformity to indicate by italics where the stress should chiefly fall.]

Evaluation. The central thought must be understood and these **three ideas reproduced :** (i) Life is neither good nor bad, but medium, for (ii) it is not so good as we wish, but (iii) better than what others wish for us. The terms and expressions matter little. [Melville omits " but medium " as essential to (i). Binet includes it, but does not specify the central thought as containing three or more subordinate ideas.]

Note whether the child fails through lack (*a*) of comprehending the abstract ideas, or (*b*) of accurate memory (rarer). Note also inventions and embellishments.

65.—Giving the Differences between President and King.

Procedure. " **There are three chief differences between a President of a Republic and a King. [Can you] tell me what they are ?** " [. . . " Can you think of any of them ? "]

Evaluation. **Two of the following differences,** apparently, must be given. [Some consider Binet required all of the first three.]

(i) A King **inherits** his crown (or, has royal blood) ; a President is elected.

(ii) A King is king for life ; a President's term of office is limited.

---

[1] " C'est cette médiocrité qui la rend équitable . . ." proved peculiarly difficult to render fairly. Most translators retain the same words, " mediocrity " and " equitable " ; but they have a more bookish ring in English ears. Dr. Simon comments : " Any slight difference in meaning would be secondary ; and your translation seems sufficiently close in difficulty and sense."

(iii) The powers of a King are greater than those of a President.

(iv) A King is not directly responsible to the people; a President is.—Added by Melville in place of (iii). ["A President is head of a republic; a King is head of a monarchy or kingdom," seems acceptable as referring to this difference; though Terman rejects it, presumably as being tautologous.]

Such differences as "a King has a crown"; "a palace," etc., are not to be regarded as "chief" differences.

[This test is obviously more suited to French and American children than to English. The third difference is hardly true of an English king.]

4. OTHER VERSIONS.

Apart from the necessities of translation, most versions of the Binet-Simon scale—for example, the Vineland Version, drawn up by Dr. Goddard, to whom the popularity of the scale is largely due—depart from the original only by an occasional attempt to improve the procedure or to amend the problems, and by the rare addition of one or two further tests. Three revisions, however, are of a more radical nature; and merit a brief notice.

The Stanford Revision and Extension.

The Stanford version[1] contains ninety tests, six for each age-level from three to ten (each test counting as the equivalent of two mental months), eight for age twelve, six each for age fourteen, for "adults" and for "superior adults," and, finally, sixteen alternative tests. Its salient virtue lies in the inclusion of many excellent tests, both fresh and familiar, intended for the higher ages. In those individual cases where Binet's original problems yield, with the unmodified procedure, an incomplete or questionable result, these accessories will be found extremely fruitful.

The new tests are as follows: For age IV., (1) discriminating forms (circle, square, triangle, etc.)—a test originally proposed by Kuhlmann; (2) easy questions ("what must you do when cold," "sleepy," "hungry?") from Binet's 1905 scale. For age VII., (3) tying a shoestring round the examiner's finger in a bow-knot (prepared model shown); (4) repeating digits from memory in reverse order—a test suggested by Bobertag—three digits for age VII., four for age IX., five for age XII., six for average adult, seven for superior adult. For age VIII., (5) marking with a pencil on a simple map the path to be followed in searching for a lost ball in a circular field entered from a gate: absence of plan fails; an imperfect plan (e.g., fan-shaped, wheel-shaded paths) is accepted for age VIII.; an adequate plan (parallel paths with no intersection or breaks, e.g., perfect spiral, concentric circles, transverse parallel paths) is required for age XII.; (6) giving similarities—a test borrowed from Binet's 1905 series; two things are to be compared for age VIII. (wood and coal, ship and automobile, etc.); three for age XII. (snake, cow, sparrow; knife-blade, penny, piece of wire, etc.); (7) defining words, with a view to an estimation (by sample) of the size of the child's vocabulary: 20 words are to be defined at eight, 30 at ten, 40 at twelve, 50 at fourteen, 65 by an average adult, 75 by a superior adult; the words are taken from a prepared list drawn up approximately in order of difficulty, ranging from "orange" and "bonfire," to "retroactive" and

---

[1] L. M. Terman, *The Measurement of Intelligence.* Harrap & Co., 1919.

FIGURE 8.

Test 63. Reversed Triangle.

(a). As presented to the child (letters not to be shown).

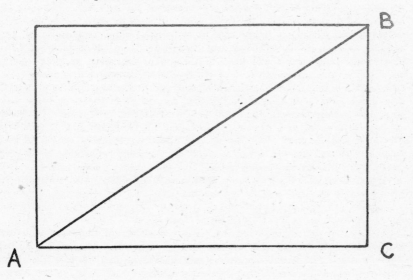

(b). As drawn by the child (letters not to be shown)

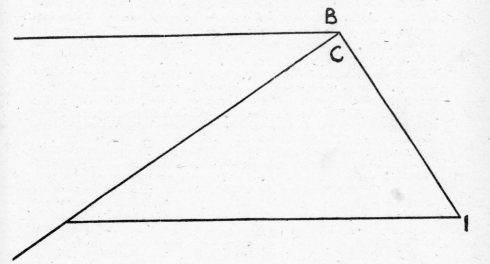

"theosophy."[1] For age X., (8) Healy's "Construction Puzzle A "—a form-board consisting of five oblong pieces fitting together into an oblong tray ; the material is an improvement upon the simple oblong card divided only into two triangular pieces, although Binet himself attempted similar puzzles with more numerous pieces and found them unsatisfactory. For age XII., (9) interpreting the morals of five well-known fables (" The Fox and the Goose," " The Milkmaid and her Eggs," etc.) ; two correctly interpreted (or the equivalent in half-credits) are accepted for age XII., and four for average adult level. For age XIV., (10) folding a paper once, twice, etc., to six times, cutting a single hole in the folded edge, and requiring the subject to infer the general rule for discovering from the number of folds how many holes there will be ; (11) three arithmetical problems (such as, " how much will seven feet of cloth cost at fifteen cents a yard ? ") ; (12) interchanging in imagination the positions of the large and small hands of a clock (supposed to point originally, e.g., to twenty-two minutes past six), and stating the time then indicated—a test first propounded by Binet in the 1905 scale, and afterwards included by Goddard and Kuhlmann. For " average adults," (13) stating how many boxes there would be if a large box contained, e.g., three smaller, each in turn containing three tiny ones ; (14) translating " come quickly " into a diagram code from memory —suggested first by Healy and Fernald, and subsequently incorporated into a revision of the Binet scale by Goddard.[2] (15) comprehending physical relations (the path of a cannon-ball ; the weight of a bucket containing water (45 lbs.) and a fish (5 lbs.) when " the water is holding up the fish " ; stating why to hit a quart can with a rifle is easier at fifty yards than at ten yards). For " superior adult," (16) an ingenuity test (given, e.g., a 3-pint and a 5-pint vessel to measure out exactly seven pints of water ; and similarly with other vessels and other quantities).

Other reforms are the addition of better or more numerous examples (e.g., for absurdities, and circumstantial problems) ; the allowance of more numerous trials ; and the provision of a more definite method of scoring (e.g., partial credits for partial success in certain tests).

The final version of the Stanford Revision reached us too late for the new tests to be incorporated into the present investigation. We are now attempting to adapt them for use with London children. It appears likely, however, that considerable modifications will need to be made, chiefly upon the following grounds.

(1) The older children, upon whose performances the Stanford Revision was based, appear to have been of a somewhat higher intellectual level than the average child in the ordinary elementary schools under the London County Council. On the other hand, the younger children appear to have been slightly more backward in the scholastic tests, owing perhaps to later

---

[1] Compare the Definition test below, p. 242.

[2] The code, said to have been largely used in the American Civil War, is of the following con-struction :—

"Come quickly" =

admission to school. Terman's subjects are said to have been drawn from schools in middle-class areas in American cities ; and, therefore, in social status, must have been distinctly superior to the average London child, and still more superior to the classes from whom defectives and delinquents are usually drawn and for whom the Binet-Simon scale has in the past been most commonly used. Terman puts the average level of the adult population at sixteen years ; whereas the recent results of the tests, as applied to recruits for the American Army, puts that level at but little over thirteen years with tests so standardised.[1]

(2) To administer the tests as revised and standardised by Terman now consumes nearly double the original amount of time—in my experience rarely less than one hour for younger children and for the brightest of the older children nearly two. The alterations are so sweeping that comparability with earlier investigations made with the Binet-Simon scale has almost vanished ; hence, little could be lost, if the scale were shortened by excising those of the original tests which are now known to be almost worthless—sex, surname, date, months, two lines, comparing faces, and the original circumstantial problems. Similarly, in translating the reading and absurdities tests, it would have been well either to have retained the Binet-Simon material in its original form—a form admittedly unsatisfactory, but still comparable with previous investigations—or else to have entirely discarded the hard prose-passage and the gruesome anecdotes.

(3) The use of American coins in the materials, and of American money-values in the problems, prevent many of the tests being transferred to English schools, in their present form and with their present age-assignments. Similarly, American phraseology and colloquialisms will need to be e'iminated. For example, the English six-year-old child would hardly understand the question : "What's the thing to do, if you're going some place and miss your car ?" or "When you notice on your way to school that you are in danger of being tardy ?" Many of the words in the vocabulary test suffer from the same disadvantage. On the other hand, the necessary alterations, particularly in the money tests and arithmetical problems, may seriously disturb the value and the level of the tests.

(4) Many of the new tests—e.g., the ball and field problem, tying the bow-knot, reversing the hands of the clock—do not, with London children, show so high a correlation as, from their ingenious character, might perhaps be inferred ; and, in any case, the procedure still seems improvable ; for example, in the second of these tests, the children are easily embarrassed by being required to tie the knot round the examiner's finger ; and, in the instructions for the first test, it is not made quite explicit that the small circle on the paper represents a large field, nor are the terms "force" and "direction" intelligible to a child barely eight, nor are all the XII.-year-old plans (e.g., the concentric but discontinuous circles) as shown on the score card really superior to all the VIII.-year-old plans (e.g., the rough but continuous spiral) ; and several in both sets are really impossible. On the other hand, many of the new tests appear to be of much value—particularly those for older and brighter children.

(5) The scale still retains a marked linguistic bias. This is shown by Terman's own observation that "in a large majority of cases the vocabulary test alone will give an intelligence quotient within 10 per cent. of that secured by the entire scale." Such problems as Porteus' maze-tests, Abelson's geometrical instruction tests, and the pictorial forms of many of the

---

[1] See, however, note on the upper limit of mental growth, p. 256.

American Army tests might well have been substituted for the feebler linguistic tests.

Nevertheless, however imperfect the Stanford Version may seem to analytic criticism, it still remains, so far as can be judged from a brief preliminary trial upon London children, the most effective, as it is the most radical, of all the foreign revisions.

The Point-Scale Method.

Yerkes's Point-Scale[1] consists of twenty exercises taken, with one exception, from the Binet-Simon series. The addition is a test which was, I believe, first used for the measurement of intelligence by myself, and which I then designated the "Analogies" test.[2] Most of Binet's information tests are omitted. And the scale as a whole loses much of its character of an instructions test, the examiner being warned not to proceed with any test until he is sure the child understands the directions.

In accordance with a suggestion of Huey's, partial credit is given to the various performances of the children according to their merit, and not invariably by the all-or-none, pass-or-fail method of Binet. Thus, for repeating three figures the child scores one mark, for repeating four figures an additional mark, and so on ; similarly in the picture tests, "enumerating" scores one mark, "describing" two, "interpreting" three. Where more than one mark is allotted by Yerkes to any one test, I have noted the fact in the instructions above under the sub-title "evaluation." The grand maximum in the Point-Scale is 100. For various ages, sexes, and social stations, norms are computed in terms of the average number of points scored ; and, having none of the fixity of an age-scale, these norms can be freely readjusted and rapidly revised. This is an unquestionable advantage. But the principle can readily be applied to the Binet scale in its usual form by merely counting the number of tests passed either actually or by implication ; and, if necessary, allowing fractions for partial success. In either case age-averages are still needed for the interpretation of the scores.

By using for partial performances entire marks or "points" instead of fractions, certain tests in the Point-Scale are given a maximum larger than unity ; and thus carry a greater weight than others. Were this weighting of the various tests determined by their diagnostic significance, the modification might be of great value. With English children, however, value and maximum score, as suggested by Yerkes, do not at all correspond. Arranging the five weights is to score at most only two points. Interpreting the three pictures—a much poorer test, neither four and a half times as good, nor four and a half times as difficult as the other—is to score nine points, nearly one-tenth of the grand maximum.

Brevity is secured by rejecting most of the tests that depend, like reading and writing, upon school instruction, or, like the coin tests, upon special experience. On the other hand, several poorer tests are still retained, e.g., suggestion (which scores three points) and comparing faces, weights, and lines. The memory tests, too, are somewhat extravagantly weighted, scoring fifteen points in all.

There is no guarantee that the points represent equal units along a linear scale. Clearly a point earned in the weights test is of more value than a point earned in the picture test. And the various age-levels are unevenly represented. Most of the tests falling in our assignments below age IV. and above age XII. are omitted. The three ages IV., V., VI. yield thirteen

---

(1) Yerkes, Bridges, and Hardwick, *A Point Scale for Measuring Ability*, 1915. (2) See pp. 234, 240.

tests ; the next three yield only seven ; for the next three, however, all
our tests (except rhymes) are retained, and the analogies are added—eleven
tests in all ; and, for ages beyond, nearly all the original tests, meagre though
they were, are dropped. Accordingly, for the two chief practical purposes—
examining borderline cases of suspected deficiency at the usual age of entrance
to special schools, and examining supernormal and scholarship children at
the older ages—the revision appears to be, for English children, no great
advance upon the original. For theoretical suggestiveness, on the other
hand, the work done with this scale, both by its authors and by those who
have since employed it, is of the highest interest and importance.[1]

The Treves-Saffiotti Method.

A modification of the Binet-Simon scale, which, among English-speaking
investigators, has attracted but little recognition, is that elaborated in Italy
by Saffiotti. The work was originally commenced in collaboration with
Treves, who died in the same year as Binet. The changes the writers have
proposed are principally two : first, the tests are to be grouped not only by
age, but also by school-class ; secondly, the children tested are to be graded
according to their success qualitatively rather than quantitatively. For
children of a given age in a given class there are allotted three sets of tests—
easy, medium, and hard. According to their success in these the children are
grouped as *deboli*, *medii*, and *forti*—dull, average, and able—and marked D,
M, or F. If time allows, the children may be tested with other sets of tests
than those immediately appropriate to their level ; and, according to their
further success in these, the children in each group are again subdivided into
three finer grades. There are thus in all nine qualitative grades—designated
most conveniently by the letters dD, mD, fD, dM, mM, fM, dF, mF, fF, *i.e.*,
dullest of the dull, average-dull, brighter dull, dull-average, and so forth.

In practice, the diagnoses obtained by this method appear, at any rate,
for Milanese children, immune from many of the disturbances to which a
mental age calculated in the usual way is liable ; in particular, they eliminate very largely the common confusion between the child who is mentally
defective, and the child who, to a degree however grave, is merely backward
educationally.[2]

Future Scales.

In England, however, it is, I think, the opinion of most of those who
have attempted to better the present condition of intelligence tests—it is
certainly my own opinion—that all departures from the Binet-Simon scale
should be either as small as possible, or else as complete as possible ; amend-
ments should be either radical or minimal. If the Binet Simon scale is to
be retained at all—and for immediate practical purposes, at any rate, it will
be retained—then uniformity can be secured, and confusion avoided, only
by returning for the time being to the exact procedure of Binet and Simon
themselves. If it is to be revised—and in the interests of future efficiency
it must be revised—then the modifications will need to be wholesale and
drastic. The three revisions just described have no title to finality ; yet

---

[1] For an excellent discussion of the Point-Scale, with results obtained from English low-grade children,
see E. O. Lewis, "The Binet and Point-Scale Methods of Testing Intelligence," *J. Exp. Ped.*, IV., March,
1918 pp. 198–202.

[2] Those unable to read Italian will find an early account of the method in *L'Année Psychologique*
XVIII., 1912, p. 327 : "L'Échelle Métrique de l'Intelligence de Binet-Simon Modifiée selon la Méthode
Treves-Saffiotti." A critical summary of Saffiotti's latest volume, *La Misura dell' Intelligenza*—a work too
little noticed in this country—will be found in the *Eugenics Review*, VIII., 4, 1917, pp. 365–373.

G

they adumbrate, however tentatively, the fitting lines for future study and research. They themselves, though sound emendations, are yet but partial emendations. The Point-Scale would have been far more effective, if it had incorporated the new tests of the Stanford Revision. The Stanford Revision would have been far more effective, if with the Point-Scale, it had ruthlessly abandoned the weakest of the original tests. Both would have been more triumphant still, if they had pursued, explicitly and without flinching, the principle that each seems tacitly to have adopted in a fitful, fragmentary fashion—the principle which I have elsewhere termed the " internal grading " of the tests.[1] In the repetition of numbers, for instance, both versions complete Binet's series by adding sets of four and six. Terman, too, is equally thorough with tests of repeating numbers in a reversed order ; and, further, carries his vocabulary test through almost every age from VIII. to Superior Adult. Such repetitions of the same form of test with regular increments of difficulty, when marked according to the method of partial credits or points, the method expressly recognised by Yerkes, and occasionally employed by Terman, virtually provide us with separate scales for separate mental functions.

Such separate scales we need, not for memory and vocabulary only, but also for all the fundamental capacities that are correlated closely with intelligence, yet remotely with each other—for perception both concrete and verbal, for delayed as well as for immediate memory, for attention both concentrated and sustained, for manual skill, for imagination, generalisation, judgment, reasoning, and the like. Such scales must be carried up through every age and stage, not merely to the thirteenth or fourteenth year with perhaps one or two maturer levels, but consistently through puberty, through adolescence, to the various grades exhibited by supernormal adults. In extracting from such scales a single measure for mental efficiency as a whole—for general intelligence, as it is currently termed—each test must be weighted, not equally or arbitrarily, but according to an empirical " regression coefficient " based upon its special correlation with intelligence itself. According to the same principles of graduation, tests of school subjects, although eliminated from the series of intelligence tests, will be separately compiled.

Nor must the influence of sex, of social status, and of educational opportunity be overlooked. Possibly, with tests of capacities more fundamental, the effect of acquired, as distinct from innate differences will be proportionately reduced. But there will remain the need for separate norms as well as for separate scales.

Only by such a scale, or such a system of scales, can we diagnose general ability with scientific exactitude. But a scheme so elaborate will demand for its completion many years of co-operative research. Meanwhile, we may enquire what degree of validity appears to attach to the method which is the most obvious temporary substitute—the Binet-Simon Scale in its original form. To this problem the following memorandum will be devoted.[2]

---

[1] See " The Measurement of Intelligence by the Binet-Simon Tests," *loc. cit. inf.*, pp. 36, 150.

[2] I have attempted to analyse and evaluate in greater detail the general principles upon which the Binet-Simon scale is based in the *Eugenics Review*, VI., 1 and 2, April and July, 1914, pp. 36–50, 140–152 (" The Measurement of Intelligence of the Binet-Simon Tests "). For this reason I have here largely refrained from entering into a theoretical discussion both of the fundamental nature of the scale and the fundamental nature of intelligence.

APPENDIX I.

List of Materials Needed for the Binet-Simon Tests.

One of the chief merits of the psychological tests devised by Binet and Simon is the extreme simplicity of the apparatus required. Many of the tests, indeed, require no apparatus at all. Such materials as are needed for the rest can nearly all be home-made. For precise results they should be prepared in exact accordance with Binet's descriptions. The pictures needed will be found in the following Appendix. If these are not to hand, other pictures of simple scenes will serve for very rough purposes ; while the "pretty faces" and faces with "missing features" could be drawn from memory, or from the descriptions below. Many of the published reproductions of the latter, indeed, greatly differ from the originals (e.g., in Winch's examples the difference between the pretty and ugly faces is more excellently brought out ; while in those of Goddard they are not so distinct) ; and several investigators have used pictures of their own choice, usually more appropriate to children, and therefore more easily eliciting "description" and "interpretation." Needless to say, very slight changes in the drawing of the pictures may make an appreciable difference in the final evaluations.

The following is a list of the materials required for the entire scale. The figures in brackets indicate the index-number of the tests for which the apparatus is required (arabic numeral) and the age to which the tests are assigned (roman numeral) :—

1. Coins : 13 pennies, 3 halfpennies, a farthing, sixpence, shilling, florin, half-crown, half-sovereign, and sovereign (or ten-shilling and pound notes). (III. 5 ; IV. 9 ; VI. 21, 25 ; VII. 33 ; VIII. 40.)

2. 5 Weights : Boxes, similar in shape, colour, and size, each $1 \cdot 5 \times 2 \cdot 5 \times 3 \cdot 5$ cm. (about $\frac{3}{8} \times 1 \times 1\frac{3}{8}$ inches), weighing respectively 3, 6, 9, 12, and 15 grams (about 1, 2, 3, 4, and 5-tenths of an ounce, or, more exactly, 46, 93, 139, 185, and 231 grains). Waistcoat-pocket matchboxes are about the correct size. They can be filled with cotton-wool, and shot (kept from rattling by melted candle-wax) until they weigh the correct amounts. (V. 19 ; X. 46.)

3. Two plain cards the size of large ladies' visiting cards (6 cm. × 9 cm., or about $2\frac{1}{2} \times 3\frac{1}{2}$ inches). One card is blackened upon one side, and then cut diagonally into two similar right-angled triangles. (VI. 26 ; XV. 63.)

4. A sheet of paper about 15 cm. (6 inches) square, folded in four like a letter ready for an envelope. In the middle of the edge, which presents but a single fold, a small triangular notch, about 1 cm. deep, is drawn. (XV. 61.)

5. Pocket-knife and door-key of familiar pattern. (III. 5 ; V. 12.) Book, table, chair, and door arranged for errand. (V. 12.)

6. Watch, showing seconds. (V. 17 ; VI. 24 ; VII. 33, 34 ; VIII. 38 ; IX. 42, 43 ; X. 46, 47, 48 ; XI. 49, 50, 51, 53 ; XII. 55.)

7. Unruled paper, pen, ink. (V. 13 ; VI. 22, 23 ; VII. 35 ; IX. 47.) Pencil. (X. 48.)

The following materials are given in the next Appendix ; they may most conveniently be cut out and inserted into a small octavo pocket-book. For some purposes, however, stout cards are preferable, one for each item. Cards are more durable and easier for the child to hold ; and if several teachers are working together at the same time, the materials may be temporarily distributed according to the requirements of each.

8. Reproductions of Binet's three engravings (Figure 9) :—

    i. (Figure 9 (a).) A man and boy pulling a cart—loaded with table, bed, basket, saucepan, etc.—up a hill leading from a large town.

    ii. (Figure 9 (b).) A man and woman seated upon a bench in a street, the woman clinging to the man who leans back limply, with head raised and eyes closed.

    iii. (Figure 9 (c).) A man in a small bare room, standing on a bed, looking out of a small window. The typical characteristics of an English convict and prison-cell are absent. (III. 6 ; VI. 29, XII. 56.)

9. Two parallel, horizontal, straight lines, 5 cm. and 6 cm. (2 inches and $2\frac{2}{5}$ inches) in length respectively, drawn in ink upon a card or sheet of paper, the longer placed about 3 cm. (1 inch) below the shorter, with its centre immediately beneath that of the other. (IV. 10.) (Figure 10.)

10. Three pairs of women's faces, all looking toward the left. Of the first pair, that on the right is much uglier ; of the second, that on the left ; of the third, that on the right. (IV. 11.) (Figure 11.)

11. A square for copying, each side measuring about 3 to 4 cm. ($1\frac{1}{2}$ inches), drawn in ink. (V. 13.) (Figure 12.)

12. Four oblong pieces of paper, 2 × 6 cm. (about $\frac{4}{5}$ × $2\frac{1}{4}$ inches), coloured bright red, yellow, blue, and green, gummed beneath one another in that order. (V. 17.) (Figure 13.)

13. A rhombus or diamond for copying, about 7 cm. ($2\frac{3}{4}$ inches) long and 4 cm. ($1\frac{1}{2}$ inches) high, with sides 4 cm. ($1\frac{1}{2}$ inches) long. (VI. 22.) (Figure 14.)

14. " See little Paul " written, as a model for transcription, in the common, sloping, large copy-book style. (VI. 23.) (Figure 15.)

15. Three faces with missing features ; the first, a man's, three-quarter face, with the mouth omitted ; the second, a woman's face in profile with the eye omitted, but the eyebrow drawn ; the third, a woman's face in profile with the nose omitted. On a separate page (or card), a full-length portrait of a woman with both arms omitted. (VII. 32.) (Figure 16.)

16. A newspaper extract, describing a fire, and printed or typed for reading. (VIII. 36 and IX. 44.) (Figure 17.)

17. Two designs to be drawn from memory, one a truncated pyramid, and the other a modified Greek-key pattern. (X. 48.) (Figure 18.)

18. Three sentences with the words disarranged. (XII. 55.) (**Figure 19.**)

19. Six cards, or better still a small home-made book containing six leaves. Each card or leaf has drawn upon it, on one side only, a pair of lines, the two lines being side by side in the same horizontal straight line. The lengths of the lines are as follows :—

	1st line.	2nd line.
(a) 1st page ..	.. 4 cm. ($1\frac{3}{5}$ in.)	5 cm. (2 in.)
(b) 2nd ,, ..	.. 5 cm. (2 in.)	6 cm. ($2\frac{2}{5}$ in.)
(c) 3rd ,, ,.	.. 6 cm. ($2\frac{2}{5}$ in.)	7 cm. ($2\frac{4}{5}$ in.)
(d) 4th ,, ..	.. 7 cm. ($2\frac{1}{5}$ in.)	7 cm. ($2\frac{1}{5}$ in.)
(e) 5th ,, ..	.. 7 cm. ($2\frac{1}{5}$ in.)	7 cm. ($2\frac{1}{5}$ in.)
(f) 6th ,, ..	.. 7 cm. ($2\frac{1}{5}$ in.)	7 cm. ($2\frac{1}{5}$ in.)

(XIII. 57) (Figure 20 (a) to (f).)

The thickness of the line for this and other tests Binet nowhere specifies. The lines in the following figures are set up with four-to-pica (three point) rules, which are nominally 1–24th of an inch in breadth. The slight absorbency of the paper, and the slight overflowing of the ink, may render the lines, as actually printed, somewhat thicker. The line used in the test-materials of the Stanford Revision appears to be about 3–128ths of an inch; that used in the test-materials for the Point Scale, about 6–128ths. For the test of memory-drawing, however, Yerkes appears to use a line which is about half as thick again.

APPENDIX II.

Pictures and other Materials for the Binet-Simon Tests.

The test-materials here appended are taken from the illustrations, or reconstructed from the text, of the original French versions. To Dr. Simon I am heavily indebted for his generous permission to reproduce the drawings here.

Some have perceived in them, or thought they perceived, a slight hastiness of choice or a slight crudity of design. Children are not so critical. It is true, the colour in Saffiotti's pictures quicken a greater interest ; the elegance of Winch's " pretty and ugly faces " appeal more to the artistic eye ; the solidity of line in Yerkes' memory-drawing test offer greater distinctness to the subject's apprehension: And all these variations may well be borne in mind by those who set themselves to construct new scales. But such changes not only reduce the difficulty, but also modify the nature, of the original task. Those who seek to preserve the wide range of comparability given by the old scale will doubtless prefer, with me, to adhere with the greatest attainable exactitude to the French materials rather than to seek a superficial finish and insert refinements of their own.

The illustrations are here printed, one on each page, and each on one side of the leaf only, with no other matter visible on that side. This is partly to avoid confusing the child, and partly to enable the examiner to cut out the essential test-materials, and transfer them, as before recommended, into a portable pocketbook. I hope it may shortly be possible to issue the entire set of materials both for the psychological and for the scholastic tests, bound with the necessary schedules and tables, in a separate and handier form.

Figure 9 (*a*).

AGES III., VI., and XII.

Tests 6, 29, and 56.

(*For instructions see pp. 26-27.*)

(i).

FIGURE 9 (*b*).

AGES III., VI., and XII.

Tests 6, 29, and 56 (*continued*).

(*For instructions see pp.* 26-27.)

(ii).

FIGURE 9 (c).

AGES III., VI., and XII.

Tests 6, 29, and 56 (continued).

(For instructions see pp. 26–27.)

(iii).

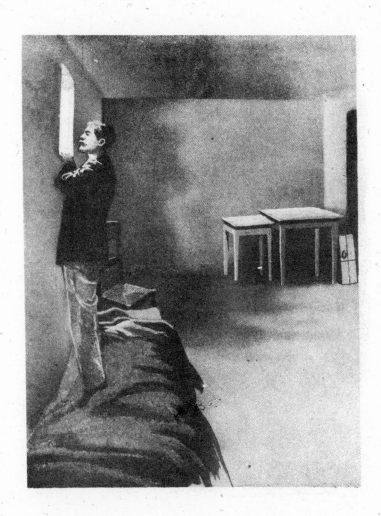

FIGURE 10.

AGE IV.

Test 10. Comparing Lines.

(For the first attempt the figure is to be shown to the child with the lines horizontal and the smaller above the larger.)

(For instructions see p. 29.)

Figure 11 (a).

AGE IV.

Test 11. Comparing Faces.

(*For instructions see p. 30.*)

FIGURE 11 (*b*).

AGE IV.

Test 11. Comparing Faces (*continued*).

(*For instructions see p. 30.*)

FIGURE 11 (*c*).

AGE IV.

Test 11. Comparing Faces (*continued*).

(*For instructions see p. 30.*)

FIGURE 12.

AGE V.

Test 13.   Copying a Square.

(*For instructions see pp.* 30–32.)

FIGURE 13.

AGE V.

Test 17. Naming Four Colours

(For instructions see p. 34.)

FIGURE 14.

AGE VI.

Test 22. Copying Diamond.

(The figure is to be shown to the child with the long axis vertical.)

(*For instructions see p. 36.*)

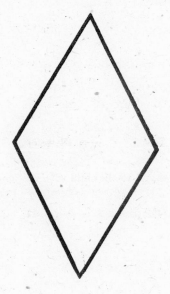

FIGURE 15.

AGE VI.

Test 23. Transcription.

(For instructions see p. 36.)

See little Paul

FIGURE 16 (*a*).

AGE VII.

Test 32. Missing Features.

(For instructions see pp. 43–44.)

Figure 16 (*b*).

AGE VII.

Test 32. Missing Features (*continued*).

(*For instructions see pp. 43–44.*)

FIGURE 16 (c).

AGE VII.

Test 32. Missing Features (*continued*).

(*For instructions see pp.* 43–44.)

FIGURE 16 (*d*).

AGE VII.

Test 32. Missing Features (*continued*).

(*For instructions see pp. 43–44.*)

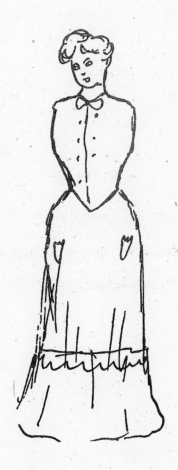

FIGURE 17.

AGES VIII. and IX.

Tests 36 and 44.   Reading and Reproduction.

(For instructions see pp. 46–47.)

THREE HOUSES ON FIRE.

LONDON,
September 5th.

A big fire last night burnt down three houses in the middle of the city.

Seventeen families now have no homes. The loss is more than 150,000 pounds.

A young barber, who saved a baby in the cradle, was badly burnt about the hands.

FIGURE 18.

AGE X.

Test 48. Memory Drawing.

figures are to be shown to the child with the truncated pyramid to
the left, and the Greek key pattern to the right. But see p. 56.)

(*For instructions see pp.* 53–56.)

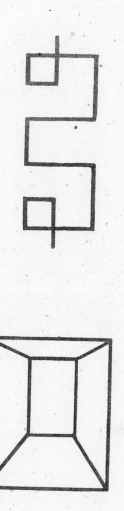

FIGURE 19.

AGE XII.

Test 55. Rearranging Mixed Sentences.

(For instructions see p. 61).

(i)

> a defends
> master dog good
> bravely his.

(ii)

> my asked paper
> the I teacher
> correct to.

(iii)

> started the for
> morning early this
> we country.

FIGURE 20 (*a*) to (*f*).

AGE XIII.

Test 57.   Suggestion.

(*For instructions see p.* 62).

K

APPENDIX III.

The Definition of Intelligence.

Need for a Formal Definition. The Binet-Simon tests claim to be primarily a scale for measuring " intelligence " ; and it is therefore natural to inquire what precisely we are to understand by this word. Curiously enough Binet himself has given no fixed or formal definition of the term ; but he has made several attempts at explaining how intelligence operates and what are its main characteristics.[1] Terman indeed declares that " it is quite unreasonable to demand, as critics of the Binet method have sometimes done, that one who would measure intelligence should first present a complete definition of it."[2]

In view of the confusion that seems to have arisen among those who have discussed the various possible definitions, I suggest that it would be useful at the outset to recall the old scholastic distinction between a " nominal " and a " real " definition : " a nominal definition is one which states how the *word* is to be used ; a real definition is one which explains the *nature of the thing* to be defined." A " nominal " definition of the term seems essential before we can consider how to measure intelligence ; a " real " definition, it is true, may have to wait for much further investigation.

Definition Proposed. In these Reports I use the word in the sense proposed in several previous articles[3] : by intelligence I understand " innate, general cognitive efficiency." This phrase incidentally seems to make explicit the idea in the minds of nearly all the earlier workers. First, it seems clear that Binet and his predecessors (Galton, for example) were seeking to measure a capacity that is " innate," " inborn," or " natural," as distinct from knowledge or skill that is acquired : (for the latter Binet himself proposed a scale of pedagogical tests). Secondly, they were attempting to measure a " cognitive " characteristic, and under " cognitive " we must include practical capacity, as well as intellectual capacity in the narrower sense. Finally, they were seeking to measure a general or all-round ability, not a special ability confined to some limited group of tasks.

The teacher has no hesitation in assuming that some such general ability exists, and is definitely recognizable. Thus, in elementary schools each pupil attends the same class or " standard " for every school subject—a high class if he is bright, a low class if he is dull ; and eventually he may be transferred either to a secondary school or to a special school on the assumption that he is exceptionally bright all round or exceptionally deficient all round. At the

---

[1] *L'Année Psychologique* 1909, pp. 1-147. In an earlier article in the same journal (1900), he had made " adaptation," resulting from attention, the chief characteristic. In this country the word had become familiar to psychologists chiefly from its use by writers on comparative psychology to describe differences in the behaviour of different animals : thus for Lloyd Morgan degrees of " intelligence " are assessed by the animal's ability to " adapt his behaviour to an environment of increasing complexity." (Cf. *Animal Life and Intelligence.*)

[2] *The Measurement of Intelligence*, 1916, p. 44.

[3] *J. Exp. Ped.*, I., 1911, pp. 93f. *Child Study*, IV., 1911, pp. 33-45, 78-100.

same time *within* a given class, or within a given form at a secondary school,
where all pupils are on much the same level for *general* ability, certain *special*
abilities seem to stand out.

The assumption of a general ability has recently been contested by Prof.
Thorndike in America and by Dr. William Brown and Dr. Godfrey Thomson
in this country. Thomson maintains that the correlation tables which at
first sight seem to imply one common or general factor can be accounted for
just as well by a number of overlapping group-factors.[1] On the other hand,
Prof. Spearman has vigorously supported the traditional notion of a " general
intelligence " (although he no longer wishes to use the term) ; but he doubts
the existence of special abilities, entering into limited groups of subjects :
such a view, he considers, is merely a relic of the old faculty doctrine, which
can find no support either in modern psychological theory or in recent
psychological experiments.[2]

Evidence for the Existence of Intelligence as thus Defined. How, then, are we
to decide between these alternative hypotheses ? To begin with, let us once
again recall a point in the logic of science. Nowhere in empirical science can
we expect a direct deductive proof of our hypotheses : we can only show
indirectly and inductively, that the hypothesis and its corollaries are consistent with the verifiable facts.[3]

First, then, it is clear that, if there is such a thing as general ability
entering into all school subjects, the marks for each of our tests should show
a fairly high positive correlation. Unless there is such a correlation, then
manifestly, by adding or averaging the marks for a large number of tests, we
should eventually obtain approximately the same final mark for every pupil.
This is an issue of fact ; and, although the earliest investigators found correlations that differed little if at all from zero, this has not been confirmed
by later work.[4]

Practically all recent investigators have found significant positive
correlations between cognitive tests of every type; and the universality of

---

(1) Thorndike, *et al.*, *Am. J. Psych.*, XX, 1909, pp. 364-369 ; Brown, *Mental Measurement*
1912 ; Thomson, *Brit. J. Psych.*, VIII, 1916, pp. 271-281. Thomson himself seems to regard the
word " intelligence " as itself merely the name for yet another faculty : as he tells us elsewhere, he
is not himself " a believer in the existence of a ' faculty ' called general ability ; and considers that
the statistical work of those who affirm this theory is of doubtful validity." Although his alternative
explanations cannot, in the present state of knowledge, be dismissed as untenable, it will be seen
that they appear to render the testing of " intelligence " impossible. Moreover, if there is no such
factor as intelligence or general ability, we cannot assume that it is inherited or innate. [It should
be added that, since this report was written, Prof. Thomson would seem to have altered his views'
since he has not only himself devised tests of general intelligence, but even initiated researches on
inborn differences in general intelligence. However, in his book on *Instinct, Intelligence, and Character*,
he states (p. 206) that " an intelligence quotient measures an *average* of the individual's intellectual
powers " ; and this definition may perhaps reconcile what to the superficial critic may appear (perhaps
quite wrongly) an inconsistency or a change of opinion.]

(2) Spearman and Hart, *Brit. J. Psych.*, V., 1912, pp. 51-84 and other papers.

(3) Thus, when Brown and Thomson complain that " a general factor is only a possible, not a
necessary explanation of the facts " (*loc. cit.*, note inserted in 1924 edition, p. 173), they are adducing
a criticism which could be applied to every explanation in empirical science.

(4) The first investigation in which Galton's correlational technique was applied to mental tests
was that published by Wissler in 1901 (*Psych. Rev. Mon. Sup.*, III). Spearman (*loc. cit.* sup., 1904)
considered that the observed correlations should first be corrected for unreliability; I should rather
urge that they should be corrected for selection. Teachers frequently complain that, when they try
intelligence-tests on their own classes, they obtain much smaller correlations than those reported by
psychologists. The answer is : a well-selected class of school children (like Wissler's classes of University students) are, in virtue of selection, a relatively homogeneous group : where there is little variation
in intelligence, there can be little covariation between the tests. The tests should be tried on complete
age-groups : (on the " Influence of Selection," see Pearson's paper with that title, *Phil. Trans. Roy.
Soc.*, CC, A, 1902, pp. 1-66).

these positive correlations is in itself sufficient to justify the assumption of a common factor entering into all the tests.[1]

But when we rule out the influence of intelligence, either by taking homogeneous classes or by the device of partial correlation, we still find small positive correlations between tests of certain types. This seems to imply the existence of special abilities or disabilities as well. In my view, therefore, the best hypothesis for the practical teacher is the double hypothesis, namely, that which postulates the presence *both* of a single general factor *and* of a small set of group factors, or, in more concrete terms, *both* of general intelligence *and* of special abilities.

Nature of Intelligence as thus Defined. Having decided, then, that a general factor underlying all cognitive tests may be reasonably assumed to exist, we now have to take up the more difficult problem of determining its actual nature.

In his first paper[2] dealing with this question, Prof. Spearman, after due consideration, rejected the " intermediate " type of test used by Binet, and preferred what American writers have called the " German procedure " (*i.e.*, using laboratory tests of elementary processes) rather than the " French " (*i.e.*, using tests of more everyday activities involving " higher intellectual processes "). As a result he was led to identify General Intelligence with " General Sensory Discrimination," and concluded that laboratory tests of discrimination (such as Galton had proposed) " have unrivalled advantages for diagnosing this central function." This is in keeping with the old philosophical view, that there is nothing in the mind which has not reached it through the senses ; and yet, as we should expect, it is not a conclusion which has been readily accepted by teachers.

Prof. Spearman's own experiments, however, had been confined to three tests of sensory discrimination and assessments of five secondary school subjects. In order to establish the existence of a general factor underlying *all* cognitive processes, it seemed essential, as I have argued elsewhere, to select tests which cover the *whole* range of cognitive ability, from the lowest and simplest sensory tests (such as those preferred by Prof. Spearman) up to the highest intellectual levels of all. When this is done,[3] we still find a common factor entering into all such processes ; but the tests which yield the highest correlations with this factor (and, indeed, with independent assessments of intelligence) are no longer the tests of simple sensory discrimination, but tests of far more complex processes. Indeed, *the more complex the process tested, the closer its correlation with the general factor of intelligence.* From this I concluded that intelligence must be essentially a synthesizing or organizing capacity ; and (to quote a later paper) the development of a child's intellectual ability appears to be " a function of the degree of organic complexity of which his attention is capable, or (in Stout's phrase) of his capacity for noetic synthesis."[4]

---

(1) In a joint paper on " General Ability, its Existence and Nature " (*Brit. J. Psych.*, V., 1912, p. 53), Prof. Spearman has proposed a mathematical " criterion " to decide between rival hypotheses as to the relations between mental tests, namely, what he calls the " intercolumnar criterion." It should be noted, however, that this is *a criterion for demonstrating not the presence of a general factor, but the absence of supplementary factors.* The only " proof " of the hypothesis of a general factor—an inductive not a deductive proof—must consist in the empirical verification of significant positive correlations between all the tests or performances into which that factor enters.

(2) *Am. J. Psych.*, XV, 1904, pp. 272, 284.

(3) Burt, *Brit. J. Psych.*, III, 1909, pp. 94-177 and later papers.

(4) *Journ. Exp. Ped.*, 1919, p. 17. This is in keeping with Ebbinghaus's view that intelligence is " an activity of combination."

Accordingly, in constructing supplementary tests of intelligence, such as those described later in this volume (Appendix III, pp. 233-257), the assumption has been that the most efficient tests will be those that elicit the most complex mental processes of which the child is capable (and, of course, which the conditions of testing permit). This principle is itself confirmed by noting which tests in the Binet Scale are most effective (see p. 218). Obviously the most successful way of synthesizing a complex set of data will be a synthesis which depends, not on mere mechanical associations, but upon logical relations. Hence the increase of intellectual ability would seem to consist essentially " in an increase in the number, variety and compactness of the *relations* which the child's mind can perceive and integrate into a coherent whole."[1] Accordingly, in my earlier attempts to test " higher mental processes," I included tests of relational activities, *i.e.*, what would popularly be called tests of logical thinking or reasoning. The simplest type is to be found in what I called the Analogies test : this " involves (i) the perception, implicit or explicit, of a relation ; and (ii) the reconstruction of an analogous relation by so-called relative suggestion " (*i.e.*, relational suggestion).[2]

Criticisms and Alternative Views. The views put forward in my earlier papers were discussed by Prof. Spearman in the course of his joint article on " General Ability, Its Existence and Nature." It is encouraging to find that Prof. Spearman himself now explicitly accepts the view that " the ' higher ' operations such as reasoning, etc., generally produce larger correlations than the sensory or motor." He argues, however, that " the rule is at once explicable by the greater complexity of these processes : for the multitude of independent specific factors must tend to cancel one another, leaving the General Factor more dominant " in the test-result (p. 69) ; and he believes that the " endeavour to identify the General Factor with synthetic power, etc." is to follow " a false track " (p. 71).

Nevertheless, further investigations, particularly by introspective methods, have only strengthened my conviction that it is the process of *combining or integrating* the subordinate processes that is the essential requirement ; and naturally integration is only possible if the processes involved exhibit some complexity. This view, it seems to me, also fits in with Sherrington's conception of the functions of the central nervous system. Those functions are, in his well-known phrase, to facilitate efficient adaptation by " integrative action." We can imagine that its capacity for integration must depend upon (i) the number of neurones ; (ii) the number of branches to the neurones ; and (iii) the systematic arrangement of these neurones and their branches ; and accordingly individual differences in intelligence may be conceived to depend upon differences in the neural architecture of the individual brain : it may be added that the microscopic study of the brains of low-grade defectives seems to bear out this view.

Further, it is natural to assume that in the same individual the nervous tissue, like every other tissue (*e.g.*, the hair or the skin), will tend to have much the same general structural characteristics throughout, though, of course, in different parts it may be more or less differentiated. And thus we

(1) " The Development of Reasoning Ability in School Children," *J. Exp. Ped.*, V., 1919, p.127.

(2) " Experimental Tests of Higher Mental Processes and their Relation to General Intelligence," *J. Exp. Ped.*, 1911, Vol. I., p. 101. The phrase " relative suggestion " was taken from Prof. Stout, and designates what might perhaps be more intelligibly called relational suggestion, *i.e.*, the suggestion of a fresh pair of correlates by a given pair standing in a given relation. These two principles—aptly renamed " eduction of relations and correlates " — form the basis of Spearman's revised theory of intelligence.

seem to have a physiological basis for interpreting the conception of a general cognitive factor.[1]

Now, if intelligence at bottom rests on a structural characteristic of the nervous system, then it is not difficult to suppose that this characteristic may be inherited. Hence we have a further reason for expecting differences in general intelligence to be inheritable, or at any rate inborn. This expectation is confirmed by empirical evidence. In several later papers I have attempted to show that measurements of the general factor, as thus defined and tested, show a high correlation (·40 to ·55) in members of the same family. It was, indeed, as a result of cumulative evidence along these lines that I ventured to give a formal definition for the term " intelligence," in keeping with its use by previous psychologists, and to offer a concrete explanation of the definition so proposed. Intelligence, therefore, I defined as an " innate, general, cognitive factor " ; and the arguments just summarized seem to warrant us in assuming that something corresponding to the definition really existed.[2]

Once again Prof. Spearman is not wholly in agreement. He accepts the evidence showing that intelligence is revealed in tests demanding new adaptations, formed by the aid of " clear awareness " (or attention), and hardly at all in tests that merely evoke old or " mechanized " co-ordinations. But, since in his view it is mechanized activities that can be simultaneously combined, whereas unmechanized activities interfere and compete, he and Dr. Hart reject the notion that intelligence is a synthetic or " combining " activity, to be explained by the structural characteristics of the brain, and prefer to identify the general factor with the brain's " central fund of nervous energy." Their conception, they believe, is really " supported by Burt's finding that the highest correlations are given by performances demanding most attention "[3] ; for, according to them, the most attentive worker is the most successful worker, because he is the worker who can concentrate most energy on his task. Whether or not differences in energy[4] are inherited, they do not say.

McDougall had previously put forward the hypothesis of a central fund of nervous energy. But for him mental energy is essentially *hormic, not cognitive* ; it underlies conative effort, and its main source is the primary emotions or instincts. Intelligence would thus correspond to the efficiency of the human machine, not (as Spearman and Hart suppose) to the energy or power available to work it : an excitable defective may be intensely active and energetic, but the behaviour is not intelligent merely *because* it is energetic.

Practical Corollaries. It must now be apparent why the modern psychologist lays such stress upon the measurement of intelligence. If intelligence is a general factor, it will enter into everything the child says, thinks, does, or attempts, both while he is at school and later on in after-life. If intelligence is innate, the child's degree of intelligence is permanently limited. No amount of teaching will turn the child who is genuinely defective in general intelligence into a normal pupil. Finally, if it is inherited, the rate of reproduction of the various groups will determine the intellectual level of the next generation. Thus, if (as some have argued) the intellectual level of pupils at present in the London schools is lower than the level attained 10 or 15 years ago, this

---

(1) Burt, *Brit. J. Psych.*, III., 1909, p. 169. *Child Study*, IV., 1911, pp. 99-100.

(2) *J. Exp. Ped.*, *loc. cit.*; *Child Study*, *loc. cit.*

(3) We are probably interpreting the term attention in slightly different ways. My view of " attention " was taken from McDougall, *viz.*, that it was an expression of the integrative, co-ordinating, or systematizing activity of the psychophysical system (*Mind*, XII, pp. 302f.).

(4) Presumably, if the terms have the same meaning as they commonly have in physics, chemistry and physiology, what is inherited must be differences in " power " (rate of doing work, *i.e.*, rate of producing or using energy) rather than in " energy " as such.

might be due to changes in the birth-rate. Hence it becomes a task of supreme importance to organize and to repeat mental and scholastic surveys such as the present at convenient intervals.

An analysis of the data procured during this survey has already revealed a striking correlation between the intelligence of school children and the occupational class from which they are drawn : arranged according to occupational classes, their average I.Q. varies from about 89 for children of casual labourers and 92 for unskilled workers up to 120 for children drawn from the higher professional classes. Now, as has been frequently pointed out, there is a definite inverse correlation between occupational class and size of family. Between intelligence and size of family the inverse correlation is even larger. The effects of these differences in birth-rate are obvious ; and it is difficult to withstand the inference that the average level of intelligence among the population as a whole must be slowly but steadily declining.[1] These deductions will need careful corroboration by further surveys carried out after (say) a ten years' interval along comparable lines.

---

[1] I have discussed this problem more fully in the Preliminary Report of a " Survey of Intellectual Ability in Different Sections of the London School Population " (1919).

APPENDIX IV.

Factor—Analysis of the Binet Tests.[1]

In selecting pupils for different types of schools, teachers and examiners have two questions to answer : first, what is the *general* level shown by each child ; secondly, does he possess any *special* ability, or disability, in this or that direction. Thus, in the County of London between 1 and 2 per cent. of the elementary school population are transferred to special schools for the mentally defective ; while at the other end of the scale nearly 13 per cent. are transferred to some kind of school offering a more advanced kind of education. Further, for these latter the education is of a more specialized type—academic or practical, artistic or technical. There are, for example, approximately 1,500 scholars holding free places in secondary schools ; more than 20,000 in central schools ; and about 2,000 holding scholarships at trade schools, technical institutes, and schools of arts and crafts. For secondary and central schools the selection is made mainly by examination at the age of 11 ; for trade schools not, as a rule, until the age of 13.

In making such selections, besides the examination-results, the teachers' reports may also be taken into account ; and in the near future, as such reports become more and more comparable and reliable, they doubtless will be, and indeed should be, given greater weight. The teacher, therefore, urgently needs some method which will enable him to detect, not only general intelligence, but also special abilities and aptitudes (assuming that there are such things). Moreover, many would argue that, if the highly gifted child is to have a fair chance at examinations of the existing type, he should be recognized by the teacher at an early age, and, so far as practicable, encouraged to develop his special talents.

The Binet-Simon scale, as we have seen, is intended primarily to measure the child's *general* level of ability. As a means of picking out the supernormal, it is certainly not so trustworthy as it is for ascertaining the defective. Nevertheless at times it may be of unquestionable value in enabling the teacher to detect the brighter pupils and to assess their level in comparable terms, especially in those cases where, owing to absence, illness, or other cause, the child's scholastic attainments are not equal to his inborn capacity. But secondly Binet himself appears to have considered that his scale might also throw light on *special* abilities or disabilities. Practical experience in some measure supports this view. Elsewhere I have described cases of young children, backward in one or more of the fundamental school subjects, where the scale as a whole often demonstrated that the pupil was not innately dull or defective, but seemed to suffer from some specialized defect of memory, itself quite possibly innate. Certainly the memory tests that Binet has included in the scale are merely tests of immediate or short-distance memory ; nevertheless, if a child's immediate or short-distance memory is weak, then *a fortiori* he can hardly be expected to show normal retentiveness over longer periods ; and memory in this sense appears to be a specialized capacity on which the fundamentals of reading, spelling, and arithmetic more particularly depend.

---

(1) Abridged from an earlier L.C.C. Report submitted to the Education Officer (1931).

135

However, the very existence of these alleged " special abilities " has been vigorously challenged by Prof. Spearman and other psychological writers. Such a notion, they contend, though still widely held by teachers and other educationists, arises merely from an unthinking acceptance of the discredited doctrine of mental faculties.[1] Prof. Spearman has summed up his view under the title of " the two-factor theory." This theory maintains that mental performances depend upon two kinds of factor only : (i) a general factor common to all performances, and (ii) specific factors peculiar to each test. In his view the specific factor " seems in every case to be wholly different from those in all the others."[2]

On the other hand, many critics of the Binet tests have objected to them just because they so often seem to depend upon special abilities or disabilities of a limited kind. Binet himself describes his tests as representing three broad categories : (i) tests of sensory or perceptual processes ; (ii) tests of memory ; (iii) tests of verbal ability ; and sometimes even seems to speak as though general intelligence was a mere sum-total of these special abilities.[3] Accordingly, it seems essential for us to determine, if we possibly can : (i) whether performances in the Binet-Simon tests do in any degree depend on specialized capacities; and (ii) if so, whether their influence is so large as to outweigh that of the general factor of intelligence.

Now, if we are to envisage, however tentatively, the possibility of *several* mental factors or abilities, then we require a more general statistical procedure. We need, in fact, not a two-factor theory, but a multiple factor theory. In my previous *Report on the Relations of Educational Abilities* (1917, p. 56) I suggested that the problem could be attacked along the same lines as has been adopted in the statistical theory of " multiple correlation " : if we could first assess the correlation of each test with the main general factor, then by means of the ordinary statistical theory we could " partial out " the influence of that factor and examine the residual or partial correlations to see whether they fell into groups which in turn had each its own general factor.[4]

Evidently in principle the same procedure should be applicable to the Binet tests, though, as I shall show in a moment, an alternative approach may here be adopted, which is simpler and perhaps more suitable. If we apply the same method of calculation as was proposed for educational tests, we shall need first of all the correlations of each Binet test with every other. With the Binet tests, however, the marks are not graded, but are expressed merely in terms of pass or fail. The correlation will therefore be measured by

---

(1) The word " specific " has led to some misunderstanding. In my earlier reports I have adopted the term " general factor " to indicate a factor covering a given *genus* of tests, and the term " special " or " specific " to denote factors limited to certain *species* only. Prof. Spearman uses the word " specific " in the sense of " peculiar to " or " unique to " : his specific factors are thus each unique to a particular test or even a particular test-performance. From the teacher's standpoint, therefore, Prof. Spearman's theory may be described as a theory of a *single* factor. Towards the end of his joint article with Dr. Hart, he certainly seems to move a little nearer to the double hypothesis for which I have always contended, and seems disposed to qualify his earlier and more sweeping statements. But his acknowledgment on this later page of " the specific correlation discovered by Burt " suggesting a memory factor (p. 75) is not quite consistent with his earlier application of his criterion to my column of figures for memory (p. 55). There the conclusion he reached was that (after due corrections have been made) the table of coefficients shows *no* evidence for a factor other than the general. However, this is not the place to press these minor criticisms : the differences of viewpoint have already been fully discussed in the report I was requested by the Chief Inspector to submit on " The Bearing of the Two Factor Theory on the Organization of Schools and Classes " (see also below, Appendix on the Classification of Pupils according to Special Abilities).

(2) *Am. J. Psych.*, Vol. XV, p. 284.

(3) For Binet's own views on the use of the correlational technique to settle the problem of mental faculties, see *Les idées modernes sur les enfants*, 1909, pp. 242f.

(4) The reader who is not familiar with this conception as applied to the results of educational tests may consult the reports and Appendix cited above. For formulae cf. pp. 272-5 below.

some form of "association coefficient," *i.e.*, a coefficient deduced from a four-fold table instead of from two columns of graded measurements. Since the tests are intended primarily to measure intelligence, and since intelligence, as we have seen, is distributed normally, the most appropriate coefficient, it would seem, is the tetrachoric coefficient described in a later appendix (p. 232).[1]

Having obtained the correlations of each test with the rest, we can go on to apply the same technique of partial correlation as was used for educational tests.[2] By way of illustration I give results for 18 tests (those for ages IV and V, together with the harder tests for age III and the easier tests for age VI : table below.). These tests were chosen because they were applied to the largest number of unselected children (853 in all). Using the same formula as before, the correlation between each test and the hypothetical general factor was first calculated from the observed tetrachoric correlations (after tentatively eliminating the effects of possible group-factors). The figures so obtained (corrected by successive approximation) are shown in the first column of the table below. On deducting the effect of this general factor from

Calculated Correlations of Tests with Hypothetical Factors.

TESTS	Gen. Int.	Verb.	Man.	Mem.	Disc.	Inf.
Naming	·30	·27	—	—	—	—
3 Numbers	·39	—	—	·17	—	·12
4 Numbers	·53	—	—	·28	—	.15
10 Syll.	·42	·13	—	·21	—	—
16 Syll.	·54	·09	—	·34	—	—
Defin.	·56	·41	—	—	—	—
Picture D.	·37	·35	—	—	—	—
Differences	·58	·43	—	—	—	—
Square	·41	—	·23	—	·16	—
Diamond	·55	—	·32	—	—	—
Divided Card	·51	—	·15	—	·12	—
2 Lines Disc.	·35	—	—	—	·19	—
2 Weights Disc.	·38	—	—	—	·25	—
4 Pence	·43	—	—	—	—	·21
13 Pence	·47	—	—	—	—	·24
Comparing Faces	·38	—	—	—	—	·26
4 Colours	·31	·18	—	—	—	—
Coins	·32	—	—	—	—	·31

NOTE.—" Gen. Int." = General Intelligence ; " Verb." = Verbal Factor ; " Man." = Manual Factor ; " Mem." = Memory Factor ; " Disc." = Discrimination ; "Inf." = General Information.

[1] Pearson has described a " phi-coefficient " which gives " the product-moment coefficient on the assumption that the presence of the character is to be considered as a concrete unit " (*Biometrika*, Vol. IX., p. 167). This is in effect the " root mean square contingency." Yule's coefficient of colligation is virtually the phi-coefficient for a four-fold table with equalized subtotals. However, for such researches as the present, neither seems quite appropriate, since intelligence is not a character that can be considered as a concrete unit. Moreover, both coefficients are affected by the total number passing the test, *i.e.*, by the difficulty of the test. Hence, when we factorize association coefficients thus computed, we find an additional and artificial factor which seems to indicate the difficulty of the test. The task of computing tetrachoric coefficients is rather laborious, but may be greatly facilitated by constructing Abacs similar to that shown on p. 231 ; the approximate value thus found from the graph can then be inserted for the squares and higher powers of r in the equation given at the top of p. 232 ; and r is then determined with considerable precision by solving the equation so obtained.

[2] With educational tests our question is : how large are the specific or partial correlations attributable to special factors in a homogeneous class ? We therefore apply Yule's formula in its original form. Here our question is : how much is contributed by the special factors to the correlations observed in the age-group ? Hence we no longer divide by the standard deviations ; and the formula becomes $r_{ab \cdot g} = r_{ab} - r_{ag} r_{bg}$: and similarly for later factors.

L

the observed correlations, groups of significant residuals were then discernible, tending to form smaller " hierarchies " of partial or residual correlations. Each of these supplementary " hierarchies " was then made the basis for determining the correlations of the tests concerned with further supplementary factors, each factor being limited in the main to a single group or cluster of tests. These additional correlations are shown in the remaining columns of the table. It will be seen that they are decidedly smaller than the correlations with the general factor.

To determine the nature of the factors, various devices may be adopted. With young children, whose introspections are scarcely trustworthy, the best procedure would be to calculate measurements for each factor, and correlate these measurements with independent assessments of the ability which we suppose each factor represents. This has been done systematically for the general factor, which we can thus identify with intelligence, and on a smaller scale for the verbal and the memory factor. But in a preliminary inquiry we shall probably not go far wrong if we seek to infer the nature of the factor from the processes apparently required to solve the related groups of tests.

The tests for later ages have also been analysed by this procedure.[1] The results are very similar. We find, besides the dominating general factor, much the same group factors as were discovered in analysing educational abilities, viz., a verbal, numerical, and manual factor ; and in addition to these there is some evidence for a memory factor, a visual or spatial factor, possibly a reasoning or relational factor, and a series of factors depending on special knowledge acquired either at school or at home.

Thus, so far as the method can be trusted, it would certainly seem (i) that the test performances depend to some extent on special abilities as well as on general intelligence ; and (ii) that the influence of these special abilities is never so great as that of the general factor of intelligence.[2]

It is instructive to note that much the same factors are discernible if we begin by correlating, not scores in the several test-items, but orders of difficulty for pupils or groups of pupils, those formed by sex or social class. First, we notice that the orders for individual girls agree much more closely with one another than they do with orders for the boys (average correlation for same sex ·78, for different sexes ·66). There is therefore an appreciable factor for sex. We can eliminate this by taking the differences between average orders for either sex.[3] Thus, instead of making a formal factor-analysis, we can reach the same results by comparing the two sets of average ranks, and noting what tests are responsible for the largest differences. We then find that the girls do better at the verbal tests and the memory tests, and the boys at the non-verbal or mechanical tests. We find equally suggestive differences on correlating or comparing the rankings for opposite social classes or for

---

[1] Detailed tables and a fuller discussion are given in the original report.

[2] The relative influence of the factors must be assessed by comparing the *squares* of the hypothetical correlations : so that the influence of these group-factors is smaller than might be inferred from comparing the coefficients as they stand. It should be noted that these " group factors" are quite distinct from Prof. Spearman's " specific factors." To assess the contribution of a specific factor, Spearman subtracts the square of the general factor from unity, and then takes the square root of the remainder. Thus, for " Differences," if there were no group factor, the correlation of the test with its specific factor would be $\sqrt{1-\cdot58^2} = \cdot81$. But, if we accept the group factor, then, assuming the factors to be independent, the correlation with the specific would be only $\sqrt{1-\cdot58^2-\cdot43^2} = \cdot69$.

[3] Cf. the method of averaging used in the Report on " Classification of Pupils according to Special Abilities " (summarized in the Appendix below, p. 449f). When we correlate the average order for the one sex with the average order for the other by taking the differences between the two, the correlation proves to be ·87. The figure may seem high ; but out of 65 tests the total of rank-differences amounts to 176 (p. 206).

normals and defectives. In all these cases the discrepancies occur in clusters ; and the clusters or groups of tests correspond with the group-factors discovered by the alternative procedures. Thus averaging orders for different classes of persons leads to much the same generalizations as factorizing correlations between tests (or for that matter between persons) : we find the same abilities and the same types.[1]

My conclusions may therefore be summed up as follows. (i) The new method proposed for determining *multiple* factors can successfully be applied to tests like those of the Binet in spite of the fact that the scores are merely dichotomous. (ii) The results show that even tests proposed for measuring intelligence depend in part on *specialized* factors,[2] and not exclusively on a single general factor, as Spearman's hypothesis would suggest. (iii) The special factors entering into groups of tests certainly contribute much *less* than the general factor, though it is wrong to suppose that their contribution is negligible or nil. (iv) The psychological factors found are much the same as those found in analysing educational abilities, but other factors often *non-psychological*, play an appreciable part. (v) That being so, Binet's principle of choosing a *wide variety of heterogeneous tests* is fully justified. Only in this way can the effects of the specialized factors be made to neutralize each other (see p. 206). It is therefore unwise to rely on a shortened scale of selected tests (as so many investigators have proposed). (vi) The neutralization will only be fully effective if a *proper balance* is observed in constructing a revised version of the scale.[3]

---

[1] For further data on these and allied questions, see *Eugenics Review*, Vol. XXX., pp. 255-260.

[2] To prove the existence of such factors, a test of significance is desirable. Following the method used by Kelley for the standard error of coefficiency corrected for attenuation, we obtain the following approximate formula for the standard error of a saturation coefficient, r :

$$\sigma_r = \frac{1}{\sqrt{N}} \sqrt{\left\{ \tfrac{1}{2}(1-2r^2)\left(1+\tfrac{1}{\bar{r}}-r^2\right) + \tfrac{1}{4}\left(1+\tfrac{1}{\bar{r}^4}\right) \right\}} \quad \dots\dots\dots\dots(i)$$

where $\bar{r}$ denotes the average saturation of the factor in question. If $r = \bar{r}$ approximately, this reduces to

$$\sigma_r = \frac{1-r^2}{\sqrt{N}} \sqrt{\left\{ 1+\tfrac{3}{4\bar{r}^2} \right\}} \quad \dots\dots\dots\dots\dots\dots(ii)$$

Thus, for the saturation of " 16 syllables " with the " memory factor " ($r = \cdot 34$), we have by (ii) $\sigma_r = 0\cdot128$. Hence the saturation is significant.

[3] In later publications I have shown how the growing list of group-factors revealed by the multiple factor method resembles the lists of " faculties " given by older psychologists and the phrenologists (cf. *Measurement of Mental Capacities*, Oliver and Boyd, 1927, where eleven are enumerated). Spearman has strongly criticized Binet's acceptance of a " crowd of faculties " (*Nature of Intelligence*, 1923) ; but in his later *Abilities* appears willing to admit four group-factors—" logical, mechanical, psychological, and arithmetical," but not apparently " verbal."

Memorandum II.

THE THEORETICAL VALIDITY OF THE RESULTS.

---

1. GENERAL SCOPE OF THE INVESTIGATION.

The Problems Investigated.

The preceding memorandum presented an exposition of the Binet-Simon tests in a form adapted for use with English children, and based upon a revised allocation of the various problems to the successive years of school life. That memorandum was concerned solely with the practical use of a practical scale ; and contained, therefore, no theoretical justification for the re-assignment of the ages, and no theoretical enquiry into the validity of the several tests themselves. The task of the present memorandum is to describe the results of an actual application of the tests, and to report in detail experiments and calculations, by which the assumptions embodied in the foregoing revision may be confuted or confirmed.

The initial aim of the whole investigation was twofold : to standardise, by an application to English school children, both the methods and the results of the scale ; and to determine its diagnostic value, as thus applied and standardised.

Such an aim involves four distinct problems. First, what changes in the actual procedure are necessitated by translating the French instructions and adjusting them for use in England ? Secondly, what averages in the final results are to be expected at each age from English school children, both normal and defective, and, more particularly, where is the borderline to be drawn between the two types ? Thirdly, how accurately do the tests, both severally and as a whole, measure the intelligence of normal and defective school children and discriminate between the two ? Lastly, what influence is exercised upon the performances, apart from age and intelligence, by various extraneous factors—by sex, by social status, by educational opportunity, and by emotional and moral disposition ?

The first and more practical problem has already been dealt with in the preceding pages. The sections that follow will be successively concerned with the three remaining questions, questions which from their general nature are more abstract and obscure.

Need for Statistical Analysis.

The distribution of intelligence among the population, like the distribution of income or the incidence of death, is a matter largely for statistics ; and in its general statistical framework the present enquiry must pursue much the same broad outlines as those adopted in my previous study of the distribution of educational ability. But as now my conclusions are addressed first of all to the practical worker, I may here dispense with a repetition at length of the methods there described ; and for details refer the enquiring theorist to that earlier work.[1]

For the statistical technicalities that still remain, some prefatory apology

---

[1] *The Distribution and Relation of Educational Abilities*, 1917. P. S. King and Son. 2s. 6d.

is doubtless due. To those unfamiliar with the recent course of educational psychology the intrusion of mathematical refinements into problems of the classroom may seem to be little short of perverse pedantry, more ridiculous and less excusable than the crotchets of the trigonometrical tailor who fitted Gulliver with a suit of clothes by means of a sextant and a theodolite. Examining children, it may be urged, is among the simplest of the teacher's daily duties ; and needs little else but common sense and rule of thumb : by many words, still more by many figures, counsel is darkened.

Such criticism has to be faced by each new application of a scientific technique to everyday affairs. To the builder and the gunner of a century ago the mathematical calculations of the modern engineer would seem the idle pastime of an arithmomaniac. To-day, before a new railway bridge can be designed or a new gun constructed, abstruse computations must be worked out, by the side of which the statistics of psychology look childish and brief. The achievements justify the means. Designed in accordance with elaborate calculations, the suspension bridge spans straits, the canti-lever estuaries, which the old empirical arch and pier could never have crossed ; the 14-inch naval gun drops projectiles, of a weight, at a range, and with an accuracy, some twenty times as great as that achieved by primitive wrought-iron, smooth-bore ordnance. While Swift was gibing at the mathe-maticians of Laputa, Newton was writing his *Principia*. The satirist may be read the more widely : but the mathematician has more profoundly changed and furthered the course of civilisation.

It has been the signal merit of the English school of psychology, from Sir Francis Galton onwards, that it has, by this very device of mathematical analysis, transformed the mental test from a discredited dodge of the charlatan into a recognised instrument of scientific precision. To the dis-regard of statistical procedure may be traced the gross divergences of standard among those who diagnose deficiency in children ; to the in-adequacy of Binet's own arithmetical formulations may be attributed at once the popularity and the confusion that have attended his diagnostic scale. Every subsequent search for an equitable test of mental deficiency, every recent endeavour to construct a scale of intelligence, whether adapted from Binet or framed afresh, has necessarily been based upon one or more of the statistical methods that re-emerge in the following discussion. Ex-perience has shown that the practical efficiency of each new scheme varies almost in direct proportion to the thoroughness of its theoretical foundations.

Version Employed.

The version of the tests with which the following results were obtained differs in no important particular from that detailed in the preceding memo-randum. The initial translation was undertaken for an enquiry commenced in 1912 in collaboration with Mr. R. C. Moore and other research students in the Psychological Laboratory at Liverpool University. The material then gathered demonstrated the need for a carefully rectified procedure. The task of revision was accordingly resumed in London, with the assistance of numerous teachers and others, as already recounted. With the scale so revised the present data were secured. More recent emendations have been too trivial to affect the general outcome.

Number and Nature of the Children Tested.

The results here reported are those derived from London children only. The children tested in London schools number over three thousand five hundred ; and comprise, first, 2,674 " normal " children, attending fifteen different departments in the ordinary elementary schools ; secondly, 729 attending seven special schools for the mentally deficient ; thirdly, 107 juvenile delinquents from remand homes, industrial schools, and elsewhere.

Of the elementary schools, eleven departments were examined by me personally, two by the head teacher, one by the teacher from a neighbouring special school, and one by the several class-teachers. In the latter school each teacher was supplied with a typed copy of instructions and with the requisite apparatus ; and the procedure was first thoroughly demonstrated and discussed. Where the marking is somewhat arbitrary, as in the drawing and the definition tests, the scripts obtained from the children were preserved, and the scores checked personally. The data thus contributed by the generous co-operation of teachers comprises about one-third of the whole amount. Owing to the wide variation displayed by social conditions in London, the inclusion of samples from schools of very different types was deemed imperative. In many cases, however, it proved unnecessary or impossible to test certain of the elementary schools throughout.

Of the special schools, all except two were examined personally. In those two the tests were conducted by the head teachers. The children aged six and seven actually attending such schools are relatively small in number. I have, therefore, incorporated results secured from children not actually attending special schools at the time of examination, but subsequently transferred thither on the ground of mental deficiency.

2. THE ORDER OF DIFFICULTY OF THE TESTS; AND THEIR ALLOCATION TO APPROPRIATE AGES.

Percentages Passing the Tests at Each Age.

The total results obtained are summarised in Tables III. and IV. These tables present, for ordinary elementary and special M.D. schools respectively, the percentage of the children in each age-group passing each of the tests. The age-groups are distinguished by age last birthday. In each, therefore, the average chronological age is $3\frac{1}{2}$, $4\frac{1}{2}$, $5\frac{1}{2}$...., not $3 \cdot 0$, $4 \cdot 0$, $5 \cdot 0$...., as in the age-groups of many previous investigators.

Before calculating the figures for normal children (Table III.) the percentages found at each school were weighted in accordance with its representative character.[1] The schools examined were first disposed into five classes—poor, below average, average, above average, and good. The criteria for this classification were partly social, for example, the economic position of the parents, and partly educational, for example, the relative number of scholarships gained annually. All the schools in a typical London borough—the borough previously chosen for my survey of educational abilities—were then similarly classified ; and thus a rough estimate was procured for the relative frequency of pupils of each type. The original percentages were then loaded proportionately by multiplying them throughout each school by the figure denoting the frequency of its type within the borough. So computed, the averages yield a more accurate picture of a random sample of London children than any results derived by examining merely a single school, however typical, or by simply averaging all schools regardless of their divergent character. Measured, for example, by the standard deviation, the general distribution of ability would, in the latter case, appear too widely scattered ; in the former, too compact.

---

[1] This " representative method of sampling " (as I termed it) was described more fully in my original report, but there is now a growing literature on this and allied procedures.

TABLE III.—ORDINARY

Number of Children at Each

Order for Normals.	Test.				3	4	5	6
	AGE III.							
1	Pointing	..	..	..	84·7	100·0	100·0	100·0
2	2 Numbers	..	..	..	82·6	98·9	100·0	100·0
3	Sex	..	..	..	75·3	93·3	100·0	100·0
4	Surname	..	..	..	73·5	94·8	99·4	100·0
5	Naming	..	..	..	69·0	91·2	99·4	100·0
6	Picture (Enumeration)	..	..	..	65·6	87·7	98·7	99·6
	AGE IV.							
7	6 Syllables	..	..	..	58·2	88·5	96·6	99·3
8	3 Numbers	..	..	..	45·3	83·2	95·8	99·3
9	4 Pennies	..	..	..	34·8	82·4	97·4	99·4
10	2 Lines	..	..	..	45·7	72·7	94·3	98·7
11	Comparing Faces	..	..	..	33·2	66·9	91·3	98·7
	AGE V.							
12	Triple Order	..	..	..	26·4	65·3	81·2	96·7
13	Square	..	..	..	11·5	70·3	85·4	97·6
14	10 Syllables	..	..	..	17·6	50·8	81·8	97·7
15	Age	..	..	..	18·0	54·5	78·7	96·0
16	Morning and Afternoon	..	..	..	13·5	51·9	79·6	96·7
17	4 Colours	..	..	..	11·9	48·6	76·0	95·2
18	4 Numbers	..	..	..	12·9	45·2	72·3	94·8
19	2 Weights	..	..	..	3·6	37·6	68·3	85·8
	AGE VI.							
20	Fingers	..	..	..	0·0	23·4	62·5	86·6
21	13 Pennies	..	..	..	0·6	32·1	51·6	85·8
22	Diamond	..	..	..	0·6	11·7	49·8	83·8
23	Transcription	..	..	..	0·0	10·5	45·2	85·0
24	Days of Week	..	..	..	0·0	17·2	44·2	81·3
25	4 Coins	..	..	..	0·0	8·0	48·8	82·8
26	Divided Card	..	..	..	1·2	19·8	47·2	80·8
27	Definition (Use)	..	..	..	0·6	21·1	46·2	72·3
28	5 Numbers	..	..	..	1·2	15·2	37·3	75·7
29	Picture (Description)	..	..	..	1·2	16·8	49·8	73·5
30	16 Syllables	..	..	..	0·6	14·6	47·8	72·7
31	Right and Left	..	..	..	0·6	11·4	52·0	75·7
	AGE VII.							
32	Missing Features	..	..	..	0·0	9·5	34·0	65·3
33	Pence and Halfpence	..	..	..	0·0	1·3	18·9	41·8
34	Differences (Concrete)	..	..	..	0·0	2·5	28·3	52·0
35	Dictation	..	..	..	0·0	0·0	7·2	45·1
	AGE VIII.							
36	Reading (2 Facts)	..	..	..	0·0	0·0	3·9	23·2
37	Easy Questions	..	..	..	0·0	0·6	9·6	31·2
38	Counting 20 to 1	..	..	..	0·0	0·0	5·7	28·0
39	Date	..	..	..	0·0	0·0	1·3	9·6
40	Change	..	..	..	0·0	0·0	0·0	10·9
41	6 Numbers	..	..	..	0·0	0·0	4·9	14·5
	AGE IX.							
42	Months	..	..	..	0·0	0·0	1·3	7·0
43	9 Coins	..	..	..	0·0	0·0	1·3	9·9
44	Reading (6 Facts)	..	..	..	0·0	0·0	0·0	3·8
45	Definition (Class)	..	..	..	0·0	1·3	3·9	16·4
	AGE X.							
46	5 Weights	..	..	..	0·0	0·0	2·6	14·3
47	Sentence Building (2)	..	..	..	0·0	0·0	0·0	5·3
48	Memory Drawing	..	..	..	0·0	0·0	0·0	2·4
	AGE XI.							
49	Absurdities	..	..	..	0·0	0·0	0·0	0·6
50	Difficult Questions	..	..	..	0·0	0·0	0·0	1·9
51	60 Words	..	..	..	0·0	0·0	0·0	4·1
52	7 Numbers	..	..	..	0·0	0·0	0·0	2·5
53	Sentence Building (1)	..	..	..	0·0	0·0	0·0	0·6
	AGE XII.							
54	3 Rhymes	..	..	..	0·0	0·0	0·0	0·0
55	Mixed Sentences	..	..	..	0·0	0·0	0·0	0·0
56	Picture (Interpretation)	..	..	..	0·0	0·0	1·3	2·5
	AGE XIII.							
57	Suggestion	..	..	..	0·0	0·0	1·3	5·3
58	Problems	..	..	..	0·0	0·0	0·0	0·6
	AGE XIV.							
59	26 Syllables	..	..	..	0·0	0·0	0·0	0·0
60	Definition (Abstract)	..	..	..	0·0	0·0	0·0	0·0
	AGE XV.							
61	Folded Paper	..	..	..	0·0	0·0	0·0	0·0
62	Differences (Abstract)	..	..	..	0·0	0·0	0·0	0·0
63	Reversed Triangle	..	..	..	0·0	0·0	0·0	0·0
	AGE XVI.							
64	Re-statement	..	..	..	0·0	0·0	0·0	0·0
65	Difference (King, President)	..	..		0·0	0·0	0·0	0·0

Age Passing the Several Tests.

	Age.							Average.
7	8	9	10	11	12	13	14	
100·0	100·0	100·0	100·0	100·0	100·0	100·0	100·0	98·7
100·0	100·0	100·0	100·0	100·0	100·0	100·0	100·0	98·5
100·0	100·0	100·0	100·0	100·0	100·0	100·0	100·0	97·4
100·0	100·0	100·0	100·0	100·0	100·0	100·0	100·0	97·3
100·0	100·0	100·0	100·0	100·0	100·0	100·0	100·0	96·6
100·0	100·0	100·0	100·0	100·0	100·0	100·0	100·0	96·0
99·2	100·0	100·0	100·0	100·0	100·0	100·0	100·0	95·1
100·0	100·0	100·0	100·0	100·0	100·0	100·0	100·0	93·6
100·0	100·0	100·0	100·0	100·0	100·0	100·0	100·0	92·8
99·2	99·6	100·0	100·0	100·0	100·0	100·0	100·0	92·5
99·0	99·2	99·6	100·0	100·0	100·0	100·0	100·0	90·7
98·4	99·2	99·6	100·0	100·0	100·0	100·0	100·0	89·1
98·2	99·2	100·0	100·0	100·0	100·0	100·0	100·0	88·5
99·6	99·2	99·6	100·0	100·0	100·0	100·0	100·0	87·2
97·3	99·0	100·0	100·0	100·0	100·0	100·0	100·0	87·0
97·8	98·9	100·0	100·0	100·0	100·0	100·0	100·0	86·5
97·8	98·6	100·0	100·0	100·0	100·0	100·0	100·0	85·7
96·1	98·9	100·0	100·0	100·0	100·0	100·0	100·0	85·0
92·2	96·4	99·1	100·0	100·0	100·0	100·0	100·0	82·0
95·3	98·6	99·3	100·0	100·0	100·0	100·0	100·0	80·9
96·6	99·0	100·0	100·0	100·0	100·0	100·0	100·0	80·5
95·6	97·6	98·3	100·0	100·0	100·0	100·0	100·0	78·1
94·8	99·0	99·0	100·0	100·0	100·0	100·0	100·0	77·8
93·9	95·6	97·6	100·0	100·0	100·0	100·0	100·0	77·5
94·0	97·2	97·6	100·0	100·0	100·0	100·0	100·0	77·4
86·2	92·2	96·0	98·5	99·0	100·0	100·0	100·0	76·7
87·2	94·2	97·1	100·0	100·0	100·0	100·0	100·0	76·6
94·0	95·6	98·8	99·5	100·0	100·0	100·0	100·0	76·4
84·7	93·6	96·8	100·0	100·0	100·0	100·0	100·0	76·4
85·3	95·2	98·6	97·3	100·0	100·0	100·0	100·0	76·0
83·8	90·1	97·1	99·8	100·0	100·0	100·0	100·0	75·9
87·3	95·6	98·6	100·0	100·0	100·0	100·0	100·0	74·2
89·5	90·4	96·8	100·0	100·0	100·0	100·0	100·0	69·1
70·6	80·0	92·9	99·1	100·0	100·0	100·0	100·0	68·8
67·3	87·2	94·5	99·1	100·0	100·0	100·0	100·0	66·7
58·2	82·1	90·5	99·2	99·6	100·0	100·0	100·0	63·1
51·7	76·5	89·3	95·4	99·3	100·0	100·0	100·0	62·8
53·6	76·0	86·1	96·0	98·3	100·0	100·0	100·0	62·0
36·4	71·4	83·9	93·5	97·6	99·2	99·4	98·4	57·6
39·1	68·2	79·3	95·4	97·3	98·4	100·0	100·0	57·4
42·5	60·2	78·2	88·5	96·6	98·5	99·5	100·0	56·9
35·3	61·6	78·6	93·5	98·3	100·0	100·0	100·0	56·3
33·3	57·2	76·0	85·8	95·4	97·7	98·8	100·0	54·6
19·3	44·5	68·4	80·2	89·3	95·7	98·1	99·1	49·9
23·6	40·4	63·8	77·0	86·6	87·0	93·5	94·1	49·0
21·0	36·1	53·5	71·9	81·4	87·4	95·0	96·4	46·6
14·7	34·4	46·3	69·3	84·3	91·3	98·0	98·3	45·2
9·8	28·9	45·7	62·0	76·9	81·1	94·5	95·4	41·4
5·2	24·4	29·3	49·2	70·3	79·2	96·3	97·5	37·7
6·3	13·1	28·2	48·6	64·6	76·5	92·5	95·0	35·6
7·6	21·6	27·0	43·6	60·4	74·3	88·8	92·1	35·0
5·8	18·8	25·5	44·6	59·4	68·9	80·3	92·3	33·2
3·1	16·5	20·4	43·0	58·1	68·7	81·5	89·2	31·8
3·4	20·2	26·6	37·3	52·0	66·4	79·3	87·7	31·1
0·9	15·3	21·4	40·1	55·1	69·5	76·3	83·8	30·2
4·6	11·2	16·6	36·7	47·5	71·7	81·5	82·1	29·6
6·9	23·6	31·4	40·1	43·1	56·2	68·0	71·4	28·9
0·9	2·2	6·7	19·6	28·0	42·8	62·5	69·1	19·4
1·8	4·3	9·7	17·4	22·0	34·1	51·0	62·3	16·9
0·0	1·1	2·6	8·7	19·6	30·5	55·8	70·5	15·7
0·0	0·0	0·0	1·4	6·6	14·7	31·7	42·1	8·0
0·0	0·0	0·0	2·6	3·4	11·4	23·7	45·4	7·2
0·0	0·0	0·0	0·7	4·1	12·7	20·2	41·3	6·6
0·0	0·0	0·0	1·4	3·4	7·3	16·2	29·2	4·8
0·0	0·0	0·0	0·0	2·3	3·6	10·3	24·6	3·4

Order of Difficulty of the Tests for Normals.

In graduating such a series of tests as this, two conditions must be obeyed. First, the tests, marking as they do successive points upon the scale, should follow one another in a fixed order of increasing difficulty. Secondly, the increase in difficulty should always be the same in amount : the intervals between each successive pair of tests, constituting as they do equivalent units of measurement, must represent equal increments of ability. Each step on the ladder must be a step upwards—and that for every climber ; and the spaces between the rungs must be of even distance. How far does the present arrangement conform to this double stipulation ? In Table III. the percentages show the difference in ease with which each test is passed by normal children ; the ranking based upon these percentages will give the order of difficulty. Is the order inflexible ? Are the intervals equal ?

The Stability of the Order of the Tests.

The tests are arranged in sequence ; and the sequence has been deduced by comparing the averages[1] of all the percentages in each of the several age-groups. The averages are shown in the last column of the table. One source of instability is immediately obvious. Within the age-groups, taken one by one, the general decline in the percentages is interrupted here and there by a momentary rise. The orders for separate years would agree neither with each other, nor with the average. These sporadic reversals are generally caused by tests learnt suddenly at a definite epoch in the child's school life—fo· example, transcription, reading, and date. At the age of three, to draw a square is harder than to give one's age, to name the colours, to distinguish morning and afternoon, to repeat ten syllables, or to echo four numbers. At the age of four, it becomes easier than these others ; and, in later years, it is performed even more readily than the triple order. By some investigators it has been alleged that " those tests are most useful which show the steepest rise in the number passing it from age to age."[2] The steep rise, however, means, in most instances, simply that the task embodied in the test is not taught to the child until he reaches a given school standard. Success in such tests is the consequence and guarantee, not of mental maturity, but of school promotion.

On the whole, however, the inconsistencies between one age and another are neither frequent nor large. A more fertile and far-reaching question lies, I think, in this : How far does the new order agree with the original order prescribed by Binet, and with the revised orders proposed by subsequent investigatiors ?

Between the arrangement presented by Table III. and the various arrangements which Binet published the correspondence is far from exact. To test the agreement more minutely, I have worked out the correlation between the various orders. The seriation obtained with London children correlates with Binet's 1908 arrangement to the extent of ·957, with Binet's 1911 arrangement to the extent of ·977, and with the order derived from Binet's own experimental data to the extent of ·964.[3] If, therefore, the present results may be accepted as a criterion, the revised arrangement of 1911 is a distinct improvement upon that of 1908. This conclusion is enforced by the correspondence that obtains between the present arrange-

---

[1] This is equivalent to taking the " difficulty-threshold " of each test to be the theoretical age at which half the children pass, and half fail in the test. See Appendix IV, pp. 439-448.

[2] W. Stern, *Die Psychologischen Methoden der Intelligenzprüfung*, 1912, p. 65. This criterion was first suggested by Bobertag, and has been accepted by Moore (*loc. cit. inf.*, p. 124) ; Moore's list of such tests, however, includes a large number that plainly depend upon school instruction.

[3] The probable errors are approximately ± ·015.

TABLE IV.—SPECIAL M.D. SCHOOLS.

Number of Children at Each Age Passing the Several Tests.

Order for Defectives.	Test.	6	7	8	9	10	11	12	13	1	Average.
1	Pointing	96·9	96·4	97·1	98·8	100	100	100	100	100	98·8
2	Surname	93·7	96·4	97·1	97·5	98·3	100	100	100	100	98·1
3	Sex	87·5	98·2	97·1	98·8	100	100	100	100	100	98·0
4	Naming	87·5	98·2	98·6	98·8	98·3	100	100	100	100	97·9
5	2 Numbers	78·1	94·5	95·7	97·5	100	100	100	100	100	96·2
6	Picture (Enumeration)	81·2	92·7	94·2	96·3	97·4	99·2	100	100	100	95·7
7	4 Pennies	71·9	83·6	94·2	95·1	97·4	99·2	100	100	100	93·5
8	3 Numbers	68·7	87·3	92·8	93·8	96·5	99·2	99·1	100	100	93·0
9	2 Lines	65·6	85·2	94·2	96·3	96·5	99·2	100	100	100	93·0
10	Square	56·2	74·5	91·3	92·6	97·4	98·3	99·1	100	100	89·9
11	Comparing Faces	46·9	78·2	88·4	88·9	91·3	98·3	97·1	98·9	100	87·6
12	6 Syllables	37·5	69·1	92·8	93·8	95·6	99·2	99·1	100	100	87·5
13	Morning and Afternoon	40·6	72·7	82·6	83·9	89·4	96·3	99·1	97·9	100	84·7
14	Age	31·2	63·6	84·1	88·9	95·6	97·2	97·1	97·9	100	84·0
15	4 Colours	37·5	67·3	75·4	86·4	93·0	98·3	97·1	100	100	83·9
16	Triple Order	34·4	70·9	81·2	83·9	89·4	97·2	96·2	96·8	100	83·3
17	10 Syllables	21·9	56·4	84·1	82·7	92·1	97·2	96·2	97·9	100	80·9
18	Fingers	25·0	45·5	72·5	82·7	90·3	97·2	98·1	98·9	100	78·9
19	13 Pennies	21·9	40·0	69·6	83·9	90·3	98·3	98·1	97·9	100	77·8
20	Definition (Use)	9·4	52·7	66·7	77·8	85·8	86·1	91·4	95·8	98·0	73·7
21	Picture (Description)	18·7	47·3	62·3	65·4	86·7	90·8	90·5	94·7	96·0	72·5
22	2 Weights	15·6	32·7	59·4	75·3	87·7	91·7	93·3	94·7	98·0	72·0
23	4 Numbers	12·5	30·9	56·5	72·8	84·9	95·4	94·3	97·9	100	71·7
24	4 Coins	12·5	25·5	53·6	70·4	83·2	93·5	98·1	98·9	100	70·6
25	Transcription	3·1	23·6	52·2	67·9	84·9	94·4	95·2	96·8	100	68·7
26	Right and Left	9·4	38·2	56·5	59·3	78·8	85·2	94·3	95·8	96·0	68·2
27	Days of Week	3·1	27·3	55·1	63·0	77·0	87·0	95·2	98·9	100	67·4
28	Diamond	3·1	36·4	47·8	61·7	74·3	88·9	96·2	96·8	100	67·2
29	Divided Card	6·2	21·8	44·9	57·9	69·0	83·3	88·6	92·6	100	62·7
30	Easy Questions	3·1	9·1	24·8	46·9	60·2	73·2	81·9	93·7	96·0	54·3
31	5 Numbers	3·1	12·7	37·7	47·8	61·1	67·6	74·3	83·0	96·0	53·7
32	Pence and Halfpence	0·0	1·8	24·6	33·3	56·6	78·7	89·5	94·7	96·0	52·8
33	Missing Features	0·0	5·5	27·5	36·2	64·6	77·8	80·0	88·3	94·1	52·7
34	16 Syllables	0·0	7·3	26·1	39·1	50·4	60·2	66·7	84·0	96·0	47·7
35	Differences (Concrete)	0·0	1·8	21·7	36·2	51·3	61·1	71·4	80·8	82·3	45·2
36	9 Coins	0·0	3·6	8·7	23·2	25·7	57·4	76·2	84·0	92·2	41·3
37	Months	0·0	0·0	1·4	17·3	29·2	45·4	70·5	80·8	84·3	36·5
38	Date	0·0	0·0	4·3	18·5	32·7	48·1	55·2	71·3	74·5	33·8
39	Change	0·0	0·0	1·4	8·6	34·5	44·5	63·8	71·3	80·4	33·8
40	Counting 20 to 1	0·0	0·0	5·8	16·0	25·7	46·3	55·2	61·7	64·7	30·6
41	6 Numbers	0·0	0·0	5·8	12·4	23·0	34·3	43·8	58·5	68·8	27·4
42	Reading (2 Facts)	0·0	0·0	0·0	4·9	9·7	23·2	36·2	44·7	49·0	18·6
43	Dictation	0·0	0·0	0·0	3·7	8·9	21·3	31·4	41·5	56·9	18·2
44	5 Weights	0·0	0·0	0·9	6·2	17·2	25·0	30·5	37·2	41·2	17·0
45	Suggestion	0·0	0·0	4·3	9·9	12·4	16·7	33·3	34·0	43·2	17·1
46	Sentence Building (2)	0·0	0·0	0·0	3·4	9·7	13·9	17·1	29·8	33·4	11·9
47	Picture (Interpretation)	0·0	0·0	1·4	4·9	15·0	15·7	20·0	23·4	25·5	11·8
48	Memory Drawing	0·0	0·0	0·0	1·2	6·2	13·0	23·8	27·7	31·4	11·5
49	Definition (Class)	0·0	0·0	2·4	4·9	8·9	14·8	17·1	20·2	23·6	10·2
50	Reading (6 Facts)	0·0	0·0	0·0	0·0	2·6	8·3	13·3	26·6	35·3	9·6
51	Absurdities	0·0	0·0	0·0	2·5	3·5	7·4	11·4	16·0	19·6	6·7
52	60 Words	0·0	0·0	0·0	1·2	9·7	5·6	6·7	8·5	9·8	4·6
53	7 Numbers	0·0	0·0	0·0	0·0	1·8	2·8	7·6	12·8	15·7	4·5
54	Difficult Questions	0·0	0·0	0·0	2·5	2·6	6·5	7·6	9·6	11·8	4·5
55	Sentence Building (1)	0·0	0·0	0·0	0·0	0·9	1·9	5·7	10·6	11·8	3·4
56	Problems	0·0	0·0	0·0	0·0	0·9	0·9	2·9	3·2	3·9	1·3
57	3 Rhymes	0·0	0·0	0·0	0·0	0·0	0·0	1·9	2·1	5·9	1·1
58	Mixed Sentences	0·0	0·0	0·0	0·0	0·0	0·0	1·9	1·1	3·9	0·8
59	26 Syllables	0·0	0·0	0·0	0·0	0·9	0·0	0·9	2·1	2·0	0·7

ment and that derived from Binet's own experiments, a correspondence closer than that subsisting between Binet's experiments and either of Binet's formal arrangements.

To collate the present order with the orders given by other investigators, and to compare each of these orders in turn amongst themselves, should yield an exquisite test of the stability of the scale. Which form of sequence accords most closely with all the rest ? In answer to this question, the correlations may be computed between the orders to be extracted from the percentage tables recorded in the published articles. Ten such tables are accessible, compiled by various authors, working in various countries.[1]

Data for tests common to both the 1908 and the 1911 series alone are to be admitted ; and, further, tests for years III., IV., and V. have to be discarded, since scarcely any writers have employed them. These restrictions leave thirty-two tests available. The correlations have been calculated by the familiar method of squaring the rank-differences. The probable errors range from $\pm \cdot 076$ for the lowest coefficient ($\cdot 625$) to $\pm \cdot 003$ for the highest ($\cdot 986$).

The coefficients are shown, arranged as a " hierarchy," in Table V. The hierarchical system strongly suggests a single " central factor," underlying, and in different proportions determining, all the various reconstructions. That " central factor " is presumably the ideal order—an order such as would be reached by applying Binet's own procedure to an indefinitely large sample, tested by an indefinitely large number of investigators, in an indefinitely large variety of countries.

Here, it will be seen, we are factorizing correlations between persons, not tests—the persons in this case being not the testees but the testers. The average correlation is $\cdot 873$— not a very high figure when correlating persons. The " saturations " (i.e., correlations of each investigator's order with the ideal order estimated by combining all) range from $\cdot 984$ to $\cdot 782$. The lowest is given by Wallin's ; but this was based on epileptics. Saffiotti's, obtained with Italians, and Bobertag's, obtained with Germans, give slightly higher saturations. The four American investigators follow next ; and two English investigators next. Binet's order naturally occupies a high position, since that formed the basis of the rest ; Goddard's is higher still, doubtless because it was the earliest of the American. The order furnished by the present investigation yields the highest saturation of all ; but that may be due partly to the

---

[1] Comparatively few of the earlier tables are given in a form which enables the order of difficulty to be determined precisely. The following are the sources of the arrangements referred to above. Even here the data had occasionally to be re-cast into a comparable form, e.g.,by assuming that tests not applied to certain children would have been passed by all or by none at certain ages. Sometimes the figures have had to be recovered from graphs printed with a scale that is not always clear.

A. Binet, " La Mesure du Niveau Intellectuel." *L'Année Psych.*, XVII., 1911, p. 150, Tableau II.

H. H. Goddard, " Two Thousand Normal Children measured by the Binet Scale." *Ped. Sem.*, XVIII., 1911, pp. 237–8, Table II.

O. Bobertag, " Über Intelligenzprüfungen (nach der Methode von B. und S.)." *Z. Angew. Psych.*, V 1911, pp. 105 seq. (Percentages *passim*, but incomplete). *Cf. ibid.*, VI. 1912, pp. 495 seq.

F. U. Saffiotti, *La Misura dell' Intelligenza nei Fanciulli*, 1916, p. 155, Tavola XXIII.

J. E. Wallin, *Experimental Studies of Mental Defectives*, 1912, p. 32, Table IV.

L. M. Terman and S. M. Childs, " A Tentative Revision of the Binet-Simon Measuring Scale of Intelligence." *J. Educational Psych.*, III., 1912. Pp. 72–3, Table IV.

A. C. Hinckley, " The Binet Tests Applied to Individuals over Twelve Years of Age." *J. Educ. Psych.* VI., 1915, p. 56, Fig. 26.

C. Schmitt, " Standardisation of Tests for Defective Children." *Psych. Monograph*, XIX., 1915, Tables I. to VII., pp. 70–77.

N. G. Taylor, " Further Data towards the Study of the Binet-Simon Scale." *J. Exp. Ped.*, III., 1916, p. 25.

R. C. Moore, " The Application of the Binet-Simon Scale to Normal English Children." *J. Exp. Ped.*, IV., 1917, pp. 121–123, Figure 5

fact that my version is the most recent, and therefore has sought to incorporate the features from all the others, Continental as well as American.

If we partial out the effect of the central factor, we are left with residual correlations that arrange themselves into two groups or clusters. The American investigators (with Binet) form one group : (their saturations are : Wallin, ·376 ; Hinckley, ·210 ; Terman and Childs, ·113 ; Goddard, ·083 ; Binet, ·033). The British and Continental form a second : (Saffiotti, —·247 ; Taylor, —·164 ; Moore, —·161 ; Burt, —·149 ; Bobertag, —·062 ; Schmitt, —·032). There is thus some common influence affecting nearly all the Americans, and apparently some other influence affecting the others. But the saturations for this supplementary factor are comparatively small : the main features are the dominance of the general factor, and the high saturation exhibited for that factor by the present arrangement.

TABLE V.

Correlations between the Orders of Difficulty found for the Tests by Various Investigators.

	Burt.	Goddard.	Binet.	Taylor.	Moore.	Terman and Childs.	Schmitt.	Hinckley.	Bobertag.	Saffiotti.	Wallin.	Average.
Burt	—	·938	·942	·975	·985	·927	·921	·892	·909	·925	·719	·913
Goddard	·938	—	·986	·928	·928	·925	·895	·923	·911	·862	·775	·907
Binet	·942	·986	—	·931	·923	·914	·911	·909	·924	·863	·756	·906
Taylor	·975	·928	·931	—	·964	·900	·933	·867	·878	·915	·690	·898
Moore	·985	·928	·923	·964	—	·912	·906	·875	·899	·911	·667	·897
Terman and Childs	·927	·925	·914	·900	·912	—	·867	·934	·870	·839	·804	·889
Schmitt	·921	·895	·911	·933	·906	·867	—	·853	·846	·872	·782	·879
Hinckley	·892	·923	·909	·867	·875	·934	·853	—	·847	·796	·833	·873
Bobertag	·909	·911	·924	·878	·899	·870	·846	·847	—	·888	·651	·862
Saffiotti	·925	·862	·863	·915	·911	·839	·872	·796	·888	—	·625	·850
Wallin	·719	·775	·756	·690	·667	·804	·782	·833	·651	·625	—	·730
Grand Average ..	—	—	—	—	—	—	—	—	—	—	—	·873

For comparability with other orders, therefore, the present arrangement is at least as satisfactory as any other, probably more satisfactory than Binet's, and quite possibly the most satisfactory of all those here examined. The orders compared, however, are confined to scales entitled to represent the Binet-Simon scale as Binet and Simon intended it. The most thorough and most recent revisions—the versions of Yerkes and of Terman—diverge too far from the original to be admissible for strict comparison. Had they been published long enough for verification over the same extent as the original schemes of Binet and Simon, I have little doubt that they might have proved as stable as either the present arrangement or any other ; only they can hardly profess to be Binet-Simon scales.

With these reservations, then, we may regard the tests, thus rearranged in order of difficulty, as marking points, fairly definite and moderately steady, along a linear scale. But stability is not enough. The gradation must be regular as well as rigid. The distances between each pair of adjacent points must everywhere be equal. Otherwise to measure intelligence by the number of tests passed would be a proceeding void of all validity. Units are not units unless each has the same size.

The Equality of the Intervals of the Tests.

The intervals between the tests can best be measured in terms of the standard deviations for the several years. Conceive a series of tests passed respectively by 50·0, 69·1, 84·1, 93·3, 97·7 . . . . per cent. of a given age-group.[1] With these frequencies, as a table of the probability integral will show, the several tests would, in a normal distribution, fall beyond the average degree of difficulty by 0, $\frac{1}{2}$, 1, 1$\frac{1}{2}$, 2 . . . . times the standard deviation. The differences in difficulty between the successive tests are thus equal, although between the successive percentages the differences—19·1, 15·0, 9·2, 4·4, ...—vary greatly. With a normal distribution the standard deviation may be assumed always to yield a comparable unit. Hence, if first expressed as the multiple of this unit, the difference observed at any one age between two tests may be legitimately averaged with the difference observed at any other age.

By means, therefore, of a table of deviates for the normal curve, each percentage[2] in the body of Table III. was first converted into terms of the standard deviation (S.D.). The differences between the figures so found, taken in successive pairs, were then averaged. Adding the average differences in series cumulatively gives the distances of the several tests from an arbitrary zero.

Thus constructed, the linear scale of tests may be depicted graphically by the graduated line in Figure 21. The vertical marks upon the horizontal line indicate the individual tests, the longer strokes showing the first tests of the several age-groups. On the whole, except toward the upper end of the series, the distribution of the tests is tolerably uniform. At age XIII. the tests begin to spread out very widely ; and they are somewhat widely scattered at age III. ; but between these limits the number in each S.D. interval, that is, in each successive unit along the imaginary base-line, approaches roughly—very roughly, it must be owned—to equality. In ages V. and VI. the tests are somewhat crowded and cramped ; and in the later ages they open out again a little too thinly. But here the paucity of the tests is partly explained and largely compensated by the progressive decrease in the magnitude and significance of the mental year when itself reduced to terms of a single standard deviation—a decrease that will emerge more clearly in the discussion below (Table IX. and p. 170). Hence, *as regards equivalence of unit, the number of tests passed provides a measure quite as valid as the number of mental years attained.*

Thus the new arrangement is about as accurate in the equality of the test-intervals as it is in the fixity of the test-order, neither approximately perfect, nor wholly precarious, but for rough purposes and provisional use, sufficiently satisfactory.

As a scientific scale the graduation of the Binet-Simon tests is not, and cannot by any means be made exact. To obtain a scale at once more stable and more uniform, a far greater variety of tests must be first assembled. Vacant intervals could then be filled ; and tests that in difficulty virtually duplicate each other could be abandoned.

Principles Determining the Age-Assignment of Each Test.

In assigning each test to an appropriate age, what is the best numerical criterion ? On this point much controversy has arisen. Binet, it would seem, started from the principle that an average child should, on attaining

---

[1] Here we are comparing imaginary percentages taken from a *column* of Table III. On p. 146 we determined relative difficulty by comparing those from each row. For fuller discussion see original report (summarized in Appendix, pp. 439*f*.).

[2] In view of the large influence exerted upon measures in terms of S.D. by a small error in extremely high or low percentages, those over 90 per cent. and those under 10 per cent. were disregarded.

FIGURE 21.

DIAGRAMMATIC REPRESENTATION OF THE TEST SERIES AS A LINEAR SCALE.

(The intervals between the tests are reduced to terms of the standard deviations of the age-groups.)

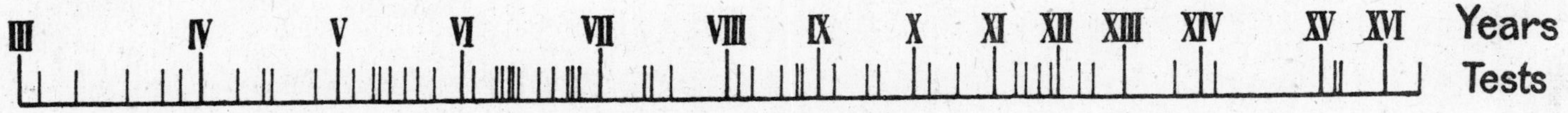

Years

Tests

III   IV   V   VI   VII   VIII   IX   X   XI   XII   XIV   XV   XVI

each birthday, perform all the tests allotted to the year then reached. This assumption carried the following corollary : every test must be passed by a majority among the children of the precise age to which it is assigned. But what proportion constitutes a majority ? Opinions conflict. Pearson and Jaederholm suggest 55 per cent. ; Terman and Childs, 66 per cent. ; Goddard, 75 per cent., "or more." To Bobertag, Binet wrote : " A test may be assigned to a given age if only 65 per cent. succeed. . . . If 90 per cent. succeed, it is perhaps too easy." An increasing number of investigators, however, have adopted a criterion of 75 per cent. for every age. But one cardinal fact all such proposals ignore. Expressed in terms of mental age, the average range of ability increases markedly from year to year. A range of five mental years (namely, from III. to VIII.) includes all the children aged five chronologically ; to include all the children aged ten, double that range (namely, from V. to XV.) is needed.[1] Hence, if a criterion of 75 per cent. be adopted at age five, a criterion of far less than 75 per cent. would be required at age ten, otherwise in the latter instance the dividing line will be removed to a greater distance above the average.

From this perplexity there is an easy escape. Let the children be grouped, not, as with Binet, by their age at their nearest birthday, but by their age at their last birthday. The age of the groups will thus average $5\frac{1}{2}$ years, $6\frac{1}{2}$ years...., respectively, not 5·0 years, 6·0 years..... Now, a correct allotment of the tests implies that in every normal group the average mental age shall coincide with the average chronological age. Clearly, to satisfy this requirement, not only must each child pass all the tests for his own year (that is, for age V., if he is five but not yet six) ; but, in addition, all the children must, on an average, pass half the number of tests for the year above (that is, for age VI.), or—to change the form of statement—half the number of children must, on an average, pass all those tests. If any chance to pass an occasional test from a yet higher age where theoretically all should fail (as age VII.), this will, in a symmetrical distribution, be counterbalanced by an occasional failure in the lower ages where theoretically all should succeed (as age IV.).[2] Here, then, is a simple criterion, uniform throughout the scale, identical for every age. *To be assigned to any given year, a test should be passed by approximately* 50 *per cent. of the children who are nominally of the year below.* Tests for age IV. should be passed by 50 per cent. of the children aged three last birthday, and so through all the series. It might perhaps seem less confusing to name such tests three-year-old tests, thus indicating that they are crucial tests for those aged over three but not yet four. For the present, however, the Binet nomenclature has been preserved. The tests in question are called IV.-year tests (Roman numerals being used according to the common convention), meaning thereby that they are tests which should all be passed before the mental age of 4·0 can be scored.

By this criterion, then, the tests have been apportioned among the several ages. It will be remarked that certain tests fall nearly midway between the two groups. Sentence building (one sentence) is passed by

---

[1] I have already drawn attention to an analogous phenomenon in the case of educational ability. See *Memorandum on Distribution and Relations of Educational Abilities* (1916), p. 31 and Fig. 5.

[2] It is important to note that, in virtue of the very peculiarity that has given rise to this embarrassment —the increase of standard deviation with increasing age—this compensation does not obtain with an equivalence absolutely exact. Suppose there are the same number of tests, say five, at each year. Then, measured in terms of the standard deviation of a middle age-group, say age ten, a test for age XII. is not as a unit equivalent of a test for age VIII., since thus measured one-fifth of a year at XII. is less than one-fifth of a year at VIII. Hence, *if the distribution of the age-group be strictly normal when its standard deviation is taken as unit, it must cease to be strictly normal when the mental year is taken as unit.*

43·0 per cent. at the age of ten, and by 58·1 per cent. at age eleven. A difference of only 1·1 per cent. in either age would have transferred the test from age XI. to age XII. On an average, it will be found, about 72 per cent. pass the tests for their own age, although in single tests the percentage varies from a little over 50 in the highest ages to all but 100 in the lowest.

Consequent Changes in Age-Assignments.

For purposes of comparison I have tabulated in an appendix[1] the various age-assignments proposed for each test by all those investigators whose data are both accessible and comparable. The table re-echoes a shrill discordance between the various utterances—a discordance which does not always catch the ears of a public somewhat deafened by the panegyrics on Binet's general scheme. One adjustment keys a test up ; another keys it down ; others, again, tune the whole gamut from a note peculiar to themselves.

With the average or commonest assignment for each test the present recommendations chime in tolerable consonance. If anything, they are flattened a trifle below the age most generally assigned : for London children the tests as graduated by the aggregate results of previous investigators would be pitched a degree too easy. *In comparison, therefore, with other children tested by the scale, the child of the London elementary school appears somewhat precocious.*

Placed against the age-assignments originally prescribed by Binet, the present results iterate and emphasise the overruling need for radical revision. At least thirty-four tests out of the sixty-five need to be reset. The table subjoined (Table VI.) enumerates the changes which involve a displacement of more than one year.

TABLE VI.—THE LARGER CHANGES IN AGE-ASSIGNMENTS.

	Binet, 1908.	Binet, 1911.	London Data.
4 Colours	VIII.	VII.	V.
5 Numbers	VII.	VIII.	VI.
Weekdays	IX.	Omitted.	VI.
6 Numbers (omitted by Binet : X. suggested by Goddard)			VIII.
Definition (abstract)	XI.	XII.	XIV.
Problems	XII.	XV.	XIII.
3 Rhymes	XII.	XV.	XII.
7 Numbers	XII.	XV.	XI.

Upon one point the present results and those of most recent investigators are in unison. The tests assigned by Binet to the lower ages appear—with the one exception of " divided card "—far too simple for London children. As a consequence, eight tests are now crowded into age V., and twelve (including, however, five omitted from the 1911 series) into age VI. ; this leaves for the higher ages only two or three apiece. On the other hand, in the higher ages Binet's assignments are perhaps a little too stern. Two tests allotted by him to age X., and two allotted to age XI., prove to be too difficult ; and are, therefore, relegated to a later year. In ages V. and VI. it might, on a hasty view, appear judicious to abridge the number of tests ; but, since during the younger ages a difference of one year has more significance than at the older ages, it becomes convenient to retain the minuter differentiation thus provided.

The new assignments introduce large alterations into the estimates of

---

[1] See Appendix I., pp. 212–15.

M

mental age as based upon the Binet-Simon tests (see Table VII.). Children whom the 1911 revision would credit with a mental age of 6·0, 7·0, and 15·0 respectively, would, according to my rearrangement, be awarded a mental age almost exactly a year below. On the other hand, a child credited by that revision with a mental age of 10·0 would now score nearly ten and a half. Doubtless the average social footing of the London child is somewhat above that of the particular subjects tested by Binet in his standardisation ; the latter are described as children of Parisian *ouvriers*, living in a district " *pauvre sans être miserable.*" But, even after due allowance for this has been granted, the differences remain considerable. They demonstrate beyond dispute how urgent a fresh calibration is, before the scale can be cited for evidence of retardation great enough to convict of mental deficiency.

TABLE VII.

The Conversion of Mental Ages based upon Binet's Original Scales into Mental Ages based upon London Age-Assignments.

Mental Age based upon Original Binet Scales.	Corresponding Mental Age according to Present Rearrangement.	
	For 1908 Scale.	For 1911 Scale.
III.	2·8	2·8
IV.	3·9	3·9
V.	4·5	4·5
VI.	5·2	5·2
VII.	5·9	5·9
VIII.	7·2	7·3
IX.	8·5	9·0
X.	10·2	10·4
XI.	11·3	—
XII.	14·0	11·7
XIII.	15·0	—
XIV.	—	—
XV.	—	14·0
Adult.	—	16·0

Explanatory Note.—A child obtaining a mental age of X. by Binet's 1911 scale will have passed thirty-nine tests in that scale—five for every mental age from III. to X., except IV., which has only four tests. In addition, he would presumably pass the nine tests assigned to various ages from VI. to IX. in the 1908 scale, but dropped in the 1911 ; and also the tests of repeating four and six numbers—tests omitted in the Binet scales, but here assigned to ages VI. and VIII.—had these various supernumerary tests been given to him. Actually, or by implication, therefore, he passes fifty tests, which, according to the key for the London assignments (Table II., facing page 19), accords him a mental age of 10·4. The other ages have been converted by a similar calculation.

Three ages in the 1908 scale (XIV., XV., and Adult), and three in the 1911 scale (XI., XIII., XIV.), have no tests awarded them in Binet's arrangement ; hence, no corresponding London assignments can be calculated.

Order of Difficulty of the Tests for Defectives.

The orders of difficulty obtained respectively with defectives and with normals are far from coinciding. The total number of special school children passing each test has already been given in Table IV. According to the fresh order indicated by these figures, the list of tests has there been re-arranged once more. The differences of position shown by each test in the two rankings have been calculated by subtraction; they are shown in

TABLE VIII.

Differences in Order of Difficulty for Normals and Defectives.

(The sign + indicates that a test is relatively easier for normals :
the sign − indicates that a test is relatively easier for defectives.)

Test.	Difference in Order.	Test.	Difference in Order.
Dictation	+ 8	3 Numbers	0
Reading (6 Facts)	+ 6	Picture (Enumeration)	0
Reading (2 Facts)	+ 6	Sex	0
Diamond	+ 6	Pointing	0
4 Numbers	+ 5	Sentence Building (2)	− 1
6 Syllables	+ 5	Change	− 1
Difficult Questions	+ 4	Date	− 1
Definition (Class)	+ 4	Pence and Halfpence	− 1
16 Syllables	+ 4	4 Coins	− 1
Triple Order	+ 4	Age	− 1
Mixed Sentences	+ 3	2 Lines	− 1
3 Rhymes	+ 3	Naming	− 1
5 Numbers	+ 3	Problems	− 2
Divided Card	+ 3	5 Weights	− 2
Days of Week	+ 3	13 Pennies	− 2
2 Weights	+ 3	Fingers	− 2
10 Syllables	+ 3	4 Colours	− 2
2 Numbers	+ 3	4 Pennies	− 2
Sentence Building (1)	+ 2	Surname	− 2
Absurdities	+ 2	Morning and Afternoon	− 3
Count 20 to 1	+ 2	Square	− 3
Transcription	+ 2	Months	− 5
7 Numbers	+ 1	Right and Left	− 5
60 Words	+ 1	9 Coins	− 7
Differences (Concrete)	+ 1	Easy Questions	− 7
Missing Features	+ 1	Definition (Use)	− 7
26 Syllables	0	Picture (Description)	− 8
Memory Drawing	0	Picture (Interpretation)	− 9
6 Numbers	0	Suggestion	−12
Comparing Faces	0		

Table VIII. arranged according to size. Here, near the head of the first column, are to be found those tests which offer relatively the hardest obstacles to the defective. These *pontes asinorum* seem to sort themselves into four or five broad classes : (1) scholastic tests of a linguistic character (dictation, reading) ; (2) tests of immediate memory (two, four, five, seven numbers ; six, fifteen, twenty-six syllables ; perhaps triple order) ; (3) reasoning tests and tests involving critical perception (absurdities, differences (class), definition (concrete), perhaps missing features, divided card, and two weights) ; (4) certain other linguistic tests requiring facility in manipulating words (mixed sentences, difficult questions, rhymes, three words in one sentence, sixty words in three minutes) ; (5) other scholastic tests depending on acquirements which should be learnt at an early period (transcription, weekdays, counting backwards, perhaps drawing the rhombus).

Toward the end of the list the plan of arrangement places those tests which, relatively speaking, prove easier for the defective. These likewise belong to several categories, tolerably distinct : (1) picture tests (particularly interpretation and enumeration) ; (2) simple money tests (change, pennies, and halfpennies) ; (3) mechanical counting (four pennies, thirteen pennies) ; (4) scholastic tests depending upon information learnt after entering the special school (right and left, months, date) ; (5) tests of general information, depending principally upon age and experience (names of coins, of colours, of knife, key, penny ; number of fingers, easy questions, definition (use), age, surname, morning and afternoon, problems, perhaps suggestion and five weights).

For many tests the shift in location is pronounced. Suggestion, with normals a test for age XIII., proves with defectives to be easier than either reading (six facts) or definition (class), which with normals are tests for age IX. Nine coins, change, and months, which with normals are also tests for age IX., prove easier for defectives than dictation, passed by normals at age VII. Accordingly, in applying the tests to defectives or to those suspected of deficiency, it will be prudent to adhere rather to the order of difficulty for special school children. Otherwise, when borderline children fail with definition (concrete) and five weights, the examiner, following the normal order, may forget they still may pass such tests as suggestion or picture (interpretation).

By a strange irony many of the tests which, on the ground of their scholastic nature, Binet rejected in his last revision (1911), stand among those that differentiate defectives most profoundly from the normal. This circumstance it is, no doubt, that has biassed many observers in favour of the earlier scale (1908). It might even, as a corollary, be claimed that scholastic tests are among the best tests of intelligence. Theoretically the claim is by no means indefensible. In practice, however, the play of specific educational abilities and of specific educational defects, still more the wide variety of scholastic opportunity and of teaching efficiency, would import into estimates deduced merely from tests of school knowledge unknown and unadjustable errors. In English special schools the children have been selected largely by reason of their inability to profit by the ordinary method of instruction. During the early ages at which most defectives are certified, such inability resolves itself, among the higher grades, into an incapacity for learning to read and write and spell with customary speed. Naturally, therefore, it is among tests of these very processes that the differences between special and ordinary schools most prominently emerge.

That *linguistic disabilities more particularly characterise the higher grades in schools for the defective* is a fact of no small moment. Practical experience confirms this observation in two ways. *In the higher classes of special (M.D.) schools the staple ground of complaint is that the children are disproportionately backward in reading : among the older children left in the ordinary elementary school it is that they are backward in arithmetic.*

Average Scores at Each Age.

The average number of tests passed at each age by children from ordinary and special schools respectively is given in Table IX. The data are plotted graphically in Figure 26 (facing page 203, continuous lines, black and red). In

TABLE IX.

AVERAGE AND VARIABILITY AT EACH AGE.

For Children of Ordinary and Special (M.D.) Schools.

Chronological Age.	Normals.				Defectives.					
	Number of Tests passed.		Mental Age.		Number of Tests passed.		Mental Age.		Average Retardation.	Average Mental Ratio.
	Average.	Standard Deviation.	Average.	Standard Deviation.	Average.	Standard Deviation.	Average.	Standard Deviation.		
3·5	7·9	3·34	3·7	0·48	—	—	—	—	—	—
4·5	16·1	5·15	4·6	0·69	—	—	—	—	—	—
5·5	24·3	6·02	5·5	0·59	—	—	—	—	—	—
6·5	32·2	5·29	6·5	0·83	11·8	1·74	4·2	0·38	2·3	64·6
7·5	37·6	5·16	7·6	1·03	18·5	2·78	4·9	0·44	2·6	65·3
8·5	43·0	4·80	8·6	1·15	24·4	5·16	5·5	0·40	3·0	64·7
9·5	46·4	4·97	9·4	1·24	27·9	6·07	5·9	0·75	3·6	62·1
10·5	50·4	4·81	10·6	1·29	32·5	6·60	6·5	0·96	4·0	61·9
11·5	53·0	4·23	11·4	1·26	36·4	6·18	7·2	1·05	4·3	62·6
12·5	55·3	3·38	12·3	1·18	39·1	4·75	7·7	0·90	4·8	61·6
13·5	57·9	3·15	13·1	1·20	41·5	5·21	8·0	1·19	5·5	59·3
14·5	59·6	2·68	13·8	·1·09	43·3	5·54	8·3	1·34	6·2	57·2

figure and table the averages shown are the usual arithmetic means. But, with tests thus unevenly distributed, the arithmetic mean scarcely yields a satisfactory index for the central tendency in the various age-groups. For the normal children averages so inaccurate would prove a grave disadvantage, since upon their averages our norms are to be based.

Among normals the fact and its causes are transparent. The members of each age-group appear distributed asymmetrically along the scale of tests; and the list of tests ceases abruptly with two or three hard tests whose age-assignment is obscure, preceded by half a dozen tests that most bright children over twelve can pass. For the older ages, therefore, the upper end of the frequency-distribution is sharply curtailed. On the other hand, the lower tail of the middle ages sprawls back through the twenty tests assigned to ages V. and VI. The two tendencies combine to drag down the arithmetic means for all but the youngest age-groups. With distributions of this stamp the median should be the more appropriate measure.

Calculation shows that for almost every year in the latter half of the age-series the medians rise above the arithmetic means by one or two units. Since each test has been assigned to its particular age-group just because it is passed by about half that age-group, and since again within a given age the tests increase in difficulty by approximately equal increments, it follows that the median for each age should fall about the middle of the tests for that age. This anticipation actual calculating verifies. With small groups, however, and with discontinuous variables, the precise determination of the median involves a procedure somewhat arbitrary. It will be convenient, therefore, to treat the central value for each age-group as falling exactly in the middle of the series of tests assigned to it. The values thus assumed rarely deviate from the calculated medians by more than 0·5.

To the standard deviations expressed in terms of tests (Table IX., column 3) small interest attaches. They are determined chiefly by the relative number of tests appropriated, as nearly equal in difficulty, to each age. Thus, among both normals and defectives, those groups with whom the many tests assigned to ages V. and VI. become crucial exhibit the largest standard deviations.

Conversion of Score into Mental Age.

In Binet's "metric scale," the outstanding novelty, the central pillar of the whole design, is the measurement of intelligence by means of age. It is an easy and alluring notion. As the woodman, who has cut down an oak, estimates the length of its life by counting the annual rings across its trunk, so the teacher can measure the mental age of a child by making with the tests a cross-section of its mind, and reckoning the number of equivalent years which its successes in those tasks denote. Thus the notion of mental development provides the final unit, as it formed the initial aim, of the Binet-Simon scale. How is the reckoning to be made ?

To convert the failures and successes into terms of equivalent years, various formulæ have been proposed. Binet's ultimate recommendation may be summarised thus : Credit the child with the highest age in which he passes all the tests ; and for every further test passed add an appropriate fraction of a year. Since in the 1911 scale there are five tests for every age (except age IV.), each test counts as one-fifth of a year. From time to time a child may also fail with a test or two from sets below the highest age in which he passes all. Should corresponding fractions be deducted ? If an unusual success is to be entered to his account, should not an unusual failure be balanced equally against him ? This Binet nowhere

FIGURE 22.

DISTRIBUTION ACCORDING TO MENTAL AGE OF CHILDREN OF ORDINARY ELEMENTARY AND SPECIAL (M.D.) SCHOOLS AT EACH CHRONOLOGICAL YEAR.

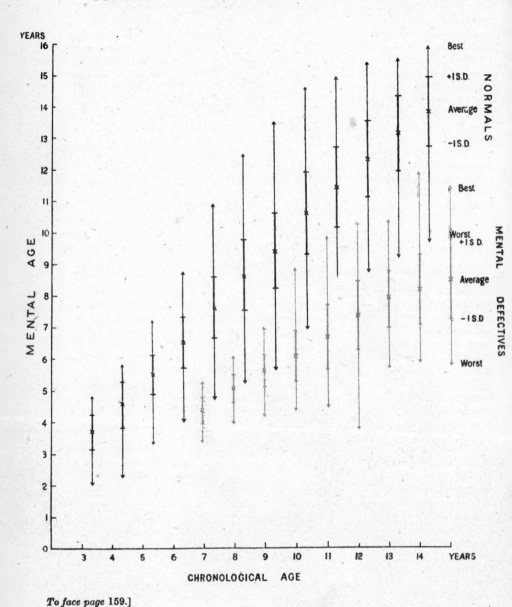

explicitly states. Indeed, he and his earlier followers evidently assumed that the breakdown would be far more sudden and abrupt than actually it proves, and that for most children the range of critical tests would be confined to one or two years at most. Later investigators, however, have demonstrated beyond question the need for carrying the child over an extended span of tests. Every test, therefore, about which there can be the least particle of doubt should be given to the child ; and he should be debited with every failure, as well as credited with every success. Such a procedure treats each success as of equal merit. Children who pass the same number of tests score exactly the same mental age, irrespective of the special nature of the particular performances in which individually they succeed or succumb. Of two children, both succeeding, let us say, with sixty tests, the one who succeeds with suggestion—a test for age XIII., but fails with definition (class) —a test for age IX., is accorded an age no higher than the one who fails with the former but succeeds with the latter. Assigned to an older age, suggestion, it is true, proves for the majority the harder test ; but to assume that it is in consequence the harder test for either of the individuals in question would involve an evident fallacy.

This general principle—the treatment of tests as convertible, colourless units—facilitates the construction of a simple index for translating the test-score immediately into a mental age and for deducing from age the number of tests that should be passed. It is shown and explained in Table II.,[1] and has been used throughout the present work.

3. THE DISTRIBUTION OF INTELLIGENCE.

Distribution of Mental Ages among Normals and Defectives.

In accordance with the age-assignments as now revised, the estimate for the intelligence of every child has been converted into terms of mental years. The numbers of normal children attaining each mental level at each age are shown in Table X. As before, percentages were first computed for each school separately, and then weighted according to its representative character before the averages in the table were finally calculated. This age-and-intelligence table may be compared with the age-and-standard table published in my memorandum on educational abilities.[2] The comparison suggests that intelligence varies more widely than school capacity, and that possibly school methods prime and prod the backward a little nearer to the average standard, but do not exploit to its utmost the inborn intelligence of the more acute. They tend to level attainments without equalising ability.

Table XI. exhibits in like fashion the distribution of ability among the special school children. It may be compared with the age-and-grade table for defectives in the memorandum on educational abilities.[3] In the present table the absence of the lowest grades of deficiency will be remarked at the older ages ; but the re-transference of brighter children to ordinary schools is not so conspicuously evident as in the table for educational ability.

The averages and standard deviations in terms of mental years are given for the several age-groups, both normal and defective, in Table IX. (columns 4, 5, 8, and 9). The data are plotted graphically in Figure 22. In this figure the vertical lines represent the total range of ability at each age, black indicating the children of the ordinary elementary schools, red those of the special (M.D.) schools. The cross near the centre of each line marks the age-average ; the arrowhead at either end the brightest or dullest child

---

(¹) Page 19   (²) Loc. cit., page 22, Table IX.   (³) Loc. cit., p. 8, Table II.

in the group. The thickened portion of the line measures a distance of + and − 1 S.D. above and below the average. Between these limits, a range in all of twice the standard deviation, fall 68·3 per cent. of a normal distribution, that is, just over two-thirds of the whole group. The diagram reveals, at every age and stage, a broad and unmistakable overlap between the children of special and ordinary schools.

Among the normals the average mental age coincides almost exactly with the chronological age, except in the older years. Here the reduction in the size of the averages for intelligence, an attenuation due to the lack of

TABLE X.

Distribution of Intelligence. Ordinary Elementary Schools.

Chrono-logical Age.	Mental Age.						
	2—	3—	4—	5—	6—	7—	8—
3 — ..	6·7	63·5	29·8	—	—	—	—
4 — ..	2·4	18·6	50·3	28·7	—	—	—
5 — ..	—	1·5	19·6	62·3	16·0	0·6	—
6 — ..	—	—	3·8	26·2	43·9	23·1	2·7
7 — ..	—	—	0·3	5·7	22·4	42·5	20·3
8 — ..	—	—	—	0·9	5·1	23·2	38·7
9 — ..	—	—	—	0·2	2·9	9·8	22·0
10 — ..	—	—	—	—	0·4	2·6	6·4
11 — ..	—	—	—	—	—	0·5	3·5
12 — ..	—	—	—	—	—	—	0·8
13 — ..	—	—	—	—	—	—	0·3
14 — ..	—	—	—	—	—	—	—
Average Chrono-Age.	3·8	3·8	4·5	5·6	6·8	7·8	8·8

higher tests, becomes pronounced. Among the special school children the amount of retardation progressively increases. The curve or trajectory of growth is for them flattened at the top. The decline insinuates that by the age of fourteen many of the defectives are nearing their mental limit.

Percentiles.

Where the distribution of measurements is normal, it is possible, when a child's measurement is known, to locate his position in a sample group purely by inference from the average of that group and its standard deviation. With the Binet-Simon scale the distribution of the nine-year-old children, measured in mental years, agrees pretty closely with the normal curve. The average for this age is 9·4, approximately nine and a half years ; the standard deviation 1·24, approximately one year and a quarter. A given child, aged nine six months ago, passes, let us say, forty-one tests ; and, therefore, has a mental age of eight exactly. He is thus retarded by one and a half years, or about $1\frac{1}{5}$ times the standard deviation ($1\frac{1}{2} \div 1\cdot24 = 1\cdot21$). From a table for the probability integral we can at once discover that in a normally distributed group approximately 11·5 per cent. will lie beyond the limit of $-1\frac{1}{5}$ S.D. This child, therefore, would rank as eighty-ninth in a series of a hundred arranged according to intelligence. Such a statement gives a clear and concrete notion of his intellectual standing.

In actual fact, I find that two children in my survey, passing this number of tests, rank as 267th or 268th in the entire age-group, which comprises just under 300 children ; they would rank, therefore, approximately ninetieth on a percentage basis.

Where, however, the distribution of the measurements is asymmetrical (as happens most conspicuously in the older age-groups when measured by the Binet-Simon scale), the tables for the normal curve can no longer be applied. The position inferred from the standard deviation would not

TABLE X—*(continued)*.

Distribution of Intelligence. Ordinary Elementary Schools—*(continued)*.

			Mental Age				Average Mental Age.
9—	10—	11—	12—	13—	14—	15—	
—	—	—	—	—	—	—	3·7
—	—	—	—	—	—	—	4·6
—	—	—	—	—	—	—	5·5
0·3	—	—	—	—	—	—	6·5
7·1	1·3	0·4	—	—	—	—	7·6
18·1	11·7	1·7	0·6	—	—	—	8·6
35·5	21·8	5·0	2·1	0·7	—	—	9·4
18·3	34·8	23·3	11·3	2·1	0·6	0·2	10·6
8·6	25·1	31·7	20·8	8·4	1·1	0·3	11·4
2·4	11·2	19·6	37·9	21·3	6·1	0·7	12·3
1·3	5·7	11·4	18·7	37·0	24·3	1·3	13·1
1·2	2·8	3·0	10·2	30·4	48·6	3·8	13·8
9·7	10·7	11·6	12·4	13·3	14·0	13·8	—

coincide so closely as above with the position obtaining in reality. And, in such circumstances, the child's position can only be deduced from tables specially compiled from the actual distribution. A mode of tabulation, convenient in form, and already much in use for measurements of children's height and weight, is that originally suggested by Sir Francis Galton, and termed by him the method of percentiles. Imagine a group of one hundred and one children arranged in inverse order of merit. The 1st or worst child will mark the zero percentile ; the 101st or best, the 100th percentile ; the 51st or middle, the 50th percentile or median (and, if the group is symmetrical, the average). The 11th, 21st, 31st,....and 91st children will mark the 10th, 20th, 30th....and 90th percentiles. Eleven measurements thus suffice to indicate the general form of distribution.

For the results of the Binet-Simon scale such percentiles are shown in Table XII. From these the approximate position of a given child in a typical series of one hundred children of the same age can be instantly read off, as soon as his test-score is known. The reader, however, should beware of inferring that equal differences between percentiles indicate equal differences in the measurement of ability. In mental age the difference between the 10th and 20th percentile is half as much again as that between the 30th and 40th. The difference between the zero and 10th may be, with age-groups of the size here dealt with, as much as one or two years (in theory, with an infinitely large group it would be infinite); while that between the 40th and 50th is but one- or two-tenths of a year.

Correlation between Mental Age and Chronological Age.

The correlation between mental age and chronological age is ·954 for the normals and ·839 for the defectives.[1] For determining from the chrono-

TABLE XI.
Distribution of Intelligence.   Special (M.D.) Schools.

Chrono-logical Age.	Mental Age.									Average Mental Age
	3—	4—	5—	6—	7—	8—	9—	10—	11—	
6 — ..	34·3	65·6	—	—	—	—	—	—	—	4·2
7 — ..	1·8	56·3	41·8	—	—	—	—	—	—	4·9
8 — ..	—	11·6	75·4	13·0	—	—	—	—	—	5·5
9 — ..	—	9·9	51·9	29·6	7·3	1·2	—	—	—	5·9
10 — ..	—	6·2	24·8	35·4	29·2	3·5	0·9	—	—	6·5
11 — ..	0·9	1·9	11·1	18·5	48·1	16·7	1·9	0·9	—	7·2
12 — ..	—	—	3·8	17·1	45·7	25·7	6·7	0·9	—	7·7
13 — ..	—	—	5·3	13·8	26·6	35·1	14·9	4·3	—	8·0
14 — ..	—	—	5·9	11·8	17·7	33·4	21·6	7·8	2·0	8·3
Average Chronological Age	6·7	7·4	9·3	11·1	12·1	13·1	13·7	13·9	14·4	

logical age the approximate mean mental age the regression equations are as follows :—

For normals,
Mental Age = (·951 × Chronological Age + ·357) years.
For defectives,
Mental Age = (·535 × Chronological Age + ·856) years.

Thus, on an average, for each chronological year the normal children advance mentally about nineteen-twentieths of a year ; and the defectives advance rather over half a year ; or, expressed conversely, to accomplish one year of normal mental progress defectives require, on an average, 1 year 10½ months.

[1] The probable errors for these coefficients are + ·001 and + ·007 respectively. The correlation ratios are as follows :—
(1) normals (a) mental age on chronological age ·953 ;
(b) chronological age on mental age ·951.
(2) defectives (a) mental age on chronological age ·841 ;
(b) chronological age on mental age ·848.
Tested by comparing the correlation ratios with the correlation coefficients, the regressions appear, among the normals, very nearly linear. With the defectives, the regression of chronological age upon mental age deviates significantly from linearity, the difference between the squares of the correlation and the ratio being nearly three times its own probable error. The averages of the various age-groups, mental and chronological (Tables X. and XI.), may be used to plot the regression lines upon a diagram. The divergencies from linearity then become plain, and prove chiefly to be due to an obvious peculiarity in the original percentage tables : the total number in each chronological age-group drops at the edge of the table (for example, after age fourteen) abruptly from 100 to zero ; whereas the total number in the mental age-groups drops more gradually. If the lower rows of Table X. were complete on the right, there would in theory be no " regression." The " average mental age " should be virtually identical with the average chronological age. In fact (as was pointed out in the Report on the Distribution of Educational Abilities) such tables are not correlation-tables of the ordinary type.

4. THE MENTAL RATIO.

Its Calculation and Constancy.

If a child's mental age be divided by his chronological age, the quotient will state what fraction of ability the child actually possesses out of the sum total of ability which at his age he should theoretically possess—both amounts being measured in terms of years. This fraction may be termed, with Stern, the child's "intelligence quotient," or, more euphoniously perhaps, his "mental ratio." It is the counterpart, in measurements of intelligence, of the figure I have termed, in scholastic measurements, the child's "educational ratio."[1]

The mental ratios of special school children are shown for each age in the last column of Table IX. They vary but little. Whereas the degree of retardation increases from 2·6 years at seven to 5·5 at thirteen, thus doubling in the course of six years, the ratios from age to age seem very nearly constant. Hence, *as a method of indicating the degree of mental deficiency, the*

TABLE XII.

Distribution of Intelligence. Ordinary Elementary Schools.

Percentiles for each Age-Group in terms of Mental Age.

Age.	0 (Worst)	10th.	20th.	30th.	40th.	50th (Median)	60th.	70th.	80th.	90th.	100th (Best)
3— ..	2·0	2·8	3·2	3·4	3·5	3·6	3·8	4·0	4·0	4·2	4·8
4— ..	2·2	3·6	3·9	4·1	4·3	4·5	4·6	4·9	5·1	5·4	5·8
5— ..	3·2	4·6	5·0	5·2	5·4	5·5	5·6	5·8	6·0	6·3	7·2
6— ..	4·0	5·3	5·9	6·2	6·5	6·5	6·7	6·7	7·2	7·7	8·7
7— ..	4·7	6·2	6·5	7·1	7·3	7·5	7·8	8·0	8·5	9·0	10·8
8— ..	5·2	7·0	7·5	8·0	8·2	8·5	8·7	9·0	9·3	10·4	12·5
9— ..	5·7	7·8	8·5	8·8	9·3	9·5	9·7	10·2	10·4	11·7	13·5
10— ..	6·8	8·8	9·3	9·7	10·2	10·4	10·8	11·3	11·7	12·5	14·6
11— ..	7·7	9·7	10·4	10·8	11·0	11·5	11·7	12·0	12·5	13·5	15·0
12— ..	8·7	10·8	11·5	11·7	12·0	12·5	13·0	13·0	13·5	14·3	15·5
13— ..	9·0	11·3	12·0	12·5	13·0	13·5	14·0	14·3	14·7	15·0	15·5
14— ..	9·7	12·5	13·0	13·5	14·0	14·3	14·7	15·0	15·0	15·5	16·0

"*mental ratio*" *may justly claim to be, for any given individual, far more useful than the statement of retardation, since it is almost independent of age.* For prognosis it is especially significant. If at the age of eight a child has a mental ratio of 75 per cent., being thus retarded by two years, we can predict that at twelve his mental level will probably be that of a child of nine, and at sixteen that of a child of twelve.

Changes in Mental Ratio among Defectives.

These claims, however, are but imperfectly realised. Although, when compared with the degree of retardation, the ratio appears throughout more constant, yet beneath this comparative stability lurks a perceptible drift towards diminution. It is small; but it is steady. The change is demonstrated most easily among the special schools. Here, at first sight, the decrease might seem attributable to the retransference of the brightest

[1] *Loc. cit. sup.,* p. 15.

defectives to ordinary schools, and the continued influx of children increasingly dull. But of recent years—at any rate, in the schools reviewed—these transferences have been rare. Further, the elimination of the worst cases proceeds as rapidly as the promotion of the best. And, since the older age-groups in the survey are preponderantly drawn from schools for elder boys and girls, schools to which the weakest defectives seldom gain admission, the children who together make up these groups can hardly constitute inferior samples of their year.

But upon this question direct evidence is of easy access. Besides simultaneously testing successive age-groups, each composed of different individuals from the last, we may test during successive years a single age-group composed of the same individuals. The same child is thus examined at different stages of his life. Data of both kinds were included in the records from the schools for the mentally deficient.

At these schools a large number of special cases have been officially referred to me, and kept under personal observation for considerable periods. Commonly such supervision entails testing the same child again and again after intervals of a year or more. By collating the results of such repeated tests it is possible to sort defectives into six classes, according as either (I) their mental age or (II) their mental ratio, (1) increases, (2) remains the same, or (3) declines. They may thus be classified (I) by mental age, as (1) progressive, (2) stationary, (3) deteriorating cases; and (II) by mental ratio, as cases of (1) accelerated or compensatory progress; (2) regular or proportional progress; (3) relative decline. It will be seen that II (1) and II (2) are subdivisions of I (1); and I (2) and I (3) of II (3).

In thirty-four of my cases the Binet-Simon tests have been annually applied over a period of six years. The average mental ratios in each of the successive years are enumerated in Table XIII.

TABLE XIII.

Mental Ratios obtained from the Same Children during Five Successive Years.

Date of Testing.		Mental Ratio
1913	..	63·7
1914	..	65·3
1915	..	64·5
1916	..	62·6
1917	..	59·8
1918	..	57·1

In all but eight individuals the mental ratio found on the last application of the tests was smaller than that found five years before. And in six of these eight the low initial grading at the commencement of the period could be clearly traced to external hindrances—weakness of health, ill-treatment at home, irregularity of attendance, unsuitable methods at the previous school—impediments that afterwards were substantially alleviated.

In one special (M.D.) school an endeavour has been made to carry out by means of the Binet-Simon tests an annual survey of all the children in attendance. The population is constantly shifting; and the largest number who remained in the school for at least a second examination comprised only some seventy-two boys and girls. These were tested in 1913 and again in 1914. Of the seventy-two children, two had remained stationary; seventeen betray an actual and absolute decline; and fifty-three could boast a definite advance in mental age—an advance occasionally approaching, rarely equalling, the actual advance in chronological age Of those who advanced, sixteen had improved mentally by more than a year in the year's interval, five by more than a year and a half. The greatest improvement was that manifested by a child aged $9\frac{7}{12}$—a boy with a bright animated presence, who at the first examination had a mental age of $7\cdot8$, and a mental ratio, therefore, of $81\cdot4$ per cent. ; at the second he had a mental age of $9\cdot5$, thus advancing $1\cdot7$ years, and increasing his ratio to nearly 90 per cent. The greatest deterioration was that shown by a low-grade child of $9\frac{8}{12}$, who at the first examination had a mental age of $5\cdot6$ (mental ratio $57\cdot9$ per cent.), and receded by $1\cdot4$ years.

Among defectives such patent examples of anomalous progress should be to the thoughtful teacher of no small interest. A change in the method of instruction is occasionally found to precede, and sometimes suffices to explain, the unexpected spurt ; those whose advance covered one mental year or more are mostly children who at the time of the first examination had been admitted to the special school but recently. In other cases some happy change in home conditions seemed responsible—a change that has of late been witnessed more frequently as a result of increased employment during the war. Five, however, are children of ten or more, who have been in attendance for several years ; and in every case, with one dubious exception, the subsequent history unequivocally suggests that the partial restoration must be connected with some deeper cause than mere accident or freak of fortune. That cause appears to be an intrinsic irregularity of mental growth. Such children are creatures of deferred maturity. Their development is not arrested ; it has been postponed. Although upon a lower plane, their mental growth runs parallel with that of many cleverer children, in whom the phenomenon is more familiar. There is many a sharp child whose cycle of growth is like that of the mulberry tree, presenting first a long delay, and then a sudden yield of flower and fruit together. Their existence is recognised in the double scholarship examination. In London at the age of thirteen a second examination has been instituted specifically for those who in the current phrase "bloom late," and whose anticipated powers, therefore, do not ripen by the age of ten. In like fashion, among the classes for defectives, time and due season will here and there disclose a sporadic "school autumnal."

There are, then, individuals whose imputed deficiency is apparent and temporary only. The initial retardation, seldom in these children very severe, is redeemed, partly, if not entirely, by a delayed and compensatory acceleration.[1] To overlook their latent possibilities, to treat them as defective for life, because stationary for a year or two, would be as mistaken as to root up a Christmas rose because it fails to blossom in the spring.

But deficiency, as well as normality, may wait until a later age to declare itself. A child of $12\frac{5}{12}$ showed a mental level in 1913 of $9\cdot6$ years, a ratio, therefore, of $77\cdot4$. On the basis of the tests even the most stringent American standard could hardly convict him of deficiency. A year later he had lapsed to a mental level of $9\cdot2$ years, a ratio, therefore, of $68\cdot7$. And when last tested at the age of $14\frac{5}{12}$, his mental age was $9\cdot4$ years, and his ratio $65\cdot3$. At this stage few would have hesitated to describe him as defective. External evidence, it may be added, rendered this diagnosis credibly certain from earlier years. Another child, aged $7\frac{7}{12}$, who at the first examination had a mental age of $6\cdot4$, at the second showed no discoverable change. He was still on the same low plane. At the beginning of the year his mental ratio, $84\cdot4$ per cent., might be thought sufficient to absolve him of deficiency.

(1) These cases seem analogous to those aptly designated by Dr. Auden instances of "larval capacity" (*Annual Report of the School Medical Officer for Birmingham*, 1912).

But at the end of the year it had dropped to 74·6 per cent. ; and in the course of five more years, by sheer increase of physical age. to barely 70 per cent. Here, however, there were tokens that the subnormality was one of temperament and character quite as much as of intelligence. I would add that, as a general rule, *such a progressive decline in the mental ratio is distinctive of neuropathic and psychopathic cases.* Where low intelligence is associated with epilepsy, whether overt or masked. the deterioration may be most profound. Where low intelligence is accompanied by temperamental instability —a conjunction seen in day schools far more frequently than epileptic complications—the symptom is yet commoner, though not so clear. Even where there is no such aggravation evident, the ratio will occasionally dwindle ; so that a child, whom at six the most rigorous would hardly dub feeble-minded, at sixteen the most tolerant could hardly deem normal. Such individuals are perhaps analogous to those described by Doll as " potentially feebleminded."[1] Almost invariably, however, during their school career they are borderland children, cases on the verge. Rarely is the transformation radical. A bright child never turns into an imbecile ; nor can a typical special school pupil climb to the height of an average normal. Indeed, in my list of suspects an appearance of latent deficiency has usually been explicable by the artificiality of our standards. Like most realities in nature, growth is irregular. Our line of demarcation is as straight and as fictitious as the equator. That certain children, whether judged by retardation or judged by ratio, veer to one side of a hypothetical boundary this year, and pass to the other side next, should be no more astounding than that a river frontier does not follow an arbitrary line of latitude, or the northern coast of Europe coincide with the Arctic circle. These vacillating nondescripts should be watched. They vex in no small measure the task of diagnosis and certification. Of the two forms, diminution in mental ratio is commoner than increase ; and among those of my cases that have shown a diminution relatively rapid, the greater portion have occurred either towards the beginning or towards the end of the school career, that is, about the ages of seven to eight or of twelve to fourteen. But neither speed nor amount of decline are, as a rule, considerable. Apart from accident, disease, or other extraneous factor, seldom, if ever, does a young child of nearly average ability grow up into a typical case of mental defect. In the few individuals that have been brought to me as clear examples of complete transition some definite disturbance has been discoverable as the underlying cause : most frequently incipient *dementia præcox.*

In view of the possibility of latent normality and latent deficiency, it is essential, particularly with children of younger ages, to supplement the evidence of the tests by evidence from other sources. Even so, to give a final diagnosis may not be justifiable until the child has been observed and tested for some months, perhaps for some years. *For cases where latent deficiency or latent normality has been suspected, but not verified, a mental clinic or observation-centre seems indispensable.* We need, as it were, a psychological dark-room where we may seclude for delicate scrutiny our undeveloped negatives.

For the seventy-two children, re-examined after an interval of a year, the average change in mental age and mental ratio is shown in Table XIV.[2] With the majority there was no question of latency. They appeared unmistakably deficient from the first ; and, so far as they have been traced, they have remained defective—at any rate in the sense of the relevant

[1] See *Training School Bulletin.* 1916, Vol XIII., No. 3, pp. 54–61 ; No. 6, pp. 159–163 ; *Clinical Studies in Feeblemindedness.* 1917. Also Goddard. *Journal of Psycho-Asthenics.* 1913. Vol. XVII., No. 4. p. 125. Florence Mateer, *Pedagogical Seminary.* 1918, Vol. XXV.. pp. 369–392.

[2] Where, owing to absence of the child or other cause, the interval between the two examinations was not exactly 365 days, the amount of change has been reduced proportionately to this basis.

Education Act—to this day. The average[1] progress made by the entire group during the year was + 0·47 mental years, a rate of barely one-half a mental year *per annum*. This figure, obtained by repeating the tests with identical children, concurs with the general result before observed, where the successive age-groups differed in respect of the individuals composing them. A progress of but half a year *per annum* implies, it will be noted, an annual increase in the absolute amount of retardation.

TABLE XIV.

Annual Change in Mental Age and Mental Ratio in the Same Children, Grouped according to Age.

Age last Birthday.	Number of Children.	1913.		1914.		Change in Mental Age.	Change in Mental Ratio.
		Mental Age.	Mental Ratio.	Mental Age.	Mental Ratio.		
7 ..	4	5·17	69·0	5·50	64·7	+ ·33	− 4·3
8 ..	15	5·01	59·0	5·79	61·0	+ ·78	+ 2·0
9 ..	15	6·06	63·8	6·57	62·5	+ ·51	− 1·3
10 ..	11	6·45	61·5	6·99	60·8	+ ·54	− 0·7
11 ..	8	7·25	63·0	7·47	59·7	+ ·22	− 3·3
12 ..	8	7·87	63·1	8·20	60·7	+ ·33	− 2·4
13 ..	7	7·63	56·5	8·03	55·4	+ ·40	− 1·1
14 ..	4	7·65	52·8	7·67	49·6	+ ·02	− 3·2

The average change in mental ratio is during a single year only −1·1 per cent. In this enquiry, therefore, the mental ratio remains pretty steadfast from one year to the next. Among the children aged eight, however, the table reveals an increase. That increase is to be traced to the salutary influence of the special methods of education upon nine or ten individuals lately transferred to the school. An analysis of the results, both here and elsewhere, divulges that *immediately after transference to special (M.D.) schools an unusual degree of progress is, as a rule, made by the younger children.* Seldom, however, does the advance equal one mental year *per annum*, the natural rate of the normal child. In the older age-groups, on the other hand, there is a conspicuous decrease. So remote are they from maintaining the normal rate of progress, that they cannot even maintain their own. This seems attributable to two factors. The boys over twelve comprise for the most part individuals not sufficiently intelligent to be transferred to an elder boys' department. They have been retained in the present school precisely because their progress has already slackened almost to a halt. Indeed, of the boys aged fourteen every one had reached his mental limit at the time of the first examination. But in the other age-groups showing the same excessive decline such low-grade boys formed only a minor proportion. A second and more general explanation must, therefore, be sought ; for neither the girls over twelve nor the children of either sex between eleven and twelve include a preponderance of low-grade types. The gradual subsidence of progress must be a universal characteristic. The lowest grades have no monopoly. Older defectives of all levels exhibit a premature loss of developmental impetus. Like a shell projected with an inadequate charge, their momentum is exhausted half-way to the target.

---

[1] In calculating the averages cited in this paragraph, the averages for the several age-groups as given in the table have first been weighted according to the number of children in each age-group. Thus, they represent the averages for the entire group of children calculated regardless of age.

N

But, it may still be asked, does not the abatement of progress, as expressed by the decrease in mental ratio, occur more frequently among the lowest grades than among the highest ? The answer is not far to seek. Higher or lower grades may best be distinguished, irrespective of age, by their initial mental ratios. According to their initial mental ratio, therefore, the children have been regrouped ; and the average change in mental age and ratio recalculated. The results are shown in Table XV. The entire number falls into three groups or sections. There is, first of all, a group of five children who possessed at the commencement of the year a mental ratio of over 80 per cent. Each of these five improved at the rate of one mental year or more per annum. *In the highest grade of special school child,*

TABLE XV.

Annual Change in Mental Age and Mental Ratio in the Same Children, Grouped according to Mental Ratio.

Mental Ratio.	No. of Children.	Change in Mental Age.	Change in Mental Ratio.
30 — 35	2	+ 1·25	+ 9·1
35 — 40	0	—	—
40 — 45	3	+ 0·59	+ 0·1
45 — 50	8	+ 0·71	+ 1·7
50 — 55	8	+ 0·53	+ 0·3
55 — 60	16	+ 0·23	— 2·7
60 — 65	10	+ 0·30	— 3·0
65 — 70	9	+ 0·56	— 0·7
70 — 75	9	+ 0·23	— 3·8
75 — 80	2	+ 0·40	— 2·4
80 — 85	4	+ 1·12	+ 2·5
85 — 90	0	—	—
90 — 95	1	+ 1·00	+ 0·8

therefore, the speed of progress may equal, or even exceed, that of the average normal. In such cases, as the last column of the table intimates, the mental ratio also expands ; and the celerity of the child's later progress cancels much of his original retardation. They may lose half their relative backwardness by recovering all the normal rate. The second group comprehends the great majority of the examinees, those with a mental ratio between 55 and 80 per cent. Here the average rate of progress is under 0·5 mental year per annum—less than half that of the ordinary child. Of the forty-six cases in this group only four children reach or surpass the normal rate—one year of mental progress in one year of actual time. In thirty-three cases the mental ratio declines ; the other thirteen, exceptions to the general tendency, occur principally among the younger representatives. Thus, with the majority of this section retardation increases, not only in absolute amount, but even relatively to age. *The progress of the typically feebleminded wanes appreciably as the end of their school career is approached :* their years of growth are few and slow. The third group comprises twenty-one children whose mental ratio was less than 55 per cent. In six, including practically all the older children in this group, the mental ratio has diminished markedly. The large remainder are really exceptions, and support the rule that they seem to transgress—the rule, namely, that the lower grades more rapidly attain their mental limit. The infraction is more apparent than real. Every case has its explanation. Many are younger children recently transferred to the special school as flagrantly backward, who during the first year under the new conditions made rapid progress, but—as later examinations prove—failed to sustain the speed with which they had begun. Some, however, seem to improve merely because there is such ample room for improvement. In a young child, with a mental ratio as low as 30 per cent., an absolute advance of much less than a single year will effect an increase of another 10 per cent. Further, on scrutinising the primary records it is evident that at least four children failed originally to do themselves justice because—like so many of the lower grades—their capacity fluctuates from day to day, and the first inspection overtook them in an unfavourable phase. Two at least appear to have failed in the first trial, largely because of the novelty of the examination ; and to have improved in the later trial, largely because the examination had grown more familiar.

The twofold influence of low-grade and increasing age is to be seen more clearly in Table XVI. This table gives the average change in retardation

TABLE XVI.

Annual Change in Mental Ratio in the Same Children, Grouped according to both Age and Ratio.

Mental Ratio at Commencement of Year.	Age at Commencement of Year.		
	8 —	9 —	10 —
55 — 60	+ 2·6	− 9·2	− 1·4
60 — 65	+ 1·8	− 2·8	− 4·3
65 — 70	—	—	− 5·5
70 — 75	+ 4·0	− 3·6	+ 0·8
75 — 80	—	0·0	+ 3·8
80 — 85	+ 4·9	+ 7·5	—

manifested by defectives of various grades at ages eight, nine, and ten—the only ages in which there are more than ten children. Figures for the highest ages and for the lowest mental ratios are not entered, because the changes in the sub-groups—represented as they would be by but one or two individuals, and influenced as they are by rare and special conditions—might obscure the general tendencies exhibited by the whole.

It will be seen that within the three age-groups enumerated a large decrease in mental ratio is characteristic of, and confined to, the lower grades and the higher years. Allowing, then, for extraneous influences that supervene in the younger ages, there is some evidence that, when identical children are re-tested, *low mental ratios tend to become yet lower with the lapse of time and the increase of age.* The numbers are small ; the cases are selected. The evidence, therefore, remains inconclusive. Further data are needed, gathered on a large scale from tests applied again and again to the same children at successive periods of school life.

Range of Individual Variability.

A point of vital consequence is the extent to which the individual children, whether normal or defective, may depart from the average for their age and category. The standard deviations for each successive year are given in Table IX., column 5. (Cf. Figure 22.) The figures are large ; and among the children of ordinary elementary schools increase with moderate regularity throughout the earlier ages. At ten the rate of increase is relaxed ; and during the later years there is, if anything, an absolute diminution. Reference to the age-and-intelligence table (Table X.) shows that the decrease in the variations may be traced to a special cause—the progressive curtailment of the frequency distributions towards the upper extremity of the scale[1] : were the Binet-Simon tests to be credited, but a handful of the older children could reach a mental age above thirteen or fourteen. This curtailment, in turn, needs explanation. It may be referred, partly to the fact that the brighter children removed at the age of eleven to central and secondary schools are but poorly represented, but chiefly to the abrupt and premature termination of the scale itself. Towards the lower extremity of the scale[2] the older age-groups spread themselves out more and more. The lower half of the distribution, which at ten and eleven extends only four mental years below the middle year, is at thirteen and fourteen dispersed over as many as five. The asymmetry is mostly an artefact. With adequate tests and adequate samples, I suspect the scattering would appear no less pronounced towards the upper end than towards the lower. Could full allowance be made for these two imperfections, the standard deviations would continue steadily to increase, although I suspect that, until puberty is approached, the rate of increase would hardly rise to that exhibited before the age of ten. At the younger ages, the large deviations at five, and again at seven and eight, presumably arise from the wide differences in the speed with which the children settle down in the novel atmosphere of infants' school or senior department ; analogous enlargements are to be found in the standard deviations for educational ability, although they fall about a year later.[3] The diminution at six may be associated with the large number of tests which children of this level may pass without altering their mental age by more than a fraction of a year. With due deduction for these factors, it seems fair to conclude that, at any rate up to the age of ten, *the standard deviation may be assumed to increase in arithmetical progression and to bear a fixed ratio to the mean or median age.* In these two features, absolute increase and relative constancy from year to year, the range of individual variability revealed in general intelligence resembles that displayed in educational ability ; here, also, as I have elsewhere pointed out, the standard deviation during the school life is almost directly proportional to age.[4] Taken in conjunction, the two characteristics explain the virtual uniformity preserved by the " mental ratio " throughout the years of growth.

On an average, the standard deviation is 11·8 per cent. of age. Thus *in intelligence, as measured by the present version of the Binet-Simon scale, children of London elementary schools tend to vary about the average for their age by exactly one year at the age of eight and a half, and throughout the earlier, if not the later, half of their school career by nearly one-eighth of their age.* The figure is large ; but it is, if anything, an underestimate.[5] In educational ability, it may be remembered, the standard deviation was estimated as about 10 per cent. of the age, approximately one-tenth. Hence, *individuals vary distinctly more in intelligence than they do in educational ability*—in effect, about a quarter as much again.

On an average, the special school children are retarded by 3·0 years

---

(1) *i.e.*, towards right hand of Table X.   (2) *i.e.*, towards left hand of Table X.
(3) For precise figures, see *Distribution of Abilities*, p. 24, Table X.   (4) *Loc. cit.*, Fig. 5, facing p. 31.
(5) The inclusion of scholastic tests and the other imperfections of the scale must tend to reduce its discriminative power. Further, this figure relates solely to the population in the Council's schools. If we included children from the professional and wealthier classes and the ineducable imbeciles and idiots the figure would probably rise to 14 or 15 years, approaching more nearly that obtained with group tests. (With recent revisions it is nearer 16.)

at eight ; and throughout the earlier ages by about three times the standard deviation of normals of the same age. If the standard deviation be taken as 12 per cent. of the age, and the deviation of the defectives be expressed as a multiple of that amount, the figure obtained is reasonably constant from one year to another. This accords with the facts just noted among the normals. The absolute retardation increases ; the relative retardation remains nearly the same. The increase in the retardation of defectives is now seen to be but a special instance of the general increase in the individual deviations among the population as a whole. Measured by the absolute units of an age-scale, *the difference between individuals, whether normal or defective, tend to appear larger as the individuals themselves grow older.*

Overlapping of Age-Groups.

The difference between the means for any two consecutive ages, when expressed in terms of the standard deviation of the lower group, averages 1·02. Thus, the annual increment is, on an average, approximately equal to the standard deviation. In the middle of the series of ages this relation

FIGURE 23.

OVERLAPPING OF CONSECUTIVE AGE-GROUPS.

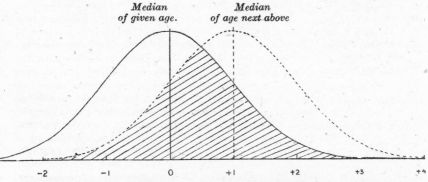

Median of given age.   *Median of age next above*

−2   −1   0   +1   +2   +3   +4   S

SCALE OF INTELLIGENCE IN TERMS OF STANDARD DEVIATION OF GIVEN AGE-GROUP.

holds with sensible exactitude ; the standard deviation at the age of eight is approximately one mental year ; and, conversely, the difference between the averages for ages eight and nine is approximately 1 S.D. This implies an enormous overlap. Throughout, one age-group trenches deeply upon its successors. Indeed, within the total range of all the children of the age of nine fall the averages of as many as eight distinct age-groups. The general extent of the overlapping is pictured schematically in Figure 23. The two curves, here assumed to be normal, intersect at a distance of only ½ S.D. from either mean. Virtually 16 per cent. of the lower age-group reach or exceed the average of the age-group next above. Measured as shown by the shaded portion of the curves, the average amount of overlap is 61·7 per cent. From one part of the age-series to another, however, the extent of encroachment differs greatly, inclining on the whole to expand. The actual amount at different ages is illustrated by Figure 22. In the lowest age-groups the overlapping sinks to 50 per cent. or less ; in higher age-groups it is much larger ; between the ages thirteen and fourteen it mounts to 77 per cent.

A mental age, therefore, is by no means so definitely determined, or so sharply limited, as Binet seemingly supposed. To measure intelligence by the yearly stages of intellectual growth is like measuring stature by means of a tape, where the lines that separate the inches are half effaced, and the figures are so broad, so blurred, and so ill-centred that any one division may easily be confounded with the next. In arbitrary terms, of course, each year of development may be defined specifically to suit the purpose of the scale. But mental age then becomes a purely artificial convention, intelligible enough for popular description, convenient enough for rough-and-ready estimates, but for scientific measurement and exact research neither indispensable nor appropriate.

Distribution of Intelligence with Standard Deviation as Unit.

The uniformity in the relative retardation enables us to condense into a single frequency diagram all the results obtained from the tests, regardless of the disparity in age among the groups examined. Expressed in mental years, the median for each normal age-group can be taken to mark the average for each age ; and the corresponding standard deviation, similarly expressed, to denote the unit of measurement. By reference to the original test-scores each child, whether from ordinary or special schools, can be re-assessed, not now in terms of mental age or mental retardation, but by degree of deviation.[1] Re-classified thus, the frequencies for each age can then be added legitimately together. The resultant totals, converted into percentages for normals and defectives respectively, are given in Table XVII.

In London the special school children form but a minute fraction of the total school population, comprising barely $1\frac{1}{2}$ per cent. of all the children on the roll at the same ages. In our present sample, however, the proportion is decidedly larger. Rightly to compare the two denominations, normals and defectives, either the number of the latter must be reduced, or the number of the former augmented, until the ratio of the one to the other is approximately as 1·5 to 98·5. This has been effected. For clearness I have imagined an aggregate population of 10,000 children, distributed in the same way as the children actually tested. Of this total, one hundred and fifty will be marked off as special school cases ; the remainder presumed to be normal. The two groups are delineated in Figure 24. The black outline depicts the normal children ; the red the defective. In principle of construction, both frequency polygons are identical with the pair already published to illustrate the distribution of normals and defectives for educational ability.[2] As before, to display columns representing fifty or one hundred children upon the same diagram as those representing two thousand or more, the vertical scale is progressively condensed towards its upper end. This has been done by making the actual heights of the columns proportional to the logarithms of the numbers indicated, instead of proportional to the numbers themselves.

This diagram, then, yields the final picture of the distribution of

---

[1] The limits of each degree or class have first been translated into terms of the tests passed by means of Table II. The smoothed or theoretical standard deviations are used (11·8 per cent. of age) ; and to obtain a finer subdivision successive halves of the standard deviation are taken as the limits for each class. The steps in the calculation, therefore, are as follows : For age six, median mental age = 6·5 years = 33 tests. Standard deviation = 11·8 per cent. of 6·5 years = 0·77 years ; $-\frac{1}{2}$ S.D. from median = (6·5 − 0·38) years = 6·12 years = 31·5 tests. Similarly, − 1 S.D. = 5·73 years = 27·6 tests. Percentage aged 6 − falling in class − 1 to $-\frac{1}{2}$ S.D. (*i e.*, passing more than 27·6 and less than 31·5 tests) = 16 normals and 0 defectives.   [2] *Loc. cit., sup.,* Figure 6, facing p. 33.

TABLE XVII.

DISTRIBUTION OF INTELLIGENCE.

Among Children of Ordinary Elementary and Special M.D. Schools.

Unit of Classification = Half the Standard Deviation of each Age-Group; i.e., approximately half a year at the age of 8-.

	Deviation.																				Total.
	-6 S.D.--5½ S.D.	-5½ S.D.	-5 S.D.	-4½ S.D.	-4 S.D.	-3½ S.D.	-3 S.D.	-2½ S.D.	-2 S.D.	-1½ S.D.	-1 S.D.	-½ S.D.	0 S.D.	+½ S.D.	+1 S.D.	+1½ S.D.	+2 S.D.	+2½ S.D.	+3 S.D.	+3½ S.D.	
Ordinary Children	—	—	—	—	—	0·1	0·6	1·7	4·7	7·4	14·8	20·7	23·7	11·6	8·2	3·3	2·0	0·8	0·4	—	100·0
Defective Children	0·3	0·5	4·0	6·7	21·1	29·5	25·9	8·8	1·3	1·5	0·4	—	—	—	—	—	—	—	—	—	100·0
Theoretical Percentage for Normally Distributed Group	—	—	·00004	·0028	0·02	0·12	0·48	1·7	4·4	9·2	15·0	19·1	19·1	15·0	9·2	4·4	1·7	0·48	0·12	0·02	100·0

intelligence, as tested by the Binet-Simon scale, among children from ordinary elementary and special (M.D.) schools.

In the curve for the ordinary elementary schools the symmetry is visibly deranged by the absence of adequate tests for the brighter children of the older ages. As is inevitable, when, to show the probable distribution of a vast population, a small sample is magnified, the tails of the curve appear somewhat blunted. The use of the theoretical standard deviation, a magnitude sometimes larger, sometimes smaller than the actual, has peaked the figure a little until in form it approaches the old-fashioned sugar-loaf perhaps more nearly than the familiar bell-shaped curve. Due allowance, however, being made for such disturbances, the diagram, if it does not corroborate, does not in any way contradict the hypothesis of "normality," the theory that ability is distributed in close conformity with the "normal curve of error."[1] From data so irregular, positive evidence to support this theory could hardly be extracted. But, where the distortion can be so readily explained, where it was, indeed, so naturally to be expected, there, I take it, to maintain that the results secured are at least consistent with, if not conclusive of, approximate normality, can be no unwarrantable extravagance.

The curve for the defectives, drawn in red, overlaps very broadly that for the normals. To compare the present diagram with its analogue in my previous memorandum is to perceive at once that *the overlap for general intelligence is far greater than for educational attainments*. In general intelligence the average for the defectives falls below the average for the normals by about 3·2 times the standard deviation. In educational attainments the former falls below the latter by over 4·8 times the standard deviation, almost exactly half as much again. The contrast endorses what I have remarked in another place. *The children of London special schools differ from normals far less in lack of intelligence than in lack of school ability.*

In general intelligence more than half the so-called defectives can readily be matched by children left in ordinary schools and therefore presumably "normal." Although our investigation was not sufficiently extensive to discover such a case, yet probably in a body of nearly ten thousand normal children, normally distributed, at least two children would be found between $-3\cdot5$ and $-4\cdot0$ S.D.; none would be discovered beyond the latter limit, unless a group of at least twice the size were examined. Beyond that same limit, however, there are no less than fifty defectives. Accordingly, to regard these fifty as simply the tail-end of a "normal" group distributed in exact accordance with the "normal" curve, would strain the laws of probability and stretch the play of chance too far. Actual inspection of many of the individual children discloses abnormalities so pronounced, defects so peculiar, as to convey that in its essential nature the condition is often pathological. No sharp distinction, however, can be erected between the pathological defectives and the extreme specimens of "normal" deviation. And a slight asymmetry in the curve for normals would, without any further assumption, account for every case.

---

[1] For the theoretical proportions mathematically deduced for a group distributed in perfect agreement with the "normal law." see bottom line of Table XVII.

Figure 24.

DISTRIBUTION ACCORDING TO GENERAL INTELLIGENCE OF CHILDREN OF ORDINARY ELEMENTARY AND SPECIAL M.D. SCHOOLS.

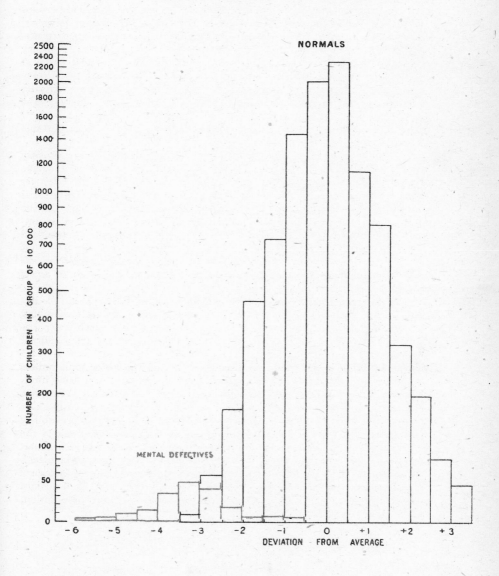

5. THE LINE OF DEMARCATION BETWEEN NORMALS AND DEFECTIVES.

Variations in Estimates for the Borderline.

I now reach the central problem of this memorandum—the line of demarcation for mental deficiency. Between normals and defectives where is the boundary to be drawn ? What proportion, in a sample thousand or ten thousand of the child population, is to be cut off for transference to the special (M.D.) schools ? On this question there has been, and still is, the acutest controversy.

For the percentage of the population which is mentally deficient, assessments made by Royal Commissions and by acknowledged experts conflict and differ almost beyond belief. They reach from under 0·2 per cent.[1] to over 5·0 per cent.,[2] that is, from about one in five hundred to about one in twenty. *One estimate thus recognises twenty-five times as many defectives as another.* Upon what scale is an education authority, such as that for the County of London, to provide, when one calculation declares that, between the ages contemplated, 22,500 children will be defective, and another only 900 ?

The incongruity springs from various sources. It arises in part from incompatible views as to what degree of unintelligence constitutes mental deficiency. The lower estimates doubtless envisage only those cases that can be regarded as definitely pathological, cases such as are encountered most abundantly in institutions and asylums. The higher estimates tend to sweep in all who would benefit by instruction in special schools, regardless of their ultimate recognition in after life as defectives in the legal sense. Partly, again, the discrepancies ensue from an unrecognised difference or opposition between alternative paths of approach. Some investigators have begun by examining first the defectives. The brightest of these they have regarded as indicating the line of partition. Others have started with normals, and have taken the limit to be marked by the dullest normal who could without aid just earn his own subsistence. Either course, divorced from its complementary, ignores the broad margin of overlapping individuals. In assuming that the dullest normal outside an institution will rank next above the brightest defective, within there lurks a simple but seductive

---

[1] In the United States Census Report on the Insane and Feebleminded in Institutions (1910) a special estimate was obtained from the public authorities in Massachusetts which included not only defectives in institutions, but also those found among the general population. On this basis it is affirmed that " if the number of feebleminded in proportion to the total population was the same for the entire United States . . . the total number of feebleminded would be over 200,000." This amounts to about 0·2 per cent. It is added that not one-tenth of these are being cared for in special institutions. Similarly, Dr. Cornell, the Director of Medical Inspection for the Philadelphia Public Schools, avers that " the number of evidently feebleminded above the age of six years may be said to be one to every five hundred of the population. These figures are conservative and have been accepted by experts for years." Estimates at Vineland give rather over 0·3 per cent.; the Departmental Committee of the Board of Education (1898), about 1 per cent.—an estimate referring to children only and excluding ineducable imbeciles ; the British Royal Commission (1904), rather over 0·3 per cent. in the general population, and 0·73 per cent. among school children only — the latter varying from 0·2 per cent. in Durham to 1·9 per cent. in Dublin. Subsequent returns by school medical officers to the Board of Education average about 0·5 per cent. Karl Pearson (1914), on the basis of various statistical returns, suggests " something between 1 and 2 per cent. among school children."

[2] This is Binet's figure (*Mentally Defective Children*, tr. Drummond, p. 8). He alleges that the proportion of defectives found in France by the Ministerial Commissions (barely 1 per cent.) is " evidently far too small " ; and cites " a special and most careful enquiry at Bordeaux " as yielding 5·17 per cent. He adds, " Probably the percentage is somewhere in the neighbourhood of five." In a publication of the United States Bureau of Education (1911) three eminent psychologists—J. H. Van Sickle, L. Witmer, and L. P. Ayres—give 4 per cent. as the proportion of feebleminded children.

fallacy. Freedom and segregation are contingent upon a multitude of factors, of which intelligence, though the most vital, is but one : the duller " normal " may have been saved by a benign environment ; the brighter " defective " may have been ruined by defect of character. There are thus two thresholds, not one threshold. The frontier is crossed at different points according as we travel from below upwards or downwards from above. With the distribution shown in Figure 24, the " ascending procedure "—to borrow a term from the psychophysicist—would locate the borderline at about —2 S.D., perhaps even closer to the average ; the " descending procedure " at —3 S.D., perhaps below.

Between these two landmarks, namely, twice and thrice the standard deviation, lie the boundaries advocated by most investigators. Binet himself looked for a retardation of two years at eight or less than eight, and three years at nine or over. This would be equivalent to a mental ratio between 75 and 66 per cent., and to a deviation between 2·12 and 2·84 S.D. In a normal distribution such limits would cut off 1·70 per cent. and 0·23 per cent. respectively. Subsequent revisions at first leant towards one or other of these two extremes, namely, a retardation of either one-quarter or one-third of age ; but later more often favoured a compromise of 30 per cent. Stern, however, in first introducing the conception of a " mental ratio," proposed a retardation of 20 per cent., which, with the present distribution, would correspond to —1·70 S.D., and cut off 4·46 per cent. from the normal group, normally distributed. On the other hand, Pearson and Jaederholm, whose statistical analysis is for method one of the most sound, and for conclusions one of the most cautious, demand evidence far more pronounced. Discussing results obtained with a special modification of the Binet-Simon scale, they write that "until the child is something like four years in arrear of its physical age, it is not possible to assert dogmatically on the basis of the most scientific test. . . ., that it is feebleminded." With their data four years answers to —4 S.D. Such a borderline would intercept "less than ½ per cent. in the normal population " ; indeed, in a population normally distributed, a proportion much more minute. Here, however, the writers are biassed almost exclusively towards the second of the two procedures. They would hesitate to consider a child defective, if he can be matched by the dullest among the normal group.

Now, in theory a normally distributed group has no lower limit. The larger the group examined, the duller will be the dullest child. In a group of infinite size the dullest normal would be infinitely dull. Similarly, with a distribution like that found for the defectives, there is no reason to regard the upper limit as abrupt or definitely fixed. A curve fitted to it is as likely to be asymptotic as to cut the base-line. Nevertheless, simplicity demands, to indicate the line of separation, a single point upon the abscissa, and a single ordinate erected at that point. What line, what point, are to be chosen ?

The Theoretical Line of Division.

I suggest that *the most natural cleavage between the two distributions is that indicated by the point where the two curves intersect.* A notched stick snaps at its narrowest part. And the two groups may be most easily severed by cutting down in the angle between the two main bulks. Here, if the overlapping branches are in reality distinct, the splicing will be thinnest.

In discussing the mental differences between other human groups—for example, between the two sexes, or between two consecutive age-groups— I have already urged the importance of this point of intersection. Where the values for the averages and standard deviations of two normally distributed groups are known, the theoretical point of intersection can speedily be ascertained by a formula derived from the classical equation for the normal curve.[1]

For the normal and defective groups the point of intersection, when thus calculated, falls at about −2·8 S.D. below the median for the normals. Mathematically determined, therefore, this is the observed line of demarcation, deduced from actual practice. At the age of eight last birthday—the age at which the largest number of candidates are presented for the statutory examination—a retardation of 2·8 years corresponds with a mental ratio of 67·1 per cent. *The practical effect, therefore, of the London organisation is to segregate the child of the special school from the child of the ordinary elementary at a level of intelligence equivalent to a retardation of about one-third of the child's age.* In our imaginary population of ten thousand this limit would mark off an additional twenty-seven of the "normal" group as fit for a special school—possibly rather more had the whole number been actually tested ; forty-one special school children it would adjudge fit for the ordinary elementary school, so far, at least, as tested intelligence is concerned.

In educational ability the point of intersection between normals and defectives, when similarly determined, lies at −3·3 S.D., that is, below the point of intersection for intelligence, by about one-half the standard deviation. For educational ability, however, the standard deviation is much smaller in relation to age. Hence, in terms of the ratio of retardation to age the borderline for educational ability differs but little from that for intelligence, being 32 per cent. of age, or rather less than one-third.

Such, or nearly such, is the actual line of separation. But to identify the actual line with the intended line is hardly permissible. The upper end of the defective group comprises individuals who have passed the scrutiny of three or four tribunals—the teacher, the school doctor or the psychologist, the certifying medical officer, and, in some cases, the medical officer inspecting for re-transference to the ordinary school. On the other hand, the lower end of the group, nominally normal, consists largely of individuals left among undoubted normals for reasons purely accidental. Some have evaded the notice, or escaped the sentence, of one or other of these examiners. A few, though duly noted and duly sentenced, are awaiting accommodation in some overcrowded special school. Hence, the high-grade defective always indicates an uttered verdict ; the low-grade normal merely the absence of a verdict. It follows that at the examinations where these judgments are delivered the retardation that is accepted as qualifying for the special school is less than a consideration of the low-grade normal might convey. The intended

---

(1) The formula used is the following : $x = \dfrac{d\sigma_1{}^2 - \sigma_1\sigma_2\sqrt{\left\{ d^2 + 2\,(\sigma_1{}^2 - \sigma_2{}^2)\,\log_e \dfrac{\sigma_1 N_2}{\sigma_2 N_1} \right\}}}{\sigma_1{}^2 - \sigma_2{}^2}$

where $x \equiv$ the distance of the point of intersection from the left-hand curve ; $d \equiv$ the distance between the two curves; N_1, N_2, σ_1 and σ_2, $\equiv$ as usual the areas of the curve and their standard deviations.

The formula follows directly from the fact that y, the ordinate at x common to both curves,

$$= (1)\frac{N_1}{\sigma_1\sqrt{2\pi}}\,e^{\frac{x_2}{2\sigma_1{}^2}} \quad \text{and} \quad (2)\,\frac{N_2}{\sigma_2\sqrt{2\pi}}\,e^{\frac{x_2}{2\sigma_2{}^2}}.$$

by cancelling $\sqrt{2\pi}$ and taking logarithms throughout to base e.

The foregoing formula is the best to use when we desire to find the borderline between two discreetly classified groups, such as normals and defectives. If instead we were given as the criterion a borderline (k) on a graded scale (y), then the best value for x is $x = k/b_{yx}$.

In applying the formula to curves that are moderately asymmetrical, I would suggest using only the intersecting halves, *i.e.*, the lower half of the upper curve and the upper half of the lower curve, and assuming these halves to be portions of normal curves whose averages coincide respectively with the medians observed, and then recalculating the standard deviations. The measurement obtained by the formula can be checked graphically by plotting the two curves from tables for the probability integral in the usual way.

line of demarcation is, therefore, nearer to the general average than the actual line. It wavers like the unsteady needle of a compass ; oscillating, for the most part, according to the personal views of each examiner, between —2·5 and —2·0 S.D., points which correspond to mental ratios of 70 and 75 per cent.

We are thus again thrown back upon the quicksand of subjective judgment. As a conceivable avenue of escape, I would advance, tentatively and to begin with, the following postulates.

First, *mental deficiency must be treated as an administrative rather than as a psychological concept.* As the relevant statutes are interpreted in practice, mental defectives comprise an indiscriminate assortment of heterogeneous types—social failures, school failures, failures in virtue of undeveloped intelligence, failures in virtue of unstable temperament.

Unstable persons, whether children or adults, occasion no small perplexity. Where the instability is a ground of social failure or a source of social menace, it may, with some plausibility, be held that the unstable person should be dealt with under that clause in the Act of 1913 which relates to " moral imbeciles "—" persons who from an early age display some permanent mental defect coupled with strong vicious or criminal propensities on which punishment has had little or no deterrent effect." But in the interpretation of this definition magistrates and others differ greatly. Viewed from the narrow loophole of psychology, the whole conception of " moral imbecility " wears a dubious legitimacy ; even in the wider field of daily practice, if " mental defect " be construed as referring to defect in intelligence alone, and if incorrigibility have to be proved for each individual case by actually administering punishment to test whether it can have " little or no deterrent effect," then the clause in question is of small utility and may work much harm. If, on the other hand, " mental " be defined not as the adjective of intelligence, but as the adjective of mind, and so taken to cover defect of temperament as well as defect of intelligence, then unstable persons, whose ability may be nearly or quite average, may yet, in virtue of their need for care and control, be dealt with as " feebleminded " rather than as " moral imbeciles." With this interpretation, *to disprove deficiency in intelligence is not necessarily to disprove mental deficiency in all its forms ;*[1] and the application of the Binet-Simon scale would, for these cases, have but a negative purport.

Cases of the unstable type account for some of the overlapping in intelligence between the ordinary and the special schools. Those, however, who are transferred to special schools on the ground, primarily or solely, of instability are comparatively rare. In this memorandum, therefore, discussion may be restricted to those who are defective, primarily or solely, in intelligence.

With these the statutes provide a further difficulty. Two definitions are offered, one for children and another for adults. Among adults the deficiency must be " so pronounced that they require care, supervision, and control for their own protection or for that of others." Among children it is sufficient that they shall be " incapable of receiving proper benefit from the instruction in the ordinary public elementary schools." The latter definition embraces a far larger proportion of the population than the former. This leads us to a second postulate : *the line of demarcation for school children must be enunciated separately from the line of demarcation for adults.*

---

[1] I have argued at greater length in favour of this highly debatable conclusion in discussing the classification of mental defectives, *Studies in Mental Inefficiency,* pp. 50 *et seq.*

The Borderline for Children.

Let us approach, first of all, the case of the defective child. As it stands, the statutory definition is too vague and indirect to be translated at once into terms of mental age. In some districts an inability to receive proper benefit from "tne instruction in the ordinary school" would include the dull and backward, for whom, as is now slowly becoming recognised, special educational provision is urgently needed, though seldom found. In more progressive areas "the instruction in the ordinary school" might comprehend such special provision; and here *many children, who might otherwise be transferred to a special (M.D.) school, would undoubtedly receive proper benefit from instruction in the backward classes of the ordinary school, and at the same time escape the unmerited stigma of mental deficiency.* Between these two alternatives the policy of different local authorities and the practice of different certifying officers tend, as is well known, to fluctuate widely.

The variations from one local authority to another are, in present circumstances at any rate, all but inevitable. But under the same local authority the standard should in justice be the same throughout. From this follows yet a further postulate: *for immediate practical purposes the only satisfactory definition of mental deficiency is a percentage definition based on the amount of existing accommodation.*[1] If in the special schools of London there is accommodation for only 1·5 per cent., then to adopt a borderline which, followed out consistently, would cut off nearly 2 per cent. is plainly indefensible. The effect of a personal standard, at variance with available provision, can only be that *less urgent cases of a higher grade that chance to be transferred at an earlier date will forestall more urgent cases of a lower grade that are presented for examination later.* This is no rare occurrence. Where a teacher or a doctor adopts some high standard of deficiency, whether borrowed from a French or American authority or based privately upon his own generous view of the children's needs, then sooner or later his milder candidates are found usurping the room of more necessitous candidates passed by a colleague who adopts a lower standard. Such lack of co-ordination is manifestly unjust. There should be one weight and one measure. To no *a priori* line of demarcation can any inviolable cogency attach. This or that percentage, this or that degree of deviation, is to be accepted solely on the humble ground of practical expediency. Once accepted, it should be complied with universally. Its merit lies not in its absolute character which is arbitrary, but in its uniform observance, which is essential. Whether a pound is worth two hundred and forty pence or two hundred and fifty matters but little. But the change returned should be the same in Westminster as it is in the Isle of Dogs.

The method of defining mental deficiency by means of the percentage of accommodation available has already been illustrated in a previous

---

[1] The ultra-logical may perhaps be tempted to deduce from my definition the corollary that areas which are without special schools must be equally free from mental deficiency: no provision, no defectives. And, when all is said, "*for immediate practical purposes*" the conclusion is surely sound. With future practical measures and even with theoretical prolegomena I am not for the moment concerned. Were those my immediate interest, I should, of course, begin by discussing what degree of social inefficiency or of anti-social conduct seemed to require administrative provision, and how far those characteristics could be attributable to psychological causes.

I should add that my formulation of a borderline holds good in the first instance merely for average conditions in an industrial area, such as that which I have been studying. Where environment and stock are better or worse, different figures would unquestionably be obtained. In the near future we shall doubtless need separate statements for rural areas and residential areas, as distinguished from highly industrialised towns, and perhaps even for the weaker sex as distinguished from men and boys.

memorandum when discussing the line of demarcation in educational ability.[1]
It was there suggested that, before a child is nominated by the head teacher
for the statutory examination for admission to a special (M.D.) school, he
should be proved to be retarded in educational attainments by at least
27 per cent., roughly one-quarter, of his chronological age. At the statutory
examination itself, were educational attainments the sole criterion, a yet
greater retardation would be required. But educational attainments are
not the sole criterion. For educational retardation may be due, not necessarily to mental deficiency, but to other factors of a very special kind—
absence from school, ill-health, or specific educational defect. Where such
conditions operate, a child may be gravely retarded in educational attainments and yet prove average or above average in natural ability; he may
in school progress seem mentally deficient, and in practical intelligence
prove unquestionably normal.

Passing over, then, for the moment those rarer and more peculiar cases
distinguished by defect in character and temperament, *the prime factor, the
essential criterion, in mental deficiency is retardation in intelligence.* And,
with the same reservation only, it ensues, that, since in London special
schools there is accommodation for 1·51 per cent. of the population during
the ages at which defectives are admitted, within this county *the mentally
defective child is to be defined as one who for intelligence ranks among the lowest
1½ per cent. of the school population of the same age.*

Between the ages of seven and fourteen, out of the conjoint population,
ordinary and special school, the lowest 1·5 per cent. will embrace all those
who fall below a deviation of −2·6 S.D. This is equivalent to a retardation
of 30·6 per cent. of age, or a mental ratio of 69·4. Accordingly, *to be considered mentally deficient on the ground of undeveloped intelligence, a child,
when tested by the Binet-Simon scale as here revised, must be backward by at least—*

> 2 *years at the age of 6 to 7,*
> 2½ *years at the age of 8 to 9,*
> 3 *years at the age of 9 to 10,*
> 3½ *years at the age of 12,*
> 4 *years at the age of 13 to 14,*

and, generally, by at least three-tenths of his age.

The precise borderline, calculated for each age upon this basis, is shown,
in terms both of mental age and of the number of tests to be passed, in
Table XVIII.

The borderline is taken as 70 per cent. of the chronological age. The
test designated as crucial for any particular age is that test which in
the order for defectives[2] most nearly corresponds with the borderline as
expressed by the number of tests passed. At the age of six and a half, for
instance, the borderline is 15·8 tests; a child who at that age can perform
fifteen or sixteen tests should be deemed normal. The fifteenth test in the
order for defectives is naming four colours; it is seventeenth in the order
for normals. A typical borderline case, therefore—though cases truly
typical are the exception, not the rule—should pass all the tests up to this
point, then break down and pass no more. At times, however, the test thus
indicated occupies in the order for normals a position widely different from
that which it holds in the order for defectives. Reciting the months, for
example, which in the former list is thirty-seventh, is in the latter list forty-
second; in the former it is below the borderline for age ten, and in the
latter above the borderline for age eleven. In such instances the test most

---

(1) *Loc. cit.,* p. 43.

(2) The test which corresponds to the borderline in the order for normals is shown above in
Schedule I., pp. 19–23.

nearly equivalent in the average or combined order is added or substituted. A child that can perform the crucial test (and, in addition, of course, all those preceding it in the order for defectives) is to be regarded as normal. The decisive criterion, however, is not the nature of the particular tests attempted, crucial or other—there is no one litmus test for deficiency at any age: the point to note in this connection is simply the total number of the tests successfully accomplished. For a nominal normality this total should at least attain the figure shown under the borderline as stated in terms of tests.

TABLE XVIII
Line of Demarcation between Normals and Defectives.

Chronological Age.	Norms in Terms of Tests.	Borderline in Mental Age.	Borderline in Terms of Tests.	Crucial Test.
3·5	8·5	2·5	3·0	Sex.
4·5	15	3·2	7·0	4 Pennies.
5·5	25	3·9	10·5	Comparing Faces.
6·5	33	4·6	15·8	4 Colours; (10 Syllables ?).
7·5	38	5·3	22·6	Transcription; (Diamond ?).
8·5	43	6·0	31·0	5 Numbers; (Missing Features ?).
9·5	46·5	6·7	33·8	Pence and Halfpence; (Differences ?).
10·5	50·5	7·4	37·4	Counting 20 to 1; (Change ?).
11·5	54·5	8·1	41·4	6 Numbers.
12·5	57	8·8	44·2	5 Weights.
13·5	59	9·5	46·5	Sentence Building (2).
14·5	61·5	10·2	49·0	Memory Drawing; (Absurdities ?).
15·5	64	10·9	52·5	60 Words; (7 Numbers ?).

On referring to Table IV. it will be seen that in terms of tests the borderline here advocated coincides closely enough with the point at which the number of defectives passing the tests begins to taper rather rapidly. In age six, for example, after the sixteenth test the percentages drop almost at a blow from over 30 per cent. to 25 per cent. or less ; and with other ages a fall equally steep is to be noticed near the level of the test assigned.

Expressed in terms of standard deviations, or in terms of mental ages, of mental ratios, and of mental retardations, a line of demarcation can have but a derivative significance, a second-hand validity. Such a figure would vary widely according to the conditions under which it were obtained. This difficulty has already been illustrated in the previous memorandum upon educational ability. When, as was there observed, the standard deviation is calculated from the normal population only, the multiple of the standard deviation required to cut off a given percentage will differ greatly from that required when the standard deviation is calculated from a population including both normals and defectives. Nor is this the only ambiguity. A bias, trifling and perhaps imperceptible, towards asymmetry in the form of distribution will introduce a large alteration into the proportion cut off from the extreme end of the tail by one and the same multiple of the standard deviation. Further, with similar tests of different abilities, and with different tests of the same ability, the standard deviation, as measured against the differences between the age-averages, is as shifting as a weather-vane. Reduced to terms of mental years, or translated into the ratio of mental years to actual age, the borderline delimiting the children of special schools from those of the ordinary elementary yields, as we have remarked, one figure for educational ability and another for intelligence ; and for intelligence it yields figures different again when measured by the Binet-Simon scale and when

O

measured by means of other tests. A borderline defective with a ratio of 70 per cent., when examined by the Binet-Simon scale, will have a ratio of but 50 per cent. when tested by graded inferences ;[1] at the age of fourteen his common sense as revealed by the former is equal to that of a child of nearly ten, but his reasoning ability as revealed by the latter is equal to that of a child of only seven. A definition of feeblemindedness expressed, like that put forward by Binet, in terms of mental retardation, or converted, like that proposed by Stern, into terms of a mental ratio, presupposes for children a fixed and reliable standardisation of age-norms, and for adults a recognised limit of intellectual growth. No such age-norms have been worked out ; no such intellectual limit has yet been measured. When both have been secured, each will still require to be perpetually ratified, and frequently readjusted, as time goes on.

From all these uncertainties the percentage borderline is virtually exempt. It does not depend upon the mode of calculation. It varies but little with the type of test employed. It presupposes neither an age-scale for the growing child, nor a mental maximum for the stationary adult. Whatever test be adopted, however the borderline be expressed, the same individuals, and therefore the same number of individuals, should be selected. This is essential. Evidently the requirement may best be satisfied by a definition stating the proportion of the number selected to the number in the total population from which the selection is drawn. The percentage formulation, therefore, is to be regarded as basal. It has, however, one drawback. At different points of the scale equal percentage differences denote equal differences in ability only where the form of distribution is rectilinear. With curvilinear distributions—those, for example, represented by normal and moderately asymmetrical curves—the percentages, as already noted,[2] must first be reduced to terms of the variability of the group, and expressed as a multiple of the quartile[3] or of the standard deviation, before the units of measurement can be manipulated as equivalent throughout. Then, and then only, will the scale employed be logically uniform, and the figures obtained be arithmetically comparable. Nevertheless, statements in terms of such units, like statements in terms of age, ratio, or retardation, must be viewed simply as a device, though unquestionably the most scientific device, for elucidating the original percentage definition, for endowing it with a convenient graduation for theoretical purposes and a concrete interpretation for practical. Such statements are not themselves fundamental.

The Borderline for Adults.

These, then, are the methods available for defining mental deficiency in children, and these their several merits. With adults a different standard is necessary. For the sake of demonstration suppose, first, that for adults the line of demarcation were the same as that for children, namely, a percentage of 1·5 and a mental ratio of 70 ; and assume, as is commonly done, that intelligence measured by the Binet-Simon scale advances but little after the age of sixteen ;[4] then, as the lower limit of adult normality, we should have a retardation of about five years and a mental age between eleven and twelve. The limit thus deduced would be impracticably high. He whose ability is inadequate for the intellectual exactions of the school may yet adjust himself without catastrophe to the practical requirements of after life. Hence, a lower and more lenient borderline is permissible for the mature. But, curiously enough, the accepted pronouncements of

---

[1] See below, Appendix IV, pp. 251-254. [2] See above, p. 150.
[3] For the definition of " quartile " see p. 337 ; for that of " standard deviation," p. 293.
[4] See note on the upper limit of mental growth, p. 256.

American psychologists dictate a line of demarcation that is higher and a standard that is more severe.

Following a scheme proposed by Goddard, the American Association for the Study of the Feebleminded placed the upper limit of mental deficiency between the mental ages of twelve and thirteen. Unquestionably for immediate practical adoption in this country such a standard is far too lofty and sweeping. It seems certainly higher than Binet's criterion. Binet's view, however, is only indirectly implied. For the diagnosis of high-grade adult defectives he selected some half-dozen crucial tests—weights, difficult questions, sentence building, definitions (abstract), picture (interpretation), and rhymes. These belong to ages IX. to XII. The other tests from these age-groups, defective adults, he thought, might pass, in virtue of mere memory and experience. Even if for all these more mechanical tests we accord them complete success, the highest grades could in theory barely obtain a mental age of twelve, probably in practice not that of eleven. Among the French defectives actually tested by Binet and Simon " the best endowed," we are told, " did not surpass the normal level of nine or ten." These earlier statements, however, are not devoid of ambiguity. More recently, in addressing the English Eugenics Society, Dr. Simon has expressed a clear and definite recommendation. " Provisionally," he says, " it may be proposed to fix at nine years the upper limit of mental debility." In sending forward for notification by the local authority the names of particular children as they leave the special school, London head teachers adopt by implication a limit lower still. At the calendar age of fifteen or sixteen children are rarely nominated—at least, on the ground of defective intelligence alone—unless their mental age is below that of eight.

My own experience tallies with this lower figure. In testing random samples of working men and youths, both at settlements in London and Liverpool and in rural districts of Warwickshire, I have met numerous individuals managing the affairs of their household and discharging the requirements of their occupation, who yet could not pass sufficient tests to attain even a mental age of eight. In a rural parish numbering about seven hundred persons—a hamlet which has a title to interest as the home of Shakespeare's grandfather before the family migrated to Stratford-upon-Avon—I have made repeated studies among inhabitants of the present generation by the Binet and other tests. Including adults and children alike, the average mental ratio for the native population is 81·6, the standard deviation being 15·7. The highest ratio is 112, obtained by the son of the village innkeeper.[1] The lowest is 38, obtained by a mongoloid girl. But many of the farm labourers in the district, like many of the dock labourers in Liverpool, contrive successfully to work and live with a mental ratio of little over 50. In towns, as well as in the country, I have found many a domestic servant of the poorer type who could pass with difficulty only tests for the age of seven. Doubtless, in domestic service, as on a country farm, the course of life is generally[2] smooth, and the conditions of existence unusually favourable. They demand no keen sagacity. They impose no strenuous exertions. They offer no irresistible temptations, and violate no

---

[1] To limit the investigation to natives, those only were tested who were actually attending, or had actually attended, the village school. The family of the schoolmaster, however, was excepted. One of his sons, who commenced education at this school, gained subsequently a science scholarship at the University of Cambridge, and later a lectureship in engineering at the University of Oxford. This family, however, was an immigrant family. On the other hand, in preceding generations the brightest individuals in the village had largely emigrated to the neighbouring industrial towns ; and the remainder had greatly intermarried.

[2] The qualification is important. Among the cases of vice and crime described below a disproportionately large number of the older low-grade female delinquents had been in domestic service ; and, in not a few instances, had encountered unusual temptations.

cherished hopes. To wash the plates or sweep the rooms, to till a field or tend a horse, are simple routine offices such as can be mastered by the intelligence of a child of nine ; and the eye of a mistress or the gossip of a village is sufficient protection against drifting into vice or lapsing into crime.

In the history of Rasselas, Prince of Abyssinia, it is related how a foolish barbarian once attempted to fly. He ascended an eminence, flourished his wings, sprang from the edge, and at once dropped headlong into a lake. But the pinions, it is added, which failed to sustain him through the air, sufficed to bear him up when he reached the surface of the water. The episode was written as an allegory ; and may not inaptly typify the fate of the defective at large. In a thin and treacherous atmosphere, at the difficult and dizzy altitude where highly civilised men, assisted by the newest machinery of a highly civilised community, alone can securely travel, and alone should venture to soar, there the simpleton, less fortunately equipped and oblivious to his ill-fortune, must crash instantly to ruin. But if he lights upon a humbler medium, dense enough and yet elastic enough, more buoyant and yet less variable, he may contrive, though quite mechanically, to support himself unaided. If in one *milieu* he falls, in the other he may float. He is there, as we say, in his element.

It is a truth which needs some insistence, because so often overlooked. A defective in a complex environment may not be defective in a simple. And the converse is no less certain. Favourable surroundings are not always to be presumed ; and, when actually present, may not perennially endure. Hence, it is advisable to watch over these milder cases lest they come to some high crisis ; and to be ready to rescue them should they slide into dangerous predicaments. With these cases, then, supervision is always expedient, though segregation is not usually essential.

Below a mental age of eight the matter is different. In this country such individuals become almost invariably parasites. This, therefore, is the *provisional* limit I propose. *As accommodation increases, as public opinion advances, the limit will doubtless rise.*[1]

Those accustomed to the higher borderlines commonly formulated for adults may be reminded that a mental level of 8·0 years, according to the London age-assignments, is equivalent to an age of eight and a half or nine, according to earlier allocations. Out of the sixty-five tests a normal adult should perform at least forty-one. The borderline tests, therefore, are those numbered 40 to 43 in the order for the defectives (Table IV.)—counting backwards, repeating six numbers, reading the prescribed passage and remembering at least two items, and writing the prescribed words from dictation. As these and the preceding tests (months, date, change, coins) are primarily tests of acquirements either in school or out of school, the failures and the successes of a borderline case are usually scattered with some irregularity about this region. Hence, as a rule, an examinee will not be accounted normal unless he can pass one or more of the succeeding tests, namely, arranging the five weights, building two sentences from three words, interpreting the pictures, drawing the two designs, or defining concrete objects by class.[2]

If, with most other writers, we take the limit of mental development, when measured by the Binet-Simon scale, to lie near age XVI., a mental age of VIII. is equivalent among adults to a mental ratio of 50. Owing to the slight tendency of the ratio to decline, the future adult defective may perhaps during school life show a ratio a little above this figure. Two reservations, however, can hardly be too often emphasised : first, no individual

---

[1] See note, p. 257. [2] Binet's selection is somewhat similar (see above p. 183). He states, however, that some of his institution patients could pass several of these tests, though none could pass three.

has a flat mental age or ratio, identical for every kind of mental function or for every type of mental test ; and, secondly, his mental age or ratio is but one of many symptoms to be weighed before his case can be finally rated as either normal or defective.[1] With adult cases, indeed, comparatively little weight will be attached in everyday practice to mere mental age. Points of a more practical order—the consideration of physique, of temperament, of home surroundings, or of actual conduct—will nearly always intervene to tip the balance, before the question of certifying the patient is finally decided.[2] But the theoretical acceptance of an ideal borderline—to be applied in practice only where other circumstances are neutral or negative—may lead, as I hope, to a broader uniformity in general standards.

If the whole of the adult population were distributed in a manner analogous to the distribution of ordinary and special school children taken as a single group, a mental ratio of 50 would cut off the lowest four or five *per mille.*. According to the investigations of the Royal Commission, between three and four *per mille* of the total population are mentally deficient. Of these, only one half are during adult life accommodated in institutions, and one quarter are permanently provided for neither by the public authorities nor by private friends. On the other hand, the rate of mortality is far higher among the mentally deficient ; and, therefore, in proportion to normals their number must rapidly diminish with increasing age. Hence, if the percentage for adults, obtained irrespective of age, be reduced to a standard age, comparable with the basis adopted for school children—for example, age sixteen—the observed figure would be once more enlarged. In the long run it would probably rise to at least one-half per cent. Now, it would appear that the cases enumerated by the Royal Commission comprehend only those requiring permanent provision and complete control, equivalent to that of, though not necessarily obtained in, an institution ; and exclude persons of a higher grade who can earn a living and attend to simple daily duties with passable success. Thus interpreted, therefore, the two estimates seem roughly to agree.

These various considerations converge toward one conclusion. From the standpoint of their adult needs, the mentally deficient children accommodated in special schools comprise three distinguishable grades. First, there are those whose intelligence will suffice for them to manage their practical affairs, though it does not suffice for them to profit intellectually by the instruction in the ordinary school. Secondly, there are those who, in addition to special instruction during childhood, will in after life need supervision or guardianship although in an even and benign environment their intelligence is sufficient for them to be allowed their individual liberty. Thirdly, there are those whose intelligence is so deeply defective that they will be unable to support themselves, unless housed in an institution, established in a colony, or provided with equivalent protection by their relatives or friends. Among the older children tested by me about 30 per cent. fell

---

[1] The curious may compare the borderline above proposed with those formulated by other investigators. In contrast to the present limiting ratio of 50, that is, half normal intelligence, Stern, who first introduced the concept of a mental ratio, assigned to the "feeble-minded "—the highest grade of deficiency—a "three-quarter " intelligence, with an upper limit of 80 ; to the second grade, namely, "imbecility," a " scant two-thirds intelligence," with an upper limit of 70. An adult with a mental ratio of 55 would be adjudged normal by the present standard, but a defective of the lowest grade—"an idiot "—by the logical consequences of Stern's. One of the most recent revisions—the Stanford Revision—considers 70 to 80 to be borderline deficiency, classifiable as dull or as defective according to circumstances, 70 to be the upper limit for definite feeble-mindedness, 50 for imbeciles, and 20 or 25 for idiots. None of these investigators, however, formulate separate ratios for adults and for children. Indeed, Stern himself applies the ratio neither to idiots nor to persons whose development has ceased ; and among the mentally deficient he considers development to cease at the mental age of nine.

[2] A summary of what may be termed supplementary sources of evidence, and some notes as to their significance, will be found in *Studies in Mental Inefficiency, loc. cit. sup.*, pp. 76–77.

into the last category, and about 38 per cent. into the first ; the remnant, about 32 per cent., into the intermediate. Such figures suggest that the entire population of the special school may be split into three nearly equal categories : the lowest 0·5 per cent. of the whole population, normal and defective, at the ages in question, are likely to form institution cases ; the next 0·5 per cent. supervision cases ; the next 0·5 per cent. purely school cases. In mental ratios these percentages indicate the following rough lines of demarcation : *below 50, institution cases ; between 50 and 60, supervision cases ; between 60 and 70, special school cases.* With adults, and with adolescents over sixteen, these limits correspond to the mental ages of eight, nine and a half, and eleven respectively.

Whether the children who are classed as mentally defective during their school career only, should be stigmatised as mentally defective at all, remains a vexed and delicate problem. In general intelligence they are, as a rule, weak. But defect connotes something more than simple weakness. It implies a weakness so profound as to demand special administrative provision. By this standard such cases are defective in scholastic ability alone, not in general intelligence. They need educational provision, but not social provision. Defect does not characterise their minds as a whole. Hence, they might, with greater justice, be designated, not mentally defective, but educationally defective.

Should such cases, then, be transferred to a special school ? So long as there is no other provision made for them it appears not only advisable, but compulsory, to commit them thither. Nevertheless, their anchorage is with the normal child rather than with those defectives who will still be accounted defectives even in after life. *When the dull and backward are recognised as requiring definite educational provision, a larger proportion of the special school cases will doubtless be accommodated in the special classes in the ordinary school rather than associated with those whose future lies for ever in an institution.*

The Borderline for Supernormality.

The poverty of the Binet-Simon tests for higher mental ages renders it idle to apply them in central and secondary schools as they have been applied in special schools for the defective. But at earlier ages the scale is not unfitted for detecting supernormality. The line of demarcation, however, has to be deduced indirectly. Evidence of two kinds is available : first, from results in the Binet-Simon tests obtained among younger children subsequently transferred to central or secondary schools ; secondly, from results in the graded reasoning tests, which are more suited for the detection of supernormal ability among older children. Upon this basis the following borderlines have been provisionally established : a mental ratio above 115 or 120 indicates central school ability at least ; and a mental ratio above 130 or 135 scholarship ability. Some elasticity in the standard is necessitated by the progressive decrease, manifested by the higher ages, in deviations toward the upper end of the scale. The lower figures (115 and 130 respectively) are more appropriate to the higher ages, and the higher figures (120 and 135) to the middle ages. A child, therefore, of seven and a half with a mental age of ten is likely to make a successful scholarship candidate.

A mental ratio above 150 is singularly rare ; and hitherto I have never, either in this research or in any other based upon the Binet-Simon scale, obtained a ratio over 160 from a child in a public elementary school.[1]

---

[1] In a private school I have recently found a boy of seven with a mental ratio of 190. Dr. Rusk in Scotland and Dr. Hollingworth in America have each described a precocity of the same order (*Child Study*, X. i. 21 ; *J. Applied Psych.* I. 101). Petzoldt defines a gifted child as one who can accomplish two years' work in one (compare Galton p. 13 *sup.*) ; and is sanguine enough to believe that 10 per cent. of German school children could achieve this progress !

6. THE RELATIONS BETWEEN MENTAL ABILITY AND EDUCATIONAL ATTAINMENTS.

The Various Influences Affecting the Tests.

A child's proficiency in the Binet-Simon tests is the complex resultant of a thousand intermingling factors. Besides the two essential items, the intelligence he has inherited, the age he has reached, a host of subsidiary conditions inevitably affects his score. Zeal, industry, good will, emotional stability, scholastic information, the accident of social class, the circumstance of sex—each and all of these irrelevant influences, in one case propitious, in another prejudicial, improve or impair the final result. To glance at the composition of the scale is to foresee its facile impressionability. Girls will figure well in the verbal tests. Errand boys and paper-boys will answer smartly in the money tests. The sullen child will at first refuse to reply altogether. The excitable child, through haste or confusion, will blunder into every trap. The truant and the invalid, having missed many lessons, will fail where print is to be read or pen is to be used. The busy little house-wife from an illiterate home, who there carries out the most intricate duties, will yet be unable to put those duties into words. The solitary child of a cultured family—profiting, perhaps, rather by daily intercourse with educated adults than by special inborn gifts—will respond with an informa-tion and a phraseology beyond anything he would spontaneously invent or acquire. Bias in such directions the very shape of the tests imparts. The examiner, therefore, who notes in the child but the one quality he means to measure, and ignores the many accidents which embarrass its manifestation, will expose his measurement to the jeopardy of gross distortion. He is like a chemist who weighs salts in a bottle without heeding the weight of the bottle itself.

Of these numerous intervening agencies the most potent is, without doubt, educational opportunity. Many of the tests—some of them with-drawn by Binet in his final revision—are sheer tests of school attainments. Reading, writing, dictation are learnt in English lessons ; counting, and addition and subtraction of money, in arithmetic lessons ; drawing from copy and drawing from memory, in drawing lessons ; the date is put at the head of every written exercise on every day of the term, and with equal regularity is never heard and never recollected on any day of the vacation. Estimated by the Binet-Simon scale, therefore, a child's apparent intelli-gence must depend in no small measure upon his class in school.

The converse is, or should be, no less true. A child's school class must depend upon his apparent intelligence. In theory, at any rate, he is classified at entrance, and promoted year by year, in accordance with what he has learnt already and with what he seems likely to learn in future. In practice, we should consequently anticipate that ability and attainment would closely correspond. In what way is this correspondence to be verified ?

The Influence of Intelligence upon Educational Attainments.

There are here two cognate problems of no slight significance. How far is educational attainment determined by intelligence, measured as above ? How far is intelligence, measured as above, determined by educational attainment ?

To the teacher the former question brings a practical appeal. How far will the finished excellence of the final product of his labours wait and depend upon an original excellence in the raw stuff upon which he has worked ?

How fully are his failures already predestined by the native refractoriness inherent in that material ?   Does the child who starts his educational career endowed with large congenital abilities rise always to the top of the class at the top of the school ; or does genius pass often undetected ?   Are the children who, year after year, get left behind near the bottom of the lowest classes doomed there irreprievably by their natural ineptitude ; or can a foundation of a solid stupidity yet be overlaid with a veneer of imparted knowledge, and tinctured and varnished with a colourable coat of super-added skill ?

To these queries our data may yield tentative replies.   Four schools in my survey were examined, not only for intelligence by the Binet-Simon scale, but also for educational attainments by means of scholastic tests. The scholastic examination embraced tests of reading, writing, dictation, arithmetic (mechanical processes and applied problems), and composition.[1] Manual tests were also attempted ; but with results too precarious to include. The children ranged in age from seven to fourteen, and amounted in number to 689—rather less than one hundred to each age-group.   For both intelligence and attainments the marks of each candidate were first converted into terms of mental or educational years ; and then, divided by the chronological age of each, were thus reduced to mental or educational ratios.   The final measurements are distributed as shown in the table annexed (Table XIX.).

Between educational ratio and mental ratio the correlation is ·738, a magnitude by no means imposing.[2]   The frequency-table itself, however, merits nearer inspection.   Several inferences emerge.   First, *the children who are most retarded mentally, appear still more retarded educationally*.   As technically backward we may regard all those who are retarded by more than 15 per cent. of their age ; and, therefore, possess a mental ratio of less than 85 per cent.   In this sense the backward comprise 59 out of the whole number.   Their average mental ratio is 79·6 ; their average educational ratio only 78·9.   The difference is a somewhat subtle one ; but when we recall that the general range of deviation is, for educational attainments, much narrower than for intelligence, the small decline assumes a large significance.   A study of the first four columns one by one shows that in each the commonest event is for a child to be lowered to an educational ratio 5 per cent. beneath his mental ratio.   Feeble ability, then, entails acquirements feebler still.

With those who, in intelligence, fall but slightly below the average, attaining ratios between 85 and 100, this tendency appears reversed.   *There is discernible an effort, and an effort by no means sterile, to coax and coach these milder dullards to a grade more closely fitted to their actual age.*   In this group alone acquired attainment is greater than inborn ability.   Their average mental ratio is 93·7, their average educational ratio 95·8.   The mental legacy which they inherit is slender.   Yet, so judiciously have their teachers invested and improved it, that the accumulated interest now exceeds the capital.

Fifteen children, having less than nine-tenths of normal capacity, can yet maintain, at least in routine work, a normal position in a normal class at school.   Seldom, however, can a child below average intelligence be raised much above the average educationally.   On the other hand, a child

---

[1] See Appendix I of Memorandum III, pp. 367 *et seq.*

[2] The probable error of this coefficient is $\pm$ ·011.   The correlation ratios are, for educational ratio on mental ratio, ·843, and for mental ratio on educational ratio ·775.   The regression, particularly in the former case, thus deviates considerably from linearity.   This, indeed, a cursory glance at the frequency-table is sufficient to reveal.

TABLE XIX.

Correspondence between Mental and Educational Ratios.

Educational Ratio.	Mental Ratio. 65-	70-	75-	80-	85-	90-	95-	100-	105-	110-	115-	120-	125-	130-	135-	140-	145-	150-	Total.
60-	2																		2
65-		3	2																5
70-		2	8	3															13
75-		1	3	10	1		1												16
80-			2	8	11	3	3	1		1									29
85-			1	7	13	16	7	2	1	2									49
90-				5	12	22	15	19	5	5									83
95-				2	10	28	41	35	23	6	1	2							148
100-					4	17	35	44	27	18	10	6	2						163
105-					1	5	9	15	21	17	11	7	2						88
110-							2	3	9	12	14	6	3	2	1	1			53
115-								1	2	6	6	3	2	2	1	1			24
120-											2	3	2	2	1	1	1	1	13
125-												2		1					3
Total ..	2	6	16	35	52	91	113	120	88	67	44	29	11	7	3	3	1	1	689

educationally below average may often display a ratio beyond average for intelligence. Only seventy-three with an educational ratio of 100 or more have a mental ratio below 100 ; only five with an educational ratio of 100 or more have a mental ratio below 90 ; while as many as one hundred and three have a mental ratio above 100 and an educational ratio below.

Passing, thus, in the third place, to those who are slightly above average, we find that the direction of the difference changes once more. For this group the average mental ratio is 106·9 ; the average educational ratio only 102·2—hardly distinguishable from the general mean. *These children, then, despite superior talent, are largely kept back scholastically,* depressed to a stage which answers more closely to their actual years. Indeed, the whole table unmasks *a strong disposition to level a child's school work up or down towards the common standard for his age.* The number of children, whose educational ratio lies between 95 and 105, and is, therefore, equalised approximately to the mean, becomes, when viewed from the standpoint of normal distribution, indisputably excessive.

On turning, lastly, to the brightest of all—those whose mental ratio is over 115—the same repression is perceptible. Their mental ratio is 123·1 ; their educational ratio 111·2. *The abler children are thus deprived of more than half their advancement and over 10 per cent. of their mental age*—a surrender tantamount, by the age of ten, to throwing to oblivion a whole year of their school life. Half a dozen in this group are prospective scholarship winners ; but the vast majority are children of good, sound, second-rate ability—such as merits instruction in a central school. Such potential candidates for central schools will evidently repay a keen attention at an early age ; and, thus watched and fostered, would, at the proper time, require selection by methods more carefully refined, and accommodation upon a scale more liberally enlarged.

The most salient cases of disparity will reward an individual scrutiny. Out of the entire group ten receive an educational ratio 30 per cent. or more below their mental ratio. The reverse, it may be noted, never occurs. No child receives a mental ratio 30 per cent. below his educational ratio.

Each of the ten by his history exemplifies some fallacy to which in their judgments either tests or teachers are exposed. The most notable is a boy aged $10\frac{5}{12}$ at the time he was tested. In intelligence, as judged by the Binet-Simon scale, he then appeared equal to a child of thirteen ; in educational attainments barely equal to a child of eight. Upon enquiry, it was learnt that, immediately after promotion to the senior department, he was forced by ill-health to be absent for the greater portion of two years. On his return he was placed in the same class as that which he was attending when he first quitted the schoolroom for the hospital. It was the class which a boy of seven or eight would naturally enter from the infants, approximately equivalent to standard I. or II. He gave no trouble ; and attracted little notice. A few months later he was tested ; and proved to be, in a quiet way, brilliant in intelligence, though in school subjects unusually ignorant. In view of his exploits in the tests, he was thrust speedily forward ; and, when last seen, at the age of eleven and a half, was making excellent progress in standard V. Indeed, except for his backwardness in arithmetic—a subject where to cover the work of four standards within fourteen months would be an incredible feat—he was sufficiently equipped for the class above.

A girl of $8\frac{8}{12}$ had a mental age of 12·5. She was then only in standard III.B. After the tests she was promoted with special rapidity. She has now, at the age of ten and a half, reached the top of standard VI. ; and is predicted by her teacher to be " a sure scholarship winner."

In the same class an older girl of $9\frac{6}{12}$ had a mental age of 13·6. She has just failed to win a scholarship—her weak subject being the paper in arithmetic. Reporting on the girl, the headmistress states : " Norah F. proved the brightest of all our candidates this year ; but was beaten by Eva H., who was certainly not so sharp." Eva H., in the Binet tests, fell a year behind her unsuccessful schoolfellow. But then, while Norah was marking time in standard III.B., Eva had already been moved to standard IV.A.

One other girl, despite a high mental ratio, was lodged in a class only level with her age. She belongs to a species, familiar since antiquity : *homo vagus et inconstans.* By her teacher she is aptly described in a single word— " unreliable." At times, roused by some rare emergency, stimulated perhaps by some fresh personality, she may respond with a flash of unexpected sprightliness. On other days her mind lies bewildered and inert. " But she does well," adds the teacher significantly, " in psychological tests and parlour games." Here evidently is an instance where the error rests rather with the Binet estimate than with the indications of the scholastic test.

There are in the table two interesting cases where the mental ratio is 120 and the educational ratio only 90. Both are emotional, inattentive children, each in a different way. The girl is excitable ; the boy reserved. The girl seeks notice, and obtains an undue share ; the boy dislikes attention, and too easily evades it. The girl is glib and plausible—indeed, her conversational gifts have earned for her in the Binet-Simon tests an estimate her general powers would hardly warrant ; the boy is taciturn, and before he will do justice to his latent capabilities must be tactfully drawn on and drawn out. Of the former the teacher says : " She answers up well enough, but is disappointing. She has no power of concentration ; and, without being lazy, she does not work." Manifestly she belongs to that perplexing type which elsewhere[1] I have tried to portray in detail—the unstable child.

The boy illustrates emotional instability in an opposite form. He is of the repressed or sensitive variety rather than of the excitable or unrepressed. He is described by his teacher as " slow and sleepy." It would be perhaps truer to call him " slow and sure." When his attention wanders, he is not asleep ; he is dreaming, giving full flight to a somewhat precocious imagination. In arithmetic he is very poor. He reads voraciously ; and spells execrably. But his compositions sparkle, even where they do not shine. There is many a quiet child with a touch of this whimsical temperament. Shy, timid, uncommunicative, yet on acquaintance most engaging, they can be brought to show their finer qualities only through patient sympathy and personal interest. In a large class they usually remain *incompris*— a little mysterious, and very much misconstrued. Just because they are pensive and visionary within, they seem outwardly aloof and unobservant. Soaring in fantasy, they see no facts. They are like those celestial beings whom the Scriptures represent as veiling their eyes with their wings.

Out of all the children in the table the cleverest is a boy aged (at the time of the examination) $8\frac{2}{12}$, with a mental age of 12·6. His mental ratio was, therefore, 154—one of the highest I have encountered in elementary schools. He was then in standard IV. In tested ability he was even with the children in standard VI. Yet, in a department organised in the usual way, to promote so young a child to so high a class would seem hardly politic. Cases of this order raise a practical issue. *May it not in the long run prove remunerative in the fullest sense to institute for supernormal children special classes analogous and complementary to those established in many schools with much success for the backward and subnormal ?*

---

[1] *Child Study,* Vol. X., No. 3, October, 1917, " The Unstable Child."

Three cases remain. They are children lately transferred from the infants' department. In every instance, the teachers report that the children have been attending the senior department hardly long enough for any opinion on their proficiency to be formed, or for any promotion into a higher class to be justified. Such reports are suggestive. *Perhaps one of the most profitable uses of an intelligence test, such as the Binet-Simon scale, might be found in examining children of youthful age and unknown ability who enter a new department from an infants', a junior mixed, or another senior school.*

These illustrations should not be misinterpreted. Not for an instant are these discrepancies adduced to asperse either the precision of the class teachers' judgment, or the efficiency of the head teachers' organisation. Indeed, where no method exists, quick, simple, and trustworthy, for assessing children's abilities, there it can be no disparagement to contend that children's abilities have not always been accurately gauged. And, when all is said, the cases of extreme maladjustment are exceptional. They number ten out of seven hundred.

Yet they are exceptions in no wise limited to the few schools studied. To submit, indeed, each of the three thousand children tested by the Binet method to a further examination in school work would have consumed an impracticable deal of time and labour. Instead, some notion of the child's educational level could always be gleaned from the standard in which he was classified, or from the report delivered by his teacher. Such larger and looser comparisons confirmed the more intensive ; they showed that the incongruities disclosed in the smaller sample would recur, proportionately multiplied, in a more extended search. On the whole, however, the leading feature here too was correspondence : class at school and ability in tests, apart from some notable divergences, approximately conform.

The Influence of Educational Attainment on the Binet Tests.

I turn now to enquire if the relation is reciprocal : whether the conformity observed is due, not merely to the child's ability determining his school attainments, but also to his school attainments determining his display of ability.

The problem is a problem in multiple correlation. Simple correlation between two variables—as between a test of intelligence and an independent estimate of intelligence—is a mode of statistical enquiry that is now familiar in educational science. But here we are unravelling a network of interlacing correlations, correlations with age and with class, as well as between tests and estimates.

Things which are correlated with the same thing become correlated with one another ; and this second-hand assimilation obscures any original likeness or unlikeness. We must, therefore, subtract from the test measurements all influence of age and of pure intelligence, in order to discover whether there still remains any direct interaction between class-standing and test-results, over and above the derivative agreement which the common factors of intelligence and age induce. A pupil passes the tests with a mental age of six. In theory his performance should argue one or other, or both, of two things. He may be young ; he may be dull ; he may at once be dull and young. Take any one of these alternatives. In view of youth or dulness or of both alike he would, of course, be relegated to a low school class. Low class and low mental age would thus be found in unison. Is some plain assumption of this obvious sort sufficient to account for the whole of such correspondences ; or is there yet in fact a further influence, an added interplay of factors which this simpler theory does not include ? Is the agreement between class and test due solely to the mediation of the two essential conditions—an age that is undoubtedly young and an intelligence that is genuinely weak—or does the child's position in school of itself recoil, reacting adversely upon the tests, limiting his performances, impoverishing his replies, and so produce a mental age artificially depressed, lower far than actual intelligence and actual years would of themselves entail ?

To detect and disengage this further possibility we should first strip away the effects of age and intelligence, and then observe if, connecting mental measurements with class attainments, there still persists, unexplained and uninduced by these twin factors, a surplus core of correlation.

The elimination of common factors such as these may be accomplished in theory by the method known to statisticians as "partial correlation," a method already employed in my earlier memorandum to analyse the relation of educational abilities among themselves.[1] Given the observed or "total" correlations between three or more variables paired in every possible way, we can, by means of a simple formula, deduct from any of the total co-efficients—for example, from the correlation between intelligence and class— the amount of correlation attributable to some tertiary factor influencing both in the same direction—for example, age. The residuary quantity is termed the "partial" coefficient.

For every child in an entire school, comprising just over three hundred pupils aged between seven and fourteen, I have secured the following measure-ments : first, the child's age ; next, his school attainments, measured by an educational examination, the results being revised by the teachers ; thirdly, his innate ability measured by special tests of reasoning,[2] the results again being carefully checked by the teachers ; and, lastly, his mental age, given directly by the present version of the Binet-Simon scale, unchecked and unrevised.

The first column of figures in Table XX. shows the six correlations subsisting between these four measurements coupled with one another in every one of the six ways possible.[3]

From these six "total" coefficients, taken each in turn, I have first of all eliminated one or other of the four factors operative. From the gross figures I have, by discount, found the net. The resulting "partial" co-efficients are given by the second column of figures in the table. A com-parison of these values at once invites several inferences. The resemblance between the Binet-Simon results and the child's school standing seems due more to the common influence of age than to the common influence of intelligence. The resemblance between the Binet-Simon results and the child's intellectual maturity, estimated independently, seems due more to the common influence of school standing than to the common influence of age. The estimates for intellectual maturity owe their correlation with school standing—a correlation by no means high even at the outset— chiefly, but not entirely, to the common influence of age. When the influence of intelligence is excluded, there still remains a correspondence between age and position in school that is unexpectedly—indeed, I apprehend, un-warrantably—close : promotion goes suspiciously with seniority. The nega-tive correlation between school standing and intelligence, obtained when differences in Binet age are eliminated, may seem odd ; but even were it larger

---

[1] *The Distribution and Relations of Educational Abilities*, p. 53 *et seq.* Cf. Appendix VI, pp. 278-284.

[2] See Appendix IV., pp. 251-254.

[3] With a group of nearly 300 children, the probable error for correlations less than ·12 ranges between + ·038 and + ·039. A coefficient under ·07, therefore, has little or no significance ; one over ·11 may be received as trustworthy.

than it is, it would not be at all inexplicable.[1] In a group homogeneous in regard to mental age, children who are older chronologically would, in a test measuring inborn intelligence rather than mere mental growth, appear duller ; yet, because they are older, the school system elevates them to a somewhat higher class. Hence the paradox of a group whose mental age is uniform : the higher the class, the duller the child.

TABLE XX.

Observed and Partial Correlations between Age, Intelligence, School Attainments, and the Results of the Binet-Simon Tests.

Factors Correlated.	Observed Coefficients.	Factor Eliminated.	Partial Coefficient (First Order).	Factors Eliminated.	Partial Coefficient (Second Order).
Tests and School Work.	·91	Intelligence.	·78	Intelligence and Age.	·61
		Age.	·68		
Tests and Intelligence.	·84	School Work.	·58	School Work and Age.	·56
		Age.	·65		
Tests and Age.	·83	School Work.	·19	School Work and Intelligence.	·13
		Intelligence.	·62		
School Work and Intelligence.	·75	Tests.	—·06	Tests and Age.	—·07
		Age.	·40		
School Work and Age.	·87	Tests.	·49	Tests and Intelligence.	·49
		Intelligence.	·73		
Intelligence and Age.	·70	Tests.	·01	Tests and School Work.	·05
		School Work.	·15		

Let us now examine the partial coefficients of the second order, coefficients, that is, obtained where two factors have been cancelled in succession (last column of Table XX).

Intelligence, it may be remembered, was observed to correlate with the Binet tests by ·84 and with school attainments by ·75. Mediated solely by intelligence, therefore, a correlation between the Binet estimates and school attainments could be predicted amounting at least to ·75 × ·84, that is ·63. The total correlation found, however, was as much as ·91. The excess is due, in part at least, to the second common factor of age. But, on eliminating also the effect of age, there is still left a substantial surplus. With both age and intelligence constant, the " partial " correlation between school attainments and Binet results remains at ·61. Of all the partial coefficients of the second order this is the largest. There can, therefore, be little doubt that *with the Binet-Simon scale a child's mental age is a measure not only of the amount of intelligence with which he is congenitally endowed, not only of the plane of intelligence at which in the course of life and growth he has eventually arrived ; it is also an index, largely though not perhaps mainly, of the mass of scholastic information and skill which, in virtue of attendance more or less regular, by dint of instruction more or less effective, he has progressively accumulated in school.*

The correlation of ·49 between age and educational attainment, left after the elimination of ability both tested and observed, confirms our

---

[1] The coefficient in question is barely twice its probable error.

previous suspicion of the undue influence of age upon school classification. The only other correlations surviving after the double elimination are those between the Binet tests, on the one hand, and intelligence and age respectively upon the other.

From the three final correlations thus furnished by the tests, and from the relevant standard deviations, can be calculated the several so-called "regressions." The regressions will indicate the relative proportions in which the three factors—age, intelligence, and school attainments—together determine a child's actual score in the Binet-Simon tests. The complete equation is as follows :—

$$B = \cdot54\ S + \cdot33\ I + \cdot11\ A,$$

where B $\equiv$ mental age according to the Binet-Simon scale,
  S $\equiv$ school attainments expressed in terms of educational age,
  I $\equiv$ intellectual ability also measured in terms of years ; and
  A $\equiv$ the chronological age.

Of the gross result, then, one-ninth is attributable to age, one-third to intellectual development, and over one-half to school attainment. School attainment is thus the preponderant contributor to the Binet-Simon tests. To school the weight assigned is nearly double that of intelligence alone, and distinctly more than that of intelligence and age combined. *In determining the child's performance in the Binet-Simon scale, intelligence can bestow but little more than half the share of school, and age but one-third the share of intelligence.* Isolated from scholastic progress and from intellectual development, age subscribes a positive but paltry portion. Its tribute is, presumably, that fund of worldly wisdom (or some fraction of that fund) which from his cradle onwards is amassed by every child, whether intelligent or unintelligent, whether an incorrigible truant or a daily attendant at school. But to achieve distinction, at all events, in a trial so academic as the Binet-Simon tests, experience must be heavily supplemented ; it must be reinforced either by the artificial aids supplied by a civilised society or by the natural stimulus of an unusual native wit. Imagine two children, aged seven and seventeen respectively, both possessing an intelligence equally normal, neither having passed a single hour in school. The younger, as a consideration of the several tests will show, might reach a mental age of six ; the older, despite ten years of seniority, barely that of nine. So barren is growth deprived of opportunity.

The Influence of Ability in Specific Scholastic Subjects.

Some data may be appended on the influence of the different topics of the curriculum, taken one by one. Between mental age and attainments in each of the subjects tested the total correlation observed is given by the first column of coefficients set out in the table subjoined (Table XXI.). For this more specific problem the influence of school class becomes of smaller interest, and might even introduce irrelevant disturbances ; accordingly, the correlations have been calculated, not for the three hundred children as a single group, nor yet for the age-groups separately, but for the several classes ; the coefficients drawn from the different classes have then been averaged. Since within each class differences in intelligence are by the very process of classification somewhat reduced, the correlations are slender. But homogeneity in a school class is far from perfect. Consequently, by the method of partial correlation such differences as there are either in age or in intelligence (estimated independently of the Binet-Simon tests) have been again eliminated. The partial coefficients are appended in the last column of the table.

On an average, the total correlations are higher for the literary subjects than for the mathematical ; and higher for the mathematical than for the manual. In manual subjects, however, estimates of attainment can rarely pretend to much fidelity. Indeed, for drawing and handwork the measurements secured with the present group are demonstrably unsound. In the literary subjects the size of the observed coefficients might seem on a cursory view to betoken for them an unusual diagnostic value. Composition, it may be thought, measures intelligence better than arithmetical problems ; reading and dictation better than arithmetical rules. It may be so. But the magnitude of the partial coefficients dispels all support that such an hypothesis might hope for in the present data. For while the Binet-Simon measurements, when age and intelligence are discounted, show little correlation with arithmetic marks, they still exhibit a pronounced and persistent correlation with the three linguistic subjects. Hence, these latter subjects form no mere passive vehicles for the revelation of general intelligence. *Linguistic ability and linguistic attainments exert upon the Binet-Simon tests a special and positive influence of their own.*

TABLE XXI.

Observed and Partial Correlations between the Binet-Simon Tests and Attainments in the Several School Subjects.

	Observed Coefficients.	Partial Coefficients (Age and Intelligence eliminated).
Composition	·63	·32
Reading	·54	·26
Dictation	·52	·21
Arithmetic (Problems) ..	·55	·07
Arithmetic (Mechanical) ..	·41	·15
Writing	·21	·01
Drawing	·15	— ·08
Handwork	·18	— ·06

7. THE APPLICATION OF THE TESTS TO JUVENILE DELINQUENTS.

The Distribution of General Intelligence and Educational Attainments among Juvenile Delinquents.

Nowhere can the factors hitherto discussed be seen so vividly in operation as among researches on delinquency. The examiner's choice of a line of demarcation, the examinee's interest and attainment in school, and, perhaps still more, the attitude and temperament of both one or the other, change and modify, in a style most palpable to the critical reader, all estimates for the proportion of delinquents presumed to be defective.

The most diverse figures, the most incredible conclusions, have been reached with the Binet-Simon scale. According to one investigator, " probably 80 per cent. of the children in the Juvenile Courts in Manhattan and Bronx are feebleminded." According to another, Dr. Goddard of Vineland, 66 per cent. of the cases in the Newark Detention Home, New Jersey, are " distinctly feebleminded." Other writers are more conservative. " The best estimate and the result of the most careful studies indicate that somewhere in the neighbourhood of 50 per cent. of all criminals are feeble-minded." " Practically one-third of our delinquent children are feeble-minded." Dr. Goring concluded that, of the convicts in England and Wales, 10 per cent. could be regarded as definitely defective—0·5 per cent. of the non-criminal population being defective in an equal degree. Finally, an estimate alike the most recent and the most guarded, based on a study of boys in Minneapolis, declares that only 1·4 per cent. of the delinquents sink below the level of the bottom 0·5 per cent. of the ordinary population, and only 7·3 per cent. below the level of the bottom 1·5 per cent. of the

TABLE XXII.—Juvenile Delinquents.

Distribution of General Intelligence at Each Age.

Chrono-logical Age.	Mental Age.										Total.
	5—	6—	7—	8—	9—	10—	11—	12—	13—	14—	
6— ..	1	1	—	—	—	—	—	—	—	—	2
7— ..	2	2	1	—	—	—	—	—	—	—	3
8— ..	—	—	1	2	—	—	—	—	—	—	3
9— ..	—	—	1	2	1	—	—	—	—	—	4
10— ..	—	—	—	1	2	2	1	—	—	—	6
11— ...	—	—	1	0	.2	3	2	—	—	—	8
12— ..	—	—	—	1	1	4	3	2	1	—	12
13— ..	—	—	—	1	2	5	3	4	4	—	19
14— ..	—	—	—	—	1	3	6	8	5	1	24
15— ..	—	—	—	—	1	1	4	9	8	3	26
Total ..	1	3	4	7	10	18	19	23	18	4	107

ordinary population. Here, therefore, are amazing discrepancies that call for re-examination.

With tests both of general intelligence and of educational capacity I have, during the last six years, examined over a hundred juvenile delinquents in London. The group consists of representative samples inspected at the Council's industrial schools and places of detention, and miscellaneous cases submitted for psychological examination by teachers, magistrates, and secretaries of colonies for delinquent children. The misdemeanour in the majority of cases was petty theft ; but the catalogue of offences includes begging, wandering, truancy, assault, sexual offences, damage to property, and being beyond parental control.

The distribution of the children according to mental age is entered in Table XXII., and according to educational attainments in Table XXIII.

The average chronological age of the entire group was 13·2 ; the average mental age, 11·3 ; the average scholastic age, 9·5—equivalent to standard III. Thus, *on an average the delinquents are retarded by nearly two years in general intelligence, and by yet a further two years—four years in all—in educational attainments.*

The measurements for each individual delinquent have also been expressed as multiples of the standard deviation of the corresponding normal age-group. The frequencies obtained at each age can thus be legitimately added ; and the totals for general intelligence and educational attainments legitimately compared. For all ages the total frequencies are given in the upper rows of Table XXIV. In educational attainments, the back-

P

TABLE XXIII.—Juvenile Delinquents.

Distribution of Educational Attainments at Each Age.

Chrono-logical Age.	Scholastic Age.										Total.
	5—	6—	7—	8—	9—	10—	11—	12—	13—	14—	
6— ..	1	1	—	—	—	—	—	—	—	—	2
7— ..	—	3	—	—	—	—	—	—	—	—	3
8— ..	—	1	1	1	—	—	—	—	—	—	3
9— ..	—	2	1	1	—	—	—	—	—	—	4
10— ..	—	—	1	3	1	1	—	—	—	—	6
11— ..	—	1	0	4	2	1	—	—	—	—	8
12— ..	—	—	2	2	3	3	2	—	—	—	12
13— ..	—	—	1	2	5	6	3	1	1	—	19
14— ..	—	—	1	4	7	9	3	—	—	—	24
15— ..	—	—	1	3	8	11	2	1	—	—	26
Total ..	1	8	8	20	26	31	10	2	1		107

wardness of the delinquent appears, at first sight, not only to be out of all proportion to his backwardness in intelligence, but also, when compared with that observed among the general school population, to be so inordinate as almost to pass belief. The more violent extremes, however, occur among children who are over fourteen. Of these, the majority have not advanced beyond the low level reached on leaving school; indeed, many have begun to recede. In general intelligence, too, the tests for these older children are not beyond cavil. Hence, in both cases the comparison will prove more valid, if limited to children of school age alone. The percentages of children who, at these years, exhibit the various degrees of backwardness or advancement are appended in the lower lines of the same table; and are plotted diagrammatically in Figure 25.

In general intelligence, among the delinquents of school age, 7 per cent. only are on or below the verge of mental deficiency; one-fifth are definitely retarded; nearly one-half fall slightly below the general average; one-

TABLE XXIV.—Juvenile Delinquents.

Distribution of General Intelligence and Educational Attainments Irrespective of Age.

(The unit is the standard deviation of the normal age-group, equivalent in general intelligence to 1 year at 8 —, and in educational attainments to 1 year at 10 —. Zero marks the average at each age.)

	Deviation.							
	−5	−4	−3	−2	−1	0	+1	S.D.
Ages 6— to 15—								
General Intelligence	—	—	6·5	30·8	44·9	15·9	1·9	per cent.
Educational Attainments ..	2·8	21·5	38·3	23·4	11·2	2·8	—	per cent.
Ages 6— to 13—								
General Intelligence	—	—	7·0	21·1	42·1	26·3	3·5	per cent.
Educational Attainments ..	1·7	8·8	29·3	36·8	21·1	5·3	—	per cent.

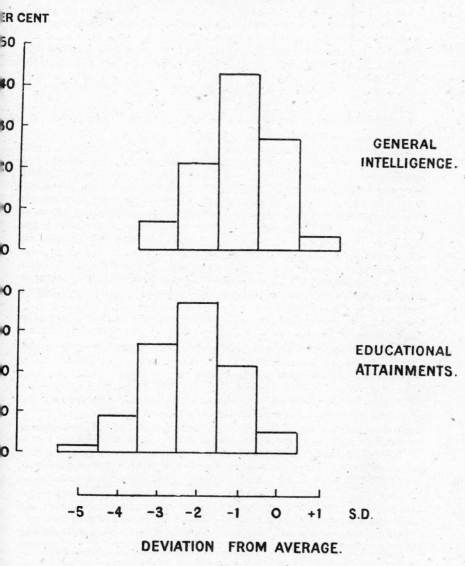

FIGURE 25.

DISTRIBUTION OF JUVENILE DELINQUENTS ACCORDING TO GENERAL
INTELLIGENCE AND EDUCATIONAL ATTAINMENTS.

(Children aged 6– to 13–.)

quarter are approximately equal to the general average ; and 2 per cent. rise slightly above. With delinquency supernormal intelligence is not incompatible ; but any well-marked degree of it is among delinquents evidently rare. In educational attainments none are sensibly above the average, and only 5 per cent. approximately equal to it ; one-fifth are slightly below ; and three-quarters are backward by over 1·5 S.D.—a large portion of these falling below the educational borderline of the mentally defective, though not themselves to be considered mentally defective from the aspect of general intelligence. Elsewhere I have advocated that a retardation of —1·5 to —3·0 S.D. (equivalent to one and a half to three years at the age of ten) should be regarded as indicative of " scholastic backwardness " in a technical sense—such backwardness requiring accommodation in special classes rather than in special (M.D.) schools. *The majority of juvenile delinquents thus appear to be technically " backward," but not technically "defective."* [1] As I have already urged, the association of juvenile delinquency with educational backwardness provides in itself a strong motive towards making special provision for the backward child during his school career.

The Correlation of Delinquency with Deficiency and Backwardness.

The relations of moral delinquency, on the one side, to mental deficiency and educational backwardness, on the other, can be most concisely compared by the statistical device of " association coefficients." A coefficient of association is a fraction, varying from zero to plus or minus unity, designed to measure the degree of correlation between attributes which are not themselves quantitatively graded. Delinquency and, for administrative purposes, even mental deficiency and educational backwardness, are such attributes. A child either is or is not delinquent ; he either does or does not require transference to a special school or special class. For deficiency both in general intelligence and in educational attainments let us take one and the same line of demarcation, namely, a ratio of 70 per cent. of age. Among the non-delinquent population this ratio would cut off about 1·5 per cent. as mentally defective and 2·0 per cent. as educationally defective. Apply this criterion to the entire delinquent group. Only 5·6 per cent. have a mental ratio less than 70 ; and presumably, therefore, are defective in general intelligence. But an educational ratio less than 70 is to be found among 42·1 per cent.—a proportion nearly eight times as large as the first. From such percentages a coefficient of association can be calculated by the aid of a simple formula. [2] Between juvenile delinquency and mental deficiency the association proves to be only ·33 ; between juvenile delinquency and educational deficiency it mounts to ·71. If we considered only the delinquents of school age, and employed for educational backwardness the technical borderline of 85 per cent., the difference would be still further enhanced. The former coefficient would sink to ·31 ; and the latter rise to ·74.

The educational backwardness of the moral reprobate may be referred to much the same causes as those which promote educational backwardness in the child who is morally normal. Irregular attendance, physical defects both general and specific, general and specific weakness in mental capacities, irregularity of growth and development, abnormality in emotional tendencies and in qualities of character as a whole—the list of factors is almost identical ; but their relative incidence is differently loaded. With the backward offender

---

[1] Throughout this section, to avoid circumlocution, I have treated the phrase "mental deficiency," in accordance with the usage of most writers on this problem, as covering deficiency of intelligence alone. Properly speaking, extreme temperamental instability, as I have argued in another place, should also, even where intelligence is unimpaired, be included under mental deficiency

[1] See Appendix II., p. 229.

instability of temperament plays a dominant rôle. The fickleness of his interests, the flimsiness of his efforts, the flightiness of his attention, conspire to stultify all intellectual progress. He displays little interest in the lessons of the classroom, little attachment to the person of the teacher or the name of his school ; and what resolution, industry, and conscientiousness he can muster is insufficient to overcome either his natural indifference or his acquired aversion. The maladjustment between the concrete bent of the individual and the abstract tasks of the school, or between a low class in the school organisation and a natural ability which is, in comparison, high, must undoubtedly react upon character. It fosters a sense of injustice ; and aggravates any instincts, nomadic, predatory, or rebellious, that may already have been inherited with an intensity too strong for control. By providing occupations and duties, in nature more congenial and in difficulty more advanced, by granting freer outlets for emotional tendencies, and a fuller play to the spirit of activity, many instinctive propensities, that would otherwise be driven to mutiny and provide motives for crime, may, when emancipated from repression and adroitly re-directed, yield energy for legitimate purposes and enthusiasm for nobler ideals and strenuous work.

The low estimate for general ability among convicts and criminals, obtained so repeatedly with the Binet-Simon scale, is largely accounted for by their educational backwardness. Upon scholastic attainments, and still more upon scholastic interests, success in the ordeal very intimately hangs. Almost equally decisive may be the conditions under which the test is applied, and the manner in which its performance is approached. For what to them must seem nothing but a resuscitated school examination, delinquents, as a rule, feel little inclination and much distaste. From the outset they assume they are more likely to fail than succeed, more likely to be reproached than commended. Examined in a remand home or in a prison, they are often labouring under an emotional strain—anxious, angry, uncomfortable, or depressed. Unless, indeed, to circumvent their suspicion and secure their goodwill special manœuvres be tactfully tried, their apparent prowess with all such tests will fall much below their veritable powers.

Children sequestered in an institution from an early age suffer from a further handicap. Brought up within the walls, perhaps, of an industrial school, governed from day to day and hour to hour by the rules of a super-imposed routine, they preserve a curious ignorance of simple practical affairs—the values of the commoner coins, for example ; they develop a sorry want of initiative, of forethought, and of self-reliance. Such a life of regulated dependence lowers their performance in the tests. Towards adolescence they may be liberated—thrown back, it may be, into a lax home and loose environment. They drift. And the constant change of employment and situation, the ingrained lack of self-direction and self-discipline, will seem to confirm the illusory diagnosis of deficiency, which their backwardness in mental tests and in school knowledge had already suggested. To argue, as I have argued, however, that they are not, except in rare instances, genuinely defective, is not to declare that they require no supervision and need no guidance. Rather it prompts the question whether a reform in the discipline of such institutions, following perhaps along the lines of the well-known experiments in self-government already made in several delinquent colonies, might not obviate the necessity for social control by training the child to control himself.

The misleading implications of quasi-scholastic tests have been exposed most transparently where I have followed up delinquents, juvenile and adult, after their emergence from the prison or remand home and on their resumption of ordinary life. In anything reminiscent of a lesson they participate reluctantly, and fail outright. But challenge them with a problem that appeals to their interest—some logical puzzle, disguised, it may be, as a brief detective story about an unsolved crime—then they will accomplish intellectual feats two or three years above the standard they exhibit in tests more academic. Dexterity, not only in carrying out their crimes, but also in managing their everyday affairs, acquits the majority of them of any suspicion of mental deficiency in the narrower sense. They may be scholastic-ally backward ; they may be emotionally unstable ; they may be morally unsound : in general intelligence they are not defective.[1]

I would not, however, deny that, unrecognised and unprovided for, mental deficiency is a grave and genuine source of crime. For example, among repeated offenders, and particularly among female offenders,[2] intelli-gence is, as a rule, of a decidedly low grade, and, on occasion, without a doubt deficient. But in the causation of juvenile delinquency—so often itself a transitory and even natural phenomenon—the share contributed by mental defect has unquestionably been magnified by those who, trusting so exclusively to the Binet-Simon scale, have ignored the factors which depreciate its results, and have adopted without criticism or misgiving the line of demarcation as currently proposed.[3]

8. *THE INFLUENCE OF SEX AND SOCIAL STATUS.*

Differences in General Ability due to Social Status.

Among the ordinary schools tested in my general investigation stand two that were selected as representing opposite extremes of the social scale.[4] Both belong to the borough chosen for my previous survey of educational abilities. One is attended by pupils drawn from families that in social status rank among the best of those sending children to elementary schools. The other is situated in one of the meanest of the overcrowded slums that cluster about the great railway termini. In Charles Booth's map of London poverty the streets from which the latter is recruited are marked as of the lowest types—" very poor " and " criminal." Those characteristics they still pre-

---

[1] To this an unintentional parallel may be found in the statements of different Americans working in the same institution. At the New York State Reformatory for Women, Bedford Hills, several studies have been made by various investigators using various methods. One examiner, using the Binet scale, reports that practically all the inmates were feebleminded , others, using only case-histories and records obtained from teachers and attendants, report that but 15 to 20 per cent. appear mentally deficient.

[2] The average mental ratio of the boys was 88·3, of the girls 82·9.

[3] In the causation of juvenile delinquency (as I endeavour to show in a series of articles in the *J. Exp. Pedagogy*, VI., i, pp. 1 *et seq.*) the preponderant psychological factors are, as a rule, not intel-lectual but emotional, not mental deficiency as revealed by tests, but repressed complexes (on a basis of temperamental instability) revealed by observation and analysis.

[4] In an inquiry carried out, with the assistance of Miss V. G. Pelling, for the Vocational Section of the National Institute of Industrial Psychology, I endeavoured to assess the average level of intelli-gence in different occupational classes : for adults the mental ratios ranged from about 83 for unskilled workers to 154 for higher professional classes ; and for children of these parents from about 91 to 120. In an analysis of birth-rates for London boroughs (" The Relation of Fertility to Social Status," 1906) David Heron has shown that there is a marked correlation between low social class and high birth-rate which has rapidly increased during the past 50 years. Our figures confirm this ; and suggest that the correlation between low intelligence and high birth-rate is still more striking. The average size of the family for children in special m.d. schools is nearly 5·0 ; for the dull and backward, 4·3 ; for central school children, 2·9 ; and for scholarship winners, 2·5. Further evidence is required to reveal how far the low intellectual performances of the poorer groups have been affected by their overcrowded homes, and how far the overcrowded home is itself an effect of the low intelligence and foresight of the parents. If, as I believe, the differences in test-results are in part the result of differences in general intelligence and if (as I have endeavoured to argue elsewhere) general intelligence as the psychologist understands it is an inheritable characteristic, then it would seem to follow that the relatively high multiplication of the less intelligent may have far-reaching consequences. But this is hardly a problem to be discussed here ; and in any case urgently demands much further research (cf. *Eugenics Review*, " The Inheritance of Mental Characteristics," IV., pp. 1-33, and other papers).

FIGURE 26.

AVERAGE NUMBER OF TESTS PASSED AT EACH AGE BY CHILDREN OF ORDINARY ELEMENTARY AND SPECIAL (M.D.) SCHOOLS, AND OF SUPERIOR AND POORER SOCIAL STATUS.

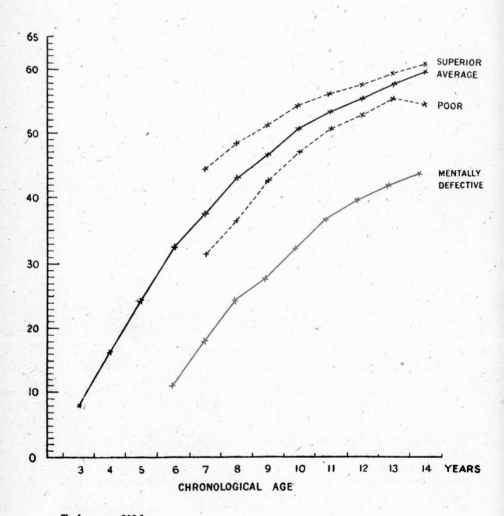

serve. In social status, therefore, the two schools may be received as typifying the best and the worst from a representative borough.

The results secured at either school are shown in Figure 26 and Table XXV. Figure 26 shows the average number of tests passed at each age in the " superior " and in the " poor " school respectively, and, for comparison, the averages obtained from the whole population. The " superior " school is nearly a year ahead of the general average (till the brighter pupils are transferred) ; the " poor " school more than a year behind.
mental years (columns 4 and 5).

TABLE XXV.

Differences due to Social Status.

Chronological Age.	Average Number of Tests passed.		Average Mental Age.	
	Superior School.	Poor School.	Superior School.	Poor School.
7 —	44·4	31·2	8·9	6·1
8 —	48·5	36·3	10·1	7·2
9 —	51·0	42·6	10·6	8·4
10 —	54·3	46·8	11·5	9·6
11 —	56·2	50·4	12·1	10·3
12 —	57·5	52·9	12·8	11·0
13 —	59·3	55·2	13·7	11·7
14 —	60·5	54·8	14·2	11·6

In other Reports[1] I have commented on the correlation of the size of the family with both low intelligence and low social class. When the two are combined, the results are still more striking. From Table XXVI. it will be seen that at the " poor " school the number of children in the family is nearly double the number at the better type of school. This incidentally must tend to impose a still harder strain on pupils recruited from the poorer classes.

TABLE XXVI.

Home Conditions of Children attending Schools of Median, Poorest, and Best Social Status.

	Poorest School.	Median School.	Best School
Average weekly pre-war income	26·4 *s.*	37·3 *s.*	49·6 *s.*
Average number of children living at home	5·2	4·1	2·9
Average number of rooms in home	2·3	3·4	4·7
Average weekly rent	5·8 *s.*	10·1 *s.*	12·8 *s.*

The backwardness of the " poor " school is likewise most obvious when the children emerge from the infants' department. It is, apparently, in early childhood that their minds wear most visibly the sharp impress of their parents' poverty. Even by the age of six or seven the difference has doubtless already decreased. It continues to dwindle, as the table shows, until the age of twelve. But during the last two or three years it once more becomes peculiarly large. This final decadence may be referred to several

---

[1] Cf. " Preliminary Report on a Survey of the School Population of a Typical London Borough " (1919) ; also Reports of later surveys to be issued shortly.

factors. Among the ill-to-do some reach early their limit of growth; others mature late. Many of the brightest, too, leave for work at an age unduly young. But, above all things, for children from the lower social strata the harder literary tests must lie for ever beyond their cultural horizon.

Averages, particularly those like the above derived from different individuals for different ages, obscure one important fact, which reveals itself not infrequently among the poorer children, when year after year the same individuals are traced and retested. This is the phenomenon of deferred development. It is a feature akin to that of "latent normality," which, as we have seen, is from time to time observable in higher grade defectives. Among the children of the slums, while most reach early what might be called their point of educational saturation, and perhaps touch their utmost limit of mental growth before their physical growth is half-completed, a few, on the other hand, commence again to develop with an exceptional speed at an age unusually delayed. They enjoy, as it were, a St. Martin's summer; and expand even more rapidly than in their natural spring. Towards the end of their school career many seem in a fair way to retrieve their previous retardation.

Emily G., for example, who lives with seven other persons in a couple of rooms in one of the meanest streets of a poverty-stricken area, was promoted to the senior school at the age of $7\frac{9}{12}$, as a small and backward child with a mental age of only 6·3, a ratio, therefore, of only 82 per cent. During the next two years she made rapid progress; and at the age of $9\frac{6}{12}$ had a ratio of 96 per cent. She then entered her chrysalis. By the age of $11\frac{6}{12}$ she had made barely half a year's progress. Her mental ratio was now only 84 per cent. Soon after this date she seemed suddenly to emerge; at $13\frac{6}{12}$ she had a mental ratio of over 100 per cent., and was among the brightest in her year.

A second girl in another school from an even poorer home, whose mental ratio before the age of twelve had never touched 90 per cent. and had appeared during the preceding two years to be diminishing, showed unexpectedly, when re-examined at the age of fourteen, an ability in various tests of intelligence approximating to that of an average child in a central school, although, of course, in scholastic tests, particularly in her knowledge of the higher rules of arithmetic she was far below.

These cases, though exceptional, are by no means rare. It is among girls of the humbler classes that this late acceleration most frequently affects my tests. With boys the slower onset of puberty, and the added stimulus of freedom, fresh work, and the earning of a wage, that comes upon them when they change from pupils into workmen, place the date of their final mental spurt just beyond the period of school life.

That children of better social status succeed better with the Binet-Simon scale is not necessarily an objection to that scale; nor is it necessarily a ground for constructing separate norms: for, by birth as well as by home training, children who are superior in social status may be equally superior in general ability. Conversely, if a child proves defective according to a scale that is otherwise authentic, the mere fact that his family is poor and his dwelling a hovel does not of itself condone his deficiency. His parents' home may be mean precisely because their hereditary intelligence is mean. Whether poverty and its accompaniments affect the child's performances in any direct fashion—whether, for example, in the Binet-Simon tests a child that inherits an abundance of natural ability may be handicapped through a lack of cultural opportunities—is a further and a separate issue. It is a recurrent problem which we cannot hope finally to solve until we have also analysed the differing effect of social status upon the individual tests, considered one by one.

Differences in General Ability due to Sex.

The averages for the two sexes are shown in Table XXVII., both in terms of tests (columns 2 and 3) and in terms of mental age (columns 4 and 5). At almost every age the girls outstrip the boys. Their superiority, however, is a very modest one. On an average the girls appear advanced by about three-tenths of a year. The difference swells to a maximum about the age of six or seven ; at ten it is reversed in favour of the boys ; but their recovery is transient ; towards fourteen the superiority of the girls is again visibly mounting. Many have seen in such figures a sign that the feminine sex matures precociously; and the suggestion is doubtless partly true, since a slight pubertal superiority of girls is also observable in other scales. It would, however, be hard to disprove that the difference may be due largely to the general preponderance of literary and verbal exercises throughout the range of tests and to the heightened preponderance of such exercises about the ages quoted : a linguistic bias would favour a linguistic sex. In tables got with other tests the differences from year to year of mental growth are less consistently maintained : the two sexes, indeed, seem during their intellectual progress to be playing a sort of statistical leap-frog, now one up, now the other, throughout their whole school course. Even here, rarely, if ever, do the differences of boys and girls reach the equivalent of half a year. Hence, to compile age-norms for the two sexes separately seems hardly needful.

TABLE XXVII.
Differences due to Sex.

Chronological Age.	Average Number of Tests Passed.		Average Mental Age	
	Boys.	Girls.	Boys.	Girls.
3 —	6·6	9·6	3·2	3·8
4 —	14·8	16·9	4·5	4·7
5 —	22·2	26·5	5·3	5·7
6 —	31·5	33·9	6·2	6·8
7 —	36·8	39·4	7·3	7·8
8 —	42·5	43·8	8·4	8·7
9 —	45·8	46·7	9·2	9·6
10 —	51·6	49·3	10·7	10·4
11 —	54·2	54·7	11·4	11·5
12 —	55·8	56·7	12·0	12·4
13 —	57·7	58·3	12·9	13·3
14 —	58·8	60·5	13·5	14·2

Influence of Social Status upon the Individual Tests.

In the tests considered singly the varying effects of sex and social status provide problems far more curious and instructive than these gross differences found in the general age-averages with the test-series as a whole.

If there were no special peculiarities in any of the tests, favouring the special abilities, interests, or experiences of either sex, then the correlation between the orders of difficulty for the two sexes should be perfect, or at any rate the correlations of the boys with the girls should be on the average at least as high as the correlations of the boys with each other, or of the girls with each other. And the same would hold true of social classes. Indeed, as I have shown elsewhere, in theory a correlational approach provides the best statistical technique for a study of such problems. But in a preliminary review we can reach pretty much the same results by the simpler and more intelligible method of finding the average order for each of the groups to be compared: (see Appendix V. to Memorandum III).

As before, social influences may be examined first. To elicit the variations in their incidence, I have calculated separately the number of children passing each test at schools attended respectively by children in better social circumstances and by children less fortunately placed. For both extremes a pair of schools have been selected—the two best and the two worst in these particulars. The differences between the rankings for " poor " and " superior " schools are given in the first column of figures in Table XXVIII.

TABLE XXVIII.

Differences in Order of Difficulty for Children differing in Social Status or in Sex.

(The + sign indicates that a test is relatively easier for children of superior social status and for girls :

The — sign indicates that a test is relatively easier for children of inferior social status and for boys.)

Test.	Differences in Order.		Test.	Differences in Order.	
	Social Status.	Sex.		Social Status.	Sex.
Picture (Interpretation)	+ 6	— 1	Differences (King, President)	0	— 1
60 Words	+ 5	— 5			
Reading (2 Facts) ..	+ 5	+ 5	Months	0	— 1
Dictation	+ 5	+ 5	Morning and Afternoon	0	— 1
16 Syllables	+ 4	+ 9	13 Pennies	0	— 2
Reading (6 Facts) ..	+ 4	+ 6	3 Numbers	— 1	+ 3
Differences (Abstract)	+ 4	+ 2	4 Numbers	— 1	+ 2
Sentence Building (1)	+ 4	+ 2	7 Numbers	— 1	+ 2
Picture (Description)	+ 4	+ 1	Sex	— 1	— 1½
Transcription	+ 3	+ 4	2 Numbers	— 1	— 2
Age	+ 3	+ 1	Differences (Concrete)	— 1	— 2
4 Colours	+ 2	+ 6	Absurdities	— 1	— 2
26 Syllables	+ 2	+ 3	Diamond	— 1	— 3
Definition (Class) ..	+ 2	+ 3	Square	— 1	— 5
Re-Statement	+ 2	+ 2½	5 Numbers	— 2	+ 3
3 Rhymes	+ 2	+ 2	Reversed Triangle ..	— 2	+ 2
Sentence Building (2)	+ 2	+ 2	Naming	— 2	+ 1
Mixed Sentences ..	+ 2	+ 2	Easy Questions ..	— 2	— 1
Definition (Use) ..	+ 2	+ 2	Date	— 2	— 1
Definition (Abstract)	+ 2	+ 1	Missing Features ..	— 2	— 1½
Days of Week	+ 2	+ 1	Folded Paper ..	— 2	— 3½
Surname	+ 2	0	2 Weights	— 2	— 4
10 Syllables	+ 1	+ 3	Difficult Questions ..	— 3	— 1
4 Pennies	+ 1	+ 2½	4 Coins	— 3	— 3
Fingers	+ 1	+ 2	Triple Order	— 3½	— 5
6 Syllables	+ 1	+ 1	Change	— 4	— 2
Picture (Enumeration)	+ 1	— 1	Divided Card ..	— 4	— 4
Count 20 to 1	+ 1	— 3	Memory Drawing ..	— 4	— 4
Right and Left ..	+ 1	— 4½	5 Weights	— 4	— 5
Comparing Faces ..	+ ½	+ 2	9 Coins	— 5	— 4
6 Numbers	0	+ 3	Pence and Halfpence	— 5	— 5
Pointing	0	— ½	Problems	— 6	— 3
2 Lines	0	— ½	Suggestion	— 10	— 7

The differences are in some cases profound. Thus, " suggestion " ranked, on an average, fifty-first in the " poor " schools and sixty-first in the " superior " schools—a difference of ten places. A difference so large might easily cause the test to appear as an X.-year test (rather a hard one, no doubt) in the former school, and a XIV.-year (rather an easy one, no doubt) in the latter school.[1]

A comparison of the differences suggests certain special factors, of ability or of experience, that in some degree seem to distinguish children from different social classes. The scale of the tests, with its many-sided, variegated features, casts searching rays upon the mental heterogeneity with which, in training children from diverse homes, the teacher has to cope.

The tests which prove relatively easier for children of " superior " social class fall principally into the following broad groups : (1) Tests requiring linguistic facility, particularly those that depend upon a wide vocabulary— e.g., giving sixty disconnected words in three minutes, building one (or two) sentences to contain three given words, finding rhymes, defining and differentiating between abstract terms, describing or interpreting pictures, defining concrete terms, and summarising a philosophical paragraph. (2) Scholastic tests, especially tests in literary subjects—e.g., the two reading tests, dictation and transcription. (3) Memory tests requiring the repetition of sentences— e.g., six, ten, sixteen, and twenty-six syllables. (Memory tests requiring the repetition of meaningless numbers show small differences in favour, if at all, of the " poor " schools.) (4) Tests depending upon items of information imparted during early life in a cultured home—e.g., surname, age, four colours, number of fingers, weekdays, right and left. In all tests of the foregoing types superiority may be much enhanced where the child is the only child or the youngest child of an educated family.

For the poorer children tests in the following categories prove relatively easier : (1) Tests depending upon familiarity with money—e.g., naming the four commonest coins, and later naming the nine commonest, adding pennies and halfpennies, and giving change. (2) Tests perceptual rather than conceptual in character, especially where manual activity is also introduced : namely, the drawing tests—e.g., memory drawing, possibly drawing the square and diamond ; the weight tests ; reconstructing the divided card, and perhaps naming common objects, as a knife, key, and penny. (3) The more practical tests generally—e.g., performing a triple errand—together with those tests which depend upon practical everyday knowledge—e.g., the easy and difficult questions and the " problems." (4) Tests depending upon critical shrewdness—e.g., noting absurdities, resisting suggestion.

This analysis, though suggestive in results, is but tentative in aim. Figures obtained from a few schools only must not be pressed. Moreover, if one item in the list ranks as relatively easier, this automatically involves an apparent increase in the relative difficulty presented by others. To seek a reason, therefore, for every test displaced would be hazardous and rash. The dominant conclusion that emerges from the differences observable is this : *It is an absolute impossibility to find for the tests an order of difficulty, fixed and universal, which shall be the same for schools of every type and for children of every class.* Confining his verification to a single school, an investigator might easily conjecture that the order here published is flagrantly in error, and readily convince himself that certain tests should be transplanted to other years. The surmise would be but partly true. Success and failure hinge upon a vast array of varying factors, a multiplicity from which sex and

---

[1] The shrewd slum child unblushingly recognises that the examiner is setting a trap for him. The child of nicer manners hardly entertains such a suspicion, and conscientiously searches for minute differences : often his mistakes have nothing to do with the *idée fixe*, which Binet expected to be the chief source of error.

social status are but a pair of instances ; so that every seriation of the tests is bound to be in some measure arbitrary. Its validity increases only with the number and the variety of the specific cases on which it rests. Every arrangement, therefore, must be relative ; none final.

Influence of Sex upon the Individual Tests.

For the two sexes the comparative difficulty of the several tests differs in a like fashion, but to a narrower extent. In the second column of figures shown in Table XXVII. the differences between the orders for boys and girls respectively are presented upon the same principles as before. A plus sign means that a test is relatively easier for the girls ; a minus sign, that it is easier, or at least relatively easier, for the boys. Only those schools have been included from which both departments were examined. Between tests which are easier for girls and those which are easier for children of a better social class there appears a singular parallel. One ground doubtless for the analogy is to be discovered in a similarity of external conditions, in the resemblance between the environment and life-history of girls as contrasted with boys, upon the one hand, and the environment and life-history of children from superior homes as contrasted with children less happily circumstanced, upon the other hand. Sheltered, supervised, detained at home, girls, like children of the better classes, incline to sedentary lives and engage in literary pursuits ; and, like those children, they consequently excel in linguistic work and conversational activities. Boys, like children of both sexes in the slums, have more to do with practical, perceptual; out-of-door pursuits. They are sent to shops with money. They are allowed to play and wander in the streets. They are encouraged to handle tools—to construct toys for amusement and articles for use. No wonder that—like the poorer child, whose lot in life for the present restricts him, and for the future destines him, to menial tasks and manual labour—boys grow more ready with hand and eye than with tongue or pen.

For the weight test and for the easier drawing tests (where the boys are superior), for the tests of reading, colours, memory for syllables (where the girls are superior), the divergences between the figures from opposite sexes are even more pronounced than the divergences between the figures from opposite social classes. Here the parallelism is most apparent. Yet there are exceptions. In memory for numbers—a type of test in which children from the more comfortable social classes are not conspicuously successful—the girls excel. In the picture tests, on the other hand, they exhibit a pre-eminence neither so marked nor so consistent as that displayed by the children of better social status. In similar fashion a few anomalies may be discovered among the performances of the boys. They do well, for example, not only in the money tests, where the poorer children likewise fare to advantage, but also in the tests of counting, where the poorer children figure ill.

Except in the infants' schools, and in one "mixed" school for junior children, the boys and girls thus tested have been educated in separate departments. Many of the differences—especially where such scholastic processes as reading, spelling, drawing, and arithmetic are involved—are but reflections of corresponding differences in the curricula ; they are due, not to inherent nature, but to social environment. The partial parallelism between sex and social differences points also to a similar cause. It hints that in both cases the special characteristics are in a large measure acquired rather than inborn. In "mixed" schools, where the boys and girls have been educated side by side—amongst others, in the junior special (M.D.) schools themselves—such differences are by no means easy to demonstrate, though even here a few deeper sex-peculiarities, as in memory and the recognition of colours and coins, seem not infrequently to recur.

It is instructive to test the foregoing differences by the statistical method of association.[1] Table XXIX. shows the values of the "coefficient of colligation" for all those tests that yield a reliable figure—a figure, that is, whose magnitude is at least three times its probable error. Numerous other tests yield figures positive but smaller, which, judged by their relation to the probable error, are presumably significant, though not implicitly to be trusted.

A plus sign indicates a positive association between tested ability upon the one hand, and either superior status or feminine sex—which, if any, is the superior sex in the Binet tests— upon the other. A minus sign indicates a negative association, that is to say, a superiority in the tests on the side of the boys, or of the poorer schools. For the sex-differences the probable errors range for the most part between ±·02 and ±·04, according to the size of the coefficient ; for the social differences they are, with coefficients of the same size, about twice as large.

TABLE XXIX.

Association between Tests and Differences in Sex and Social Status.

Test.	Coefficients of Colligation (ω).	
	Intelligence and Social Status.	Intelligence and Sex.
Reading (2 Facts) ..	+ ·28	+ ·18
Dictation	+ ·28	+ ·09
60 Words in 3 Minutes ..	+ ·22	+ ·13
Reading (6 Facts) ..	+ ·24	+ ·11
26 Syllables	+ ·18	+ ·15
4 Colours	+ ·18	+ ·12
Sentence Building (1) ..	+ ·20	+ ·08
Picture (Interpretation)..	+ ·23	+ ·02
Memory Drawing	+ ·11	— ·10
Pennies and Halfpennies..	+ ·10	— ·13
9 Coins	+ ·05	— ·11
5 Weights	+ ·03	— ·12
Suggestion	— ·13	— ·21

The table, where it quotes a test, confirms the differences already elicited by the method of rank comparison. Where it omits a test, it warns the reader that the conclusions which the differences in rank then prompted are not irrefragably proved. Sharpest and surest are the differences that arise between tests associated with the feminine sex positively and tests associated with it negatively. With superior status but one test is negatively associated, namely, suggestion. In suggestion, and in suggestion alone, the poorer children commit fewer errors, both relatively and absolutely, than the children in happier circumstances. With this one exception, throughout the series of tests, whether specified in the table or not, there is to be traced an association, unobscure and unequivocal, between social status and tested ability. This was inevitable. As we have seen, the poor children lag by

---

[1] For a brief explanation of this method and of the coefficient of colligation, see Appendix II, p. 229.

one or two years behind those of superior social status. Between social status and intelligence the average coefficient of association is, for the whole set of tests, + ·15. Accordingly, in examining the varying incidence of social factors for the tests separately, the pertinent figure is not the absolute magnitude of the coefficient, but its divergence above or below this value of + ·15. The positive coefficient of + ·10, exhibited in the first column by "pennies and halfpennies," proves, it is true, that actually the better-class children succeed better at this test than the poorer ; but its smallness also implies—and this is its real bearing and significance—that relatively they do not succeed as well with it as they do with most of the other tests. With reading, and the seven tests that follow, they succeed disproportionately and doubly well. So used, the colligation coefficient flings into brighter relief the more prominent of the distinctions already foreshadowed by the method of rank-differences ; and guarantees their validity.

Taking them all in all, however, we may, I think, with justice infer that the variations in the influence of sex and in that of social status are, when measured in this way, neither many in number nor profound in degree. Tests, indeed, like those cited in Table XXIX. exemplify the type of mental process that may well be abandoned in framing a scale intended to apply indifferently to both sexes and to all classes.[1] But they are exceptional. Sex differences and social differences exist, of course, within the mind as well as without it : in character, in interests, and in emotional disposition girls differ much from boys ; and in the absolute level of general intelligence, as a whole, children of better homes excel children from poorer. But, in the relative development of intellectual capacities, considered specifically one by one, girls and boys, children from better homes and children from poorer, diverge, the one group from the other group, in but a few stray instances and then to but a narrow or negligible extent. Such group-differences as can at these points be detected appear dwarfed and swamped by contrast with the immensity of individual differences. That a scale of universal applicability, so far as sex and social status are concerned, is no impracticable chimera, seems evident. Even upon the Binet-Simon tests these two conditions exert nothing like the influence maintained by the factors studied previously—educational attainment, and general goodwill.

Slight and slender as they are, however, the nature of the differences illuminates their origin. It confirms our previous suspicion. Facility in reading, counting, spelling, in the reckoning of money, in the use of words—these and the other special aptitudes enumerated are just such qualities as might be deduced from the peculiar environment and the peculiar traditions amid which the two sexes and the two social groups respectively live and move. If, then, the specific superiority is in either case not inherent but superimposed, may not the general superiority shown by the better-class children be also acquired rather than hereditary ? Does it not emanate from environmental advantages quite as much as from talent inborn ?

In a valid measure of pure intelligence accidents of opportunity should have no weight. Hence, if these conjectures be well grounded, we should be forced to concede a large allowance to the poorer child before we permit ourselves to accept his weak performance as the sign and seal of mental

---

[1] It may be noted that several of the tests enumerated in Table XXIX. follow closely one upon the other in the final order of difficulty already accepted (Table III.). Finding sixty words in three minutes and sentence building (one sentence) are both tests for age XI., and are both specially easy for girls and children of superior social status. Both are linguistic tests. The three tests that follow in age XII. have also the same linguistic character. Dictation and reading (two Facts), again, are similar and adjacent tests. Hence, at these two levels boys and poor children are alike somewhat unfavourably handicapped. Conversely, the fact that both the tests for age XIII. and two out of three of those for age X. are relatively easy for boys and for poor children, makes these levels relatively harder for girls and children of superior status to surmount.

defect. And although, with its strict justice tempered thus by merciful concessions, we may provisionally rely upon the Binet-Simon scale, we should yet spare no effort to construct a scheme that shall be immune to environmental agencies, and no longer prejudiced by the lack of a prosperous history or the want of a cultured home.

9. THE DIAGNOSTIC VALUE OF THE TESTS.

The Validity of the Scale as a Whole.

The veracity of the scale for the diagnosis of intelligence forms a problem that is fundamental. It is a problem upon which few direct observations have as yet been published. How closely does the estimate of a child's intelligence, when measured by the scale as a whole, tally with what is known from prolonged and independent experience ? How effectively does each single test, by the successes or the failures it induces, discriminate between high and low degrees of intelligence ? Do the several tests differ widely from each other in such effectiveness ? If they do so differ, which items are the most effective of all, and which if any, are worthless ? These are vital issues, questions upon which, strangely enough, experimental evidence is still scarce and scanty.

How far, in the first place, do the pronouncements of the scale in its entirety agree with the best judgments available from some independent source of admitted value ?

There is no standard of comparison which can surpass or supersede the considered estimate of an observant teacher, working daily with the individual children over a period of several months or years. This is the criterion I have used. In certain schools the class-teachers were asked to rank the children known to them in an order of general intelligence, compiling separate lists for children in separate age-groups. General intelligence was defined as inborn all-round mental ability. In asking for estimates, emphasis was laid upon two facts : first, that practical out-of-school common sense should be weighed quite as attentively as scholastic ability ; and, secondly, that proper discount should be allowed for age. In grafting together the lists from different classes for children belonging to the same age-group some trouble was experienced. In theory it may be legitimate to assume that, at any rate among children born in the same year, every one in a higher standard is brighter than any one in a lower standard, no matter how low the former child may be placed within the high standard, no matter how high the latter child may be placed within the low. In practice the rule has many exceptions. There exists much overlapping, however unjustifiable, even with children of the same age-group. Nevertheless, in the schools examined, a class-teacher could usually be found who had at some time or another been acquainted with all the members to be compared from separate class-lists, and who could, as it were, dovetail their names into a continuous order of merit. With her aid a single composite series was drafted ; and the head-teacher was always good enough to check and rectify the final ranking.

Correlations with Intelligence among Normals.

With such an order, the order furnished by the Binet-Simon scale was correlated by the usual method of rank-differences. The average coefficients obtained from the different departments in the ordinary elementary schools are given in column 2 of Table XXX. For the senior children rankings were submitted from four departments. Each older age-group, therefore,

Q

comprises about two hundred children. For groups of this number the probable error ranges from about ± ·02 to ± ·05. For children under six the age-groups comprise barely sixty cases each. The probable error here soars to the region of ± ·10 to ± ·14. Hence, below this age the coefficients afford but very rude approximations.

TABLE XXX.

Correlations between Tests and Teachers' Estimates.

Age.	Ordinary Elementary Schools.		Special (M.D.) Schools
	Binet-Simon Tests.	Reasoning Tests.	Binet-Simon Tests.
3—	·33	—	—
4—	·37	—	—
5—	·40	—	—
6—	·56	—	·55
7—	·71	—	·70
8—	·62	—	·77
9—	·48	—	·68
10—	·53	·78	·56
11—	·57	·81	·62
12—	·60	·64	·49
13—	·35	·59	·53
14—	·41	—	·64

Correlations were obtained in a similar way for the children in the special schools (column 4 of Table XXX.). Here, owing to the small size of the groups, the probable errors are large throughout. They range, for all but the extreme ages, between ± ·03 and ± ·06.

Among the normal children, the average correlation between the mental ages, as measured by the Binet-Simon tests on the one hand, and the estimates of intelligence as given by the teachers on the other hand, amounts to barely ·50. If the order for the tests is based upon mental retardation or intellectual ratio, instead of upon mental age, the coefficients change but little. This is inevitable; since within one and the same group the chronological age for the several members varies only within the latitude of twelve months. Possibly in certain schools and certain classes a slight and unavoidable inaccuracy in the teacher's estimates has somewhat reduced the coefficients. This certainly has occurred among the infants. With infants, indeed, all tests and all estimates are bound to be more or less unsatisfactory. But, even with the most ample allowance for sources of error such as these, the scale can by no means arrogate over all other methods for measuring intelligence a sustained, indisputable supremacy. As a control experiment certain reasoning tests—a revised version of the tests previously described by me under the title of Syllogistic Problems[1]—were applied to the same children, and the results correlated with the same observational estimates. These tests are suited for older children only. But at every age available for comparison the correlations which they yield are higher than those furnished by the Binet scale. They average ·70 as contrasted with ·51. With these age-groups, therefore, the teacher's judgment, however inexact, cannot be impugned as the sole cause of the depreciation in the coefficients. If his estimates are correct enough to admit a high correlation in the one

---

[1] *J. Exp. Ped., loc. cit.*, I, 2, p. 101. Cf. also Appendix IV., p. 251.

experiment, they cannot be so incorrect as to generate a low correlation in the other. The inaccuracy lies not with the teacher, but with the test. Hence, *with children in ordinary elementary schools, the Binet-Simon tests, as tests of intelligence, prove but moderately successful.*

Correlation with Intelligence among Defectives.

Among the defectives the correlations between Binet-Simon tests and teachers' estimates rise, with one or two exceptions, to a much higher point. They average ·62, as contrasted with ·53—the figure secured by averaging the coefficients obtained for the corresponding age-groups among the normals. Here, at least among the younger children, the results obtained by the Binet-Simon tests would compare not at all unfavourably with results obtained by other tests.

Once again we may enquire whether peculiarities in the estimates supplied by the teacher are not more responsible than peculiarities in the estimates supplied by the tests. Do not the high correlations among the defectives suggest that here the teachers' estimates may be singularly dependable, just as the low correlations among the normals hinted that there the teachers' estimates might be at fault? This is easily checked. By correlating the estimates of one teacher with that of a second we obtain a measure for the veracity of both. Accordingly, two independent estimates were, whenever possible, secured. Curiously enough, the correlations between the teachers' estimates—the "reliability coefficients," as they are commonly termed—proved to be smaller in the special schools than in the ordinary. In the former they averaged ·81, in the latter ·89. So conspicuously do defectives differ the one from the other that it should seem, indeed, a facile task to rank them ; yet those differences are themselves so anomalous, and affect various capacities in manners so diverse,[1] that, unless the two judges view the children from an angle identically the same, large discrepancies in the judgments may be discovered, and larger deviations from the actual fact may very plausibly be suspected. In any case, the superiority in the correlations among the defectives is too great to be credited simply to a superiority in the standard by which the test-results are tried. Hence, it may with some probability be inferred that *as a test of intelligence the Binet-Simon scale is more trustworthy with defectives than with normals.*

The efficiency of the tests differs at different points upon the scale to no small extent. For normals the tests yield the most accurate measurements at the calendar ages of six, seven, and eight ; for defectives at the mental ages of V., VI., and VII. The superior accuracy at these levels seems traceable rather to the number than to the intrinsic excellence of the tests allotted to these years. With tests as with armies, where a few efficient units fail, a multitude of less efficient units may push home. At the ages of XI. and XII. the coefficients again increase. Here it is, as will be shown later, that the tests which are inherently the most valuable happen to be placed. *The estimates appear least reliable in the middle of the scale, namely at ages IX. and X., and towards the extreme ends, namely, at ages II. to V., and ages XIII., and XIV.*

The Validity of the Several Tests considered Singly.

The general merits of the Binet-Simon method as a whole are no longer contested so hotly as once they were. Most psychologists would concede to it a moderate utility ; few would allow that the earlier pretensions had been vindicated to the full. The agreement has been reached, not so much by

---

[1] Cf. *Distribution and Relation of Educational Abilities*, pp. 63 and 64.

tangible figures and palpable results, as through the vague but cumulative impressions of a great and growing band of authoritative workers. The conclusions in the foregoing paragraphs bring but a fresh reinforcement to a view already prevailing. Touching the collective value of the tests, therefore, taken in their entirety, nothing need be added to what I have already urged elsewhere.[1]

The relative value, on the other hand, of each test-item opens up a new enquiry, an enquiry far more complex in character, far more suggestive in results, and far more obscure in approach. There is, in the whole procession of researches to which the Binet-Simon scale has given birth, no question at once so manifestly fundamental and yet so generally ignored.

The Coefficient of Association.

The method most effective for attacking this problem is not, at the outset, obvious. With Binet's marking a single test yields no graded order. The children either pass or fail. The commoner methods of calculating correlations are, therefore, applicable no longer. In technical language, the relationship is one of " association " rather than of " correlation." Accordingly, some form of " association coefficient " alone seems to offer a fair measure of the correspondence to be investigated.

The application of this concept is new in psychology. Already, however, we have seen minor occasions for its use. In measuring the connection between delinquency and deficiency, between tested ability and sex or social status, its convenience has become plain. But it is in estimating the efficiency of mental tests, particularly mental tests of the dilemma type, that such a coefficient is most sorely wanted. Here, therefore, a brief note may be inserted to explain its nature and possibilities in this regard.

Suppose, first, that no relationship of any kind obtains between superiority in intelligence and success in tests. We should then expect the same proportion of successes among the normal children as among the defective, and the same proportion of defective children among the successful as among the unsuccessful. The degree of association would be zero. Suppose, however, that all the normal children succeed, and all the defective children fail. Then the association might be regarded as complete. Its most natural measure would be + 1. The two cases are hypothetical limits. In practice we are but rarely confronted with a complete correspondence ; and never can we be sure that it is completely absent. Most frequently we encounter intermediate degrees. Here, therefore, intensity of association will be measured by a fraction, by an index varying between zero and unity. Now, it is not sufficient to compare the percentage of defectives passing with the percentage of normals passing ; and to treat the excess of the latter over the former as the measure of association. This is evident upon reflection. Consider a specific case—a deficit of say 40 per cent. in the proportion of defectives passing. The inference is that the test is satisfactory. But such a figure would be far more significant where the proportion of normals passing was 99 per cent. (and that of defectives, therefore, 59 per cent.), or again where it was 41 per cent. (and that of defectives, therefore, 1 per cent.), than where it had some intermediate value, say 70 per cent. (and that of defectives, therefore, 30 per cent.).[2] A more technical mode of comparison, some method of weighting

(1) *Eugenics Review*, July and April, 1914, " The Measurement of Intelligence by the Binet Tests."

(2) This fallacy is committed in almost every one of the rare researches that have essayed comparisons upon this point. Measured by the coefficient described below, the association would be ·66 in the first two cases, and only ·40 in the latter. I have said that the former case is more significant. I am not sure that it would be more reliable. In practice it is always well to avoid such extreme dichotomies.

these different possibilities, is, therefore, needed. For this purpose various formulæ have been proposed. The one I have found most serviceable is that devised by Mr. Udny Yule, and termed by him the "coefficient of colligation." This coefficient becomes identical with the difference between the percentages of normals passing and defectives passing in one special case, the curious case of symmetry, where the sum of these two percentages is equal to one hundred, and where the proportion of normals that pass is the same as the proportion of defectives that fail. If, for example, 70 per cent. of the normals and 30 per cent. of the defectives pass, and, therefore, by symmetry, 30 per cent. of the normals and 70 per cent. of the defectives fail, then 70 minus 30, that is, 40, would be the coefficient of colligation. The condition of symmetry is rare in practice; but theoretically it proves a convenient one to adopt as a standard; and all other cases can by a little arithmetic be reduced to comparable terms. The coefficient has thus a clear and concrete meaning; and the calculation is simple.[1]

By this method, then, the diagnostic value of each test may be gauged. The test may be examined from three points of view : first, its accuracy in distinguishing defectives from normals ; secondly, its accuracy in distinguishing brighter children from duller among normals ; and, thirdly, its accuracy in distinguishing the less deficient from the more deficient among defectives.

The Diagnosis of Defectives as Distinguished from Normals.

The object for which the Binet-Simon scale was originally contrived, the purpose for which it has been most commonly used, is the discrimination of the defective from the normal child. This is its prime function. How effectively does each test contribute to this aim ? The question can be answered by a comparison of the data recorded in Tables III. and IV. Take, for example, the dictation test—the test which, judged by rank-differences,[2] appeared relatively the hardest for the defectives. In the special schools only 18·2 per cent. passed this test. In the ordinary schools 88·1 per cent. of the children of the same ages passed this test.[3] Calculated as described above, the coefficient of colligation is + ·71. Its purport, roughly expressed, is that, other factors such as age being presumed to be equal, there is a reasonably high probability that, of two children thus tested, one failing and the other passing, the one who fails is defective, and the one who passes is normal. For one solitary test, therefore, the differentiation so furnished must be acknowledged as fairly refined.

The coefficients computed in this way for the several tests are exhibited in Table XXXI. In that table the first column of figures may be accepted as measuring the efficacy with which any given test sifts and separates the children into normal and defective. Tests assigned to the first three and last three age-groups (III., IV., and V.—XIV., XV., and XVI.) do not lend themselves to this method of calculation, since, between the ages considered, the former are passed by practically all the genuine normals, and the latter by no genuine defectives.[4]

---

(1) cf. p. 229. As Table XXXI. shows, when obtained from the selected group only, such coefficients should be corrected by Pearson's formula.　　　　(2) Page 155, above.

(3) In either case the average cited is the average of the percentages for the several age-groups—those given in the body of the table—not the percentage based on the total of the actual number passing at each age. The latter would give undue weight to the largest age-group in either set of schools.

(4) As one or other of the proportions approximates either to 100 per cent. or to zero, the possibility of error rapidly increases ; and the coefficient, which then tends to be high, is apt to be illusory. This occurs in cases of two kinds : First, with tests so easy that the normals from the comparable age-groups all pass, except for one or two accidental failures ; and, secondly, with tests so hard that special school children all fail, except for one or two accidental successes. The accidents may be due to the presence in the special schools of a

For the tests included in the table the average degree of association is ·54. The figure implies that, on an average, for any given test, if the proportion of normals failing were the same as the proportion of defectives passing, then of the failures .77 per cent., or about three-quarters, would be defective, and the remainder normal.[1] This is but a moderately good result. On referring to the detailed figures it is plain that *many of the individual tests are of comparatively little value.* In suggestion, 36 per cent.—more than one in three—of the failures would, under the above condition, come from the normal group. Naming coins and months, describing and interpreting pictures, answering the easier practical questions, defining concrete terms by use, are somewhat surprisingly poor ; tests which, like these, depend largely upon experience apparently reveal intelligence only through a dim, distorting medium. On the other hand, some of the linguistic tests seem to offer bright if broken glimpses of it, as through fragments of clear glass. Mixed sentences and rhymes, for example, and (though the coefficients are here not so high as might have been expected) sentence-building, difficult questions and absurdities, provide, with older pupils, an excellent opportunity of watching the working of their minds. Next to these, the scholastic tests— dictation and reading (two and six facts)—and the memory tests—sixteen syllables, five and seven numbers—appear definitely to mark off the ordinary from the special school children. But, as in many cases the defective children were originally nominated for special schools on the very grounds of incapacity for scholastic work, of general inability to learn, and as in some cases they were actually transferred after an examination largely resembling the Binet-Simon method, the evidence thus elicited is hardly conclusive.

Diagnosis of Intelligence among Defectives and among Normals.

The problem of diagnostic value may be approached by two other paths. Since the children of the special schools range from high-grade imbeciles up to ability which is nearly average, the value of each test may be judged by the delicacy with which it distinguishes the duller defectives from the less dull. And since the ordinary schools contain numerous children whose intelligence as tested differs little, if at all, from that of many a so-called defective, a further corroboration may be sought in the accuracy with which each test discriminates the dullest normals from the brighter.

In either type of school the teacher's ranking for intelligence provides a standard of comparison. To increase its reliability, particularly where separate lists for consecutive school classes were mortised together, the larger discrepancies between the original order and the order derived from the Binet-Simon scale in its entirety were closely scrutinised and discussed in detail with the teachers. With their assistance a revised order of merit was then constructed for comparison with the results supplied by each individual test.

---

child normal in intelligence, or to the presence in the elementary school of a child either defective, but not yet transferred, or possibly so nervous as to make slips with tests he should pass. With such extreme percentages the addition of one or more accidental cases will sometimes reduce the coefficient by 10 or 20 per cent. ; their elimination would raise the coefficiency to unity, since, by the definition here adopted, when all the normals pass or all the defectives fail the association is complete, regardless of the proportions failing or succeeding in the opposite group. For these reasons the tests for the ages specified in the text were omitted.

Even if the diagnosis were valid only in one direction, tests revealing such high associations would be of inestimable value, provided that the line between success and failure was natural and sure But that line is both arbitrary and uncertain. With the Binet-Simon tests, as with most mental tests, there are in the actual performances degrees of success and degrees of failure. Of these the marking takes no account. The division it draws is thus purely conventional. A happy chance may tilt a borderline child into nominal success, and bad luck tip him into nominal failure.

[1] Since $77 - (100 - 77) = 54$.

TABLE XXXI.

Coefficients of Colligation (ω) between Success in Tests and Intelligence as Estimated by Teacher.

Test.	Defectives and Normals.	Defectives.	Normals.
Mixed Sentences	·80	·71	·58
Absurdities	·58	·64	·61
Difficult Questions	·62	·52	·46
Sentence Building (1)	·63	·48	·50
3 Rhymes	·77	—	·40
Definition (Abstract)	—	—	·42
Dictation	·71	·61	·31
Memory Drawing	·51	·58	·41
Missing Features	·58	·47	·40
Count 20 to 1	·53	·51	·43
Differences (Concrete)	·50	·49	·47
Reading (6 Facts)	·62	·49	·32
Re-Statement	—	—	·38
60 Words	·62	·40	·39
Transcription	·64	·49	·29
Diamond	·64	·39	·37
Definition (Class)	·60	·41	·39
Differences (Abstract)	—	—	·37
Pence and Halfpence	·48	·48	·42
Change	·43	·50	·44
5 Weights	·46	·47	·42
16 Syllables	·62	·36	·35
5 Numbers	·64	·38	·31
Right and Left	·46	·47	·40
26 Syllables	—	—	·34
Reading (2 Facts)	·65	·40	·29
Sentence Building (2)	·54	·43	·34
4 Numbers	·61	·37	·34
13 Pennies	·61	·43	·29
Differences (King, President)	—	—	·32
Problems	·68	·35	·26
Triple Order	—	·35	·41
6 Numbers	·48	·33	·36
Fingers	·56	·35	·28
Picture (Interpretation)	·38	·46	·31
Divided Card	·49	·39	·31
6 Syllables	—	·32	·32
4 Pennies	—	·34	·31
Reversed Triangle	—	—	·30
Easy Questions	·32	·45	·30
9 Coins	·32	·40	·31
10 Syllables	—	·33	·29
Square	—	·31	·30
Folded Paper	—	—	·31
4 Coins	·56	·30	·23
3 Numbers	—	·31	·27
Definition (Use)	·43	·29	·29
Comparing Faces	—	·31	·25
Days of Week	·57	·23	·20
2 Numbers	—	·29	·25
Picture (Description)	·45	·28	·24
Date	·53	·19	·22
2 Weights	—	·29	·24
4 Colours	—	·33	·21
Picture (Enumeration)	—	·26	·25
Morning and Afternoon	—	·29	·23
2 Lines	—	·27	·24
4 Numbers	—	·27	·24
Naming	—	·24	·25
Pointing	—	·24	·24
Months	·39	·22	·16
Age	—	·26	·22
Sex	—	·20	·23
Surname	—	·25	·18
Suggestion	·28	·18	·15

On a cursory view the foregoing method for extracting a coefficient of association might seem to be inapplicable. An order of merit does not split a group into two distinct portions, as a test will divide it into those who succeed and those who do not. Each test, moreover, draws the line of division at a different level—one may cut off ten per cent., another forty or fifty. Even had the teachers been asked to bisect each age-group into bright and dull, the point of cleavage being determined once and for all, the mere fact that one test cuts the group near the centre and another near the extreme end, while the teachers' division remained constant, might alter the magnitude of the coefficient quite apart from the merits of the test. To obviate these difficulties the following principle was adopted. The teachers' list was divided into two sections ; and for each test the division was made afresh. The point of separation was always chosen so that the brighter section contained, as nearly as possible, the same number of children as had passed the test. Thus, if with a given test thirty children are successful out of sixty, complete association requires that these thirty shall be the top thirty in the teacher's list for intelligence. On this basis, and with these preliminaries, the colligation coefficient was, by the formula given above, computed for each age-group separately, and the several coefficients then averaged.

The average coefficients are shown for each test in the last two columns of Table XXXI. For all the tests attempted by both defectives and normals the grand averages are ·37 and ·32 respectively. Thus the agreement between test and teacher's estimate proves somewhat closer among the defectives than among the normals. But, *with the exception of absurdities and mixed sentences, the value of any single test, as a criterion of normal intelligence, proves singularly low.* And, as was perhaps to have been prophesied, the broader the grouping, the better the result : with the primary division of the whole population into defectives and normals, the proportion of failures and successes shows a nicer correspondence than with further separation of these two smaller and selected groups into more intelligent and less intelligent sub-divisions.

Conclusions as to Relative Value of the Several Tests.

In order of their efficiency, as revealed by each of the three coefficients, the several tests have been ranked, re-ranked, and ranked again. In Table XXXI they are arranged in the order furnished by averaging the three gradings thus obtained.

Judged in this way, suggestion, as a test of intelligence, appears consistently worthless. Many of the simple " general information " questions asked of the younger children—age, sex, surname, knowing features, common objects, colours, time of day, and date—have also but a nugatory value. Contrary to the predictions of many, the picture test, prized by Binet as one of his best, yields, in all three forms, indifferent results. Mere discrimination of pairs of lines, weights, or faces, and—at any rate, with normals—memory for the shorter series of numbers and for the days of the week and the months of the year, have likewise little to do with intelligence.

Of all the tests the most effective are absurdities and mixed sentences : this result admirably bears out the views of the nature of intelligence I have offered in previous reports. There are perhaps some thirty more that can claim a moderately high validity. To classify[1] the more satisfactory tests according to their apparent psychological nature is a somewhat difficult task. They look, to a casual glance, most heterogeneous. In general, they number tests which necessitate neither mere memorized knowledge nor yet mental

---

(1) See Report on a Factor-Analysis of the Binet Tests, where it was shown that the special factors influencing the tests can only be eliminated by including tests of many different kinds.

capacity or skill of any simple kind, but rather the application of that knowledge and the use of that skill in the solution of original problems. Among the money tests, the more serviceable—adding pennies and halfpennies, and giving change—belong manifestly to this type. So, too, counting backward is far more effective than straightforward counting ; and to state the day before yesterday, or the day after to-morrow, would prove a test of much greater utility than Binet's request to recite in their accustomed order all the days of the week. In some the logical element is conspicuous—as in absurdities, difficult questions, definition of abstract terms, and of concrete terms by class, stating differences between concrete and abstract terms, and summarizing a philosophical sentiment. Judged by the teachers' estimates, practical or non-verbal tests—such as observing missing features, drawing from memory, drawing a rhombus, arranging weights in order, and perhaps performing a triple order—should be accorded greater weight in the selection of defectives. On the other hand, the scholastic tests of reading, writing, and spelling, and the harder memory tests, though good, are not so trustworthy as our previous comparison of defectives with normals allowed them to appear. The high diagnostic value of finding rhymes, of finding sixty words in three minutes, and of finding a single sentence containing three given words, implies perhaps that a test of inventiveness or of fertility in association might form a symptomatic exercise. In the cruder puzzle tests, where blind chance, obvious traps, and simple catches have freer play—left hand, right ear, divided card, cut paper—the correlation with intelligence seems attenuated or obscured.

The heterogeneous nature of the more valuable tests is quite consistent with the hypothesis of a common intellectual factor—a central function radiating, in various directions and in different degrees, through all mental activities of whatever kind ; and it points with no unsteady finger to the need for determining, by adequate modes of experiment and statistics, the utility of each individual test regarded as a measure of that function. The more profitable lines of advance, the more fertile regions of research, what types of test deserve most study, what kinds of mental function are most significant, this the foregoing conclusions, and the results gathered by the way, may serve in some measure to suggest.

10. SUMMARY AND CONCLUSION.

The evidence furnished by actual applications of the tests has now been analysed. In its light, the arrangement of the scale and the validity of the method, as revised and re-standardised in my first memorandum, has been fully examined and freely discussed. The outstanding conclusions may be recapitulated in the following terms.

For normal London school children the age-assignments for the several tests differ widely from those prescribed by Binet. Binet's own distribution has had to be stiffened for the earlier years, and eased for the later. In his original arrangement the tests for younger children were much too easy ; those for older children a little too hard ; while for adolescents and supernormals there were, and still are, practically no fit tests whatever. In the new arrangement here presented, the final order of difficulty seems moderately stable, and the increments of difficulty moderately uniform, except for the extreme ages. For normals the order of difficulty bears a general resemblance to the average order suggested by previous investigators ; but differs in certain essentials from that given in the French and the leading American recensions. For defectives the order of difficulty departs significantly from that obtained for normals ; and the differences imply that the tests are not tests of pure capacity.

Between normals and defectives the line of demarcation has been provisionally fixed, for children, at a mental ratio of 70 per cent., and, for adults, at a mental age of eight.

Numerous factors affect the measurement of a child's intelligence by means of the Binet-Simon scale. Sex influences it but little ; social status rather more ; educational, and particularly linguistic, attainments more profoundly than any other factor measurable with exactitude ; while qualitative conditions, such as temperament and emotional attitude, affect it in a degree that is too variable to fix and too elusive to define. Among delinquents, indeed, paucity of educational attainments and peculiarities of emotional attitude will debase their performances and impoverish their replies to a degree that may be gravely deceptive ; and, unless duly discounted, may engender an unwarrantable suspicion that the bulk of them are mentally defective.

In diagnostic value the single tests differ vastly. Many are scholastic ; most are linguistic ; few yield a high correlation with intelligence. The numerous educational tests have an occasional value ; the rarer tests of reasoning a permanent value ; and some tests, such as suggestion, no value at all. In discriminating the child of the special school from the child of the ordinary school, the scale as a whole is tolerably successful ; in grading the special school children amongst themselves it is almost as efficient ; in grading the normal children amongst themselves it is less accurate than other tests that are now to hand ; and in detecting supernormal ability it is altogether invalidated by the anomalies and the lacunæ among the problems for the higher mental years.

Such conclusions will be thought but a faint and faltering recommendation for the Binet-Simon scale. But is there any better scale to fill its place ? The ordinary function of such tests should be to estimate intelligence among children backward in attainments and still young in age, but in other respects forming for the examiner an unsolved problem, an unknown Perhaps. This requirement can no longer be deferred. For such a purpose the Binet-Simon scale is unquestionably superior to the unaided judgment of the examiner ; for such a purpose, too, there is as yet, besides the Binet-Simon scale, no other method available, at once surpassing it in simplicity, equalling it in accuracy, or approaching it in prestige. Workers untrained in a psychological laboratory feel instantly that here is a non-technical instrument which they can understand and apply. By its aid the intelligence of tens of thousands has been tested and measured—young and old, supernormal and defective, moral and immoral, the convict in jail and the pauper in the almshouse, rural labourers and university students, schools by the hundred, army recruits by the battalion, in short, men, women, and children from almost every sphere of life. Pending the construction of some more scientific scale, whose validity has been as widely tested and whose authority is as generally revered, the Binet-Simon scale must, for rough and practical purposes, still hold and monopolise the field.

But its value should not be overrated ; and its temporary adoption should not be suffered to block the path of further enquiry. The unwarranted claims advanced on its behalf by votaries in foreign quarters have among academic psychologists in this country become a commonplace and a byword. The routine examiner, it is true, busy with practical diagnosis, remains generally unconscious of the frail foundation upon which his standards of comparison repose. But the rigourist and the precisian have been disposed unflinchingly to abandon—at any rate, for scientific purposes—a scale whose worth is so ill attested, and whose construction is so feebly based. In its place they look for the elaboration of some fresh scheme, established anew upon investigations, broader and more detailed, into the reliability, the variability, and the significance of the numerous mental tests that are now ready to hand.

Such a quest is imperative. But it will entail long years of co-operative research. The period will be longer still before the fruits can command the measure of popular recognition already accorded to the present scale.

Meanwhile, when new buildings have not been finished, it is wiser to repair than to demolish the old. While waiting for the slow and sure, we must make shift with the rough and the ready. The need is urgent ; the field is vast. Throughout the country there is a cry for a practical mental test—for a handy method, which can be immediately applied by teachers, doctors, and social workers ; for a snapshot instrument which can be easily manipulated by the routine examiner, engrossed with the administration of the Mental Deficiency Acts and too pressed to await the experience or the appliances of a laboratory ; for a pocket rule, which will furnish diagnostic measurements in terms of some plain concept, like the mental year, obvious, moderately exact, and instantly intelligible to a magistrate or a jury, to whom the technicalities of percentiles and standard deviations would be esoteric gibberish. To satisfy such a demand, scientific exactitude may pardonably be postponed for the prompt delivery of an acceptable, workable substitute. And such a substitute, provisional yet ready-made, is to be found in the Binet-Simon scale.

APPENDIX I.

AGE-ASSIGNMENTS FOR THE SEVERAL TESTS.

In Table **XXXII.** I have collected the age-assignments suggested for the several Binet tests by the results of the chief preceding investigations. Three shorter compilations, similar in aim, have been published—an American by Carleton Bell, a German by Meumann, and an Italian by Saffiotti. From these the present differs chiefly by the addition of data more recently published, including more particularly those of eight or nine English investigators. With the exception of the earliest, English investigations, even when available at the time of publication, have been almost entirely ignored by the foregoing compilers.

In comparing the various age-assignments then available, the American compiler stated that " there is a surprising agreement in the results of the different investigators." Such a conclusion could hardly be drawn from the present compilation. Indeed, my chief object in publishing such a collation as the table which follows is to emphasise the absence hitherto of any acceptable set of age-assignments. If anything, the figures minimise the discrepancies ; for often, when an investigator had no data whatever, and sometimes even when he had obtained contradictory data, he has still pronounced his adherence to Binet's own assignment. But even Binet's own assignments, it will be seen, differed considerably from each other and from those indicated by his experimental data.

The ages entered below are, in the first place, those expressly suggested by the investigators themselves, whenever such assignments are recorded in their published articles. A difficulty, however, arises when the investigator departs, without explanation, and sometimes apparently by oversight, from his avowed criterion. Moore, for example, adopting a 70 per cent. criterion, definitely retains Binet's age-assignment for counting four pennies and describing pictures, although in his tables nearly, if not quite, 100 per cent. pass the test at the preceding age. In such cases I have seldom ventured to correct the assignments given by the investigators themselves. On the other hand, where no assignment is so given, I have myself inserted in brackets any suggestion that seemed deducible from the investigator's own figures and criteria. Where neither assignment nor criteria are suggested by the investigator himself, I have, after the practice of previous compilers, used a 75 per cent. criterion.

The following abbreviations are used :—

Ad. = adult.

a = altered ; *i.e.*, the test referred to was modified considerably by the investigator named.

e = judged by the investigator specified to be too easy for the assignment proposed in Binet's 1908 scale, and therefore to be assigned to an earlier unspecified age.

h = judged by the investigator specified to be too hard for the assignment proposed in Binet's 1908 scale.

r = rejected by the investigator specified as unsuitable.

s = considered by the investigator specified to be too much influenced by school attainments.

t = considered by the investigator specified to be too much influenced by training.

m = considered by the investigator specified to be too mechanical.

From a study of the table two obvious conclusions may be drawn. First, a reinvestigation of the age-assignments was urgently desirable. Secondly, such assignments will probably require to be investigated afresh for different conditions and different localities.

Of the sixty-five tests, only four are assigned to the same age-group by all investigators. These are without exception three-year-old tests which have not been scrutinised very thoroughly or by very many experimenters. With these exceptions, for not one test is there complete agreement as to the age to which it should be assigned. For eight tests, again mostly tests which but few investigators have used, the assignments differ only by one year. The commonest result, occurring in some fifteen cases, is for a test to be assigned now to a year above, now to a year below, the original or the average assignment—thus fluctuating over a range of three years. In about the same number the assignments spread over a range of four years; and in almost as many cases, namely, fourteen, over a range of five. Three tests—definition (abstract), building one sentence out of three words, mixed sentences—have a range of six years; four tests—absurdities, seven numbers, three rhymes, twenty-six syllables—a range of seven; the test of five weights has a range of eight years; and that of sixty words a range of nine.[1] Several of these extremes are explicable by differences in procedure. This explanation, however, is neither the sole nor the chief one. The procedure for memorising seven numbers is fairly definite, and simple to comply with; yet, while Binet assigns it to age XV. and Miss Johnston to adult years, such reliable investigators as Bobertag and Miss Taylor assign it to age X. Progress from year to year being more conspicuous at a younger age, the fluctuation in the range for tests at this period is much smaller. Yet even so straightforward a test as naming the four primary colours is assigned by Miss Taylor and by Decroly and Degand to age IV., and by Binet, Bobertag, Saffiotti, and others to double that age, namely, to age VIII. The two most stable tests appear to be counting backwards and pointing to right and left.

As a rule, the age-assignments based on the present investigation conform fairly well with the most usual assignments of previous investigators. In four tests, however, an assignment is suggested which has never been put forward before. In two cases the novelty is perhaps accidental. Six syllables, now shown as the easiest test for age IV., has, by the few who have pronounced upon it, been assigned hitherto to age III., the age prescribed by Binet. Twenty-six syllables, assigned sometimes to XI. or XII., sometimes to XV. or Adult, has never been awarded the intermediate age of XIV. But for suggestion no previous investigator has obtained an age-assignment so high as XIII.,[2] or for change one so low as VIII. The innovations may be due to accidents of the investigation or to peculiarities of London children. It is an issue which further research can alone decide.

---

[1] Adult age is here throughout counted as equivalent to age XVI.

[2] My results would agree with Miss Taylor's in making this test far easier than Binet believed, were it not for the conscientious efforts of my older and brighter subjects to find minute differences as described above (p. 207). The ease of " Change " appears to be due partly to the practical familiarity of the London child with money values and shopping and partly to the emphasis placed at an earlier age in London schools upon problem arithmetic, often illustrated in concrete form by real or imitation coins.

TABL

AGE-ASSIGNMENTS FOR THE SEVERAL TESTS

Test.	Binet and Simon.					Decroly & Degand.	Goddard.	Wallin.	Bobertag.	Chotzen.	Johnston.
	1905	1908	1909	1911	1911 (L. & M.)	1910	1911	1911	1911	1911	1911
AGE III											
Pointing	III	III	III	III	—	e	III	—	—	—	—
2 Numbers	III ?	III	III	III	—		III	—	—	—	—
Sex	—	IV	IV	IV	—	t	IV	—	—	—	—
Surname	—	III	III	III	—	t	III	—	—	—	—
Naming	IIIa	IV	IV	IV	—	e	IV	—	—	—	—
Picture (Enumeration)	IIIa	III	III	III	—		III	—	—	—	—
AGE IV											
6 Syllables	—	III	III	III	—	—	III	—	—	—	—
3 Numbers	V	IV	IV	IV	—	—	IV	—	—	—	—
4 Pennies	—	V	V	V	—	t	V	e	V	V	—
2 Lines	Va	IV	IV	IV	—	—	IV	—	—	—	—
Comparing Faces	—	VI	VI	VI	VII	III	VI	—	VI	VI	VI
AGE V											
Triple Order	—	VI	VI	VII	VII	III	VI	h	VI	VII	V
Square	—	V	V	V	—	—	V	—	V	VI	—
10 Syllables	—	V	V	V	—	—	V	—	V	V	—
Age	—	VI	VI	—	—	t	—	h	VI	VII	—
Morning and Afternoon	—	VI	VI	VI	VI	—	VI	—	VII	IX	VIII
4 Colours	—	VIII	VIII	VII	VIII	IV	VII	e	VIII	VIII	VI
4 Numbers	—	—	—	—	—	—	—	—	V	—	—
2 Weights	V	V	V	V	—	—	V	—	V	V	—
AGE VI											
Fingers	—	VII	VII	—	—	t	—	e	VII	VII	—
13 Pennies	—	VII	IV ?	VI	VII	m	VII	e	VI	VII	VI
Diamond	—	VII	VII	Vi	VII	—	VII	h	VIII	VIII	VII
Transcription	—	VII	VII	—	—	s t	—	—	VIIr	VIII	—
Days of Week	—	IX	IX	—	—	m	—	e	VIII	IX	—
4 Coins	—	VII	IV ?	—	—	m	VIII	e	VIIa	VIIa	—
Divided Card	—	V	V	V	—	—	V	h	VI	VII	—
Definition (Use)	V	VI	VI	VI	VI	III	VI	—	V	V	VI
5 Numbers	VII	VII	VII	VIII	IX	—	VIII	h	VII	IX	VIII
Picture (Description)	—	VII	IV ?	VII	VII	—	VII	h	VII	VII	VII
16 Syllables	VII–XI	VI	VI	—	—	—	—	h	VI	VII	—
Right and Left	—	VI	VI	VII	VII	—	VI	—	VII	VII	VII
AGE VII											
Missing Features	—	VII	VII	VIII	VIII	—	VII	—	VII	VII	VIII
Pence and Halfpence	—	VIII	VIII	VII	VIII	—	VIIIa	—	VII	VIII	VII
Differences (Concrete)	VII	VIII	VIII	VIII	VIII	e	VIII	—	VIII	IX	—
Dictation	—	VIII	VIII	—	—	s t	—	h	VIIr	IX	—
AGE VIII											
Reading (2 Facts)	—	VIII	VIII	—	—	s t	—	—	IX ?	IXa	—
Easy Questions	VIIa	X	X	IX	IX	—	X	e	VIII	VIII	X
Count 20 to 1	—	VIII	VIII	VIII	VIII	s t	VIII	h	VIII	IX	IX
Date	—	IX	IX	VIII	VIII	—	IX	—	IX	X ?	X
Change	—	IX	IX	IX	IX	—	IX	h	IX	IX	—
6 Numbers	—	—	—	—	—	—	X	—	X	—	—
AGE IX											
Months	—	X	X	IX	IX	m	IX	—	(X)	(X) ?	IX
9 Coins	—	X	X	IX	IX	—	X	e	X	X	XI
Reading (6 Facts)	—	IX	IX	—	—	—	—	h	(Xa)	Xa	—
Definition (Class)	—	IX	IX	IX	X	—	IX	h	IX	IX	X
AGE X											
5 Weights	XIa	IX	IX	X	XII	V–VI	IX	h	IX	X ?	X
Sentence Building (2)	—	X	Xa ?	X	XII	XI	X	—	X	—	XIII
Memory Drawing	IX–XI ?	—	—	X	XII	—	X	—	—	—	—
AGE XI											
Absurdities	—	XI	XII	X	XII	VI	XI	—	XI–XII	—	XIII
Difficult Questions	VII–XIa	X	X	X	XII	—	X ?	—	XI–XII	—	XI
60 Words	—	XI	XII	XII	XIII ?	e	XI	h	—	—	XII
7 Numbers	—	XII	XV	XV	—	—	XII	h	X	—	Ad.
Sentence Building (1)	XII ?	XI	XII	XII	XII	—	XI	—	XI–XII	—	XV

XXXII.

ACCORDING TO DIFFERENT INVESTIGATORS.

Shrubsall	Terman & Childs	Carleton Pell	Kuhlman	Strong	Dumville	McIntyre & Rogers	Eltes	Winch	Taylor	Saffiotti	Moore	Stanford Revision	Burt
1911	1912	1912	1913	1913	1913	1914	1914	1914	1916	1916	1917	1917	1919
III	—	—	III	—	—	—	—	III	—	—	—	III	III
IV	III	—	IV	—	—	IV	—	IV	IV	—	IV	III	III
h	—	—	III	—	—	—	—	III	—	—	—	III	III
IV	III	—	IV	—	—	IV	—	III	IV	—	IV	III	III
h	III	—	III	—	—	—	—	III	—	—	—	III	III
h	—	—	III	—	—	—	—	IV	—	—	—	III	IV
IV	III	—	IV	—	—	IV	—	IV	IV	—	IV	III	IV
—	IV	—	V	—	IV	IV	IVa	IV	IV	—	IV	IV	IV
IV	III?	—	IV	—	—	III	—	IV	IV	—	IV	IV	IV
—	IV	VII	VI	VI	V	IV	V	Va	V	VI	V	V	IV
e	IV	VI	VI	VII	IV	V	V	VI	VI	VI	V	V	V
—	IV	—	V	—	IV	V	VII	V	V	VI	V	IV	V
h	V?	—	V	—	V	V	rVa	r?	—	VI	V	(IVa)	V
—	V?	—	VI	VII	—	VI	VI	—	VI	—	V	V	V
—	V	VIII	r	VI	V	VI	V	V	IV	VIII	V	VI	V
—	VI	—	v	—	V	—	IV	V	IV	V	—	IV	V
—	III	—	v	—	—	V	V	VI	VII	V?	VI	V	V
—	VI	—	VII	—	—	VI	—	VI	—	—	—	VII	VI
—	VI	VII	r	VI	VII	VI	—	V	VI	VIIIa	VI	VI	VI
—	VII	VII	VIII	VI	VI	VII	VII	VII	VI	VIII	VI	VII	VI
VI	VII?	—	r	VIII	VI	VI	VI	VI	VI	—	—	—	VI
e	VII?	—	r	VIII	—	VI	VI	VI	—	—	—	VII	VI
—	VII	—	VII	—	—	VII	VIIa	VIII	VII	—	—	VI	VI
—	IV	—	V	—	VI	V	VII	VIII	VII	VIIIa	V	V	VI
—	IV	—	VI	VI	VI	VI	—	VI	VI	VII	VI	V	VI
—	VIII	—	VII	VIII	VI	VI	VI	VI	VI	VIII	VI	VII	VI
—	VII	—	VII	VI	VI	VI	VI	VI	VI	—	VII	VII	VI
—	VII	—	—	—	VII	VII	Va	VIII	—	—	—	VI	VI
VIh	VI	—	VI	VII	VI	VI	—	VI	VI	—	VI	VI	VI
—	VII	—	VII	VI	VIII	VI	VI	V	—	VIII	VII	VI	VII
—	IX	—	VIII	IXa	VIII	IX	VIII	VII	VII	X	VII	(IXa)	VII
—	VIII	—	VIII	VI	VII	VIII	—	VII	VII	VII	VII	VII	VII
—	VIII	—	r	—	VII	—	VII r	—	—	—	VIII	VIII	VII
h	IX?	—	r	X	—	IX	r	—	—	—	VIII	VIII	VIII
—	IXa	—	X	X	—	X	VIII	VII	VIII?	VIII	VIII	VIII	VIII
he	VIII	—	VIII	IX	IX?	IX	—	VII	VIII	VIII	VIII	IX	VIII
—	IX	IX	IX	X	IX?	IX	—	r	VIII	VIII	IX	IX	VIII
—	X	X	IX	XI	—	IX	—	VIII	IX	XI	IX	IX	VIII
—	X	—	IX	XI	—	—	—	—	—	—	—	(Xa)	VIII
—	—	—	VIII	IX	—	X	r	—	IX	IX	IX	IX	IX
—	X?r	—	IX	VII	—	X	—	—	IX	—	X	(VIIIa)	IX
—	XII?a	—	r	r	—	IX	(IXa)	—	—	IX	—	(Xa)	IX
—	—	X	IX	X	—	XII	X	—	IX	—	X	VIIIa	IX
—	IX	—	IX	X	—	XII	VIII	—	X	VIII	IX	IX	X
—	XI?	XI-XII	r	XI	—	X	—	—	X	—	IX	IX	X
—	X	—	X	XI-XII	—	—	—	—	IX	—	IX	X	X
—	XII	XI-XII	XI	XI	—	XII	—	—	XI?	XI	X	X	XI
—	XI	XI-XII	r	X	—	X	—	—	X	(XI?)r	X	X	XI
—	XV?	XIII-XIV	XI	VII-VIII	—	XV	—	—	XI	—	XI	XI	XI
—	XIII	—	XII	XII	—	XIII	—	—	XII	—	XI	(XIVa)	XI
—	X	XIII-XIV	X	XI	—	X	—	—	XII	—	XI	—	XI

Test.	Binet and Simon.					Decroly & Degand.	Goddard.	Wallin.	Bobertag.	Chotzen.	Johnston.
	1905	1908	1909	1911	1911 (L. & M.)	1910	1911	1911	1911	1911	1911
AGE XII											
3 Rhymes	IX+	XII	XV	XV	—	—	XI	e	XI-XII	—	XV
Mixed Sentences	—	XI	XII	XII	XII	—	XI	h	XI-XII	—	XIII
Picture (Interpretation)	—	XII	XV	XV	—	—	XV	—	—	—	—
AGE XIII											
Suggestion	XI	—	—	XII	—	—	XII	—	—	—	—
Problems	—	XII	XV ?	XV	—	—	XII	h	—	—	—
AGE XIV											
26 Syllables	—	XII	XV	XV	—	—	XII	h	X	—	XV
Definition (Abstract)	IX ?	XI	XII	XII	XIII ?	XIII	XII	h	XI-XII	—	XIV
AGE XV											
Folded Paper	XII	XIII	—	Ad.	—	h	Ad.	h	—	—	—
Differences (Abstract)	—	XIII	—	Ad.	—	h	Ad.	h	—	—	—
Reversed Triangle	—	XIII	—	Ad.	—	h	Ad.	h	—	—	—
AGE XVI											
Re-Statement	—	—	—	Ad.	—	—	Ad.	—	—	—	—
Differences (King, President)	—	—	—	Ad.	—	—	Ad.	—	—	—	—

The following are the several references in which the data utilised above are to be found :—

(1) Binet, A., and Simon, Th., *The Development of Intelligence in Children.* (Transl. by E. S. Kite, from *L'Année Psych.*, 1905, pp. 245–336.) Pp. 93–139 with relevant tables. (The age-assignments are often neither precise nor explicit ; and in consequence my interpretation of them differs from the convenient tabulation given by Saffiotti, *loc. cit. inf.*, Tabella I., pp. 62 *et seq.* ; cf. Tabella XVIII., pp. 118 *et seq.*)

(2) *Id., ibid.* (from *L'Année Psych.*, 1908, pp. 1–90). Table on pp. 238–9. (" Right and Left " is omitted by oversight.)

(3) Binet, A., *Les Idées Modernes sur les Enfants*, 1909, p. 126. (Some of the assignments are so curious as to suggest printer's errors.)

(4) Binet, A., *loc. cit. sup. sub* (1) ; (from *L'Année Psych.*, 1911, pp. 145–201). Table, p. 276.

(5) *Id., ibid.* Table II., p. 279. (Taken with a 75 per cent. criterion, following previous compilers. Data obtained by Levistre and Morlé.)

(6) Decroly, O., and Degand, J., *Archives de Psych.*, 1910, pp. 81–108.

(7) Goddard, H. H., *The Binet-Simon Measuring Scale : Revised Edition*, 1911. Table on pp. 10–11. (The compiler states that the arrangement "embodies our own experience, while following Binet's order as closely as we can." Goddard's tables of actual figures—see *Ped. Sem.*, 1911, pp. 232 *et seq.*—would give, with a 75 per cent. criterion, larger and more numerous divergences.)

(8) Wallin, J. E. W., *Experimental Studies of Mental Defectives.* Table VIII., p. 49 ; cf. also pp. 43–44 *et seq.*

(9) Bobertag, O., " Über Intelligenzprüfungen nach der Methode von Binet und Simon." *Z. f. angew. Psych.*, V., 1911 ; VI., 1912. Table on p. 523 ; supplemented by Tables on pp. 441 and 472 *ibidem, ap.* Chotzen, *loc. cit. inf.* (The tables do not quite tally, *e.g.*, as regards assignment of Definition (Class), Picture (description), 5 Weights, Reading.)

XII—*continued.*

	Terman & Childs.	Carleton Bell.	Kuhlman.	Strong.	Dumville.	McIntyre & Rogers.	Eltes.	Winch.	Taylor.	Saffiotti.	Moore.	Stanford Revision.	Burt.
11	1912	1912	1913	1913	1913	1914	1914	1914	1916	1916	1917	1917	1919
	—	—	XII	XI	—	XIV	—	—	XIV	—	XII	IXa	XII
	XII	—	XI	XII	—	Ad.	—	—	XII	XIV	XII	XII	XII
	XV	—	XI	—	—	XII	—	—	XIII	—	XII	XII	XII
	XII	—	XII	h	—	—	XV	—	X	—	XII	—	XIII
	XIII	—	XII	h	—	XIV	—	—	XIV	—	XIV	XIV	XIII
	XII	—	XIIa	h	—	Ad.	—	—	Ad.	XII	(XV ?)	—	XIV
	XIV?	XIII–XIV	XI	XII	—	Ad.	—	—	XIII	—	(XV ?)	XIIa	XIV
	—	—	XV	—	—	Ad.	—	—	—	—	(Ad. ?)	(Sup. Ad.)	XV
	—	—	XV	—	—	Ad.	—	—	—	—	(Ad. ?)	Ad.	XV
	Ad.	—	XV	—	—	Ad.	—	—	—	—	(Ad. ?)	—	XV
	Ad.	—	XV	—	—	—	—	—	—	—	(Ad. ?)	(Sup. Ad.)	XVI
	Ad.	—	r	—	—	—	—	—	—	—	(Ad. ?)	XIV	XVI

(10) Chotzen, F., " Die Intelligenzprüfungsmethode von Binet-Simon bei Schwachsinnige Kindern." *Z. f. Angew. Psych.* VI., 1912. Table on p. 441.

(11) John·ton, K. L., "M. Binet's method for the Measurement of ·Intelligence : Some Results." *Journ. Exp. Ped.*, I., 1, 1911, pp. 25 *et seq.* (Assignments inferred from figures given for tests mentioned as ill placed. Where no data are recorded we are presumably to infer that the writer agrees with the 1908 age-assignments, although I have not ventured in such cases to insert those assignments on this slender assumption.)

(12) Shrubsall, F. C., "The Examination of Mentally Defective Children." *School Hygiene*, 1911, pp. 613 *et seq.* This investigation, one of the earliest undertaken in this country, is especially suggestive for those examining special school cases, and is by no means as well known as it should be.

(13) Terman, L. M., and Childs, S. M., "A Tentative Revision and Extension of the Binet-Simon Scale." *J. Educ. Psych.*, III., 1912. Table on pp. 277–8. (Meumann and Saffiotti have followed J. C. Bell, *loc. cit. inf.*, who, writing at an earlier date, was forced to deduce the age-assignments from the earlier table of figures published on pp. 72–3 of the same *Journal.*)

(14) Bell, J. Carleton, " Recent Literature on the Binet-Simon Tests." *J. Educ. Psych.*, III., 1912, p. 107. (Recommendations deduced from previous investigators' assignments. Where no ages are mentioned the writer would apparently agree with Binet's 1911 arrangement ; as, however, he has no new data, I have not ventured to add his authority for the old assignments. There has been some confusion about this compilation. It is attributed sometimes to C. J. Bell and C. Hood (Meumann and Saffiotti) and sometimes to Catherine Bell (Saffiotti). Students who refer to Saffiotti's Tabella XVIII. should observe that in the *erratum* on p. 278 he withdraws his use of these assignments.)

(15) Kuhlmann, F. " A Revision of the Binet-Simon System." *J. Psycho-Asthen., Mon. Suppl.*, 1912.

R

(16) Strong, A. C. "Three Hundred and Fifty Children measured by the Binet-Simon Scale." *Ped. Sem.*, XX. 4., 1913, pp. 485 *et seq.* Table IX, pp. 509–10.

(17) Dumville, B. "A Trial of Binet's Tests on Five-Year-Olds." *J. Exp. Ped.*, II., 2, 1913. (Assignments in third table on p. 116, supplemented from first and second tables *ibid.*)

(18) McIntyre, J. L., and Rogers, A. L. "The Measurement of Intelligence in Children by the Binet-Simon Scale." *Brit. J. Psych.*, VII., 3, 1914. (Table VII., p. 284.)

(19) Eltes, Mátyás. "A Binet-Simon-féle intelligencia-vizsgálat eredménye magyar gyermekeken." *A Gyermek*, VIII., 1914, pp. 257 *et seq.*

(20) Winch, W. H. "Binet's Mental Tests." *Child Study*, VI., 7, 1913, and following numbers.

(21) Taylor, N. G. R. "Further Data towards the Study of the Binet-Simon Scale." *J. Exp. Ped.*, III., 4, 1916. Table A, p. 265.

(22) Saffiotti, F. V. *La Misura dell' Intelligenza nei Fanciulli.* Tabella XVIII., pp. 118–123.

(23) Moore, R. C. "Age-Scale Methods of Measuring Intelligence." *J. Exp. Ped.*, V., 2, 1919. Table XII., p. 97. (Supplemented by data in previous article, *ibid.*, IV., 1917, pp. 114 *et seq.*)

(24) Terman, L. M. *The Stanford Revision and Extension of the Binet-Simon Scale*, 1917.

(25) Burt, C., *hoc op.* Table III., p. 132–3.

Of the earlier collations cited in the text that of Carleton Bell is to be found *loc. cit. sup.* (14), Table, pp. 104–5. It reviews only the half-dozen investigations then available. Meumann (*Vorlesungen zur Einfuhrung in die Experimentelle Pädagogik.* 2te Aufl., 1913. Pp. 273–5), practically repeats Carleton Bell. Saffiotti (*loc. cit. sup.* (22). Tabella XVIII.) repeats Meumann with the addition of about half a dozen more recent studies. Owing to the ease with which misprints and misunderstandings creep into such tables, I have endeavoured, as far as possible, to go for my own compilation to original sources ; but have found the other collections—particularly Saffiotti's—of great assistance in checking or supplementing my own deductions from earlier work.

APPENDIX II.

ON THE CALCULATION OF COEFFICIENTS OF ASSOCIATION.

The conception designated in the text by the name association, and the formulæ for expressing the degree of such association in quantitative terms, may best be understood by reference to a table on the following plan We wish to determine the degree of interdependence, let us say, between deficiency, on the one hand, and delinquency (or sex, social status, success at a given test), on the other hand. In such a case we have two main lines of classification, each line dividing the total population into two classes— a negative and a positive, each line crossing the other, and so yielding four sub-classes. Thus :—

TABLE XXXIII.

Fourfold Table to illustrate the Conception of Association.

		FIRST CLASSIFICATION (*e.g.*, according to Morality).		TOTALS.
		POSITIVE (*e.g.*, Delinquent).	NEGATIVE (*e.g.*, Non-Delinquent).	
SECOND CLASSIFICATION. (*e.g.*, according to Intelligence.)	POSITIVE (*e.g.*, Defective.)	Positive-positive (*e.g.*, Defective-delinquents) P_p	Positive-negative (*e.g.*, Defective-non-delinquents). N_p	$p = P_p + N_p$
	NEGATIVE (*e.g.* Non-Defective).	Negative-positive (*e.g.*, Non-defective delinquents) P_n	Negative-negative (*e.g.*, Non-defective non-delinquents) N_n	$n = P_n + N_n$
Totals		$P = P_p + P_n$	$N = N_p + N_n$	$P + N = p + n =$ $P_p + P_n + N_p + N_n$

The formula used in the foregoing memorandum for calculating the degree of association is as follows :—

Coefficient of colligation (ω)

$$= \frac{1 - \sqrt{\dfrac{N_p\, P_n}{P_p\, N_n}}}{1 + \sqrt{\dfrac{N_p\, P_n}{P_p\, N_n}}},$$

229

where $P_p \equiv$ the number from the positive subdivision of the second classification (p, *e.g.*, defectives) that is found in the positive subdivision of the first classification (P, *e.g.*, delinquents) and $P_n \equiv$ the remainder of the latter (*e.g.*, non-defective delinquents) ; $N_p \equiv$ the number from the positive subdivision of the second classification (p, *e.g.*, defectives, as before) that is found in the negative subdivision of the first classification (N, *e.g.*, non-delinquents) and $N_n \equiv$ the remainder of the latter (*e.g.*, non-defective non-delinquents). The probable error of this formula is as follows :—

$$\text{p.e.} = 0 \cdot 6745 \; \frac{1 - \omega^2}{4} \sqrt{\frac{1}{P_p} + \frac{1}{P_n} + \frac{1}{N_p} + \frac{1}{N_n}}$$

It is convenient to express the subdivisions of the two main classes as percentages, thus putting P and N both $= 100 : 5 \cdot 6$ per cent., for example, of the delinquents and $1 \cdot 5$ per cent. of the non-delinquents, are defective. P_n then $= 100 - P_p$; and $N_n = 100 - N_p$. The coefficient can thus be obtained at once from two proportions or percentages only ; in the above instance it is consequently unnecessary to discover what percentage of the defective and non-defective population are delinquent.[1] Accordingly, I have constructed a graph which enables the investigator to read off at a glance the approximate value of the association coefficient directly two such percentages are obtained (Figure 27).

In educational enquiries there are numerous problems that require the determination of some such measure of association. In the foregoing memorandum many instances have already been encountered, notably in estimating the value of individual tests for mental deficiency. Other occasions arise where it is required to estimate the influence upon educational progress of new methods of teaching or special conditions of school work, *e.g.*, open-air classes, free discipline, etc. In all such cases it should be observed that at least two proportions are essential. Too often teachers, for example, are content simply to record a marked progress in the group selected for the experiment without reference to progress under normal conditions. Plainly (to revert to the instance employed above), however large be the number of defectives among the delinquents, this can yield no indication of any association between the two conditions until we know the number of defectives among the non-delinquent population. A control-group is indispensable.

The reader should realise that there are other ways of determining associations from data in the above form. In Yule's *Introduction to Statistics* a simpler coefficient Q is suggested, the formula for which is identical with the above except for the omission of the signs for square-root. I have calculated many coefficients for tests and other mental functions by both formulæ, and in most cases found ω to be more satisfactory. Q is much larger than ω, *e.g.*, for $\omega = \cdot 5$, $Q = \cdot 8$. With Q the differentiation among the higher values will thus be disproportionately small. To those more familiar with such coefficients of correlation as r, Q yields results that are confusingly high. ω, on the other hand, possesses this advantage : it is mathematically equivalent to the product-sum correlation, r, for the corresponding symmetrical fourfold table,[2] *i.e.*, for the case where each of the four main classes,

---

[1] Working from the other two percentages might even give widely different coefficients. It should be noted that a coefficient of unity might mean either that all delinquents are defective (which would be nearly true of deficiency in educational attainments) or that all defectives are delinquent (which is grossly untrue of defectives either in general intelligence or in educational attainments), or in both.

[2] Calculated, however, it should be added, as if the distributions were not normal but rectilinear, that is, as a correlation of ranks where the ranking runs to no more than two places, and without any correction whatever for treating what may in fact be continuous variables, distributed more or less normally, as though they involved the mere addition of discrete units.

FIGURE 27   231

ABAC TO DETERMINE FROM TWO GIVEN PERCENTAGES THE CORRESPONDING COEFFICIENT OF ASSOCIATION.

N_p expressed as a percentage of N.

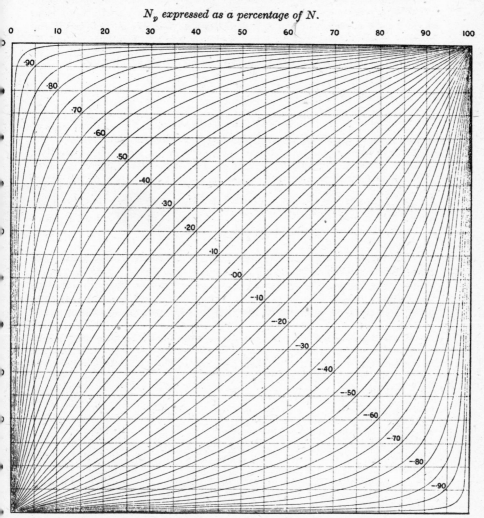

EXAMPLE.—A puzzle test is passed by 71 per cent. of normals and only 27 per cent. of defectives, a difference of 44 per cent. A maze test is passed by 98 per cent. of normals and 60 per cent. of defectives, a difference of 38 per cent.

In which test is failure more closely associated with deficiency?

71 per cent. is found on the left-hand vertical. An imaginary horizontal is carried from this point towards the right to meet an imaginary vertical dropped from the point corresponding to 27 per cent. on the top horizontal.

The two imaginary lines intersect between the curves for ·40 and ·45, but much nearer the latter.

The association coefficient is, therefore, approximately ·44.

Similarly coordinates for 98 and 60 per cent. intersect on the curve for ·70.

Contrary, therefore, to the suggestion that might be drawn from the crude percentage-difference, failure in the maze test is far more closely associated with deficiency. The puzzle test is comparatively worthless.

whether positive or negative, contains the same number of individuals, namely, half of the grand total, and thus $P = N = p = n$, and where, accordingly, $P_p = 100 - N_p = N_n$, and $P_n = 100 - P_p = N_p$.

The Tetrachoric Correlation (r_t). Pearson has criticized Yule's original coefficient, Q; and stated that "On the whole, r_t seems to me the most satisfactory coefficient of association." The determination of r_t, however, involves an elaborate calculation, as may be seen from its formula,

$$\frac{N_n}{P+N} = \tau_0 \tau'_0 + \tau_1 \tau'_1 r + \tau_2 \tau'_2 r^2 + \ldots + \tau_n \tau'_n r^n + \ldots$$

where τ and τ' are functions of $\dfrac{N}{P+N}$ and $\dfrac{n}{P+N}$, the more usual of which can be read off from published tables of the "tetrachoric functions."

$\mathrm{Sin}\left(\dfrac{\pi}{2}\omega\right)$ might be used as a rough approximation to r_t. Indeed, in the symmetrical fourfold table that is formed from a "normal" correlation by taking the points of division between P and N, p and n at the medians, the correlation can be shown mathematically to be

$$r_t = \mathrm{Sin}\left(\frac{\pi}{2}\omega\right).$$

Thus ω (Yule's "colligation" coefficient) and r_t are related somewhat as R (Spearman's "footrule" coefficient) and r. The tables for converting r into R, published in Whipple's *Manual of Mental Tests* (p. 44) and Thorndike's *Mental Measurements* (p. 226), can be used for obtaining r_t approximately from ω, provided the points of division are not far from the medians.

Since the distribution of intelligence is approximately normal, it might be thought at first sight more advisable to use r_t, or $\mathrm{Sin}\left(\dfrac{\pi}{2}\omega\right)$ as an approximation to r_t. But where the points of division lie far from the medians, as in some of the cases discussed above, these coefficients give values that may be illusively high. For corroboration, instead of dividing the children into two groups, first, according to imputed deficiency or non-deficiency and then according to failure or success in the test of ability, we can mark or rank them individually for imputed ability and use the biserial formula. In the cases thus verified the correlations then obtained in the ordinary way as a rule lie between ω and r_t or $\mathrm{Sin}\left(\dfrac{\pi}{2}\omega\right)$, sometimes below the former, and usually nearer the former than the latter.[1]

---

[1] A critical discussion of this and other coefficients suggested for measuring association will be found in *Journal of Royal Statistical Society*, Vol. LXXV., 1912 (G. Udny Yule, "On the Methods of Measuring the Association between Two Attributes"). The coefficient of colligation is there described. As, however, in Mr. Yule's *Introduction to Statistics* the coefficient is but briefly referred to, and the formula not given, it has seemed advisable to explain it at some length above.

Criticisms of the various association-coefficients will be found in *Biometrika*, Vol. IX., 1913, Nos. 1 and 2 (K. Pearson and D. Heron, "On Theories of Association").

To avoid misconception I may add that I use the colligation coefficient ω only as a rough measure for rough experimental tests. To determine the precise relation between general intelligence and the mental functions tested, we should, I believe, first cast our tests into an "internally graded" form. As indicated in the text, this could be done in detail for most of the problems in the Binet-Simon scale. The product moment coefficient could then be directly computed. Where "internal grading" is out of the question, or alters the issue, then for final conclusions tetrachoric r should be calculated at length and other suitable formulæ used as controls. Graphs, similar to that on p. 231, can be constructed for finding r_t, but different graphs will be needed for different "lines of division."

APPENDIX III.

SUPPLEMENTARY TESTS OF INTELLIGENCE.

A. WRITTEN AND GROUP TESTS.

In this and the following appendices I have added sample test-sheets and material for the more effective and better known tests of intelligence which may be used as supplementary to, or in place of, the Binet-Simon scale. Those contained in the present appendix are drawn up for use as written, group tests. The test material may be duplicated by a copying press ; the copies will be distributed to the class ; and, after due explanation and illustration of the test by means of blackboard examples, the entire class will thus be able to work through the exercises simultaneously in writing. With young children, by whom the art of expressing ideas in writing is but recently acquired, such a procedure will not yield the most successful results. Hence, collective tests are best reserved for the preliminary testing of older and brighter children[1]; with children under the age of ten and below the level of Standard IV. the results will correlate less highly with intelligence. The easier tests, such as the opposites and completion (story) tests, give results tolerably satisfactory about this level ; the harder tests, such as the synonyms, definitions, and completion (argument) tests, will be found appropriate only for pupils in the top standards.

The most convenient method of measuring performances with such tests is to assign one mark for each correct answer, and fractions—one-quarter, one-half, and three-quarters—for answers that are partially correct. What answers are to be accepted as completely correct and what answers are to be credited with the various degrees of incomplete correctness—these are problems that must be left to the individual examiner's discretion. For greater precision, I myself employ a detailed key containing all the likely alternatives, all the answers, in fact, actually given by children I have tested ; and am thus able to award always the same mark for the same word. Such keys are too lengthy to be published here ; and too elaborate for the occasional needs of the busy teacher.

Subjective evaluation could be reduced to a minimum by the following modifications. Instead of leaving a blank to be filled in by the child, the test-sheet may present for each question three or four alternative answers, and the child is required to indicate by underlining which he considers correct, or by erasure which he considers incorrect. The use of a stencil or partly transparent sheet, to be laid upon the test papers so as to show through only the correct words, will render the marking perfectly automatic. Unfortunately, this procedure eliminates the element of spontaneous invention and creative thought ; and thus, while increasing the mechanical precision, decreases the intrinsic value, of the test so used.

Owing to the inevitable variations in the marking of different teachers who may use the tests in their present simple form, and in view of the limited

---

[1] For purposes of junior county scholarship examinations a special committee at Bradford, working largely with earlier forms of my present test-sheets, concluded that the most effective tests would be Opposites, Analogies, Completion (discontinuous), and Graded Reasoning (written). These were, accordingly, employed. See, for an interesting account of one among several such experiments, the *Annual Report of the Bradford Education Committee*, 1920. Several other education authorities are now preparing to experiment upon similar lines with group tests of intelligence in their scholarship examinations.

On the trustworthiness of group-tests I may perhaps refer to my early article (*J. Exp. Ped.* 1911, p. 93), which showed that with older children such tests were in many ways quite as effective as individual tests.

range of years over which the tests are applicable, complete tables of age-norms would be unnecessary or even misleading. In Table XXXIV. (p. 250), therefore, I give only rough averages calculated regardless of sex. And for a like reason I have not thought it worth the necessary time and space to elaborate and print a set of standardised instructions as to procedure or marking. Teachers, indeed, will probably prefer, not to adopt the materials and instructions as here printed, but to modify them to suit the needs of their own particular pupils ; and then compile each his own set of typical results. As the tests can be carried out upon large numbers simultaneously, those who use them will have no difficulty in rapidly obtaining for their own schools data for age-averages, standard deviations, and borderline performances.

The materials for the majority of the tests are identical with those used

TABLE XXXIV.
Norms for Supplementary Tests—A. Group Tests.

The units for the first seven tests are the number of words correctly written or the number of questions correctly answered ; for the absurdities, the number of absurdities discovered ; for the mazes, the mental year.

	Opposites	Analogies	Synonyms	Definitions	Instructions	Completion (Story)	Completion (Argument)	Absurdities	Maze
0—	—	—	—	—	—	—	—	—	7·3
7—	—	—	—	—	—	—	—	—	8·5
8—	10·2	[3·8]	[4·8]	—	[5·8]	[12·2]	[2·8]	[8·8]	9·1
9—	18·5	6·1	[8·3]	[2·6]	10·1	18·8	[5·2]	[10·2]	9·8
10—	29·4	8·3	14·6	[5·9]	14·9	29·7	[9·3]	11·2	10·6
11—	35·8	16·8	21·2	8·1	18·3	32·6	11·1	13·4	11·5
12—	39·3	19·2	26·1	13·0	20·4	34·8	14·6	16·6	12·3
13—	42·6	21·0	32·2	19·7	22·3	36·4	19·3	18·7	13·2
14—	45·2	22·5	35·4	25·3	23·8	37·9	22·6	20·6	13·8

in my previous investigations. A fuller account of the results to be expected and the ground upon which the tests have been chosen will be found in earlier publications dealing with these researches.

It will be noted that all the tests in the present category are linguistic in form ; all are, therefore, characterised by the limitations and disadvantages which stamp all linguistic tests. Accordingly, estimates based upon them should be supplemented and checked by measurements obtained with tests which—like the maze tests of Appendix IV (3) are of a more concrete and practical type.

For this purpose, however, and for the purpose of testing younger children who cannot read, most of the present tests may, with a little ingenuity, be cast into pictorial form. For example, in the analogies test, instead of the words " glove," " hand," " hat," pictures of these objects may be shown ; and instead of writing the answer " head," the child may be required, not perhaps to draw a " head," but to indicate out of several alternative drawings—of a head, a foot, a boot, and a bonnet—which is the correct one. Or, again, instead of pictures, simple geometrical forms of various sizes may be used, either drawn and painted, or cut out in card, and the child will with this material work through such relations as would be indicated by the words : "The large square is to the small square as the large circle is to .... ?" Or, "The red, erect triangle is to the green, inverted triangle as the red, erect pentagon is to .... ?" Similarly, for the

---

(1) A useful version of the " non-verbal analogies test " consists of a two-way series, in which one item in a 3 × 3 (or 4 × 4) set of numbers or shapes (arranged as on p. 244) has to be inserted by the child : (now known as the " matrix " test).

opposites test, instead of writing down " black " as the opposite to " white," the child will select a black card from an assortment of various colours, and pair it with the white card. Instead of defining names he will define the use of actual objects shown. Instead of writing words of a similar meaning, he will pair together, from an assortment of cards, pictures of objects having a similar purpose—such as a knife and a fork, ink and a pen, a cart and a horse, a railway carriage and a locomotive. Instead of completing a printed story he will complete a dissected picture ; or place a series of pictures (cut, for example, from the *Busch Bilderbogen*) in the right order, to tell a story. Instead of pointing out the absurdities in a printed story he will point out absurdities in a picture or series of pictures—a chair with three legs, a horse pushing a cart, a see-saw impossibly balanced. In every case the pictorial material should be so selected as to call forth the power of reasoning. Success in the ordinary jig-saw puzzle, for example, depends chiefly on luck, ingenuity, and perseverance, in matching experimentally a number of shapes and colours ; but by cutting out in their entirety particular objects represented in the picture—the windows from the station, the engine that draws the train, the wheels from the carriages, the smoke from the funnel—a pictorial completion test can be devised that depends upon the perception of significant relations—the very essence of reasoning—rather than upon the lowlier processes of trial and error.

1. OPPOSITES.

The instructions for this test are : " Against every word write another which means the opposite of the printed word." The stimulus-words here given, a hundred in all, have been carefully chosen, standardised, and arranged. The words are moderately easy ; and nearly equal in difficulty. Hence, the test is adapted for use as a speed test. The children will be told to start and stop at given signals, and to work as quickly as they can. Each opposite correctly inserted receives one mark ; fractions are allowed in rare cases for an attempt moderately or dubiously successful.

In obtaining the norms given in Table XXXIV only the first fifty words were used, and the time limited to five minutes. This allows the second fifty words to be used in a subsequent test, either for reliability, or to test improvement after a given interval. With the second fifty the norms obtained are about 2 per cent. lower.

The material for the present test has been carefully selected and standardised by means of a special investigation. As an illustration of the method used for such a purpose, and as a guide to those who wish to attempt the standardisation of other tests for themselves, I append a detailed description of the procedure and criteria used.[1]

Numerous lists have been drawn up by different investigators for use as opposites tests.[2] None of these were found entirely satisfactory. A preliminary set was, therefore, compiled, which included all the published lists, and contained in all over 300 stimulus words. It was given in the form of shorter series, to approximately 400 boys and 400 girls. The following determinations were then made for each stimulus-word : (1) the number of omissions, (2) the number of different words supplied, (3) the frequency with which each different word occurred. On the basis of these calculations our final words were ultimately chosen and arranged.

---

(1) In carrying out the enquiry I am especially indebted to the assistance rendered by Mr. Corkhill and Mr. Moore, two of my research students in the psychological department of the University of Liverpool.

(2) The most important of the earlier investigations, together with samples of their test-materials, are given in Whipple's *Manual of Mental and Physical Tests*, Vol. II., pp. 79–89.

The following criteria were employed in compiling the standard lists :—

1. At least fifty, preferably one hundred, words of approximately equal difficulty are required when used for written tests with a fixed time-limit. Short lists, containing twenty only, as those of Wells and Woodworth, do not differentiate sufficiently between the children tested.

2. The average level of difficulty sought must, therefore, not be too low. It would be impossible to devise longer lists so uniformly easy as those of Wells and Woodworth.

3. The upper limits of difficulty must not be too high. Unfamiliar words like " loquacious," " obnoxious " (Thorndike's list) must be discarded ; and, in general, words which produce a high proportion of omissions must be eliminated : e.g., " pull " suggested no opposite, correct or incorrect, to 25 per cent. of the children, " help " suggested none to 23 per cent., " please " none to 32 per cent., " approach " none to 53 per cent., " virtue " none to 8C per cent.

4. That word is preferable which elicits the same response from different children with the highest frequency, e.g., " soft," " north," " dirty "—the only words suggesting the same response to over 99 per cent. of the children answering.

5. That word is preferable which elicits from different children the smallest number of different responses. Simple words like " joy," " glad," " give," " little," possess an enormous variety of alternative opposites. Of all the stimulus-words used, " funny " gave the largest variety of replies—" serious," " sad," " stern," " solemn," " gloomy," " glum," " dismal," " miserable," " dull," " grave," " sober," " staid," " quiet," " sedate," " proper," " depressing," " stupid," " insipid," " wearisome," " tedious," " boring," " tiring," " dry," " sulky," " mournful," " awful," " bad-tempered," " grim," " tragic," " instructive "—thirty-one in all. In discrete reaction tests, a frequent explanation of delay with girls of copious vocabulary was : " I could not make up my mind which it was best to say."

6. Words eliciting only two or three opposites should, however, be discarded, if these occur with about equal frequency, e.g., " begin " – " end " (42 per cent.), " finish " (40 per cent.) ; " under " – " above " (39 per cent.), " over " (35 per cent.) ; " morning " – " night " (38 per cent.), " evening " (33 per cent.), " afternoon " (27 per cent.).

7. Cases involving difficulties of spelling or grammar must be omitted, e.g., " profit " – " loss " (27 per cent.,—4 per cent. erased or corrected), " apostle " (often incorrectly spelt or respelt, 2 per cent.), " brave "—" coward " (25 per cent.), " cowardice " (5 per cent.), " cowardness " (2 per cent.), " clever "–" dunce " (10 per cent.). A slight grammatical change often makes a considerable improvement, e.g., " loss "–" find " (32 per cent.), " lost "–" found " (98 per cent.).

8. Each word should be capable of only one interpretation, e.g., " left " may be understood as the opposite either to " right " (49 per cent.) or to " taken " (21 per cent.). " Simple " is understood as the opposite to " hard " or " difficult " (20 per cent.), to " complex," " compound," " complicated " (13 per cent.), to " clever," " wise " (11 per cent.), to " proud," " haughty," " grand," " great," " rich " (10 per cent.), " fussy," " gaudy," " smart," " ornamented " (8 per cent.).

9. Words eliciting as a frequent opposite merely the same word preceded by " not " or a negative prefix or suffix should (with occasional exceptions in the latter cases) be discarded, e.g., " guilty "–" not guilty " (girls, 24 per cent. ; boys, 1 per cent.), " happy "–" unhappy " (68 per cent., followed by a marked increase in use of " un- " with the ensuing words).

10. Words possessing both contraries and contradictories should be avoided, e.g., " nobody " – " somebody " (65 per cent.), " everybody " (16 per cent.).

11. Words should be avoided which suggest circumlocutions, neologisms, or other time-consuming ingenuities, e.g., " please," " no, thank you " (15 per cent.), " I'll make you," and similar phrases (8 per cent.), " approach " – " get away from " (6 per cent.), " get far away," " deproach," " inapproach," " disapproach," " re-proach " ; " parent " – " transparent " (3 per cent.).

12. Words where the most frequent reply is not the true opposite should be avoided, e.g., " son " – " daughter " (63 per cent.), " father " (12 per cent.).

13. Words where the replies differ greatly in the two sexes should be avoided, *e.g.*, " child " :—

Reply ..	"Man."	"Woman." "Lady."	"Adult."	"Father." "Mother."	"Baby."	"Parent."	Omissions.	
Boys ..	43	1	32	0	0	6	18	per cent.
Girls ..	14	30	26	7	5	2	2	per cent.

Similarly, " servant " (boys, " master " ; girls, " mistress "), " cheap " (boys " dear " ; girls, " expensive "), " busy " (boys, " lazy " ; girls, " idle ").

14. Several words suggesting the same opposite should not occur in the same list, *e.g.*, " long," " tall," " big " (the last two in immediate succession in the lists of Bonser, Simpson) ; " glad," " happy " (Simpson, Whitley). " Slow " repeatedly does duty as opposite to " fast," " quick," " rapid," " sudden," " swift," and even to " busy," " active," " clever."

15. No word should be a possible opposite of another word in the same list. *e.g.*, " soft," " rough " (Simpson, Whitley).

16. Of any pair of opposites, both terms should be tried as a stimulus-word in the standardisation experiments, and that word selected which best conforms to the foregoing conditions, *e.g.*, " fluid " yields twenty-eight different responses, the commonest being " solid " (31 per cent.) ; " solid," on the other hand, yields only nine, " liquid " (72 per cent.) being the most frequent, " hollow " (13 per cent.), " gas," or " gassy " (10 per cent.) the commoner alternatives ; but even this ambiguity is sufficient to cause its rejection, and the entire group is eliminated.

Judged by these principles, the words in Wells' and Woodworth's standardised list are far superior to any other set, except that they are too few and perhaps a little too mechanical. In my trials of this test, however, " dead " and " slow " furnish too many synonymous replies, coming 108th in order of variety of response. " Male " was several times passed over, provoked many meaningless replies, and was often taken as a misprint for " mate " (hence, " foe," " enemy," " traitor," " unmate," " himself," as opposites). Their criterion, too (quickness of reaction time), does not seem entirely satisfactory, *e.g.*, " day " (among their easiest of all) gives ten different responses ; " soft " (unstarred) gives only one response.

According to these criteria, we eventually selected 100 stimulus-words, arranged as below :—

Test 21[1].—Opposites.

	Answer.		Answer.
1. Old....................		21. Sunrise	
2. Poor....................		22. Brother	
3. Big		23. Borrow	
4. Early		24. Clean	
5. Long		25. Common	
6. Easy		26. Warm	
7. Inside		27. Tight	
8. Pretty		28. Mountain	
9. Boy		29. Father	
10. Wet		30. True....................	
11. Kind		31. Shut....................	
12. Winter....................		32. Female	
13. Woman		33. Few	
14. Slow....................		34. Heavy	
15. White		35. Multiply	
16. Upwards		36. Absent....................	
17. Loud		37. Moving	
18. Crooked................		38. Question	
19. Cheap		39. Now	
20. Busy		40. Polite....................	

([1]) Tests 1 to 20 are scholastic; see Appendix I., pp. 367 *et seq.*

Answer.   *Answer.*

41. East ....   71. Near ....
42. Enemy ....   72. Lowland ....
43. Nobody ....   73. Within ....
44. Glad.....................   74. Smooth ....
45. Top ....   75. North ....
46. Possible ....   76. Forget.................
47. Come ....   77. Large ....
48. Front ....   78. Over ....
49. Day ....   79. Narrow ....
50. Tame ....   80. Sober ....
51. Less ....   81. Tender ....
52. Great ....   82. Lost...................
53. Love ....   83. Obey..................
54. Sell ....   84. Soft ....
55. Low ....   85. Nice ....
56. Blunt ....   86. Careless ....
57. Yes ....   87. Town..................
58. Win ....   88. Complete ....
59. There ....   89. Left ....
60. First ....   90. Happy ....
61. Noisy ....   91. Laugh ....
62. Best ....   92. Well ....
63. Strong.................   93. Stand ....
64. Asleep ....   94. Evening .
65. Land ....   95. End ....
66. Thin ....   96. Little ....
67. Me ....   97. Slanting ....
68. Dislike ....   98. Dark ....
69. Backwards ....   99. Stale ....
70. Wrong.................   100. After ....

2. ANALOGIES.

I have taken the title for this test from an Aristotelian term which means " proportion."[1] The exercise is, in fact, " rule of three " in words instead of in numbers. The essential instructions are : " In the blank space provided for the answer, fill in a fourth word standing in the same connection with the third word as the second word does with the first." The task, however, should be explained and illustrated with not more than three simple examples, worked upon the blackboard, before the papers are attempted. As with the opposites test, the list is best divided into two series ; and each carried out as a speed test. Table XXXIV. gives results obtained in five minutes.

Test 22.—Analogies.
Answer.

1. Prince *is to* Princess *as* King *is to* .... ?
2. Pencil *is to* Drawing *as* Brush *is to* .... ?
3. January *is to* February *as* First *is to* .... ?
4. Sailor *is to* Soldier *as* Navy *is to* .... ?
5. Moon *is to* Earth *as* Earth *is to* .... ?
6. This *is to* Here *as* That *is to* .... ?
7. Day *is to* Midday *as* Night *is to* .... ?

---

[1] A test of this form was first used to measure intelligence by Mr. Moore and myself at Liverpool. It has since been widely employed for this purpose ; and has been inserted into one or two revisions of the Binet-Simon scale.

Answer.

8. Little *is to* Big *as* Dwarf *is to* .... ?
9. Foot *is to* Leg *as* Hand *is to* .... ?
10. Neighing *is to* Braying *as* Horse *is to* .... ?
11. Heat *is to* Cold *as* Summer *is to* .... ?
12. I *is to* Mine *as* You *is to* .... ?
13. Table *is to* Wood *as* Window *is to* .... ?
14. Dining-room *is to* Bedroom *as* Eating *is to* .... ?
15. Coffee-grounds *are to* Coffee-pot *as* Tea-leaves *are to* .... ?
16. Sheep *is to* Mutton *as* Pig *is to* .... ?
17. East *is to* West *as* Day *is to* .... ?
18. Penny *is to* Copper *as* Nail *is to* .... ?
19. Hour *is to* Minute *as* Minute *is to* .... ?
20. Bicycle *is to* Tricycle *as* Two Wheels *is to* .... ?
21. Straw *is to* Hat *as* Leather *is to* .... ?
22. White *is to* Snow *as* Black *is to* .... ?
23. Cloud *is to* Rain *as* Sun *is to* .... ?
24. Spider *is to* Fly *as* Cat *is to* .... ?
25. Uncle *is to* Aunt *as* Brother *is to* .... ?
26. Liquid *is to* Solid *as* Water *is to* .... ?
27 Little *is to* Less *as* Much *is to* .... ?
28. Grandfather *is to* Husband *as* Grandmother *is to* .... ?
29. Tuesday *is to* Wednesday *as* Wednesday *is to* .... ?
30. Evening *is to* Morning *as* Supper *is to* .... ?
31. Wash *is to* Face *as* Sweep *is to* .... ?
32. Tailor *is to* Baker *as* Clothes *is to* .... ?
33. Pale Yellow *is to* Deep Yellow *as* Pink *is to* .... ?
34. At Home *is to* Abroad *as* England *is to* .... ?
35. Fire *is to* Hot *as* Ice *is to* .... ?
36. Cork *is to* Water *as* Balloon *is to* .... ?
37. Robin *is to* Swallow *as* Winter *is to* .... ?
38. Man *is to* Woman *as* Boy *is to* .... ?
39. Steamer *is to* Pier *as* Train *is to* .... ?
40. Sky *is to* Blue *as* Grass *is to* .... ?
41. Once *is to* One *as* Twice *is to* .... ?
42. Cat *is to* Fur *as* Bird *is to* .... ?
43. Library *is to* Books *as* Greenhouse *is to* .... ?
44. Gulf *is to* Sea *as* Cape *is to* .... ?
45. Houses *are to* Bricks *as* Cathedrals *are to* .... ?
46. Three *is to* One *as* Yard *is to* .... ?
47. Oyster *is to* Shell *as* Banana *is to* .... ?
48. Good *is to* Bad *as* Long *is to* .... ?
49. Eat *is to* Bread *as* Drink *is to* .... ?
50. James *is to* Jimmie *as* William *is to* .... ?
51. Seeing *is to* Eye *as* Hearing *is to* .... ?
52. Fruit *is to* Orange *as* Vegetable *is to* .... ?
53. Lily *is to* Flower *as* Oak *is to* .... ?
54. Trunk *is to* Elephant *as* Hand *is to* .... ?
55. Sit *is to* Chair *as* Sleep *is to* .... ?
56. Half-sovereign *is to* Gold *as* Bullet *is to* .... ?
57. Cradle *is to* Baby *as* Stable *is to* .... ?
58. England *is to* London *as* France *is to* .... ?
59. Small *is to* Large *as* Mouse *is to* .... ?
60. Eat *is to* Fat *as* Starve *is to* .... ?
61. Chew *is to* Teeth *as* Smell *is to* .... ?
62. First *is to* Last *as* Beginning *is to* .... ?

Answer.

63. Sweets *are to* Sugar *as* Cakes *are to* .... ?
64. Church Bell *is to* Church Service *as* School Bell *is to* .... ?
65. Float *is to* Sink *as* Cork *is to* .... ?
66. Farmer *is to* Gardener *as* Farm *is to* .... ?
67. Kitten *is to* Cat *as* Lamb *is to* .... ?
68. Honey *is to* Milk *as* Bee *is to* .... ?
69. White *is to* Good *as* Black *is to* .... ?
70. Knitting *is to* Girls *as* Woodwork *is to* .... ?
71. Legs *are to* Horse *as* Wheels *are to* .... ?
72. Nasty *is to* Nice *as* Medicine *is to* .... ?
73. Mewing *is to* Cat *as* Barking *is to* .... ?
74. Blood *is to* Flesh *as* Gravy *is to* .... ?
75. Pen *is to* Write *as* Knife *is to* .... ?
76. July *is to* June *as* February *is to* .... ?
77. Pigtail *is to* Chinamen *as* Curly Hair *is to* .... ?
78. Purse *is to* Money *as* Grate *is to* .... ?
79. Skirt *is to* Girl *as* Trouser *is to* .... ?
80. Glove *is to* Hand *as* Boot *is to* .... ?
81. Tears *are to* Sorrow *as* Laughter *is to* .... ?
82. Japanese *is to* Japan *as* Turk *is to* .... ?
83. Healthy Cheeks *are to* Red Roses *as* Clean Teeth *are to* .... ?
84. Mowing *is to* Hay *as* Reaping *is to* .... ?
85. Lion *is to* Animals *as* Rose *is to* .... ?
86. Infantry *is to* Cavalry *as* Walking *is to* .... ?
87. Cabbage *is to* Kitchen Garden *as* Tulip *is to* .... ?
88. Silver *is to* Spoon *as* China *is to* .... ?
89. Skating *is to* Winter *as* Bathing *is to* .... ?
90. Breakfast *is to* Dinner *as* Dinner *is to* .... ?
91. Cornfield *is to* Corn *as* Orchard *is to* .... ?
92. Dawn *is to* Morning *as* Twilight *is to* .... ?
93. Possessions *are to* Wishes *as* A Bird in the Hand *is to* .... ?
94. Button *is to* Glove *as* Lace *is to* .... ?
95. Tallow *is to* Candles *as* Oil *is to* .... ?
96. Nose *is to* Face *as* Toe *is to* .... ?
97. Cold *is to* Hot *as* North Pole *is to* .... ?
98. Flying *is to* Birds *as* Swimming *is to* .... ?
99. River *is to* Sea *as* Fresh Water *is to* .... ?
100. King *is to* Emperor *as* Kingdom *is to* .... ?

3. SYNONYMS.

A synonym test is a natural complement to a test of opposites or antonyms ; and the two have been used in conjunction in the American Army tests.

For the following test the instructions are simply as follows :—

"Against each word write another word which expresses, as nearly as possible, the same meaning." A time limit may be imposed, if desired. The words employed in this test were selected in accordance with definite principles from Roget's *Thesaurus of English Words and Phrases ;* and reference to the classified lists of synonyms there published will greatly facilitate the marking.

Of all forms of "controlled association," this test perhaps approximates most closely to the familiar test of "free" or "uncontrolled association." The replies may, therefore, be classified upon lines analogous to those in use for the latter ; and will then be found to throw much light on specific capacities and perhaps still more on temperamental tendencies. Of these the following deserve special notice : namely, a disposition to choose colloquial, pedantic, or obvious words ; short, simple, Anglo-Saxon words, or long, intellectualistic, romance words (Latinisms) ; words objectively accurate, or words emotionally vivid ; words in familiar use, and therefore frequently selected by others, or peculiar, "individual" and "egocentric" words, rarely selected by others ; and, again, rigid adherence to the same part of speech as that suggested by the stimulus-word, or careless divergence ; wide or narrow vocabulary ; and consistent variations in these respects for stimulus-words of special types—e.g., for common and rare words, for relatively abstract and relatively concrete words, for psychological and nonpsychological words, words of censure and praise, and so forth. Special interests will be largely deducible from the significance attached to the more general or ambiguous words ; but for this purpose the test should include a freer admixture of relatively concrete words, such as those in the following test, which, indeed, may also be used as a synonym test.[1]

Test 23.—Synonyms.

Answer.		Answer.	
1. Active		26. Inquire	
2. Affectionate		27. Insane	
3. Anger		28. Knowledge	
4. Assert		29. Nasty	
5. Attend		30. Obstinate	
6. Bad		31. Obvious	
7. Beautiful		32. Pleasure	
8. Begin		33. Poor	
9. Cause		34. Proud	
10. Change		35. Real	
11. Clever		36. Reject	
12. Cloth		37. Sign	
13. Collection		38. Slow	
14. Curious		39. Spoiled	
15. Deceive		40. Succeed	
16. Decide		41. Superior	
17. Destroy		42. Tempt	
18. Difficulty		43. Timid	
19. Fasten		44. Trouble	
20. Free		45. Untruth	
21. Funny		46. Useful	
22. Great		47. Vulgar	
23. Hidden		48. Weak	
24. Honest		49. Wish	
25. Important		50. Work	

4. DEFINITIONS.

The following test correlates highly with intelligence among older and brighter school children. It was framed as a test of "general knowledge" ; and in vocational examinations has been found to throw considerable light upon the range of information and direction of interests among young

([1]) I have given a preliminary account of the possibilities of this and the following test in *Child Study*, 1915, Vol. VIII., No. 1, p. 11. In revising the above I have been particularly indebted both to Miss May Smith and to Mr. E. R. Mason-Thompson, who have had a wide experience in applying such tests to adults of various ages and of different levels of culture.

adults. Two words have been chosen from each of twenty-five of the commonest branches of knowledge. The words of a pair are printed below on the same line. In assessing the results, however, many of these doublets may again be classed together into a smaller number of overlapping groups—scientific, artistic, linguistic, literary, recreational, commercial, domestic, etc.

In administering the test, the words should be hectographed in a single column, not in pairs as below, with at least one clear line between each word. The instructions are : " Write against the following words, as briefly and accurately as you can, what you think to be the meaning of each." A time limit may be employed, if desired ; but is not recommended, as it decreases the comparability of deductions as to special interests, and handicaps the careful and detailed writer.

Test 24.—Definitions.

Answer.	Answer.
1. Tropical	26. Latitude ....
2. Barrister	27. Trustee ....
3. Millinery	28. Gusset ....
4. Steeplechase	29. Tee ....
5. Balance	30. Invoice ....
6. Charter	31. Renaissance ....
7. Platoon	32. Howitzer ....
8. Tragedy	33. Sonnet ....
9. Minim	34. Fortissimo ....
10. Cancer	35. Tuberculosis ....
11. Junket	36. Consommé ....
12. Ensign	37. Tonnage ....
13. Molar	38. Cranium ....
14. Grease-paint	39. Libretto ....
15. Mammal	40. Ruminant ....
16. Mercury	41. Ether ....
17. Fauteuil	42. Cinch ....
18. Frieze	43. Chancel ....
19. Magnet	44. Barometer..............
20. Octagonal	45. Ratio ....
21. Pollen	46. Tuber ....
22. Landscape	47. Fresco ....
23. Cue	48. Stalemate ....
24. Planet	49. Satellite ....
25. Postmortem	50. Auf Wiedersehen ....

5. GRADED INSTRUCTIONS.

The various so-called " Instructions " or " Mixed Instructions " tests are based on the view that the measurement of a number of different mental activities provides a better test of intelligence than the measurement of only one mental activity. The questions here used have been roughly graded in order of increasing difficulty. Most of the questions indicate a type that might well be made the basis of a homogeneous series of questions, were it so desired. Since the material is graded and not uniform in difficulty, the test is best applied without a time-limit.[1]

---

[1] A test of this type has been widely used in America ; and from some of the copies there in use a few of my questions have been drawn, though all have been regraded. For a similar test in oral form see below pp. 303, 374, et seq.

Test 25.—Instructions.

1. Put a dot under this line : ——————————————

2. Write a capital letter S in this square :

3. Cross out both A's in the word " ADA."

4. Write ten (in figures) in the largest square :

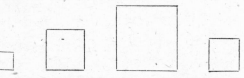

5. Make a girl's name by adding one letter to "Mar   ."

6. If you have had your supper to-day, write Y for yes ; if not, write N for no. ......

7. John has four big beads—white, red, green, and blue. He has given the green one to Tom ; and the white and blue ones to Jane. Write down which he has kept ? ....

8. What do I need to light a fire beside matches, coal, and wood ? Write the first letter of the word only. ....

9. Suppose it were Sunday to-day. What day would it have been the day before yesterday ? ....

10. What number follows next but one after 19 ? ......

11. If February comes after January, make two crosses here ...... ; but if not, make one cross here. ......

12. Suppose your mother were ill and sent you for the doctor, but you found it was raining. Think what you should do : (1) Wait until the rain has stopped ? (2) Get a mackintosh or umbrella, and go at once through the rain ? (3) Go to the post office and telegraph to him ? (4) Ask your little sister to go instead ? Write here the number of the correct answer. ......

13. Draw a line under the word which contains the first letter of the alphabet more times than any other word does : **cap, Adam, atlas, black, almanac, bluebottle.**

14.[1] Put a figure 1 in the space which is inside both the triangle and the square, but not inside the circle ; put a figure 2 in the space which is inside the square, but outside both the circle and triangle.

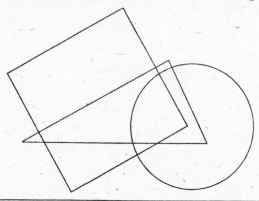

[1] ¼ a mark is allowed for each part of this question.

S

15. "It takes about ...... minutes to boil an egg." A number is missing from this sentence ; if it is more than 10, write it here ...... ; if it is less, show the number by making strokes here. ....

16. Cross out the three wrong words in the following sentence : "**Most motor-cars are driven by wind, steam, petrol, gas.**"

17. A **wheel** is part of a **cart** ;
An **foot** is part of an **inch** ?

If one sentence only is correct, cross out the last word in the incorrect sentence ; if both are true, write your name here............. ; otherwise do nothing.

18. Fill in the missing word : "Daisies, tulips, lilies, and buttercups are all ...."

19. In the following sentence only one word out of the last five is needed. Put a ring round the word that is right : "Nights are longest in *June, summer, jellyfish, winter, Hampstead.*"

20. Draw a line from the corner marked A, passing across the first square, between the second and sixth squares, between the sixth and seventh squares, under the seventh square, between the eleventh and twelfth squares, and across the sixteenth square to the corner marked B.

A

1	2	3	4
5	6	7	8
9	10	11	12
13	14	15	16

B

21. In the following words find one letter which is contained in only three of the words, and then cross out the remaining word which does not contain that letter :

heap, April, drake, lark.

22-23.[1] Write down four more words made up (like the first two words) out of three or four of the following letters : A, E, R, T.
(1) **ate**, (2) **tare**, (3) ......, (4) ...... (5) ......, (6) ......

24. Read these words ; and think what their meaning would be if they were in the right order :

people church dance go to to.

If the sentence is untrue, put a line round the word which makes it wrong. But if the sentence is true, cross it all out.

---

(1) Half a mark is awarded for each correct word.

25.[1] In the picture below you are looking at the reflection of a clock and some words in a mirror. What do the words say ?............

What would be the actual time, if you could turn round and look at the clock itself ? ....

COFFEE ROOM

6. COMPLETION.

This test is based upon the well-known *Combinations-Methode* devised as a test of mental efficiency in school children at the request of the educational authorities of Breslau by the late Professor Ebbinghaus. I give two samples. The first, like the material used by most investigators, including Professor Ebbinghaus himself, is in the form of a simple narrative. It is, in fact, taken from Stevenson's fable of *The Two Matches*. The completion of stories, however, depends more upon visual imagination than upon reasoning ; and experiments show that the same method applied to an abstract argument gives far higher correlations with intelligence. The second passage, therefore, is more philosophical in character. It forms the opening paragraph of Bacon's *Essay on Revenge*. An ethical discussion is of all abstract arguments perhaps the easiest for children to follow. Nevertheless, the present passage presents considerable difficulty to all but those in the highest standard of the elementary schools, or of central or secondary school merit.

The instructions are as follows : " In every blank space fill in one word, and one word only, to complete the sense of the story " (or " of the argument "). No time limit is imposed.

The missing-word device is applicable to tests of almost every form. In disconnected form—consisting of a set of separate sentences only—it often provides a quick and convenient form of test dealing with informational subjects, such as science or history—a form, too, which is more reliable, and easier to evaluate, than the customary list of questions or request for essays.

Test 26.—Completion (Story).
THE TWO ......(1)......

One......(2)......there was a traveller in the wood in California, in the......(3)......season, when the......(4)......were blowing strong. He had ridden a......(5)......way, and he was......(6)......and hungry, and dismounted from his......(7)......to smoke a......(8)...... But when he......(9)......in his pocket, he found but two......(10)...... He struck the......(11)......and it would......(12)......light.

([1]) No mark is awarded for correctly reading "coffee room"; this is inserted for demonstration only.

" Here is a......(13)........state of things ! "......(14)......the traveller.

" Dying for a......(15)......; only one......(16)......left ; and that certain to miss fire. Was there ever a creature so......(17)......? And yet," thought the traveller, "suppose I......(18)......this match and......(19)......my pipe, and shake out the......(20)......here in the grass—the......(21).......might catch on......(22)......for it is...... (23)......like tinder ; and while I snatch out the flames in front, they ......(24)......evade and run behind me and......(25)......upon yon bush of poison oak ; before......(26)......could reach it, that....:.(27) ......have blazed up ; over the bush I see a pine tree hung with...(28)....; that too would fly in fire upon the instant to its topmost......(29)...., and the flame of that long torch—how would the trade wind take and brandish ......(30)......through the inflammable forest ! I......(31)......this dell roar in a moment with the joint voice of the wind and......(32)...... I see......(33)......gallop for my......(34)......, and the flying con-flagration chase......(35)......outflank me through the hills ;...(36)... see this pleasant......(37)......burn for......(38)......, and the cattle ......(39)......and the springs dried up and the farmer......(40)...... and......(41)......children cast upon the world. What a world hangs upon this moment ! "

With that he struck the......(42)......and it......(43)......fire.

" Thank......(44)......! " said the......(45)....., and put his ......(46)......in his pocket.

Test 27.—Completion (Argument).

Of ......(1)......

Revenge is a......(2)......of wild justice, which the more man's nature runs to, the......(3)......ought law to weed it out. For as for the first wrong, it......(4)......but offend the law ;......(5)......the revenge of that......(6)......putteth the law out of office.

......(7)......, in taking revenge a......(8)......is but even with ......(9)......enemy ; but in passing it......(10)......he is...... (11)......; for it is a......(12)......part to pardon. And Solomon, I am sure,......(13)......: " It......(14)......the glory of a man to ......(15)......by an offence."

That which is past is......(16)......and irrecoverable, and wise men have enough to do with things present and to......(17)...... Therefore they do but trifle with themselves that labour in......(18)......matters.

There is......(19)......man doth a wrong for the......(20)...... sake ; but thereby to......(21)......himself profit, or......(22)......, or honour,......(23)......the like. ......(24)......why should I be ......(25)......with a......(26)......for loving himself better than ......(27)......? And......(28)......any man should do....(29).... merely out of ill-nature, why, yet it is but......(30)......the thorn ......(31)......briar, which......(32)......or scratch, ...(33).....; they can do no other.

The......(34)......tolerable sort of revenge is for those wrongs ......(35)......there is no law to remedy ; but then let a man take ......(36)......the revenge be such......(37)......there is..:...(38)..... law to punish ; else a man's......(39)......is still beforehand, and it is two for......(40)......

Key.

TEST 26—(COMPLETION : STORY).

(1) Matches	(13) strange	(25) seize	(37) farmstead
(2) day	(14) thought	(26) I	(38) days
(3) rainy	(15) smoke	(27) would	(39) roasted
(4) trades	(16) match	(28) creepers	(40) killed
(5) long	(17) unfortunate	(29) bough	(41) his
(6) tired	(18) strike	(30) it	(42) match
(7) horse	(19) light	(31) hear	(43) missed
(8) pipe	(20) dottle	(32) fire	(44) Heaven
(9) felt	(21) grass	(33) myself	(45) traveller
(10) matches	(22) fire	(34) life	(46) pipe
(11) first	(23) dry	(35) and	
(12) not	(24) might	(36) I	

TEST 27—(COMPLETION : ARGUMENT).

(1) Revenge	(11) superior	(21) purchase	(31) or
(2) kind	(12) prince's	(22) pleasure	(32) prick
(3) more	(13) saith	(23) or	(33) because
(4) doth	(14) is	(24) And	(34) most
(5) but	(15) pass	(25) angry	(35) which
(6) wrong	(16) gone	(26) man	(36) heed
(7) Certainly	(17) come	(27) me	(37) as
(8) man	(18) past	(28) if	(38) no
(9) his	(19) no	(29) wrong	(39) enemy
(10) over	(20) wrong's	(30) like	(40) one

Note.—Since the foregoing Appendix was set up in type, several sets of collected group-tests—the "Terman," the "Otis," the "National Intelligence Scale"—have reached this country from America ; and their titles should be added to the bibliography below (p. 460). With the assistance of a small number of British teachers and psychologists, I am testing the applicability of these scales—duly modified to eliminate American peculiarities—to school children in this country. Professor Terman has also given his generous permission for us to attempt an English re-standardisation of his "Stanford Version" of the Binet tests. We should gladly welcome the co-operation of any who are experimenting with these several scales.

Booklets containing bound blanks for the foregoing tests (slightly revised), together with instructions for marking the results, may now be obtained from the *National Institute of Industrial Psychology* (329, High Holborn, London. W.C. 1). For testing the general ability of intelligent adults I may be permitted to recommend the question-papers constructed by me in 1920 for the Civil Service Commission. The tests are similar to the foregoing; but harder in difficulty and more easily marked. They have been drawn up in five alternative booklets of equal difficulty. It is hoped that the results based upon an examination of 10,000 candidates, may shortly be published.[1]

---

[1] The results are summarized in *Ann. Rep. Brit. Ass.*, 1923, pp. 218f. The tests are now issued in the form of a revised booklet, called " Group Test No. 33 " by the N.I.I.P., present address, Aldwych House, Aldwych. A booklet for children is published by the University of London Press.

APPENDIX IV.

SUPPLEMENTARY TESTS OF INTELLIGENCE.

B. ORAL OR INDIVIDUAL TESTS.

The following are the oral or individual tests of intelligence, other than those of Binet and Simon, which have been found most satisfactory in the foregoing investigation.[1] The first two are suitable only for children who can read and understand simple printed matter, *i.e.*, who are above the educational level of standard I. But for such children, especially for older and brighter children about scholarship age or scholarship standard, they appear to give results distinctly superior to those obtained by the Binet-Simon scale.

1. ABSURDITIES.

This test may be used for a written group test as well as for an individual oral test. For a group test with this material the instructions are as follows : " This story is full of ridiculous and impossible statements—words or phrases which contradict each other or the rest of the passage. Some persons have found twenty or thirty absurdities. Cross out the words or phrases which you think are absurd." No time limit is imposed.

More fruitful results, however, will be obtained with an oral procedure, since then the child can explain the reasons for his criticisms. This method was employed to obtain the results recorded in the table (p. 234). The child is first asked to read the passage through to himself, without further explanation. Younger children should read the passage aloud, so that the examiner can, if necessary, assist them with the harder words. The child is then asked if he notices anything peculiar about the story. Usually, he has remarked the absurdities in the last sentence, even if he has not smiled at the earlier ones. He is then told that the story is full of such absurdities, that some persons have found as many as twenty or thirty, and that he is to find as many as he can. He is now required to read the whole through a second time, aloud, beginning with the title ; and instructed to point out each absurdity as he notices it. If, through some misapprehension, he is content with discovering only one or two in the first paragraph, and then hurries on with the reading, he is asked if that is all he can find, and reminded that there are a large number in every paragraph. One mark is given for each absurdity spontaneously discovered by the child. The criticism of legitimate or possible statements on the ground of fancied absurdity—*e.g.*, a denial that the moon might be visible in the daytime—is, of course, not to be counted.

Like a completion-test, an absurdity test can be also cast in discontinuous form, consisting of a number of separate unconnected sentences, each of which (or some of which) contain some inconsistency or absurdity. This is the form adopted by Binet. But the number of examples employed by him—five in all—is far too few. American investigators have collected a larger number ; interspersed them with a number of statements which are not impossible or absurd ; and require the child to mark those which he considered absurd. The procedure, however, is cumbrous, since even if the child's marks are distributed by mere chance the probability is that 50 per cent. would be correct.[2]

(1) See p. 212.   (2) Dr. Ballard, however, has since constructed a valuable scale of absurdities graded and discrete in form.

Test 28.—Absurdities.

A Sunday in France.

Ten years ago on a pleasant summer's afternoon in the middle of January, 1916, the twelve o'clock express from Scotland was rushing past the busy terminus of the Great Western Railway at twelve miles an hour.

A clean-shaven young Englishman, of about fifty years of age, stepped lightly from one of the first-class carriages and hurried slowly down the platform with both hands in his pockets, carrying a heavy bag, and gaily curling the tips of his moustache. His strange voice suggested that he was a native of Germany, born and bred, no doubt, in Paris ; and by his dusty shoes I gathered he had walked over from New York that very morning.

There was not a cloud in the sky ; and, as the rain was still falling heavily, he took off his mackintosh and strolled out into the crowded streets of the city. The ripening fields of corn through which he passed were turning golden as the sun set in the south. The square semi-circle of the new moon shone brightly in the heavens overhead. The evening shadows grew shorter and shorter in the twilight. And a few minutes later, with a burst of splendour, the day dawned.

He was standing on London Bridge watching the grey waters of the Severn rush northwards out to sea, and listening to the bleating of the sheep on Hampstead Heath. A few feet above his head an aeroplane was standing still in the sky ; and beyond in the cloud a bright red seagull, with its four broad wings outspread, could be seen flying invisibly above the Dutch mountains. The clock on the dome of St. Paul's struck the hour. One, two, three, he counted, and then ten more strokes. "It must be just half-past eleven," he said ; "no wonder I am thirsty. I must call at a greengrocer's for a glass of salt beef."

2. GRADED REASONING TESTS.

Of all the supplementary tests here given the following is, in my view, by far the most efficient. It is particularly suitable for older and brighter children. It consists of brief questions, preceded by the data necessary for answering those questions. From the premises thus given, the solution to each problem can be deduced by ordinary logical inference. No special knowledge, apart from that which is the common property of all normal children at the ages tested, is expected or required. Empirically it is found that reasoning tests of this character form the best tests of intelligence, so far as intelligence can be tested by tasks of a single kind. It should be remembered, however, that, if time allows, it is always better to use tests of several different types, and not limit the examination to one form, however excellent in theory.[1]

There are in the present series seventeen problems. They are arranged in order of difficulty ; and allocated in groups to successive mental ages, two to each year. The principle adopted for the age-assignments resembles

[1] A fuller account of the construction and use of the tests will be found in *Journ. Exp. Ped.*, Vol. V. Nos. 2 and 3, 1919, pp. 68 *et seq.* The appendix there published contains fifty such tests, suitable for a more precise differentiation. Those used in the present investigation and printed below consist of what is there described as the "short series." Where it is desired to obtain a more accurate estimate of a child whose mental level is already approximately known, for example, in testing children within the same school standard the supplementary questions contained in the fuller list of fifty are usually necessary.

that suggested above for the Binet-Simon scale ; but is somewhat simpler in its application. It is, in fact, that which is recommended in the next memorandum for the standardisation of educational tests.[1] Each problem is assigned to the age at which 50 per cent. of the children can successfully answer it, not, as in the Binet-Simon scale, to the age next below. Age is taken as age last birthday. Thus, half the children between age 8·0 and age 9·0, averaging therefore 8½ years, should pass the tests headed " 8 years." Theoretically, therefore, a child on its eighth birthday passes all the tests above the heading " 8 years " and none of the tests below that heading. At 8½ he passes half the tests immediately below that heading—that is, one out of the two in the short list here given for age 8.

The conversion of the test-score into equivalent age or *vice versa* also follows a simpler rule. Each test counts as half a year, zero falling at 6½. Hence, the norm for any age is approximately twice the corresponding school standard. The averages actually obtained at each age are given to the nearest unit[2] in Table XXXIV. together with scores roughly demarcating children of Central School and scholarship merit. With these tests there is

TABLE XXXIV.
Norms for Supplementary Tests—B. Individual Tests.

iverages and Borderlines for Reasoning Tests (Short List).

Age last Birthday.	Approximate Average.	Borderline for Central School Ability.	Borderline for Scholarship Ability.
7 —	2	5	8
8 —	4	7	10
9 —	6	9	12
10 —	8	11	14
11 —	10	13	16
12 —	12	15	17
13 —	14	16	17
14 —	16	17	17

at any one age a far greater range of individual variation than with the Binet-Simon tests. Thus a high-grade " defective " of fourteen, who reaches a mental age of nearly eleven with the Binet-Simon tests, and can read fairly fluently, is yet unable to do more than one or two of the simplest reasoning tests allotted to ages seven or eight. On the other hand, one of the brightest children I have met in the ordinary elementary schools of London (she is the daughter of a headmaster in the Council's service, and has since been awarded a Christ's Hospital Scholarship) scored, when tested at the age of $9\frac{5}{12}$, a mental age of 14·5 with the reasoning tests, but only 13·6 with the Binet-Simon tests.

As with the Binet-Simon tests, each child is to be examined individually and orally.[3] The same general procedure, and the same method of recording the results, may be observed.

(1) See below, p. 299.

(2) For fuller tables and preciser figures see *J. Exp. Ped., loc. cit.*, p. 121. The round numbers place the borderlines for ages 10- and 11-, and perhaps for age 9-, a little too low. The exact numbers lie about midway between the figures given and the next unit; *e.g.*, the borderline for scholarship ability appears to lie, on an average, at about 14·4 ; but, of course, must vary in different schools and under different circumstances.

(3) For an interesting group experiment with these tests in written form, see M. M. Fairgrieve, " A Mass Test with Intelligence Questions," *J. Exp. Ped.*, VI., i., pp. 27 *et seq.* The written form, however, is inevitably less successful, since then the child does not always grasp that he is intended to deduce the answer from the premisses, and, further, the examiner loses the opportunity for insight into the child's methods by means of cross-examination.

The questions are to be read by the child himself. For younger children it is more convenient to have each problem cut out and pasted, or else clearly typed, upon a separate card. The problem is handed to the child with the following explanation : " Will you read this, please ? At the end you will find a question. When you have read the question, look carefully again at what is printed above it, and try whether you can think out the answer." The younger and duller children should read each problem aloud. Those of higher level (standard III. or above) need only read aloud the first few. If unable to pronounce a particular word, or if unfamiliar with its meaning, a child may be assisted. When it is clear that the child understands his task, he should be left quietly puzzling over the question, forgetful, as far as possible, of the examiner's presence. As soon as the answer is given, it is accepted with a word of praise, and the child asked to give his reasons. If answer and reasons are incorrect, the child is then asked to try again, until he either succeeds, or fails in four successive attempts. Every child should work forward from the easiest example until he fails on at least three consecutive problems.

One mark is given for each test correctly answered and correctly reasoned. The additional trials should not exceed three in all for one test. For each unsuccessful attempt a quarter of a mark is deducted. A fraction— as a rule, a quarter, a half, or three-quarters respectively—is also deducted for an ill-expressed reason, an inadequate reason, or no reason at all.

Test 29.—GRADED REASONING TESTS.
(Short List.)

1.   Tom runs faster than Jim :
        Jack runs slower than Jim.
    Which is the slowest of the three ?

7 Years.

2.   Kate is cleverer than May :
        May is cleverer than Jane.
    Who is the cleverest—Jane, Kate, or May ?

3. I have bought the following Christmas presents : a pipe, a blouse, some music, a box of cigarettes, a bracelet, a toy engine, a bat, a book, a doll, a walking-stick, and an umbrella.
My brother is eighteen : he does not smoke, nor play cricket, nor play the piano.
I want to give the walking-stick to my father, and the umbrella to my mother.
    Which of the above shall I give my brother ?

8 Years.

4.   I don't like sea voyages :
        And I don't like the seaside.
    I must spend Easter either in France, or among the Scottish Hills, or on the South Coast.
    Which shall it be ?

5. The person who stole Brown's purse was neither dark, nor tall, nor clean-shaven.
The only persons in the room at the time were—
    1. Jones, who is short, dark, and clean-shaven :
    2. Smith, who is fair, short, and bearded :
    3. Grant, who is dark, tall, but not clean-shaven.
        Who stole Brown's purse ?

9 *Years.*

6.   Three boys are sitting in a row :
     Harry is to the left of Willie :
     George is to the left of Harry.
    Which boy is in the middle ?

7. In cold, damp climates, root crops, like potatoes and turnips, grow best :
   In temperate climates, there are abundant pastures, and oats and barley
    flourish :
   In sub-tropical climates, wheat, olives, and vines flourish :
   In tropical climates, date-palms and rice flourish.
        The ancient Greeks lived largely on bread, with oil instead of
   butter : they had wine to drink and raisins for fruit.
        Which climate do you think they had ?

10 *Years.*

8.   There are four roads here :
   I have come from the south and want to go to Melton.
   The road to the right leads somewhere else :
   Straight ahead it leads only to a farm.
        In which direction is Melton—North, South, East, or West ?

9. The doctor thinks Violet has caught some illness.
     If she has a rash, it is probably chicken-pox, measles, or scarlet
      fever :
     If she has been ailing with a cold or cough, she may develop
      whooping-cough, measles, or mumps.
   She has been sneezing and coughing for some days : and now spots are
    appearing on her face and arms.
        What do you think is the matter with Violet ?

11 *Years.*

10. Where the climate is hot, gum-trees and rubber will grow :
    Heather and grass will grow only where it is cold :
      Heather and rubber require plenty of moisture :
      Grass and gum-trees will grow only in fairly dry regions :
    Near the river Amazon it is very hot and very damp.
        Which of the above grows there ?

11. Father has just come home in a brand new overcoat : there is clay on
     his boots and flour on his hat.
    The only places he can have been to are Northgate, Southgate, West-
     gate, or the City; and he has not had time to go to more than
     one of these.
    There is no clay anywhere in the streets except where the pavement
     is up for repair.
    There are tailors' shops only in Southgate, Westgate, and the City.
    There are flour mills only in Northgate, Westgate, and the City.
    I know the roads are not being repaired in the City, though they may
     be in the other places.
        Where has father been ?

12 *Years.*

12. I started from the church and walked 100 yards :
I turned to the right and walked 50 yards :
I turned to the right again and walked 100 yards.
How far am I from the church ?

13. Field-mice devour the honey stored by the humble-bees : the honey
which they store is the chief food of the humble-bees.
Near towns, there are far more cats than in the open country.
Cats kill all kinds of mice.
Where, then, do you think there are most humble-bees—
in the neighbourhood of towns or in the open country ?

13 *Years.*

14. A pound of meat should roast for half an hour :
Two pounds of meat should roast for three-quarters of an hour :
Three pounds of meat should roast for one hour :
Eight pounds of meat should roast for two hours and a quarter :
Nine pounds of meat should roast for two hours and a half.
From this can you discover a simple rule by which you
can tell from the weight of a joint for how long it
should roast ?

15. What conclusion can you draw from the following facts ?
Iron nails will not float in a pool :
A cup of pure gold dust weighs nearly twenty times as much as a cup
of water of the same size :
If you drop a silver sixpence or a copper coin into a puddle, it will sink
to the bottom :
A cubic inch (about a tablespoonful) of water weighs less than half an
ounce ; a cubic inch of brass weighs over two ounces :
A leaden weight will drop to the bottom of the ocean.
Sum up all these observations in one short statement of the
following form : " Most —— are —— —— —— "

14 *Years.*

16. John said : " I heard my clock strike yesterday, ten minutes before the
first gun fired. I did not count the strokes, but I am sure it struck
more than once, and I think it struck an odd number."
John was out all the morning from the earliest hours : and his clock
stopped at five to five the same afternoon.
When do you think the first gun fired ?

17. Captain Watts and his son James have been found shot—the father in the
chest and the son in the back. Both clearly died instantaneously.
A gun fired close to the person —as, for example, when a man shoots himself—will blacken and even burn the skin or clothes : fired from a
greater distance, it will leave no such mark.
The two bodies were found near the middle of a large hall used as a rifle
range. Its floor is covered with damp sand, which shows every foot-
print distinctly. Inside the room there are two pairs of footprints
only. A third man standing just outside the door or window could
aim at any part of the room : but the pavement outside would
show no footmarks

Under Captain Watts' body was found a gun : no such weapon was found near James.

In each case the coat, where the bullet entered, was blackened with gunpowder, and the cloth a little singed.

Captain Watts was devoted to his son, and would have died sooner than harm him purposely : hence it is impossible to suppose that he killed him deliberately, even in self-defence. But some think that James secretly disliked his father, and hoped to inherit his fortune at his death.

> (1) Was Captain Watts' death due to murder, accident, or suicide ?
>
> (2) Was James' death due to murder, accident, or suicide ?

3. THE PORTEUS MAZE-TESTS.

Mazes and miniature labyrinths have been used freely to study both speed and manner of learning among animals. Power to learn, educability, is for some writers the very definition of intelligence. And it is, therefore, natural that what has proved so successful for the investigation of educability in animals should also be adopted as a possible test for intelligence in the child. Such a test would have the great advantage of being embodied in non-linguistic material, and requiring other than a merely verbal manifestation of general capacity.

For this purpose the only systematic set of maze-tests is that arranged by Dr. Porteus, Director of Research at the Vineland Training School in America. The mazes, eleven in number, are reproduced on the following pages.[1] They have been chosen to form an age-scale upon principles similar to those that underlie the Binet-Simon tests.

The procedure which I recommend, slightly modified from that of Dr. Porteus, is as follows : For all children above the level of the infants' school, the examiner begins with the maze for age V. The child is told to "suppose this is the plan of the paths in a garden. These lines are walls which you cannot get over. Start with the pen from the mark at the top, and find your way out of the garden by the quickest path. Show me, first of all, any openings that you can see." (The two openings are indicated.) "All the other paths are blocked. Don't go up any of the blocked turnings. Go down this path from the top, and then out by the *first* opening you can find." To avoid marking the paper, the child uses a dry pen or a pointed stick. After he has once begun, he should not lift his pen from the paper.[2]

With the succeeding patterns the openings are not pointed out first of all. Emphasise that the child must find his way out without turning up any of the blocked paths; and, as soon as he enters a blind alley and has discovered that he is blocked, do not allow him to correct his mistake by retracing his path, but bring him back to the starting point for a second

---

[1] I have to thank Dr. Porteus for his courteous permission to reproduce these figures. An earlier version has already been published in this country in the *Journal of Experimental Pedagogy* (Vol. III., No. 2, p. 113) ; but the mazes there shown are in an unrevised form, and are printed on a scale too reduced for actual use. The tests originally assigned to ages V., VI., and XIII. have now been transferred to ages IV., V., and XIV. respectively. In place of the earlier unsatisfactory VII.-year-test two new tests have been inserted for ages VI. and VII. (not differing, however, as I think, widely enough from each other in difficulty). And in the patterns retained a few slight changes have been introduced, apparently to fit them a little more closely to the levels required. The tests, as thus revised, are described and discussed in full in a recent monograph published by the Vineland Training School, *The Porteus Tests : Vineland Revision*, September, 1919.

[2] Dr. Porteus requires the child to mark his path visibly in pencil. This entails a fresh sheet for every child, and, with the same child, after every error. For such a procedure blanks in large quantities can be obtained from the Extension Department of the Training School, Vineland, N.J.

trial. If for some reason—for example, a suspected accident in a successful second trial—a third attempt seems needed, invert the diagram and treat it as a new test.

Dr. Porteus states that the tests need be continued only until the child entirely fails with two successive mazes. I suggest that, unless it is plainly evident that the remainder are too hard, each child should be allowed to attempt every maze.

The following method is recommended for scoring the results. One mark is awarded for each test correctly performed on the first trial. Half a mark only is allowed if a second trial is necessary for success. To the total number of marks thus gained, add four marks for presumable success in imaginary tests for ages I. to IV.; the result will give the child's score roughly in terms of a mental age. There is no test for age XIII. But four trials are allowed with the mazes for ages XII. and XIV. With that for age XII. a full mark is allowed for a success in any of the first three trials ; and half a mark for a success in the fourth. But with that for age XIV. two marks are allowed for a success in the first trial ; and for every further trial needed half a mark is deducted : thus a child who does not succeed until the second trial scores only one and a half, and so on.

With the patterns for ages III. and IV. the child has simply to follow the general shape of the figure by drawing his pencil between the two lines. The examiner demonstrates by visibly drawing with his pencil on a separate copy. In the pattern for age III. the child passes if he does not cross the lines, or cut off corners, in more than three places ; in that for age IV., if he does not cross the lines more than twice. In either case, a full mark is allowed for a success in either one of the two permissible trials. With the maze for age V. half a mark is deducted if the child passes out of the second, or lower, opening.

For English children the standardisation does not appear altogether perfect. The percentage in each age-group, passing the tests assigned to their own year, differs much from maze to maze. For example (counting two half-successes scored by two different children as equivalent to one full success scored by a single child), only 62 per cent. of the children aged 5 pass the maze for age V., while as many as 84 per cent. aged 8 pass the maze for age VIII.; and, indeed, even by modifying the given mazes slightly, or selecting mazes afresh from a new and larger series, it would be difficult to hit upon an evenly graduated scale containing only one test to mark the exact median for each year. Hence, I suggest that the mazes as a whole be regarded as forming a single graded test-series, roughly increasing in difficulty, rather than as marking definite mental ages. In Table XXXIV. I append norms for London children. For strict comparisons mental ages should be deduced from these. But it will be seen that those obtained by the simpler method and upon the original assumptions differ only by a fraction.

In any case, the examiner should endeavour to observe the cause of the child's failure. Here, as elsewhere, the significance of the test lies quite as much in the child's method of attack as in his ultimate achievement. The cause may be an intellectual one. The child may become confused; his power of systematic attention may be unable to cope with a task so complex ; he may be unable to follow with his unaided eye the longer paths and more devious routes, or he may fail to retain the results of his observation so as to guide the movements of his hand ; he may be unable to plan, or to profit by his past mistakes. Quite as commonly the cause is partly emotional. The child may be over-confident, or careless ; he seems unable to take thought beforehand, or too dashing and impulsive to carry out his thoughts.

The peculiar value of the tests lies in the fact that the material is non-linguistic. Many borderline cases of suspected mental deficiency, particularly slow and steady dullards with a manual or industrial bias, fail hopelessly with the Binet-Simon scale, and yet unexpectedly succeed with the maze tests ; and, conversely, many of the more unstable type, girls especially, who answer glibly with the former, have not the prudence, the forethought, the maintenance of attention and alertness which the latter demand. The maze-tests, therefore, supplement, though they cannot, I think, supplant, the other scales in a profitable way. It is perhaps in estimating social as distinguished from educational efficiency that they will be found most helpful.

Note on the Average Upper Limit for the Development of Intelligence.—It will be noticed that the Porteus tests, like the version given above for the Binet-Simon scale, make no provision for the years beyond sixteen ; and so, by implication, seem to set an upper limit to the growth of intelligence at about that age.[1] I have indeed, in the text (p. 170) explicitly taken the mental age of 16 as representing the average level reached by normal London adults. Terman, in the Stanford Revision, and most other investigators, have made a like assumption. Influenced, however, by the low average revealed with the Binet tests among American recruits (13·5 years), the latest suggestions infer that mental growth must cease two or three years earlier than has hitherto been believed ; and propose, in calculating the mental ratio for adults, a divisor of 13 or 14.

With this extreme deduction my own results hardly conform. Apart from the immense accession of acquired knowledge and skill, setting aside, too, the gradual emergence of new powers of character and feeling, which the process of adolescence seems to confer, there can, indeed, be little doubt that, after the age of leaving school, the further development of natural intelligence is, in most persons, far smaller than is commonly thought. Nevertheless, the opposite assumption—that intelligence grows by equal annual increments up to the beginning of puberty, and then abruptly ceases—is equally mistaken. The error perhaps comes largely from supposing that a limit found with tests of one or two restricted types can be assigned as a fixed flat highwater-mark for intellectual processes of every observable kind.

My present conclusion is based, not upon experiments with the Binet-Simon scale, but upon supplementary tests of intelligence, such as those above described. My data are incomplete and provisional.[2] They have been obtained, not only from students in Universities and Training Colleges, who are, of course, of supernormal grade, but also from adults in various spheres of life, who from their educational history may be regarded as median or average specimens of the ordinary elementary school class. Enquiries begun in the new continuation schools, whereby the same individuals will be tested and re-tested year after year, may, I hope, eventually return a conclusive reply.

It is not sufficient to compare, age by age, as is so commonly done, merely the average number of marks obtained, or the average number of questions answered (the procedure illustrated in figure 26) ; for there is nothing to show whether the units are of equal magnitude throughout the scale or whether the last test-questions are hard enough, easy enough, or graded finely enough, to differentiate the averages for the later years. The original measurements must first be converted into terms of the standard deviations of the relevant age-groups (as was done in constructing figure 21).

I have, therefore, taken as zero the average performance of children aged nine—the age about which the standard deviation is approximately equal to the annual increment or mental year. I have treated the standard deviations for all the age-groups as theoretically equivalent, both to one another, and to the standard deviation (mental year, or annual increment) at nine, which thus becomes the unit for the successive age-averages, expressed as divergencies above or below the average nine-year level. Thus measured, the averages for the years between five or six and twenty-two or twenty-three, when all the test-results are amalgamated in a single series, lie nearly upon a logarithmic curve. The following equation roughly fits the line of growth obtained :—

$$A = 4 - 10^{\frac{15-a}{10}},$$

where $A \equiv$ mental level (expressed as above), and $a \equiv$ chronological age.

This curve is asymptotic. By the form of its equation it progressively approaches a horizontal line 4 units above the arbitrary zero, that is, a level above the mental age at nine by four times the mental year at nine. If, for purposes of measurement, the mental year remained as large throughout the next few years, this might

[1] Dr. Porteus, as I understand, is now experimenting with mazes for adults of higher intelligence.

[2] They will, I hope, be published very shortly elsewhere in fuller detail than can be given here.

seem to imply that the upper limit of intellectual growth was the mental age of thirteen (9+4). But, as we have seen, the annual increment decreases steadily.[1] It is, however, still discernible and still measurable, not only after the calendar age of thirteen, but (particularly when we compare test-results from adults in the twenties) even after the age of sixteen ; yet, as contrasted with the standard deviation, though theoretically significant, it becomes negligible in practice.

Attempts at constructing an absolute curve of mental growth, however, are at present likely to be of academic interest only. For practical purposes it is far more instructive to express the growth curve in terms of mental years. On this basis a logarithmic curve gives a first rough approximation for the later stages (ages 7 to 17). To fit the earlier stages (ages 0 to 7) we may use an inverted logarithmic curve. When we join the two curves into one, we obtain an S-shaped curve, not unlike the cumulative ogive obtained from the normal distribution. This in turn suggests a speculative hypothesis as to the nature of the growth-process which I have developed elsewhere.

With certain simplifications it is not difficult to arrive at an analytical expression which will yield a first approximation to the double curve. Let us suppose that the rate of growth at any moment, dy/dt say, is more or less proportional (i) to the amount of growth already achieved, and (ii) to the amount of growth that remains to be achieved, i.e., (i) to the distance the child has travelled from zero growth, and (ii) the distance he has yet to travel to reach maximum growth, i.e., maturity. Then

$$\frac{dy}{dt} = k.y.\,(1-y)$$

where l represents maximum growth and k a constant dependent on the unit of scale. This suggests that mental growth during the earlier ages is governed by a " law of compound interest " and during the later by a " law of diminishing returns." If we measure both time and growth from the midpoint (age of maximum speed), and changing the scale, we may write

$$\frac{dy'}{dt'} = (1 + y')\,(1 - y')$$

The solution of this (cf. D. A. Murray, *Int. and Diff. Calculus*, p. 415) is

$$y' = \tanh t',$$

so that the values of y' can be found from a table of hyperbolic tangents.

But if we put $x = 2t'$ we can express this very conveniently as

$$y = \frac{1}{1 + e^{-x}}$$

An equation and a curve of this type—known as the " logistic " or " Malthusian curve "—has frequently been suggested for describing the growth of populations both of human individuals and of other organisms, e.g., cells. But the relations between the logistic curve, the curve for the hyperbolic tangent and the cumulative normal curve, have not to my knowledge been previously pointed out.

The fit so obtained, however, is not altogether satisfactory : the observed data suggest a curve that is (i) less sinuous (nearer to a straight line between ages 5 and 11); and (ii) not necessarily symmetrical. A more elastic expression can be obtained by taking for the index in the exponential term a series of powers of x. I then find that

$$y = \frac{15}{1 + e^{-\cdot27x + \cdot0025\,x^2 - \cdot0025\,x^3}}$$

gives a reasonable fit.

This suggests taking an age of 15 or thereabouts (on a conventional scale of mental years) as the limit for the normal child. It does not follow that 15 should be used as a universal divisor in obtaining a mental ratio for older youths or adults. The common figure of 16 is undoubtedly too high. If mental ratios are to be used at all at these older levels, I suggest a changing divisor, devised to keep the ratio equal (so far as possible) to that obtained during childhood. However, on all these points further research is needed.

---

[1] Since, during a large portion of the school year, the standard deviations, measured in terms of age, are in arithmetical progression (see p. 158), it should seem perhaps that the annual increments, measured in terms of the standard deviation, would be in harmonical progression. The curve, however, deduced on this basis rises too high to fit the figures for the later years.

The non-mathematical reader, who finds himself bewildered by the technicalities of my general argument may perhaps best seize my meaning if he turns to figure 21 (p. 151) and notes that (up to the age of XIII. or XIV.—the rest of the diagram is untrustworthy) the intervals between successive years become smaller and smaller, and the longer vertical lines dividing them become more and more closely packed. An artificial illustration of more regular condensation will be seen in the scale-divisions to the left of figure 24 (p. 162) ; the scale is, in fact, here actually logarithmic. If now in figure 21 he supposes the ages after XII. or XIII. to get telescoped upon each other in the same even way, he will realise at once that the year-intervals towards the age of twenty, though still discoverable, would become negligibly small, and so ultimately disappear.

FIGURES 28 TO 38.

Test 30.—PORTEUS MAZES.

FIGURE 28.   YEAR III.

Allow demonstration, 2 trials, and 3 errors.

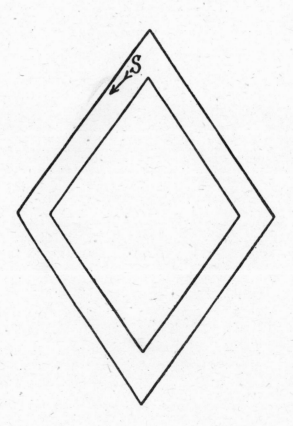

FIGURE 29. YEAR IV.

Allow demonstration, 2 trials, and 2 errors.

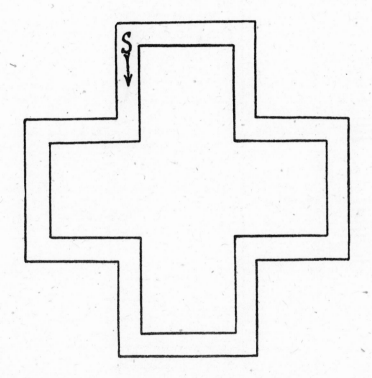

T

FIGURE 30. YEAR V.

Demonstrate openings: deduct ½ mark for 2nd trial.

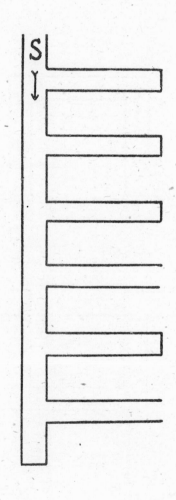

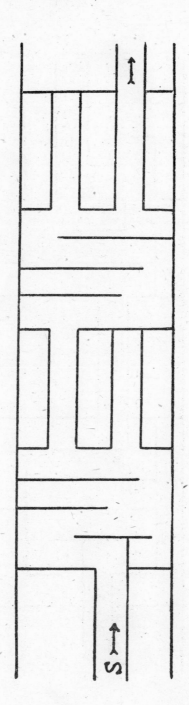

FIGURE 31. YEAR VI.

No demonstration : deduct ½ mark for 2nd trial.

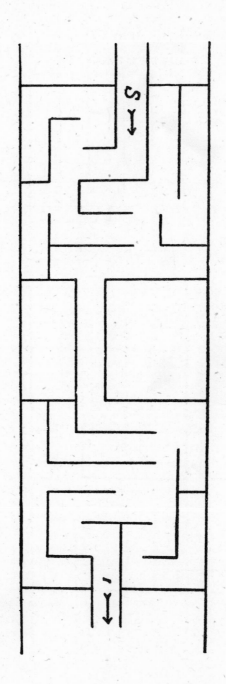

FIGURE 32. YEAR VII.

½ mark for 2nd trial.

FIGURE 33. YEAR VIII.

½ mark for 2nd trial.

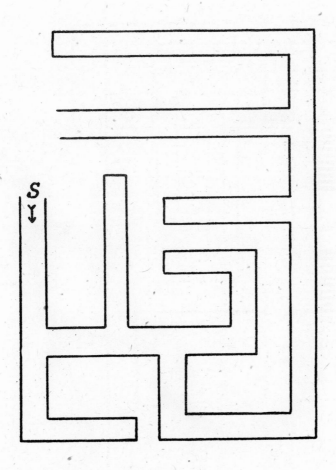

FIGURE 34. YEAR IX.

½ mark for 2nd trial.

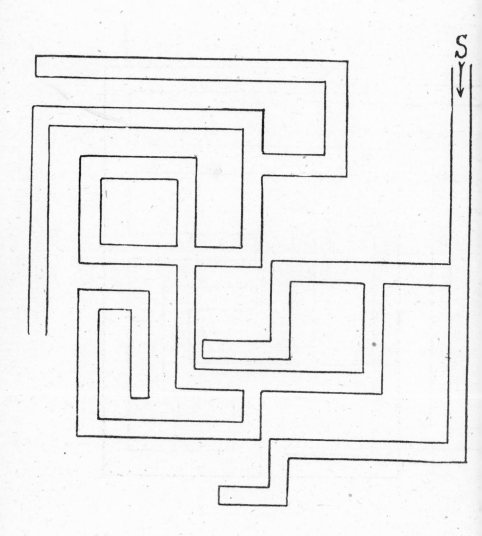

FIGURE 35. YEAR X.

½ mark for 2nd trial.

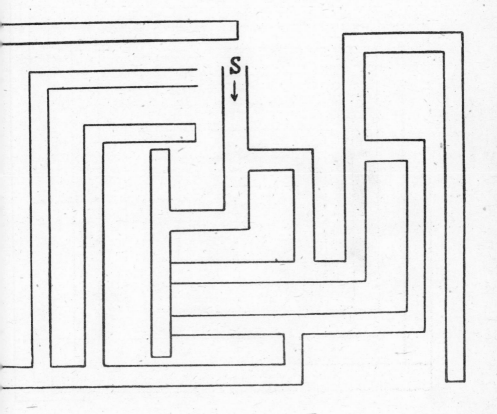

FIGURE 36. YEAR XI.

½ mark for 2nd trial.

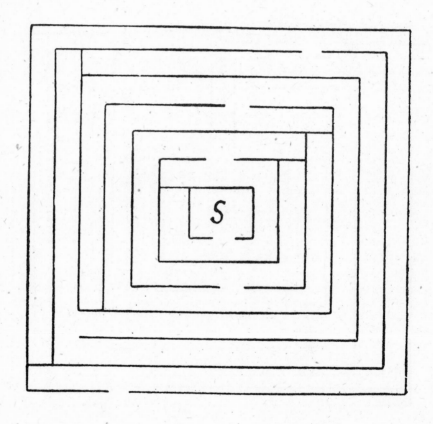

FIGURE 37. YEAR XII.

1 mark for 1st, 2nd or 3rd trials ; ½ mark for 4th trial.

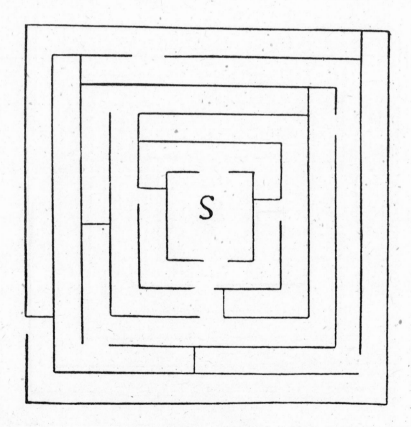

FIGURE 38. YEAR XIV.

2, 1½, 1, ½ marks for 1st, 2nd, 3rd, 4th trials respectively.

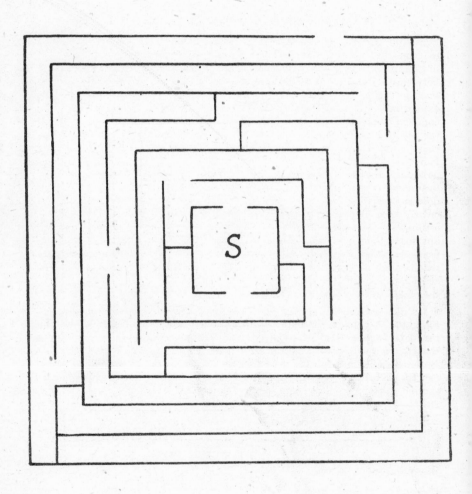

APPENDIX V.

Accuracy of the Supplementary Tests.

Criticisms of Previous Demonstrations. For the teacher the most convincing evidence that the new tests described above will provide trustworthy estimates of the pupils' general intelligence will consist in the actual correlations between the results of the tests and the assessments of intelligence made by teachers themselves ; and this was the criterion I relied on in my earliest experiments. To the psychologist, however, the problem will seem too complex to be conclusively settled in that fashion. "How," he asks, "does the teacher who supplied you with assessments for intelligence know that there is any such thing ? " The correlations of Cattell, Thorndike and their fellow-workers have failed to substantiate its existence ; and, though their methods were considered faulty by Prof. Spearman, Prof. Spearman himself has since expressed grave doubts.[1] Intelligence, he argues, has so many different meanings, and includes such a " superposed mass of obscurity and error," that it would be better to drop the word altogether. Teachers' estimates " vary according to the criterion they happen to adopt," and are apt to include a variety of mental qualities that do not fall within the psychologist's conception. More particularly, it is added, their assessments tend to show a strong scholastic bias : they are influenced more by the child's actual attainments than by his innate capacity, and thus depend largely on the child's docility, industry, and memory.

Prof. Spearman therefore concludes that, instead of using the teachers' estimates to explain the experimental data, it would be better to use the test-data to elucidate the teachers' estimates, " which reveal all the faults that might have been expected from their origin in lay psychology. . . . Burt himself, for instance, found that certain teachers' estimates, instead of exactly coinciding with his General Factor as indicated by the experiments, showed a strong tendency to base themselves on power of memorizing " (*loc. cit.*, p. 67). And even those who, unlike Prof. Spearman, accept the term " intelligence " have voiced somewhat similar objections. Would it not be better, they ask, to assess each child's all-round ability by his total perform-ance in all the experimental tests employed ? In that way the relative efficiency of each particular test could be measured by its agreement with the sum total of the lot.

Correlations of Separate Tests. With much of these criticisms I wholly agree ; but I do not find them decisive. No doubt, it is the task of the educational psychologist to check and refine the practical teachers' conceptions and rough-and-ready procedures. No doubt, too, many teachers take too narrow a view of what intelligence should really mean. Nevertheless, in my experi-ence, once an adequate definition or explanation has been given, the majority

---

[1] *Brit. J. Psych.*, V., 1912, p. 66.

of the more thoughtful observers are able to give broad and unbiased assessments, which may serve at least as useful starting points. But the best reply to these preliminary questions, and the best proof that the two interpretations of intelligence are approximately identical, are to be found in a detailed comparison of the test-results, on the one hand, with the teachers' estimates on the other.

The group tests described above were applied to 843 children aged 10.0 to 13.0 (including a due proportion of children from central and secondary schools) ; the individual tests to 251 children aged 10.0 to 12.0[1]. To avoid the influence of age, the correlations were worked out separately for each age-group, and then averaged. In the tables below (Tables XXXV. A and B) I have followed my previous practice and given the correlations of *each* test (a) with the hypothetical general factor ; and (b) with the teachers' assessments for general intelligence. It will be seen that the order of magnitude is much the same for both sets of coefficients, but that the correlations with the general factor are invariably higher. That we should expect, seeing that all the tests were carried out at about the same date and refer to much the same limited type of situation. And, if the agreement between the results of each test taken singly and the assessments of the children's own teachers falls short of perfect identity, then, I venture to suggest, it is at least conceivable that the psychologist's brief tests may be as much at fault as the prolonged observations of experienced judges.

From the standpoint of rigorous demonstration the most cogent procedure of all would be to calculate the amount of (a) the hypothetical general factor possessed by each child, by taking a *weighted* sum of the test-marks, and then to correlate this calculated figure *directly* with (b) the teacher's assessment.

The Calculation of Weighted Estimates. Yule's formulæ for partial correlation furnish the procedure required.[2] Adopting his notation we have to find an estimate of X_1 (the general factor) on the basis of n tests ($X_2, \ldots X_n$). We can do this by setting up what he terms the " characteristic equation "

$$X_1 = a + b_2X_2 + b_3X_3 + \ldots + b_nX_n.$$

By the method of least squares we can then determine the best values for the coefficients $b_2, b_3, \ldots b_n$ (which he terms " partial regression coefficients "). All we need are (i) the correlations of each of the ($n - 1$) tests, $X_2, X_3, \ldots X_n$, with each other and (ii) the correlation of each of the tests with the hypothetical general factor.

Accordingly, having computed the appropriate weights, I have found the weighted total of the marks for the various tests employed (*i.e.*, the estimated values for X_1) by this equation, and correlated these estimates with the teacher's direct assessments for " intelligence," defined as above. I then find that for the children tested the correlations average 0.82 for the written group tests and 0.87 for the individual tests—correlations appreciably higher than those given by the Binet-Simon tests.

The Calculation of the Regressions. For those who wish for fuller details a brief explanation is desirable to show how the weights have been obtained. The crux of the adapted method lies in the preliminary determination of the correlation between each test and the hypothetical general factor. For this

---

(1) The individual testing was carried out with the aid of Miss Bradshaw and Miss Grant, to whom I am much indebted for assistance in the calculations. Earlier versions of the tests had been applied at Liverpool schools with the assistance of Mr. R. C. Moore : (see *J. Exp. Ped.*, *loc. cit.*, I., pp. 101f. ; a full discussion of the tests and correlations will be found in Mr. Moore's thesis).

(2) *Introduction to the Theory of Statistics*, 1910, pp. 230 *et seq.*

purpose I have here employed the same formula as was proposed in my previous Report (*Distribution and Relation of Educational Abilities*, 1917, p. 53). And since the imperfect correlations suggest that the tests themselves may in part depend on irrelevant specialized abilities (memory, speed, verbal ability, spatial perception, or capacity for quick and skilful movement), I have at the same time adopted the supplementary device there used, namely, calculating the residual or specific correlations and testing their significance by the probable error.

In the printed report the algebraic proof and the technical justification for these further formulæ were omitted. But, since several teachers have inquired how they were reached, it may be convenient to incorporate the fuller account[1] here : to those who are familiar with the work of Udny Yule and others on " multiple " and " partial " correlation, the derivation both of the formulæ and of the procedures will be sufficiently evident without further discussion.

Algebraic Proofs. All that is necessary is to modify the principle of partial correlation so that it can be adapted to the case where the relevant and irrelevant factors which are to be successively partialled out *must be deduced from the correlated data themselves* instead of from an external rating or " criterion." Let us begin, as the familiar proof of the Bravais-Pearson formula begins,[2] by supposing that any pair of correlated variables, x and y say, may be conceived as linear functions (*i.e.*, weighted sums) of a number of independent causal factors, $g, h, \ldots s, t$: so that we can write

$$x = w_{xg}g + w_{xh}h + \ldots w_{xs}s + w_{xt}t \ldots\ldots\ldots\ldots\ldots\text{(i)}$$

$$y = w_{yg}g + w_{yh}h + \ldots w_{ys}s + w_{yt}t \ldots\ldots\ldots\ldots\ldots\text{(ii)}$$

(where some of the weights may be zero). Here we are weighting factor-measurements to obtain test-measurements, not vice versa. From this the usual proof proceeds to demonstrate that the best value for the correlation will be

$$r_{xy} = \frac{\Sigma xy}{\sqrt{\Sigma x^2}\sqrt{\Sigma y^2}} \ldots\ldots\ldots\ldots\ldots\text{(iii)}$$

Now let us express the right-hand side of this equation in terms of the original factors. For simplicity, we will first of all suppose that each variable depends upon *one* common factor only (g), together with *one* specific factor peculiar to itself (s or t). Then the weights attached to all the other factors will be zero ; and we have

$$x = w_{xg}g + w_{xs}s, \ldots\ldots\ldots\ldots\ldots\text{(iv)}$$

$$y = w_{yg}g + w_{yt}t. \ldots\ldots\ldots\ldots\ldots\text{(v)}$$

Accordingly, substituting these values in equation (iii), we obtain

$$r_{xy} = \frac{\Sigma(w_{xg}g + w_{xs}s)(w_{yg} + w_{yt}t)}{\sqrt{\Sigma(w_{xg}g + w_{xs}s)^2}\sqrt{\Sigma(w_{yg}g + w_{yt}t)^2}} \ldots\ldots\ldots\text{(vi)}$$

---

[1] *Annual Report of the Psychologist*, 1914, Appendix I.

[2] The reader will find a simple and accessible version of this proof (based on Prof. Pearson's original memoir) in the Appendix to Caradog Jones's *First Course in Statistics*, 1920, pp. 276f.

But by hypothesis $r_{gs} = r_{gt} = r_{st} = 0$, and therefore $\Sigma gs = \Sigma gt = \Sigma st = 0$. Consequently we have, on multiplying out,

$$r_{xy} = \frac{w_{xg}w_{yg}\Sigma g^2}{\sqrt{w^2{}_{xg}\Sigma g^2 + w^2{}_{xs}\Sigma s^2}\;\sqrt{w^2{}_{yg}\Sigma g^2 + w^2{}_{yt}\Sigma t^2}} \quad \ldots\ldots \text{(vii)}$$

But, by the same procedure, we have

$$r_{xg} = \frac{\Sigma(w_{xg}g + w_{xs}s)g}{\sqrt{\Sigma(w_{xg}g + w_{xs}s)^2}\sqrt{\Sigma g^2}}$$

$$= \frac{w_{xg}\sqrt{\Sigma g^2}}{\sqrt{w^2{}_{xg}\Sigma g^2 + w^2{}_{xs}\Sigma s^2}} \quad ; \ldots\ldots\ldots\ldots \text{(viii)}$$

and similarly

$$r_{yg} = \frac{w_{yg}\sqrt{\Sigma g^2}}{\sqrt{w^2{}_{yg}\Sigma g^2 + w^2{}_{yt}\Sigma t^2}} \quad \ldots\ldots\ldots\ldots\ldots \text{(ix)}$$

Substituting from (viii) and (ix) in (vii), we obtain

$$r_{xy} = r_{xg}r_{yg} ; \ldots\ldots\ldots\ldots\ldots\ldots\ldots \text{(x)}$$

and if x, y, g, s and t are all in " standard measure," so that

$$\Sigma x^2 = \Sigma y^2 = \Sigma g^2 = \Sigma s^2 = \Sigma t^2 = 1,$$

$$w_{xg} = r_{xg} \text{ and } w_{yg} = r_{yg} ; \ldots\ldots\ldots\ldots \text{(xi)}$$

in that case the correlations of x and y with the general factor are identical with the weights or " regression coefficients " w_{xg} and w_{yg}.

Equation (x) provides in my view the best expression for the theoretical table of correlations we should expect if all the correlations depended upon a single factor only. It was regularly used to reconstruct the tables printed in my previous book on *Distribution and Relations of Educational Abilities* and in several earlier papers.

If we envisage the possibility (even without accepting it as a fact) that *more than one* general (or partly general)[1] factor exists, we can easily generalize the foregoing proof. Starting afresh with equations (i) and (ii), and following precisely the same algebraic argument, we obtain

$$r_{xy} = r_{xg}r_{yg} + r_{xh}r_{yh} + \ldots\ldots\ldots\ldots\ldots \text{(xii)}$$

where g, h, $\ldots$ denote the multiplicity of factors.

Now, if we have n tests (x, y, z, $\ldots$ say) instead of only two, we shall have analogous equations for all possible pairs. Accordingly, reverting for a moment to the simplest possible case, namely, that there is only one common factor entering into the n variables, then (using k to denote any one of these variables), we have at once from (x)

$$\Sigma r_{xk} = r_{xg}\Sigma r_{kg}$$

$$\text{and } \Sigma\Sigma r_{kk'} = \Sigma r_{kg}\Sigma r_{k'g} = (\Sigma r_{kg})^2$$

(where k and k' both denote x, y, z, $\ldots$, so that $\Sigma r_{kg} = \Sigma r_{k'g}$).

Thus

$$r_{xg} = \frac{r_{xg}\Sigma r_{kg}}{\sqrt{\Sigma r_{kg}\Sigma r_{kg}}} = \frac{\Sigma r_{xk}}{\sqrt{\Sigma\Sigma r_{kk'}}} \quad \ldots\ldots\ldots\ldots \text{(xiii)}$$

---

[1] By a " partly general " factor I mean one that is shared only by a limited group of the tests, not by all, *i.e.*, what are conveniently called group-factors. We have provided for these by assuming that some of the weights, such as w_{yh}, w_{zh} (say) may be zero.

This " simple summation " formula was given in my 1917 Report (p. 53, equation iii). And it is the formula I have used in calculating the " correlations with the general factor " shown at the foot of Table XXXV. A below.

With several factors we have from equations (i) and (ii)

$$r_{xg} = \frac{r_{xg}\Sigma r_{kg} + r_{xh}\Sigma r_{kh} + \dots}{\sqrt{\Sigma(r_{kg})^2 + \Sigma(r_{kh})^2 + \dots}} \qquad (xiv)$$

To apply equation (xiii) in such a case we must consequently assume that Σr_{kh}, etc. $= 0$. That means we must assume that, for the particular set of tests on which r is based, the residual correlations r_{kh} are distributed, like errors, symmetrically about an expected value of zero.[1] Once we have determined the correlations with the general factor, the calculation of the required regressions follows in the usual way.

The Definition of a Hierarchy. There are two ways in which this procedure differs from that originally suggested by Prof. Spearman ; and, where my conclusions differ from his, it is therefore possible that he would decline to accept them.[2] First, his conception of the hierarchy seems to be broader than mine, and to turn primarily on the " order " of the coefficients, not on their actual size : his requirement is that it should be possible to arrange the table so that " the value always " (*i.e.*, in every row or column) " becomes smaller as the eye travels to the right or downward " (*Am. J. Psych.*, XV., p. 275). He apparently would admit as perfectly hierarchical *any* table in which the columns (or rows) were themselves in perfect correlation (see *Brit. J. Psych.*, V., p. 54, where he applies this alternative method to my own table). He points out that this columnar criterion could be deduced from what he calls " Burt's equation." It does not, however, follow that, if the columnar criterion is satisfied, then my equation will of necessity also be satisfied. Thus he and his students accept as hierarchical a table in which the coefficients are in arithmetical progression, though such coefficients could not be obtained by my multiplication formula (x). Moreover, it would be quite impossible to reconstruct his own table of intercorrelations, even approximately, by multiplying the saturation coefficients that he gives (*Am. J. Psych.*, *loc. cit.*, pp. 276 and 291), *i.e.*, by using the method proposed in my 1909 article. *If* the multiplication gives a good approximation, then, it appears, he would acknowledge the hierarchical order as proven. If it does not, then he would still insist on applying the broader intercolumnar test before rejecting the table as not hierarchical.[3]

---

[1] If we prefer to minimize not the mean of the deviations but the root-mean-square of the deviations, then (as explained below) we must weight each row of observed correlations by the correlation with the general factor. We then have

$$r_{xg} = \frac{\Sigma r_{kg} r_{kx}}{\sqrt[3]{\Sigma(\Sigma r_{kg} r_{kx})^2}} \qquad (xv)$$

This gives the largest weight to deviations (or systematic " errors ") of the highest correlations, which, as is well known, have relatively small sampling errors.

[2] I fancy we also differ about the conclusion to be drawn, when that is strictly formulated. I hold that a perfect hierarchy would only prove the *absence* of group factors ; Spearman holds that it proves the *presence* of a general factor.

[3] As I have shown elsewhere, this intercolumnar formula can be modified to fit the narrower conception by taking the product moment of the correlations as they stand instead of the product moments of their deviations from the column-mean.

The Saturation Formula. Secondly, Prof. Spearman has objected to equation (xiii) on the ground that it assumes a knowledge of the " self-correlations," r_{xx}. (My procedure is to insert approximate values for these self-correlations, and adjust them by successive approximation until we obtain $r_{xx} = r^2_{xg}$.) He therefore suggested an ingenious alternative formula which avoided this assumption. Anything which would avoid this assumption seemed to me at the time a great improvement; but I now doubt whether the particular formula he proposed to substitute is altogether satisfactory. In deciding between the merits of the various formulæ that may be proposed,[1] I venture to suggest that we should accept that equation which gives the best fit to the observed results as judged by the principle of least squares, just as we should in seeking any other form of average. If that be admitted, my own equation would seem to give the better working value, *i.e.*, to yield not merely *a* common or " general factor " but what I have called " the *highest* common factor."[2] However, in practice, the differences obtained by these various formulæ are too small to make any serious differences to the conclusions eventually drawn.

The Statistical Significance of the Deviations. As suggested in previous Reports, the decision as to whether any given table is or is not " hierarchical " will depend upon the statistical significance of the deviations of the " observed coefficients " from the " theoretical values " (cf. Tables XVIII. and XIX. in the 1917 report). Thus to determine whether the discrepancies are due to some further significant factor, *h* say, we can calculate each deviation (or " residual correlation ") by the formula

$$r_{xy \cdot g} = r_{xy} - r_{xg}r_{yg} \qquad \text{(xvi)}$$

and then test its statistical significance by the probable error of the original correlation. This was the procedure adopted in my 1909 article.[3] For example,

---

(1) It is not difficult to devise alternatives. Formula (xiii), it will be seen, is virtually equivalent to taking the ratio of (*a*) the arithmetic mean of the coefficients in a column; and (*b*) the root of the arithmetic mean of all the coefficients in the table. With a perfect " hierarchy " (as I define it) exactly the same value can be obtained by taking the ratio of the *geometric* means; and in this case (as the reader can easily show) the self-correlations are no longer necessary. Unfortunately, however, with empirical correlations a single coefficient that is approximately zero will be sufficient to throw out the whole calculation.

(2) A formal proof can readily be given by adapting the ordinary proof of the partial regression formula which is based on the familiar device of least squares. This leads either to a weighted or an unweighted mean according to the requirements laid down : the closest fit of all is given by the equation already cited ((xv) above), but this is a little cumbersome for general use. (For the method, cf. W. W. Johnson, *Theory of Errors and Method of Least Squares*, pp. 91f. ; in the determinantal equation, reached by this method (*loc. cit.*, p. 100), the symmetrical determinant represents table of correlations and the second members are the correlations with the general factor.) Prof. Karl Pearson would prefer to treat such problems by the method of moments. But here the results reached are the same or nearly the same, according as we include higher moments or not : strictly speaking, the " highest common factor " of all would seem to require the inclusion of all possible moments. (I am much indebted to Dr. Ritchie-Scott and Dr. W. F. Sheppard for suggesting these approaches to the problem, and for checking the proofs given in my previous Notes.)

(3) " Experimental Tests of General Intelligence," *Brit. J. Psych.*, III., pp. 161-2, Tables V. and VI. I still recommend this procedure for beginners and for preliminary trials or checks : but, when it is employed, we must remember that, in a table of 20 residuals, a residual that is three times its own probable error is likely to occur once by sheer chance. A more succinct procedure is to calculate the p.e. or s.d. of the residuals and compare that with the theoretical p.e. or s.d. expected if the true residual correlations are zero. [It would be still more in keeping with modern statistical procedures to compare variances rather than p.e.'s or s.d.'s : since the second variance is laid down by hypothesis, we should use the chi-squared distribution rather than the F-distribution : and greater accuracy is ensured if the observed and the hypothetical correlations are converted to *z* (=tanh⁻¹*r*) before subtracting.]

in Table XXXV. A, if the two Completion tests had only a single factor in common, namely, the hypothetical general factor, we should expect the correlation between them to be ·925 × ·854 = ·790. Actually it is ·834. The residual of + ·044 is more than six times the probable error. Hence there must be some special factor common to this group of two related tests. Most of the other residuals, however, appear to be well within the range of the fluctuations to be expected from chance.

If we desire to estimate the amount contributed to the observed correlation by factors other than g (*i.e.*, the amount of $r_{xy} \cdot g$) *for the group actually tested*, then equation (xvi) indicates the best mode of calculation. If, however, we desire to estimate the amount of partial or specific correlation to be expected *in a group homogeneous as regards the general factor* (*e.g.*, in a well-selected class where all the children are on about the same level for general intelligence), then we must divide by the standard deviations. We then obtain

$$r_{xy \cdot g} = \frac{r_{xy} - r_{xg} r_{yg}}{\sqrt{1 - r^2_{xg}} \quad \sqrt{1 - r^2_{yg}}} \qquad \text{(xvii)}$$

which is Yule's ordinary formula for partial correlation. This yields a larger figure for the residual correlation ; and explains why to the teacher in the classroom the effects of the more specialized factors seem so conspicuous.

When we go on to compute the correlations of each test with the next common factor, h, we can use precisely the same formula as before (xiii). If we apply it to the whole table of residuals, then—as in calculating an ordinary mean deviation, so in calculating what is virtually the mean deviation of correlations—we must disregard the negative signs (*i.e.*, reverse the signs for those tests or columns which have a negative saturation with this second factor). When both first and second factors are based on the whole table, we shall obtain negative correlations between certain items and the second factor. This seems legitimate in dealing with temperamental characteristics, where current psychology classifies persons in terms of contrasted types or tendencies (cf. W. Stern, *Differentielle Psychologie*, pp. 481f.). It may even be plausible in dealing with educational interests and attainments (cf. 1917 Report, p. 58). But (so far as we know) innate abilities are seldom antagonistic or compensatory. Here, therefore, it seems better to seek supplementary factors limited to certain groups of tests alone. We shall then base the general factor saturations on the observed correlations for tests which share no special ability in addition to the one general factor. This entails an obvious modification in the mode of calculating the divisor in equation (xiii) ;[1] and was the procedure used for calculating the correlations with the general factor in Table XXXV. B.

In Table XXXV. B, it will be found, there are a number of significant residuals suggesting special abilities within certain groups of tests.[2] These

---

(1) Let A denote the sum of the saturations for tests a, b, and c ; D the sum for d, e, and f ; G the sum for g and h. Then we should expect the sum of the correlations of a, b, and c with d, e, and f to be equal to the product AD. Similarly for the other two sets. Hence to calculate a divisor such as A, we have $A^2 = \dfrac{AD \times AG}{DG}$, with similar equations for the other divisors. (This principle can be extended to tables where there are more than three groups : for, when we pool groups of similar tests by averaging or summing their correlations, these averaged or summed correlations will form a hierarchy, except of course for the sums in the diagonal of the pooled table ; so that the formulæ for a hierarchy of single coefficients will apply to a hierarchy formed of summed coefficients.)

(2) It thus conforms to the imaginary case described by Prof. Spearman and Dr. Hart in their recent article (*loc. cit.*, Table, p. 57), which, they believed, was rarely, if ever, to be found in tables of test-correlations available at the time they wrote.

W

are not unlike those described in my previous reports.[1] From introspections and objective assessments of pupils doing exceptionally well or badly in these groups, I infer that the factors may plausibly be identified with verbal ability, visual ability, and manual speed and dexterity. But from the size of the hypothetical correlations it will be seen that they play a comparatively small part as compared with that of the general factor.[2]

---

[1] A convenient test for the presence and location of such " group factors " is readily deduced from the " principle of simple summation." Estimate the self-correlations as usual ; then divide the entire correlation table into submatrices, according to the expected lines of separation between the group-factors. Let R_{vv} denote the sum of the 9 correlations of the 3 verbal tests with each other ;

R_{vv} the sum of the correlations of verbal and visual tests ; and so on. Then, if $R_{vv} > \dfrac{R_{vv}\ R_{vm}}{R_{vm}}$,

R_{vv} contains a group-factor. $Eg.$, in Table XXXV. B, $7 \cdot 912 > \dfrac{6 \cdot 066 \times 3 \cdot 487}{3 \cdot 064} = 6 \cdot 904$. (Cf. footnote 1, p. 275.)

[2] If the non-mathematical teacher finds the algebraic proof on pp. 271-2 difficult to follow, I suggest he thinks the problem out in verbal terms, along the lines of my 1909 article ($l.c.$, pp. 159f.): $e.g.$, if the contribution of the General Factor to Reading is $\frac{1}{2}$, and to Spelling $\frac{1}{2}$, then the resemblance of Spelling to Reading will be $\frac{1}{2} \times \frac{1}{2} = \frac{1}{4}$; hence the importance of the contribution of the General Factor to Reading will be proportionate to the sum of the correlations of Reading with all the other tests. The formula finally deduced from this argument (eq. xiii.) Spearman cannot accept, because it assumes a knowledge of the self correlations. These, however, can be found by successive approximation, and the formulæ Spearman would substitute are not valid if group-factors are present.

TABLE XXXV.

Correlations for Supplementary Tests (843 Children).

A.—Group Tests (843 Children).

TEST	1	2	3	4	5	6	7
1. Completion (Argument)	(·856)	·846	·834	·752	·723	·739	·655
2. Analogies (Written) ..	·846	(·804)	·772	·710	·768	·697	·672
3. Completion (Story) ..	·834	·772	(·729)	·726	·671	·668	·591
4. Definitions	·752	·710	·726	(·676)	·645	·672	·623
5. Synonyms	·723	·768	·671	·645	(·648)	·631	·618
6. Instructions	·739	·697	·668	·672	·631	(·640)	·624
7. Opposites	·655	·672	·591	·623	·618	·624	(·550)
TOTAL	5·405	5·269	4·991	4·804	4·704	4·671	4·333
General Factor ..	·925	·901	·854	·822	·805	·799	·741
General Intelligence ..	·813	·746	·780	·763	·662	·745	·631

B.—Individual Tests (251 Children).

TEST	a	b	c	d	e	f	g	h
a. Reasoning ..	(·970)	·944	·851	·797	·703	·651	·670	·574
b. Absurdities ..	·944	(·942)	·828	·678	·680	·644	·548	·603
c. Analogies (Verbal)	·851	·828	(·754)	·683	·655	·575	·581	·511
d. Analogies (Non-Verbal)	·797	678	·683	(·726)	·781	·687	·526	·550
e. Completion (Picture)	·703	·680	·655	·781	(·895)	·763	·543	·487
f. Porteus Maze..	·651	·644	·575	·687	·763	(·666)	·505	·453
g. Dotting ..	·670	·548	·581	·526	·543	·505	(·679)	·654
h. Alphabet Sorting	·574	·603	·511	·550	·487	·453	·654	(·632)
General Factor	·934	·867	·827	·817	·775	·716	·683	·645
Verbal Factor	·310	·438	·251	—	—	—	—	—
Visual Factor	—	—	—	·268	·543	·382	—	—
Manual Factor	—	—	—	—	—	—	·461	·461
General Intelligence	·807	·716	·755	·683	·691	·667	·517	·429

APPENDIX VI.

The Contribution of Schooling to Binet Scores.

In the foregoing Memorandum and in the more detailed report on which the account here given was based, I attempted to compare the influence of innate ability and school environment on the Binet tests by the aid of partial correlation. This section (pp. 193-195 above) led to a prolonged controversy, which deserves a reference here. A fuller discussion may throw some further light on the difficulties involved in interpreting this useful statistical technique and in formulating the conclusions that may be drawn from it. Both those who attacked my statement and those who defended it seem to have read more into my words than was really meant. Unfortunately, in abridging my original report for incorporation in a semi-popular volume like the present, I had omitted many of the technical reservations, and, in my eagerness to emphasize the limitations in the Binet tests which the analysis appeared to reveal, I went beyond what the evidence actually cited would warrant : I assumed, of course, that the majority of my readers would be familiar with other contributions bearing on the same point. These supplementary arguments therefore require a brief recapitulation here.

Bagley, who accepts my conclusions, has pushed them to an extreme. In an early paper on " Democracy and the I.Q.", and later in his book on *Determinism in Education* (1925), he is good enough to refer to my brief analysis as " the only thoroughgoing attempt to determine what schooling contributes to intelligence as determined by tests " ; and quotes the figures given in the text as showing that " not less than 54 per cent. of whatever it is that is measured as native intelligence turns out to be the result of experience and training " (*loc. cit.*, pp. 18, 75f., 135f.). He accordingly goes on to protest against the " common psychological doctrine " that innate endowment " sets a limit to a child's educability " ; and, in his article at any rate, gives the impression that, in his own opinion, " human mentality alone among biological traits is not subject to biological variation," or, if it is, then the amount of that variation is so slight as to be negligible.

Those for whom this Report was primarily intended were already aware of my views on this further issue. In several previous contributions on " Experimental Tests of General Intelligence," I had applied factor-analysis to the results of cognitive tests, and had shown that the general factor underlying them appeared mainly innate. In this memorandum my contention was merely that *the Binet Scale in the form in which it was then being used* furnished a very inadequate measure of this innate factor, and was largely affected by schooling. I had no intention of arguing that variations in

278

intelligence itself, as a sound psychological assessment would measure them, are ".merely the result of experience and training."

Bagley's further inferences naturally drew heavy criticism ; and, doubtless because my view was taken to be the same as his, my own interpretation was criticized on similar grounds by several American writers.[1]

The chief objection of these critics is to my introduction of phrases implying causation. Regression coefficients, they say, " show merely the average change in the dependent variable for unit change in the independent variable." Holzinger and Freeman, for example, construct an alternative equation : " School work = ·69 Binet — ·05 Burt + ·47 Age " ; and add it would be " at least as reasonable to suppose that the ability which determines the child's Binet score is also responsible for the quality of his school work, as to suppose that the quality of his school work is responsible for his Binet score." They then proceed to argue that " if the Burt score measures intelligence, it is a kind of intelligence which is of no practical importance, since its regression for school work is zero." These, they say, are their two main points of disagreement. But in fact there would seem to be several points at issue between these writers and myself.

1. *The Introduction of Causal Interpretations.* As regards the primary significance of the coefficients themselves, there is, I fancy, no difference between us. " A correlation coefficient," we are told, " yields no information in regard to causes" : similarly, a regression equation only enables us to make estimations, and " an effect will yield as good an estimate of its cause as a cause yields of its effect." With all this I heartily agree : indeed, I have urged much the same points elsewhere myself.[2] But the corollary to my mind is not that we can never look to the relative strength of our regressions to indicate the relative strength of the causes, but rather that, in order to decide what are the causes, and what functions are most appropriate to indicate their relative strength, we require access to *antecedent sources of knowledge.* Here my preliminary specification of the variables concerned provides a

---

(1) Gates, A. I., and Lasalle, J., *J. Educ. Psych.*, XIV., 1923, pp. 577-589 ; Holzinger, K. J., and Freeman, F. N., " The Interpretation of Burt's Regression Equation," *J. Educ. Psych.*, XVI., 1925, pp. 577-582, and *id.*, " Rejoinder on Burt's Regression Equation," *ibid.*, XVII., pp. 384-386. A reply from Godfrey Thomson is given in the same volume (pp. 300-308).

(2) These points were clearly stated in the longer report, which was necessarily abridged for inclusion in the Memorandum. I there described Yule's method in detail, and quoted his account of the interpretation of partial regression coefficients : *viz.*, " the magnitude of the coefficient b_2 gives, in fact, the mean change in X_1 " (the variable to be estimated) " that is associated with a unit change in X_2 " (one of the variables on which the estimate is to be based) " when all the remaining variables are kept constant." " The relative influences of the three factors are indicated by the regression equation " (Yule, *Introd. to Theory of Statistics*, 1912, pp. 230, 245. Cf. also Burt, *Eugenics Review*, VI., pp. 36f., 40f.).

In the earlier article, suggesting the use of partial regressions, I had stated that their *primary* function was (assuming linear relations) to give as exact an estimate or prediction as possible, not to measure the " relative influence " of causal factors, which is only a derivative inference. For the latter purpose, as was pointed out in my report, they can only be regarded as a rough and preliminary guide.

As regards the objections to importing causal phraseology, this kind of criticism is extremely common in discussions of inductive arguments. In factor-analysis (as noted above) critics are fond of showing that, in some particular instance, an inductive argument, when treated as a deductive argument, involves apparent fallacies. My own view on the general logic of the matter is briefly as follows. In all such arguments we must take into account, not only the *a posteriori* information furnished by the experimental results, but also the *a priori* knowledge which we possess apart from the experiment. Many of the objections by Holzinger, Freeman and others could thus be sustained only if we suppose that knowledge of the variables concerned is confined to what can be extracted from the figures.

knowledge, rough and inexact no doubt, of the causal factors at work. Indeed, to make their point, Holzinger and Freeman have to alter that specification.

This requirement seems obvious when we think what other equations could be constructed from the data. We might, for example, as Holzinger and Freeman point out, set up the following regression equation (I give it in their terms) : Age = ·15 Binet + ·51 School Work + ·03 Burt. Now would my critics argue that because the weighting for school work is so large, therefore " it is equally reasonable to suppose that the quality of a child's school work determines his chronological age " ? Evidently not : in this case we might use the regression to guess the child's age from his various scores, but we should not think of suggesting that the scores caused or " contributed to " his age. A projectile is fired with a muzzle velocity of I, and a following wind, S ; after a certain time, A, it has reached a specified distance from its starting point, B. Having regard to the units of measurement, we find (using a linear equation by Taylor's theorem as a first approximation)

$$B = aS + bI + cA.$$

Would Holzinger and Freeman declare that, since we can deduce other equations, like

$$cA = B - aS - bI,$$

therefore we cannot distinguish between causes and effects ? And that if we tried to do so, it would be as fair to say that the distance travelled is responsible for the time (or for the wind or the muzzle velocity) as that the latter are responsible for the distance travelled ?

To the reader who has not the context in my book before him, the argument of Holzinger and Freeman has doubtless seemed more plausible because (as I have just observed) they tacitly change the designation of one of the variables : what in my regression equation I called " Intelligence " (*i.e.*, innate general cognitive ability) they call " Burt " ; and they treat the assessment for " Intelligence " as though it was merely another test-score. Now this assessment was intended to give the best available estimate " of the amount of intelligence with which he (each child) is *congenitally endowed*." I was not here concerned to demonstrate that, with this group of children, my own test would yield a somewhat better estimate of this quality than the original Binet scale : I assumed that as already proved. But, what is more important, as stated on p. 193, I did not take my test-results just as they stood. They were carefully discussed with the teachers, and freely corrected whenever it seemed likely that the teacher's view of the relative merits of his own pupils gave a better estimate than the crude test-marks. Some kind of test was essential as a basis, to render the assessments of teachers from different classes comparable one with another.

No doubt, even so the assessments of " Intelligence " were not absolutely perfect. At this particular school, however, I believed that, when checked and revised, they provided as good an estimate of innate capacity as could possibly be obtained. Now, if we are justified in assuming (as the argument explicitly postulates) that what is designated " Intelligence " *tout court* forms a reasonable indication of congenital endowment, then it is plainly absurd to suggest, as Holzinger and Freeman have done, that we might just as well suppose that the " Burt score " is the joint effect of the Binet score and of the scholastic score as that the Binet score is the joint effect of the scholastic score and the " Burt score " : for this would be equivalent to maintaining that congenital endowment was an effect of school teaching.

2. *The Prediction of School Attainments from Binet Scores.* If our immediate object were to " predict " a child's *present* or *actual* school attainments from a single type of test, then I should again accept the comments of Holzinger

and Freeman. But, of course, that was not the purpose for which I was recommending the Binet scale to teachers or school medical officers. Indeed, here once again the criticisms urged by these and other writers seem largely due to the fact that they have overlooked the particular points I was concerned to demonstrate in this section. Holzinger and Freeman, for example, " conclude that for predicting quality of school work the Binet test should be used in preference [to Burt's reasoning test], and that the latter will not improve the forecast when the Binet result is already known." But this particular section was not dealing with the problem of " predicting quality of school work " in the sense here meant : I had already discussed the value of the Binet tests for that purpose in the preceding section (see pp. 187f.). Here my primary object was to adduce empirical evidence for two improvements in the scale which I eventually wished to make.

First, the *original* Binet scale (with which alone this Memorandum dealt) included a large number of tests of school attainments as such (*e.g.*, the tests of copying script, of reading, of dictation, of arithmetic, etc.). My contention was that in this respect the Binet scale required a good deal of excision, and that the proper place for questions on school attainments was in a series of separate standardized scholastic tests, not in a scale of tests for innate intelligence : in my next version they were in fact eliminated. Secondly, I wanted to urge that, even with this elimination, the Binet Scale could only be relied upon for children who had received the *usual amount of training in school and home*. In those days truancy was quite frequent in London schools ; and it was not impossible for a child who was only moderately dull to be diagnosed as certifiably deficient, because his mental age with the Binet scale fell below the borderline for mental deficiency. For such cases, I maintained, the teacher or school doctor should supplement the Binet scale by using tests of a different type—the Porteus Mazes, the picture completion tests, the non-verbal analogies, and other tests which are commonly dubbed " performance tests."

In support of these proposals my reasoning ran as follows. Consider first a school class (say, a junior class in a " central school ") where all the pupils have approximately the same chronological age and the same innate intelligence, but (since they are drawn from different elementary schools) differ appreciably in reading, spelling, composition, and arithmetic. Then, if the Binet scale consisted of a set of pure and perfect tests of intelligence, unaffected by school teaching, each of the pupils should receive the same mental age. But they do not. Their Binet scores differ considerably ; and, what is more, the differences show a fairly high correlation with the pupils' marks for school attainments. The inference therefore is that the Binet scores depend, to a larger extent than the Binet-testers of that day believed, on the child's school attainments, which in turn we may suppose depend on numerous factors, such as special aptitude, interest in school work, regularity of attendance, efficiency of previous teaching, and the like. Can we generalize from these observations ? Would the same result hold good, not only in a central school, but of any homogeneous group at every level, and, if so, how great, on the whole, is the influence of school knowledge as compared with that of innate intelligence ?

My suggestion was that these further questions could be answered by eliminating differences in age and intelligence statistically, by partial correlation, instead of actually, by selecting homogeneous groups. On calculating the " partial correlation " between the Binet scores and the estimates for school work, with Age and Intelligence eliminated, I obtained a coefficient of ·61. Since with over 300 cases such a figure is fully significant, it seemed definitely to demonstrate that the scores with the original Binet tests depend on other factors beside sheer intelligence and chronological age. In the Memorandum I tried to give this argument a concrete shape by imagining two persons, of normal intelligence, one a child of 7, another a youth of 17 (*i.e.*, an adult in the sense that mental maturation is complete), both of whom had acquired no school knowledge whatever, and estimating what score they would have on the Binet tests. Giving them no marks for every problem requiring school knowledge, I calculated that the former would get a mental age of barely 6 and the latter one of barely 9 (p. 195).

The influence of schooling and of accumulated worldly knowledge was not entirely denied by the supporters of the original Binet scale ; but they held that it was too slight to affect such matters as certification for mental deficiency or scholarship awards. Hence it seemed essential to secure some rough evaluation of its relative amount. Accordingly, I suggested that, as Yule had done, we might take the regression equation to " indicate the relative influence of the three factors " (Yule's wording, *loc. cit.*, p. 245). Let me quote from the fuller Report. " The average child in this school " (where the assessments were obtained) " had a chronological age of rather over 10 : let us put it at 10·0 exactly. Further, since a typical school had been chosen, the average intelligence and the average school attainments would also be measured by a " mental " age of 10·0. Now consider a dull and backward child whose chronological age is 11·0, but whose mental and scholastic ages are only 10·0. Our equation tells us that his Binet age would be 10·11. Again, take another child, backward but not dull, whose chronological age *and* mental age are 11·0, but whose scholastic age is still 10·0 : we estimate his Binet age as 10·44. Thirdly, consider a normal child whose chronological, mental, and scholastic age are *all* 11·0. His Binet age will be 10·0 + 0·11 + 0·33 + 0·54 = 10·98. . . . Conversely, suppose a school doctor, after examining a child of 10, who had lost a good deal of schooling owing to illness or truancy, found that the boy had a mental age of only 7 ; the doctor would have to remember that possibly quite one-half of this deviation of − 3 years might be the effect, not of innate mental deficiency, but of ignorance of reading, spelling, writing, and arithmetic ; only one-third might be due to innate dullness."

3. *The Value of Other Tests*. Holzinger and Freeman also argue that a test, such as that which they designate " Burt," " will not improve the forecast [of school work] when the Binet score is already known," for its partial regression coefficient is approximately zero : " intelligence which is unrelated to school work is not the sort of capacity which we usually have in mind when we use the term." Here, it seems to me, it is my critics who are misinterpreting the partial regression coefficient. Because the partial regression coefficient is zero we cannot conclude that the " Burt score " is unrelated to school work ; in fact, what they call a " Burt score " is correlated with school work to the extent of ·75. What the zero coefficient tells us is that, when we have based our estimate on the Binet score, the inclusion of the Burt score will not produce any further improvement in our estimation. If we dropped the Binet score, we could, of course, make quite a good estimate on the Burt score and age alone.

Part of the fallacy arises from the substitution of the word " forecasting " for " estimating." I venture to suggest that, if we *really* want to " forecast " a child's school attainments, *i.e.*, to predict his *future* attainments under appropriate teaching instead of estimating his *present* attainments as a result of past teaching, then the new type of test might be even better than Binet.

My conclusions seem to have been fully confirmed by later researches. Mr. Hugh Gordon, one of His Majesty's inspectors of schools, examined 80 canal-boat children with the Binet-Simon Scale. With these tests their average mental ratio proved to be 69, just below the borderline for the defective. From this we should "forecast" that nearly 50 per cent. could not achieve school attainments above those of the feeble-minded. At my suggestion, one of my research students, Miss Frances Gaw, then tested the same group with a set of performance tests. The average mental ratio rose to 82. Barely one in ten appeared to be feeble-minded ;[1] and the rest appeared manifestly capable of much greater educational progress with more adequate educational provision (a forecast which was subsequently verified with those for whom such additional provision could be arranged).

4. *The Contribution of Innate Ability to the Revised Binet Scale.* Let me repeat that these statements about the influence of schooling on Binet ages refer primarily to the original version in which tests of reading, writing, and arithmetic were included ; they do not hold (at least not so strongly) of the later revisions from which these scholastic tests have been excluded. But even after we have eliminated the influence of schooling, we still have to consider whether other sources of general information, particularly the home environment, may not contribute an appreciable element, possibly quite as much as innate ability.

This brings me to a final point, which, I fancy, has not been sufficiently considered in the discussions I have cited. Granted we are concerned with causal influences, what is the best function to choose for measuring their relative strength ? I took the partial regression coefficients as affording the best available indication (sufficient, it seems to me, for rough practical arguments) because in those days there appeared to be no better type of function. In the light of our later work I should now prefer to make two modifications : (i) I should prefer, by using factor-analysis or an appropriately selected sample, to re-define the causal influences so that they form independent (*i.e.*, uncorrelated or orthogonal) factors ; (ii) I should prefer, for most purposes, to measure the relative strength of these factors by their contributions to the total variance.

To express the proportionate contributions of a number of causal factors in simple additive form, suitable for purposes of calculation and deduction, it is much better to deal with factors that are virtually uncorrelated, wherever we can, because we then eliminate the awkward cross-products that represent their mutual interaction. Thus, for a rigorous argument, we should either take as our population of reference a group in which the measurable variations in heredity, home environment, and teaching efficiency have little or no correlation, or else reduce the measured variables to terms of uncorrelated factors by some process of factor analysis. Further, if we are to generalize the additive process, it is better to add contributions that combine to form the variance instead of adding contributions that combine to form raw marks, because the former lend themselves much more readily to mathematical manipulation. Thus, in more recent analyses, what we have commonly analysed is not the crude deviation, but the "variance" (mean *square* of the deviations). Starting with the partial regression equation in standardized form we can express the variance as the sum of a series of squares and products of regressions, which are conveniently called "coefficients of determination," and include "joint" or "indirect" determinations when the components or "independent" (*i.e.*, given) variables are correlated. This change to an

---

(1) Gordon, H., "Mental and Scholastic Tests among Retarded Children," *Board of Education Pamphlets*, 1923, No. 44 ; Gaw, F., *Brit. J. Psych.*, XV., 1925, p. 390.

equation which involves measuring the relative strength of causal factors by expressions involving squares or sums of squares is rather like the change from " force " to " energy " in measuring the strength of physical causes.[1]

In a later investigation, using this mode of assessment with results obtained with the London revision of the Terman-Binet tests, we calculated that the respective contributions to the total variance could be approximately expressed as follows : (A) " Nurture," 22 per cent., consisting of (A1) schooling 7 per cent., and (A2) home environment 15 per cent. ; (B) " Nature," 74 per cent., consisting of (B1) parental inheritance 41 per cent., and (B2) other hereditary or congenital influences 33 per cent. ; (C) other factors, 4 per cent.

As was pointed out in my 1917 Report (p. 67) educational classification reduces variability to three-quarters or even one-half. My proposal to correct for this by inverting Pearson's generalization of the partial correlation formula has been criticized on similar grounds. But it is strongly confirmed by the figures in Table XXXI. I have, however, discussed this problem more fully in my *Report on Junior County Scholarship Examinations* (App. I. Correlations from Select Groups, 1934).

---

[1] In the familiar formula for Multiple correlation, $R^2 = \beta_{01}r_{01} + \beta_{02}r_{02} + \ldots$, where R^2 is the total variance due to the tests $1, 2, \ldots, \beta_{01}r_{01}$ gives the total contribution (direct and indirect) of test 1, and so on. In the equation $\beta_{01}r_{01} = \beta^2_{01} + \beta_{01}\beta_{02}r_{12} + \ldots, \beta^2_{01}$, gives the direct contribution and $\beta_{01}\beta_{02}r_{12}$ the indirect. $2\beta_{01}\beta_{02}r_{12}$ will be the coefficient of joint determination and give the indirect contribution of both tests 1 and 2.

In my view expressions based on an analysis of variance should not wholly take the place of those involving the unsquared regression coefficients. In particular it should be noted that, for those who are unaccustomed to think in terms of variance, the resulting figures are apt to make the importance of supplementary factors seem smaller than it really is. Thus, if $x = \cdot71a + \cdot50b + \cdot40c + \cdot30d$ (the four factors a, b, c and d being uncorrelated), the contributions to the variance will be 50%, 25%, 16% and 9%, so that a contributes over 5 times as much to the variance as d, although the " weight " of a is little more than twice as much as the " weight " of d. In several minor Reports and later Laboratory Notes I have discussed the precautions that must be observed in applying and interpreting the partial correlation technique and the allied technique of correction for selection. Here, as elsewhere, a correct interpretation is, in my view, only attainable if we take into account antecedent, extrinsic, or *a priori* knowledge, as well as the intrinsic or *a posteriori* knowledge extracted from the data furnished by the *ad hoc* experiment : the causal structure of the phenomena must be borne in mind as well as the quantitative assessments themselves. In particular, a straightforward interpretation of Yule's formula for $r_{xy.z}$ is only strictly permissible, if we know (from antecedent information) that the whole of z is contained in x and y. Let the reader compare different structural compositions for the three variables considered : *e.g.*, $x = g + x', y = g + y', z = g + z'$; or again $x = g + h, y = h + i, x = i + j$; or again, $x = g + h + x', y = g, z = h$; and then contrast the resulting partial correlations with the results obtained if $x = g + h + x', y = g + h + y'$, and $z = g$. The requisite condition is rigorously fulfilled when $z = $ age, and age is then partialled out. But with most of the other empirical variables that we desire to eliminate by the partial correlation technique, the causal pattern tends to be more complex : in such cases the results of the technique are apt to be misleading if its limitations are not kept in mind. (Useful discussions will be found in Kelley, E. L., *J. Educ. Psych.*, XX., pp. 119-24, and Snedecor, G. W., *Statistical Methods*, pp. 282f.)

The reader will get a clear notion of the effect of factor-composition on correlations and regressions, if he constructs an " overlap diagram," similar to those suggested by Guilford, *Psychometric Methods*, pp. 365, 460 ; or by Thomson, *Factorial Analysis of Human Ability*, p. 11. A possible pattern to fit my own regression equation has been suggested by Thomson, " The Interpretation of Burt's Regression Equation," *J. Educ. Psych.*, XVII., 1926, pp. 300-308. One further warning should be added. Variance also measures heterogeneity. Hence the contributions of factor-variance to total variance, expressed as a variance-ratio, depend not only on the relative strength of the postulated causes, but also on the relative heterogeneity of the population. Consequently, for discussions like the present, the correlations must be obtained from (or referred to) some standard type of population, *e.g.*, an unselected age-group or a random sample drawn from such a total age-group.

Memorandum III.

TESTS OF EDUCATIONAL ATTAINMENTS.

1. *NEED AND USES OF SCHOLASTIC TESTS.*

For the measurement of school progress there is no scheme of tests, widely used and popularly recognised, claiming the same position and enjoying the same prestige as the Binet-Simon scale for the measurement of native intelligence. In collaboration with Monsieur V. Vaney, Binet and Simon did, indeed, attempt what they styled a "barometer of instruction "—a set of graded exercises in reading, spelling, and arithmetic.[1] But the tests were compiled upon a rougher plan ; and were of necessity suited only to those educated in French schools, speaking and writing the French language, and using the French systems of weights and measures. In other countries they have attracted little notice.

At first sight, it might seem that teachers need no assistance from psychologists in assessing educational attainments ; they can make their own class tests. Nor is the presumption altogether mistaken. Where qualitative estimates are concerned, the intuitive judgment of the experienced teacher is likely to be both surer and speedier than the laborious deductions of the statistical psychologist. But in quantitative exactitude it is no longer the same ; here the records of the practical teacher appear—not always, indeed, without advantage—to drop short of the high ideals of theory. This has been demonstrated by scientific studies upon the validity of school marks ; and more recently,[2] in America, there has arisen an eagerness, perhaps too great an eagerness, to supplement traditional examinations by psychological tests, and to apply the new statistical methods to the survey of educational systems.

The aim of such tests and surveys should not be to criticise. They are weapons of enquiry, not of inquisition. Their office is to serve the teacher, not to rule him ; to enable him, in fact, to do more easily what already he desires to do, but can now do only with difficulty, or not at all : that is, to assess —independently of all personal or subjective standards, whether his own or those of an external scrutineer—the comparative level of his individual pupils or of his class taken as a whole. For the rest, it is to be remembered that if he deviates from quantitative exactitude, such exactitude is not his immediate

---

[1] See, for example, Binet and Simon, *The Development of Intelligence* (1905), translated by E. Kite p 70 *et seq.* ; and *id.*, *Mentally Defective Children*, translated by W. B. Drummond, p. 54.

[2] It is now nearly twenty years since Rice applied the first scientific test of educational attainments to measure improvement in a definite school subject—spelling ; and just ten years since Thorndike published the first graded scale to measure a definite school product—handwriting. For the literature of later investigators, see bibliographies contained in the volumes cited in Appendix IV. (p. 460). The chief disadvantage of the American scales, apart from differences of idiom and values for money, weights, and measures, is that, as explained below, the averages and norms are usually given only for school-classes or "grades," not for age-groups.

business. The examinations of the teacher should be adaptable to the shifting needs of the moment ; hence, he follows *the method of the extemporised test*. The psychologist seeks universal comparability and numerical precision ; he, consequently, is bound to *the method of the standardised test*. Each procedure has its special uses, its special merits, its special shortcomings. Each can find something to learn from the other.

Psychologists, physicians, social investigators, and other officers who, without themselves being school teachers, desire from time to time to gauge the school attainments of the child, are compelled, by the exigencies of their work, either to adopt, or to evolve for themselves, some simple scheme of educational tests. To them, as well as to professional teachers, my own attempts, imperfect as they are, may be of some small interest and service.

The selection described in this memorandum includes the various scholastic tests used for the preceding enquiry and cited from time to time in the foregoing pages. Both in general character and in age-assignment, the test-questions and test-material are virtually identical with those employed in my previous investigation upon the distribution and relations of educational abilities. The age-averages or norms, therefore, may be accepted as defining, in concrete detail and with rough exactitude, the level of the several units—educational " ages," " standards," or " grades "—in terms of which school attainments were then measured and reviewed.

Purpose of Present Scale of Tests.

The object of the tests is to provide a set of scales measuring, as scientifically as possible, the attainments of individual children in all the fundamental subjects of the elementary school curriculum. Especially have I had in mind the purpose for which hitherto such tests have been mainly used in this country, namely, to determine the scholastic abilities of borderline cases found in, or recommended for, the special (M.D.) schools. The series contains, first, the complete test-sheets, questions, and other materials needed for administering the tests ; and, secondly, a set of tables for deciding whether the performance of any given individual child corresponds with the average for normal children of his years, whether it deviates from that average by more than the average or " standard " deviation, whether it approaches the borderline dividing the normal from the mentally deficient, or, finally, whether it descends to, or even sinks below, the average for deficient children of equal age.

The Age-Basis in Scholastic Tests.

The conception underlying each of the scales is that of an " educational age." Throughout I have sought, however tentatively, to construct such tests as may permit the examiner to measure attainments in terms of what may be called—in a broader sense than usual—" mental years." The figures give, as it were, a time-table of intellectual progress. They seek to indicate in quantitative terms, first, at what differing rates children of diverse types, the slow-coach and the non-stop express, the lumbering goods truck and the first-class train, pass the chief stations along the various routes of the educational journey ; and, secondly, how far each one, with its particular freight of fuel and pressure of steam, may be expected to travel toward that distant terminus, which forms the destination of all, but which few will reach.

The unit of the mental year is, I admit, a conception suited only to a preliminary enquiry. In America scales and norms for scholastic abilities have been based almost exclusively upon averages, not for each age, but for each class, for the successive " grades," as they are termed. This is as though

we in this country were taking figures merely for the several "standards." [1]
To gather data on this basis avoids, no doubt, the troublesome dislocation
of classes that the sorting out of ages (when the same tests are not given
throughout the school) must inevitably entail. But the composition of
"grades" in America, like that of "standards" in England, varies so much
from school to school that the results must always be of uncertain significance
even in the country where they were got, and in all other countries of no use
whatever.

A few American psychologists, however, following Professor Thorndike's
enterprising lead, have endeavoured to find a unit more scientific than
either age or grade—a unit that shall be demonstrably of equal value
throughout the scale. In any series of problems, the interval of difficulty
which separates problem number one from problem number two should,
it is said, be identical in magnitude with the interval of difficulty which
separates problem number two from problem number three; and so
throughout the series. The ideal is praiseworthy; but the methods may be
questioned. The statistical technique, evolved for selecting such test-problems,
differs with different investigators and for different subjects; in every
instance it is cumbrous and abstruse. [2] Certainly, for the uncompromising
precision of a scientist's research, a technical unit, intelligible only to the
initiated—the "probable error," the "percentage difference," or the
"standard deviation "—must in the end be unavoidable. But, for ordinary
use in ordinary hands, something simpler, something speedier, something
self-evident is wanted. The unit must embody an everyday conception,
some formula in origin less pedantic, in application more practical. Accordingly, for the busy teacher and the visiting psychologist the "mental year,"
however crude, would seem, as a unit, to be sufficiently exact, as it is eminently serviceable. Laboratory tools are for the laboratory; the journeyman
carries a pocket footrule, not a micrometer screw.

The Schools Tested.

The figures in the tables are derived from the examination of somewhat
slender numbers. A single investigator is necessarily confined, with so large
a range of tests, to a narrow range of schools; and, whenever he revises his
test-questions—a process inevitable in the early phases of his work—he must
sacrifice all his preceding data and base his finished tables solely upon figures
got by the new material.

In the final experiments nineteen ordinary elementary schools or departments have taken part, and eleven special (M.D.) schools. These contain in
all rather over five thousand normal children, and rather under fifteen
hundred mentally deficient children. In many instances, however, it became
impossible to give the whole series of tests throughout the entire department.
But, so far as was possible, complete age-groups were selected. As a rule,
the total number of representatives for any one year may be taken as about
five hundred for the normals, and about one hundred and fifty for the defectives. At the youngest and oldest ages, both among normals and
defectives, the numbers were very much smaller; in consequence, for the

---

(1) The Code of Regulations for Elementary Schools, issued by the Board of Education some thirty
years ago, enumerated rough standards of attainments to be expected in the various classes, which thus
acquired a name which only recently they have begun to drop. The formulation of such minimum standards,
in itself a useful piece of work, was, as there given, too vague and tentative to do more than confer some
definiteness of aim. The system of examination and of payment by results, which were associated with this
discarded scheme, still unfortunately cause many older teachers to look with suspicion upon all attempts to
discover norms and to define objectives. The interest of the statistical psychologist, it is hardly necessary
to affirm, lies in something altogether different from the purposes of the code. (2) But cf. p. 150, 439f.

extreme periods of school life, the figures offer but the rudest approximation.

In thus selecting a comparatively meagre sample of the total population, it has been necessary to make some allowance for limitations in scholarship, in social status, and in age, which inevitably characterise pupils in particular schools and particular school classes. The ordinary elementary schools chosen for the experiments represent, with certain exceptions, median schools for their borough.[1] To this end all the schools in the borough were first ranked in a rough order of merit according to the general level of the pupils' attainments. Merit was deduced principally from the performances of the children in the preliminary examination for junior county scholarships, and from the number of scholarships attained annually in the final examination. The schools placed in or near the middle of this series were selected as medians. To these typical schools were added four schools of an exceptional type, namely, the school in the poorest neighbourhood, the school in the most prosperous neighbourhood, a school in a moderately poor neighbourhood, and a school in a neighbourhood moderately well-to-do. The data obtained from these and other sources were ultimately weighted, upon the principle described in discussing the Binet-Simon tests, in proportion to their representative value.

Within a circumscribed area special schools are few. They offer no such opportunity for systematic choice. I have, however, endeavoured to include special schools recruited from both the poorer and the better social classes.

In calculating averages and standard deviations for normal children at the older years, I have admitted representatives of those transferred to Council Central schools and of scholarship winners at Council Secondary schools ; and have attempted to weight data from these sources in just proportion. For the ages of 11 — and upwards, therefore, the norms are somewhat higher than could be obtained in ordinary elementary schools alone, since these commonly surrender the best of their oldest pupils. Similarly, for the older defectives, I have striven to weight the figures derived respectively from junior schools and from schools for elder boys and girls, so that the composite result eventually obtained should approximate to the true average for a random sample.

2. PRACTICAL CAUTIONS AND SUGGESTIONS.

A few practical suggestions and warnings may be added for those who wish to employ these or similar scales for special purposes in their schools.

(i) Provisional Nature of the Scale.

This is, I believe, the first attempt to construct a systematic set of scholastic tests and norms for English school children.[2] It follows that the results are only provisional. Their value is limited ; their accuracy low. If a child, hitherto deemed normal, deviates below the standard here tabulated as average for his age, the examiner will not too hastily conclude the child must therefore be backward. When the thermometer registers sixty degrees, and the pools are frozen, it is always possible that the instrument

---

[1] Owing to the fact that in the course of my previous survey many of the tests had been given in an earlier and unrevised form in the median schools of the borough then reviewed, it proved necessary to include for some of the final tests, median schools from an adjacent borough. The special schools were also situated in the same two boroughs ; and comprised those to which the ordinary elementary schools in question commonly transferred their defective cases.

[2] Since this was written, Dr. Ballard has collected and published a large number of tests, both of educational abilities and general intelligence, many of them tests of his own constructing, in his admirable volume on *Mental Tests* (Hodder and Stoughton, 1920).

may be at fault—particularly if it be the first manufacture of an apprentice hand. Already, in diagnoses based upon the Binet-Simon tests, we have seen the risks to which a too submissive loyalty is blind. And, in foreign schools, faith in a fallible test-scale, as in something beyond appeal, has greatly impaired the value which early efforts at educational measurement, cautiously accepted and critically appraised, might conceivably have possessed. He, therefore, who applies these methods to some class or school, and thinks he has discovered a mote, should first consider whether a beam may not lurk in the test. The eye of science, no less than the eye of the body, has its *muscæ volitantes*—quivering flecks that seem to lodge upon the faces of our friends, but prove when re-examined to be mere illusory projections of some little opacity in our own apparatus of vision.

(ii) Practical Uses and Limitations.

Nevertheless, pending the construction of some more valid scale, even the present compilation may have a practical as well as a theoretical use. Tests are time-savers. They cannot pretend to greater accuracy than the considered sentence of the observant and experienced teacher, judging his own old pupils. But observation is slow, and experience an affair of years. The young teacher who has not yet based his expectations on prolonged experience, the new teacher who has not yet had opportunity for protracted observation, may by means of such devices be helped swiftly to some provisional conclusion. To the verdicts even of the shrewdest judge the method may have something to contribute : for without such a method we possess in educational measurement no personal equations—no formula measuring the estimate of one teacher against the estimate of a different. The lack is crucial. It is like the option of twenty francs or twenty marks when one is ignorant of the rate of exchange.

Tests should provide a universal currency ; or at least some first approach to it. When the headmaster of one school says his pupil is " fair," and the headmaster of a second says his candidate is "excellent," the two reports, as they stand, are incommensurable. What is " fair " in Lewisham or Hampstead excels even " excellence " in Bermondsey or Bethnal Green. We have first to equate the teachers' standards before we can equate their reports. But if both use the same tests and quote the same terms—" with such a scale the child is so many years above or below the normal average "— then a valid comparison has already been instituted. And, for most purposes, I believe, the tests will furnish a statement of general and specific school attainments probably more trustworthy and certainly more precise than could be got with the same expenditure of labour from unaided impressions and improvised examinations. To test the general level of an entire class, to reveal the teaching efficiency of a school as a whole, they are perhaps not wholly to be trusted. But for measuring the more extreme degrees of backwardness or advancement among individual children they may, I fancy, be of positive service.

For norms obtained upon so limited a scale as the present, a wide margin should be allowed for error of measurement. Unless a child, or a group of children, differs from the stated averages by one year at the very least, little significance can be affixed to the divergence. If possible, when testing individuals, a teacher should always examine the remainder of the age-group in the same school, or, at any rate, a sufficient normal sample. This holds with especial force for those accepting a scale worked out in a particular London district, and applying it either to schools in the provinces or to localities in London itself poorer or less poor than the district here surveyed. So great, indeed, are local differences in school attainments, whether due as in some cases to differences in social and economic status, or as in others to differences in teaching method, that a child's performances should never be judged except by comparison with others of his age who have had equal opportunities and an equal chance, alike at school and at home.

(iii) Teachers' Own Scales.

It follows that every teacher should prepare his own series of tests and his own scale of norms. He should, in any event, hesitate before adopting, blindly and bodily, someone else's ready-made scheme. An instrument of his own forging, if framed upon scientific principles, will be far more suited to his peculiar requirements. Teachers are too modest. From time to time some external examiner introduces a new test. The teacher infers that the device enjoys some occult efficacy to which nothing of his own could ever aspire. He borrows the test. He may adopt and adapt it for purposes of teaching. The next time it is used in an examination, either by himself or by the originator, its whole significance is destroyed or changed ; to the child the task is now as stale and familiar as any class-room commonplace. Medical officers who examine cases of suspected deficiency find that such tests as those in the Binet-Simon series, once they have been popularised, become rapidly useless for their special ends. Abroad, the same fate has already overtaken tests of school attainments. If, therefore, any body of teachers or educational investigators are studying the value of a particular test-sheet, it is better, as a rule, that the questions contained in it should be left to the investigators themselves. They should not be applied, forthwith and indiscriminately, by any whose curiosity happens to be stirred. Those prosecuting the enquiry will welcome the co-operation of others who may be interested. But then, that the procedure may be correct in detail and comparable as a whole, the original investigators should be approached before, not after, the results are secured.

If any wish to test the merits of the present series, I personally shall respond most gratefully either to criticisms, or to requests for minuter explanations. Our next efforts, I would urge, should be addressed primarily to two problems : first, to the perfection of the tests themselves, both by selecting additional questions and by improving the form of the questions already selected ; and, secondly, pending the construction of a better and more diversified series, to the standardisation of the measurements of age-averages and variability, by repeating the present sets, with all their imperfections, upon a more ambitious scale.

(iv) Application of Scales to Syllabuses.

Indirectly and within limits, such a series as the present may prove helpful and suggestive in the compilation and criticism of syllabuses of class instruction. Too often, in place of a detailed formulation of aim, the class-syllabus contents itself with vague recommendations touching method alone. As an illustration, I may quote an extract from a scheme of work drawn up for a particular class in a particular school for mental defectives.

" *Arithmetic.*—Analysis of numbers with the four rules up to 99. Stress to be laid on addition, subtraction, and multiplication, rather than on division. Special attention to subtraction ; method of decomposition to be used. Mental to precede written work ; exercises in the concrete to be fully used ; but care to be taken to lead up to an abstract idea of number and to guard against figures being used mechanically and unintelligently."

The theoretical principles that animate such precepts are unexceptionable ; they are rational, all too rational. But the precepts themselves dictate almost exclusively points of practical method. They remind us of the reasoning of M. Tomès in *L'Amour Médicin* : " I think with Artemius. Whether he cures his patient or kills him is of no consequence, so long as his treatment follow the correct rule. A dead man is a man dead ; and we are sorry for him. But if rules are to be broken, who shall answer for the consequences ? " The old psychology ordained correct rules of method, rules deduced from the supposed nature of the human mind as such, and the supposed self-evidence of some universal ideal. If there chanced to be some particular mind so deeply defective as to be incapable of approaching that ideal, so much the worse for that particular mind ; everyone was sorry for it ; but it had to be sacrificed, not the rules, nor the ideal. The new psychology takes a humbler stand. It is concerned with individual minds, not with mind in general. It is content to define the limited powers of this child and of that, not the ultimate potentialities of children as such. It seeks to formulate aims proportioned to those limited powers, not the ideal aims of an ideal school in an ideal society. And, taking care to state precisely the end to be achieved, it will, for the present, leave the means to take care of themselves. Of method, a region of research as yet all but unvisited and totally unexplored, the psychologist of to-day knows less than the teacher. And of rules of method the psychologist is tempted to say with another professor of medicine : " Each case must be a rule to itself." Method should be individualised, not universalised ; adaptable as clay, not rigid like a clamp ; evolved progressively from week to week, modified for this pupil, and reversed for that, not written down, once for all cases and occasions, in a book.

Of the class for which the syllabus quoted was drawn up all but two failed, and will for ever fail, to form an " abstract idea of number." Two succeeded. Four at least found it easier to manipulate figures " mechanically " than to understand the " exercises in the concrete." Thus the dietary which was one child's meat left another child starved, and, had it been forced upon a third, would have poisoned its mind against the whole subject. Respecting manner of instruction and mode of approach, therefore, no rigid directions should be laid down. To generalise, to prescribe, and to dictate, to attempt to deduce at the beginning of the term, from *a priori* presumptions, an ideal procedure that is to be applied throughout the term, regardless of unforeseen developments in the future, regardless of individual idiosyncrasies from moment to moment, to the children in a mass—such a plan, even with the most homogeneous class of defectives, would be fatal, were it not futile. The one merit of such prescriptions is that almost inevitably they are too vague to be injurious, too general to be restrictive.

Method, then, may wisely be left to the class teacher to determine, who in his turn will leave it to be determined by the children's needs, to be unfolded from lesson to lesson by the progressive self-revelation of each individual mind. On the other hand, an exact enunciation of results to be looked for would be, not only possible, but helpful. To the class teacher it would be no small service, if the head master, after due consultation with his assistants and due examination of the class, formulated, in terms of tests and marks, the aim he considers should be kept in view : " in addition so many columns of such and such a character to be added in such and such a time with at most such and such a percentage of error " ; and so forth. His statement might announce the average he expected the class to achieve ; or it might specify the minimum beneath which even the meanest pupil should not fall ; or it might indicate both. It would not exact the same attainments from every one, as though each inherited the same capacity, and as though all, therefore, could make similar progress at the same flat rate.

X

What has been said of arithmetic observations might be applied to reading, and indeed to any subject measured by our tests. In reading, the class syllabus not infrequently imposes a preference for some special method —the " Phonic," the " Nellie Dale," the " Look-and-say," or what not ; while the results to be attained by the method are passed over, unnoticed or ill defined. Here, once more, the norms may bring precision.

With the mentally deficient the most successful plan is usually the policy of a limited objective ; and the tests may well aid in stating that objective, and in defining its limits. Indeed, throughout in the foregoing suggestions I have had chiefly in view the special (M.D.) class. But their application may doubtless be extended. In constructing the schemes of work for the backward they have certainly proved serviceable ; whether they are applicable to syllabuses for normal classes, it is perhaps beyond my province to decide. But, even in the ordinary school, a trial would be worth the making. It is an axiom that the plan of instruction should be adapted to the age and ability of the children to be taught. Lessons and level should correspond. Take an ordinary London child of a given age—say nine and a half. What degree of accomplishments in reading, spelling, and arithmetic may we, with the greatest probability, presuppose ? What further amount may we seek fairly to have added by the end of the ensuing year ? Hints for the answer to such questions may be extracted in much detail from a perusal of the various scales. We may safely assume from them that already at the age specified he can spell such words as " towel " or " touch " ; we may hope that in a few months he will spell such words as " surface," " saucer," and " succeed " ; if we set him words like " conceited " or " occasion," he will probably, even after twelve months' drudgery, still blunder. Similarly, from the arithmetic scales we may discover what problems in money he can attack, and what type of bill or invoice he may be taught ; problems in the measurement of time, of equal complexity, will, for at least a year or two. remain beyond his grasp.

With a child of average ability to aim at attainments well above the average will be usually unavailing and sometimes dangerous ; what are to be considered average attainments the tests and tables show. Similarly, with children of ability above or below the average, the aim should be correspondingly high or low ; and once more the tests will intimate in detail what a child who is backward by two years can barely do, and what a child who is two years ahead may be taught with profit.

Arguments, however, founded upon this limited basis should be received with proper reserve. The problems have been selected upon statistical grounds, not from a priori deductions. The words proposed for the measurement of reading, spelling, and dictation were picked, not because they are the words that should specially be taught, but because they form appropriate or suggestive tests. The examples set in the arithmetic papers are published, not as model questions, but solely because they happened to have been answered by 50 per cent. of the children at the age specified. Whether these or other exercises are the best to teach at this age, whether these or other formulæ should be used in framing examination papers, are distinct issues. to be decided only after a distinct research.

(v) The Danger of the Average considered as a Norm.

Equally, too, the standards of attainment are norms only in the statistical sense. They represent actual averages and actual medians, not ideals. If asked to point to an average child, the class teacher commonly selects one who suffers from no disabilities. He thinks of the normal child as one who, without being obviously supernormal, is entirely free from abnormalities. But, in an environment so distant from perfection as that of a typical London borough, the average child has many disabilities, and the majority might be by a precisian dubbed abnormal, at least in the sense that they fall short of perfect normality. Hence, most teachers and educationists will, I suspect, view with a shock of surprise the low level of the norms now given. They should remember always that the norm, as here defined, is approximately a median, that is, a mediocre measurement or performance which cuts the entire group into two halves numerically equal, those above average and those below. Hence, it approaches an unsatisfactory or inferior performance as nearly as it approaches a satisfying or superior performance, neither more nor less, being itself but neutral and indifferent. Like the bare watershed that divides the sterile slopes of the foggy north from the fertile terraces of the sunny south, it inclines of itself to a preponderance neither of brightness nor of dullness, but has an equal share of each. If a child or a school reaches merely the average here given, that in itself is little cause for gratification. In a good school or a good neighbourhood, it would be a reason for dismay. A norm such as this is not an ideal or standard to be aimed at ; it is the scantest minimum, short of which the verdict "below par," "definitely inferior," must be pronounced.

In thus printing only median samples and average figures, there is, I am sensible, a lurking danger. A minimum wage, officially recognised, tends in its practical operation to become, or at least to limit, the maximum wage. So, too, in educational statistics : when nothing but averages are published, a risk arises lest all better performances tend to be depressed towards conformity with those averages. The figures printed here, however, are put forward simply as a record of facts, not as the formulation of an aim—a guide, perhaps, but not a goal. To be completely useful, indeed, such a scale should comprise for every age, not only average achievements, but best and worst achievements, together with typical achievements at even intervals between these two limits. But the publication of further samples the narrow compass of this memorandum inexorably forbids. Standard deviations I have invariably given throughout ; and their unexpected size shows how artificial a thing is the list of averages against which they are set. If the reader desires some indication of a genuinely good performance, he may add the standard deviation to the average ; and take their sum as marking a figure which only the best 16 per cent. of a typical age-group reach or surpass : add twice the standard deviation to the average, and only 2·3 per cent, in a random sample will be found to pass the total.[1]

(vi) Specific Disabilities.

The examiner should always discriminate between children who are backward in most subjects and children who are backward in one subject, or one limited group of subjects, alone. A child, for example, who suffers merely from a specialised disability in reading and spelling, such as so-called "word-blindness," is to be carefully distinguished from one who is in every respect mentally defective.

---

[1] For those unfamiliar with statistical nomenclature, the standard deviation may be defined as the average of the divergences of individual children (duly weighted by squaring) from the arithmetical average for their age-group. It indicates the limit between which approximately the middle two-thirds of that group will fall. For example, in the graded reading test sixty-four words are, on an average, read by boys of ten. The standard deviation is fourteen. Hence, about two-thirds of the boys of that age read more than fifty words and less than seventy-eight words. Unless, therefore, a boy of ten can read such words as "theory," "reputation," "philosopher," he cannot be considered a remarkably good reader.

As 1 have shown in memoranda previously published,[1] educational attainments depend largely upon capacities of two kinds : first, a common or general capacity, entering into every subject in different degrees, but best exhibited in those that need thought-processes of a higher order, such as the comprehension of reading-matter among young children, and, among older children, problem arithmetic and literary (or rather logical) composition ; secondly, specific capacities—such as arithmetical ability, linguistic ability, manual ability, and musical ability—entering only into a small group of subjects. A child who is deficient in the former will be backward in all subjects—most backward in those subjects most dependent upon this central capacity (such as the subjects first named), least backward in those subjects least dependent upon it (such as manual and musical subjects). A child who is deficient in one of the specific capacities alone will be backward in the limited group of implicated subjects, and in none but these.

If the teacher compares the individual results, obtained from a group of boys of the same age and about the middle of their school career, with the different scholastic tests, he will have little difficulty in verifying for himself the joint operation of capacities of these two orders. To establish their existence scientifically, to disengage their several influences, statistical methods based upon the calculation of correlations (such as are illustrated in the memorandum cited) must be employed. The application of such methods through all classes and in all departments yields a further twin conclusion : namely, that the relative influence of the more general capacity is greater, first, in earlier years as contrasted with later ; and, secondly, (though perhaps less certainly) among girls as contrasted with boys. To procure from one and the same group of children clear statistical evidence of the interplay of both general and specific factors, it seems best to confine the experiment to boys about the level of standard V. With younger children, and particularly, it would appear, with younger girls, one can often demonstrate little but the existence of the general factor ; with older school children, and particularly with college students, little but specific talents or specialised interests.

From this it should follow that in younger years—below the age of about ten—it must be peculiarly difficult to diagnose a special or localised disability, as it is undoubtedly difficult to discover special or localised talents. Specialisation is, during early childhood, the exception rather than the rule. Young turtle, said Epicurus, is every kind of meat in one—fish, fowl, pork, venison ; but old turtle is just plain turtle. Similarly, the young child contains in fresh and dormant essence the germ of every faculty. Age alone betrays our idiosyncrasies.

Like special abilities, then, special disabilities often fail to declare themselves until a later age. Nevertheless, the teacher should always take into consideration their possible existence. Many young children committed to special schools for the mentally deficient prove afterwards to have been cases of specialised defect, especially defect in linguistic subjects, such as reading and spelling. To assist the diagnosis of such cases, a systematic comparison of test-results in the several subjects, each with each, should invariably be made ; it may be achieved most simply and most clearly by a chart, by plotting the results graphically in the form of what I have termed elsewhere a "psychograph."[2] I shall append to my discussion of the several tests case-studies, obtained by such means, and illustrative of special disabilities in the more important subjects of the curriculum.

---

[1] See *Distribution and Relations of Educational Abilities*, p. 46 et seq., and earlier papers.
[2] See *Distribution and Relations of Educational Abilities*, Fig. 9, pp. 64–5.

(vii) The Analysis of the Psychological Causes of Backwardness.[1]

To diagnose the mere fact of backwardness in some particular subject' even to measure its amount, is still not sufficient. The teacher should also analyse within that subject those special aspects or elements of it in which the child is peculiarly weak. As a means to this, he may adopt one or other of the devices suggested already for analysing backwardness in non-scholastic abilities.[2] To compare performances in the specific processes entering, for example, into arithmetic, the results for each sum can be tabulated according to the scheme employed for comparing specific aptitudes revealed by the Binet-Simon tests.

The most useful plan is that of cross-classifying the marks, by children and by tests, in a row-and-column table. The test-questions may be entered by number along the upper margin, and the names of the children, preferably in order of their general abilities, down the left-hand edge. A mark for each performance is then placed under the number of the test against the name of the child. The totals of the rows indicate relative performances of the children ; the totals of the columns, the relative difficulty of the tests for this particular group. If from extensive experiments it is known that for most children all the tests are equally hard, or that for most children the order in which the several tests are entered is the order of increasing difficulty, then the special weaknesses of this particular class, and of particular individuals in this class, are patent at a glance. It may become manifest, for example, that subtraction is much weaker than multiplication, or that easy sums dealing with time are worked less accurately than harder sums in long-measure ; that "phonic" words are badly read, or that "look-and-say" words are badly spelt.

Such a device may be applied to tests of almost every subject. There are other devices which are specially applicable to certain subjects alone. These I shall discuss under the appropriate headings.

But the examiner should go further still and test the underlying psychological capacities. His end is only reached when he has probed beneath the scholastic abilities and scholastic defects, and has, wherever possible, observed and measured the deeper and simpler functions, the elementary intellectual processes, that together make up the activities of school. He should remember always that linguistic ability and arithmetical ability, even the ability to read and to add, are themselves highly complex functions ; and that in mental life there are always more ways than one of learning to do one thing.

It is here that mass teaching, with its employment of a uniform method and its insistence on uniform results, fails most conspicuously. Too many children, who, under the methods of class instruction generally in vogue in the ordinary elementary school, make little or no progress, are set down as mentally defective ; and are assumed, therefore, to be inherently incapable of learning the primary subjects of the elementary curriculum. Nor is this misconception confined to the ordinary school. In the special schools also, just as there are many struggling with reading and number who should be turned aside on to concrete and practical work, so there are not a few who, while rightly held to the formal subjects, are yet limited to the rudiments, capable of climbing yet kept at the foot, simply through failing to make headway by the time-honoured track.

I am not, of course, contending that this is a universal characteristic, or even a common mark, of the current education in special or elementary schools ; nor have I so much in mind the inexperienced teacher as the

---

[1] For an analysis of the non-psychological causes of backwardness, I may refer to my previous memoranda. (*Distribution of Abilities*, pp. 37 *et seq.*   [2] See above, pp. 4 and 11.

ineffective system—that system of collective instruction which has long been traditional, but which is now being valiantly thrown over by the enterprise and efforts of masters and mistresses themselves. Many, indeed, will still argue that, since individual teaching and small classes cannot at present be provided for all, they should, therefore, when available, be devoted specially to those children among whom they are likely to be most remunerative—namely, to the supernormal. But the argument is fallacious. It may well be maintained that what the supernormal need is not individual teaching, but rather an ampler opportunity for individual work.

Yet, even for the backward, individual teaching may be no less wasteful —it will, indeed, be more wasteful—than class teaching, unless it follow the appropriate method. And the appropriate method can only be discovered by an intensive study of the special needs of each particular child. Individual teaching, in short, presupposes individual observation. The teacher must rid himself of the assumption that for a given subject there is one sound method ; and test each method afresh upon each backward individual. The sound method for a child is that method by which he learns most successfully ; and what is sound for one child, or even for most children, may be unsound for the remainder.

How, then, are we to discover the method best adapted for each individual ? In the first place, as I shall later explain in greater detail in dealing with the several subjects, special tests may reveal what in a given child are the mental capacities we may most successfully rely upon, and what we cannot entirely trust. Let me here emphasise that it is not sufficient to discover disabilities. We are too prone to look for backwardness and to emphasise deficiency. In the most backward and in the most defective we should still search also for unusual abilities and special gifts, gifts and abilities that may compensate for defects, that may offer help to appropriate training, and hold out hope for a successful development. As it is, such gifts in the less favoured child are left too often to waste, since, being neither sought for nor suspected, his special talents pass unnoticed.

> " The jewel that we find we stoop and take it
> Because we find it ; but what we do not see
> We tread upon, and never think of it."

For the rest, the teacher may well adopt the plan pursued, often half unconsciously, by his most successful colleagues, the plan which may be termed experimental teaching. Essentially it consists of individual instruction carried out by constantly varied devices and by widely diversified methods ; but it is to be accompanied always by a close observation of the child's spontaneous method of attack, and by a detailed study of the ways which the child can, does, and will by preference, follow and adopt in learning a given piece of work ; and it is to be succeeded always by an intensive training in the most defective operations by means of the least defective mental channels.

(viii) The Need of Permanent Records for Each Child.

Last of all, let me urge, not only the need of periodic testing whether by the same teacher or by successive teachers, but also the preservation of the records, and their transference from one teacher to another as the child is moved from class to class. Too often the personal knowledge gleaned by his first teacher, through individual attention, through daily study and a year's experience, is lost when the child is promoted to a fresh class or leaves for a fresh school ; and the discoveries have to be made all over again. Rather the old records should become the basis of new observations ; and, as the child develops, as he passes from standard to standard, from department to department, from school to school, and, finally, from school to his ultimate vocation, his *dossier* or 'personal file' should go with him, and form the basis of the advice and guidance offered to him when selecting his appropriate employment.[1]

3. *INSTRUCTIONS FOR THE SEVERAL TESTS.*

The tests which it has been possible to print below are a selection only. They are not intended, as they stand, to form a complete or closed system for scholastic examinations. Rather they have been chosen as samples or illustrations of the most important types of test and test-procedure. I have, for example, given but one standardised passage for continuous reading, believing that other passages, suited to younger or duller children, can readily be standardised in the same way by the teacher for himself. Nor, as a rule, will the practical examiner attempt to apply every type of test to each given case. For quick, preliminary estimates the graded reading test (Test 1) and the mental arithmetic test (Test 8, abbreviated) will be sufficient in oral interviews; and the spelling test (Test 6) and the written arithmetic tests (Tests 9 and 10) will be sufficient in written examinations. But additional tests may be needed in making a more intensive study of the difficult or doubtful cases revealed by this cruder survey.

Detailed instructions follow for the successive tests. For convenience in practical use, however, the test-materials and tables of norms are bound together in an appendix at the close.

(i) READING.

Reading may be tested for at least four different qualities : for mechanical accuracy, for fluency or speed, for expression, and for comprehension.

As customarily regarded by the teacher, reading means reading aloud ; and it is upon the third of the above qualities—expressiveness—that attention is principally focussed. Reading in the classroom has been usually, and often still remains, an " elocutionary display." Fluency and mechanical accuracy, it is true, are both of them pre-conditions of expressiveness ; and expressiveness itself very largely is a sign and pledge of comprehension. He who reads the wrong words, or reads the right words only after hesitation and without understanding, cannot soar to an eloquent delivery ; but apt modulation and appropriate emphasis argue an intelligent grasp. Nevertheless, even so considered, expressiveness affords a measure, but indirect and dim, of the most important aspects of reading through the least important ; and, as usually assessed in school, its worth is further prejudiced by the inveterate practice of testing in rotation different children upon successive passages, and so intercepting them, according as the child's turn falls first or last, in different stages of preparation and rehearsal.

The essential purpose of reading is to decipher the knowledge, thoughts, and feelings of another mind. It is primarily a matter of interpretation. Comprehension is thus, with older children, by far the most noteworthy element to test, as it is by far the most ignored. But the younger child is in reading preoccupied chiefly with the mechanical components, with the correct and rapid association of the " sound "[2] of the word with its visible symbol in print. Under present teaching methods, perhaps under all teach-

---

(1) Here I dismiss the wide subject of vocational psychology very summarily, since I have recently set out the above proposals more fully in my chapter on " Vocational Diagnosis in Industry and at School," in B. Muscio's *Industrial Administration ;* see esp. pp. 108 *et seq.*

(2) Strictly speaking, for the child it is usually the movements of utterance, actual or imagined, that are recalled. Intelligibly enough, teachers speak of this as the " sound " of the word. But much faulty method ensues from confounding a kinæsthetic or motor image with an auditory.

ing methods, the further association of visible sign with meaning—an indirect association springing from the joint association of both with "sound"— becomes automatic only at a stage comparatively advanced. Among younger children of elementary schools, therefore, and among all backward and borderline cases, it is the mechanical aspect of the reading process—uttering a certain sound on seeing a certain sign in print—that in general calls for testing.

Tests in reading may be usefully classified in various ways according to procedure. They may, in the first place, be either group tests or individual tests. If the children are to read silently, they may conveniently be tested simultaneously and in class. If they are to read aloud, each must be tested singly, privately, and in succession. In tests of reading the predilection of American investigators is for the silent or group procedure ; and, certainly for learning, silent reading is a peculiarly useful, as it is a peculiarly neglected, means of daily exercise. The disregard of silent practice is exposed in almost every type of reading test. In oral tests the child taught by purely oral practice is habitually watchful, not for meaning, but for words of whose pronunciation he is uncertain. In silent tests, the incipient movements of his lips while he is reading, and his sudden oblivion of the context when he is asked to recite the substance, betray an attention concentrated upon articulating sounds and upon that alone. For periodic examinations, however, as distinct from daily practice, silent reading is of relatively trifling worth. Much of the information conveyed by the modulation and inflexion of the child's voice—by the tone, the timbre, the rise and fall, the intelligent emphasis, and sympathetic note, all that expresses, not reading capacity only, but power of mind and quality of temperament—is of necessity sacrificed. Even for the measurement of reading capacity itself (as the figures from my comparative experiments at Liverpool [1] show) silent reading, with all but the oldest and brightest children, elicits results neither self-consistent nor secure. Indeed, for testing mechanical accuracy and mechanical speed, as distinct from speed and accuracy in seizing the thought, reading aloud and alone is all but inevitable.

There is a further classification. The matter read may be either continuous or discontinuous. In the second case, the test sheet contains a list of disconnected words : it provides what may be termed a vocabulary test. In the former case, the test-sheet usually consists of a connected passage of prose. Lastly, in degree of difficulty, either kind of test may be uniform or graded, according as the words throughout are equally easy, or become progressively harder.

(a) Graded Vocabulary Test (Accuracy).

[Test 1.]

In principle, mechanical accuracy could be measured by a simple vocabulary test upon the following plan. Find the hardest word the child can read correctly ; by implication he is presumed able to read all the words that are easier than this word ; the total number of words that, actually or by implication, he thus appears able to read, forms, when expressed as a proportion or percentage of the total number of words in the whole English language, a convenient measure for his accuracy in reading. For a practical test we cannot toil through the whole of Webster's dictionary. We must, as a dealer would in sampling corn, restrict ourselves to specimens culled from various fields. The list on pages 368 and 369 contains one-hundred words which should be read by the average child before the age of fourteen, that is, before

---

[1] See *Journ. Exp. Ped. (loc. cit. sup.).* " Experimental Tests of General Intelligence."

leaving the ordinary elementary school. The words are arranged in average order of increasing difficulty. The child, therefore, is to read each word in succession until he can read no more. The number of words correctly read measures his reading ability, and may be taken as expressing the ratio of words he can now read to those he should be able to read at the end of his school life. With the brighter, older child this ratio may well exceed 100 per cent. Ten additional words are, therefore, appended for a hypothetical age-level beyond fourteen, making 110 words in all.

The words are printed in a type which conforms, or nearly conforms, to the requirements of the British Association Committee on School Reading-Books.[1] To each age, from four to fourteen, ten words are assigned. These were eventually selected as words which are read by approximately one-half —between 40 and 60 per cent.—of the age-group specified.[2] By virtue of this arrangement a child so tested can at once be awarded a mental age for reading. Of the children aged between ten and eleven, for example, about one-half can read the ten words from "economy" to "atmosphere." At ten and a half, therefore, the average child reads half of these ten, and by implication the sixty easier words preceding them, sixty-five words in all. Consequently, a score of sixty words indicates a mental age for reading at ten : seventy, one of eleven ; and so on, according to the formula :—

$$\text{Reading Age} = \left(4 + \frac{\text{Words}}{10}\right) \text{Years.}$$

From the age thus calculated the child's backwardness in reading can be immediately deduced in mental years.

The words set out in the list below have been empirically selected, by several stages of reduction, from an assortment of over two thousand words, tried and retried with over two thousand children. These words, in turn, were selected principally from the children's own vocabulary as reconstructed from their original compositions. Regular or "phonic" words, and irregular or "look-and-say" words, were alike inserted. And, to test the powers of the child in attacking words entirely strange, there were added at almost every level a few words altogether outside the dialect of the ordinary reading-book. Still further to reduce the undue benefits of chance familiarity, inflected word-forms—principally derivatives in "-ed" and "-ing" and "-ly"—were freely interspersed.

The reading ages of four and five pretend to little more than a conventional significance, since at this period a child may not have received even his first lesson in reading. With pupils of such an age or stage, therefore, it will be wiser simply to declare, as is so often done with children of a low grade or from a special school, that they can read so many two- or three-letter words ; and for this purpose the test to be described later will yield statements more detailed and more precise.

Even where ability is unknown and undetermined, it is still, of course, superfluous to ply the child with each of the one hundred and ten words. It will be sufficient to give him the first word in each line or age-group until he fails or falters ; and then to test him with all the words in the preceding group and with those that follow until he fails outright with about ten con-

---

[1] *British Association Annual Report*, Dundee, 1912, pp. 295–318, "Report on the Influence of School Books upon Eyesight."

[2] This method of numbering the age-assignments follows that suggested for the reasoning tests on page 238, not that of Binet. The mental ages as calculated above, however, are entirely comparable. A child who reads sixty-eight words obtains a mental age of 10·8, whether we term the words from the sixty-first to the seventieth XI.-year words (according to Binet's nomenclature, because when the child reads them all he scores an age of eleven) or 10-year words (as here, because they are crucial for children aged ten last birthday).

secutive words. Certain individuals fail erratically and succeed sporadically. With them wide-range testing is essential. In such a case, after the child has failed with a consecutive ten, time and tedium are saved, if the examiner then asks him to pick out any other word he knows and directs his attention along the remaining lines by pointing one by one to the rest of the words.

Results obtained with this test are to be found in Table XXXIX. Averages and standard deviations for each age are given, separately for children of either sex in the case of ordinary elementary schools, and for both sexes combined in the case of the special (M.D.) schools. Among normal children an unmistakable sex-difference is to be observed. Indeed, as is now generally recognised, girls outstrip boys not only (as here) in accuracy of reading, but also in every aspect of that subject—in fluency, in comprehension, and in expressiveness. In the present investigation, since the results have been procured from boys and girls segregated from the age of seven in two distinct departments, the sex-divergence during the senior ages is even wider than that remarked in my previous enquiries at Liverpool, where the results were obtained from mixed departments.[1] The difference is greatest among children living in better social circumstances; and is, as a rule, comparatively small among the less fortunate. In the former case, the sedentary life and literary occupations of the girls allow them to make the most of books, newspapers, adult conversation, and the other means of intellectual culture available in their homes; while domestic duties and unhealthy conditions seem alike to tell most heavily upon the frailer sex, in the latter. Social differences are thus quite as marked as sex differences. Between schools in better neighbourhoods and schools in poorer neighbourhoods the difference in reading (as stated in my previous memoranda) may amount, especially among the girls, to as much as the equivalent of a mental year.

From boys, therefore, and from poorer children of either sex, a mental age in reading, calculated as above, may be accepted at a level lower than would be accepted from girls, or from children from good homes, before deficiency in this subject is inferred. For strict exactitude separate age-norms should be employed for the two sexes, and perhaps should be re-calculated for different social classes.

Between the average for normals and for defectives there is a well-marked interval. Reading, indeed, is the subject in which children of London special schools are currently reputed to be most backward. Nevertheless, as I have already hinted, the diagnostic value of reading tests, at any rate in their more mechanical form, is partly illusory, and largely overrated.

(b) Letters and Figures.

[Test 2.]

For general purposes the foregoing test of reading seems by far the simplest and most handy of those I have to offer. Yet for measuring the meagre attainments of the lowest grades—testing, for example, the reading capacity of young borderline defectives—it is by no means sufficiently refined. The ten or twenty words assigned in it arbitrarily to ages three and four may be for such children all too hard, or, if not too hard, still too few in number and too narrow in range, to provide effective differentiation. For such cases the three following tests are designed.

With the lowest grades of all it is necessary to test first and upon a proper system their knowledge of the letters of the alphabet and of the Arabic numerals. The test-sheet printed in regulation type on page 370 may be

---

[1] *Journ. Exp. Ped.*, 1911, I., 2, "Experimental Tests of Intelligence," p. 111. Cf. also *ibid.*, I., 5 "Mental Differences between the Sexes," p. 370

used for this purpose. With older and brighter children it is at times desirable to try their power with figures and fractions of a more difficult order. Specimens of these are accordingly included.

In reading letters and figures a child's performance varies so much according to the time at which he entered, and the period for which he has attended, the infants' department or the special school, that it is useless to attempt a table of norms. Very roughly, it appears that 90 per cent. of the letters and simpler figures are correctly read by the average normal at the age of 6·0, and by the average defective at 9·0. The former should learn them after six to nine months' teaching in the ordinary elementary school ; the latter after twelve to eighteen months in the special school.

(c) Two- and Three-Letter Monosyllables.

Speed (with Normals) and Accuracy (with Defectives).

[Test 3.]

While accuracy is best tested with graded material, speed is best tested with material that is throughout, as nearly may be, uniform in difficulty, and lies, from beginning to end, well within the capacity of the child whose speed is to be measured. For reading, such material is provided by Test 3. The same test-sheet may also be used to measure mechanical accuracy in those low grade cases who have mastered the letters of the alphabet but are still wrestling with the simplest words. This, indeed, was my original design in framing the present test.

In the progress books kept by teachers, and upon the record cards filled in by medical officers, the reading attainments of younger defectives are not infrequently conveyed by the remark that the child knows " most two-letter words " or " a few three-letter words." This is a very convenient index in such cases. Ambiguity, however, may arise when those who refer to such records are left in ignorance as to what particular words were used in the test, and what particular number is implied by "few" or "most." If the words used by the examiner are always the same, if the number correctly read is stated explicitly in figures, and if the words known by the child are assumed to be the easiest in the list, then the statement becomes exact.

By systematically combining, in groups of two and three, all the letters of the alphabet, and rejecting all unpronounceable collocations and all " nonsense syllables," we readily obtain a complete and exhaustive inventory of the two- and three-letter words in the English language. From a test designed for defectives we plainly must expurgate all obsolete words (as " ye," " thy," " wot," " eke "), all unfamiliar proper names (as " Cid," " Usk "), and all interjections (as " oh," " ho," " ah," " ha," " lo," " tut "). Words that differ very much for different individuals in their comparative familiarity, notably the less common personal names (" Tim," " Pat," " Eva "), should, even with normal children, likewise be discarded. The remaining words may be arranged (apart from a few undesirable juxtapositions) in the order of difficulty as determined by experiments upon defective and younger normal children.

A list of words, thus selected and thus arranged, is given on pages 372 and 373. In an English dictionary there are about five hundred words of this length, thirty-three being two-letter words, the remainder three-letter words. I have retained one hundred and eighty of the latter and twenty of the former, two hundred in all. To ascertain the number of such words that the child can read, it is usually sufficient for him to work through the test from the beginning until he breaks down upon practically every word in a line. Since,

T

however, such words differ but little in difficulty, the child should be asked
if he can find any other words that he knows, and his eye should be guided
along the next three or four lines.

In testing accuracy of reading with material such as this, the measurement of ability will be the total number of words upon the sheet which the
child can read. The figures on the right-hand margin of the test-sheet will
be found to facilitate counting ; they indicate the total number of words
in the foregoing portion. If thought desirable (and perhaps it always is
desirable with children whose reading vocabulary is extremely small), the
number of two-letter words correctly read can be stated separately. The
two measures, for two-letter words and for two- and three-letter words, when
thus obtained, if multiplied by three or divided by five respectively, will
roughly express the percentage which the child can read out of the entire
number of such words. Thus, at the age of seven and a half a borderline
child can read the first thirty words on the sheet, twenty-two of which are
two-letter words. He can, therefore, read about 66 per cent. (3 × 22) of all
two-letter words in the language, and under 2 per cent. ({30 — 22} ÷ 5) of all
words of three letters or less (Table XL.).

In this way we can measure the beginner's reading ability by its extent
or range. Its speed or fluency can be measured with the same test-material
by observing the time required to read a given amount, or the amount read
in a given time. Following Dr. Ballard's procedure, before the child begins
the test I expressly instruct him to read as rapidly as possible ; and then
record the number of words correctly read in sixty seconds.[1] Thus obtained,
the results should be closely comparable with those gathered upon an extensive scale by Dr. Ballard and his co-workers.[2]

In practice, both speed and range can be measured during a single
experiment. After the examiner has noted the number of words correctly
read within the first minute the child is simply required to continue, as
described above, until he utterly fails.

Detailed results obtained with this material will be found, for accuracy
of reading, in Table XL., and, for speed of reading, in Table XLI. As
regards speed, it is convenient to observe that the average child of ten

[1] It is wise, I find, to remind the investigating teacher that a minute cannot be exactly measured by observing a minute-hand. Hence, a watch which, like most women's watches, is unsupplied with a second-hand, is useless for this test. Indeed, both for this and for the preceding test a stop-watch or stop-clock, if obtainable, should be employed.

A period so short as a minute leaves room for a relatively wide margin of error. But the eye-movements required to fixate each successive word are so contrary to normal action that, when maximum speed is sustained for a longer period, this test is apt to induce excessive ocular fatigue. Hence, a brief test remains preferable.

[2] In elaborating this form of the test my debt to Dr. Ballard's pioneer investigations will be obvious to all who are conversant (as every teacher should be) with his pregnant articles. My test-sheet, originally compiled for a somewhat dissimilar purpose—to study, namely, the range of defectives in reading, rather than the speed of normals—appears to differ from Dr. Ballard's in the following respects : Four-letter monosyllables (as "rock"), and dissyllables, whether of three or four letters (as "any," "upon"), are alike excluded ; the words are graded, not by length—all two-letter words preceding all three letter words, and all three-letter preceding all four-letter words—but in order of average difficulty for defectives regardless of length (thus in my series "eat" and "dog" precede "van" on the ground of greater ease ; in Dr. Ballard's they follow it) : an endeavour has been made to exhaust all the easier three-letter words before having recourse to harder, such as "act" or "fur." For completeness I have given averages for every year including those from nine to thirteen ; but I entirely agree that for such higher levels the test, particularly with the material thus still further simplified, is ill adapted. My material, it will be seen, embraces far less variety : it is, therefore, less suited for older normals. On the other hand, for young or low-grade special school children, it seems more appropriate. Owing, it may be, to the elimination o post-ponement of more difficult words, my examinees show a slightly higher average speed. Here, however, it should be observed that Dr. Ballard's results were gathered from over twenty thousand children, and have, therefore, a title to far greater veracity.

The reader will find the test-sheet and norms for Dr. Ballard's test, together with a suggestive discussion of the significance of speed-tests in reading with discrete material, in Child Study, 1909, Vol. IX., No. 1, p. 1.

reads at the rate of about a hundred monosyllables per minute. For accuracy I give no age-norms derived from normals, since by ordinary children simple two- and three-letter words are practically all learnt within a few weeks. Indeed, for normals the gradation in difficulty is almost too gentle to be perceived. For them the test-material is virtually of the uniform or ungraded type ; and, therefore, well fitted for testing speed.

In speed the odd divergence between the two sexes, first noticed by Romanes with continuous prose, is evident at almost every age. That sex whose tongue is reputed the more fluent in daily speech yields also the more facile readers. The defectives, it would seem, are backward in speed even more than in accuracy.

(d) Graded Directions Test (Comprehension).

[Test 4.]

This monosyllabic medley provides a simple test for speed and accuracy ; it offers nothing for comprehension. To be equally simple, a comprehension test is best framed upon the principle of a " directions " test. Here the criterion of intelligent reading is not power to reproduce from memory the substance of some fictitious story or some abstract argument, but ability to carry out from a printed order some concrete practical instruction.

A series of such directions are given on pages 374 to 377. Each order should be typewritten or printed upon a separate card. A card is handed to the child with an explanation such as the following : " Read what is on this card ; and then do what it says. You need not read it aloud to me ; but you must do what it tells you." If, as often happens from the novelty of the demand or from the shyness of the child, no response is made, the examiner may add some further word of encouragement : "The card contains a little message like a postcard or letter ; it asks you to do something for me." With the first test card it may even be necessary to suggest that the direction be read aloud, and to enquire in detail : " Where is the pen ? " " What are you to do with it ? " Only then will a subdued examinee summon heart to touch an article on the examiner's desk in the examiner's presence and offer it to the examiner in person. In fact, throughout the series, in dealing with very young or very backward children, it may often prove expedient not to insist too stringently that the reading be silent, but freely to embolden the child to make some movement of response without expressly intimating what the response should be.

In these early stages of learning to read, doing is the best test of under-standing. At a later stage, saying may supersede doing ; for a verbal reply to a problem consumes less time than the actual execution of an order, especially when, as on this higher footing, the injunction must of necessity be somewhat complicated. The test may then approximate to the " instruc-tions " test and to the " reasoning " or " syllogistic problem " tests given above for measuring intelligence.[1]

An interesting modification of this test may be constructed by using pictures for the response. This form is convenient for problems intermediate in difficulty between those requiring a practical response and those requiring a verbal response. Showing the child an illustration of the well-known fable, the examiner says : " Read this little story to yourself." (The story runs : " Once a hunter caught a lion in a net ; but a mouse nibbled the ropes, and set the lion free.") " Now show me in the picture who was caught in a net ? . . . Who caught him ? . . . Who set him free ? " For a class test, the teacher who is a skilful draughtsman may draw and

---

[1] See pp. 243 and 251 et seq.

hectograph the picture, with the questions or instructions, suitably modified, written beneath. The instructions may now run : " Find in the picture who set the lion free, and draw a ring around him " ; or, with other pictures, mutilated as in Binet's " missing features " test, the child may be instructed still in silence by the printed matter, to " put a long tail on the mouse . . ." ; ". . . an eye in the lion's head . . ." ; " a feather in the man's cap. . . ." With series of problems graded in difficulty, this pictorial form of the instructions test will prove extremely helpful to the class teacher in examining young children ; for the purposes of an external examiner, however, it is, perhaps, too much influenced by previous training in kindred tasks. For this reason, and in view of the cost and difficulty of reproducing the requisite pictures, I give no samples of the test in this form ; but leave it rather to the ingenuity of the inventive teacher.

At the most advanced stages of all, whatever type of response be required, a test of this general character, particularly if composed of a discontinuous series of tasks, is converted almost inevitably from a specific test of reading capacity into a general test of intelligence. In the relevant literature, instruction tests and problem tests alike appear, now in pedagogical articles as tests of reading, now in psychological manuals as tests of intelligence. In their more developed forms both tests were designed specifically for the latter purpose ; for the latter purpose they are by nature more appropriate ; and, accordingly, for the latter purpose they should, at least when of a more complex character, be, on the whole, reserved.

For an individual examination in intelligent reading, then, a " directions test " seems suited only to those who have just mastered the elementary mechanics of that process. For children varying in mental age from about 6·0 to 8·0, for children at the stage of standard I.—a standard which has perhaps the widest range of all—and, above all, for older borderline defectives, such as are examined for possible retransference to an ordinary elementary school, this type of test is eminently adapted. In compiling the test-material, therefore, I have included as many as five questions for ages 6 − and 7 −, and one only for each of the remaining ages. Owing to the time needed to apply such tests, the latter have been but roughly standardised upon small groups : they will be required only for rare and special cases— for example, an older backward child who shows an unexpected facility in this particular test. A larger series of harder " directions " for higher levels will be found on page 231, to be used as a written, group test of intelligence, rather than as an oral, individual test of reading. The power of intelligent reading, among children who are well advanced, is to be tested, not with a disjointed instructions-test, but rather with a single connected passage of prose, such as is supplied by the test which follows.

Averages, standard deviations, and borderline scores are given in Table XLII. The figures for older normal children are inserted merely for comparison with those obtained at the same ages from the defectives. The test is not intended for use with normal children above the age of nine. Among normals, the greater emotional shyness of the girls and the greater practical readiness of the boys tend at certain ages to obliterate, and even to reverse, the direction of the sex-difference elsewhere observed in reading tests. In this test defectives are peculiarly backward ; and their rate of progress, as compared with that shown by normals, is singularly slow. The defectives advance at the rate of about one question per year. The first half-dozen questions, which require five years for the average defective to master, are accomplished in little over a year by the normals. For backward and defective children, therefore, the number of test-questions needful to determine their mental level is, in this instance, larger than would be necessary to determine the mental level of the ordinary children. But for the same reason the test, when applied to such borderline cases, has a high discriminating power.

(e) Continuous Prose Test (Speed, Accuracy, Comprehension).

[Test 5.]

The foregoing tests have been concerned with reading either at its simpler levels, or in its most mechanical aspect—the ability to pronounce isolated words quickly and correctly on seeing their printed symbols. At higher stages, however, the other aspects of the reading process are at least equal in importance. Preferably for judging fluency, inevitably for judging expressiveness and comprehension,[1] the material to be read by older and abler children must be continuous ; it should form a single consecutive passage of intelligible prose. For these three aspects, therefore, the extract printed on page 379 has been used in the higher classes of the ordinary school It may also be used to test the fourth aspect, mechanical accuracy, in reading connected matter as opposed to isolated words.

The paragraph is taken, with trifling simplifications,[2] from Ruskin's *King of the Golden River*, a tale which sometimes figures in reading-books for intermediate standards. The chosen portion advances progressively in difficulty both as regards words and as regards thought ; and is thus adapted to testing, both in accuracy and in understanding, a fairly broad range of ability. Further, the quoted question, the descriptive close, and the variety of emotions delineated, give added play for expressive utterance.[3]

The results obtained with this test are presented in Tables XLIII. to XLV. The figures show the averages and standard deviations found, in each age and sex among the children of ordinary elementary schools, for fluency, for accuracy, and for comprehension. With a continuous passage these four aspects of the reading process may be assessed by the following means.

Fluency is measured most simply, as before, in terms of speed ; and, indeed, for intermediate as for lower levels of ability, speed of reading forms a simple and convenient index of attainment. But among older children, the fast reader is often a careless gabbler ; the more intelligent and more expressive take their time. The rate should be timed unobtrusively, otherwise the child may infer that he is expected to read at maximum velocity. Whenever owing to the difficulty of some word, the child hesitates, a pause of five seconds is allowed ; the child is then assisted, and the need for prompting reckoned an error. In the table the figures given for speed are the number of seconds required to read the whole excerpt of 193 words or 259 syllables. Allowing for the unusual difficulty of the last few lines, the figures given, when divided by two, may be taken as approximately indicating the time required to read a hundred words.

Accuracy and inaccuracy are indicated by the total number of mistakes made in reading the passage. Slips rectified by the child spontaneously do

---

[1] A discontinuous vocabulary test (see pp. 241 and 242) may be used for testing comprehension of isolated words. But such a test is a test of knowledge rather than of reading. When we say that a child can read such words as " metaphysical " or " philanthropic," we do not usually imply that he is therefore acquainted with their meaning.

[2] Chiefly the substitution of English names, Tom and William, for German, Hans and Schwartz.

[3] It is impossible in any but prose specially manufactured to obtain a very wide range of difficulty. Accordingly, I have artificially constructed a graded passage, increasing in difficulty from sentences of the simplest monosyllables to sentences beyond the scope of all but the brightest readers of thirteen. The piece was prepared for a co-operative research upon errors in reading ; and has been published with this object by the Child Study Society (see *Child Study*, 1915, Vol. VIII., No. 5, p. 93). For general use as a rapid test, however, it is far too lengthy ; nor does it afford much scope for comprehension. Norms for accuracy in this test will, I hope, shortly be published in that Society's journal.

not count as faults. To avoid prolonging the time of reading, the teacher should never interpose to correct an error, except when the reader is embarrassed or delayed by his own vague consciousness of an unlocated blunder. Unless the examiner has the passage by heart, it is advisable to follow the child, word by word, upon a second sheet ; otherwise, errors that do not clash with the gist of the passage—for example, the substitution of " green " for " grey " in line 16, the omission of " again " in line 9 or in line 11 and of " for " in line 14—may pass unnoted.

Expressiveness could be permanently standardised by selecting median readers, and causing them to read the passage aloud before a dictaphone. This I have attempted for every age. I have not, however, ventured to re-mark complete age-groups by means of the age-scale so obtained ; and consequently for expressiveness no averages or standard deviations are here tabulated.

Comprehension of a continuous prose passage may be measured by various methods. Simplest and commonest is that of reproduction. The child is required to relate *viva voce*, or to set down in writing from memory, the substance of the passage just read. His account may then be assessed either by reckoning the number of unit ideas correctly reproduced—the procedure adopted by Binet and Simon (tests 36 and 44 of their scale) ; or, more simply, by crossing out erroneous words and phrases, and counting the total number of written words remaining. However the exercise be marked, the procedure in itself is not very exact ; and, in any case, affords a test of memory rather than of comprehension. One child may precipitate, as it were, whole clauses, word for word, without ever having absorbed a particle of their meaning. Another may omit an entire block of sentences, not because he has read them without grasping them, but because, through the relative unimportance of the contents, through the distraction of writing and spelling, or, it may be, through some inexplicable freak of recollection, he fails for the moment to recall a paragraph that he fully comprehends.

A child's power to extract the meaning from what he reads does not depend exclusively upon an intellectual act, upon a cold capacity for understanding the words and statements presented to him in print. Emotional, imaginative, and even moral propensities equally act their part. I have already suggested[1] that many of the mistakes made by a child in reading have an emotional rather than an intellectual origin ; and that they are often wrongly interpreted by teachers, who, according to the prevalent tradition, treat education as a purely intellectual process ; that they are, in fact, parallel to those lapses of speech and memory, the slips of the pen, and the trippings of the tongue, which in adults have been shown by psycho-analysis to be so richly symptomatic of the profounder secrets of the individual's mental attitude.

To verify this view when the matter read by the class is reproduced by each child independently, would be difficult except for the expert analyst. But the processes at work may be clearly demonstrated by a simple device which magnifies the general tendencies like a microscopic lens. Every teacher is familiar with the game of " gossip," which under various names and in various forms has been exploited in infant schools and kindergartens. Upon this game an instructive experiment can be modelled. One child alone reads the story in the printed original. That child's version is handed to the second child to read and reproduce. The second child's version is handed to the third ; and so on, in series, until the last child writes out a story which has passed progressively through the minds of every member of the class. If the class is animated by a fairly uniform spirit of literary

---

[1] *Child Study*, loc. cit., p. 93.

composition, little by little the divergence between the printed original and the successive reproductions widens ; until at length the final version, thus distorted and transformed by a cumulative sum of tiny modifications, may eventually emerge unrecognisable. If, on the contrary, the class be inspired with a fairly homogeneous ideal of scientific fidelity, the lack of change will be no less striking.[1]

Very easily in such class experiments, less clearly in the independent reproductions of the isolated child, two antithetical types or tendencies may be discerned. One type may be loosely termed " positivist," the other " imaginative."[2] The tendency of the first is to condense, to simplify, to generalise—to give a brief, bald *précis* of definitely recollected facts, unaltered and unadorned. The tendency of the second is to embellish and elaborate, to rationalise and vivify, to construct a concrete and interesting narrative, with every detail picturesque and every incident explained.

I give below two extreme instances of these respective tendencies. The first version contains but fifty-seven words. Its errors are errors rather of fact than of falsification. The second contains 285 words—actually longer than the original ; it is, indeed, amid numerous experiments of this kind almost the sole example in which I have not found the final reproduction to be much abridged.[3] The theme of the story and most of the incidents have been radically altered. A study of the changes will immediately reveal the part played by emotional factors—by the children's own half-conscious wishes, interests, and ideals, or by their half-conscious adoption of what they take to be the wishes, interests, and ideals of their teacher and examiner.[4]

---

(1) This device, which may be termed that of " serial" or "cumulative reproduction," has been employed by E. J. Swift in a single experiment with a class of American adults for a different purpose, namely, to demonstrate the worthlessness of second-hand testimony (see *Psychology and the Day's Work*, pp. 309–312). It is interesting to find that even with adults "at the eleventh version the story may be said to have lost all resemblance to that with which they first began," and that the original version of 131 words was reduced to an epitome of twenty-one. More recently, with a group of Cambridge adults, Mr. Bartlett has employed the same technique to investigate the effects of introducing a legend derived from one sphere of culture, that of primitive savages, into another sphere of culture, that of civilised intellectual adults. (*Folk-Lore*, xxxi., 1920, pp. 30 *et seq*., "Experiments in the Reproduction of Folk Stories.") Once more, it is instructive to note that the changes introduced into the modified versions clearly illustrate the mechanisms which, as psycho-analysts maintain, largely underlie the distortions of rumour.

(2) This distinction is, to my view, of special interest to the teacher ; and under different names is constantly recurring in psychology. In psycho-analysis the reader will at once recall Bleuler and Jung's distinctions between " directive " (or " realistic ") and " autistic " (or " phantastic ") types of thinking, and between " extro-verted " and " intro-verted " types of mind (based perhaps on Freud's two principles or motives of " reality " and " pleasure ") ; in French psychology, Binet's " objective " and " subjective " types, and his " *simplistes* " and " *interpretateurs* " ; in American psychology, James' " associative " and " reasoned " types of thinking ; in German psychology, Müller's " perseverating " and " non-perseverating " types, Meumann's " fluctuating " and " fixating " types, Pfeiffer's " associative " and " apperceptive " types ; among scientific writers, Ostwald's " classical " and " romantic " types ; among literary writers, Schiller's " naïve " and " sentimental " types. I need hardly add that most reproductions belong to a mixed or intermediate type, one tendency perhaps predominating, but never excluding the other.

(3) The passage as set for this experiment was slightly longer than the extract printed below ; it contained 212 words. The sentence which, in Ruskin's original narrative, follows the phrase " spear-like pine " (" Far above shot up red splintered masses of piled-up rock, jagged and shivered into hundreds of queer forms ") was at first retained, only to be discarded in the later tests. I should add that, in the class that produced the second and most singular version, both teacher and pupils (particularly those who handled the story last of all) were unusual in both temperament and ability. I must also record my indebtedness, not only to the various teachers who used my reading-test for the above enquiry, but also to Mr. J. C. Flügel and Mr. F. E. Bartlett, who have been good enough to read the children's reproductions, and, either in correspondence or conversation, to make valuable criticisms and suggestions in connection with this experiment.

(4) The psycho-analyst will at once be reminded of Freud's analysis of the psychology of fantasies and dreams, and of Jung's analysis of the psychology of rumour. In the latter, he may remember, cumulative reproductions, given by a class of girls for a dream related by one of their number, are shown to continue and to complete the processes at work in creating the original dream. He will, too, perceive a close analogy between the mental tendencies at work in the elaboration of dreams and those at work in the above re-elaboration of Ruskin's story. The final version may be compared to the " manifest content " of a dream ; the original narrative to the " dream material." In the progressive conversion of the latter into the former the following dream-like operations perhaps deserve attention.

Y

CUMULATIVE REPRODUCTION.
(I.) 19 Boys, aged 12 and 13, Standard VII.
Final Version.[1]

There were two brothers, and one of them was in prison. The other, whose name was Tom, passed by the prison and jeered at his brother and showed him a bottle of holy water. This made his brother furious, but Tom took no notice and went on his way. He was trying to find the Golden River.

CUMULATIVE REPRODUCTION.
(II.) 16 Girls, aged 12 and 13, Standard VII.
Final Version.[1]

There were two young brothers who were rather poor, named Tom and Dick. Dick was a happy lad, but Tom was very ill-tempered. And one day he stole something and was sentenced to a term of imprisonment. One day

It is, first of all, to be remarked that all of the changes appear to have been made unintentionally and most of them to have been made unconsciously : the child sincerely believes himself to be reproducing the real purport, if not the identical words, of the version he has received. Of the numerous modifying processes, the most conspicuous is that which, in dream-analysis, would be termed "secondary elaboration." This in turn involves, as its most constant instrument, a process of "rationalisation." Attempts are repeatedly made to supply reasons for facts which in the version received are merely stated without explanation : a theft is invented to explain William's imprisonment ; a draught of wine is invented to explain the strange appearances of the rocks and crags, the original reason—the light of the rising sun—having been suppressed. The unfamiliar and the unpleasant is often omitted or repressed. Much of the alteration, however, is generally attributable to the fact that the less clever children, who handled the story in the middle of the series, dropped out many of the connecting phrases ; and related what they recalled in the order in which they recalled it, regardless of the true logical or chronological order. At this stage, the versions had much of the bizarre inconsequence that marks the majority of dreams. Later hands, at once more critical and more inventive, re-systematised the story. Several incongruities, however, still remain : for example, the brothers are said in the first sentence to be poor, but in the last paragraph to live in a mansion.

Isolated words, if vivid, may be correctly remembered. Like most emotional ideas, particularly the exciting and the pleasant, they have what I have elsewhere termed "suggestive dominance" ("The Development of Reasoning,' loc. cit. sup., p. 126). Whether in themselves trifling or essential, they persist in the memory ; and are then apt to be fitted, by a process which the psycho-analyst would term "displacement," into an incorrect context, or supplied with a fabricated context to give them a satisfactory meaning. "Cliffs" suggest a seashore ; "oil" makes its appearance because one of the children used the word "anoint." By the punning process so common in subconscious fantasy-making, the reference in the original to Tom's "spirits" appears to have partly suggested that he drank the wine ; the "spear" to which the pines are compared becomes an instrument which almost literally cleaves the rock. Except that the quoted portion of the dialogue is put into oratio obliqua, the general tendency is for the incidents to become even more concrete and more dramatic than they are in the original. Unfamiliar phrases and incidents are throughout assimilated to those more familiar to the child : according to Ruskin, Tom shook the bottle of water before William's eyes to taunt him ; by the children this is rapidly converted into shaking his fist at him, or the water (later, oil) over him, or dashing the bottle to the ground. Similarly, Holy Water, unfamiliar to most Protestant children, becomes transubstantiated into Holy Wine. Although the matter is read silently and rewritten silently on paper, auditory confusions are common : e.g., "holy water" becomes "golden water," and the "massy mountains" become "mansions." The amalgamation of the phrases "Golden River" and "Holy Water" into a single phrase, "Golden Water"—later improved into "golden oil"—is an evident instance of "contamination." Proper names are readily confused, forgotten, or misinterpreted : William first becomes "Dick" ; and a later hand inverts the two characters ; the "King of the Country" becomes "King Charles"—an intrusion from an historical novel read on the same day. As in dreams, incidents, persons, and objects are apt to be repeated or multiplied : there are in the final version three visits to the prison instead of one ; the bottle of water appears first as "Holy Wine" and then as "golden oil" ; the "King of the Golden River" (from whose stream, according to one child, the Holy Water has been taken) suggests the "King of the Country" and the "Holy Man." The "Holy Man" is evidently a composite personality : a little questioning at once revealed that, with the King of the Golden River, had become fused various recollections from accounts of the Ascension, from a visit to Faust, and from a legend of a hermit who lived by a well. Above all, the children's deep-rooted desire to have for every story a happy ending and a simple moral has had free play : the prisoner escapes ; and the attempted reformation apparently succeeds. The fantasies embodied in the story thus represent the fulfilment of primitive wishes. Nor would it be difficult to argue that the wine and the water, Dick and Tom, and the several incidents in the story, could be taken as symbolic of certain fundamental moral ideas common to the children's minds. ([1] For the correct original see below, p. 379.

Dick visited his brother in prison, and his brother said, "Hullo, my brother, have you brought a pardon from King Charles ?" Dick said he had not, and then Tom lost his temper and shook his fist. When Dick saw how rebellious his brother was, he went to a holy man and told his tale to the man. He received a flask of holy wine with instructions to give his brother to drink. After expressing his thanks to the holy man, he again visited his brother and bade him drink the holy wine ; but Tom in another fit of passion dashed the flask against the wall. So Dick turned sadly away, and, as he felt tired, he sat down on the seashore and drank what was left of the foaming wine. Then suddenly the cliffs seemed to go into all sorts of queer shapes and went red and misty and split in two as though pierced by a spear, and out of the smoke he saw the form of the holy man ascending. Then the holy man gave Dick a cruse of golden oil, and Dick felt happy again.

So he went back to the prison and sprinkled the golden oil on to the bars, and they flowed into a hundred pieces, and so Tom was able to escape, and as Tom and Dick were going home to their mansion, Dick said to Tom, "If you would only keep your temper, we should all be very comfortable."

As a rapid test of sheer intellectual comprehension, then, the method of reproduction has serious failings. Dissected phrase by phrase, such a version may disclose suggestive information on the qualitative characteristics of the writer's temperament ; but, however carefully marked, it does not lend itself with much readiness or precision to the quantitative assessment of the writer's power of understanding.

The difficulties involved in the method of simple reproduction may be met and partly overcome by the use of two accessory devices. The child may be supplied with an abstract framework of the narrative, either in the form of a series of questions, or else in the form of a series of incomplete statements. He has then to furnish the pivotal words—the cardinal ideas on which the meaning of the remainder hinges, the unessential words and the general fabric of the context being delivered to him ready-made.

In the first form, the method of interrogation supplants or supplements the method of reproduction. For the present test a list of twenty questions has been drawn up dealing with the matter of the piece selected ; it will be found on pages 380 and 381. For each correct answer the child receives one mark. He may first be desired, if it be so preferred, to give his own account unprompted ; in this account the statements which answer questions in the list may then be awarded one mark each ; and the questions not so answered may be subsequently put to him. This double procedure— spontaneous reproduction (*Bericht, récit*) followed by an interrogatory (*Verhör, questionnaire*)—has been adopted in tests of "capacity to report" by Binet, Stern, and others ; and by them has been recommended for more general employment.

In the other procedure for checking comprehension a series of incomplete printed statements is substituted for explicit oral questions. Its central principle it borrows from the celebrated test of intelligence bequeathed by the late Professor Ebbinghaus, and described above as a "completion test."[1] This test, even in its earliest shape, where the intact passage was

_____

(1) See pp. 245-7.

never seen but only reconstructed by the candidate, was still a test largely of comprehension in reading ; it has, in fact, been so utilised for the measurement of linguistic ability by American investigators. Others have found in it virtues, not possessed by the commoner catechistic method, for estimating knowledge acquired, and for testing information gathered upon specific topics from previous reading or instruction. Indeed, the artifice is clearly one which might be exploited by teachers more freely in their own examination papers. Quite recently, Courtis in America, and Ballard in England, have ingeniously adapted the same contrivance specifically for testing comprehension in reading.[1]

In my own test, on account of difficulties in marking such completion-exercises, I have adhered to the former plan, to the oral questionnaire. Those that favour the missing-word device may readily construct their own test-sheets by deleting the obvious key-words from the narrative as printed in full below ; for accurate results, after the children have perused and laid aside the intact passage, the mutilated text, printed or mimeographed, is to be completed from memory by writing the correct words in the spaces left ; for the roughest purposes, such stories may be simply given as an exercise in dictation, certain words being omitted in the recital by the teacher and left for the children to insert as they proceed.

In testing the child's power of comprehending what he reads, whatever form of reproduction be subsequently used, it will be desirable always to warn the child before reading the original that he will afterwards be examined on the subject matter. Handing him the printed extract, the examiner will say : " Read this to me aloud ; and afterwards I shall ask you some questions about it," or, " Afterwards I shall ask you to write out the story for me in your own words." But, whatever preliminary instructions be given, and whatever method be employed, irrelevant factors will now and then intervene with the most unexpected results. Often the slow, inaccurate reader, who has wrestled strenuously with the mechanical difficulties of the passage, will remember far more than the fluent, easy, or expressive reader. At times, despite the most explicit warning, even the best readers may become so immersed in the customary task of attending to articulation and expression, and to these alone, that they fail utterly to reproduce a single item from the story. The same result may ensue from the " emotional confusion," which. with many nervous or excitable children, is in an oral interrogatory yet more evident than in a written reproduction. In such cases, I supply for them the answers to the first two or three questions. Often this will suddenly recall at least some of the more memorable incidents—usually the fact that one of the men was in prison ; and these in turn will gradually bring back to mind the main events in the story.

The questions on pages 380 and 381 are printed in logical, or at least chronological order, regardless of the importance of the items with which they deal. Younger and duller children, however, if catechised first and at some length upon details possessing small interest for them, are apt to become disheartened and bewildered ; and to forget what little they might otherwise have remembered. With such children, therefore, it is advisable to postpone the harder questions to the end ; the figures in the second column of the interrogatory indicate the inverse order of difficulty. Where, however, strict comparability is essential, for example, in testing children from a single class, the same order should be rigidly preserved for all.

---

[1] Courtis has employed a modified form of the completion-test, already familiar in this country for testing intelligence. Instead of empty spaces, alternative words are printed in special type, and the child has to delete all except the correct word in each group. This simplifies the marking ; but has special disadvantages of its own.

In difficulty, the passage here set for reading is suited primarily to children of intermediate age or of intermediate ability. To test with precision the reading capacity either of the younger or duller children, or of the oldest and brightest, stories, or other reading matter, adapted more specifically to their plane of thought would be desirable. For defectives, in particular, Ruskin's story is far too hard. In the special school a few children of exceptional reading ability may, it is true, succeed in reading the passage, not without expressiveness. But, as a rule, even the brightest defective needs well over three minutes to work through it; requires prompting or correction for well over fifteen words; and answers barely three questions intelligently.[1]

Backwardness of Defectives in Reading.

In every test of reading, and, above all, in tests of comprehension, the defective ranks decidedly below his general plane of intelligence, even when intelligence is judged by a semi-linguistic scale, like the Binet-Simon tests. His mental age for reading is but little over 80 or 85 per cent. of his mental age for intelligence. In after life such a child will seek his information from sources other than books. I have made enquiries on this point among the defective and borderline adults whom I have tested; and, of those showing a mental age of only eight, barely 12 per cent. have continued their reading after they have left their school. Below this general level, a servant, a farm hand, or a dock labourer scarcely ever opens the pages of a book or glances at the columns of a newspaper; if he receives a letter, he asks a friend to read it. Accordingly, to teach reading in a special school to children whose mental ratio is less than 50 per cent. is simply to squander time and energy.

Even with those whose mental ratio falls between 50 and 60 per cent., reading should be limited to grasping the sense of common words and the meaning of brief passages. To work through paragraphs of printed matter is an exercise that should be forced on none but the brightest or the inguistically gifted. A child who, after a fair opportunity, fails to reach in reading half the attainments that belong to the normal child of the same calendar age may well be trained through other avenues.

Analysis of Backwardness in Reading.

If a child is backward in reading, the teacher, having examined him with reading tests in order to measure the degree of his backwardness, should then, in order to ascertain the cause of his backwardness, examine him with tests of purely psychological functions. Much will already have been conjectured. Hints as to the inner nature of this cause will probably have been gleaned by the way from the child's relative proficiency in the different kinds of reading tests—in tests of accuracy, of speed, and of comprehension; from the class of error to which the child is most prone—errors with regular "phonic" words, or errors with irregular "look-and-say" words; from the child's performances in tests of other linguistic subjects; and, above all, from a vigilant attention to his natural procedure when actually reading. Such deductions should now, if possible, be confirmed by tests of specific capacities—of sight and hearing, of perception and discrimination, of imagery and retentiveness, whether visual or auditory, of memory, whether immediate or delayed, mechanical or logical, and, finally, of rational analysis and rational synthesis. One of the most fruitful experiments lies in an actual

---

[1] A simpler story may also be used. But my aim is to illustrate the more important uses of the more valuable types of test, not to provide tests for all possible eventualities.

endeavour to teach the child to read by varied methods—the instruction being in the first instance undertaken, not for the direct improvement which it may induce in his reading capacity, but for the oblique illumination which it may cast upon the particular means that seem best adapted—and least adapted—to his particular form of disability.

Reading is a complex process. It presupposes for its efficient accomplishment the integrity of a large number of more elementary functions ; and is, in turn, itself a relatively elementary constituent in a process, or group of processes, yet more comprehensive—processes which may generically be termed linguistic ; for effective teaching, still more for effective diagnosis, reading is not to be divorced from other linguistic activities—from writing, spelling, and composition. It is, therefore, to be measured neither as an unanalysed unit, nor as an isolated whole.

If the child proves to be backward in such a subject as reading or spelling, the teacher should first hold in mind two truths : the one, that any single mental function (as visual memory or memory for sounds) that enters as a subordinate component into the total process of reading may by its own ineffectiveness render ineffective the larger process in its entirety ; the second, that one or another of many different mental functions may assume the office of the ineffective function, if only the means of teaching and the mode of learning be appropriately changed. The duty of the teacher, therefore, is to find first what element is out of gear, and then to seek another element to fill its place.

He will enquire, to begin with, whether the cause of the backwardness is extrinsic—due to ill-health, irregular attendance, or an illiterate home ; or, on the other hand, intrinsic—due to causes residing in the child himself. If it is intrinsic, he will proceed to ask : is the disability predominantly moral or temperamental—due to lack of industry or lack of interest, to want of motive or to want of care—or is it predominantly intellectual ? And if intellectual, is it but one of many symptoms of an all-pervasive backwardness, crippling general intelligence in each of its many forms ; or is it a specific disability affecting the linguistic subjects alone, or, it may be even, simply reading alone—suggesting, in fact, what is, in extremer cases, sometimes designated " word-blindness " ?[1] In such a case, is the backwardness due perhaps to defective sensation—to partial deafness, or to imperfect vision uncorrected by appropriate spectacles ? Is it due to defective perception—to an imperfect analysis of forms seen or of sounds heard, of words uttered by his own lips or of movements traced by his own hand ? Is it due to a difficulty in retaining these sense-perceptions, or rather the memories

[1] Strictly, the term " word-blindness " denotes a condition, most commonly occurring as the sequel to an apoplectic stroke, where a hæmorrhage destroys a portion of the visual area of the brain, and so leaves the patient destitute of memories for word-forms as seen. The patient sees black marks upon white paper but fails to recognise them as standing for sounds or ideas ; views them as an unlearned Englishman might view a text in Greek. It has been supposed that an analogous condition might exist from birth ; that, owing to imperfect development of the same portion of the brain, the child might be unable to store up, in the shape of memories, word-forms as seen. For the existence, however, of such " congenital word-blindness " the evidence is far from conclusive. When, therefore, a child is definitely backward in some linguistic subject— backward in that subject by at least 30 per cent. of his age, and in that subject twice as backward as in any other school subject or in general intelligence (for so would run my definition of " specific disability ") —it still seems wiser to speak only of " special disability in reading " (or spelling, or whatever the subject may be) ; and, instead of assuming some gross cerebral defect, such as post-mortem inspection could alone reveal, to proceed further, and enquire by actual experiment to what particular defects in various alternative mental functions the disability is to be ascribed. Of the possible defects enumerated in the text, the commonest seem : (1) failure to discriminate between similar visible forms, especially symbols differing chiefly in the order, orientation, or internal arrangement of their component parts ; (2) failure to remember a series of sounds in their due order ; (3) failure to associate visible symbol and audible sound in the absence of any comprehensible connection.

of the forms, sounds, and movement-feelings fully sensed and distinctly perceived ?

And, if the difficulty be a difficulty of memory, it must further be recollected that memory, too, is of many forms. Some children may be unable to evoke memory-images of a particular kind ; many visualisers cannot call up sounds ; many audiles cannot visualise ; many carry memories best in a motor form—a recollection of movements traced by the hand, or of postures assumed by tongue and lips. Others, again, are defective in recognition-memory ; they can evoke images, that is, they can imagine ; but they cannot identify. Some have poor short-distance memories ; some poor long-distance memories. Some have poor rote memories ; and learn bare facts only after an exceptional amount of drill. Some have poor rational memories ; and learn empirical data better than logical principles. Each of these different modes of memory should be separately tested. Very frequently the weakness lies in long-distance mechanical memory : the central difficulty is to preserve for long periods the arbitrary associations between the several abstract symbols—between the word as seen, as uttered, as heard, and as written—or between any of these abstract symbols and the concrete meaning symbolised (whether that meaning be apprehended clearly as a visual picture or implicitly as definable through words), or, finally, between the several elements which comprise one and the same abstract symbol, which are apprehended in one and the same mental form, and which require to be associated in the correct and proper order, for example, the successive letters of a given word.

There is, it will be seen, a bewildering network of interweaving associations. And, as the electrician will disengage and inspect in turn every relay in a faulty circuit, so the teacher should test each type of connection, one by one, between all possible pairs—visual with articulatory, visual with graphic, auditory with articulatory, auditory with graphic, articulatory with visual, articulatory with graphic, ideational with graphic, with visual, with auditory, and with articulatory. He must note which mode of association is feeblest, and so tends to throw the whole series out of action. He must also note which mode is most easily formed, most permanently retained. He will then in his teaching appeal to the stronger, and distrust the weak.

But even here the analysis is not yet at an end. The mind is something more than a consecutive string of associations. It is a hierarchy of systems with systems. Every mental process is to be conceived rather as the functioning of a complex mechanism than as the mere percolation of a simple conduit. Every act of learning consists in the organisation of a mental schema—of a "neurogram" or a "psycho-physiological disposition," to borrow the technical jargon—not in the mere addition of one link to another endwise in a long chain. The mind of the backward or defective child is pre-eminently weak in this very capacity for mental organisation, in the constructing of such psychical systems. He fails not so much in power to associate as in power to integrate ; not so much in the capacity to hook, as it were, "C" mechanically on to "A" and "A" mechanically on to "T," as in the capacity to synthesise in order the letter-sounds, "C—A—T," both with each other and with the letter-forms, and the two groups in turn with word-form and word-sound as a whole, and each and all with meaning—with mental picture, or generic idea—until the whole arrangement can operate as a compound unit of implicitly apprehended parts.

Such, then, are the various functions which should be observed and tested before a complete diagnosis can be made of the cause of backwardness in reading.

Cases Illustrative of Backwardness in Reading.

One or two samples of this specific form of disability I append in illustration. Cases where the backwardness is in origin extrinsic and non-mental —due to absence from school or to ill-health [1]—I shall pass wholly by. The instances below are chosen rather to exemplify how, and by what tests, such failings may best be diagnosed. As a rule, it will be seen, the analysis of itself points the way to an appropriate, and often a successful, remedy : to disclose the cause is to discover the treatment.

Case I.   *Boy, Age* 12$\frac{8}{12}$.   *Class*, Standard IV.

Intelligence Tests. Binet, 11·6[2] ; Reasoning, 11·3 ; other Tests, 11·9.

Educational Tests. Reading: Graded Vocabulary, 7·5 ; Directions 7·7 (guesses words from dominant letters ; hearing names or sounds of letters spelt out does not help). Spelling (Graded Vocabulary), 7·0 ; errors show confusion between words similar in form, but different in sound ; *e.g.*, " beard " or " bead " for " bread," " point " for " paint," " paint " for " print." Arithmetic : Mental, 9·6. Problems (with assistance in reading the questions), 10·0. Mechanical, 10·2. Four Rules, 11·4. Writing, 10·6. Drawing, 10·4. Handwork, 10·2. Composition, 6 (?). Informational subjects, 10·5. General Knowledge, 12·0.

This boy, in spite of only slight backwardness in intelligence and reasoning, is two and a half years backward in arithmetic and manual subjects ; and five or more backward in linguistic subjects.

Psychological Tests. Vision : sight normal ; perception and immediate memory for forms good for level of intelligence. Hearing : acuity, normal ; perception, discrimination, and recognition of sounds, poor, especially if sound long and complex ; auditory memory (immediate) very poor—fails to repeat in numbers (age VI.) and sixteen syllables (age VII.). Muscle sense : motor co-ordination, poor ; but motor memory, good. Enunciation : very poor and indistinct,—the defect partly motor, partly auditory : can correct errors if he hears short sentences slowly and clearly repeated to him. Articulatory memory, good. Associative Memory (long distance) : good for level of intelligence. Learning nonsense syllables and arbitrary symbols : 11·5 to 12·0. Logical Memory : 12·0 (only a little poorer with passage read to him).

Interest, Industry, etc.: good. Health and Home Circumstances : fair only.

Diagnosis. The defect is here chiefly in auditory perceptions and memory : the child has been taught chiefly by the phonic method, and has been unable to analyse and retain the sound-values of letter- and word-forms. His motor powers, either oral or manual, afford no subsidiary assistance. His mechanical memory and his industry have enabled him to make good progress in the fundamental rules of arithmetic ; and his backwardness in other forms of arithmetic is doubtless due chiefly to his detention in a low class on account of his reading disabilities.

Treatment. To rely primarily on his visual and articulatory memory, assisted by his mechanical memory, reasoning power, and interest ; and to train intensively his defective articulation and feeble auditory powers, especially analysis of phonetic values.

---

[1] Backwardness specifically in reading is often due to illness or absence between the ages of six and eight It is during this period that the ordinary child is taught to read. If he fails to learn to do so then, he s still, on grounds of age, transferred at the usual time from the infants' department. Once in the senior school, he meets with nobody who feels it his business, or perhaps with nobody who feels himself able, to teach a child the rudiments of reading ; and so he lingers on, and a few years later appears, in a very literal sense, word-blind. [2] Test-results throughout are given in mental years.

Progress (after one year's training). Reading, 9·5, Spelling, 8·8: (improvement at nearly twice the normal rate). Arithmetic (Mechanical), 11·2. Problems (with assistance in reading), 11·0.

Case II. *Boy, Age* 11½. *Class*, Standard IV.

Intelligence Tests. Binet, 11·4 ; Reasoning, 10·8 ; other Tests, 11·1.

Educational Tests. Reading : Graded Vocabulary Test, 8·2 ; Directions, 7·8. (Errors greatest with irregular words : endeavours to reconstruct word from sound-values of letters ; but frequently guesses blindly and commits reversals ; recognises a word most easily when it is spelt aloud to him.) Two- and Three-letter words : fairly accurate, but very slow (speed, 7·8). Spelling, 8·0. Errors : phonetic spelling ("pickser" for "picture," "plesent" for "pleasant ") and reversals ("saw" for "was"). Dictation : 8·9. Arithmetic : Mental, 9·1 ; Mechanical, 10·0 ; Problems, 9·6. Writing, Drawing, Handwork : 11·0 to 11·5. Composition : amount, 10·8 ; quality, 10·0.

Psychological Tests. Visual and Auditory Acuity, and Motor Control : normal or nearly so. Imagery : Visual, poor ; Auditory, good. Visual analysis (describing a picture while present) : fairly good ; Visual report (describing picture from memory) and Visual recognition : very poor, about 9·0 : (in dealing with objects shown tends mentally to note their characteristics in words ; failed badly in Binet's Test of Memory Drawing.) Mechanical long-distance memory : not good (10·2) Interest poor : believes he will never read.

Diagnosis. Specific backwardness in reading and spelling due to poor analysis and memory of visible word-forms. Arithmetic suffers from weak memory for arbitrary associations and deficient reasoning.

Treatment. To rely on auditory memory and analysis : increased emphasis on phonic method. Additional drill and revision for memory work. Intensive training of visual analysis. Individual work to secure full attention, and remove the discouraging consciousness of persistent failure.

Progress (after one year). About eighteen months' improvement in reading. Somewhat less than a year's progress in spelling and arithmetic No improvement in visual memory.

(ii) SPELLING.

For spelling, as for reading, the test-material may be either discontinuous or continuous. It may consist of a catalogue of isolated words ; or it may be taken from a consecutive piece of prose. The former may be termed a vocabulary test ; the latter a dictation test. In practice, either test discloses, together with obvious merits, special disadvantages.

(a) Graded Vocabulary Test.

[Test 6.]

For general purposes the most serviceable test of spelling is supplied by a graded vocabulary—a list of words increasing in difficulty by equal degrees, and classified on an age-basis akin to that adopted for the analogous test of reading. Such a test is printed below on page 382. As before, the words chosen are those successfully spelt by approximately one-half of the specified age-group.

For spelling, however, the series begins at a year later than for reading, namely, at a theoretical age of five ; and there are only one hundred words. The regulations of the earlier Board of Education Code implied that children should be able to spell the words they read. But to spell a word is harder than to recognise it when spelt already in print. " Emergency," for example, is correctly read by 43 per cent. at the age of eleven ; it is not correctly spelt by such a proportion until the age of thirteen : there obtains, as it were, an interval of orthographic latency. At the earlier ages the delay is not so great ; but it is still perceptible : for the first few years after commencing to read and write it averages about twelve months. The latent period, however, is longer with common irregular words, such as are learnt by "look-and-say" methods, than with words constructed according to rule, and learnt by phonic principles, or, it may be, not so much learnt as deduced. At the same level the same words, therefore, cannot be used both for reading and for spelling.

When administering the test, the teacher should employ as wide a range of test-words as possible. To set a child or a class only the ten words assigned to the corresponding mental age is not enough. The words for the age below and for the age above should at least be included. In dictating the list, each word should be pronounced separately. The enunciation should be quite distinct and moderately slow, without, however, any dislocation of the syllables. The words may be repeated if necessary ; but are not to be enshrined in an illustrative context. No time-limit is imposed.

One mark is awarded for each word correctly spelt. To find the total score, take the number of crucial words, actually dictated and rightly spelt, and add to them the number of all the easier words, which in the list precede those dictated, but were not themselves dictated because presumably known. Thus derived, the score may be regarded as roughly indicating the percentage that the child can now spell out of the total number that should form his entire spelling and reading vocabulary at the age of leaving school. From this total score a mental age for spelling can be calculated, as for reading, by the following formula :—

$$\text{Spelling Age} = \left(\frac{\text{Words Correct}}{10} + 5 \right) \text{Years.}$$

From the mental age, in turn, the child's backwardness can, if required, be directly computed.

Results in the usual form are given in Table XLVI. In spelling, defectives appear particularly backward ; and normal boys, especially during senior ages, appear backward as compared with normal girls.

(b) Dictation Test.

[Test 7.]

To test spelling simply by a disjointed list of unmeaning words has evident disadvantages. In such a test the accuracy of the examinee varies considerably with the clearness of the examiner's enunciation. Further, with homonymous words inevitably, and with all words in a lesser degree, the correct spelling is associated, and rightly associated, with the sense as closely as with the sound. Moreover, the type of spelling-capacity that is required for practical purposes is the ability to spell words automatically, when the attention is diverted to the purport of the total context, rather than riveted on the orthography of the isolated unit.

Accordingly, a second test has been attempted. In the test material given on page 383 the words are strung into phrases or sentences which carry some degree, although perhaps a low degree, of meaning. As distinguished from the discontinuous vocabulary test described above, which, according to the common but narrow usage of the phrase, might be styled *par excellence* a "spelling" test, this continuous type of test answers to the exercise familiarly termed "dictation."

In order to secure test-material suited to diagnosing a wide range of mental ages, it is preferable, with spelling as with reading, to employ a passage which begins with the easiest words, and in the sequel gradually increases, or at least materially varies, in difficulty. Unfortunately, to construct a coherent paragraph solely of hard words, without introducing easy connecting words, is as arduous as to build a firm wall of bricks without mortar; and with such a composite structure the young child, who neither attempts, nor understands the hard, long words, is apt to omit or to misspell even the short and easy connectives. Indeed, for him, this portion of the test, if given at all, degenerates once again into an exercise with disconnected vocables.

There are various expedients. Partly, though not entirely, the difficulty may be mitigated by counting, not the number of correct words, but the number of correct letters. This method of evaluation carries an additional advantage. From a comparatively brief test it extorts far more information; and it differentiates, with minuteness and precision, even those borderline defectives who make abortive attempts at numerous two- and three-letter words, but fail utterly to spell more than one or two such words with complete correctness.

Another device is to embed the test words in an explanatory sentence. The majority of passages that the teacher uses for dictation in class are selected, if they are selected deliberately at all, for the sake of but a few crucial words. The rest of the material is but rubble to give these words connection and support: it supplies to them a context and a meaning; but, as a test of spelling, it is in itself largely, if not wholly, otiose. Indeed, it is no uncommon device for the examiner to mark, and sometimes even for the children to write, only the critical word in each sentence. Some ingenuity in the examiner, and some sacrifice of coherent thought in the test, may, in part, at any rate, obviate the need for so cumbrous a proceeding; and sentences may be compacted out of words, of which every one is a serviceable test-word. The passage printed for Test 7 below is a verbal breccia of this sort. It is an agglomerate rather than a conglomerate. Into the last few lines, to impart some semblance of cohesion to the sesquipedalian posers, I have, indeed, admitted, what Dr. Johnson himself could not have excluded, one or two stray articles and particles. But, with these exceptions, every word has been carefully chosen, and expressly inserted, because it seemed fitted for the purpose of the test; there is no superfluous cement.[1]

In dictating the passage, I would advise, simply for uniformity, the following procedure. Read each sentence completely through before the children attempt to write. Then dictate the portion thus read, very slowly, in phrases of two or three words, repeating each phrase a second time after an interval of about two seconds. The phrase may be repeated a third time, if this is especially requested. Incline throughout to a pronunciation colloquial rather than pedantic, the "e" in the last syllable of "kitten," "sentence," "model," excellent," the first "a" in "acceptable." and the first "u" in "picturesque" and the last in "adventure," should all be given the

---

[1] My latest trials, however, reveal such weaknesses as the reader will himself easily suspect. The monosyllables in the final section, few as they are, are sufficient to introduce substantial variations in the measurement when the test is placed in different hands. Nor is the sacrifice of sense, however unavoidable, entirely to be condoned. Originally, to quicken a childish interest, the passage propounded a simple riddle and announced a reward for its solution, in the manner of a newspaper advertisement. To ensure a better standardisation, the wording had to be altered, and what little sense existed has since almost evaporated. Dictated in unconvincing accents the test may elicit no better achievement than if it were in form what it is in fact—a mere catalogue of words. Those who fail to construct a better test upon these principles or to devise better principles for another type of test may find the present passage, with all its imperfections, interesting and helpful, if they consistently adhere to their own method of dictating the test, where they cannot precisely follow mine. It may be, however, that every test, framed upon lines such as the above, is bound to prove, as the present instance too plainly suggests, more elaborate than efficient, over-ingenious and under-exact.

U

interdeterminate sound. Similarly, " ci " should be pronounced " shee " or " sh." Final " d " and " s," though clearly articulated, should not be over-stressed.

One mark is to be given for each correct letter. The constant counting up of every letter would be a slow, laborious process. Accordingly, the material has been so contrived that, in all but the final paragraph, the clauses contain exactly some round number of letters, such as ten or twenty.

Averages, standard deviations, and borderlines for the several ages are given in Table XLVII.

Backwardness of Defectives in Spelling.

In spelling and dictation, the defective ranks far below his level for intelligence : the difference is greater even than for reading, probably greater than for any other subject. His mental age for dictation is less than 80 per cent. of his mental age for intelligence, even as assessed by the Binet-Simon scale, and probably less than three-quarters of that mental age as it would be assessed by a scale exempt from all linguistic bias. Among the low-grade adults whom I have tested, spelling is much worse than among special school children of the same mental level. With such persons, exact orthog-raphy is the last thing to be learnt, and the first thing to be forgotten. Yet, even if they cannot spell, they can still write. Of the adults, indeed, showing a mental age of only eight, barely 7 per cent. can compose even the simplest letters. But at the mental age of nine as many as 37 per cent. attempted to write. For generalisation the groups tested are too small and hetero-geneous. But it is clear that, with individuals of undoubtedly low grade, difficulties in the mechanics of spelling do not always hinder spontaneous writing in the way that difficulties in the mechanics of reading usually preclude spontaneous reading. As with reading so with spelling, it is assuredly both useless and wasteful for the special school to inflict the labour of spelling lessons upon any of the children whose mental ratio is below 50 per cent., or even upon the majority of those whose mental ratio is below 60 per cent. Among the latter, however, there may be not only a few individuals showing special linguistic ability, but also a few individuals showing special graphic interest—the desire to express themselves and to communicate with others by means of writing. With these, therefore, the writing lesson should not be discontinued on the ground merely of an ineradicable weakness in spelling.

But with them, and indeed with most defectives, it would probably be wiser to aim in spelling at the barest essentials alone, to abandon the hours of drudgery and drill with harder irregular words, and even to rest satisfied, for the simple communications such simple minds attempt, with a simplified or phonetic orthography. If, therefore, in spelling, after individual testing and teaching, the child has not acquired at least half the attainments of a normal child of the same calendar age, forgo all formal attempts to teach a flawless orthographic exactitude.

Analysis of Spelling Errors.

In the diagnosis of a child's disability in spelling, a statement of the type of error to which he is prone contributes a datum quite as suggestive as the measurement of the degree of backwardness to which he has lapsed. Accordingly, to assist this qualitative analysis, I subjoin two empirical classifications of the spelling errors most commonly encountered. The first classification is drawn up from the standpoint of the error made ; the second from the standpoint of the individual making the error. In neither classifica-tion are the subdivisions logically exhaustive or mutually exclusive. But a system theoretically perfect would contain many subdivisions over-crowded, which for practical uses should have been split ; and would leave many subdivisions virtually empty, wherever the specified errors, though logically conceivable, were actually rare.

SCHEDULE III.
Classification of Spelling Errors (A).

1. *Visual Substitution.* The incorrect letter resembles the correct letter[1] in visible form : *e.g.*, " hiny " for " king," " gueem " for " queen."

2. *Motor Substitution.* The incorrect letter involves similar movements to those made in forming the correct letter : *e.g.*, " duelln " for " queen."

3. *Auditory Substitution.* The incorrect letter resembles the correct letter in audible sound : *e.g.*, " celekt " for " select." An important sub-group in this class is one which may be designated *Homonymous Confusion* ; words having the same sound, but a different spelling, are incorrectly substituted one for another : *e.g.*, " their " for " there," " hear " for " here," "too " for "two," "road " for "rode," and *vice versa*.

4. *Motor Omission.* One of two letters requiring similar movements is omitted : *e.g.*, " gld " for " glad." Sometimes a single stroke only is omitted : *e.g.*, " cone hone " for " come home." (The omission of one duplicated letter, an error especially common in words containing two pairs of duplicated letters, may be classified either here or under auditory omission : *e.g.*, " occurence," " embarass," and that facile slip of the teacher himself—" accomodation.")

5. *Auditory Omission.* One of two letters resembling each other in sound, or contributing to the same sound, is omitted. The more important sub-types are : (i) Omission of " silent " consonants : *e.g.*, " rythm " for " rhythm," " morgage " for " mortgage," " shipwrect " for " shipwrecked." (ii) Omission of portions of diphthongs : *e.g.*, " receved " for " received." (iii) Omission of silent (lengthening) " e " : *e.g.*, "receivd " for " received."

6. *Initial Omission* (usually motor ; but often with *Condensation,* and then frequently visual). The initial letters of a word are omitted, usually when the preceding word ends with similar letters, the two words being then run together in one : *e.g.*, " theeth " for " the teeth."

7. *Final Omission* (usually auditory). The last letter of a word is omitted, usually when the following initial has a similar sound : *e.g.*, " he ask to " for " asked," and, with *Condensation,* " alright " for " all right," doubt-less influenced by the analogy of " always."

8. *Motor Insertion.* A letter, usually involving similar movements to those of the correct letter, usually inserted immediately before or immediately after the correct letter : *e.g.*, " globle " for " globe."

   Motor insertion (and, less frequently, other types of error) are occa-sionally determined by habit (*Assimilation*) : *e.g.*, " pronounciation," "similiarity "—due, not to faulty pronunciation, but to greater mechani-cal familiarity with " pronounce " and " peculiar."

9. *Auditory Insertion.* An incorrect letter, having, or contributing to, the same sound as the correct letter, is inserted : *e.g.*, " seleckt " for " select."

---

[1] For brevity the term " letter " is used throughout as including not only single letters, but a com-bination of letters having a single sound, such as might otherwise be represented by a single letter, in short what may be technically termed a " phonogram."

10. *Motor Transposition.* Two correct letters, usually adjacent letters, are transposed, the result being usually an incorrect sound. but seldom a transposed sound : *e.g.,* "siad " for "said," "salior " for "sailor," " mountian " for " mountain," " guage " for " gauge."

Where the order of the letters in a word is reversed, the error is often described as *Inversion : e.g.,* " no " for " on," " god " for " dog," " saw " for " was," and *vice versa.*

11. *Auditory Transposition.* Two correct letters, or more commonly sylla-bles, are transposed, the result being an erroneous transposition of sounds : *e.g.,* " Put the cerely in the scurrily " for " celery in the scullery." (Where the transposition of sounds is not a temporary lapse, most apparent auditory transpositions are due to faulty pronunciation. Here, therefore, it is not always possible to classify the error, immediately and with certainty by mere inspection.)

12. *Duplication.* A single letter is erroneously duplicated. Such duplica-tion may be perseverative : *e.g.,* " merrilly " for " merrily " ; or antici-patory : *e.g.,* " dissappoint " for " disappoint " ; or transposed : *e.g.,* " paralele " for " parallel," and " merilly " or " meerily " for ͥ" merrily."

13. *Repetition.* A combination of letters, sometimes a complete word, is erroneously repeated. (Usually motor, *e.g.,* " merrilily " for " merrily." Sometimes auditory, *e.g.,* " precisision " for " precision," " neigherbor-hood " for " neighbourhood.")

14. *Anticipation.* A letter or, more commonly a syllable, is inserted or substituted from the following syllable (" intra-verbal " anticipa-tion) : or word (" inter-verbal " anticipation, usually with " contami-nation," *i.e.,* the correct and incorrect syllables contain one or more identical letters) : *e.g.,* (*a*) intra-verbal : " husdband " for " husband," " neucleus " for " nucleus " ; (*b*) inter-verbal : " pictard card " for " picture card."

15. *Perseveration.* A letter contained in a preceding syllable or word, usually some dominant element in it, is incorrectly inserted or substi-tuted, frequently with " contamination " : *e.g.,* (*a*) intra-verbal : " pro-trect " for " protect " ; (*b*) inter-verbal : *e.g.,* " the theeth " for " the teeth."

16. *Faulty Pronunciation* (Articulatory Errors[1]). The incorrect letter cor-rectly represents this child's incorrect pronunciation :—

(*a*) Omission of sounds[2] : *e.g.,* " Febuary " for " February," "Artic " for "Arctic," " twelth " for " twelfth."

(*b*) Insertion of sounds : *e.g.,* " heighth " for " height."

(*c*) Transposition of sounds : (i) of syllables (*i.e.,* complex sounds) : *e.g.,* " pernemant " for " permanent," and perhaps " cerely " for " celery " ; (ii) of letters (*i.e.,* elementary sounds) : *e.g.,* " persent " for " present."

(*d*) Substitution of sounds, usually vowel sounds : (i) with accented vowel sounds : *e.g.,* " Voilit " for " Violet " (the second " i " illustrates

---

[1] Articulation is, of course, a motor process. But to avoid cumbersome technicality I have (as is commonly done) used the term " motor " throughout as equivalent to " grapho-motor " or " hand-motor " ; and I here use the more familiar term " pronunciation " in place of the phrase " articulatory-motor processes." I am not, therefore, introducing a new principle of division, as the change in phraseology might at first sight suggest.

[2] I use this familiar term for what is to the child really an " articulatory unit " rather than an audible sound.

the following sub-group) ; (ii) with unaccented vowel sounds ; a large group capable of further subdivision according to the sounds confused : *e.g.,* " a " for " e," " e " for "i," and *vice versa ;* especially common with " indeterminate ' e ' " and sounds resembling it : *e.g.,* " sentance " for "sentence," "fountin " for "fountain," "privelege " for "privilege."

For diagnosis, it is further important to classify spelling errors as belonging to one or other of the following broader groups, arranged according to the tendencies of the person making the error rather than according to the nature of the error made. To identify errors under these further heads, it is, as a rule, necessary first to repeat the same or similar tests, although with experience it becomes possible to identify the child's errors tentatively by mere inspection. To the teacher it will be at once evident that the different types of error, when detected, need each a different procedure or method to ensure their ultimate correction.

SCHEDULE IV.
Classification of Spelling Errors (B).

I. *Lapses :* the child knows the correct spelling, but fails for the moment to reproduce it. If the same test is repeated, the same error is not, as a rule, repeated ; and if the child's attention is called to the misspelt word. he will rectify it without further information or fresh instruction. Such " slips of the pen," such errors of " carelessness "—as they are often inadequately called—form by far the commonest type of error. As a rule, a lapse exhibits only a single error in a single word ; and the words so misspelt are easy and familiar. The errors classified above as motor—whether of omission, insertion, substitution, or condensation—are, as a rule, lapses. The errors classified as auditory rarely occur as lapses.[1]

II. *Extemporisations :* the child does not know the correct spelling, and, therefore, invents—usually from analogy with the construction of more familiar words—an impromptu spelling of his own. If the test is repeated, the same word is erroneously spelt, but the form of the error is not, as a rule, the same. Something new is improvised. Thus in five successive

---

[1] Lapses in spelling, like lapses in reading (see above, p. 306), prove frequently, especially in older and well-educated persons, to be due to what may loosely be termed a psycho-analytic mechanism. A young adult girl, quite normal and intelligent, who is under my observation at the moment, spelt "origin" three times in the same essay as " origan." Requested to spell it aloud, she said, "o, r, g, a, n—'origin'; oh, no; that's ' organ.' O, r, i, g, i, n." Having thus realised the misleading association she has never misspelt the word since. In a similar way, by free association, "annalyse" (an incorrigible error for "analyse ") suggested "Anna ; a foreign coin; and another one whose name I forget—ru—? . . . India! I've often amused myself by fancying I was an Indian girl in a previous life." The misspelling was now cured. After hunting up the word "consciousness" in a dictionary, she repeatedly transcribed it "conscienceness." She had looked for "conscience" and "conscientiousness." Most of these words she could spell orally with perfect exactitude; but she explained: "My hand is always doing things I know it shouldn't, when I'm thinking of something else."

Cases of this type sometimes rationalise their mistakes by expressing their ingrained impatience of petty orthographic conventions ; and this impatience in its turn seems often a symptom of a deeper and more general intolerance. dating from the earliest years, of nursery rules and regulations. Their writing is usually as slovenly as their spelling, almost by a half-obstinate defiance. Literary composition is for them not a thing to be confined by pedantic restrictions as to times and seasons, or ways and means; rather it is a spasmodic discharge of inner desires upon worthless sheets of paper. A neurotic delinquent of ten spelt well when she wrote well ; and when she wrote badly and spelt badly (the products were then commonly smudgy letters of abuse) what she wrote was, in a double sense, unfit to read. Students of Dr. Ernest Jones' *Papers on Psycho-Analysis* (second ed., pp. 664 *et seq.*) will immediately divine the character of the complex at work. I should like here to acknowledge my indebtedness to my friend Mr. J. C. Flügel, who has always willingly discussed with me this and similar points that have arisen during my analysis of such cases as the above ; and from his wide psycho-analytic knowledge and experience has generously made most helpful criticisms and suggestions.

exercises the same child spelt the word "necessary" as follows : "nessecery," "nessessery," "nessisery," "nessery," "nessecry." Misspellings that show several errors compressed into a single word—the word written being often at first sight a meaningless jumble of letters—are, as a rule, extemporisations. The individual errors are of various types ; but those classified above as auditory generally preponderate.

III. *Habitual Errors :* the child appears to have learnt an incorrect form, which has become fixed, in place of the correct form. If the test is repeated, the same error recurs, time after time, with the same word. Thus, a second child in five successive tests invariably wrote "necesary." In the "extemporary error," the child has failed to form any association whatever between the sound of the word and the way it is to be spelt ; in the "habitual error," the child has formed and fixed an association, but it is an erroneous one. In such cases there are in the same word seldom more than one or two errors ; and usually the errors belong to the types classified above as auditory. Habitual errors of a motor type exist, but appear less frequent ; one child, for example, persistently substitutes "y" for "g," "h" for "k," and "l" for "b," thus showing a tendency to motor substitutions of three kinds. It may be noted that the common practice of teaching spelling through dictation is apt, with those members of the class for whom the passage dictated is too hard, to induce false extemporisations which, through repetition, rapidly become ingrained as habitual errors.

IV. *Idiosyncrasies :* many children are addicted to some one characteristic type of blunder. Again and again the same error is repeated in different forms or in different words. A young and backward child, for example, will incessantly invert words. A high-grade defective once wrote : "I *was* the *god* go *of* the cat *no* the *tale*" (the sentence dictated was : "I saw the dog go for the cat on the table "). Out of the five misspellings four were inversions. Subsequent tests displayed the same propensity. Another child is reported constantly to add a final mute "e" to words, particularly before plural "s" : *e.g.*, "whome," "oures," "perhapes" ; and another to insert epenthetic consonants, usually anticipating a consonant normally occurring toward the end of the same word : *e.g.*, "wringing," "husdband."[1] In the errors made by the girl mentioned above (footnote ([1]), p. 321) more than 40 per cent. involved (as she put it) "making the big words bigger" by a repetition of internal letters, syllables, or sounds : *e.g.*, "ingenuiniuty," "precisition," "neigherborhood," "bigography." A tendency to repeat or to omit whole words or whole syllables is another, more common form of idiosyncrasy. Apparent idiosyncrasies in spelling may also be produced by faulty pronunciation, such as occurs in local dialect or in speech impediment.

Analysis of Backwardness in Spelling.

The diagnosis, then, which is based upon an examination in spelling should be partly quantitative and partly qualitative. It should give, first, the marks or measurements obtained in the tests, noting what is the individual's "orthographic age," degree of backwardness, or "ratio" ; secondly, it should state the type of error to which he is most liable—whether, for example, his errors are the lapses of a careless speller, the improvisations of an ignorant speller, or the fixations and idiosyncrasies of a speller inherently and habitually bad ; and, again, whether the errors are chiefly omissions, insertions, or substitutions, and whether they are principally motor, visual, or auditory.

([1]) For these two cases I am indebted to Miss Hollingworth.

These statements the examiner can deduce from spelling tests alone. But his end is not attained until he has directed both his tests and his observations to discover what special psychological disabilities prompt and promote these errors. From the nature of those errors he will have already gathered hints as to the directions which he may most profitably explore ; and, following the methods described for backwardness in reading, he will proceed to analyse the extent and nature of the psychological disability, to discover what defects in more elementary processes condition it, and to search for stronger mental functions which may be relied upon to do the office of the weaker.

Case Illustrative of Backwardness in Spelling.

Case III. *Girl, Age* 10$\frac{1}{12}$. *Class*, Standard III.

Intelligence Tests. Binet, 10·0 Reasoning, 10·4. Other Tests, 10·1.

Educational Tests. Reading, 9·7. Spelling, 7·6 (errors largely phonetic). Dictation, 7·8. Arithmetic : Mental, 9·0 ; Mechanical, 9·4. Problems, 9·8 (method usually correct ; but working often inaccurate). Fundamental Rules, 8·8. Writing, Drawing, and Handwork, about 9·5 (somewhat slovenly) Composition, about 9·0 (handicapped by gross spelling errors).

Psychological Tests. Visual acuity, Perception, Imagery, Memory (immediate), unusually good for mental level. Auditory perception and memory somewhat poor. Motor control, poor. Long-distance mechanical memory for arbitrary associations, very poor for every type of stimulus. Logical memory, good. Emotional temperament.

Diagnosis. Special backwardness in spelling, due more particularly to weak long-distance memory.

Treatment. To rely less on phonic method, and more upon "look-and-say" methods in reading. To attach meaning to arbitrary associations— *e.g.*, to explain reasons for orthographic anomalies, and use mnemonics. Special mechanical drill in spelling by the alphabetic method, and in addition and multiplication tables. Special instruction in technique of memorisation. Eurhythmic training (proved impracticable).

Progress. After one year, an improvement equivalent to eighteen months' normal progress in spelling and fundamental rules. Work still somewhat inaccurate.

(iii) ARITHMETIC.

Tests of arithmetic may be classified upon a basis analogous, though not identical, with that adopted for tests of reading. They may be divided, first, into graded and uniform tests ; and, secondly, by a cross-division, into individual and group tests. In arithmetic, as in reading, the range or scope of attainments is best measured by test-material graded in difficulty ; the ease or speed of working by test-material approximately uniform in difficulty. Graded tests of arithmetic incline towards one or other of two procedures, namely, oral or written. A completely oral test is necessarily an individual test ; a written test may be, and usually is, a group test. Ungraded or uniform tests are, in arithmetic, though not in reading, nearly always written tests.

In arithmetic, more than in other subjects, teachers are prepared to define, precisely and without hesitation, the attainments to be expected at successive ages. In arithmetic, therefore, I supposed that graded tests would prove the most easy of all such tests to construct. They have proved the most arduous. In no subject are children so influenced by the range of instruction and so responsive to the degree of practice in the specific processes ; and in no subject do those influences now so obstinately defy prediction. Teaching, instead of unifying the grading, renders it more unstable. Pupils of a given age who, with a particular group of problems succeed in only 10 per cent. at the beginning of the term, may succeed in 90 per cent. when the instruction for that term is concluded. Much will hinge upon the phrasing of the tests. Children are as dependent upon the inculcated formula as the door of Ali Baba's cave upon a " Sesame " in the spell. Recast the question to fit the customary *cliché ;* change but one synonym for another, alter but the order of the clauses : and every pupil in the class will work the sum correctly, where before almost every one had blundered.

The old uniformity has passed away. In various directions and in differing degrees, most schools have departed from the earlier recommendations of the Board. Its code no longer, like a steam-roller, levels all results. Syllabuses and schemes of work differ greatly in different schools ; teaching methods diverge still more. The proportion of mechanical arithmetic to problem work, of mental arithmetic to work on paper, varies enormously with different teachers. In girls' departments, in schools in poor neighbourhoods. in the youngest classes of ordinary schools, in the older classes of special schools, many innovations in the teaching of this subject have been fostered and fostered rightly. In London other factors co-operate. Here the raising of the age at which children enter the infants' department or are transferred to the seniors', there the migration from a school with one scheme of work to a school with a different scheme, and almost everywhere the recent system of double promotions, have deepened a diversity already profound, and made liberty essential. It is not my duty, even were it my desire, to criticise these changes from the standpoint of administrative efficiency or of educational value. But plainly what makes so laudably for freedom and variety in teaching will militate against uniformity and finality in the standardisation of tests.

Above all, tests in arithmetic have proved extremely sensitive to disturbances of social conditions. There is, indeed, no subject of instruction but has been unsettled by the war ; but arithmetic, in virtue of its exacting call upon the most delicate functions of the mind, has been dislocated more than any. It was the Belgium of the school curriculum. It suffered first ; it suffered most ; it suffered more conspicuously than all. The havoc of fatigue, of insufficient sleep, of excitement, shock, and strain, of change in teachers and in the sex of teachers, was, as a rule, seen earliest in arithmetic. At one period, indeed, the whole grading of my problems had to be materially reduced, and the general requirements of my norms to be repeatedly relaxed. In consequence, as pre-war conditions are gradually resumed, the age-assignments for the graded tests will become too easy ; and, for uniform and graded tests alike, the standard deviations will probably be found too large, and the average attainments will certainly appear too low.

(a) Mental Arithmetic (Accuracy).

[Test 8.]

For individual tests an oral procedure is the most convenient ; but it is also the one most exposed to disturbing influences of various kinds.

In the completely oral test the examiner announces the question *viva voce.* The child works the sum (as the phrase goes) " in his head " ; and then returns the answer *viva voce.* Such an exercise is familiarly known as " mental arithmetic."

A test of " mental " arithmetic need not be exclusively oral. The reply may be given by the child in writing ; the question may be presented in chalk upon the blackboard or in print upon paper. Provided the child sets down nothing but his answer, the work is still said to be "mental." A group test in mental arithmetic may, therefore, be carried out by distributing printed question-sheets, with blank spaces opposite each question for the child to insert the answer. As a rule, a time-limit will be imposed ; and the measure will be in terms of speed. This form of test was adopted in my experiments at Liverpool ; it has already been described elsewhere ; and here need not further be discussed.

The test in mental arithmetic set out below[1] was designed for use as an individual and completely oral test. With older children, above the level of standard I., the tests may also be used as a group test, the questions being given orally, but the answers written down. With this modification, the performances will be slightly inferior to those obtained in an individual interview and with a purely oral procedure.

The test-material has been compiled according to the principles propounded for the graded test of reading. There are ten problems for each age-group from age four to age fourteen, thus making 110 in all. They are picked from a much larger assortment ; and have been chosen as being those which are correctly answered by approximately 50 per cent. of the age to which they are assigned. They are disposed in average order of difficulty.

The child, however, should not be given those problems merely which are allocated to his own chronological age. If time allows but ten problems to be set, it will be wiser to select those which correspond to his mental age, as inferred from his school class or "standard," or from tests of another kind. But, if possible, the harder problems for the year below, and the easier problems of the year above, should at least be included. If the child's mental age is totally unknown, it may be advisable first to work upwards from the series three or four years below his chronological age, giving a problem from each year until the child fails. By choosing one problem only from every set, the whole collection can be telescoped into a brief progressive test of twenty graded problems, suitable for rough and rapid assessments. Mental arithmetic is an activity which is much impaired by fatigue. Hence, to give more than ten or fifteen problems at one sitting will seldom be expedient.

In administering the test each question is to be recited to the child clearly, slowly, and with due emphasis. If necessary, the question may be repeated once. The child himself should not see the question. Nothing is to be written in explanation by the examiner, either on paper or on the blackboard ; and nothing (except—in a group-test—the answer) is to be written by the child.

There is no time-limit. When the test is given in class, care should be taken to allow ample time even for the most tardy to arrive at the best answer he can.

The measure of ability consists in the total number of problems correctly answered, whether actually or by implication.[2] If desired, this total can be converted into a mental age by an equation similar to that used for reading. Averages and standard deviations for normal boys and girls, and for defectives, are given in Table XLVIII. The arithmetical superiority of boys—a superiority which is familiar to all teachers, and which I have already discussed both in reporting experiments at mixed schools[3] and in my memorandum on sex-differences in arithmetic—finds a clear echo in the figures for all but the earlier years. At younger ages the difference tends to be abolished, if not reversed. At this period, not only are the children of both sexes taught together in a mixed department for infants, but also there may be traced among the girls a temporary advantage in all oral work—

---

[1] Pp. 384-388.　　[2] The suggested exercises for children under four are not to be reckoned.

[3] *Journ. Exp. Ped.*, loc. cit. sup., I., 2, p. 111 ; cf. also I., 5, p. 373.

an advantage which in a "mental" test may more than counterbalance any slight deficiency of inborn arithmetical powers: it should be remembered, too, that experiments in mixed schools disclose throughout school life an innate difference far smaller than is commonly assumed. As stated in my earlier memoranda,[1] the arithmetic results obtained from schools in good neighbourhoods may be more than a year ahead of those obtained from schools in poor neighbourhoods. In schools from poor neighbourhoods, owing doubtless to the influences already noted in discussing sex-differences in reading, the girls are, almost invariably, much inferior to the boys ; but in mixed schools in good neighbourhoods, it would seem that, given an equal amount of practice, sisters may, in childhood at any rate, calculate with greater accuracy and greater celerity than their brothers. Differences such as these, associated with sex and social status, recur in all tests of arithmetic ; but are perhaps most marked in oral tests.

Defectives are certainly backward in mental arithmetic to a deplorable degree ; yet not to a degree so extreme as might perhaps have been expected. Much of their daily lessons is worked in the form of oral problems ; and, where the question involves a simple sum in concrete money values, the petty transactions of the older defective, in the shop and in the street, place him, as compared with the younger normal of equivalent mental age, at a relative advantage. Elsewhere he is an infant among youths ; here he is a youth among infants.

All the arithmetic tests proved troublesome to standardise ; but none so refractory as the graded series of mental problems. With written work, at all events about the middle of the school career, the arithmetic papers for external examinations, such as those for the Junior County Scholarship, create, notwithstanding the variety of syllabuses, a certain measure of uniformity. But with mental arithmetic even this slight levelling influence is absent. And in this branch of the subject, particularly with the problems for the oldest age-groups, and most of all with the problems for the youngest, the standardisation recorded below is doubtless somewhat precarious. For the youngest of all, indeed, it proved impossible to base the age-assignments solely upon the data obtained from normal children of four or five. Among children of such years, differences in the conditions of teaching—in the schemes and methods of the infants' department, in the age at which children enter school, in the character of the informal instruction given at home—all these have a large and disproportionate influence ; and the results obtained are equally capricious. Accordingly, the order and grouping of the easier tests has been founded predominantly upon the work of defective children of the corresponding mental ages.

In actual practice it is more instructive to examine children at these primitive levels with simple apparatus and with concrete tasks. The nature of such material, however, would hardly submit itself to standardisation here ; and, indeed, should vary with the character of the appliances with which each young child is familiar. Consequently in the present series, such problems alone have been included as require no apparatus.

(b) Written Tests (Accuracy).
[Tests 9 and 10.]

The written tests for arithmetic[2] consist of ten examples for each age graded upon much the same principles as before. Since written work is rarely attempted with children before the mental age of 7 — (standard I.), no examples appear for the lower years. Even with the series for age 7 — the children will tend to work the problem-sums mentally. As the test is

---

([1]) *Distribution of Educational Abilities*, p. 65.   ([2]) pp. 389-393.

definitely an examination in paper work, the children should be left to read the questions for themselves ; and, no matter how simple the computation, should display all their working. But at the lower stages some latitude in these respects—at the discretion of the examiner and according to the teaching-methods in vogue—may be conceded without scruple. In testing a defective, for example, isolated words or phrases that he cannot read for himself may be read to him.

For simplicity of scoring, one mark is granted for each correct answer. If the answer is incorrect, no partial credit is awarded for propriety of method or for accuracy in subsidiary operations.

At each age the ten examples include five " mechanical " sums and five sums in " problem " form. The two types may be distinguished thus. In the " mechanical " sum there is, as a rule, but one main operation ; the operation belongs to a familiar and well-practised type ; and its nature is clearly indicated in conventional fashion either by symbols or by the manner in which the figures are set out. In the " problem " the pupil is required first to determine for himself what operations are to be performed ; and, according to the intricacy of the problem, two or more different operations, two or more " steps," may be needed. A test of the former type is a test almost entirely of specific habits, of arithmetical automatisms ; and reasoning emerges solely, if at all, in the criticism of the final results, when obvious absurdities are checked. A test of the latter type demands, or should demand, in order that the circumstances of the question may be rightly visualised and the suitable process rightly selected, a wider play of imagination and a deeper exercise of reasoning. At times the problem is a problem only in name. Where the question itself belongs to a stereotyped class, certain cues or catch-words are apt to touch off an appropriate mechanical response ; the word " altogether " acts as a cue for the addition table ; the word " left " or " remainder " as a hint to subtract : the effort, in fact, may be as blind and unreasoning as clicking the trigger of a gun already aimed. Between mechanical work and problem work, therefore, the distinction is relative rather than complete.

In their ability to work examples from these two categories, children of certain types differ much from one another. For the analysis of arithmetical deficiency in individual cases, the distinction is one of the most penetrating that can be drawn. Accordingly, in printing the tests, the two kinds have been arranged in separate series ; and averages are recorded for each kind apart. But in administering the tests it will, as a rule, prove more convenient to set the problem-sums for a given age immediately after the mechanical sums for that age, and before proceeding to the mechanical sums for the next age.[1] Owing to the greater dependence of written arithmetic upon syllabuses and upon the scope of the teaching generally, a narrower range of testing than would be necessary for reading or for spelling is admissible where these conditions are known. As before, a child should never be tested only with sums appropriate to his age. But, in general, to avert deterioration through fatigue, one set—five sums only—will be sufficient to set at a single sitting. If for an unknown individual a speedy judgment is wanted, and several sittings are therefore precluded, one mechanical sum and one problem sum, chosen from each of the three ages which are, respectively, below, equal to, and next above the child's presumable level—six sums, therefore, in all—will give a crude approximation. For a selected group of

[1] If the two types be set as alternatives, and the child allowed to choose of each pair *either* a problem sum *or* a mechanical sum (of equal difficulty), light will be thrown upon two temperamental factors, initiative and preference for routine tasks. The psychology of the " optional question," however, has hardly yet been analysed. See, for an experiment with non-scholastic questions, I. E. Ash, *Ped. Sem.*, XIX., 4. " The Conditions and Correlates of Mental Inertia."

known individuals, already assembled into a fairly homogeneous class, the ten sums allotted to the mental age equivalent to their standard will yield a finer differentiation. Usually, however, it will be practicable—always, indeed, it will be desirable—to include at least one additional series : the sums for the mental age above, in a good school ; in a poor or average school, those for the mental age below.

For the "mechanical" tests, copies of the sums should be printed in large type, or hectographed in a clear hand ; and the sheets distributed to the children. Upon these sheets the children may work the examples, and enter the answers, without transcribing either answer or sum. For the "problem" tests similar copies of the several questions will again be distributed ; but the working will be done, and the answers shown, upon a second blank sheet. If the printing or hectographing is impracticable, the sums may be first copied from the blackboard by the children themselves. But with this plan extraneous factors may easily interfere with the results— errors in copying the problem, increased analysis of the problem, loss of interest through familiarity with the problem, and general fatigue, due to the prolongation of the whole task. In no circumstances should the questions be dictated, since children, especially when young, understand a sentence, if it is read aloud to them, much more surely than when it is left for them to read silently to themselves.

Total scores and mental ages may be derived as before. Results are given for the mechanical and problem tests separately in Tables XLIX. and L. Girls and defectives appear most backward in problem tests. By both groups, as we have seen, processes that involve mere mechanical rote memory are likely to be better accomplished than those that demand reason-ing. In problem work, however, the backwardness of the defectives is not so glaring as might have been anticipated. Reasoning, it might be thought, is the supreme manifestation of intelligence ; and in reasoning, of all mental processes, the defective is most deficient. Hence, not without justice, teachers who themselves have never taught in a special school expect problem arithmetic to be the weakest subject of the defective. There is this, however, to be borne in mind : that, for such a child, many of the simpler so-called problems are mere mechanical repetitions, with concrete examples, of pro-cesses in which he has already been thoroughly drilled. Indeed, his chief trouble is to comprehend what he has to read, not to work out what he has to compute. Correct calculation turns simply upon the appropriate functioning of an automatic habit, not upon a process of reasoning spontaneously initiated and logically pursued. Where genuine and original reasoning is really required, the defective breaks down instantly. On the other hand, the so-called "mechani-cal" sum, though dependent almost wholly upon specific memories and habits, is for the same mental age often somewhat more complex than the nominal "problem." It is purely abstract ; it evokes no picturable scene or setting ; it presents no concrete case to control or check the child's thoughts when they slip into a channel that issues in an absurd or impossible answer. To such lapses the defective is perpetually prone. And thus his score for mechanical arithmetic is expressive, not of meagre attainments only, but also of a general unreliability, of an ineradicable lack of accuracy.

(c) Fundamental Rules (Speed).
[Tests 11 to 14.]

With the foregoing graded tests, children who lack proper training—for example, delicate or delinquent individuals who have attended school irregu-larly—often produce results strangely below their true capacity. For these and many other causes exercises embracing only the four fundamental rules may yield a more equitable test. Samples of test-sheets that may be compiled with this object are appended on pages 394 to 397.[1] In constructing them, I have endeavoured to obey a definitely formulated scheme. Consequently, for each rule or process it is possible to compose an unlimited number of test-sheets that in difficulty shall be virtually equal.

The principles underlying the scheme of construction were briefly as follows : first, that all available figures and all available combinations of figures, taken in pairs, should be used, as far as possible, with equal frequency ; and, secondly, that each figure and each pair should be scattered evenly over the paper in an order determined by artificial " chance." With these precautions the level of difficulty becomes, on the whole, uniform throughout the paper ; and any child, after working through the first quarter (or, with certain types of sum, the first half) of the sheet, has added, subtracted, multiplied, or divided all possible pairs of numbers up to nine, once each. For addition every other column involves " carrying." Similarly, for subtraction half the pairs involve " borrowing." In the division sums there are no remainders.

The children work the sums upon sheets already printed. Five minutes are allowed for each paper. The examples are plentiful enough to occupy the quickest of the children for the whole of the time. The measure of ability is the number of processes correctly worked in the period allotted—for addition the number of columns correctly added, for the other processes the number of pairs correctly subtracted, multiplied, or divided ; that is, as a rule, the number of correct figures in the answer, counting, in the case of addition, the "hundreds" as part of the "tens" figure, and, in the case of multiplication, the "ten thousands" as part of the "thousands." To facilitate marking, the sums are printed in rows of five or ten ; so that for each line of correct answers the child scores, in every type of sum, exactly twenty marks.

To be mechanically efficient, calculating, like reading, demands correct and rapid work ; and, like reading, it may be marked for both accuracy and speed. Following the practice of previous investigators, efforts were at one time made to separate quality from quantity, to score the papers first for the number of mistakes, and then for the amount accomplished in a given time. Further experiments revealed that a trustworthy mark for accuracy can be attained only after repeated tests upon the same individual. Measured by the coefficient of correlation for successive tests, the reliability of papers in the fundamental rules, when marked for accuracy alone, seldom rises above ·35 ; and is, in general, but little over half that of the same papers marked for speed. On the other hand, in estimating the accuracy of a class or age-group as a body, as distinct from the accuracy of the component individuals, a single test-paper will ordinarily produce results reasonably secure.

Expressed as a percentage of the total amount worked, the proportion of error diminishes with age. The figures are given in Table XXXVI. For the separate ages the decrease is uneven ; the first three age-groups and the last three have, therefore, been combined.

---

[1] These test-sheets were originally drawn up for an investigation carried out by a Committee appointed by the British Association to enquire into the mental and physical factors involved in education. A full account of the results will be found in the *British Association Annual Report*, Newcastle Meeting, 1916 pp. 307-325.

Once more I would refer the reader to the suggestive article of my friend and colleague, Dr. Ballard (" Norms of Performance in the Fundamental Processes of Arithmetic, with Suggestions for their Improvement," *Journ. Exp. Ped.*, 1914, Vol. II., No. 6, p. 396). The results recorded in my previous memorandum (*Distribution and Relation of Educational Abilities*, pp. 68-77) were obtained with sheets reprinted for that purpose from Dr. Ballard's tests. The test-sheets here described were drawn up to meet certain minor criticisms urged against Dr. Ballard's tests by various investigators (see *Journ. Exp. Ped.*, 1916, Vol. III., No. 5, p. 318 *et seq.*).

The detailed instructions for drawing up comparable sheets, though simple, are too lengthy to be printed here. Any who wish to construct such sheets may obtain the full instructions by communicating with me at the Education Offices of the Council.

TABLE XXXVI. ARITHMETIC.

Four Fundamental Rules.

Percentage of Error

Age.	Addition.	Subtraction.	Multiplication.	Division.
7 – to 9 –	15·0 %	18·3 %	17·1 %	20·2 %
11 – to 13 –	8·3 %	7·5 %	6·7 %	4·6 %

The percentages are high. But the demand for speed encourages slips, and excludes revision. At the same time, had the original unit of marking been the final answer instead of the process or column, the percentages, particularly for addition, would have been larger still : the tiniest error makes the whole sum wrong. If, on the contrary, the unit had been the single step (for example, adding two digits only), the figure would have been, at any rate for addition, far smaller. Among the four rules measured as above, subtraction is worked most inaccurately. The reason is transparent : "borrowing" never becomes completely automatic. This peculiar inaccuracy, and its cause, are still more evident in using Dr. Ballard's subtraction sums, in which "borrowing" is introduced for every pair of numbers. But in mechanical sums of every type the amount of sheer inaccuracy is often surprising. Where the whole sum is marked as a single unit, where the length of the sum is appropriate to the level of the child, and where the working is carried out under conditions exacting maximal speed, there, throughout the various classes, high standards as well as low, nearly one-quarter of the answers are wrong. The practical import of this is patent : accuracy is largely a result of drill—of daily practice in making and keeping the fundamental operations automatic ; such drill is very often dropped in the higher classes. A theoretical corollary emerges as well : in an arithmetic test, set to estimate ability rather than mechanical correctness, to mark for accuracy alone is to defeat the aim of the test.

Accordingly, in compiling norms for the present papers, accuracy and speed have not been kept apart, but amalgamated, as above described, into a single measure for the double quality. Norms are given in Tables LI. to LIV.[1]

Among the children of ordinary elementary schools, girls are decidedly inferior to boys in subtraction and division. In addition, and still more in multiplication, they are often superior. The disparity originates chiefly in the dependence of these latter tasks upon rote memory for tables, rote memory being a capacity in which boys always yield to girls. A pubertal decline in accuracy, doubtless transitory, is to be perceived in the figures for the later years. At about the age of thirteen, even where the averages themselves do not actually sink below the highest of the preceding years, the rate of annual increase, up to this point rapid and uniform, begins, in almost every instance, suddenly to abate. A re-inspection of the scripts reveals that the drop is due to an increase in error rather than a diminution of speed. It is a feature that may be remarked in many tests ;[2] and seems, as a rule, to overtake girls somewhat earlier than boys.

---

[1] More detailed results, illustrated diagrammatically, will be found in the British Association *Report*, *loc. cit. sup.* It should be added that norms obtained in subtraction are peculiarly dependent upon the particular method of instruction adopted. As a rule, at any rate in earlier years, averages from schools where the method of "equal addition" is adopted are superior to those obtained from schools where the method of "decomposition" has been taught. For drill the new "Courtis Practice Tests" will be found suggestive.

[2] Tests of spelling and handwriting, as well as all tests of mechanical arithmetic, show this increase of unsteadiness at puberty; and the phenomenon is perhaps not unrelated to what I have termed the phase of repression in drawing (see below, p. 350). Those interested in the educational psychology of adolescence would find here a fruitful problem for research in secondary and continuation schools.

The performances of defectives in these tests vary considerably according to teaching. Of all four mechanical rules, subtraction with borrowing is the one where the backwardness of the defective is most pronounced. Division, as a rule, is learnt by normals, as well as by defectives (when it is learnt by defectives at all), at a later stage than the other three processes ; here, therefore, comparison is dubious : in the main, it appears to be a process that is disproportionately hard for the young normal as compared with the young high-grade defective, and disproportionately hard for the old low-grade defective, as compared with the old normal. In multiplication, and particularly in addition, the inferiority of the defective is perhaps less marked than in any of the tests we have considered hitherto. Doubtless, the cause is in part that which was cited to explain the diminished inferiority of the girls—namely, the dependence of these processes upon mere mechanical memory.

Backwardness of Defectives in Arithmetic.

Although in the various branches of rudimentary arithmetic the defective seems thus to be more amenable to instruction and drill than he is in the linguistic subjects, yet for the figure-work of after life he relies upon his school attainments to an even narrower extent. Among the low-grade adults whom I have tested, those about the mental age of twelve would usually fumble for pencil and paper to make a computation that the normal person works within his head ; those under the mental age of eleven would hardly ever exploit their power to add or subtract, to multiply or divide, on paper ; those under the mental age of ten do not even trust their memory for the addition or multiplication table, but do all by counting ; the only school knowledge they retain consists in the well-worn equations of the tables of equivalents—the number of pence in a shilling, of shillings in a pound, of pints in a quart, and a few other simple conversions falling daily within their experience. And in most instances they work by trial and error. Watch an elder boy in a special school handing out books to a desk of half a dozen children ; or a girl setting a table for as many persons. Seldom does the child reason : " Six and myself make seven ; I must fetch seven books " or "seven knives and as many forks." Each works by trial and error. The boy takes down a pile of books, and hands out one to each till all have one. The girl fetches " a knife for Florrie and a knife for May " ; and then has to go back again because " Florrie wants a fork." Number as learnt in the arithmetic lesson remains an exercise apart, a feat laudable enough in itself for a defective, but never spontaneously brought to bear, because the necessary intelligence—the power to foresee, to plan, and to apply—is lacking to the low-grade mind.

Unless, therefore, a child has a mental age for general intelligence equivalent to at least 60 per cent. of his chronological age he should never, in my opinion, be burdened with formal lessons in arithmetic. The simplest facts of number should alone be taught him, always in connection with the practical needs of practical life. Save for exercise in reading common symbols —such, for example, as may be seen on the tickets in a grocer's window—and perhaps in writing them, too, he need have nothing to do with paper. This proposal, it will be noted, is advanced irrespective of the child's abilities or attainments in number work itself. Since the lower levels of arithmetical work may be so readily mechanised, a defective may, with practice, counter-feit a mental age in arithmetic tests well above his mental age with tests of general intelligence ; and yet the mechanisms thus so laboriously constructed in his brain will be as worthless to him as a typewriter to a house-dog.

Analysis of Backwardness in Arithmetic.

With a child who is not deficient generally, but only backward specifically in arithmetic, some endeavour should be made to discover the probable cause. If carried out in detail, the more purely psychological exploration will follow lines much the same as those laid down for reading : the examiner will test in detail short-distance memory and long-distance memory, rote memory and logical memory, and the association between the various ways —visual, auditory, articulatory, and graphic—in which numbers and their symbols may be apprehended and learnt. In addition to all this, particular powers of reasoning—analysis, abstraction, comparison, synthesis, deduction —both with con. rete and tangible material and with symbolic and abstract material, should be tested and compared. By such methods, a child who is backward in mechanical arithmetic may be shown to suffer primarily from a more radical defect in some particular form of memory ; and a child who is backward in problem arithmetic from a more radical defect in some special form of reasoning.

But, on the whole, I have found such purely psychological tests less helpful than intensive tests of particular arithmetical operations. Arithmetic as practised in the ordinary elementary school may be regarded as little more than a huge bundle of specific habits and memories. Hence, with the poor arithmetician the problem for the teacher is often simply this : to find which particular habit or memory is not operating as smoothly and as automatically as it should. The ordinary class exercises convey little to the teacher, because they deal, for the most part, in mere repetitions of the same rule. But results obtained by such tests as the foregoing will prove a vast quarry of information for him who knows how to extract it. Consider the graded tests. Almost inevitably they fall, as it were, into a spiral scheme. We begin with simple addition ; and then pass to other fundamental rules. Presently addition recurs in the form of a money sum. Later there are weights and measures to be added. And, on still higher planes, there appear first addition of vulgar fractions, and then addition of decimal fractions. In the problem sums addition occurs again in an applied form, or as a partial step in a complex process. Analogous cycles are to be found for subtraction, multiplication, and division. The same simple processes keep reappearing in a more and more elaborate disguise, like the supernumerary actors at a cheap suburban theatre that come round and cross again in different dress. By thus comparing similar operations upon successive planes we may frequently discover where the central difficulty hides. Often an entire class is peculiarly backward in subtraction, or, it may be, in division ; and this backwardness appears and reappears throughout the scale in every test of the defective process. The analysis may be pushed yet further. Graded tests may be constructed to examine solely the defective operation. In division, for example, we may test efficiency at the following levels : in mechanical work, (1) the division table, or, it may be, the power to apply the multiplication table to the task of division—the table being regarded as a set of specific memories and tested with special reference to the pairs that are notoriously hard to learn ; (2) simple division, involving two operations, but no carrying and no remainders ; (3) simple division, with carrying, and (4) with remainders ; (5) simple division, with zero in the divisor ; (6) division by factors, without and (7) with remainders ; (8) long division, without carrying or other difficulties ; (9) long division, with zero difficulties ; (10) long division with carrying, but where the trial divisor is the same as the first figure of the true divisor, and the trial quotient the same as the true quotient ; and, finally, cases (11) where the trial divisor is one unit larger than the first figure of the divisor, (12) where the trial quotient is one unit larger than the true quotient, and (13) where both difficulties are combined ; and so forth. Again, in problem work, we may test the child's power of interpreting the situation described in each question, of discovering whether it is one that calls for the operation of division ; this power depends largely upon a right understanding of such phrases as " divide x by y," "share x among y," " how many y in x ?", and the like. Here the child need not work out the example in full ; but simply indicate, in a mixed series, where he would divide, and where multiply, add, or subtract.

A similar, but simpler, set of tests, in mechanical and problem form, might be made out for subtraction, examples being so chosen as to detect whether the difficulty arises from special cases of " borrowing," or from particular methods of instruction, as that of " decomposition "—methods that often create special difficulties for special individuals. The same may be done for the not uncommon weakness in vulgar fractions. Take, for example, addition of pairs of such fractions. Examples for each of the following types, graded in complexity, may be constructed :—(1) $\frac{1}{3} + \frac{1}{3}$; (2) $\frac{2}{3} + \frac{2}{3}$; (3) $\frac{1}{3} + \frac{1}{6}$; (4) $\frac{1}{3} + \frac{5}{6}$; (5) $\frac{2}{3} + \frac{5}{6}$; (6) $\frac{1}{3} + \frac{1}{4}$; (7) $\frac{2}{3} + \frac{3}{4}$; (8) $\frac{1}{4} + \frac{1}{6}$; (9) $\frac{3}{4} + \frac{5}{6}$. Frequently it will be found that a pupil's weakness is confined to one particular type or group of types. And, thus located, the failing can readily be remedied by giving him further practice in that type, or explaining to him more thoroughly the meaning of the process which he has but partly understood. After testing, concentrate the drill, which should be short, sharp and systematic, upon those children and those pro-cesses that are shown to need it. Let each child keep, and aim at outdoing, his own daily record. As soon as re-testing shows that intensive drill is no longer fruitful, let it be dropped before it is stale.[1]

Cases Illustrative of Backwardness in Arithmetic.

Case IV. Girl, Age $13\frac{2}{15}$, *Class*, Standard VI.

Intelligence Tests. Binet, 13·0. Reasoning, 13·4. Other Tests, 13·0.

Educational Tests. Reading, 13·6. Spelling, 13·1. Arithmetic : Mental, 11·6 ; Mechanical, 11·2 ; Problems, 11·8 ; Fundamental Rules, 10·8. Writing, Drawing, Handwork, about 12·5. Composition, about 13·5.

Psychological Tests. Visual memory, poor (fails in memory drawing) ; auditory, fairly good. Mechanical memory : immediate, fairly good (recalls seven numbers) ; delayed, very poor.[2] Logical memory, good. Industry, not very great. Dislikes sums.

Diagnosis. Special disability in mechanical arithmetic, due chiefly to weak long-distance memory, other factors co-operating.

Treatment. Drill in arithmetic tables ; relying especially on auditory memory. To teach child to reason out tables and rules, where unable to rely upon memory. Practice in mechanical rules of arithmetic with special incentives.

Progress (after six months). Fundamental rules (intensively practised), 11·6. Barely normal progress in other subjects. (Treatment commenced too late ; child's interest flagged.)

---

[1] The analysis and classification of errors in arithmetic form an obscure and almost untouched field of research. I shall not enlarge upon it here. A suggestive study upon this problem, however, will be found in a paper by W. Scott, *Journ. Exp. Ped.*, 1916, Vol. III., No. 5, p. 296, "Errors in Arithmetic."

[2] This case illustrates the fact that "memory" in all its forms, particularly delayed memory, cannot be safely inferred simply from the tests of immediate memory provided by the Binet-Simon scale.

Case V. Boy, Age 13$\frac{1}{12}$. *Class,* Standard V. (promoted on account of age).

Intelligence Tests. Binet, 11·2. Reasoning, 8·5. Other Tests, 10·7.

Education Tests. Reading: Graded Vocabulary, 12·2; Comprehension, 10·9; Directions, about 11·5. Spelling, 10·4 (errors for the most part non-phonetic; many instances of "visual confusion." Poor in attacking unfamiliar words, however regular). Dictation, 10·1. Arithmetic: Mental, 9·8; Mechanical, 10·3; Problems, 8·7; Four rules, 11·0 (many errors, especially in subtracting with borrowing, and short division). Writing, Drawing, Handwork: 11·5 to 12·0. Composition: amount, 9·7; quality, 10·7.

Psychological Tests. Visual and auditory acuity, motor control : normal. Imagery : visual, poor ; auditory, average. Visual analysis, visual report, and visual recognition (picture tests and blot tests), very poor. Mechanical memory : short distance, good (*e.g.*, repeats seven numbers, twenty-six syllables) ; long distance, fairly good. Reasoning, extremely poor. (See above under tests of intelligence. Fails badly in " absurdities " and " difficult questions " ; also fails in " memory-drawing," " change," and " nine coins.")

Diagnosis. The boy was presented as mentally deficient, chiefly on the ground of backwardness in arithmetic, together with a history of several childish reactions in practical matters. The tests show that his backwardness in arithmetic chiefly affects problem work, and, to a less extent, all work in money sums and sums dealing with long measure. He is peculiarly dull in reasoning powers and in higher thought-processes generally. This is aggravated by the fact that he is almost entirely unable to visualise concrete situations, as he has been taught to endeavour to do. Constructive imagination is also deficient (note his meagre compositions, fair in quality as far as they go). He is an only child in a fairly comfortable and cultured home ; and has not been allowed to mix much with other children, or to undertake practical tasks or errands ; but rather encouraged to stay at home and read.

Treatment. Mechanical memory to be exploited to the full for compound rules in arithmetic. Problem work to be approached through practical tasks and manual work. Spelling to be taught by alphabetic method, and memorisation of rules. Independence and initiative to be cultivated at home. Psycho-analysis, to determine whether the inability to reason is fundamental, or due rather to an unconscious mental regression to an early phase of childhood.

Progress (after six months). Little advance shown in tests, except reading (directions), spelling, and mechanical arithmetic ; and improvement here traceable to direct influence of training. The co-operation of his home seemed successful in increasing self-reliance ; perhaps some improvement in this respect was to be ascribed to a superficial psycho-analysis which pointed to infantile fixations, especially, a latent wish never to grow up. The lack of reasoning seemed based upon a vicious circle : it was in part congenital ; but a painful consciousness of inherent stupidity had created a wish to remain in situations where reasoning and initiative need never be required ; and this, in turn, deprived these higher functions of the exercise needful for their development. The boy left school before further progress or further re-examination could be made.

Case VI. Boy, Age 10$\frac{5}{12}$. Class, Standard II.

Intelligence Tests. Binet, 10·8. Reasoning, 10·6. Other Tests (Opposites, Analogies, etc., with time-limit), 9·4.

Educational Tests. Reading: Graded Vocabulary, 10·1; Comprehension, 10·3; Directions, about 11·0. Spelling, 9·7. Arithmetic: Mental, 9·9; Mechanical, 8·3; Problems, 8·5; Four rules, 7·8 (practically no errors). Writing, Drawing, Handwork, about 11·0. Composition: amount, 8·5; quality, 10·5.

Psychological Tests. Visual and auditory acuity: good. Motor control: slow but good. Imagery: visual, good; auditory, average. Visual analysis and report: slightly above average. Visual recognition: slightly below average. Logical memory: very good. Immediate mechanical memory: good (repeats twenty-four syllables and seven numbers correctly in all three trials. Draws designs correctly from memory). Long-distance memory: poor. Speed tests: very poor (pronounced sensory type in reaction-time experiments. Only gives twenty-eight words in three minutes. Builds one sentence in three words, but requires nearly two minutes. Fails to count backwards, because he reasons out the reverse order. Cannot name months correctly in fifteen seconds).

Diagnosis. In general intelligence, this boy is equal to, if not above, the average level for his age. But his speed of reaction in almost every form of activity is extremely slow; and his rote-memory feeble. Hence, in the formal subjects of the school curriculum, he appears, upon a superficial view, to be extremely backward, especially in arithmetic; and has, in consequence, been kept back in a class lower than his general intelligence and reasoning powers would warrant. There is perhaps a slight temperamental complication: an outward appearance of emotional apathy and lethargy seems to over-compensate for a repressed excitability.

It should be noted that the Binet-Simon tests give no direct evidence of the memory defect, since in them the reproduction experiments are all of the immediate form.

Treatment. To be promoted as rapidly as possible to a class more nearly level with his age. A special allowance of time in class to enable him to work his arithmetical exercises correctly. Special exercises for speed; and, as an experiment, a course of training in memory. More reliance to be placed on his excellent reasoning powers—*e.g.*, in teaching spelling, and arithmetical rules; but constant drill and revision for tables and spelling. Freer discipline.

Progress (after one year). Speed in arithmetic much improved (nearly two years' progress in twelve months with test of "four rules"). Little or no improvement in rote memory as such; but defects in mechanical long-distance memory less noticeable owing to a constant tendency to exploit ingenious mnemonic devices, largely home-made, but perhaps encouraged by efforts at "memory training." Rivalry and efforts to beat his own record have proved powerful motives. Now appears fit for standard V.; and in Binet tests and reasoning tests is grading half a year in advance of his calendar age.

(iv) WRITING.

Tests of ability in handwriting have to do with at least two distinguishable aspects: first, with speed; and, secondly, with quality—a term which will here include, not legibility only, but general æsthetic character as well.

(a) Speed of Writing.
[Test 15.]

With nearly every form of activity it is possible, in testing a given individual, to measure ·maximum speed with greater certainty than average or ordinary speed. In handwriting, therefore, speed may be tested most effectively at its highest. The examiner will require the children to write, as rapidly as they can, some sentence that they know by heart ; and will afterwards count the number of letters written by them in a given time. In the exercises here reported, the sentence set consisted of the first line of the nursery jingle—" Mary had a little lamb "; the time-limit was two minutes. Pencils and singly ruled paper were employed throughout ; and all were instructed to begin a fresh line with each repetition of the word " Mary." To avoid hesitation through ignorance of spelling, children below the level of standard IV., before the test began, first copied the words from the blackboard, letter by letter, at the head of their papers.[1]

The results are tabulated on page 435 (Table LV.). The figures represent the total amount written in the period of two minutes. To obtain the rate in terms of letters per minute, the figures should be halved.

The sex-difference, which I have already noted as existing even in mixed schools,[2] is here strongly marked. The girls write faster at every age.

Between normals and defectives there is an unusual amount of over-lapping. In this test, therefore, a margin of 50 per cent. should be allowed on either side of the nominal borderline. At age ten, for example, sixty is given as the borderline. But several defectives of ten can write over ninety letters in the time allotted ; while even a right-handed normal of that age may be found who fails in the same time to write thirty.

(b) Quality of Writing.
[Test 16.]

Excellence of handwriting is a qualitative characteristic ; and, as such, can be measured in quantitative form only by recourse to some statistical device. Two principles may be adopted, either separately or in combination : first, that of analytic marking ; and, secondly, that of general impression. According to the one, marks will first be assigned to particular features enumerated upon some prearranged scheme—letter formation, general neatness, uniformity of slope, and so forth ; and the total score will be taken as measuring the child's performance. According to the other principle, the performance will be judged in its entirety, and compared with some standardised sample or set of samples—marks being awarded as the whole cumulative impression suggests that its merit approaches, or falls short of, the standard.

Upon an elaboration and a blend of both principles the scale annexed is based. The children were required to write, as carefully as possible, in ink upon unruled paper, first, a prescribed sentence containing all the letters of the alphabet ; and, next, all the capital letters in order. The scripts written

---

[1] In Starch's American investigation (*Journ. Educ. Psych.*, VI., 2, 1915, pp. 106 *et seq.*) the same specimen was used for both speed and quality. The children were enjoined to write as well and as rapidly as they could. Two minutes were allowed for the test.

In my own earlier measurements of handwriting (*Journ. Exp. Ped.*, I., 2, 1911, pp. 98 *et seq.*), as in the more recent and more extensive tests carried out by Dr. Kimmins (*Child Study*, IX., 5, 1916, p. 63), the children were required to write for five minutes. With maximum speed, however, wrist fatigue very rapidly supervenes, if the test is prolonged for such a period.

Norms obtained under such different conditions differ greatly. Average speed is by definition slower than maximum speed. But the shortness of the period in such experiments as Starch's considerably increases the apparent rate.

[2] *J. Exp. Ped., loc. cit.*, p. 111. Cf. also *ibid.*, I., 5, p. 371, " The Mental Differences between the Sexes."

by children of the same age were then, first of all, ranked in order of general legibility; where general legibility appeared approximately equal, they were ranked in order of general æsthetic merit; where both legibility and æsthetic merit, judged hitherto by general impression, appeared approximately equal, the samples were compared in certain detailed aspects taken one by one; and the sample excelling in a majority of these aspects was rated most highly.

From the whole series thus graded nine specimens were then extracted: (1) the first or best; (2) the last or worst; (3) the middle specimen or 50th per cent. in the whole series (the "median"); (4) the middle specimen of the upper half of the series (the 25th per cent., or "upper quartile," marking a distance of $1 \times p.e.$ above the median or average); (5) the middle specimen of the lower half of the series (the 75th per cent., or "lower quartile," marking a distance of $1 \times p.e.$ below the median); (6) the 10th per cent.; (7) the 91st per cent.; (8) the 3rd per cent.; and (9) the 98th per cent., representing respectively $2 \times p.e.$ above and below, and $3 \times p.e.$ above and below, the median.[1]

We thus secure scales for measuring individuals of a given year in terms of the average and variability of their own age-group. Since the unit of variability is the same throughout the scale, it may be assumed that the intervals between successive specimens are equal.

The publication, however, of nine specimens for every age space forbids. Accordingly, the medians alone are reproduced. As a matter of fact, the poorer specimens of the highest ages are, in the main, comparable with median specimens of certain lower ages. Adjacent age-groups overlap enormously. The median for one age falls nearly always between $1 \times p.e.$ and $2 \times p.e.$ below the median for the age above. Hence, for rough purposes, we may content ourselves with one continuous scale measuring children of all years, instead of a number of distinct p.e. scales, each allotted to a different year. The samples reproduced in Figures 43 to 52 are selected from manuscripts written by children themselves; and represent median or typical specimens for each age. By a comparison, therefore, with these illustrations, the teacher can broadly assign to any given pupil a mental age for handwriting.

The comparison is to be made according to the procedure already described. The criteria are, first, legibility; secondly, general æsthetic quality; thirdly, superiority in specific aspects or details (for which, see schedule below). For comparisons in respect of the last criterion the specimens here given are barely adequate. A single example cannot be expected to depart from a model of perfection to exactly the same extent in every detail. Further, for different types of calligraphy perfect models would themselves deviate from the particular types upon which the specimens printed below were based. It follows, therefore, that the teacher should himself construct his own scale, inserting, if possible, separate series for different aspects—for slant, size, heaviness, spacing, and the like.[2] Such a detailed scale, with the aid of the schedule on page 338, will facilitate, not merely the measurement of the general level of a pupil's handwriting, but also the diagnosis of his particular faults; and, if the comparison be renewed from time to time, will stimulate an improvement in the details thus brought into focus. For repeated or

---

[1] "P.e." denotes "probable error," or "quartile deviation." $1 \times p.e. = 0·6745 \times S.D.$, the two expressions—quartile deviation and standard deviation—being different units for measuring the same thing, namely, the average degree to which the individual members vary above and below the average for their group. The reader unversed in statistical terminology will note that half of the entire age-group falls between the limits marked by (4) and (5), i.e., between plus and minus $1 \times p.e.$ from the median.

[2] As soon as the new "manuscript" hand has been established a sufficient time, a scale for this will become imperative, since here the age-averages are far above what would be expected from the specimens appended below for the cursive style.

comparative records the headings of the schedule may be made the basis of a score-card, which will enable pupil as well as teacher to locate flaws and chronicle progress.

To the teacher whose faith is in practical experience, such methods will savour of exaggerated pedantry. Their use may be defended by reference to their admitted value in other fields of observation. In judging grain and live-stock, for example, farmers and agriculturists have for long used detailed schedules and score-cards to secure more accurate and precise results. And what is not too elaborate for adjudicating the points of cattle is surely not too refined for measuring the capacities of children.

SCHEDULE V.

Analysis of Quality of Handwriting.

1. *Size.*

(a) Too small. (b) Too large. (c) Not uniform. (d) Variations in specific types of letters (capitals, letters looped above, below, etc.). (e) Variations in specific parts of the specimen (ends of words, etc.).

2. *Slant.*

(a) Too sloping. (b) Too upright (for the style adopted). (c) Sloping backward. (d) Not uniform. (e) Variations in specific types of letters. (f) Variations in specific parts of the specimen (ends of line, of page, etc.).

3. *Line.*

(a) Too heavy. (b) Too thin. (c) Irregular. (d) Up- and down-strokes insufficiently distinguished. (e) Small unintentional deviations (tremulous, jerky, etc.). (f) Larger, intentional deviations (crooked backs, etc.).

4. *Alignment.*

(a) Irregularity of bottoms of small letters. (b) Of tops of small letters. (c) Of specific types of letters (capitals, loops, i-dot, etc.). (d) Of specific parts of specimen (dropping of end of line, etc.).

5. *Spacing of Lines.*

(a) Too close. (b) Too wide. (c) Not uniform. (d) Affecting specific types of letters (confusion of loops and tails of adjacent lines). (e) Affecting specific parts of specimen (crowding at bottom of page).

6. *Spacing of Words.*

(a) Too close. (b) Too far apart. (c) Not uniform. (d) Specific tendencies (joining certain words, or certain final letters, to following words, etc.).

7. *Spacing of Letters.*

(a) Too close. (b) Too wide. (c) Not uniform. (d) Variations in specific letters (capitals, etc., separated from rest of word). (e) Variations in specific parts of specimen (crowding at end of line).

8. *Formation of Letters.*

(a) General form. (b) Smoothness of curves. (c) Parts omitted. (d) Parts added. (e) Parts not joined. (f) Specific letters and parts of letters (capitals, loops, dotting i, crossing t, junctions, etc.).

9. *General arrangement.*

(a) Margins—top, bottom, left and right. (b) Centring (of headings etc.). (c) Indentation of paragraphs, etc.

10. *Neatness.*

(a) Erasures. (b) Blots and smudges. (c) General carefulness.

11. *Posture.*

Position—(a) of pen ; (b) of hand ; (c) of paper ; (d) of body.

To obtain comparative tables for quality of writing, every child's paper has been compared with the median samples and assigned a mental age. The averages and standard deviations given in Table LVI are expressed in terms of these mental ages. The girls, it will be seen, write a fairer hand than the boys. Between normals and defectives the difference is comparatively small.

Left-handedness.

For backwardness in handwriting, which is itself so often attended by backwardness in drawing, handwork, and other manual subjects, an illustrative case will be found, described in detail, on page 357 below. And here, in place of systematic analyses of further instances, I prefer rather to illustrate more particularly the two commoner causes of disability in this direction—namely, left-handedness, and choreic (or quasi-choreic) motor inco-ordination.

In assessing a child's handwriting, either for speed or for quality, it is important to consider whether he may not be left-handed. The frequency of left-handedness is far commoner than is generally supposed. In the schools tested I have found the following percentages :—

TABLE XXXVII.

Incidence of Left-handedness among Normals and Defectives.

		Ordinary Elementary Schools.	Special (M.D.) Schools.
Boys	..	.. 6·2 per cent.	13·5 per cent.
Girls	..	.. 3·9 ,,	10·3 ,,
Average	..	.. 5·1 ,,	11·9 ,,

By left-handedness I mean a natural tendency (whether congenital, or induced post-natally by accident or other changes in the hand or its neuro-muscular apparatus) to undertake new dexterities with the left hand rather than with the right. The criterion used, therefore, was not merely the habitual method of using the pencil or pen, but the power to deal cards, to throw or pick up a ball, to cut with a knife or scissors, to hammer or bore, to turn a handle or wind cotton round a reel, more easily with the one hand than with the other. Of children thus convicted of left-handedness, only 64 per cent. among the girls and 81 per cent. among the boys appeared to use the left hand to write with at school. Hence, judged by a writing test alone, the percentage of left-handed children would appear too small; and, moreover, would seem to decrease enormously with age.

Owing, therefore, to the ambiguity of the term and the frequency of the phenomenon, I decided not to eliminate left-handed children before undertaking my calculations or making my samples; but only to require the child to write with whichever hand he could write fastest and best.

I may draw attention to the fact that left-handedness appears far commoner among boys than among girls—being, indeed, among normal children in the infants' school almost twice as common with males as with females. Boys, however, appear to correct, or to grow out of, this habit somewhat more readily than girls. Left-handedness is more than twice as common among defectives as among normals. But it is by no means rare among bright and imaginative children of emotional disposition. Its incidence, indeed, seems greater among those children who are temperamentally neurotic, whether normal, supernormal, or defective in general intelligence. It is among this limited group that the premature enforcement of right-handed activities appears to conduce to stammering; and, as a rule,

A*

stammering is but one, although the most conspicuous, of several consequent disturbances in the more delicate adjustments of the nervous system. Of the left-handed children examined by me, 9·1 per cent. actually showed some such defect of speech at the time ; and nearly twice as many, 15·4 per cent., were reported to have stammered or stuttered in the past. Of the 9·1 per cent., four out of five were demonstrably of a neurotic or unstable type ; and such a condition—in some instances, it must be admitted, appearing rather as a consequence than as a cause of the speech defect—was inferred or suspected in nine out of ten.

It is important, therefore, that the nervous left-handed child should not be forced to use his right hand at an early age. Since the apparatus of civilisation is arranged for a right-handed populace, the teacher will do well in most other cases to encourage right-handedness before the opposite habit has become too firmly fixed ; but such efforts ought to be discontinued immediately, should any neurotic symptoms arise. The seemingly left-handed child, who is not so much dexterous with the left hand, as *gauche* with both left and right, is an evident case for right-handed training. But with the child who not only proves genuinely left-handed, but also appears left-legged, left-eyed, and generally (as it is sometimes wrongly put) left-brained, such training is, as a rule, utterly profitless.

A connected feature of handwriting which sometimes causes anxiety to the young child's teacher is inverted writing or mirror-script (see Figure 39). Of mirror-script the most notable and most sustained example is to be discovered in the quaint and cryptic-looking notes left to posterity by Lionardo da Vinci. His manuscripts are, almost every one of them, written from right to left, *more Hebraeorum* (see Figure 39, A, (4)). Reflected in a glass they can be readily deciphered. It is said that in his later years, if not before, he suffered from a partial paralysis that afflicted his right hand ; and presumably, to write his hieroglyphic manuscripts, he used the left.

There are very few school-children, who, when first beginning to write or print, do not from time to time reverse their letters : *b* and *d*, *q* and *p*, which form mirror-images of one another, and *N*, *S*, *Z*, which to the un-analytical eye appear symmetrical (like *A*, *H*, *I*, *M*, *O*, *T*, *U*, *V*, *W*, *X*, and *Y*) but yet in fact are not, these are the characters that most frequently become reversed. Both here and in other tasks, lateral directions, as right and left or East and West, are always more readily confused than vertical directions, as up and down or (on the map) North and South. And in writing, the rarer vertical inversions, and the commoner lateral reversals seem alike attributable to an independent functioning of the nervous centres for visual or motor control. The successive movements, with their varying changes of direction, are all or nearly all of them, relatively to one another, correctly performed ; but the absolute orientation of the whole result upon the page is wrong—either because the child starts with his pen from an incorrect point (*e.g.*, upon the line instead of above it—(cf. Figure 39, B, (5))—or towards the right-hand margin instead of towards the left—(cf. Figure 39, A, (3)), or else because the whole motor mechanism, being arranged symmetrically rather than similarly for opposite sides of the body, unwinds itself, as it were, automatically, or by ingrained habit, without special guidance, either preceding or concurrent, by a visual image or by a schematic visual apprehension—(cf. Figure 39, A, (3) and (4)).

As a transitory phase mirror-script is far commoner among normal children in the infants' school than is ordinarily believed ; as a rule, however, it persists only for a few days or weeks. It is chiefly, but by no means entirely, to be seen among left-handed children, particularly those who have learnt to write with their right hand. It is far commoner among girls. In the special

FIGURE 39.

Examples of Mirror-Script and Inverted Writing.

[Written in course of ordinary class work by Left Handed Normals
with the Right Hand, except
A (3) *(written at request with the Left Hand) and presumably,* A (4).]

A. Lateral Inversion ("Mirror Writing"). [To read, hold this
and the following pages before a mirror].

1. Girl, aged $7\frac{2}{12}$.

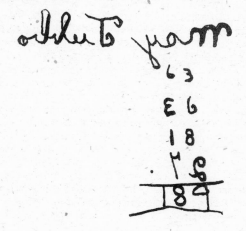

2. Boy, aged $5\frac{11}{12}$.

3. Girl. aged 12$\frac{10}{12}$.   (Backward in all but handwork.)

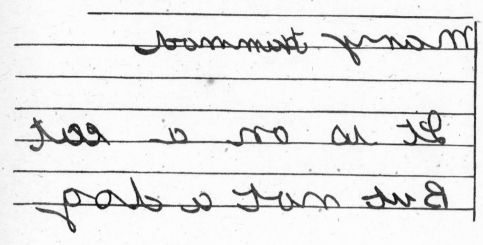

4. Lionardo da Vinci (b. 1452), *Dell' Anatomia* (Windsor MSS. Fogli B. 15 recto. Compare also *Arundel MS.* 263, exhibited as No. 42 in Case XI in the Manuscript Saloon of the British Museum).

[Reads "a b sono musscoli ul|timi latitudinali [che]|e panichuli [di] ne q̊|li [*i.e.*, quali] essi si cov̊ertano pa|s(s)å con angolo retto sot|to i longitudinali a m"; *i.e.*, "*a b* are the last latitudinal muscles [that], and the membranes [from] into which they change pass at right angles beneath the longitudinal (muscles) *a m*."]

B. Vertical Inversion ("Inverted Writing").

5. Boy, aged $6\frac{8}{12}$.   (The name should read "J. Stacey.")

6. Girl, aged $6\frac{4}{12}$.   (Should read: "The man came to Johnnie.")

Note to Figure 40 overleaf.

It will be found instructive to examine the characteristics of the specimens point by point according to the details enumerated in Schedule V., p. 338. Observe more particularly (1) the general irregularity of size and slope ; (2) the irregular and excessive thickening of the down-strokes, especially where effort is marked ; (3) the highly irregular alignment ; (4) the irregular spacing of letters—lateral wrist movements being usually excessive, but occasionally insufficient, and so producing a sprawling hand with occasionally crowded strokes ; (5) inco-ordinate and often incomplete letter-formation, due especially to jerky strokes and a fine tremor (the spasmodic movements are particularly noticeable in the loops and at the beginnings and ends of the letters ; and sometimes carry the nib completely off the page) ; (6) blots, smudges, and corrections ; (7) attempted control is sometimes successful, but often simply increases the involuntary movements : in the effort, the penholder is rigidly grasped, and the first child steadies the right thumb with the knuckles of the left hand.

In the reproductions overleaf the finer and more tremulous up-strokes and side-strokes appear, upon the present paper, somewhat thicker and firmer than the originals. Signs of tremor can thus be distinguished only by close inspection.

It should be noted that samples from choreic, and indeed from nervous and unstable children generally, vary greatly from day to day and from week to week. For example, a boy aged ten was brought to me by his father on account of periodic fits of wandering and uncontrollability. On examining his old exercise books at school I found that he also showed periodic fits of bad work, the variations being most conspicuous in his handwriting. Here one page might be as well written as that of a child of eleven ; another worse than that of a child of seven. And the aberrations in writing synchronised very closely, over the whole of the preceding year, with the aberrations in behaviour. (Cf. the neurotic delinquent described above, p. 293, footnote (1) ad fin.). These instances show how fallacious it is, especially in temperamental cases, to draw final generalisations, as regards either handwriting or any other subject, from a single cross-section of the mind taken at one moment only.

FIGURE 40.—Examples of Choreic Handwriting.

1. Girl, aged 10 8/12. (Mental age = 13·1 years ; Educational Age = 11·4 years. Backwardness due chiefly to 18 months' absence between ages of 6½ and 8.)

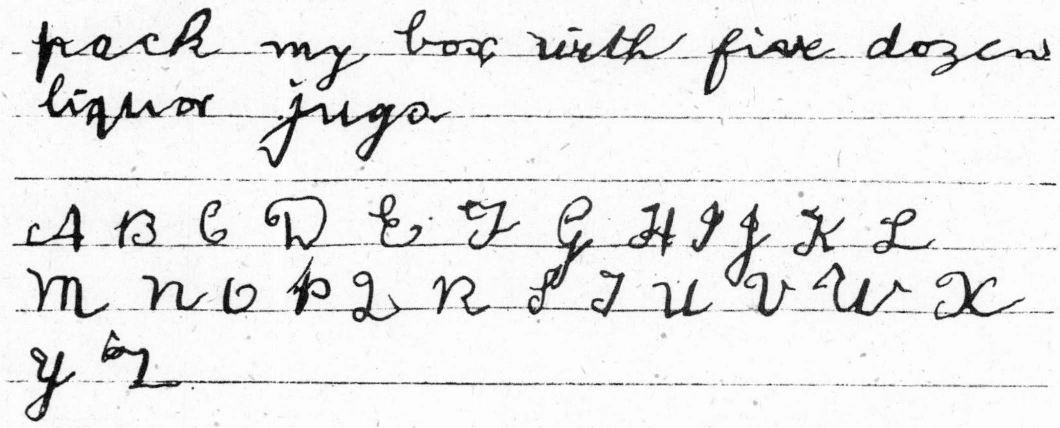

2. Girl, aged 11 1/12. (Mental Age = 10·6 years ; Educational Age = 9·8 years.)

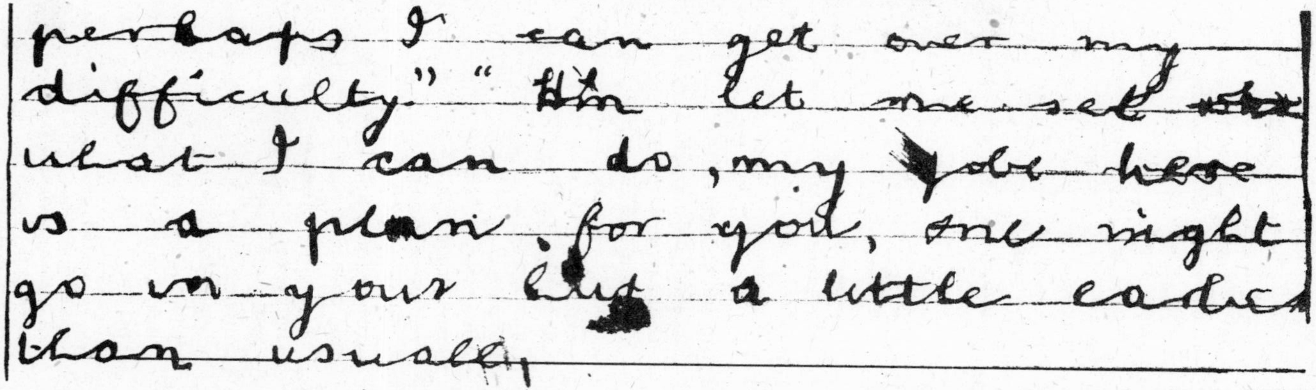

(M.D.) schools examined by me, 7·1 per cent. of the boys and 13·6 per cent. of the girls showed a tendency to mirror-writing in certain letters or figures, or under certain conditions (*e.g.*, where required to write with the left hand, or to commence at the right-hand margin of the page ; compare sample 3 of Figure 39). Teachers report that the spontaneous dropping of such peculiarities, and particularly the spontaneous change from left hand to right hand in writing and drawing, frequently concurs with a marked acceleration in general progress both among young normals and among defectives.[1]

Next to left-handedness, the commonest cause of backwardness in hand-writing is to be sought in the motor inco-ordinations, nervous in origin, that characterise chorea and more general forms of emotional instability. In Figure 40 I append in facsimile two typical specimens of choreic script. With children of hysterical constitution, slovenliness in handwriting, like im-patience of spelling (see above, page 321), is often traceable by psycho-analysis to what I may call a deep-rooted anti-neatness complex, dating from infancy. To the same complex Dr. Ernest Jones has ascribed "the tendency to reverse letters and words in writing" among adults.[2]

(v) DRAWING.
[Test 17.]

" Painting," says one of Wilde's characters, " is a mode of autobiography invented for the use of the illiterate." Drawing, it might with equal truth be added, is a mode of self-revelation peculiarly adapted to those who cannot express their mental powers through the usual media of writing and speech. Tests of drawing come thus to be among the most valuable we possess. They do not, indeed, in my experiments, show such high correlations with intelligence or educational ability as are evinced by some of the foregoing tests, or, indeed, as have been claimed by early enthusiasts who deduced *a priori* what they could not discover by statistics. Nevertheless, they have one advantage over most of our other tests, whether tests of intelligence or tests of attain-ments : they do not depend upon an acquired power to manipulate abstract symbols, such as words or numbers. They are not linguistic ; they are not arithmetical. On the contrary, they open avenues to strange places in the childish mind, provinces that otherwise would remain untouched and un-explored. Drawing gives a penetrating glimpse into the child's powers of imagination and construction—of imagination, in terms of real things visual-ised, rather than of mere words uttered ; of construction, in the sense of self-expression through the hand as guided by the eye. Unlike most tests of manual construction—modelling, building, and handwork generally—it has two unique inducements : it requires no special apparatus, and brings with it no special perplexities in marking for quality and in standardising samples. A picture gallery of sketches, all dealing with the same subject, all executed by the same individual as year by year he passes from infancy to adolescence, will provide a valuable and vivid self-history which all can understand, a memoir (as it were) of the growing artist's mind, of his mental, manual, and imaginative development. Nor will such a collection be without interest to the child himself. If the drawings are bound by each young draughtsman into a portfolio of his own, which shall not be too ruthlessly handed round by the teacher for the delectation of visitors, then an unfailing spur to

---

[1] On the whole subject, see the recent and admirable paper by Dr. James Kerr ("Left-handedness and Mirrored Writing," *School Hygiene*, Feb. and May, 1920). I may also refer to the excellent article by Dr. Ballard ("Sinistrality and Speech," *J. Exp. Ped.*, I., 1912, pp. 298 *et seq.*) and to the newer researches of Mr. Hugh Gordon ("Left-handedness and Mental Deficiency," *Brit. Psych. Soc. (Educ. Sect.)*. Abstract of paper read May 12, 1920. See also *Brain*, XLIV., March, 1921).

[2] *Papers in Psycho-Analysis*, 2nd ed., p. 675.

progress will be derived from the natural efforts of the child to beat his own best record.

Quality of drawing I have sought to measure upon principles akin to those laid down for quality of handwriting. The children were asked to " draw a man." No time-limit was enforced. This subject was selected for several reasons : first, it is seldom practised in school ; secondly, as previous studies have shown, the sketches at different ages are distinguished by fairly definite peculiarities, and these peculiarities in turn reflect the outstanding features of drawing generally in its several and successive phases ; thirdly, during the greater portion of the school period every child delights to draw the human figure, and no child doubts its ability to do so.

I would not venture, with Ruskin, to contend that in lessons upon drawing the child's practice should be limited to exercises purely voluntary and spontaneous.[1] But I may perhaps urge that, both for teaching and for testing, instructors of the art might, in a more liberal measure, exploit the natural interests of the younger child, and introduce at an earlier stage human and animal subjects. Occasional practice, indeed, in the tracing of lines and curves, of geometrical designs and decorative arabesques, has its value for teaching ; and even for testing I have found endeavours to reproduce an intricate geometrical pattern correlate highly with intelligence, if not with drawing ability. Such a task, with its demand for visual analysis and synthesis, resembles the Porteus maze tests ; and, like them, accommodates itself very readily to an age grading. But, for a rapid test of drawing ability as such, a subject with an instinctive appeal is far more effective. Indeed, not infrequently a child, previously rated as incompetent both in school subjects generally and in the traditional work of the drawing class, discovers an unsuspected vein of talent, when assayed with a test that gives his native powers and interests a fuller scope and freer play.

As in quality of writing, so for quality of drawing, an age-scale may be formed by selecting the median sample from each year. A series of such samples is reproduced below (Figures 53 to 64, pages 411 to 422). It provides a graphic illustration of the pictorial evolution of man as mirrored from year to year in the developing mind of the child.

Merely to compare by general impression a given drawing with such an age-scale is, of course, a gross and clumsy method of weighing its merit. With a view, therefore, to more exact measurements, I have, in drawing as in writing, compiled, for each year separately, scales in terms of the quartile deviation (" probable error ") ; and have constructed a schedule of characteristics to be compared. Unfortunately, space precludes a reproduction of the separate year-scales and of any detailed schedule here. Every teacher who desires to measure drawing capacity with precision should himself attempt such scales for all the commoner objects drawn in school. The scales would in turn suggest analytic schedules enumerating those technical details in which weaknesses most frequently appear, and upon which teaching might most profitably be concentrated.

Progress in drawing shows successive changes in kind as well as in degree. It resembles, not so much the uniform accretions of the inanimate crystal, as the spasmodic growth of some lowly organism, one whose life-history is a fantastic cycle of unexpected metamorphoses. Each advance follows a different line from the last. If, for every age, the investigator collects, instead of one solitary sample, a typical set all approximately median, and then compares his age-groups serially, he becomes quickly sensible of a well-defined course of development, which moves, not merely from a low grade

---

[1] *The Elements of Drawing.* 3rd ed., p. ix.

through higher grades to the highest, but from one unique phase to another, through a series of transformations marked, no less characteristically, by distinct and determinate features. The several stages have been studied and described, with some disagreement in detail, by American investigators. And, amid certain peculiarities not unexpected (among others a slight precocity)—all attributable to differences in childish experiences and in teaching methods, much the same phases reappear in age-scales derived from the drawings of London children. Confined as they are to a single sample from each successive year, the half-dozen pictures printed below can afford but a meagre notion of this evolution. I may, therefore, pardonably append a more detailed commentary in words. To those already apprised of previous work upon this subject what I have to say will be far from new. Nevertheless, the leading points deserve reiteration. They illustrate most aptly how experiments at successive ages unfold the line of mental progress ; they demonstrate most vividly how instruction in drawing, in spite of recent reforms, is still based upon logical principles deduced *a priori*, instead of upon generic principles gathered from observation at first hand.

For convenience, I may perhaps mark off some six or seven distinguishable steps. There is, however, no sudden transition or break. One phase glides imperceptibly into the next, as dawn passes into morning and morning into noon. From the items enumerated in my description the enquiring teacher will find it easy to reconstruct the schedule I have used. If then for every age he calculates the percentage among the drawings in school that show each of the features specified, he will arrive at a suggestive cross-tabulation, which will depict, more precisely than any words could do, the artistic progress of the children in his charge. Upon a similar tabulation (which, I hope, may be submitted later, when the data are more complete) the following generalisations are, for the most part, based :—

(1) The first stage may well be named the STAGE OF SCRIBBLE. As expression through speech begins with half-automatic cries and babblings, so graphic expression begins with half-automatic scratching and scrawling of pencil upon paper. The scribbling stage may begin as early as the age of 2— ; it often swells to an eager interest about the age of 3— ; and may persist, even for some months after the child has entered the infants' school, until about the end of the child's fifth year. To teachers the details of this stage are familiar rather from the products of low-grade defectives than from those of younger normals. In both the general trend is much the same.

The whole stage may be subdivided into three or four component periods. The phase begins with (*a*) a period of *purposeless pencillings*, enjoyed chiefly for the muscular movement, which, significantly enough, is first made usually from right to left. This leads to (*b*) a period of more *purposive pencilling*, in which the results themselves become a centre of attention, and may be given a description or a name as chance likeness or fanciful caprice dictates. At the third period (*c*) the pencillings are *imitative*, mimicking the adult draughtsman's general movements more often than copying any drawn original or natural model. Through all these periods a study of the products of such scribbling indicates, what direct observation of the child at work confirms, that motion is being gradually refined : wrist-movements come to dominate over arm-movements, finger-movements over wrist-movements. But the overmastering interest is still muscular rather than visual; there is as yet but small control by sight. Towards the mental age of four, the scribbling becomes, as it were, (*d*) *localised* (Figure 54 ; *cf.* also Figure 53). The child seeks to reproduce specific parts of the subject of his drawing. He scratches first this portion, then that portion, regardless of their relative disposition within the whole ; and rarely so much as approaches an exhaustive enumeration of all the essential parts. At first the scrawl may be quite unrecognisable without the aid of the child's own utterances, as he works now at this feature, now at that. Here, as everywhere in child-study, it is of the utmost importance, not only to scrutinise the finished product, but also to observe the child in the act of creation ; his ways must be watched as well as his works. The phase of localised scribbling is, however, a transitional period leading to the next stage.

(2) Usually by the age of four an increasing tendency has emerged to limit activity to single movements, instead of making rhythmically repeated oscillations ; and so to produce single lines, often admirably continuous and firm, in place of massive scribbling (Figure 54 ; cf. also Figure 55). This, then, is a stage of LINE, though hardly yet of form. The change, of course, is greatly affected by instruction at home or at school.[1] Visual control is manifest, at first sporadically, and then with a steady progress. The scrawls come slowly to resemble definite objects. The favourite subject has now become, even more exclusively than before, the human figure ; and the drawing soon begins to show (Figure 54) almost invariably a rude circle for the head ; nearly as frequently a pair of dots for the eyes ; usually a pair of single lines to represent the legs ; more rarely a second rude circle for the body ; and, more rarely still, a second pair of lines to represent the arms ; feet, indeed, which are found in nearly 50 per cent. of my drawings at four, and in over 90 per cent. at five, appear earlier than body and arms. The eyes may be placed outside the circumference of the face (Figure 54) ; the arms may sprout from the head (Figure 55). A proper synthesis of the parts at this stage is usually unattainable, and often unattempted. Juxtaposition seems to suffice.

(3) About the mental age of five the child enters on a period of DESCRIPTIVE SYMBOLISM (Figure 55); and by the age of six (Figure 56) the form, or at least the general plan, of the human figure is now reproduced with tolerable accuracy, though only as a crude symbolic scheme. There is little attention to the shape, and still less attention to the relative proportions of the several parts. Stiff geometrical contours still satisfy the child just as well as the soft irregular forms of nature (Figures 57 and 58). The head may be circular, oval, or square ; the body, circular, oval, square, triangular, or bottle-shaped. The arms and legs are represented at first by single lines ; but between the ages of six and seven there is an increasing tendency to show their contour by two lines approximately parallel. The several features are localised in the roughest way. Each adheres to some conventional form. The eye—which is always prominent—may be represented by a dot, by a circle, by a dot in a circle, or a dot under a semicircle. The fingers may radiate from a point like the rays of a star, or from a line like the prongs of a trident ; they may be (to borrow terms from the botanist) crenate, lobate, palmate, or digitate. Similar conventions are employed for nose, mouth and feet. Knees, elbows, and neck are, until a much later stage is reached, conspicuously absent. Except for the addition of a feathered hat and a transparent skirt, the same schema does duty for woman as for] man. Laid horizontally, with limbs appropriately rearranged, it serves, with equal felicity, drawn large, for a horse or a cow ; drawn small, for a cat or a dog. The general schema assumes with different children somewhat different types ; but the same child clings pretty closely, for most purposes and for long periods, to the same favourite pattern. If the subject to be drawn is before him, it matters little whether that subject—the examiner,

[1] American writers appear to over-emphasise the child's early predilection for line and outline as opposed to mass. The apparent difference, however, may be due in part to peculiarities of English instruction, particularly during recent years.

for example—stands, sits, presents a full face, a profile, or his back ; the portrait is the same. Indeed, at this stage and during much of the next, a few will look at the copy or model only once ; most will not look at all.

(4) After the child has been at school for a year or two there is an effort at greater realism, a REALISM, however, which is at first still DESCRIPTIVE rather than depictive, logical rather than visual. Drawing is still a form of silent language, not a form of art. The child sets down what he knows, not what he sees ; and is still thinking, not of the present individual, but rather of the generic type. He is trying, by his pictures, to communicate, or perhaps merely to express, and sometimes only, it would seem, to catalogue, all that he remembers, or all that interests him, in the subject to be drawn. He does not pretend to represent that object, as it appears to his eye in a single moment, or from a single point of view. Though still generalised, the schemata become gradually more true to detail and to fact. The items, however, are suggested more by the association of ideas than by the analysis of percepts.

An early change, usually commencing about the age of seven, is that from full-face to profile (cf. Figures 57 and 58)—the face as drawn by the normal right-handed child turning usually to the left (Figures 58, 59, 60, 61, 62, 64, and contrast 42). At the age of six, nearly 70 per cent. of the drawings are full-face ; at the age of eleven, nearly 70 per cent. will be profile. As is well known, all the parts do not undergo this transition at the same time (Figure 41). The face (as shown by the outline of the nose) turns first ; but for long the two eyes may be visible on the same side. Later, the body (as shown by the buttons) rotates to the left ; but the two arms may still extend in opposite directions. The drawing is thus a monstrous hybrid of two incompatible aspects—half profile, half full view. Some portraits, indeed, may show the same feature by both methods ; and thus exhibit, like some malformed image from Hindoo mythology, two mouths, two noses, and three or four gesticulating arms.

Perspective, opacity, foreshortening, and all the consequences of singleness of viewpoint, are still disregarded. Clothes are drawn ; but usually appear diaphanous—the outlines of the body, legs or arms shining, as it were, through the coat, the trouser, or the sleeve (Figure 59), the crown of the head through the substance of the hat (Figure 58). There is a gathering interest in decorative details. Buttons, hats, pipes, cigarettes, beards, moustaches, sticks and umbrellas, pockets and watch-chains, attract increasing notice ; and, as each comes to the focus of attention, it may borrow, for a while, an exaggerated size and a preposterous richness (Figures 59, 61, and 62).

(5) By the age of nine or ten the increasing demand for realism brings with it a great improvement in technique. Hitherto the child has drawn chiefly from memory and imagination ; he now inclines to trace or copy the drawings made by others, and even spontaneously to draw from nature. There is an effort to portray the external semblance of the object as it is seen by an unsophisticated vision. And thus the stage of logical or descriptive realism yields to one of VISUAL REALISM (Figures 60 and 61). The child no longer confounds what he knows with what he sees ; he has recovered what may be called the native innocence of the eye.

We may distinguish, first, (a) a two-dimensional sub-phase. The drawing of the whole and of its parts is attempted only in outline ; and aspects are predominantly chosen that can be readily transferred to two dimensions (Figure 60). But gradually—very largely by studying or redrawing from copies—solidity is attempted. The figure appears at first in silhouette ; then in relief ; and, only after a long delay, in the round. This marks (b) a three-dimensional sub-phase (Figure 62). The three-quarter view is during the school period attacked but rarely. Particular types are now delineated—a soldier or a sailor ; later particular individuals—" Charlie Chaplin," " Teacher," or " King George " ; and the title may be subscribed in ornamental lettering (*cf.* Figure 63). The figures, too, instead of floating in the air, are given a line or two of ground to stand on (Figure 60, *et seq.*), perhaps a background to stand up against (Figure 64). Into the better drawings action is freely introduced (Figure 62) ; and, later on, there are constant efforts seen best on a comparison of different drawings by the same individual, not only to characterise, but even to dramatise the subject of the sketch.

Landscapes are now not infrequently attempted. Hitherto, endeavours to represent a complicated scene would produce jumbled panoramas, half maps, half juxtaposed vignettes, like the illustrations of the early chroniclers, either disregarding space altogether, or giving a curious bird's-eye view. By the age of eleven, however, there is considerable attention to overlapping and to perspective ; and later, particularly among the brighter children, a little shading and an occasional foreshortening. A properly placed horizon is rarely to be seen before the last of the stages here to be described.

(6) A phase of REPRESSION follows. It overtakes most children during the prepubertal period, somewhere between the eleventh and fourteenth years, setting in most commonly about the age of thirteen (Figure 63). With many there is a danger of arrest at an even earlier stage. Near the termination of school life the drawings often show an apparent deterioration or regression, a regression which, in my view, is by no means to be ascribed solely to the fact that the brightest pupils have left the elementary departments. It is part of the child's natural development. Progress, where it appears, is now at best laborious and slow. The young draughtsman seems disillusioned and discouraged ; the confidence, the keenness, so requisite for realistic renderings, has left him. In some instances, at least, as analysis and psycho-analysis show, the repression is to be ascribed to emotional rather than to intellectual changes. But the factors that thus so strangely stifle the earlier and almost universal enthusiasm are always manifold, and sometimes obscure : increased power of observation, increased capacity for æsthetic appreciation, augment, no doubt, an increasing self-consciousness and an increasing self-criticism, due partly to other causes. From expression through drawing, and through movement generally, interest is transferred to expression through language ; and the fascination of the pencil, if it survive at all, lives rather in an attraction towards geometrical and purely ornamental art, and in a preference for conventional patterns and decorative designs. Among the spontaneous drawings of children, nearly 80 per cent. at the ages of six and seven are drawings of human figures ; the remainder depict animals, plants, horses, ships, and miscellaneous objects of still life ; conventional designs are virtually non-existent. At the ages of thirteen and fourteen the order of preference is almost exactly reversed : conventional designs are commonest ; the human figure rarest of all.

(7) Under free and natural conditions, graphic ability tends, it would seem, to rise to new life during early adolescence ; and the last stage may be denominated one of ARTISTIC REVIVAL. The drawings are now made to tell a story (Figure 64) ; or, if still mere portraits, they approximate more to the methods of the professional artist, being, for example, limited to the head and shoulders instead of embracing the full length (*cf.* Figure 63). From about the age of fifteen onwards, drawing for the first time blossoms into a genuine artistic activity. In adolescent girls, new-found æsthetic interests preponderate—a love of richness in colour, of grace in form, of beauty in line. Among youths, the recrudescence of draughtsmanship may find a technical or mechanical outlet. By many, however, perhaps by most, this

FIGURE 41.

Drawing by Backward Girl (Aged 7½⁹₁₂).

Showing " Mixed Profile."

The contour of the head, particularly the nose and hair, are in profile; the two eyes, two arms, two legs, two rows of buttons show a front view; note also, that while the nose turns to the left, the feet turn to the right; and there are two mouths and no ears.

FIGURE 42.

Median Sample for Mental Defectives (Age 10–).

final stage is never reached. The talented few, indeed, come to this point at a somewhat earlier chronological age. But it is, in my experience, not easy to diagnose with. any certainty, among individual children, special artistic poweis before this phase is entered—that is, not before the calendar age of eleven even in the most precocious.

Such, then, or nearly such, is the general course which the development of ability in drawing seems to pursue. The teacher who attempts to assign to a child a rough mental age for this subject will probably find it helpful to bear in mind the foregoing details, as well as to compare the product to be assessed with the samples reproduced below. It should be noted, however, that deviations above and below the average show other characteristics than those of mere immaturity or precocity in the natural line of development.

It would not be difficult, were this the place, to deduce from these particulars a practical body of recommendations respecting the teaching methods most appropriate to each age and stage. But the corollaries will be sufficiently obvious. The natural tendencies of mental growth should be followed, not forced ; here as elsewhere compliance rather than constraint should be the watchword. We have to do with an activity of such burning interest for the young child that some have fancied it rises from an inborn racial instinct ; we must beware, therefore, of cooling or dimming that ardour, or of allowing it to become extinguished before its full progress is achieved. The tedious grammar of drawing must be postponed until the need for it is felt ; and the child should be suffered to draw what he knows he wants to draw, not what we think he ought to draw. In the earlier stages we may assist him to a better feeling for proportion, without insisting upon rigid correctness or excessive symmetry ; in the latter stages we may supply him with copies that will lift him over the technical difficulties which he is beginning to feel and face, without, however, forcing models upon him prematurely at a time when he draws rather from what he imagines than from what he sees. And at every stage, in drawing as in all other subjects, we should strive to keep slightly ahead of, but never to outdistance, the mind of the child as he proceeds from phase to phase.

To obtain comparative tables for quality in drawing, the method adopted for quality in handwriting has again been utilised. By reference to the median samples, the drawing of each child has been awarded a mental age ; and from these mental ages the averages, standard deviations, and borderlines have been computed (see Table LVII). In drawing, even among normal children, boys are eminently superior to girls ; and among older children of special schools the difference is still more pronounced. Although, as I have elsewhere shown, the correlation between ability in drawing and general ability is, among boys, and particularly among older boys, by no means large ; yet among girls, and particularly among younger girls, it is in no way negligible.[1] Of all special scholastic abilities, that which underlies drawing is (with the exception of music, which falls outside our present scope) the most easily verified. Yet among girls the specific talent for drawing is small, and plays but a slender part. A young girl's drawing depends largely upon her general ability. Consequently, for the diagnosis of intelligence, to rely, in part, at any rate, upon accomplishments in drawing is somewhat safer with a girl of eight than it would be with a boy of twelve.

The correlation between drawing and intelligence is not altogether linear ; that is to say, the inferences from one capacity to the other cannot

[1] This, doubtless, is a special instance illustrating two general facts, which I have already emphasised above (p. 294): namely, that the general mental factor pervading all scholastic activities predominates in a greater measure, first of all, during earlier years as contrasted with later, and, secondly, among girls as compared with boys.

be drawn with equal security in either direction. Among children, intellectual ability usually connotes graphical ability; but graphical ability does not necessarily connote intellectual ability. Pupils who appear most intelligent in other lessons are, as a rule, above the average in the drawing lesson; on the other hand, pupils who are extremely backward in the more academic subjects—in reading and spelling, in arithmetic and composition—not infrequently display much ability in drawing and handwork. A teacher in an older class containing, as he believes, many backward boys, will be tempted to revise his judgments concerning many of them when he has given the whole group a set of tests in manual dexterity. As for prediction, most children who show artistic talent in later life prove to have drawn well in earlier years. But, even by the age of eleven, there are many children whose latent artistic powers have not yet ripened; and, inversely, there are many children whose talents, although of fair promise before the pre-adolescent stage is reached, experience an unforeseen repression or arrest, and so fail to redeem their early pledge.

The divergences, both in merit and method, between the drawings of boys and girls have so impressed the earlier investigators that some of the most eminent[1] urge for the two sexes courses entirely separate. In my own investigations, it is rather the divergences already existing between the two courses that has been largely responsible for the divergence in the results. In boys' departments, for example, a greater proportion of time is allotted to this subject—a factor too easily overlooked by external enquirers. Thus the plea wears the appearance of a circular argument: the difference in the curricula is cited as the cause of the difference in skill; the difference in skill is urged as a reason for a difference in curricula.

In part, however, it must be owned, the sex-difference seems undeniably innate. It affects the drawing of subjects not taught in the drawing lesson; and it affects different aspects of the drawing process in different ways. Girls have a keener eye for colour; boys have a steadier hand for form. Girls are contented to draw still life, to sketch flowers and landscapes; boys prefer scenes of activity and movement, such as games and battlefields. Girls copy objects that are actually in front of them; boys turn for their subjects to imagination and invention. Girls excel in delineating minute particulars; boys in conveying a general impression of the whole. In the fulness of detail, both as regards the incidents in the story to be illustrated, and as regards personal peculiarities like those of dress, girls everywhere surpass boys. They reach the decorative stage earlier; and are cunning in conventional design. On the other hand, they display less vigour, less humour, less originality. They are comparatively weak in the sense of proportion and in the production of perspective. They stay longer at the more primitive phases; and their development is more open to a premature arrest.

With either sex, particularly after the infants' department has been quitted, the standard deviations are high. Not only does instruction fail to level aptitudes; but those natural aptitudes, by virtue of inborn individual peculiarities, vary unusually in their range.

Defectives, it is often remarked, excel in drawing. Their excellence, however, has been over-rated. It is relative, not positive. It appears only when their drawings are contrasted with their own feeble performances in other school subjects, not when they are set beside the drawings of the normal child. Compared with drawings from ordinary schools, those obtained in the special school resemble the work of normal children two or

---

[1] Kerschensteiner, for example, at Munich.

three years younger. The majority of defectives suffer an arrest during what I have distinguished as the fourth period. Some never reach it. Few advance beyond it.

There are, however, in the drawings of defectives special differences in kind and character, as well as a general deficiency in degree; so that it is usually quite possible to distinguish the drawing of an older defective from that of a younger normal child (*cf.* Figure 42). These differences well deserve study. They may perhaps be most briefly epitomised by saying that the drawings of the defective are apt to include inconsistent features characterising phases of development which among normals are distinct and even remote. Thus in the defective's portrait of the human figure the face may be a mixed profile, as at stage four; the body may be a hard square, as at stage three; the arms may be omitted, as at stage two. Such a composite, indeed, is not rare among normals. But, on to this mixed and primitive scheme, the defective will fit a mass of detail which the normal child seldom observes until the mental age of eleven or twelve—a Hohenzollern moustache, buttons and pockets of unusual type or arrangement, a packet of a particular brand of cigarettes with the name ostentatiously displayed; and upon and around the whole he may weave a profusion of rhythmic decoration for a background, such as a normal child rarely attempts till near the stage of puberty. The odd, incongruous product reminds us of those urchins who strut the poorer streets, clothed in the discarded garments of relatives of almost every age.

The symbolic and decorative elements which, with the normal child, are chiefly confined to certain stages of development, are to be found at almost every phase in the drawings of the higher-grade defective; and, owing to his greater command of the pencil, they are pushed to such bizarre degrees as to tinge most of the portraits with a quality of caricature. Schemata also tend to predominate throughout. A defective of thirteen or fourteen may still draw for the body a symmetrical oblong or triangle, with semicircles at the sides for arms, and parallel straight lines at the lower corners for the legs; and, if a ruler is handy, the human figure may be ingeniously ruled in lines perfectly straight; the hands may be constructed of rays in a fashion no less geometrical; and in every limb and feature the schematic character seems almost perversely accentuated. Decoration is exaggerated at nearly every stage. The hair may be a chain of loops or curls. The clothes (which are nearly always transparent) may be covered with rows of buttons, or with patterns of criss-cross lines or chequered squares. All this grotesqueness is enhanced by the fact that the sense of relative size and position is extremely poor. The head may be larger than the body; the arms may be as long as the entire figure. The eye, drawn elaborately perhaps with radiating eyelashes, may appear in the middle of the cheek; and the ear below the eye. Further, there is frequently an impression conveyed of something unfinished; one arm may be shaded, but the child has forgotten to shade the other; and the whole figure may be mathematically symmetrical except for one arm or one leg, which shows a sudden change of schema, or perhaps is missing altogether.

The striking feature of the defective's drawing is thus a want of proportion—a want of proportion not merely in the amount of space, but also in the amount of attention and labour, bestowed upon the several parts. The original, implicit apprehension of the whole, which, as a determining tendency or *idée directrice*, should control and harmonise the work upon the various portions, tends to dissolve and vanish; and the artist is carried away at a tangent, to elaborate, with perverted intricacy, some subordinate detail that for the moment engrosses his interest.

B*

(vi) HANDWORK.

[Tests 18 and 19.]

Ability in manual construction is, of all school capacities, the most perplexing to assess. Standing, as it does, apart from other scholastic activities, related, as it is, to tasks of industrial life, it is plainly a capacity of unusual significance. Its measurement, therefore, is a subject eminently suited for research by the specialist teacher.

In the present enquiry, the test-material chiefly consisted of wooden-building blocks of various sizes and shapes. As with other tests, the exercise has taken one or other of the twin forms that constantly recur—either that of a qualitative test of merit or that of a quantitative test of speed.

In the speed test (Test 18) a model of a "house," erected with a dozen blocks, was put before the child. He was given a duplicate set of twelve similar pieces ; and was asked to reproduce the model in front of him as quickly as he could. The time required to build an exact copy was accepted as the measure of his efficiency. If his first trial was inaccurate or incomplete, he was instructed to continue, and eventually assisted, until the product was correct in every point. An error, or an inability to construct certain portions without help, thus counted by extending his total time.

In the qualitative test (Test 19) the child was given thirty blocks and enjoined to make what he chose—the best thing he could think of. The product was marked for merit according to an arbitrary scale based on a comparison with the average productions of normal children of each age.

Tables LVIII and LIX show the results for the two forms of the test. There is a striking sex-difference, particularly in that form of the test which calls for the spontaneous invention of an original design. The boys are quicker and more creative. The difference between normals and defectives of the same age, compared with that discovered in most of the preceding tests, is small. Indeed, so great is the overlapping that the formulation of a borderline would be grossly misleading.[1]

For the measurement of individual children, as distinct from the calculation of averages, the test, in both its forms, proved highly unsatisfactory. Often, from one day to another, a child's time in the speed test and his marking in the qualitative test would fluctuate widely. A model of a dozen pieces, too, which young children and defectives can put together, seemed far too simple to elicit individual differences of ability among older normal children. For the latter I have preferred to take some plates and bolts from a meccano outfit, or a dozen interlocking strips from a set of miniature building planks ; and then to require, as before, first a timed reconstruction from a pattern, and afterwards an original design. But with all forms of material bought from toy-shops the child's performances are influenced by previous practice—by work or play with bricks, blocks, clay, building apparatus, and similar media at home or at school.

For more recent experiments, therefore, I have assembled materials of a more homely and more varied form—match-sticks, wooden discs made from cotton reels, pieces of tin, strips, sticks, and blocks of different sizes, and a little plasticine so small in amount that it is available for joining rather than for modelling.[2] The pieces have been so selected that fairly

(1) Owing to the time occupied by this test and the numerous modifications introduced in the endeavour to improve it, the figures given are based upon very slender numbers—about fifty cases for each age-group among both normals and defectives. Further, since the weakest individuals among the lowest ages failed entirely to reproduce the model or to construct a design of their own, it has been necessary here, as in analogous instances occurring more rarely in other tests, to deduce approximate averages and standard deviations from the median and quartiles and the general form of the curve of distribution.

(2) In the most recent form the wood and metal are bored and pointed for junction. This makes the suggestion of designs still more limited and specific and eliminates the possible effects of familiarity with plasticine.

definite objects, ranging from a three-legged stool to a four-wheeled waggon, suggest themselves for construction. By photographing a number of median samples for each age, the marking can be rendered reasonably objective. The whole task turns more upon ingenuity than upon familiarity with purchased toys ; and familiarity with any one particular medium is discounted by the great variety. Apart from direct instruction in toy-making, a child is likely to have had experience in such rough and varied materials, only if he has himself, by virtue of a native interest or inborn talent, exploited the possibilities of household odds and ends in making playthings at home.

To present this or, indeed, any other test of original construction in sufficient detail for practical use would need many pages of print, and many illustrations of typical products. But the tests remain as yet in an experimental form and at a tentative stage. Consequently, a full description here would hardly be justified. This composite material, however, seems to point to the most profitable direction for future research.

In assessing handwork for girls I have commonly made use of the same material as I have employed for boys. With girls, however, I have also attempted, upon a more limited plan, tests of ability to sew. After several experiments it appeared that a practical scale of sewing ability was best limited to speed and neatness in making a few simple, standard stitches with some simple, standard material. The construction of completed articles— handkerchiefs, bags, and garments—was found to involve a test far more lengthy and far less reliable. The children were accordingly required to hem, gather, oversew, and back-stitch pieces of calico ; and median samples for each age were selected as before. The ability to sew, however, depends so largely upon practice and instruction, and is, in consequence, so much more limited in diagnostic significance, that again I give no detailed results.[1]

Case Illustrative of Backwardness in Handwork.

Case VII. Boy; Age $12\frac{5}{12}$. Class, Standard VI.

Intelligence Tests. Binet, 10·6 (fails in memory-drawing and five weights ; has unusual trouble with missing features and divided card ; his drawing of a diamond just passes). Reasoning, 10·8. Other Tests, 11·0.

Educational Tests. Reading, 10·5. Spelling, 10·7. Arithmetic : Mental, 10·8 ; Mechanical, 10·2. Problems, 10·8. Fundamental Rules, 10·0. Composition, 11·0. Writing, 8·5. Drawing, 7·5. Handwork, 7·0.

Psychological Tests. Motor control and co-ordination, exceedingly poor. Visual memory, poor. Delayed mechanical memory, rather poor. Other forms of memory, good. Temperament, somewhat unstable : emotional and impulsive.

Diagnosis. The child's backwardness is largely due to early ill-health (rheumatism). It will be noted that, unlike the typical backward child, he is better in subjects demanding reasoning than in the more mechanical subjects. His chief deficiency, however, is for manual work. This is partly due to weakness of muscles and of muscular control ; but is doubtless further aggravated by an inability to visualise the concrete things he is copying or constructing. No definite outbreak of chorea could be traced ; but he presents many resemblances to the sub-choreic type.

---

[1] I am especially indebted to Miss V. G. Pelling for advice and assistance in attempting these sewing tests. The teacher who wishes to attempt such scales for herself will find a suggestive experiment recorded by Miss Katherine Murdoch in *The Measurement of Certain Elements of Handsewing* (Columbia University : Teachers' College Contributions to Education). The scale there given is illustrated by photographed samples ; but the samples are not selected upon an age basis ; and the scale itself has still to be standardised.

Treatment. Largely physical, to improve general health, muscular strength, and co-ordination. Special coaching in formal subjects. To use intelligence and reasoning rather than blind trial and error in dealing with concrete problems. As an experiment, practice in tests of visualisation.

Progress. In reading and arithmetic he has made nearly two years' progress in the course of a year ; in spelling, somewhat less. Handwriting has somewhat improved with improvement of health (level roughly 10·0) ; but still shows signs of fluctuation with health and weather. In drawing and handwork he has barely made half a year's progress. No clear improvement in visualisation as such.

(vii) COMPOSITION.

[Test 20.]

That which of all school tests is at once the most fertile and the most fascinating still remains for notice. English composition, like handwork or handwriting, may be marked both for speed and for quality. But with this subject the same exercise may serve for the measurement of both features.

In the present enquiry the topic chosen for the children's essays was " School." This title was selected, out of many others, because it announces a subject interesting and well known to all school children ; and, moreover, affords something familiar and concrete to the young and to the dull, and, at the same time, offers itself to a broader treatment and more abstract discussion in the hands of the oldest and ablest.[1] Exactly half an hour was allowed for the task. The children were informed of the time-limit at the outset. After twenty-five minutes had elapsed a warning was given that the papers would be collected in five minutes.[2] No emphasis, however, was laid upon the necessity for speed or for amount.

Strange as it may at first sight appear, the mere amount written is instructive. Indeed, among young or backward children, speed of composition forms, as a rough measure of performance, no bad index of ability (Table LX). In speed, too, there is between the two sexes a remarkable divergence. Even upon paper, girls are more voluble than boys.

Quality of composition, however, is far more significant than quantity ; and provides not only for linguistic ability, but also for educational capacity, and indeed for intelligence generally, a test infinitely superior. With composition, as with handwriting and drawing, qualitative excellence can best be measured by the method of samples. Here, as for the other subjects, I have constructed " probable error " scales for each age. Of the various specimens, however, which constitute the scale, my limits again permit me only to reproduce the most essential. The medians alone, therefore, will be quoted. These are printed without change of spelling or punctuation, on pages 423 to 426. Norms for quality, in terms of mental age, are shown in Table LXI.

The common method of marking compositions—to ignore positive excellences, to note only definite faults, to count the number of such faults, and to subtract that number from an arbitrary maximum—is from a scientific standpoint almost worthless. On the other hand, the pupils will gain

---

[1] The word " School " should be written on the blackboard. Both children and teachers have a curious tendency to alter this title : it constantly becomes " Our School," " My School," " The School," " School Life," and so forth—modifications which, of necessity, vitiate many of the comparisons subsequently to be made. It is hardly necessary to add that no preparation is permitted. The subject should not be stated until the last moment, when, all general instructions having been given, and the papers having been duly headed, the test-period is about to commence.

[2] The omission of this warning, especially in the absence of a visible clock, obliterates most of the formal perorations. The children simply break off when the expiration of the half-hour is announced.

considerably if symbols be affixed in the margin drawing attention to the type of fault, and if from time to time they be allowed to relieve the teacher's labour by marking each other's exercises.

A schedule of items to be noted and faults to be overcome will be found of great service both in assessing literary merit and in teaching literary technique. Such a schedule should include not only (1) the more mechanical aspects of composition—as writing, spelling, punctuation, grammar, syntax ; but also (2) the more strictly literary aspects of composition—as range, correctness, and appropriateness of information, of vocabulary, and of rhetorical devices ; and, above all, (3) the logical aspects of composition—that is, the general organisation of ideas, as revealed by the unity, the complexity, the relevance, and the sequence of sentences and of paragraphs, and, indeed, by the intellectual structure of the essay as a whole. To print a detailed schedule for English composition, analogous to that given above for handwriting, would require a disproportionate allowance of space. From the headings here briefly enumerated the experienced teacher can readily elaborate his own.

A rapid reference to the samples reproduced will discover a progress, fairly definite and tolerably well sustained, in most of these special characteristics.[1] None perhaps is more suggestive than the use of connectives and conjunctions. Thought is synthetic ; and the growing richness of mentality unveils itself in the growing fullness and complexity of its expression in words. Sentences to begin with are simple and asyndeton. But co-ordinating conjunctions, particularly " and," are inserted at an early stage. Temporal conjunctions (" when," " as," " while ") appear later ; and, later still, conjunctions of cause (" because " and " since ") and contingency (" if " and " unless "). At first, each sentence starts a fresh subject. At the age of seven there are as many topics as there are clauses. The whole essay is a bald list of unassorted remarks, as incoherent and disjointed as a leaf from a grocer's catalogue. A year or so later, two or three consecutive sentences may sustain the same proposition ; but there is still a persistent tendency to revert, illogically and irrelevantly, to a point already done with. At the age of eleven or twelve, the essay is subdivided into sections ; and separate themes have separate paragraphs. Even with children comparatively young, however, the compositions may open with a brief preamble—usually a definition of school or an announcement of its purpose. But they do not so much formally conclude as suddenly leave off. Only the oldest indulge in a definite close—an inference drawn or a moral appended. To introduce, it would seem, is easier than to perorate ; the overture more natural than the finale.

The changes in the child's intellectual outlook are clearly mirrored in his compositions. Throughout school life, it is evident, his comprehension of space relations is gradually widening. His horizon becomes enlarged ; his world more systematically arranged. And, by somewhat later stages, it would appear, his notion of time pursues a parallel development. There is, too, a constant progress in the degree of generality or abstraction which his mind can envisage : the concrete conception of school as one particular building, his own school, yields to a more general conception of school as a class or type of building ; and this in turn gives way ultimately to an abstract conception of school as a social institution.

One cardinal symptom is the length of the sentences. Owing largely to the multiplication of conjunctions, the sentence tends to expand with an

[1] A brief but most suggestive study of children's compositions will be found in a paper by C. W. Kimmins, *Journ. Exp. Ped.*, 1916, Vol. III., No. 5, pp. 289–295, " Methods of Expression used by London School Children."

increase of ability or with an advance in age. From seven to fourteen, the average number of words in the sentence grows steadily from about six or seven to about sixteen or seventeen (Table LXII). Compared, however, with averages to be found among recognised authors, even the highest of these figures is low. For most modern writers the averages lie between twenty and forty. An average below the former impresses the reader as jerky and snappy ; an average above the latter as cumbrous and diffuse. With children, indeed, length of sentence forms a good index of the span of verbal synthesis—that is, of power to organise thought in units of high complexity, and to formulate those units in words. It is, in consequence, a rough measure of literary ability ; the longer the sentence, the abler the writer. But with adults, perhaps, this generalisation should be reversed or, at any rate, qualified. Among University students, for example, the habitual propensity of the jejune essayist is to ramble and sprawl. Only the practised pen forms sentences short and crisp, like the utterances, let us say, of Mr. Masefield. Macaulay's sentences are notoriously curt. Their average, indeed, outruns the average even of our oldest children, amounting to approximately twenty-three words. Nevertheless, few authors are more abrupt. Macaulay's editor, Jeffrey, would not infrequently import upwards of three hundred words into a single period.[1] Ruskin is often as voluminous. Yet all are classics. Hence, to the literary apprentice, as every manual of rhetoric would insist, no standard measure for the perfect English sentence can be offered or prescribed. With a like restriction, the averages given in our tables are to be looked upon as facts observed, not canons to be obeyed. There is no virtue in uniform brevity ; no skill in unrelieved length. The one rule is to be " infinitely various " ; to condense, to expand ; to blurt, and then to amplify ; to balance lengthy statements with a series of brief ; and to set off the staccato emphasis of the short, sharp phrase against the complicated harmony, long-drawn and subtly suspended, of the periodic paragraph ; to be ever altering, as it were, the dimensions of the block, yet still to preserve the effect of a neat and solid structure. Even during school age this delicate interchange may be traced among the more felicitous writers. Note, for a case in point, the dexterous management of sentence-length in the essay quoted on the opposite page. It will be found, in fact, both in English lessons and in English literature, that, as regards the length of sentences, it is a high mean variation, far more than any particular average, that stamps the pleasing stylist.[2]

4. EXTREME RANGE OF INDIVIDUAL VARIATION.

Of all school subjects, English composition is the one in which individual variation is widest. Neither reading nor writing, nor spelling nor dictation, nor mechanical arithmetic nor problem arithmetic, nor manual subjects nor informational subjects, can show, as against the annual progress from one year to another, so large a standard deviation for the same year. It is evident in every table for this subject (Tables LX. to LXII.). Composition, therefore, lends itself admirably to demonstrating, in concrete and impressive form, a fact which I have so often emphasised, but which, through lack of space, I am unable to illustrate for every test and for every age—namely, the incredible range of ability over which individual children in the same age-group are scattered and dispersed.

As a representative age I may perhaps select age 10 —, a year which

---

[1] For example, in the well-known passage on the genius of Shakespeare—a curious contrast to Mr. Masefield's remarks upon the same subject.

[2] Fifteen to fifty words are the extremes generally quoted as serviceable limits (e.g., by Brewster *The Writing of English*, p. 167). Macaulay's *Essay on Milton*, however, contains several sentences of only five words, and two or three of nearly one hundred.

marks the middle of the senior school career, and forms for the brightest pupils the final phase before the elementary school is exchanged for the secondary or the central. For this age I shall take, from among all the elementary school children of a single borough, two specimens of composition from the two extremes of ability, one from the keenest and one from the meanest, the best essay and the worst essay that I have as yet encountered.

I shall quote first the composition of a girl aged $10\frac{8}{12}$. Judged by my tests she is, out of a school population averaging in this borough about three thousand for each age-group, the cleverest child in her year. A girl of high mental powers and of still higher mental promise, in tests of intelligence thoughtful and observant, clear in describing what she observes, and cogent in arguing what she has thought out, in tests of attainment quick and accurate, a good linguist, a good mathematician, deft with the needle, neat with the pencil, and, above all, a constant and omnivorous reader, she appears, alike in general ability and in the special subjects of the school, foremost among these thousands.[1] Her essay, written in class, was prompted by a picture-postcard of G. F. Watts' *Hope*. For eliciting both intellectual and tempera-mental qualities, pictures of this kind furnish most effective material. Her exercise on *School*, though good, was not unique.

HOPE.

Sublimely, majestically sorrowful she seems. Yet her name is Hope. Cowering low, not in submission to Fate, but longing for happiness, she sits, blindfolded; and fingers, lovingly and musingly, the one vibrating string of her lyre, striving to create sweet melody. The first beam of sunshine is kissing her feet; and in her inmost soul she wonders whether the time will come when it will kiss her drooping head.

She is the good spirit of the world, and the ruler of the minds of those who dwell in it. In the darkest hour of night she visits us, and helps us to wait patiently for dawn and the light.

Hope cannot read the future. But the morning star, the eye of Heaven, is a prophet; and though Hope cannot see it, she feels its light shining in her heart. It puts into her soul dreams of happiness, thoughts of the realisation of her ideals, and the winning of eternal bliss.

In the most unhappy moments of the life of man, she comes to him, drives away despair, and teaches him patience. She is like a sparkling and refreshing fountain to a thirsty flower, or a light seen in the darkness by some weary footsore traveller.

The style of this essay in a girl of this age is perhaps not of a kind to be too zealously encouraged. In its language, in its sentiments, in its literary flowers and figures, it is all too plainly touched by the influence of the child's favourite writer at the moment—a well-known authoress of mystic novels. Nevertheless, the piece bears many marks, both obvious and recondite, of

---

[1] With the supplementary intelligence tests, with my reasoning tests, and with tests of special scholastic attainments, her mental quotient was, in the main, curiously uniform, namely, about 155 per cent. With the Binet-Simon scale it was somewhat lower. But at this plane such a figure has no precise significance.

a mind peculiarly original, a skill in the use of words that is all her own. I may perhaps pause for a moment over one only of the more elusive. Those familiar with Prof. Saintsbury's *History of Prose Rhythm* will recognise in the child's diction many of the rhythmic types which he notes as recurrent in classical prose of the highest and most aspiring order. Take, for a revealing instance, her second paragraph. It consists of two sentences balanced one against the other. Each of these sentences in turn contains two co-ordinate clauses, similarly balanced in a fashion almost biblical, and ending respectively in an anapæst ("ŏf thĕ wŏrld ") and a dactyl ("dwĕll ĭn ĭt "), and then in a dactyl ("vīsĭts ŭs ") and an anapæst ("ănd thĕ līght "). This intricate polyphony is succeeded by a curt contrasting statement of five words only, which ushers in a paragraph of four sentences, each progressively lengthened through seven, thirteen, sixteen, and thirty-one syllables, the whole closing in a triple parallelism. The *ionic a minore* undertone, so constant an accompaniment of romantic writing, is throughout curiously insistent, like a contrapuntal melody in a fugue. It sustains the four clauses of the second paragraph ("ănd thĕ rūlĕr / ŏf thĕ mīnds ŏf / thŏse whŏ dwĕll ĭn . . ." etc.) ; while in the final paragraph the rocking of the cradle heard above the lullaby becomes almost too obtrusive. From start to finish, and above all in these two paragraphs, a pleasing prevalence of liquid consonants, and a skilful variation of broad vowels, still further heightens an effect, not wholly inappropriate, of a consolatory music.

To trace in a child's exercise subtleties such as these must strike many as far-fetched and fanciful. Let the reader, however, search, even in the best of our average selections below, for definite rhythm or vowel-melody, Their absence will be manifest to the most sceptical ear. At the same time, if the present piece be read in direct succession to a fragment penned on a similar theme by an adult professional hand—Chesterton's analysis of the same picture in his book on *Watts*,[1] or (*si parva licet componere magnis*) Pater's consummate rhapsody cast in the same pæonic metre on the mystical masterpiece of Lionardo [2]—then the shortcomings, the immaturities, the blemishes even, of the child's prose impress themselves immediately. There is none of the ingenuity of Chesterton in the thought ; none of the hard and brilliant enamel of Pater in the style : merely the simple reflections of a clever girl expressed in somewhat sentimental language—reflections a little beyond the writer's real experiences, language a little too lofty for the thought that it clothes. Yet, despite all the limitations of her ideas, despite all the labouring of her style, how many children, aged barely eleven, educated only in a Council school, could produce so exquisite a trifle ?

Not many yards from the school attended by this young genius lives a boy who, among all the " normal "[3] children of the same age, resident in

[1] pp. 97 *et seq.*

[2] *The Renaissance*, 1912 edition, p. 130. Note the curious similarity in rhythm. "Shĕ ĭs ōldĕr / thăn thĕ rŏcks / ămŏng which shĕ / sĭts ; lĭke thĕ vămpīre /, shĕ hăs bĕen deăd / mănў tīmes, ănd / leărned thĕ sĕcrĕts / ŏf thĕ grăve ; ănd / hăs bĕen ă dīvĕr / ĭn dĕep seăs, ănd / keĕps thĕir făllĕn / dăy ăbŏut hĕr /."

[3] In previous papers (*J. Exp. Ped.* I, 1912, p. 281) I have pointed out how a child's "apperception" of a picture may throw unexpected light on his interests and temperament. A schedule of points to be noted in the *form* and in the *content* of his compositions (similar to, but more comprehensive than, that outlined on p. 359) is essential, if a systematic study of individual traits is to be made. In this way, by taking the compositions on the picture *Hope* (and other problem-pictures of a more realistic kind), and compiling frequency-data, Miss Charleston has shown how even under classroom conditions, personal attitudes and vocational interests may be revealed. For intensive study an oral composition (taken down in shorthand) is, of course, better still. The procedure has called forth some scepticism from English teachers. But may I remind them that literary critics themselves have employed statistical analysis for comparing peculiarities of style, not only to verify the authenticity of writings, but also to deduce the psychological characteristics of the writers ? [I may add that more recent work on the " interpretation of pictures " and on " rankings of pictures " shows that such devices are particularly suggestive in the examination of neurotics and delinquents : see *The Subnormal Mind*, p. 330.]

Those who wish to compare results from their own pupils in class may conveniently use the coloured picture-postcards published by Messrs. Eyre and Spottiswoode. They should see, however, that the star and the single string are both distinct ; and that the title " Hope " is printed (or written in) below the reproduction.

the same borough, is poorest for composition. His essay, composed under precisely similar conditions, with the same picture in front of him and with the same allowance of time, reads, or rather runs, as follows :—

> Wos a pon a tim a putr of a lrg sitndan was out a bot
> ro stne no. (" Once upon a time a picture of a girl sitting
> down without any boots or stockings on.")

This boy has made during the last three years but little advance. The following essay on " School," written by him at the age of $12\frac{1}{1}\frac{0}{2}$, as part of my general survey, excels the preceding in one clear point : it at least contains a verb and forms a sentence :—

SCHOL.

> I lick Schol very mock dno and Scpl in a myines wen
> we have Scpch. (" I like school very much and and
> specially in the morning when we have scripture.")

A comparison with the average samples on page 423 will show that this effort falls well beneath the productions even of a mediocre child of seven.

The pair of essays on *Hope* supply a vivid illustration of the vast range of individual differences to be discovered within the limits of a single year. Those who are intimate with none but good schools will accept the first essay without demur ; they will find the second incredible in a normal child of ten. Those who are conversant only with poor schools will readily admit that they have seen performances almost, though perhaps not quite, as illiterate as the second ; but will insist that the first has been inspired, or at least edited, by an older hand. Few, I suspect, are acquainted with both extremities of the scale. The two samples are, of course, exceptions. Yet they are not outstanding exceptions. In a large and truly representative collection of the writings of children of ten, a few will be found nearly as admirable as the first, a few almost as mean and pitiful as the second ; and between these two extremes the rest of the series might be marshalled in an order of diminishing merit, passing from one end of the scale to the other through barely perceptible gradations. So wide, so varied are the abilities of individual children at the same chronological age.

5. RELATIVE BACKWARDNESS OF DEFECTIVES IN THE VARIOUS SUBJECTS.

As the last problem in this long review, it may be of interest to glance back through the catalogue of tests, and to enquire in what particular subjects of the ordinary school curriculum mentally defective children appear most backward and in what subjects their backwardness seems least pronounced. For a reply, the reader may first compare the set of tables brought together in the third appendix (pp. 427-438). These tables, as they stand, suggest that apart from a few notable exceptions, the differences in backwardness, revealed by the different tests, are by no means large. For an exact comparison, therefore, it becomes essential that the results should be drawn from the same group of children throughout. For this purpose, I have, accordingly, selected data from those children only who were examined each in every one of the foregoing tests. The average of their marks I have converted, at each chronological year, into a mental or "educational" age ; and from this again I have computed an "educational ratio," which will express the educational age as a percentage of the chronological.

With the low averages obtained from the youngest children such computations and conversions would be highly untrustworthy. I have, accordingly, retained none but children aged 10·0 and upwards ; and have also rejected children but recently transferred to a special school. The total number thus remaining is slender. It comprises 143 children. With a sample so small any distinctions by age or sex would be invalidated by a huge margin of error. Hence, in Table XXXVIII. the figures are shown for the entire group in the form of a single average educational ratio for each test. For many readers an "educational ratio" is an abstract and unusual concept. To lend it a significance more practical and more concrete, I have reconverted the ratios into the presumable mental ages to be attained at the age of 14·0, the year of leaving the ordinary elementary school.[1]

A comparison of the figures suggests the following conclusions. Children of London special schools are most backward in linguistic subjects[2]—in spelling, in intelligent reading, and in composition (the last a subject barely coming within the limits of their range). They are least backward in manual subjects—in handwork, in drawing, and in writing. In arithmetic their abilities vary with the type of sum. In the mechanical use of memorised tables—in addition and multiplication—they are, indeed, moderately accurate, though insufferably slow ; in subtraction and short division (the latter, again, hardly entering within the compass of their curriculum) they are lame and lamentably weak. Easy oral problems, dealing with simple money sums, they can solve with a measure of success ; such work is alike mechanical and concrete. Written exercises in the four rules, whether simple or monetary, the older defectives can also attack, though with an ample proportion of inaccuracy. But where the problem has to be read, where the scheme and type of working has to be discovered, where genuine reasoning, novel applications, and abstract processes of two or more steps are involved, there they fail utterly. And, no matter what the subject be, when speed is demanded, their incapacity becomes as sadly apparent as that of a wooden-legged cripple when his companions break into a run.

The above comparisons apply to the majority of children in special schools ; they do not apply to all. Among the brighter defectives, reading, so far from being the task in which they are most backward, is not infrequently the subject in which they acquit themselves best of any. Yet even here it is in mere mechanical accuracy and in mere mechanical speed that they excel, much more than in genuine comprehension. A few, contrary to the general trend, reach a high speed in simple addition—a feat, however, no less mechanical. On referring to the detailed tables for these two subjects, the reader will observe that, whereas in most subjects the borderline for ages twelve to fourteen rarely rises much above a mental age of nine years, in reading it is fixed at about ten years, and in simple addition at eleven. On the other hand, for composition, for written arithmetic (particularly problems), and for simple division, the borderline tends to be low. Here, between normals and defectives, the amount of overlapping is scanty—much

---

[1] The special school teacher who attempts to check these figures by his experience will probably find them either too high or too low, according to the type of school with which he is most familiar. If he compares them with a typical group aged fourteen in a school for elder boys, he will consider my figures too low. If he compares them with the older children left behind in the junior school, he will consider them too high. He must remember that the figures are deduced by calculations from an eclectic sample of younger children.

[2] On the other hand, Binet has stated that "sub-normal children, whom we have brought together in the special classes, are all weak in number work, much weaker than in spelling or reading" (*Intelligence of the Feebleminded*, p. 95). Such a broad generalisation, however, must not be pressed too closely. As we have noted at various points, much depends upon (1) the grade of defective accepted ; (2) the age at which the diagnosis is made ; (3) the particular school subjects upon which the diagnosis chiefly turns ; (4) the kind of number work to which such a statement refers.

less, indeed, than a comparison of the respective averages would imply. Probably the mental age assigned for these subjects to the average defective, somewhat magnifies, by its nature and size, his apparent attainments. At the corresponding mental level the young normal child is just learning the rudiments of these subjects ; but he is learning them with great rapidity. The defective, on the contrary, learns them with laborious slowness—in truth, by comparison, with a diminishing speed. In these subjects, if we are to contrast the backwardness of the average defective with the attainments of the average normal of his own chronological year, we ought rather to measure it in terms of the standard deviation for the normal age-group. This procedure, though cumbersome, would be more equitable and fair ; it is, however, too elaborate for my present data, and too technical for my present exposition.

TABLE XXXVIII.

Relative Attainments of Children of Special M.D. Schools in Tests of the Chief Subjects of the School Curriculum.

Subject.	Educational Age at Fourteen.	Educational Ratio.
Dictation	6·3	45·3
Spelling	6·5	46·7
Reading (Comprehension)	6·8	48·9
Composition (Quality)	7·0	50·3
Reading (Speed, Discontinuous)	7·1	50·8
Simple Subtraction (Speed)	7·2	51·4
Arithmetic (Problems, Written)	7·2	51·7
Composition (Speed)	7·4	52·6
Reading (Accuracy)	7·5	53·3
Simple Division (Speed)	7·6	54·1
Simple Subtraction (Accuracy)	7·7	54·7
Simple Addition (Speed)	7·7	55·1
Arithmetic (Written, Mechanical)	7·8	55·6
Reading (Speed, Continuous)	7·8	55·9
Simple Division (Accuracy)	7·9	56·5
Arithmetic (Oral)	8·0	56·8
Simple Multiplication (Speed)	8·0	57·4
Simple Addition (Accuracy)	8·1	57·9
Writing (Speed)	8·4	59·7
Simple Multiplication (Accuracy)	8·5	60·5
Writing (Quality)	8·7	62·1
Drawing	9·1	64·9
Handwork	9·8	69·7
Average Educational Age and Ratio ..	7·7	54·6
Average Mental Age and Ratio (Binet-Simon scale)	8·1	57·6

The foregoing comparison is not altogether barren of practical corollaries. In the school curriculum the main obstacles for the defective arise from the fundamental aspects of the linguistic subjects, most of all, perhaps, from spelling. Might it not, therefore, be judicious, with all save those who possess special linguistic abilities, to aim in these particular subjects (as I have already urged in detail above) only at the barest essentials ? We must not be too easily seduced by the gloss of surface achievements, by a semblance of progress in the pages of a copybook, or the glib recitation of a lesson of the classroom. We must remember there will be an echo of education in the fine phrases of a parrot, if only its cage has been fortunately placed.

In handwork, in oral problems, and in rote arithmetic, on the other hand, the relative excellence of the defective is more genuine; and springs more immediately from the relative powers of the pupil. But here also they are enhanced by the educational methods of the teacher, which rightly accentuate and exploit these powers. At the same time, since mental speed is largely, even among low-grade intelligences, a matter of training and drill, the slow performance of defectives throughout the curriculum suggests that systematic practice, systematically renewed, might yield a sudden and sustained acceleration, and so reduce, if it did not remove, this disproportionate lethargy. But again the data are too meagre to bear the weight of such conclusions. Nor was it here my purpose to develop them at length; but only to illustrate by what means and with what prospects they may be deduced from such enquiries.

6. CONCLUSION.

And thus I am led to reiterate at the close what I have emphasised from the beginning, that the scales are only tentative. Each test, in its present condition, is to be regarded as a venture rather than as an achievement, as a provisional and imperfect illustration rather than as a finished and final product. It is put forward as a stimulus to the enquiring teacher, as a starting-point for further research, not as a ready-made instrument, calibrated, patented, warranted exact. If the tests are now somewhat prematurely published, it is in the hope that they may improve and profit by criticism, not that they may be used as touchstones for the criticism of the work of others.

From the need for a preliminary sketch or preparatory design, the scientist is no more exempt than the artist. The sculptor, before he and his fellow-workmen set the plaster for the full-sized metal cast, kneads a miniature statuette in cheap and plastic clay. Such a studio model is all I have roughed out. There is plenty to retouch, to refashion, to remould. No one can mistake a raw and clumsy figurine for a polished effigy in bronze.

To attempt a complete collection of standardised scholastic tests will be assuredly to undertake a colossus. To perfect such a series will be a task beyond the power of any solitary investigator, experimenting only in a few selected schools. It must be the self-appointed duty of a large band of co-operating enquirers—expert teachers, examining each his own pupils according to some prearranged scheme, pooling the results from a wide variety and a large number of departments, constantly criticising one another's test-questions, constantly checking their own age-norms, reviewing and revising the whole in the light both of general teaching experience and of special knowledge of special subjects. The sooner such research proves these scales to be worthless, the sooner will their aim have been achieved.

CYRIL BURT.

9th June, 1920.

APPENDIX I.

MATERIALS FOR READING, SPELLING AND ARITHMETIC TESTS.

Test 1.

READING (ACCURACY).

Graded Vocabulary Test.

For test material, see over-leaf.

For Instructions, see pp. 298-9. For Norms, see Table XXXIX., p. 427.

Age last Birthday						Number of words
4-	to	is	of	at	he	10
	my	up	or	no	an	
5-	his	for	sun	big	day	20
	sad	pot	wet	one	now	
6-	that	girl	went	boys	some	30
	just	told	love	water	things	
7-	carry	village	nurse	quickly	return	40
	known	journey	terror	obtain	tongue	

8–	shelves scramble twisted beware commenced scarcely belief steadiness labourers serious				50
9–	projecting fringe luncheon nourishment overwhelmed urge explorer trudging events motionless				60
10–	economy formulate exhausted contemptuous renown universal circumstances destiny glycerine atmosphere				70
11–	perpetual emergency humanity perambulating ultimate apprehend excessively domineer theory reputation				80
12–	physician fatigue philosopher melodrama autobiography constitutionally champagne encyclopedia hypocritical efficiency				90
13–	melancholy exorbitant influential terminology palpable mercenary contagion fallacious binocular microscopical				100
14–	atrocious phlegmatic refrigerator unique alienate eccentricity ingratiating subtlety poignancy phthisis				110

Test 2.

READING (LETTERS AND FIGURES).

For Instructions, see pp. 300-1.

O S A X T E M B K

I C R L P D G N H

W F U Z V Y J Q

s o a i m e t x f

c n v h g u b k l

j r z d y p w q

1 3 2 5 4 8 7 9 0 6 10

12 18 14 11 13 19 15 17 16 20

26 39 50 74 100 132 576 1,000 1,498 1,927

10,000 500,000 1,000,000 72,967 8,104,035

$\frac{1}{2}$ $\frac{1}{4}$ $\frac{2}{3}$ $\frac{11}{20}$ $2\frac{5}{8}$ 0·1 2·5 10·001 0·17 6·3

Test 3.

READING (SPEED ; AND, WITH DEFECTIVES, ACCURACY).

Discontinuous Ungraded[1] Test. Two- and Three-Letter Monosyllables.

For test material, see over-leaf.

For Instructions, see pp. 301-2. For Norms, see Table XL. and
XLI., pp. 427 and 428.

---

[1] The words are graded for defectives ; but for normal children are practically uniform in difficulty throughout.

C*

					Number of words
go	is	at	so	cat	5
to	on	the	we	it	10
he	in	of	my	an	15
up	by	be	and	me	20
do	if	too	dog	as	25
us	you	for	see	am	30
no	or	man	Tom	but	35
ran	ox	not	can	she	40
mat	sun	has	boy	pen	45
box	bat	bad	his	did	50
hat	pig	say	had	wet	55
sat	day	ten	rat	bee	60
run	fox	jam	was	get	65
sit	hot	big	hen	her	70
out	all	men	top	red	75
two	pot	bed	let	pat	80
Sam	fed	fat	leg	got	85
Ned	pin	are	net	one	90
cup	pet	pan	fun	may	95
old	now	who	bit	six	100

					Number of words
sum	saw	pit	cap	hop	105
dad	hit	lot	lad	wee	110
ink	sad	set	Bob	off	115
met	egg	nor	fan	cow	120
lip	tea	ill	yet	fit	125
pay	beg	pop	sea	led	130
end	bag	lay	how	put	135
joy	ham	dot	buy	lit	140
far	log	new	fix	way	145
eat	fly	ram	mix	win	150
yes	toy	tin	map	arm	155
bar	our	Jim	hip	hay	160
nut	rag	sin	sow	tub	165
ice	why	ask	car	cry	170
gun	bid	sky	fin	rap	175
rum	bun	jug	fry	sip	180
jar	van	toe	cot	dim	185
jet	tip	wit	rot	mob	190
mew	lap	lie	dig	tap	195
oak	fog	air	vex	ark	200

Test 4.

READING (COMPREHENSION).

Graded Directions Test.

For Instructions, see pp. 303-4. For Norms, see Table XLII., p. 428.

Age 5.–

1   # Get me a pen.

Age 6.–

2   **Put a pin in the box.**

3   **Give the box to me and sit down.**

4   **Put two more pins into the box, and one near it on the table.**

5   **Lift your hands above your head, and look at me while I count 5.**

5   **Pick up the box again; shake out the pins; then give seven pins to me, holding them in your left hand.**

7   I have something in my pocket which I use to tell the time. Do not say what it is called; but tell me how many hands you think it has.

8   Open my book at page 8. Put the pencil between the leaves of the book. Shut the book. And then say to me: "I have done what you asked."

9   Take this card with you and do all that it tells you. First, go outside the room. While you are outside, change the card into your other hand, and then come back and put the card on the table.

10   " So the shepherd brought his flock to the market; and the animals were sold to make mutton, after their wool had been cut off to make cloth."
What kind of animals were they?

11   Turn with your face toward the window before you read the rest of the card. When I tap, walk two steps away from me. When I tap again, raise your empty hand. When I tap the third time, do nothing. At the fourth tap, bring me the card.

Age 8.-[1]

12

Here, she, believe, queen.

Each of these words has the letter " e " in it.

Tell me which contains it the largest number of times.

Age 9.-[1]

13

" The greenest buds of May,
    The brightest flowers of June,
To me are never so gay,
As a brown October day,
    With its golden sheaves,
    And its crimson leaves,
And Autumn tints of decay."

Which month does the writer think the most beautiful—May, October, or June?

Age 10.-[1]

14

Look at the figures below. Cross out every 3 that comes after 4, except when the 4 follows an 0.

1 2 3 1 2 4 3 5 4 3 6 7 0 4 1 8 0 4 3 9
7 4 3 1 2 3 0 4 3 4 3 1 2 3 4 5 6 7 8 3

([1]) These headings simply indicate that of the children tested approximately 50 per cent. at the ages specified were able to answer the questions indicated. There are, however, great variations from school to school in the relative difficulty of such questions; and, of course, a single question is not sufficient to decide a mental age. The reasons for appropriating only one question to each of the higher ages are noted above, p. 304.

For the last two questions paper ruled in ½-in. or ¼-in. squares is issued.

Age 11.—[1]

15   "Yesterday," said Mrs. Jones, "our cook and the gardener had a race : and to my surprise the gardener won."

"What surprised you ?" said Mr. Smith. "Surely you expected the man to beat the woman ?"

"Yes," said Mrs. Jones, "but he didn't. You see our gardener is a land girl: and the cook is a Frenchman who used to work in a hotel kitchen."

Mr. Smith laughed. "Of course," he said, "I naturally thought your cook was a . . . . , and your gardener a . . . ."

Read Mr. Smith's last remark aloud, putting in the missing words.

Age 12.—[1]

16   Take the squared paper and the pencil. Place a capital letter O on the fifth square in the top row. Now make a cross in the third square of the next row, unless there are more than six squares in this row, in which case you should write the first letter of your surname in the last square of the third row.

Age 13.—[1]

17   Suppose that the blue lines on the paper are streets. With your pencil start from the black mark, and go straight on in the direction of the arrow, until you come to the fourth turning to the right. Go down this, take the third turning to your left and stop at the very next cross road.

---

[1] See footnote [1] on preceding page.

Test 5.

READING (COMPREHENSION; ALSO SPEED, ACCURACY, AND EXPRESSION).

Continuous Prose Test.

For Instructions, see pp. 305-11. For Norms, see Table XLIII., to XLV., pp. 429-30.

On his way out of the town he had to pass the prison, and as he looked in at the windows, whom should he see but William himself peeping out of the bars, and looking very sad indeed. "Good morning, brother," said Tom, "have you any message for the King of the Golden River?" William ground his teeth with rage, and shook the bars with all his strength; but Tom only laughed at him, and advising him to make himself comfortable till he came back again, shouldered his basket, shook the bottle of holy water in William's face till it frothed again, and marched off in the highest spirits in the world. It was, indeed, a morning that might have made anyone happy, even with no Golden River to seek for. Level lines of dewy mist lay stretched along the valley, out of which rose the massy mountains— their lower cliffs in pale grey shadow, hardly distinguishable from the floating vapour, but gradually ascending till they caught the sunlight, which ran in bright touches of ruddy colour along the sharp crags, and pierced, in long, level rays, through their fringes of spear-like pine.

Test 5—continued.—READING (Comprehension.)

Continuous Prose Test.

INTERROGATORY.

For Instructions, see p. 282. For Norms, see Table XLV., p. 402.

For Instructions, see p. 282. For Norms, see Table XLV., p. 402.

Order of Question.	Order of Difficulty.	Question.	Answer.
1	3	The story is about two people. What were their names ?	Tom.
2	6	And the name of the other ?	William. *(If both names are given in answer to the first question, the reply counts 2 marks.)*
3	8	Were they related to one another, or were they only friends ? *(If " related " is not understood, repeat question, substituting " Did they belong to the same family ? ")*	Brothers.
4	1	Where was William ?	In prison. *(For " at the window " allow only ½ marks, unless the child can specify that it was a prison window.)*
5	15	What did Tom say to William when he first saw him ?	Have you a message for the King ? *(For " from the King " allow only ½ mark.)*
6	9	How did William reply ?	He was very angry ; or he gnashed his teeth ; or shook the bars.
7	13	Did Tom lose his temper, too ? What did he do ? *(If the child replies, " he shouldered his basket," or " he just went on his way," ask, " What did he do first ? ")*	No. He laughed ; or started taunting or teasing him. *(For " no " alone, allow only ½ mark.)*
8	18	What else did Tom say to William ?	Make yourself comfortable ; or Wait there till I come back.
9	4	How was Tom feeling that day ?	Happy. Pleased with himself.
10	12	What time of day was it ?	Morning.

READING (Comprehension)—*continued*.

Order of Question.	Order of Difficulty.	Question.	Answer.
11	2	What kind of weather ?	Bright ; *or* beautiful ; *or* misty ; *or* sunny.
12	19	Where had Tom come from ?	The town.
13	5	What was he setting out to find ?	The Golden River. (*If the child replies* " the river " *or* " the King," *without being able to specify further, allow only* ½ *mark.*)
14	7	What was he carrying ?	A bottle.
15	11	What else ?	A basket.
16	10	What was in his bottle ? (What kind of water ?)	Holy water (*often given in reply to No. 14, in which case the answer scores 2 marks.*)
17	17	What did Tom do with the bottle as he left William ?	Showed him the water ; *or* shook it in his face ; *or* shook it till it frothed. (*No mark for* " threw the water at William.")
18	14	What sort of country was Tom walking towards ? What could he see in the distance ?	Mountains ; a valley ; a rocky country.
19	16	Could he see the whole of the mountains very clearly ? Why not ?	No. Because of the mist (*or* shadow).
20	20	What sort of trees were growing on the edge of the rocks ?	Pines.

Test 6.—SPELLING.

(Graded Vocabulary Test.)

For Instructions, see pp. 315-6   For Norms, see Table XLVI., p. 430.

Age.

5 — a   it   cat   to   and
the   on   up   if   box

6 — run   bad   but   will   pin
cap   men   got   to-day   this

7 — table   even   fill   black   only
coming   sorry   done   lesson   smoke

8 — money   sugar   number   bright   ticket
speak   yellow   doctor   sometimes   already

9 — rough   raise   scrape   manner   publish
touch   feel   answer   several   towel

10 — surface   pleasant   saucer   whistle   razor
vegetable   improvement   succeed   beginning   accident

11 — decide   business   carriage   rogue   receive
usually   pigeon   practical   quantity   knuckle

12 — distinguish   experience   disease   sympathy   illegal
responsible   agriculture   intelligent   artificial   peculiar

13 — luxurious   conceited   leopard   barbarian   occasion
disappoint   necessary   treacherous   descendant   precipice

14 — virtuous   memoranda   glazier   circuit   precision
mosquito   promiscuous   assassinate   embarrassing   tyrannous

Test 7.—DICTATION (Continuous Graded Test.)

For Instructions, see pp. 316-8. For Norms, see Table XLVII., p. 431.

	No. of Letters.
It is on a cat, but not a dog.	(20)
I saw her run by in the wet.	(40)
She came to seek or steal	(60)
a bird's nest in the grass—	(80)
the cruel little kitten !	(100)
I have asked forty girls	(120)
this puzzle. None failed	(140)
Imitate their industry.	(160)
Explain every sentence.	(180)
Employ beautiful style.	(200)
Should your solution be	(220)
satisfactory, I believe	(240)
thoroughly acceptable	(260)
prizes will be bestowed,.	(280)
designed for either sex—	(300)
pianos, sewing machines,	(320)
ingenious model yachts,	(340)
forfeited photographs,	(360)
excellent bicycles for	(380)
picturesque adventure,—	(400)
an emphatic sign,	
genuine if miscellaneous in character.	
of our conscientious appreciation	
of your unique proficiency.	(500)

ARITHMETIC.

Graded Oral Test : Mental.

[Test 8.]

For Instructions, see pp. 324-6 For Norms, see Table XLVIII., p. 431.

Below the Educational Age of 4–.

For children at the lowest mental levels, *e.g.*, defectives of a mental age of 3–, and young normals who have never been to school, exercises of the following types may be recommended to test their "sense of number" :

1. Show the child 1, 2, 3 or more fingers : ask him to do the same.

2. Show the child 3 or more beads, (*a*) arranged in some simple pattern like the pips upon a domino, (*b*) arranged in a single line (much harder) : ask him to pick out the same number.

3. Show the child a given number of beads, and ask him to hold up the same number of fingers ; and *vice versa*.

4. Try the same exercises through other sensory channels : *e.g.*, make him reproduce a given number of taps on the table, of taps on his own hand, of rhythmic movements impressed upon his arm—the child's eyes being shut.

5. Make him repeat after you the numbers in order—*e.g.*, "1, 2, 3"—progressively increasing the length of the series.

6. Ask him to name without counting small numbers of fingers, beads, taps, etc. ; and to compare without counting the size of larger but unequal groups ("which is the bigger ? ")

7. Make him count aloud, pointing with his finger, larger number of objects, arranged in rows.

8. Make him arrange beads in a row in a definite and recurrent order according to colour : *e.g.*, 1 red, 3 blue, (2 yellow), 1 red again, and so on.

9. Make him build up 2 groups ("one for you and one for me") containing a given number of beads in each.

10. Make him divide a given heap of (say) 6 beads into 2 (or 3) equal groups.

Age 4–.[1]

1. How many fingers do I hold up ? (Showing 2.)

2. If I hold up one more, how many will there be ?

3. Count how many fingers there are now. Count them with your finger. (Holding out four with each hand.)

4. Let me hear how far you can count—one, two, three,...... (To pass, should recite the cardinal numbers to 10 at 4½ years, to 19 at 5½, to 21 or beyond at 6½ or above.)[2]

---

[1] The ages by which the earliest and latest sets of questions are denominated are convenient and conventional rather than exact (see p. 326). Tests below the age of 4— are not included in the totals given in the tables.

[2] The higher ages refer primarily to chronological ages of backward and defective children.

5. If you had 3 pennies in this hand, and then I gave you 1 more, how many would you have altogether ? (Hold out the child's hand that he may visualise the money.)

6. Suppose you had 2 pennies, and lost 1 : how many would you have left ?

7. How many are 7 and 1 more ?

8. How many halfpennies would you want to buy a penny bun ?

9. Two and two more ?

10. If I gave you 3 sweets and you ate 2, how many would you have left ?

Age 5-.

1. If you had 5 nuts and gave 1 away, how many would be left for yourself ?

2. If you had 3 beads in this hand and 2 beads in this one, how many would that be altogether ?

3. Take 2 from 4. How many would be left ?

4. How many halfpennies are there in a penny and a halfpenny ?

5. What are twice 2 ?

6. How many farthings would you want to buy a penny ball ?

7. 5 and 2 more. How many is that ?

8. Four boys have given me a halfpenny each. How many pennies is that worth ?

9. I once had 4 pet mice in a cage. One died : one ran away : and one was eaten by the cat. How many were left ?

10. A boy caught 4 fish on Friday and 3 on Saturday. How many fish did he catch altogether ?

Age 6-.

1. How many do 6 and 3 make ?

2. What are 5 two's ?

3. Take 5 pence from 7 pence. How much would be left ?

4. How many ears are there on 3 donkeys ?

5. How many farthings are there in 2d. ?

6. Write down (in figures) 35.

7. How much is one half of 4 ?

8. I have 3 pockets and 3 apples in each. How many is that altogether ?

9. I put 2d. in my money-box every morning before I go to school. How many pennies shall I have saved in 3 days ?

10. I had 9 eggs in a basket, and smashed 3. How many were left ?

Age 7-.

1. My brother has picked 6 nuts, my sister has picked 10, and I have picked 18. How many have we got altogether ?

2. 12 girls have a farthing each. How many pennies is that ?

3. How many ½d. stamps can I buy for 9d. ?

4. I started with 14 marbles, and I have won 26. How many have I now ?

5. I have 2s. to divide among 4 children. How much should each have if all are to have the same amount ?

6. How many days are there in 6 weeks ?

7. My brother is 4 ft. high. How many inches is that ?

8. On a tram there were 50 people who each paid 1d. fare. How much (in shillings and pence) did the conductor take altogether ?

9. If treacle were 8d. a pound, how much would ¾ lb. cost ?

10. Yesterday we went blackberrying. I picked 21 berries, and my brother ate 12 of them. How many were left ?

Age 8-.

1. A boy had 20 marbles. Afterwards he won 3 and lost 5. How many had he then ?

2. How many penny stamps can I buy for 7s. ?

3. Mother gave me 2½d. Father gave me twice as much. How much have I altogether ?

4. I have 22 farthings in a bag. How many pennies is that worth ?

5. In an infants' school there were 99 boys and 60 girls. How many more boys than girls were there ?

6. Norton is 36 miles away. What would the fare be at 1d. a mile ?

7. Tommy collected 32 tram tickets. 18 are white, and the rest are pink. How many pink ones has he ?

8. How many beans must be taken from 47 to leave only a dozen ?

9. I have an empty album that will hold 100 picture post-cards. I have been to 6 different towns during my holiday, and at each I bought ten picture post-cards. How many more must I collect to fill the album ?

10. Add together a farthing, a halfpenny, a sixpence, a shilling, and half-a-crown.

Age 9-.

1. Jack weighs exactly 100 lbs. His sister weighs 81 lbs. How much heavier is Jack ?

2. I have been for a week's holiday. I spent 6d. a day while I was away. How much should I have left out of 4s. ?

3. I bought 9 penny stamps and 7 halfpenny ones. How much change should I have from 2s. ?

4. When oranges were 2 a penny, how many could I buy for half-a-crown ?

5. Tom had 31 sweets. And 9 boys have each given him 7 more. How many has he altogether ?

6. I had 12s. and I have spent 5s. 11½d. How much have I left ?

7. How many ounces are there in 1¾ lbs. ?

8. My bookshelf is 3½ ft. long. How many books will it hold if each is 1 inch thick ?

9. Share 1s. 3d. equally among 10 boys.

10. I have cut 1 ft. of tape into pieces 1½ ins. long. How many pieces have I made ?

Age 10–.

1. I get 6d. an hour: and I work 8 hours a day. How much can I earn in 5 days ?

2. If apples were 4 for 3d., how many could I buy for 3s. ?

3. I must be at the station a quarter of an hour before my train starts. It starts at five-and-twenty to one. When should I be there ?

4. My brother was born in 1899. How old will he be in 1930 ?

5. Take 100d. from £1. How much is left in shillings and pence ?

6. I bought 10 pairs of boots at the rate of a guinea for a single boot. How many pounds did the 10 pairs cost ?

7. What is the difference between one-half and one-quarter of £8 8s. 8d. ?

8. I posted a penny post-card every day in January. How much did the postage amount to ?

9. My brother is 21 years old. I was born when ho was 10. Add both our ages together.

10. What would be the total postage for 9 letters, 9 post-cards, and 9 circulars at 1½d., 1d., and ½d. respectively ?

Age 11–.

1. Write down 2·25 as a vulgar fraction in its lowest terms.

2. A servant earned £26 a year wages. How much was that a week ?

3. How much is seven-tenths of half-a-crown ?

4. Divide 15s. 5½d. by 7.

5. How many minutes from ¼ past 6 to ¼ to 8 ?

6. A man walked 2 miles in 30 minutes. How many hours would 20 miles take him ?

7. How many months will there be between 1st January, 1920, and 31st December, 1924 ?

8. My neighbour drinks ½ pint of cider at dinner and ½ pint at supper. How long will a 7-gallon cask last him at that rate ?

9. If 3 glasses cost 4½d., how many can I get for 2s. ?

10. How many words are there in a book of 100 pages, at 20 lines to a page and 10 words to a line ?

Age 12–.

1. What fraction of £1 is a third of 1s. ?

2. A wall is 30 ft. long and 4 ft. high. How much would it cost to whitewash it at ½d. a square foot ?

3. The church door is 50 ft. away, and I step 2¼ ft. In how many steps can I get to the church ?

4. 129 rackets at 5/- each ?

5. How many lbs. and ozs. in ·75 of 2 lbs. ?

6. A man bought 100 oranges for 5s. 16 were bad. He sold the rest at a shilling a dozen. How much profit did he make ?

D*

7. I bought a football for 12/– and sold it for 15/–. What was my gain per cent. ?

8. What is the shortest length of silk from which I can cut off either 4 inches, 6 inches, or 8 inches an exact number of times ?

9. Divide 3/– among 2 boys so that one has 8d. more than the other.

10. How many pieces of a foot and a quarter can I cut from 5 yds. ?

Age 13–.

1. What is the average of 6 inches, 7 inches, 9 inches, and 1 ft. ?

2. A motor goes 3 times as fast as a horse. The horse goes 36 miles in 6 hours. How long will it take the motor ?

3. Simple interest on £300 for 3 years at 5 per cent. ?

4. $4\frac{1}{2}$ ozs. at 2/8 per lb. ?

5. 3 boys can eat a pudding in 10 minutes. How quickly can 12 boys eat it ?

6. How many times is one-sixth contained in $13\frac{1}{2}$?

7. What is $2\frac{1}{2}$ per cent. on £4 ?

8. My little garden is 7 yds. square ; my sister's is 5 yds. square. By how many square yds. is mine bigger than hers ?

9. How many sq. yds. of paper will just cover a table 6 ft. long and 3 ft. broad ?

10. Multiply ·5 by 2·4 and divide by 3.

Age 14–.

1. How many labels $2\frac{1}{2}$ in. by 2 in. are needed to cover a sheet 10 in. square ?

2. If a train goes 30 miles in $1\frac{1}{2}$ hours, how far will it travel in $4\frac{1}{4}$ hours ?

3. If 6 men do a piece of work in 15 days, how many men must I employ to get it done in 10 ?

4. A blackboard is 3 ft. broad and 4 ft. long. How many inches of wire would just go round the edge ?

5. One-third of my stick is in the water ; one-quarter is in the mud ; 15 inches is above the water. How long is the stick ?

6. Add the cube of 5 to the square root of 121.

7. I want to cover these square boxes or cubes completely with gold paper. How many sq. yds. shall I need ? There are 3 boxes : and each edge measures 2 ft.

8. In what proportion must rice at 7d. a lb. be mixed with rice at 4d. a lb. to make the mixture worth 5d. a lb. ?

9. My father is 45 years of age, and I am 21. At what age was my father 3 times as old as I ?

10. If 2 hens lay 2 eggs in 2 days, how many eggs will 6 hens lay in 6 days ?

ARITHMETIC (Written Graded Test : Mechanical.)

[Test 9.]

For Instructions, see pp. 326-8. For Norms, see Table XLIX., *p.* 432.

Age 7-.

1. 2 1
    3 7
    1 8
    3 6
    —————

2. 61 — 38.
3. 953 × 4.
4. 2s. 1d. + 1s. 3d. + 10d.
5. 1s. 5d. × 3.

Age 8-.

1. 9 6 8 7
    1 2 0 9
      8 3 4
    3 6 2 0
    2 1 7 5
    —————

2. 5) 1 0 8 5

3. From £9 15s. 9½d.
    Take £3 17s. 5¼d.
    —————

4. £   s.   d.
    1 18   4¼
    3   9   6½
    2   5   7¾
        3   4
    —————

5. £1 13s. 5d. × 3.

Age 9-.

1. From 9,084½ take 3,597½.
2. £   s.   d.
    42 16   7¼
     3 19   8½
    18   7   4¾
    25 10 11
    —————

3. $98,467 \div 84$.

4. *Bill.* 1½ lbs. of Butter at 1/– per lb.
   Milk for one week at 2d. per day.
   2 doz. Eggs at 1½d. each.

5. How many farthings in £2 17s. 6½d. ?

Age 10–.

1. $2233 \cdot 6 \div 8$.

2. £61 13s. 7¾d. $\times$ 64.

3.
yds.	ft.	in.
35	2	11¾
8	1	9½
12	0	7¼
73	2	5¼

4. How many pounds in 1 ton 6 cwt. 0 qr. 0 st. 3 lbs. ?

5. $\frac{1}{10} + \frac{1}{5} + 8 \cdot 5 - 0 \cdot 2$.

Age 11–.

1. If 14 yds. of calico cost 5s. 3d., what is the cost of 35 yds. ?

2. $5 \cdot 281 \times 0 \cdot 047$.

3. $2\frac{7}{15} + 1\frac{20}{21} + \frac{16}{35} - \frac{12}{105}$.

4. Express $\frac{2}{3}$ of 7s. 6d. as a fraction of £1.

5. Find the value of 3 tons 10 cwt. 2 qrs. at £5 10s. 0d. per ton.

Age 12–.

1. If it takes 16 men 28 days to do a piece of work, how long will it take 21 men to do it ?

2. Simplify $\dfrac{4236 \cdot 4 \times \cdot 008}{1 \cdot 0591}$

3. Find the L.C.M. of 48, 28, 50, 51.

4. Find the simple interest on £560 for 22 years at 2¾ per cent.

5. Find the sum of $1 \cdot 7$ of 5 lbs. $+ 3 \cdot 75$ of 1 lb. 4 ozs.

Age 13–.

1. Simplify $\dfrac{\frac{1}{3} + \frac{1}{4} + \frac{1}{5} + \frac{1}{6}}{2\frac{3}{4} - 1\frac{5}{8}}$

2. Find the average of 2 tons 6 cwt. 3 qrs. 3 lbs., 3 tons 17 cwt. 2 qrs. 7 lbs., 2½ tons, 15¾ cwt., and $1 \cdot 125$ tons.

3. An article which cost £33 6s. 8d. was sold for £37 10s. 0d. What was the gain per cent. ?

4. At what rate per cent. will £306 5s. 0d. produce £1 0s. 5d. per month ?

5. Find the cost of papering a room 30 ft. long, 25 ft. wide, and 12 ft. 6 in. high with paper 1 ft. 6 ins. wide at 10d. per yard.

Age 14–.[1]

1. The following table gives the sums assessed for Income Tax for the last five years of the last century. Find the totals for the several years.

Years	Land and Houses	Business	Investments	Salaries	Totals
1895–6	145,917,380	271,768,638	36,394,180	33,878,682	—
1896–7	147,329,579	284,400,461	36,127,937	35,806,653	—
1897–8	148,146,174	303,598,980	35,966,088	37,499,958	—
1898–9	153,110,123	318,555,003	36,703,116	39,861,208	—
1899–1900	153,875,858	332,149,361	36,165,000	42,678,520	—

2. Which is the greater, and by how many grams—a thousand kilograms or $\frac{49}{50}$ of a ton ?   [1 gram = ·035 ounce.]

3. Make out the following contractor's bill, deducting 5 per cent. discount :

To 300,000 bricks at 35s. per 1000.

,, 240 tons lime at 25s. per ton.

,, 670 yd. gravel at 12s. 6d. per yd.

,, 250 yd. sand at 17s. 6d. per yd.

,, cartage lime at 1s. 6d. per ton.

,,   ,,   sand and gravel at 9d. per yd.

4. Find, to the nearest penny, the difference between the Simple and the Compound Interest on £6310 15s. 0d. for 3 years at 4 per cent. per annum.

5. The area of a square is 1722·25 sq. ft. Find (in yards, feet, and inches) the length of the side.

ARITHMETIC (Written Graded Test : Problems).

[Test 10.]

For Instructions, see pp. 326-8. For Norms, see Table L. p. 432.

Age 7–.

1. There are 7 oranges in my basket, 11 in yours. and 9 in Jack's. How many are there altogether ?

2. I have 12 apples. How many more must I buy to make 20 ?

3. How many legs are there on 9 sheep ?

4. 12 Germans attacked us. We shot 6 ; and 2 ran away. How many were left to be taken prisoners ?

5. Share one shilling equally among 6 children. How much would each have ?

Age 8–.

1. This strip of tape is 1 ft. 4 ins. long. How many inches can I cut it up into ?

2. I have just smashed 17 eggs ; and have 43 left. How many dozen did I have to begin with ?

3. How many sixpenny pop-guns can I buy with four shillings and six pence ?

4. I have bought a cake for 1s. 2d., and some jam for 5d. How much change ought I to have out of 3 shillings ?

5. In the front of my house there are five windows, with nine panes in each. Some boys have broken several panes. Thirty are left unbroken. How many want mending ?

[1] The age assigned to these problems is purely conventional, and is intended merely to mark a further year's instruction in arithmetic beyond the stage of age 13– (Standard VII).

Age 9–.

1. I have lost a purse containing a pound note, 3 ten-shilling notes, half a crown, 4 sixpences, and 9 halfpennies. How much have I lost altogether ?

2. If I can buy two pounds of red paint for 6d., how much shall I pay for 7 lbs. ?

3. On Fido's grave we raised a mound of stones. Mother put 50 pebbles, and my six brothers and I put 11 each. How many stones were there in the heap ?

4. Mary had 3 times as much money as John. John had sixpence more than Harry. Harry had half a crown. How much had they altogether ?

5. My wife and I have just bought tickets for Liverpool. How much change have we left out of a five-pound note ? (Fare to Liverpool, 32s. 6d. each.)

Age 10–.

1. Tom had 13s. 9d., Jack had 6s. 11d., and Nellie had 17s. 7d. With this money they bought their mother a present, and received 2s. 6d. back as change. What did the present cost ?

2. Altogether there are 34 medals in these two boxes. One contains 8 more than the other. How many are there in each box ?

3. The King left Windsor at 10 minutes past 10 this morning, and reached London at a quarter to twelve. How long did the journey take him ?

4. I have just bought 3 jars of raspberry jam at 1/1½ a jar ; 3½ lbs. of butter at 1/2 per lb. ; 5 lbs. of tea at 1/10 per lb. ; 7 lbs. of sugar at 2½d. per lb. How much have I left out of £2 ?

5. How high is the floor of my room from the ground floor of the house ? There are 14 steps on the staircase leading up to it, and each step rises 6¼ inches.

Age 11–.

1. In 1916 the Germans and Austrians had at least 2,600,000 fighting against Russia, 1,800,000 fighting against France, England, and Belgium, and 400,000 fighting against Italy. Let us suppose that altogether they had 6,000,000 available as soldiers. How many were left to be called up later on ?

2. A postman told me this morning that he walked 19 miles a day for 6 days a week and 8 miles on Sunday. How many miles will he walk in a year ?

3. Write down the figures 789 in every possible way : 789, 798, etc., and add up the total.

4. A rich and a poor girl live together and pay 17s. 6d. per week for their room. The rich girl agrees to pay twice as much as the poor girl. How much does each pay ?

5. If an aeroplane can fly from here to Norton in 45 minutes, how long would it take to fly to Easton and back without stopping ? (Distance to Norton, 40 miles ; to Easton, 18 miles.)

Age 12–.

1. A statue in plaster of Paris weighed 6 stns. 6 lbs. when it was completely dry. In drying, plaster of Paris loses water to the extent of three-fifths of its weight. What was the original weight of the statue when soft and wet ?

2. How many penny stamps will just cover a sheet of foolscap paper ? (A sheet of foolscap measures 12¾ in. by 8 in. ; a penny stamp is 1 in. by ¾ in.)

3. The average age of 6 children is 14 years 8 months. The oldest is 18 years old. What is the average age of the remainder ?

4. Under the National Insurance Act Mrs. Smith received a sickness benefit of 7s. 6d. a week for 26 weeks, and afterwards a disablement allowance for 5 years 2 months at 5s. per week. What was the total amount received ?

5. A soldier's step is 2½ ft. At quick march he takes 108 steps per minute. How far could he march in 3 hours ?

Age 13–.

1. Mr. Miles' classroom is 24 ft. long, 17 ft. 6 ins. wide, and 10 ft. high. By the regulations each child must have on an average at least 100 cubic feet of air space. How many children can he accommodate ?

2. If a frog spends 15 per cent. of its time in the water, and lives to the age of 16 years, how many days does it spend on land ?

3. How many hours do you spend at lessons in one term of 13 weeks ? (Lessons from 9.15 a.m. to 12 noon in the morning, and from 2.10 to 4.25 in the afternoon, with ten minutes' play in the morning and ten minutes' play in the afternoon.)

4. How long will it take an English cruiser steaming at ½ mile per minute to overtake a German battleship 10 miles ahead of her, if the battleship steams at ¼ mile per minute ?

5. The foreman earns 32s. per week and his two assistants 25s. per week each, and the 10 men under him earn 16s. per week each. What is the average wage expressed as the decimal of £1 ?

Age 14–.[1]

1. Last week I burnt 12 tons of coal at 64s. a ton. I then bought a large quantity of coke at 48s. a ton, and mixed it with the remainder of the coal in the proportion of 3 parts coke to 5 parts coal. I find I use only 11 tons a week of the slow-burning mixture. How much money a week am I saving by this method ?

2. A cube of marble whose edge is 1½ ft. in length is lowered to the bottom of a deep rectangular tank, 5 ft. 6 in. long and 4 ft. 3 in. broad. The tank is part of a fountain, and is usually about half full of water. How much was the surface of the water raised by the complete immersion of the stone ?

3. Last July the average temperature from the 9th to the 16th (including both these days) was 65·8° ; and from the 10th to the 17th (including both these days) it was 67·5°. On July 9th it was 65° What was it, therefore, on July 17th ?

4. Travelling from Aytown to Extown, 40 miles away, a man ran his car at 20 miles per hour. At Kewtown he stopped for 10 minutes for more petrol ; and at Veetown, 5 miles further on, he had to return to Kewtown for a pump he had forgotten. At what steady speed would he have to return from Extown to Aytown (without any stoppages) to take the same time coming back as he did going ?

5. From a cistern which is ⅚ full 300 litres of oil leak away. 700 litres are then added, and the cistern is found to be ⅞ full. How many gallons will it hold ? [1 gallon = 4·54 litres.]

---

(1) See note, page 291.

ARITHMETIC (Written Ungraded Tests).

[Tests 11 to 14].

Four Fundamental Rules.[1]

For Instructions see pp. 329-30. For Norms, see Tables LI.-LIV., pp. 433-4.

Test 11.   (i) ADDITION.

9 2	4 5	3 6	8 4	4 6	2 3	7 8	9 6	3 4	6 2
2 7	3 7	9 3	7 8	9 2	6 4	2 3	8 9	6 2	5 9
5 4	9 8	5 2	5 3	7 9	5 8	9 2	6 8	5 9	7 7
9 5	7 6	3 4	6 9	4 8	2 5	3 5	7 4	8 6	8 6

7 6	3 8	2 5	8 3	9 7	7 9	2 7	4 5	7 9	9 5
9 8	5 9	3 6	5 2	5 8	6 4	5 4	7 9	5 3	6 3
5 3	9 7	8 3	6 7	4 6	5 3	6 9	6 2	6 8	3 9
4 8	4 5	9 5	8 9	8 5	7 6	2 5	9 6	3 7	4 2

8 5	4 6	8 9	3 5	2 5	6 7	5 9	5 4	9 4	3 6
6 8	5 7	4 7	8 4	4 2	7 2	3 2	2 9	3 7	4 5
2 4	8 4	2 4	4 2	3 7	9 6	8 5	3 6	6 8	8 4
7 3	3 9	9 7	2 3	2 2	5 3	7 7	9 8	5 9	4 2

5 3	8 7	4 9	5 4	7 9	5 2	7 2	2 3	5 8	8 2
4 5	9 6	8 6	6 3	4 8	7 4	8 3	9 8	9 6	3 6
3 7	2 8	7 5	8 6	2 5	8 9	4 6	3 9	2 5	4 7
8 4	6 3	9 3	5 2	5 9	6 4	5 9	6 7	3 4	9 8

6 9	5 8	6 7	9 7	3 4	9 2	4 3	6 8	6 8	2 3
2 5	8 7	8 9	4 5	2 5	7 5	2 6	9 5	3 4	7 9
9 2	3 2	7 5	7 3	7 3	4 6	9 5	4 9	2 5	9 4
8 7	5 9	2 6	5 2	6 4	3 7	6 8	7 3	4 2	2 8

[1] The test-sheets, printed for the children, should, of course, be set up in type considerably larger than the above,—12 point at least, with modern face.

Test 12. (ii) SUBTRACTION.

9 8 0 2	7 7 2 1	4 9 4 4	3 2 0 8	5 8 3 1
6 2 4 6	1 8 4 1	1 2 9 5	1 7 3 8	3 6 7 6
8 7 8 1	8 0 7 9	3 2 5 3	5 1 0 6	8 7 5 6
5 7 9 5	4 5 9 9	2 1 9 5	2 8 9 2	3 5 6 9
9 6 5 3	7 6 3 4	7 8 1 2	5 0 1 4	4 9 5 2
3 8 7 3	4 6 4 8	3 1 7 8	1 6 9 4	2 8 8 9
7 2 0 6	6 2 6 5	9 2 3 1	9 8 4 3	9 1 3 6
2 3 2 1	3 5 7 5	1 2 8 2	1 7 6 9	7 4 6 5
6 4 0 3	9 4 0 5	9 1 0 7 .	5 8 2 2	7 0 2 9
4 3 1 8	5 7 8 4	4 3 7 6	1 8 9 3	3 3 7 2
5 7 0 1	8 5 0 2	9 6 4 0	4 4 3 8	3 4 0 2
2 6 9 4	3 7 4 2	5 4 8 1	1 5 7 2	1 4 2 5
7 1 0 9	7 9 1 6	5 0 3 9	6 0 5 4	8 5 1 8
4 2 6 3	2 9 5 8	3 7 4 8	2 8 6 3	1 5 9 9
6 8 3 5	6 2 5 7	7 3 6 4	4 6 7 8	8 6 7 0
3 4 6 9	1 6 8 7	5 3 7 9	2 9 8 7	6 5 9 5
9 3 4 6	8 2 1 2	7 5 3 1	9 2 1 3	9 1 1 4
1 9 6 6	5 8 3 1	1 4 5 7	6 4 8 2	4 1 6 7
3 9 5 2	8 0 6 5	9 7 0 3	9 4 2 7	6 6 8 1
2 8 9 8	6 5 7 4	6 5 4 9	2 7 9 6	4 6 9 6

Test 13.   (iii) MULTIPLICATION.

2 4 9 8	7 5 2 8	9 4 8 2	3 5 7 4	2 6 3 8
2	3	4	5	6

8 2 6 5	9 5 8 7	5 7 6 3	6 7 5 3	3 7 4 9
7	8	9	4	7

7 5 4 9	2 9 6 8	3 4 6 9	4 9 2 8	3 7 5 6
6	5	3	9	2

2 6 3 4	5 6 8 9	5 3 9 2	7 6 2 9	8 5 2 7
8	2	4	5	8

8 7 5 6	3 9 5 7	7 6 5 9	4 5 9 3	4 3 9 2
6	6	9	3	7

3 5 4 8	4 8 2 3	6 8 7 4	6 4 2 8	3 2 7 4
5	9	4	6	2

7 2 8 6	4 9 3 6	2 8 4 7	5 9 2 8	8 4 9 3
3	8	5	9	3

9 6 2 7	8 6 3 4	3 5 8 7	3 6 4 7	6 8 5 2
7	4	6	8	2

5 9 2 7	7 4 6 3	5 3 6 9	4 6 9 2	8 2 9 5
4	9	5	6	8

7 4 9 3	3 4 5 8	5 2 6 7	2 9 3 8	4 7 5 6
2	7	3	6	4

Test 14. (iv) DIVISION.

2)16738	3)13749	4)33500	5)47670	6)44568

7)60844	8)53832	9)57168	3)22887	8)66760

2)14850	9)43182	7)52045	4)38492	6)39234

5)34135	3)17796	9)66141	6)31722	8)27832

7)37086	5)21475	4)26156	2)12494	5)18930

2)19670	7)26348	3)23592	9)77868	4)19488

8)46608	6)56184	7)32151	8)67936	6)37710

9)70668	4)38608	3)11874	5)16340	2)15186

3)19281	8)61080	6)44634	2)16492	9)84924

4)26936	7)43946	5)47285	4)11752	6)28536

APPENDIX II.

MEDIAN SPECIMENS OF HANDWRITING, DRAWING, AND COMPOSITION FOR EACH AGE.

FIGURES 43 TO 52.

WRITING (QUALITY): (TEST 16)

Median Samples for Each Age

Facsimile reproductions, original size.

For description, see page 337.

FIGURE 43.

AGE 5-.

FIGURE 44 (a).

AGE 6-.

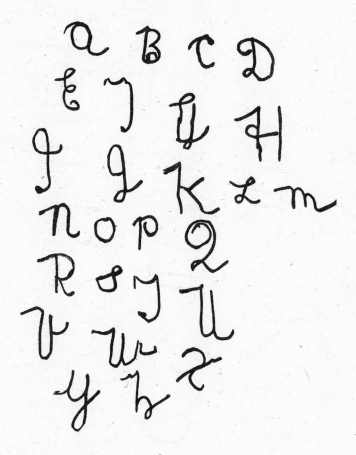

FIGURE 44 (*b*)

AGE 6– (*continued*).

FIGURE 45.

AGE 7-.

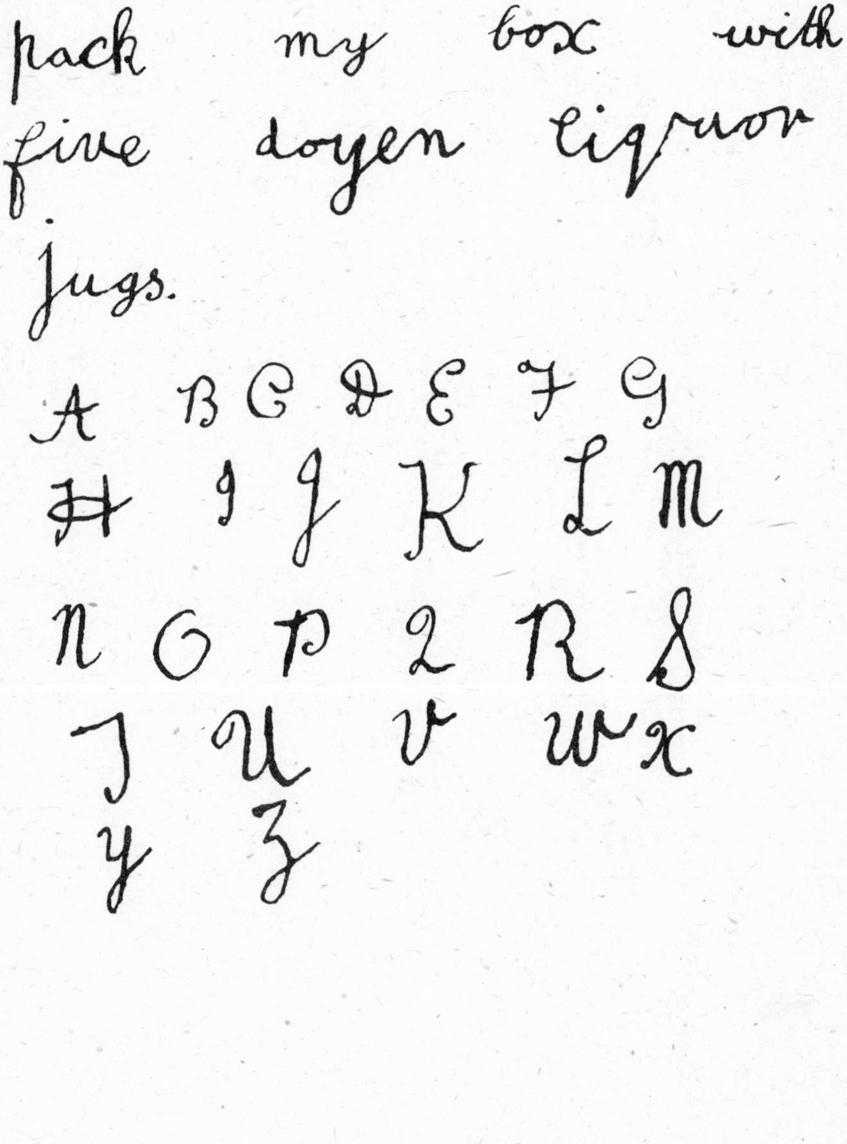

pack my box with
five doyen liquor
jugs.

A B C D E F G
H I J K L M
N O P Q R S
T U V W X
Y Z

FIGURE 46.

AGE 8-.

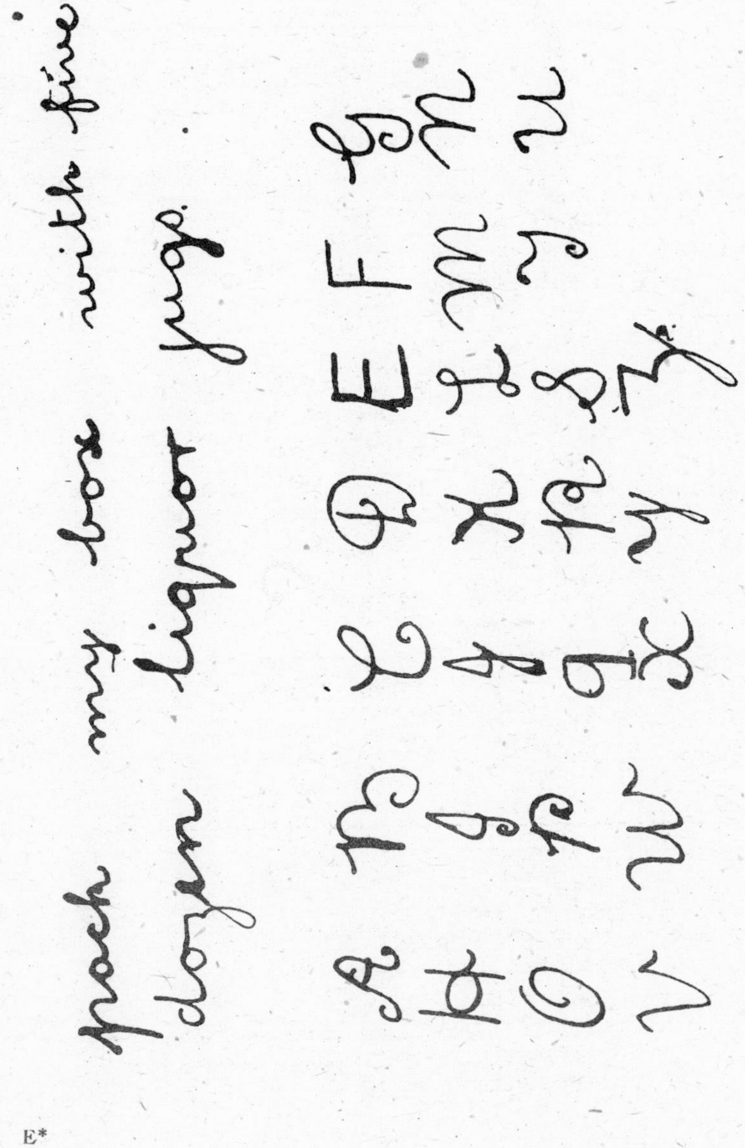

pack my box with five
dozen liquor jugs.

E*

FIGURE 47.

AGE 9-.

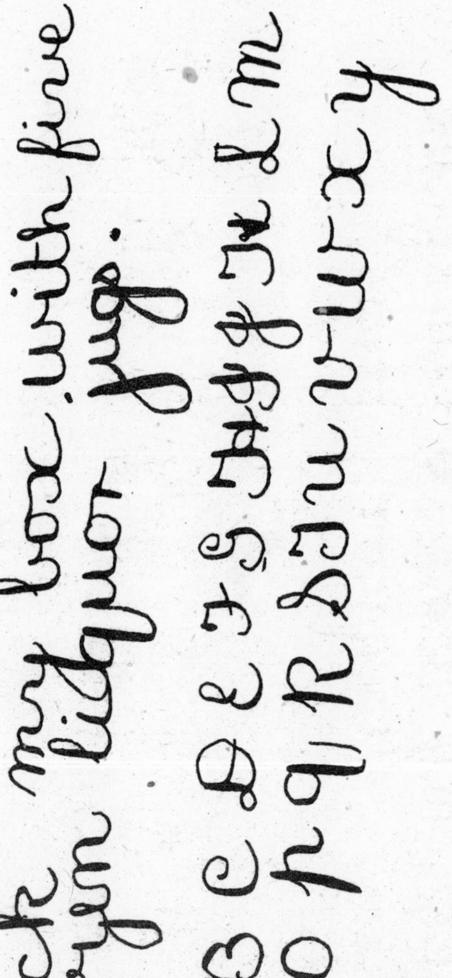

pack my box with five
dozen liquor jugs.

A B C D E F G H I J K L M
N O P Q R S T U V W X Y
Z

FIGURE 48.

AGE 10-.

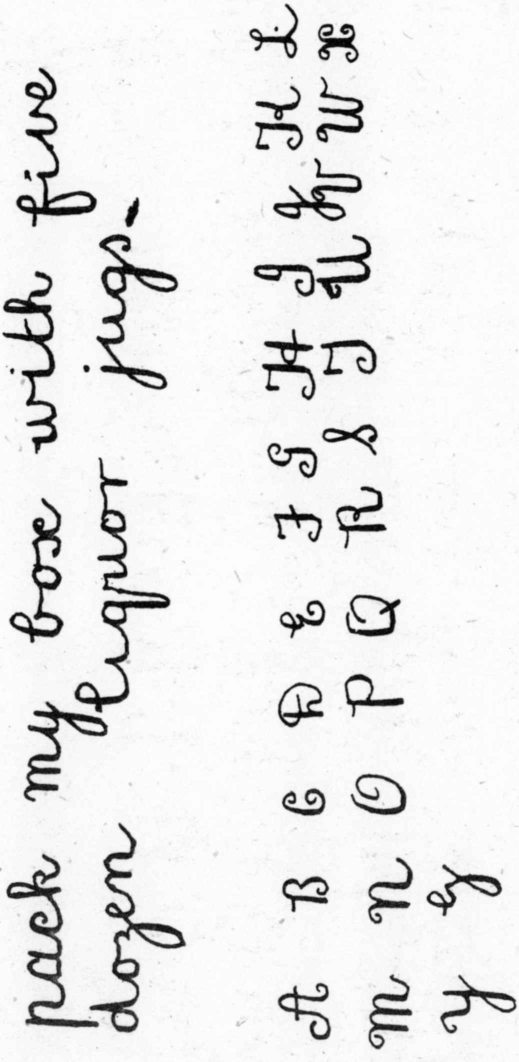

pack my box with five
dozen liquor jugs-

A B C D E F G H H L
M N O P Q R S T U V W X
Y Z

FIGURE 49.

AGE 11-.

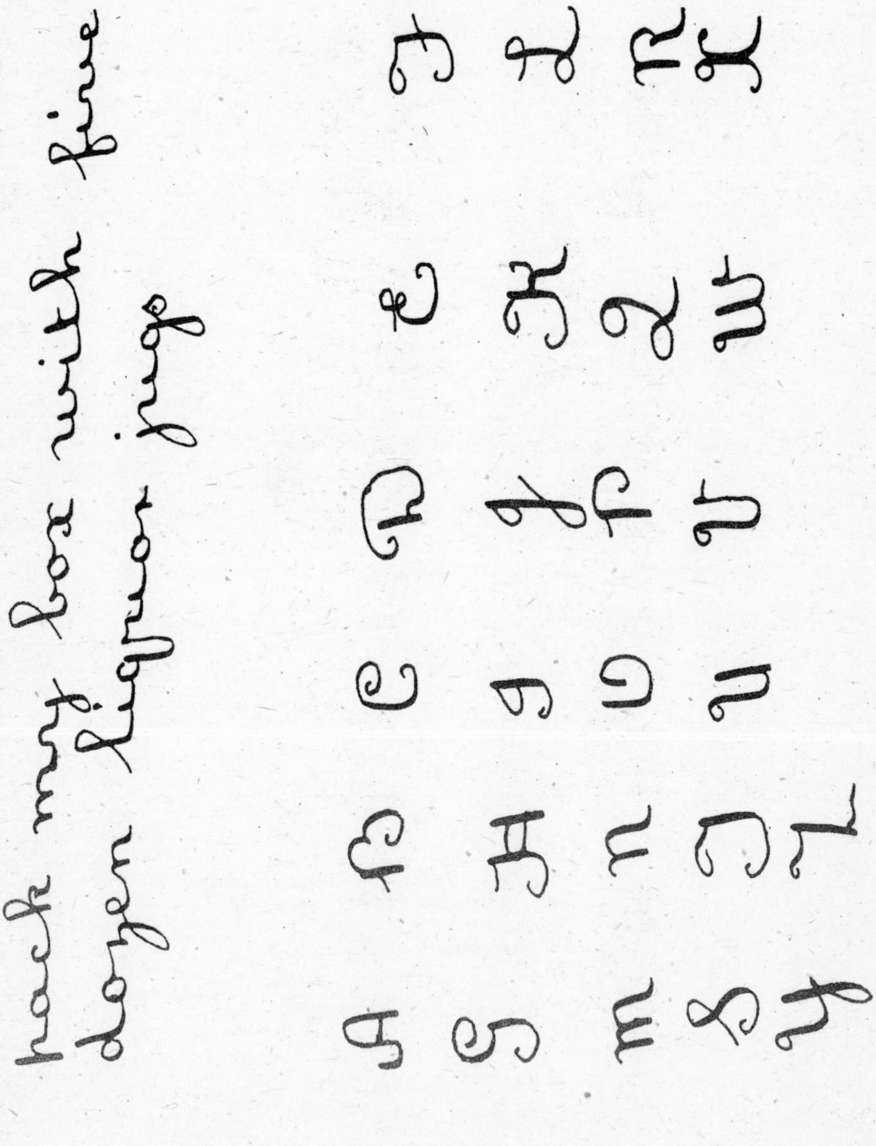

pack my box with five
dozen liquor jugs

FIGURE 50.

AGE 12-.

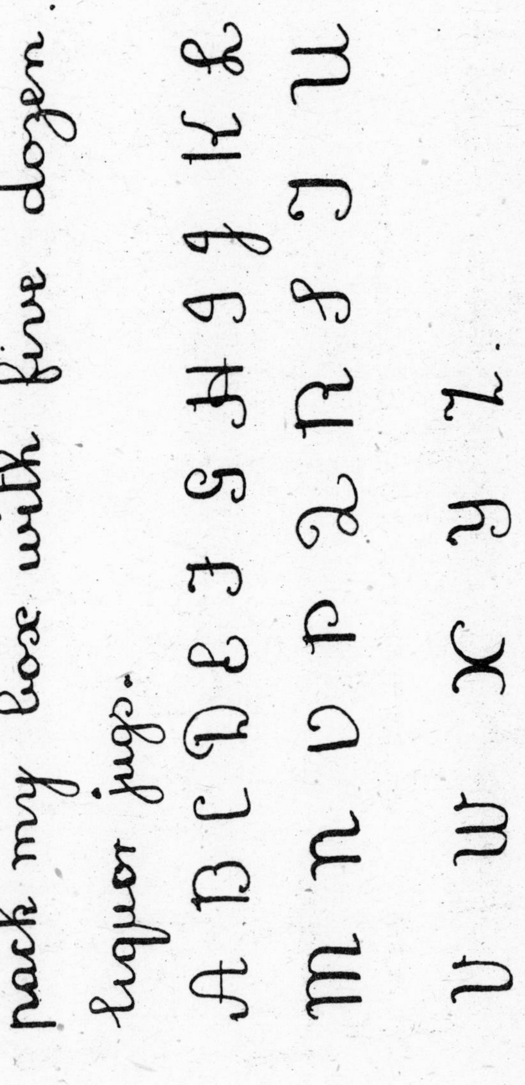

pack my box with five dozen liquor jugs.

A B C D E F G H I J K L M N O P Q R S T U V W X Y Z

FIGURE 51.

AGE 13.

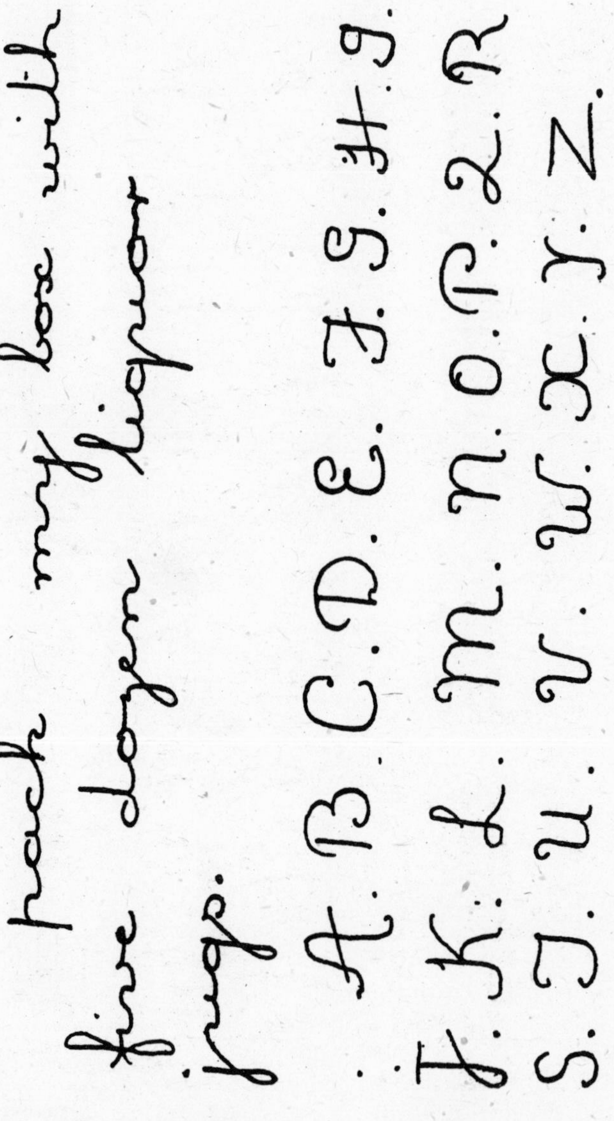

FIGURE 52.

AGE 14-.

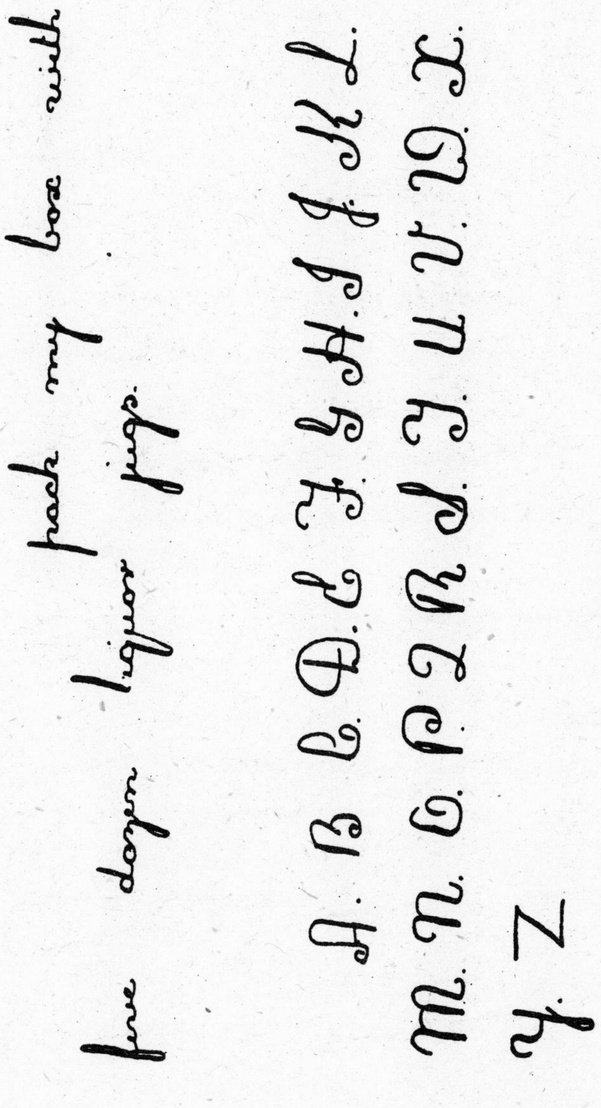

five dozen liquor jugs.

pack my box with

For description, see pages 346 to 353.

Figures 53 to 64.

DRAWING (QUALITY): (TEST 16)

Median Samples for Each Age.

Facsimile reproductions, original size.

For description, see pages 346 to 353.

411

FIGURE 53.

AGE 3-.

FIGURE 54.

AGE 4.

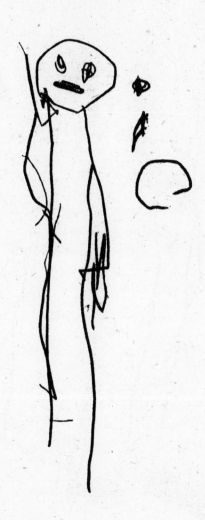

FIGURE 55.

AGE 5-.

FIGURE 56.

AGE 6-.

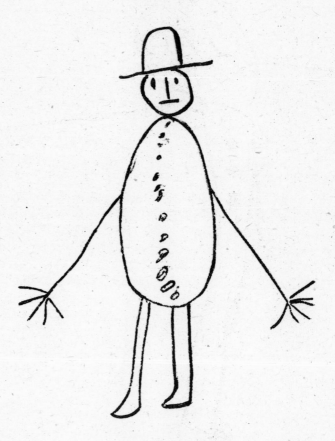

FIGURE 57.

AGE 7-.

FIGURE 58.

AGE 8–.

FIGURE 59.

AGE 9-.

FIGURE 60.

AGE 10-.

FIGURE 61.

AGE 11-.

F*

FIGURE 62.

AGE 12–.

German Soldier

FIGURE 63.

AGE 13–.

KING GEORGE

FIGURE 64.

AGE 14--

COMPOSITION (Median Samples for Normal Children of Each Age).

[Test 20.]

See pages 358-9.

Age 7-.

We do singing in school.
Sometimes we have sums
our school is very nice
We have riting in shool.
our techers are very nice

Age 8 -

SCHOOL

We come to School evry day. I like going to School,
And I like doing lesons. Their are a lot of teachers
And their are a lot of boys in our room, at School
we lern reading and speling and somtimes we have panting
We must not be late for School
When it wet we go in to the hall to play
some days we do drill.

Age 9 .

COMPOSTION.

SCHOOL

I like school very much because we have nice lessons. I
like painting and sowing best of all I am making a night-
gound. Today I have been doing sums. I do mony[1] sums
in this class. Then we do righting and then we have play
and then we do some more lessons. In our room there is a
blackbord and cubbords and desks and inkwells and there
is pictures on the wall. Miss....is the Headmisstreses name
and miss....is the name of my teachers name. She is a
very kind teacher friday if we been good our teacher
tells us a story.

Age 10-.

SCHOOL.

We go to school to learn. The lessons are sums,
Dictation, spelling, and drawing and there are teachers to
teach us. We do arithmetic every morning. On Tuesday
we do histry and on friday (half)[2] afternoon we do drawing.
In some schools, there are three halls one for the boys and
girls and infants. I go to the....school I am in Class 5

---

[1] Money   [2] The first syllable of "afternoon" misspelt and erased.

standard 4. At playtime we go out into the playground to play but when it rains we stay in. When it snows we can go sliding, because there is a tap in the playground and the water frezes. The school I go to is a very big biulding it has very near a thousand children I like arithmetic very much and it is my faverit lesson. We are learning a very interresting piece of poetry which is called The (s) Spanish armada, it tells us about Drake and about a fight at sea

Age 11-.

COMPOSITION.

SCHOOL.

School is a good place for boys and girls to go to. Generaly they go every morning and afternoon to learn History and Gography and do arithmetic and a lot of other things. It is a good thing that we have schools, because if we did not have them we could not go out to work because we could not read or write. There are seven classes in our school and the headmasters' room. The boys have got a big playground so have the girls, but the infants have got the smallest playground. We come to school every morning when the bells rings After we had our names called we start work. Every morning we have scripture. After scripture is over we have Arithmetic. We go Swimming at a quarter past two on every Wensday, most boys in our class can swim. It teaches us to try and save lives if we can swim. Another lesson I like is Drill because it strenthens your body. Sometimes we practice Fire drill which sometimes is nessesary. Prizes are given for best work.

Age 12-.

" SCHOOL."

I am now going to tell you about school. We have to go to school every day until we are fourteen, then we go out to earn our own living. I am nearly thirteen now and I shall soon be leaving school. I shall be sorry as I am very fond of school.

I think school is very useful for girls because if we learn all our work well it helps us with our education. Our school has a very good name and we ought to be proud of it.

We have very interesting lessons, but I think the chief lesson I like best of all is history because it tells us about the kind of things we had in olden days.

When children first start school they go to a part

what we call the infants, there they have rocking horses and beads to thread on string. Soon they are put in another class and then when they have learnt enough they go into the Big Girls and in the Big Boys if it is a boy. We go to school at 9 a clock and come home at twelve for our dinner, and go back again at 2 and then go home to tea at half past four. Each teacher has a class and every year we go up into a higher class. On Tuesday our headmistress takes us for litrature.

Age 13-.

COMPOSITION ON SCHOOL.

Schools are big buildings all over London where we are taught to learn special subjects which we will want to know about in after life. Our parents pay taxes, out of which they help to pay for us to go to school.

At school there are two or three divisions. 1) The Girls 2) The Infants 3) The Boys. At our school we have nine classes with teachers. There are different kinds of schools, such as Private Schools, secondry Schools, and Council Schools. In some countries there are no schools and the poor people grow up ignorant.

A child can get in school at five years of age and leave at fourteen but this will soon be altered. When you are fourteen if you have been good at your work and attendance, the headmaster gives you a good reference. Some boys go in for schollarships, if they win they go to a higher school. If they nearly win they go to a central school where they stay till they are sixteen.

There are different sorts of lessons, Grammar, Composition, Science, Drill, Drawing, Arithmetic, and English.

I have read many different books at school such as "John Halifax, Gentleman." "Westward Hoe!" "Robinson Crusoe," and "History Books." "John Halifax," describes the life of a poor, friendless boy till manhood.

My favourite subjects are :—science and crayon or pastal drawing.

On the whole schools are very useful places.

Age 14-.

ESSAY ON "SCHOOL."

A school is a large building with many rooms in it ; they are built for children to be educated. There are usually three stories ; the "infants" on the bottom floor, the "girls" next and the boys up the top.

King Alfred the Great first invented schools and the first one was built in his time. In the present day children can go free but in Alfred's time only the Lords and Barons sons and daughters could go because the poorer class of people could not aford to send their children to school.

Another reason why we are sent to school is, that if we leave we may be able to go out to work and get on in the world when we are older. It is also a good thing to have school because it keeps some children out of the streets.

There are different kinds of schools for instant L.C.C. Schools, Central Schools, Colleges, etr. In College the boy's sleep there. There sleeping place is called a dormitry. And they have studies four boys to one study. Only rich men's sons go to College. There are also night classes of an evening where older children go, some learn typewriting and some learn Shorthand and "french."

We have arithmetic which is very useful when we go out to business. We have painting and drawing which is very useful for any one who wants to go in for that sort of work. Some boys go in for Sports which I think is very good exercise.

Thus I think School is the most important training a person can possibly have, it is also the happiest time of life.

APPENDIX III.

TABLES OF NORMS FOR THE VARIOUS SCHOLASTIC TESTS.

TABLE XXXIX.

Test 1.—GRADED READING TEST (Accuracy).
Vocabulary Test.
Number of Words Correctly Read.

Age.	Boys.		Girls.		Mental Defectives.		Borderline.
	Average.	Standard Deviation.	Average.	Standard Deviation.	Average	Standard Deviation.	
5—	15·1	7·3	13·2	5·4	—	—	—
6—	23·2	12·1	25·3	10·3	2·0	1·8	5
7—	33·4	15·3	38·9	17·8	3·8	2·1	11
8—	42·8	13·1	49·1	16·1	6·7	4·5	18
9—	54·3	15·0	58·7	14·2	11·0	6·1	23
10—	64·5	14·2	66·7	13·5	19·2	8·3	35
11—	73·6	13·7	76·0	12·0	25·3	9·5	42
12—	82·5	12·6	86·3	10·1	28·4	12·1	51
13—	91·4	12·3	96·8	14·2	31·3	11·4	58
14—	[101·6]	[9·9]	[103·4]	[11·3]	34·3	11·9	70

TABLE XL.

Test 3.—DISCONTINUOUS UNGRADED READING TEST (Accuracy).
Two- and Three-Letter Monosyllables.

Number of Words Correctly Read (Without Time Limit).

Age.		Mental Defectives.		Borderline.
		Average.	Standard Deviation.	
6—	..	[0·6]	2·8	13
7—	..	2·3	6·2	30
8—	..	8·2	12·4	65
9—	..	21·4	19·0	106
10—	..	52·8	24·1	134
11—	..	93·6	30·9	168
12—	..	124·8	28·8	183
13—	..	161·7	34·3	190
14—	..	183·9	29·7	194

TABLE XLI.

Test 3.—DISCONTINUOUS UNGRADED READING TEST (Speed).

Two- and Three-Letter Monosyllables.

Number of Words Correctly Read in One Minute.

Age.	BOYS.		GIRLS.		MENTAL DEFECTIVES.		Borderline.
	Average.	Standard Deviation.	Average.	Standard Deviation.	Average.	Standard Deviation.	
6—	22·2	18·6	25·6	15·5	[0·0]	[0·6]	[2]
7—	52·4	22·1	57·3	24·2	[1·1]	[1·6]	[8]
8—	65·0	15·4	71·1	18·5	[4·0]	[3·8]	17
9—	82·5	21·4	86·3	15·3	12·3	5·7	26
10—	100·8	19·5	103·5	17·4	18·8	9·1	33
11—	108·7	13·8	112·8	13·0	25·7	10·8	41
12—	119·5	14·3	123·4	11·7	31·9	13·9	50
13—	123·6	9·9	128·9	12·6	35·6	11·2	58
14—	127·3	8·2	130·7	11·3	38·5	12·3	64

TABLE XLII.

Test 4.—READING : (DIRECTIONS TEST : Individual Examination).

Comprehension.

Number of Directions Rightly Performed.

Age.	BOYS.		GIRLS.		MENTAL DEFECTIVES.		Borderline.
	Average.	Standard Deviation.	Average.	Standard Deviation.	Average.	Standard Deviation.	
5—	0·8	1·1	0·5	0·8	—	—	—
6—	3·9	2·2	3·2	1·9	—	—	—
7—	9·4	3·8	9·0	4·3	[0·0]	[0·3]	1
8—	12·1	3·1	12·4	3·4	0·3	[0·4]	2
9—	[13·2]	[2·3]	[13·9]	[1·9]	0·8	0·6	3
10—	[14·8]	[1·5]	[15·1]	[1·2]	1·4	0·9	4·5
11—	[15·7]	[1·1]	[15·5]	[1·0]	2·5	1·3	7
12—	[15·9]	[1·2]	[15·8]	[1·3]	3·9	1·8	9
13—	[16·2]	[1·1]	[16·3]	[1·3]	4·9	2·2	11
14—	[16·4]	[1·4]	[16·1]	[1·2]	5·6	1·9	12

TABLE XLIII.

Test 5.—READING (CONTINUOUS PROSE).

Speed.

Time in Minutes and Seconds.

Age.			Boys.		Girls.	
			Average.	Standard Deviation.	Average.	Standard Deviation.
7—	..	..	[4' 24·3″]	[141·3″]	[4' 12·2″]	[124·9″]
8—	..	..	2' 55·6″	81·7″	2' 43·5″	67·8″
9—	..	..	2' 1·4″	60·2	1' 54·7″	52·6″
10—	..	..	1' 31·5″	31·3	1' 26·4″	35·0″
11—	..	..	1' 18·2″	16·3″	1' 16·4″	20·5″
12—	..	..	1' 11·4″	4·6″	1' 12·3″	4·4″
13—	..	..	1' 7·6″	3·8″	1' 8·8″	3·4″
14—	..	..	1' 5·7″	1·9″	1' 4·3″	2·1″

TABLE XLIV.

Test 5.—READING (CONTINUOUS PROSE).

Accuracy.

Number of Errors.

Age.			Boys.		Girls.	
			Average.	Standard Deviation.	Average.	Standard Deviation.
7—	..	..	[24·5]	[18·2]	[23·4]	[21·3]
8—	..	..	15·9	15·1	14·7	12·2
9—	..	..	9·6	8·2	8·1	10·0
10—	..	..	3·1	4·6	2·3	4·3
11—	..	..	2·1	2·5	1·9	3·1
12—	..	..	1·6	1·3	1·4	1·1
13—	..	..	0·8	0·8	0·7	0·5
14—	..	..	0·4	0·6	0·2	0·6

TABLE XLV.

Test 5.—READING (CONTINUOUS PROSE).

Comprehension.

Number of Questions Correctly Answered.

Age.	Boys.		Girls	
	Average.	Standard Deviation.	Average.	Standard Deviation.
7—	[4·1]	[2·0]	[4·4]	[1·9]
8—	7·9	1·5	7·8	2·1
9—	9·4	1·6	9·8	2·5
10—	11·9	2·1	12·2	2·4
11—	12·6	3·2	13·1	2·6
12—	13·8	3·1	14·2	3·0
13—	14·8	2·6	15·5	2·5
14—	15·7	3·1	16·0	2·6

TABLE XLVI.

Test 6.—SPELLING.

Number of Correct Words.

Age.	Boys.		Girls.		Mental Defectives.		Borderline.
	Average.	Standard Deviation.	Average.	Standard Deviation.	Average	Standard Deviation.	
6—	16·7	5·1	14·2	4·3	0·0	0·0	0
7—	26·5	6·4	26·9	6·5	0·2	1·3	1
8—	35·6	8·6	35·8	6·9	2·1	2·1	6
9—	44·7	8·0	46·2	7·3	4·2	3·2	15
10—	52·3	9·8	58·4	10·3	7·9	6·4	22
11—	61·2	11·5	69·0	9·7	12·3	7·6	29
12—	73·0	12·4	77·2	10·6	15·9	5·9	34
13—	80·6	11·3	86·9	12·2	19·7	7·1	37
14—	91·8	8·7	93·2	10·4	21·8	6·2	39

TABLE XLVII.

Test 7.—DICTATION.

Number of Correct Letters.

Age.	Boys.		Girls.		Mental Defectives.		Borderline.
	Average	Standard Deviation.	Average.	Standard Deviation.	Average.	Standard Deviation.	
6—	68·6	50·9	63·6	46·8	0·0	0·0	0
7—	131·8	52·7	134·3	48·5	0·7	2·1	6
8—	216·3	73·3	227·4	65·2	7·3	6·3	23
9—	309·0	63·5	313·5	82·4	19·5	13·2	52
10—	362·5	58·6	364·2	51·6	28·3	16·2	70
11—	397·4	45·2	405·2	39·1	42·5	15·4	115
12—	440·9	32·8	451·7	40·7	51·2	21·6	121
13—	467·7	47·2	476·1	29·1	61·8	26·2	141
14—	478·1	31·3	482·9	34·4	72·3	27·5	164

TABLE XLVIII.

Test 8.—ARITHMETIC (Oral Test).

Number of Sums Correctly Answered.

Age.	Boys.		Girls.		Mental Defectives.		Borderline.
	Average.	Standard Deviation.	Average.	Standard Deviation.	Average.	Standard Deviation.	
4—	3·8	6·2	4·1	5·7	—	—	—
5—	14·3	8·5	15·0	7·3	—	—	—
6—	25·2	9·2	24·8	8·9	1·3	3·6	7
7—	34·8	10·5	35·2	9·6	4·9	4·5	11
8—	46·6	10·6	44·3	11·3	9·8	8·3	16
9—	56·5	11·4	35·4	11·9	13·2	11·7	23
10—	67·7	12·1	64·6	13·2	18·5	16·4	31
11—	75·3	10·3	72·9	9·1	24·2	18·2	40
12—	86·4	9·6	83·7	9·8	30·6	20·3	48
13—	94·2	11·2	93·5	10·7	34·8	17·3	55
14—	103·2	8·3	102·8	11·1	38·3	18·8	60

TABLE XLIX.

Test 9.—ARITHMETIC (Written Test).

Mechanical.

Number of Sums Correctly Answered.

Age.	BOYS.		GIRLS		MENTAL DEFECTIVES.		Borderline.
	Average.	Standard Deviation.	Average.	Standard Deviation.	Average.	Standard Deviation.	
7—	2·7	4·1	2·9	3·8	[0·0]	[0]	[0]
8—	7·3	5·3	7·6	5·0	[0·0]	[0]	[0]
9—	12·5	5·1	12·1	4·9	[0·1]	[0·4]	[1]
10—	18·1	5·8	17·3	5·3	0·4	0·8	4
11—	73·0	4·3	20·6	4·6	1·8	0·9	6
12—	26·4	4·8	24·2	4·1	2·8	1·4	10
13—	30·5	4·5	28·4	5·3	4·2	2·7	13
14—	33·8	3·9	29·3	5·9	5·3	2·6	14

TABLE L.

Test 10.—ARITHMETIC (Written Test).

Problems.

Number of Sums Correctly Answered.

Age.	BOYS.		GIRLS.		MENTAL DEFECTIVES.		Borderline.
	Average.	Standard Deviation.	Average.	Standard Deviation.	Average.	Standard Deviation.	
7—	2·5	3·9	2·8	4·1	[0·0]	[0]	[0]
8—	8·6	5·1	7·4	4·7	[0·0]	[0]	[0]
9—	13·9	5·4	11·5	5·3	[0·0]	[0·4]	1
10—	17·8	6·2	15·4	8·0	[0·2]	[1·3]	3
11—	24·3	5·1	19·7	6·7	1·1	2·5	7
12—	29·7	4·8	24·1	5·6	2·6	3·4	9
13—	32·8	5·6	28·8	6·2	4·4	3·1	11
14—	34·5	4·2	30·0	5·9	5·0	3·2	12

TABLE LI.

ARITHMETIC. (Four Fundamental Rules.)

Test 11.—(i.) Addition.

Number of Correct Figures in Answers ("Hundreds" counting as part of "Tens").

Age.	Boys.		Girls.		Mental Defectives.		Borderline.
	Average.	Standard Deviation.	Average.	Standard Deviation.	Average.	Standard Deviation.	
6—	6·9	2·2	6·7	2·5	0·0	0·2	0
7—	9·7	3·0	9·5	3·6	0·0	0·4	0
8—	13·8	5·2	14·4	8·0	0·7	0·8	2
9—	17·8	8·1	17·6	6·3	1·8	1·1	3
10—	21·4	8·5	22·5	7·3	3·9	2·3	8
11—	24·7	9·8	27·4	9·4	6·5	3·5	12
12—	29·6	11·2	32·2	9·7	9·2	6·2	17
13—	32·5	9·3	30·8	13·1	13·4	5·7	22
14—	33·6	10·1	31·9	15·2	16·5	6·7	29

TABLE LII.

ARITHMETIC. (Four Fundamental Rules.)

Test 12.—(ii.) Subtraction.

Number of Correct Figures in Answers.

Age.	Boys.		Girls.		Mental Defectives.		Borderline.
	Average.	Standard Deviation.	Average.	Standard Deviation.	Average.	Standard Deviation.	
6—	7·2	4·8	7·5	3·0	0·0	0·0	0
7—	18·7	7·2	18·3	11·2	0·0	0·3	0
8—	28·3	13·2	27·0	13·6	0·4	1·2	3
9—	34·7	16·3	34·8	18·4	1·3	2·3	4
10—	43·8	20·4	42·4	19·2	4·9	5·7	9
11—	50·2	26·6	48·3	21·7	7·7	6·2	16
12—	56·0	19·8	54·8	22·8	11·1	7·8	27
13—	61·7	22·6	59·9	24·8	17·3	6·9	33
14—	68·5	24·2	64·7	26·1	20·1	8·3	39

TABLE LIII.

ARITHMETIC. (Four Fundamental Rules.)

Test 13.—(iii.) Multiplication.

Number of Correct Figures in Answers (" Ten Thousands " counting as part of " Thousands ").

Age.	BOYS.		GIRLS.		MENTAL DEFECTIVES.		
	Average.	Standard Deviation.	Average.	Standard Deviation.	Average.	Standard Deviation.	Borderline.
6—	5·6	2·9	5·8	2·1	0·0	0·0	0
7—	14·1	6·5	14·5	7·4	0·0	0·0	0
8—	25·9	9·6	26·8	13·7	0·0	0·5	2
9—	32·8	15·7	33·2	17·6	1·6	1·1	3
10—	43·9	25·1	44·1	18·0	2·8	2·6	8
11—	50·2	24·3	48·4	20·5	4·7	3·2	14
12—	56·3	19·4	57·1	26·7	8·7	6·3	24
13—	66·1	21·0	65·4	25·2	14·4	7·1	35
14—	71·5	22·8	73·0	26·3	19·6	8·4	43

TABLE LIV.

ARITHMETIC. (Four Fundamental Rules.)

Test 14.—(iv.) Division.

Number of Correct Figures in Answers.

Age.	BOYS.		GIRLS.		MENTAL DEFECTIVES.		
	Average.	Standard Deviation.	Average.	Standard Deviation.	Average.	Standard Deviation.	Borderline.
6—	0·0	0·0	0·0	0·0	0·0	0·0	0
7—	5·1	6·1	5·3	6·8	0·0	0·0	0
8—	15·2	11·3	14·7	9·6	0·0	0·0	0
9—	19·1	15·2	18·7	13·3	0·0	0·2	1
10—	28·3	19·0	27·2	16·1	0·4	0·6	4
11—	34·2	23·1	31·1	22·3	1·0	1·3	6
12—	38·7	18·3	38·2	20·1	1·9	2·4	10
13—	45·4	19·8	44·6	21·7	3·1	3·7	13
14—	53·3	16·9	53·5	24·4	4·4	4·6	18

TABLE LV.

Test 15.—WRITING (Speed).

Number of Letters Written in Two Minutes.

Age.	Boys.		Girls.		Mental Defectives.		Borderline.
	Average.	Standard Deviation.	Average.	Standard Deviation.	Average.	Standard Deviation.	
6—	20·7	15·6	19·9	18·6	[3·2]	[4·8]	8
7—	43·7	22·8	52·3	26·7	7·9	6·1	8
8—	72·4	28·8	81·1	24·3	12·5	12·3	19
9—	100·6	40·9	109·4	38·2	27·9	20·4	41
10—	128·0	39·0	141·7	37·7	38·1	33·5	60
11—	150·1	38·3	166·2	35·0	48·2	32·5	84
12—	171·8	41·8	179·9	54·3	61·7	38·7	110
13—	183·7	52·4	185·4	58·2	76·8	43·6	135
14—	184·2	45·6	191·2	61·7	81·2	32·8	160

TABLE LVI.

Test 16.—WRITING (Quality).

Expressed in Terms of Mental Age.

Age.	Boys.		Girls.		Mental Defectives.		Borderline
	Average.	Standard Deviation.	Average.	Standard Deviation.	Average.	Standard Deviation.	
5—	5·4	0·8	5·6	0·9	—	—	—
6—	6·4	0·9	6·7	0·7	[4·8]	[1·0]	5·9
7—	7·5	0·8	7·6	1·1	[4·8]	[1·9]	6·8
8—	8·5	1·0	8·5	0·9	5·4	1·6	7·5
9—	9·4	1·2	9·6	1·2	6·2	1·3	8·6
10—	10·3	1·3	10·6	1·2	6·9	1·5	9·4
11—	11·3	1·1	11·7	0·9	7·5	1·5	10·2
12—	12·2	1·2	12·6	1·1	8·1	1·8	11·2
13—	13·2	1·1	13·5	1·4	8·6	1·7	11·6
14—	14·1	0·9	14·6	1·0	8·9	1·2	12·4

G*

TABLE LVII.

Test 17.—DRAWING (Quality).

Expressed in Terms of Mental Age.

Age.	Boys.		Girls.		Mental Defectives.		Borderline.
	Average.	Standard Deviation.	Average.	Standard Deviation.	Average.	Standard Deviation.	
5—	5·4	1·0	5·6	0·8	—	—	—
6—	6·5	0·9	6·4	0·7	4·3	0·9	6·0
7—	7·4	1·0	7·5	0·8	4·9	1·9	1·5
8—	8·6	1·1	8·4	0·9	5·4	1·8	7·4
9—	9·7	1·2	9·2	1·1	6·2	1·2	8·3
10—	10·7	1·4	10·3	1·3	6·8	1·5	9·2
11—	11·6	1·1	11·4	1·2	7·6	1·9	10·3
12—	12·7	1·3	12·1	1·4	8·3	2·4	11·2
13—	13·4	1·4	13·5	1·3	8·9	2·2	11·8
14—	14·1	1·2	14·6	1·5	9·3	2·0	12·5

TABLES LVIII.

Test 18.—HANDWORK (Speed).

Time Taken in Seconds to Reproduce Models of Twelve Pieces.

Age.	Boys.		Girls.		Mental Defectives.		Borderline.
	Average.	Standard Deviation.	Average.	Standard Deviation.	Average.	Standard Deviation.	
6—	113	63	106	78	—	—	—
7—	77	47	79	51	176	41	103
8—	62	31	61	36	125	32	71
9—	51	28	56	29	101	28	62
10—	46	29	48	32	85	23	55
11—	42	27	44	24	66	18	39
12—	38	21	41	28	57	21	44
13—	31	25	34	23	53	16	45
14—	32	19	33	26	49	14	32

TABLE LIX.

Test 19.—HANDWORK (Quality).

Quality of Original Product Graded in Terms of Equivalent Mental Age of Normals.

Age.	Boys.		Girls.		Mental Defectives,		Borderline.
	Average.	Standard Deviation.	Average.	Standard Deviation.	Average.	Standard Deviation.	
6—	6·6	0·9	6·3	0·8	—	—	—
7—	7·5	0·9	7·4	0·9	4·3	2·1	6·0
8—	8·8	1·1	8·3	1·0	5·3	1·7	7·0
9—	9·8	1·2	9·1	1·3	6·4	1·3	7·7
10—	10·9	1·4	10·2	1·6	7·6	1·7	8·8
11—	12·3	1·5	11·6	1·3	9·0	1·8	10·4
12—	13·1	1·3	12·0	1·5	9·9	2·3	11·5
13—	14·4	1·5	12·8	1·6	10·3	2·1	12·0
14—	14·2	1·3	13·8	1·5	10·1	1·7	12·5

TABLE LX.

Test 20.—COMPOSITION (Speed).

Essay on "School".

Number of Words Written in Half an Hour.

Age.	Boys.		Girls.		Mental Defectives.		Borderline.
	Average.	Standard Deviation.	Average.	Standard Deviation.	Average.	Standard Deviation.	
7—	21·2	19·3	27·2	26·1	—	—	—
8—	61·8	27·7	76·5	30·8	—	—	—
9—	99·4	44·6	104·6	52·0	—	—	—
10—	137·3	56·3	152·6	63·5	[2·5]	3·2	6
11—	156·8	48·2	184·7	59·7	[4·3]	5·1	16
12—	192·6	52·4	213·3	64·7	12·6	14·6	48
13—	216·1	65·8	239·2	68·9	18·3	16·0	63
14—	231·7	59·1	262·4	66·5	25·1	20·5	77

TABLE LXI.

Test 20.—COMPOSITION. (Quality)

Essay on "School."

Quality in Terms of Equivalent Mental Age.

Age.	Boys.		Girls.		Mental Defectives.		Borderline.
	Average.	Standard Deviation.	Average.	Standard Deviation.	Average.	Standard Deviation.	
7—	7·3	1·2	7·8	1·3	—	—	—
8—	8·3	0·9	8·6	1·1	—	—·	—
9—	9·2	1·0	9·7	1·3	—	—	—
10—	10·1	1·3	11·0	1·6	—	—	—
11—	11·1	1·3	11·8	1·4	[6·0]	1·7	6·9
12—	12·0	1·5	13·1	1·7	6·7	2·0	7·5
13—	12·7	1·6	14·2	1·8	7·4	2·2	8·1
14—	13·9	1·5	14·8	1·5	6·9	1·9	8·5

TABLE LXII.

Test 20.—COMPOSITION (Length of Sentences).

Essay on "School."

Average Number of Words per Sentence.

Age.	Boys.		Girls.		Mental Defectives.		Borderline.
	Average.	Standard Deviation.	Average.	Standard Deviation.	Average.	Standard Deviation.	
7—	5·7	1·6	7·3	2·3	—	—	—
8—	7·8	2·4	9·1	2·6	—	—	—
9—	11·3	1·9	11·5	2·3	—	—	—
10—	13·3	2·7	13·3	1·8	5·3	1·3	8
11—	14·1	1·8	14·6	1·7	6·1	1·5	9
12—	14·9	2·0	15·4	1·9	7·0	1·8	11
13—	15·7	1·6	15·9	2·1	7·8	1·9	12
14—	16·2	1·7	16·9	2·4	8·4	1·6	13

APPENDIX IV.

Age as a Unit of Measurement.

In the preceding tables and throughout this work, not only the Binet tests for measuring intelligence, but also the scholastic tests for measuring attainments have been standardized in terms of an age-scale. A few words are therefore necessary to state how far, and for what purposes, this particular device is justifiable.[1]

The Determination of Mental Age. The basic principles proposed in this volume for determining mental ages, particularly the method suggested for assigning the several test-problems to their appropriate years (p. 140) have found fairly wide acceptance. To rely *solely* on the 50 per cent. rule proposed in the text would have certain disadvantages : it would yield mental ages that are a little too high at the earlier levels and a little too low in the higher levels. Towards the ends of the total age-range, therefore, slight adjustments have to be introduced, along the lines described below, by taking into account the percentages of passes at other ages. The best practical method is to determine the difficulty of each test in terms of an equivalent age by a procedure such as that described on p. 150.

Defects of Mental Age as a Unit of Measurement. In this volume, as in earlier papers,[2] I have criticized the limitations of " mental age " as a unit of measurement, and suggested an alternative method. Further evidence appears to confirm the conclusions then expressed : namely (i) for research purposes the standard deviation of an unselected (*i.e.*, a genuinely random) sample of a standard population, itself carefully defined, provides the best unit : in the case of children this will mean a complete age-group or a representative sample of such an age-group ; (ii) on the other hand, for rough practical purposes a mental age (or, up to puberty, a mental ratio) provides a unit which, in spite of its imperfections, is at once useful and intelligible ; it is readily understood by teachers and others, and further is specially convenient where, as in school organization, the classification goes largely by age or maturity. This double view (howbeit with a varying emphasis, on the relative disadvantages of one method or the other) has since been endorsed by many different writers. And what I have called " standard measure " (often termed by other writers the sigma-score, the z-score, or the T-score)

---

(1) The original report dealt with this problem at some length ; but it has been largely re-written in order to take into account more recent criticisms and suggestions. In particular, my proposal to determine the age-assignment of the tests, not by Binet's principles, but by analogy with the use of a formal psychophysical method for determining sensory thresholds, has called forth both criticisms and requests for the fuller explanation.

(2) " The Measurement of Intelligence by the Binet Tests," *Eugenics Review*, VI., 1914, pp. 36-50, 140-152.

has, with minor modifications, met with increasing acceptance for research purposes. Thus McCall's well-known T-scale (*How to Measure in Education*, 1922) takes one-tenth the standard deviation of 12-year-olds as the fundamental unit. For English children 12 is not a good age to choose, since so many have by that age been removed to central and secondary schools : my own preference was to take the S.D. of the 10-year-olds, when a standard age-group was desirable.

A few writers, however, have been more emphatic in their criticisms. Thurstone, for example, suggests that we should " discard the awkward mental age concept," and the I.Q. along with it, and urges that " percentile standing should be used instead,"[1] though he admits that " for many studies it might be preferable to use the sigma standing." The use of percentiles has of late come into more frequent use ; but I should prefer to regard the S.D. scale as basic, and the percentile rating as secondary (though in many cases, especially where the distribution is skewed, the former would have to be deduced from the latter).[2] Both in this book and in the previous volume (*Distribution of Educational Abilities*, 1917, pp. 32f. and 49f.) the use of an S.D. scale, defined when necessary by percentiles, has been fully illustrated.[3]

The Metrical Problems. Before constructing an age-scale, like that formed by the Binet tests, we have to reach a decision in regard to two essential questions of procedure. First, how are we to measure the difficulty of the tests in years ? Secondly, how are we to measure the ability of the child in years ? Now, as I have noted above, with tests (like most of those in the Binet scale) where there are only two types of answer—right or wrong—the problem of procedure is essentially the same as that involved in measuring a sensory threshold by such devices as the " limiting method " or the " method of right and wrong cases."

Let us recall the problem as it appears in the ordinary text-book when dealing with the estimation of sensory acuity. Two compass-points are placed simultaneously on the skin of the arm : at three inches they can easily be distinguished as two ; then the task is made harder and harder by diminishing the distance between the points, until the examinee eventually fails. If his breakdown is sudden and complete, then his discriminative ability will be measured by some figure between the narrowest interval that he *can* discriminate and the next interval which will be the broadest interval that he *cannot* discriminate. But if there are irregular recoveries, then the problem becomes more complicated, and some plausible convention has to be devised for deducing the most appropriate measure.

---

[1] " The Mental Age Concept," *J. Educ. Psych.*, XXXIII., 1926, p. 277. (A more recent discussion of special interest is to be found in M. W. Richardson, " The Logic of Age Scales," *Educ. Psych. Meas.*, I., 1941, pp. 25-34 : the criticisms, however, appear to rest on somewhat dubious assumptions.)

[2] Pintner has also expressed the same preference of standard measure to percentiles (*Intelligence Testing*, 1924, p. 80) ; Terman and Merrill (*Measuring Intelligence*, p. 27-28) adopt the same view as to the relative merits of standard measure and mental ages.

[3] To avoid minus signs I suggested adding 5 to the marks in standard measure ; to avoid decimals one can then multiply either by 2 or by 10 : the former gives a scale with 10 as mean and 2 as S.D. (analogous to the school teacher's common scale with 20 as a maximum) ; the latter, a scale with 50 as mean and 10 as S.D. (analogous to the University examiner's common scale with 100 as a maximum. Cf. *Distribution of Abilities*, p. 49 ; *Backward Child*, p. 26) ; doubling the latter gives a scale analogous to the I.Q. scale. Note, however, that if a normal distribution is desired, the standardized marks should be derived from the percentiles, not by dividing the mark obtained by the S.D. [It may be added that the unit now called the " probit " is obtained in much the same way : the " probit " of a proportion or percentage is the corresponding unit normal deviate increased by 5 (Bliss, C. I., " Method of Probits," *Science*, LXXIX., 1934, pp. 38-39).]

To the ordinary reader the following example will be more familiar. **We**
desire to measure a child's athletic ability by a high jump. A horizontal **bar**
is placed at successive heights ; and the greatest height successfully cleared
is then taken as indicating the child's ability, provided he fails to clear any
height that is greater still. If he happens to succeed with some of these
harder trials, then once again some convention must be prescribed : we may,
for example (much as Binet does with his memory and weight tests), enjoin
a certain number of repetitions with the *same* tasks (*e.g.*, a bar placed repeatedly at the same heights), and demand a certain percentage of successes.

The Binet problem presents one important difference from that encountered in the ordinary psychophysical test. With most of the Binet tests there
is no independent measure to indicate the increasing difficulty of the task.
It is as if we were working in the dark, and could not see to measure the
heights of the bar or even observe whether each position was really higher
than the last. In such a case we might attempt to assess the objective
difficulty of clearance by trying the various positions again and again with
groups of different stature or age, and noting what proportion in each group
successfully cleared the bar at each position.

What conventional procedures or " processes " (as they are technically
termed) can be suggested for our present purpose ? Where we are dealing
with the measurement of sensory acuity, we have already to hand a number
of accredited techniques devised by a succession of psychological investigators, and we can choose the most convenient according to the degree of
exactitude we require. Now, almost any of these can be adopted, with or
without some minor modification, for the metrical problems encountered
in constructing test-scales for higher mental processes. Thus to measure
the ability of the child, we may adopt some version of the limiting method
(" serial exploration by minimal changes ") ; and to measure the difficulty
of the tests, we may use some version of the method of right and wrong cases
(" constant method ").

It is the latter problem that presents the greatest novelty. Here we have
to measure the acuity of the test, not of the testee ; and the changing
" stimuli " that we use to elicit a " response " from the test are (paradoxically
enough) the children of different chronological ages. Thus the usual form of
the psychophysical problem is inverted. Moreover, just as equal differences
between heavier weights are harder to discriminate (in virtue of Weber's law),
so equal differences between successive years are hard for the tests to discriminate at the older ages. Consequently, the scale of chronological ages
cannot, except for rough purposes, be accepted as constituting an objective
or " absolute " scale just as it stands.

Measuring the Difficulty of Tests by Exact Age Assignments. Let us consider
an imaginary test applied to children of all ages, from birth onwards ; and
let us express the proportion of failures or successes at each age by decimal
fractions instead of percentages. We can regard these proportions as speci-
fying the requisite " psychometric function." Thus, suppose the following
relevant results have been obtained (Table LXIII.)

TABLE LXIII.

Calculation of Difficulty of a Test in terms of Mental Age.

Age	Failures	Successes	Frequency Distribution (f)	Age (x)	fx
$\frac{1}{2}$	1·00	0·00			
$1\frac{1}{2}$	1·00	0·00	·20	2	·40
$2\frac{1}{2}$	0·80	0·20	·30	3	·90
$3\frac{1}{2}$	0·50	0·50	·30	4	1·20
$4\frac{1}{2}$	0·20	0·80	·20	5	1·00
$5\frac{1}{2}$	0·00	1·00			
Total	3·50	2·50	1·00		3·50

Since (as we see from column 3) 50 per cent. pass at the age of 3 to 4, we might at once conclude that $3\frac{1}{2}$ represents the median age, and treat this age as expressing the difficulty of a test in terms of the age-scale. But with a more irregular distribution we should need to take into account the figures obtained at all ages. We should then draw up a non-cumulative frequency distribution (column 4), and work out the average in the familiar way[1] (see last two columns) : but time is saved if we use Hardy's summation method,[2] and simply add the number of failures as shown in column 2 (headed " failures ") : this at once gives 3·50 as the average mental age. Actually the cumulative percentages most frequently tabulated are those giving, not failures but successes (column 3) : these correspond to a row of the observed percentages set out in Table III. of the second memorandum (pp. 144-5). We can use these just as readily. We have simply to subtract the total determined from this series (2·5) from the borderline-age marking the termination of the series (6·0) ; we then obtain the same average age for the test as before : $6·0 - 2·5 = 3·5$.

Thus take tests 22 and 29 from the Binet-Simon scale (" Diamond " and " Picture Description "). From Table III. we see that both these tests are passed at age $5\frac{1}{2}$ by almost exactly half the children (49·8 per cent.). Calculated as above, the average age-level, however, is 5·63 years for test 22 and 5·84 years for test 29. This method of determining difficulty, it will be seen, is equivalent to taking the total or average percentage of passes or

---

(¹) This might be regarded as a further extension to the Binet scale problem of Spearman's proposed extension of the ordinary method to the problem of sensory thresholds : (Spearman, " Method of Right and Wrong Cases without Gauss's Formulæ," *Brit. J. Psych.*, II., 1908, pp. 227f.).

(²) The method of cumulative summation was first applied to the calculation of " moments " (mean, s.d., etc.) by Sir G. Hardy : it is described and illustrated in Palin Elderton, *Frequency Curves and Correlation*, 1906, pp. 19f. [It is a little puzzling to find Guilford stating that with this method " the probable errors are determined with great difficulty " (*Psychometric Methods*, p. 209,) since the cumulative method can be adapted quite as easily for the standard deviation as for the mean.]

failures as forming a linear scale of difficulty-values.[1] (The standard deviations can be computed according to the same principles : these, it will be found, increase with increasing age; thus " 2 Weights " has an S.D. of 1·40, and " 5 Weights " one of 2·45 : but, after allowing for this increase, the best test will generally be that which has the smallest standard deviation.)

Accordingly, without making any assumptions as to age-equivalents, we may take the total or average percentage as it stands to determine the order of difficulty of the tests. As stated in the text, this was the basis on which the new order, given in Table III, was actually drawn up (see p. 146).

The simple 50 per cent. criterion, proposed for determining the approximate age-assignment, can be justified as follows. Tests whose difficulty is measured by an age-value anywhere from over 6·00 up to 6·99··· will in theory be passed by 50 per cent. of the children having the age specified (*i.e.*, age approximately 6½). Tests whose difficulty is measured by an age-value anywhere from 7·00 up to 7·99··· will similarly be passed by 50 per cent. of the children having these higher ages (*i.e.*, age approximately 7½). Now suppose a child passes all the former group of tests and fails in all the latter. Evidently his mental age should be 7·0 exactly. Thus, if we adopt Binet's convention for naming the ages, we shall be led to allocate all the former tests to an age of VII and all the latter to an age of VIII. With the test-problems for the educational tests[2] (*e.g.*, the words for the vocabulary tests in Reading and Spelling, the sums for the tests of mechanical or problem arithmetic) the same principles were adopted ; but here Binet's convention for naming the ages was not retained. Instead, any test obtaining an average age of 6·00 to 6·99··· (for example) was given an age of " 6— " : this means " 6·00 to 6·99··· inclusive, with an average of 6½." If the distributions were symmetrical, the 50 per cent. rule would give the same figure, since the median and the average would coincide. However, as will be seen from Table III., the percentages, read horizontally, give a definitely asymmetrical curve. Hence, with the Binet tests (and occasionally with the educational problems) it was found better to locate a 50 per cent. passing point by smooth-

---

[1] Adding the percentages for the 12 age-groups in Table III. we obtain for test 22 a total of 937·3 ; or, converting percentages to decimal fractions, 9·373. The borderline marking the end of the series is the termination of the last age-group, namely, 15·0 (since the age-group containing children aged 14 last birthday extends from 14·0 to 15·0 years). The " average age at which the test is passed " (defining this to mean the age at which in theory 50 per cent. of the children would pass and 50 per cent. fail) is therefore 15·00 — 9·37 years = 5·63 years (see Table , LX.IV). Similarly for test 29, the total is 916·4, and the " average age " 15·00 — 9·16 = 5·84. Of course, for more exact determinations the percentages, or the corresponding deviates, should first be weighted, according to the principles worked out by Müller and Urban, and the " threshold " calculated by least squares (for the stock psychophysical procedure, see Guilford, *loc. cit.*, p. 177).

The method described above, however, is not applicable to tests for the earliest or latest ages without some more or less speculative device for completing the figures for the cumulative curve by extrapolation at either end. Hence, for the purpose of arranging tests in order of difficulty, it would seem best to rely solely on the percentages actually observed, and to take their total or averages. Thus for tests 22 and 29 the average percentages are (937·4 and 916·4) ÷ 12 = 78·1 and 76·4. Where the data are complete the average percentages give the same relative intervals as the average ages ; and consequently, in arranging the order of the tests, the former yields the simplest and most objective procedure.

[2] The reader familiar with my earlier reports will remember that it was in connection with these educational tests that the application of a " psychophysical method " to the present type of test was originally proposed : it was there used for selecting items, as well as for grading them. For those problems the suggestion was not only more obvious, but more plausible. In applying it to the Binet scale I expressly commented on its limitations—comments which my critics seem to have overlooked.

ing the ogive, rather than to rely exclusively on a calculated arithmetical mean.[1]

Indeed, as indicated in the footnote above, the differing variability of the differing ages, as well as the skewness of the distributions, renders these simple arguments a little untrustworthy, if we want to determine the relative difficulty of the several tests with the greatest possible accuracy. It was for this reason that, in examining the equality of the intervals between successive tests, I proposed to convert the percentages into terms of the standard deviation as unit : with this procedure we work vertically down the columns of Table III. instead of horizontally across the rows. The effect is that the data are treated as indicating a series of overlapping normal frequency-curves on the same base-line (cf. Fig. 23, p. 171). Thurstone[2] has described a modification of the same principle, leading to an " absolute scale," and has calculated from my data not only the absolute values for the means and standard deviations, but also an absolute zero. The reader will find a succinct account of the method (with results taken from my table above on p. 145) in Guilford, *Psychometric Methods*, pp. 440f.

Measuring the Ability of the Child by an Exact Age Equivalent. To determine the child's intelligence in terms of the Binet scale, the method recommended in this volume was to count up the number of tests passed by each child, and translate his score into an equivalent mental age by means of the key shown in Table II. (facing p. 19). With later versions of the scale, where there is the same number of tests for each year (usually five), each test passed counts as one-fifth of a year. Accordingly, a simpler but equivalent method is to take the highest year at which the child passes all the tests, and then add one-fifth of a year for each additional test passed.

Much the same underlying principles are adopted for converting test-scores in the educational tests to terms of an educational age. But here we usually have to do with tests where the scores may more easily be regarded as forming a continuous, graded scale. Thus, in the test for Speed of Writing, if a child writes 128 letters in two minutes, he can be given a mental age of $10\frac{1}{2}$ for this test, since that is the number of letters written by boys aged 10 last birthday (Table LV., p. 435). With tests where an equal number of problems is assigned to each age (*e.g.*, the vocabulary tests for Reading and Spelling), the conversion is effected by means of a formula, which has the superficial appearance of a simplified regression equation smoothing average performances at each successive year (pp. 299, 316). Strictly speaking, how-ever, the formula is not a regression equation, for it makes no allowance for

---

[1] It may be noted that the deviate corresponding to the 50 per cent. borderline is the deviate which can be estimated with greatest precision : it marks the point at which (in the language of current statistics) the " quantity of information " is greatest. I may add that the problem of esti-mating the difficulty of a test-item from the percentage of children passing is closely analogous to the problem of estimating the lethal strength of a drug from the percentage of animals surviving after the administration of known dosages. Hence the " probit method " recently developed by Bliss and others for purposes of toxicological research can readily be applied to problems of psychometry. The probit method may be regarded as a refinement of what psychologists know as the " constant process " : Bliss's weights (Fisher and Yates, p. 49) are virtually the Urban-Müller weights (Guilford, p. 543) tabulated for deviates instead of for percentages. The chief difference is that, in order to obtain estimates of " maximum likelihood " for the parameters, the empirical deviates are replaced first by " provisional " and then by " working " deviates (or " probits ") according to a method of successive approximation. The working procedure is clearly described by Fisher and Yates, *Statistical Tables,* pp. 8-11 ; cf. also Fisher, *Design of Experiments*, pp. 235f., Garwood, *Biometrika*, XXXII., pp. 46-58. With my own data I found that the probit method gives practically the same order of difficulty except for tests at the beginning and end of the scale. Miss Sharp, however, has used the newer method at my suggestion with data for the Terman revision, and concludes that it may introduce definite improvements where the data are few or the curve of percentages irregular, and will yield larger and more trustworthy estimates for the standard error.

[2] *J. Educ. Psych.*, XVI., 1925, pp. 433-451, and *Psych. Rev.*, XXXV., 1928, pp. 175-197 (a " growth curve," based on the present data, is there shown in Fig. 11, p. 196).

the phenomenon of regression : it is a convertible equation, like that for translating the height of a column of mercury (measured in inches) into terms of atmospheric pressure (measured in dynes per sq. cm.) or vice versa. To the psychological student, who is often more familiar with the use of regression equations, the procedure seems a little questionable : does it not imply a *perfect* correlation between test-scores and age ? Since this criticism has frequently been put to me in reference to my method of scaling the tests, a word or two seems desirable on this point. Briefly, I may say that, in my view, the question is answered by distinguishing between the purposes for which the equations are required. But a summary of the arguments used in the fuller report may usefully be repeated here.

Conversion of Test-results to Terms of Mental Age. In the preceding volume I had discussed the determination of *educational* age from chronological age, and vice versa, and gave regression equations for calculating the one from the other (l.c., p. 24). Similar problems arise with *mental* age. Thus, for certain purposes we may require either (i) to determine chronological age for which a given test-score is the average score ; or (ii) to predict or estimate the average or most probable chronological age of the individuals who make that given test-score. Now, as is well known, when the correlation between age and score is not perfect, the line showing average age for given scores is different from the line showing average score for given ages. Thus, if we know the child's chronological age and want to predict his test-score, we should use the regression of test-score on age ; if we know the child's test-score and want to estimate his probable chronological age, we should use the regression of age on test-scores.

Accordingly, the student, acquainted with these statistical maxims, inquires why, in converting test-scores to terms of age, we do not use an equation of the latter type, in order to find the most probable chronological age, that is, the average chronological age, which corresponds to any given test score. The answer in my view is that we are not seeking to predict or estimate the child's *chronological* age : that, of course, is something we know exactly without any error of measurement and without any need to predict. Our aim is to determine the child's *mental* age. In fact we are merely converting a test-performance from one set of units to another. No doubt, if we wanted to predict a Binet mental age *from some other test*, a regression equation would be appropriate. But when the child has actually done the Binet tests, his Binet mental age is merely a way of stating what he has actually done. If a youngster of 10 passes and fails in those tests in which the average 10-year-old pass and fail, then his mental age *is* 10. And similarly with the educational tests : our argument is not : "Tommy has a score of 50 tests right ; the average age of the children who get 50 tests right is so-and-so ; therefore Tommy's probable chronological age is so-and-so." It is rather : "Tommy has a score of 50 ; children aged 10½ have an average score of 50 ; therefore in mental maturity Tommy belongs to that particular class of children."[1]

---

[1] Thurstone apparently regards this argument as involving a " logical somersault," and, if forced to use a mental age, would prefer the " second and less popular definition of mental age," *viz.*, that which defines it as " the average chronological age of all children who make the test score of this particular child " : (however, as stated above, he would rather discard the " ambiguous " concept of mental age altogether : *loc. cit. sup.*, p. 273). Thomson, on the other hand, believes that " Thurstone's two definitions of mental age are practically identical," because the two regression lines virtually coincide (*J. Educ. Psych.*, XXXV., 1928, p. 413). My own reply would be a little different. Thurstone, I fancy, misstates the problem : it is not a problem of regression at all. My argument was really based on the principle followed in fitting lines for scale-conversions in other sciences : there a common method is to take the " principal axis," much as we do in factor-analysis when using the method of least squares : (cf. Yule and Greenwood, *Proc. Roy. Soc. Med.*, VIII., 1915, p. 113 Pearson also appears to accept this principle for certain cases ; cf. *Phil. Mag.*, II., pp. 559f.).

I have used the phrases " average 10-year-old" and " average score" in the broader, popular sense, as meaning the "*typical* 10-year-old " or the "*typical* score." We still have to ask, therefore, which form of measurement will give the best indication of what is typical—the median, the mode, or the arithmetical mean. Now, as I pointed out in my previous report on educational abilities, the theoretical bivariate distribution for age and ability (calculated from the theoretical normal frequency distribution in Table XXXII. of that report) is not elliptical, like the typical correlation-table, but fan-shaped. And, as I have noted again in dealing with tables which are based not on theoretical calculations, but, like Table III. above, on empirical data, the distributions along the rows and columns are apt to be markedly skewed. Admittedly, even in the theoretical distribution, the mean educational age for each chronological age, and the mean chronological age for each educational age (given in the margins of Table XXXII.), do not precisely correspond, but rather suggest two diverging lines. But the special peculiarity of such tables is that a person cannot have a chronological age that is less than zero, whereas he can have one of 70 or even higher. Similarly, he cannot have an educational age that is less than zero, but he can go on adding " school standards " or " educational years," as his knowledge accumulates up to the end of his life. Thus in either case the arithmetical mean becomes unduly shifted by the long upper tails. The same holds good of the results obtained with intelligence tests (cf. Table X. above and footnote 1, p. 162).

Accordingly, in comparing the two series of measurements, chronological on the one hand and educational on the other, it would seem better to employ not the mean but either the median or the mode. If we examine the modal ages in the table, we shall find the correspondence much closer (though even here the calculated modes would not correspond exactly). On these grounds, therefore, in seeking the most convenient approximation, it might seem better to take an equation based on modal ages rather than on means. This would be virtually equivalent to assuming an increase of one whole mental year for every chronological year, and vice versa, *i.e.*, of assuming a single conversion-line, following the highest ridge in the frequency distribution, instead of two regression-lines. For practical purposes, however, I incline to keep mainly to the median, if only because it falls between the mode and the average, and thus, when no simple measure is perfectly exact, would appear to yield the most convenient compromise.

When we turn from educational ages to mental ages (*i.e.*, intelligence-ages), the situation is not quite the same, because, while attainments go on increasing all through life, intelligence ceases to mature appreciably after the age of puberty. Nevertheless, the parallel is sufficiently close to warrant the same argument being used to defend the adoption of a mental age as ordinarily defined and assessed. But in conclusion may I repeat that I regard the mental age merely as a rough and ready concept, and I entirely agree that, however defined, it is not a unit for rigorous scientific research ?

Note on the Probit Method. Table A. below illustrates the calculation of the 50 per cent. age-threshold and its sampling error by the probit method. The notation, formulæ and general arrangement are taken from Fisher and Yates, *Statistical Tables* (pp. 8-11, esp. Table 2). Test 22 (Diamond) has been taken as an example.

The " empirical probits " are obtained from Fisher and Yates, Table X. The " provisional probits " are then found by provisionally fitting a straight line to these empirical figures, either graphically or mentally : the equation used here was $Y = 0.15 + .85x$. The " working probit " is obtained by the equation $y = (Y + Q/Z) - (1 - p)/Z$, the values for $Y + Q/Z$, Z, and w (weights, here printed to three figures only) being taken from Fisher and Yates, Table XI.

The figures obtained from the final regression equation are so close to the " provisional probits " that no further approximation is necessary. We thus conclude that the 50 per cent. threshold value is $M = 5.613 \pm 0.049$. With the simpler method described on the preceding page we should have had (from column 3) $x = (10.0 - \Sigma p) = (10.0 - 4.373) = 5.627$: the difference is little over 0.01.

The S.D. is simply $1/b = 1/0.876 = 1.142$: (calculated by cumulative summation from column 3 the S.D. would be

$$\sqrt{2\Sigma(\Sigma p') - \Sigma p(1 + \Sigma p)} = \sqrt{2 \times 12.387 - 4.373\,(5.373)} = \sqrt{1.278} = (1.131).$$

The regression coefficient, b, thus gives a good measure of the precision of the test as judged by its power to discriminate ages.

The standard sampling error of the threshold by the familiar formula would be $\pm 1.142/\sqrt{N} = \pm 0.047$ (where N is the average number tested per group) ; by Fisher's fuller formula it is ± 0.049.

The assumption of normality can be assessed by calculating the correlation $r_{xy} = 0.969$. Since the number of pairs correlated (7) is so few, we cannot test the divergence $1 - r^2_{xy} = 0.0614$, by the ordinary probable error. But we can calculate χ^2, which here $= (1 - r^2_{xy}) \Sigma (y^2) = 31.6$. The simplest mode of calculation is shown in Table LXIV. A. As there are only five degrees of freedom, χ^2 is undoubtedly significant. Thus either the relation between age and test-performance is not very satisfactorily expressed by a straight line or else the responses given by the pupils in the several age-groups are not entirely independent.

The psychological reader will find it instructive to compare the procedure shown in Table LXIV. A. with that commonly followed for the " constant method " (e.g., Woodworth, *Experimental Psychology*, Table on p. 413 : " Constant stimuli with two response categories : fitting normal ogive, using Müller-Urban weights.") He will find that the formulæ for M. and S.D. are algebraically identical. But the working procedure is here a little simpler ; and the introduction of " provisional probit " has the advantage of yielding a " maximum likelihood " solution for the two constants.

TABLE LXIV.

To Illustrate Probit Method of Calculating Test Constants.

Age (x)	Number (n)	Proportion Passing (p)	Empirical Probit	Provisional Probit (Y)	Weight (w)	Weight including Number (nw)	Working Probit (y)	(nwy)	(nwxy)	(nwy²)	(nwx)	(nwx²)
3·5	106	·006	2·49	3·1	·154	16·3	2·75	44·8	156·9	123·3	57·05	199·8
4·5	184	·117	3·81	4·0	·439	80·7	3·83	309·1	1390·9	1183·8	363·15	1634·2
5·5	227	·498	4·99	4·8	·627	142·4	4·99	711·0	3908·2	3545·8	783·20	4307·6
6·5	242	·838	5·98	5·7	·532	128·6	5·96	766·5	4978·8	4568·1	835·90	5433·4
7·5	261	·956	6·71	6·5	·269	70·2	6·68	468·9	3517·0	3132·5	526·50	3948·8
8·5	253	·975	6·96	7·4	·062	15·6	6·65	103·7	882·1	689·9	132·60	1127·1
9·5	248	·983	7·12	8·2	·008	2·0	7·12	14·2	135·3	101·4	19·00	180·5
TOTAL		4·373				455·8		2418·2	14969·2	13344·8	2717·40	16831·4

$\Sigma nwx = 2714 \cdot 4$; $\bar{x} = 2717 \cdot 4/455 \cdot 8 = 5 \cdot 962$. $\Sigma nwy = 2418 \cdot 2$; $\bar{y} = 2418 \cdot 2/455 \cdot 8 = 5 \cdot 305$

$$\begin{array}{lll}
\Sigma nwx^2 = 16831 \cdot 4 & \Sigma nwxy = 14969 \cdot 2 & \Sigma nwy^2 = 13344 \cdot 8 \\
\bar{x}\,\Sigma nwx = 16200 \cdot 7 & \bar{x}\,\Sigma nwy = 14416 \cdot 9 & \bar{y}\,\Sigma nwy = 12829 \cdot 5 \\
& & \Sigma(y^2) = 515 \cdot 3 \\
\Sigma(x^2) = 630 \cdot 7 & \Sigma(xy) = 552 \cdot 3 & b\Sigma(xy) = 483 \cdot 7 \\
& & \chi^2 = 31 \cdot 6
\end{array}$$

$$b = \frac{\Sigma(xy)}{\Sigma(x^2)} = \frac{552 \cdot 3}{630 \cdot 7} = 0 \cdot 876$$

$$(Y - \bar{y}) = b(x - \bar{x})$$

i.e., $Y - 5 \cdot 305 = 0 \cdot 876 (x - 5 \cdot 962)$

or $Y = 0 \cdot 876x + 0 \cdot 082$

When $Y = 5 \cdot 0$, $x = 5 \cdot 613 \ (= M)$.

APPENDIX V.

Classification of Pupils According to Special Abilities.[1]

Controversial Views. One of the most pressing problems of educational organization is the allocation of pupils to advanced education of specialized types, particularly the selection of children for secondary schools and trade schools respectively. At a recent Conference of Teachers it was contended by several teachers that in London the existing scholarship system tends to cream off the brighter children at the age of 10-11 regardless of any special bent for technical as distinct from scholastic work, so that, when the examinations for trade schools are held, those who might make good technicians have already been transferred to secondary schools. On the other hand, one or two psychological speakers replied that Prof. Spearman's two-factor theory had shown that " the teacher's distinction between intellectual and technical types is a popular application of the faculty theory," and that the notion of specialized abilities has now been disproved by recent experimental researches : consequently the only legitimate classification of pupils will consist in grading them according to their general ability.

The evidence collected during the present survey appears more in keeping with the impressions of the practical teacher than with the conclusions of the laboratory investigators. As was stated in my previous *Report on the Junior County Scholarship Scheme* (Appendix I), many eminent opponents of Prof. Spearman's theory, like Prof. Karl Pearson, Dr. William Brown and Dr. Godfrey Thomson, have strongly criticized his proof of the existence of a single general factor ; and Thomson has even maintained that mental performances can be satisfactorily explained in terms of a number of overlapping special abilities, without postulating any general factor whatever. The view reached in my previous reports has been that both conceptions are required. This conclusion emerges still more clearly when we turn from the study of high ability or special talent to that of mental disability and defect : there can be little doubt that educational backwardness is due in some cases to deficiency in general intelligence, but in others to a more limited deficiency in certain specialized capacities—verbal, arithmetical, manual and the like. At the same time it must be owned that far more evidence is needed on this problem ; and the following suggestions are put forward as indicating how rough and ready modes of estimation, current among school-teachers and examiners, may be refined, so as to lead to more adequate statistical techniques.

Example. The principles I have proposed may best be understood in terms of an imaginary but concrete example. For simplicity let us suppose that we are concerned with four pupils only, and that the headmaster wishes to decide which (if any) are sufficiently bright to be awarded some kind of scholarship, and which of these are suitable for a secondary and for a trade school respectively. He sets them a combined scholarship examination in four typical subjects of the ordinary curriculum—Arithmetic, English,

---

[1] Abridged from my earlier report on " The Bearing of the Factor Theory on the Organization of Schools and Classes." Cf. also Appendix above on " Factor Analysis of the Binet Tests."

TABLE LXIV. A.

Analysing Marks in Scholarship Examination.

	Brown	Green	Smith	Jones	Total	Averages	Average Deviation
Arithmetic	27	8	8	9	52	13	−7
English	29	14	10	15	68	17	−3
Total : Academic ..	56	22	18	24	120	30	−10
Drawing	31	9	23	29	92	23	+3
Handwork	33	17	23	35	108	27	+7
Total : Practical ..	64	26	46	64	200	50	+10
Total : All Subjects ..	120	48	64	88	320		
Average : All Subjects..	30	12	16	22		20	
Average Deviation ..	+10	−8	−4	+2			0

TABLE LXIV. B.

Correlations between Tests.

	Arith.	Eng.	Draw.	Hand.	Total	Av.
Arithmetic ..	1·000	·965	·563	·509	3·037	·759
English	·965	1·000	·510	·541	3·016	·754
Drawing	·563	·510	1·000	·933	3·006	·751
Handwork ..	·509	·541	·933	1·000	2·983	·746
Total ..	3·037	3·016	3·006	2·983	12·042	·753
1st Factor ..	·875	·869	·866	·859	3·469	·867
2nd Factor ..	·465	·477	−·465	−·477	·000	·000

TABLE LXIV. C.

Marks as Deviations about Averages.

	Brown	Green	Smith	Jones	Average All Pupils
Arithmetic	+ 4	+ 3	− 1	− 6	0
English	+ 2	+ 5	− 3	− 4	0
Average : Academic	+ 3	+ 4	− 2	− 5	0
Drawing	− 2	− 6	+ 4	+ 4	0
Handwork	− 4	− 2	0	+ 6	0
Average : Practical ..	− 3	− 4	+ 2	+ 5	0
Average : All Subjects	0	0	0	0	0

Drawing and Handwork. The marks obtained by the pupils are, we will assume, those set out in Table LXIV. A. To determine who is the brightest, his natural course is to add each boy's marks for all four subjects, and compare the totals or averages. To determine who is most suitable for a trade school as distinct from a secondary school or vice versa, he can compare the totals for the two academic school subjects (Arithmetic and English) with those for the two practical subjects (Drawing and Handwork). From this double calculation he would doubtless conclude that Brown and Jones were the brightest of the four (total marks 120 and 88 respectively), and (perhaps with less assurance) that Brown was the best suited for the academic work of a secondary school and Jones for the practical work of a trade school.

The psychologist, however, must inquire : what is the justification for these two common procedures ?

1. *The Assumption of General Ability.* As regards general ability the answer seems obvious. Unless there is some common " general factor " entering into all four subjects, we should expect the process of addition to even out the individual variations in each separate subject, and in the long run (*i.e.*, with a large number of tests instead of only four) we should inevitably find that every boy tended to get approximately the same total or average.[1] In that case it would be absurd to attempt any differentiation on the basis of the total marks. As it is, however, we find that the boy who has the highest total for *all* subjects tends to be well above average for *each* subject ; and there are corresponding tendencies discernible in the other pupils. Thus, the justification for the process of averaging is to be found in the close agreement (or " correlation ") of the marks for each separate subject with those for every other subject and with the total. It is no doubt his frequent impressions of this widespread correlation or agreement between performances in different subjects that has led the experienced teacher to assume that there must be some *common ability* entering into all the tests.

To secure a formal verification of this assumption, therefore, the obvious procedure is to carry out an explicit and systematic calculation of the correlations between all possible pairs of tests (Table LXIV. B.). Were there no real connection between the several subjects, we should expect these calculated correlations to be of negligible size : they would seldom be exactly zero, but there would be as many negative correlations as positive. Now with nearly all tests of intellectual efficiency what we actually find are positive correlations, usually quite large in amount, between any and every pair we like to take.

Here then is the reason why we may legitimately add or average marks for all subjects in order to obtain a single composite mark for each boy's all-round ability.

Weighting, Intentional and Unintentional. At this point a further question of some practical consequence arises. In calculating these totals or averages, should every subject be given the same weight ? In my previous report (*Distribution and Relations of Educational Abilities*, p. 52), I showed that certain tests, such as English Composition and Arithmetic, revealed a much closer correlation with general intelligence than other tests, such as Handwork and Drawing. This supports the common practice of giving a greater weight to tests of the former kind than to tests of manual subjects such as Drawing or Handwork.

---

[1] There would, of course, always be some small " accidental " differences. Hence the statistician would require first to investigate whether the differences actually obtained were statistically significant. I should now propose, therefore, that the significance of the differences should be checked by Prof. R. A. Fisher's new technique known as the " analysis of variance " (*Statistical Methods for Research Workers*, 1925).

H*

To discover what weight has actually been given in an examination like that described, the simplest method would be to add the marks, not for pupils, but for subjects (Table LXIV. A., last 3 columns : for greater accuracy we ought also to compare the range of marks, or best of all the average range, *i.e.*, the mean deviation or standard deviation ; but these figures will generally vary with the totals, since both depend largely on the maximum allotted to each subject). In the above table of marks, we see that the highest totals are given, not to Arithmetic or English, but to Drawing and Handwork. Could we be sure that the marking had been really objective (*e.g.*, based on number of questions or test-items correctly solved), we should go on to infer that the latter subjects (or at any rate the tests for the latter subjects) were easier. In the same way, on adding scores for separate questions in the Binet scale, we conclude that the test which furnishes the largest number of right answers is the easiest, and that which furnishes the fewest the hardest.

The Difficulty of the Tests. But once again the process of adding marks implies an assumption. When we declare that one test is harder than another, we mean that it is harder for nearly all the pupils ; and that in turn implies that the order of difficulty of the several tests is much the same for all. Evidently this assumption can be checked, like the last, by calculating the inter-correlations ; but here we shall correlate the order of tests for each pupil, instead of the order of pupils for each test.

This somewhat novel mode of correlation was adopted, it will be remembered, in our inquiry into the stability of the Binet scale (page 149); there we found that the correlations were all positive and all fairly high. This demonstrates the existence of a new kind of " general factor "—a factor which is not a mental " ability " at all. When we correlated tests, the " general factor " was a general mental capacity required for all the tests : now, when we correlate persons tested, the " general factor " is the general order of difficulty—it is, in fact, an average of the individual orders. But once again in theory it would be better to take a weighted average instead of averaging the orders just as they stand. However, the theoretical weights differ so little that the simple average of the orders yields a final order of difficulty almost indistinguishable from that obtained by the more elaborate process of weighting. Accordingly, throughout this volume I have represented the factor of difficulty, both for particular groups and for general population, by an order which has been obtained by averaging the several rankings just as they stand. In estimating general ability from marks in various subjects the tests should obviously be so set or marked that their difficulty is approximately the same.

2. *The Assumption of Special Aptitudes.* We now turn from the two main or " general " factors to the problem of supplementary factors. This brings us to the second of the broader questions that we posed at the outset. How far is the headmaster justified in assuming the existence of special abilities or special types ? To study this further issue we must begin by eliminating the influence of the two general factors we have already discovered—the general factor of intelligence and the general factor of difficulty. The simplest and most obvious way to do this is to reduce all the marks to deviations about the average for each subject and the average for each pupil. All the averages will then be changed to zero. Accordingly we subtract first the average for the whole group (20), then the average deviation for each pupil (*e.g.*, $+10$ for Brown), and finally the average deviation for each subject (*e.g.*, $+7$ for Handwork) : thus Brown's mark for Handwork will be $33 - 20 - 10 - 7 = -4$. (To make the figures still more closely comparable we might go on to

divide by the standard deviations, so as to secure the same average range for every row or for every column ; but, to avoid over-elaboration, we shall ignore this further refinement here.)

The deviations or " residual marks," obtained in this way by deducting the effects of the two " general factors," are shown in Table LXIV. C. From these figures it is now easy to see that the tests group themselves into two main clusters or types, namely : (i) the written or academic tests ; and (ii) the practical or manual tests. Similarly the pupils group themselves into two main classes or types, corresponding to the classification of tests, namely, an academic type suitable for the secondary school, and a practical type suitable for the trade school.[1]

What then is the formal justification for such classifications ? The answer is clear. To justify our procedure we must once again calculate the correlations. The correlation between the residual marks for English and Arithmetic is positive and moderately large ; and so is that between those for Drawing and Handwork. On the other hand, the correlations between either of the written tests, on the one hand, and either of the practical tests are negative. Precisely the same result is reached, if we calculate the correlations between residual marks by pupils, instead of by tests. The marks obtained by Brown and Green show a positive correlation ; so do those obtained by Smith and Jones ; but the correlation of either of the first pair with either of the second is negative.

The Partial Correlation Technique. It is obvious that, if we had tested a large batch of pupils, running into hundreds instead of only four, this process of subtracting average marks would be extremely laborious. But the same end can be reached by adopting the device of partial correlation. A partial correlation coefficient, such as $r_{ab \cdot g}$ (a symbol which is used to denote the correlation between a, Arithmetic say, and b, English say, after g, the general factor has been partialled out) is simply the correlation between the residuals[2] $x_{a \cdot g}$ and $x_{b \cdot g}$ (where $x_{a \cdot g}$ denotes the residuals obtained by subtracting from the observed values of x_a the effects of x_g, these effects being measured by the regression of x_a on x_g, i.e., $x_{a \cdot g} = x_a - r_{ag} \dfrac{\sigma_a}{\sigma_g} x_g$; and similarly for $x_{b \cdot g}$).

The figures entered in Table LXIV. C. are estimates for these residuals. Evidently, when we have a large number, the appropriate method for finding the best weights will be virtually the same as that for finding " partial regression coefficients ;" and the quickest procedure for eliminating the influence of general intelligence would be, not to subtract the calculated averages from the raw marks, but to subtract the calculated correlations from the observed coefficients. We are thus able to " partial out " the general factor, and then examine what we may call the specific correlations (i.e., the residual or partial correlations) to find evidence for specific factors.[3] This procedure has the further merit of introducing, by implication, an improved system of weighting both for the general factor and for the residuals. Table LXIV. B. shows the calcu-

---

(1) The appearance of a systematic pattern of plus and minus signs does not of itself constitute evidence for the existence of such types. In a formal inquiry it would be necessary first to demonstrate that the residual deviations were significant. With the correlation technique we should test the significance of the residual correlations, as illustrated in the researches quoted in the text. With simple averaging this can now be conveniently done by Fisher's method of analysing variance.

(2) This follows immediately from Yule's equations 2 and 7, or 8 and 3 ; *Introduction to Theory of Statistics*, 1912, pp. 234-236.

(3) I should remind the reader that I have used the phrase " specific factor " to denote a factor common to particular *species* of tests (the " general factor " being a factor common to the whole *genus*) : Spearman uses the phrase " specific " to mean peculiar to a *single* test : (cf. previous Appendix on Factor Analysis of the Binet tests, p. 136, footnote 1).

H*

lated correlations with the first or general factor—" saturations " as they are
sometimes termed ; and at the foot the resulting " saturations " with the
special factor after the former has been partialled out.[1] Since it is based on
the theory of " multiple correlation," I have called this procedure the method
of " multiple factors." Detailed illustrations have already been given in
previous reports (e.g., *Report on the Distribution and Relations of Educational
Abilities*, 1917, pp. 53f.).

Averaging and Correlating by Pupils and by Tests. It is, moreover, evident that
we should reach much the same results whether we begin by correlating tests
or by correlating pupils. If, as is usually the case, we have a large number of
pupils but a comparatively small number of tests, then the speediest method
is to correlate tests. But where, as with the Binet scale, we have a large
number of tests, then it is commonly quicker to correlate pupils rather than
tests, or to adopt some equivalent mode of averaging. In my previous studies
of the difficulty of the Binet tests and of the differences attributable to sex
and social status, it will be remembered that two procedures were adopted :
first, I took typical representatives of each type of pupil, and then correlated
the orders for the several types ;[2] but secondly, it was shown, much the same
results are reached in a speedier and more intelligible fashion if we compare
simply the average marks (or orders of merit) for boys and girls respectively,
or for the two extreme social classes. The advantage of the latter procedure
is that, instead of selecting a few typical pupils for purposes of correlation, we
can base our analysis on all the children available : obviously, to correlate
the orders of difficulty for every child that has been tested when the total
number runs into several hundreds would be an impracticable task.

The figures obtained by averaging the *observed* marks for each pupil have,
as we have seen, a different meaning from those obtained by averaging the
observed marks for each test : and consequently, as already noted, the
general factor obtained by correlating pupils has a different meaning from
the general factor obtained by correlating tests. But when we average
residual marks, the types resulting are the same, whether we work by pupils
or by tests ; and similarly when we correlate residual marks or, (what amounts
to the same thing) extract factors from the residual or partial correlations,
then the factors obtained in either case relate to the same kinds of special
ability, whether we correlate by pupils or by tests.

The Nature and Influence of Special Abilities. However, these " special
abilities " must not be envisaged as necessarily forming simple and discrete
" faculties." They may denote highly complex characteristics ; and their
composition may quite possibly vary from one child to another. The " factors"
are thus to be regarded rather as statistical principles, useful for the practical
purposes of description, classification, and prediction ; they do not necessarily
consist of isolated functions of importance in the analysis of the theoretical
constitution of the mind. In particular the secondary or supplementary
factors—group factors, as they may be called—seem to represent groups or
clusters of tests or tested subjects which merge one into the other, and so
producing the phenomenon which was termed in my previous report "cyclic
overlap."

The reader may perhaps find it clearer to picture the relations thus
revealed if they are represented geometrically by a diagram instead of

---

(1) The method used is that described in the Appendix above in connection with the factorization
of group tests of intelligence (Appendix V, " Accuracy of the Supplementary Tests").

(2) *Preliminary Reports to the Chief Inspector on the Use of the Binet Scale with London Children*.
In that report, at each age level, 16 pupils were taken, namely, 8 boys and 8 girls—4 of each sex being
drawn from the more cultured classes and 4 from the poorer and less cultured classes.

numerically by a pattern of coefficients. In my analysis of educational tests, it appeared that the subjects of the curriculum could be divided antithetically into first (A) a verbal and (B) a non-verbal group, and then that each of these could be subdivided into (A1) a linguistic or word-recognition group and (A2) a literary or composition group, and again into (B1) a mathematical and (B2) a manual group. This implies that, so far as the specialized abilities are concerned, the relations of the subjects tested can be expressed by a two-dimensional circular diagram with the Composition factor marking the North pole and the Manual factor the South pole, while the Linguistic and Mathematical factors form the West and East poles. Thus, in virtue of their cyclic relationship each subject can be placed appropriately on the circumference of the circle, so that those having the largest positive specific correlation with each other are closest to one another, and those having the largest negative specific correlation would be almost opposite to one another. In this way the angular distance between two subjects can be made to represent inversely the specific correlations between them : (cf. the " clock diagram " in Fig. 8, loc. cit., p. 59). Evidently, if 0° denotes perfect positive correlation, 90°, zero correlation, and 180°, perfect negative, then the natural function to take is $r = \sin (90° — \theta) = \cos \theta$, where θ denotes the angular distance between the two points. Distance from the centre can be used to indicate the effect of the general factor (cf. K. Pearson, *Grammar of Science*, p. 436).[1]

Dr. Maxwell Garnett has since given a formal proof that, under certain conditions, the " correlation is equal to the *cosine* of the angle ; " and has further formulated the precise requirements to be fulfilled before three or more tests can be represented by a diagram on a single two-dimensional plane, or more generally by points on a sphere of a specified number of dimensions.[2] In virtue of these equivalences, those who prefer to express or to picture numerical relations in terms of co-ordinate geometry can thus do so with exactitude. The reader will find it instructive to attempt similar analytic diagrams to represent the relations of the Binet tests assigned to a given age or adjacent group of ages.

In virtue of this overlap it is clear that what we have called " types " or groups of pupils and of tests must not be envisaged as clearly separated, mutually exclusive classes. " Types," like " factors," merge into one another by insensible gradations. Nevertheless, they appear sufficiently well marked to justify the teacher and the general mode of educational organization in introducing some kind of classification at any rate for selected pupils at the later ages. Thus the tests described in the foregoing memorandum may serve the purpose, not only of assessing the level or " mental age " of the child in each of the subjects and of grading him according to his general educational attainments, but also of classifying him according to what may be called his educational " type."[3] If we accept the provisional scheme proposed above, it will yield first a broad classification into verbal types, (which include the linguistic and the literary) and non-verbal. The latter then appear to subdivide into a mathematical or scientific type and a manual or technical. This view, however, must be considered as provisional and

---

[1] The same type of circular diagram was used to represent the interrelations of emotional factors : cf. *Brit. Ass. Ann. Rep.*, 1915, p. 696. As explained in a previous paper, the principles were suggested by Pearson's diagrammatic representation of partial correlations in terms of spherical trigonometry. To represent the general factor as well as the two bipolar factors on a flat surface one can employ globular or gnomonic projection, or the stereographic nets supplied to schools for making maps of the terrestrial hemispheres. These representations will only be exact if we are justified in assuming that the sum of the squares of the factor loadings for each test may be taken as (or raised to) 1.

[2] *Brit. J. Psych.*, IX., 1919, pp. 347f.

[3] The tests on which the correlations printed in my previous report (*loc. cit.*, Table XVIII.) were based were virtually the same as those described in the foregoing memorandum.

tentative only. The commonest type will be the average type, *i.e.*, the children whose general and special abilities are all of them pretty close to the average. With rare exceptions children before the ages of 11 or 12 show little signs of deviating markedly towards one specialized type or the other ; and, in any case, it must be repeated, the " types " are only tendencies. Moreover, much of the specialization appears to be a specialization of interest rather than of aptitude ; and even up to the end of adolescence interests are liable to change considerably.

Thus, if the results so obtained can be trusted, it would seem that at the age of the junior county scholarship examination any final classification according to special abilities would probably be premature.[1] The whole subject is a matter for further inquiry ; and the foregoing methods, it is hoped, may be of assistance to the increasing number of teachers in the Council's service who are seeking to contribute to educational science by undertaking scientific investigations as research-students or in other capacities.

In conclusion, let me insist on two final points, already mentioned in passing. First, the present Reports have been concerned solely with intellectual qualities; but the modern teacher should be concerned quite as much with his pupils' temperament and character as with their intelligence or scholastic achievements. Secondly, the methods here described for investigating intellectual qualities can be applied equally well to other aspects of the child's personality. The use of partial correlation to discover multiple factors, the measurement of emotional maturity by a developmental age, the assessment of qualitative characteristics with rating-scales defined by percentiles and checked by standard specimens, and above all the adoption of analytic schedules to supplement vague subjective judgments—all these devices will be found as valuable for temperamental traits as for intellectual. Only by carefully controlled procedures such as these can the investigation of character-qualities be removed from the field of mere personal impression, and carried out in an exact, objective, and scientific way. The supreme requirement is to observe every aspect of the child's personality, and then combine the piece-meal analyses into a synoptic picture of the whole.[2]

[1] I have discussed this subject more fully in my *Preliminary Report on the Selection of Pupils for Secondary, Technical and other Schools.*

[2] A standard scheme for personality-schedules is given in *The Measurement of Mental Capacities* (1927, p. 8, cf. p. 29).

[I have attempted to summarize results to date in my article on " The Assessment of Personality." *Brit. J. Ed. Psych.* XV., 1946, pp. 107-121.]

APPENDIX VI.

SELECTED REFERENCES.[1]

Instructions for Giving the Binet-Simon Tests.

1.—BINET, A., and SIMON, TH.—*The Development of Intelligence in Children.* Translated by Elizabeth S. Kite. Publications of the Vineland Training School, New Jersey, 1916. pp. 336.

> (Chapters iv. and v. are American translations of the original 1908 and 1911 scales as published in *L'Année Psychologique*, xiv., pp. 1 *et seq.*, and xvii., pp. 145 *et seq.*)

2.—BINET, A., and SIMON, TH.—*A Method of Measuring the Development of Intelligence in Young Children.* Translated by Clara H. Town. Chicago Medical Book Co., 1913. pp. 82.

> (An authorised American translation of Binet's final instructions for giving the tests, with the theoretical discussions contained in the preceding articles, as published in the *Bulletin de la Société Libre pour l'Étude Psychologique de l'Enfant*, x., April, 1911.)

3.—MELVILLE, N. J.—*Testing Juvenile Mentality.* Lippincott Co., 1917. pp. 142.

> (A carefully compiled practical handbook describing a "uniform" method for giving the tests to American children. The order recommended is somewhat involved.)

Revisions of the Binet-Simon Tests.

4.—YERKES, R. M., BRIDGES, J. W., HARDWICK, ROSE S.—*A Point Scale for Measuring Mental Ability.* Warwick and York, 1915. pp. 218.

> (Contains materials and directions for using the Point Scale, with results of its application to normal and defective individuals.)

5.—TERMAN, LEWIS M.—*The Measurement of Intelligence.* G. G. Harrap and Co., 1919. pp. 362.

> (An explanatory guide for the "Stanford Revision and Extension.")

6.—TERMAN, L. M., LYMAN, G., ORDAHL, L., GALBREATH, N., and TALBERT, N.—*The Stanford Revision and Extension of the Binet-Simon Scale for Measuring Intelligence.* Warwick and York, 1917. p. 179.

> (Analysis of results of applying the Stanford Revision to over 1000 children. Detailed discussions of the relation of intelligence to sex, social status, school ability, etc.)

Cf. also Goddard, Bobertag, Winch, Saffiotti, cited below, Nos. 34, 8, 32, and 10.

---

[1] The references I have selected deal for the most part either with British work, or with studies of the Binet-Simon scale, with which hitherto British work has been chiefly concerned. References to foreign work upon mental and scholastic tests of other kinds are readily accessible in the bibliographies contained in Nos. 35, 36, and 39.

My indebtedness throughout this volume to earlier investigators will be evident to all who are familiar with the literature of the subject, or who turn to the books and papers quoted here. In the text it would have been impossible to make more detailed acknowledgments to the work already carried out upon every individual test ; and I was desirous not to overburden my semi-practical discussions with yet more numerous footnotes. The scientific student, who takes up a test of any one particular species, will find it easy, by following up the fuller references inserted in the volumes chosen below, to put himself in touch with the principal researches.

Untranslated Literature.

7.—MEUMANN, E.—*Vorlesungen zur Einführung in die Experimentelle Pädagogik.* Verlag von W. Engelmann, 1911–14, pp. 726 + 800 + 919.

    (Vol. ii., pp. 130–300, summarises work on the Binet scale up to date of writing, and gives suggestions for improvement of the tests.)

8.—BOBERTAG, O.—" Über Intelligenzprüfungen nach der Methode von Binet und Simon." *Zeitschrift für Angewandte Psychologie,* 1911, v., pp. 105–203 ; 1912, vi., pp. 495–538.

    (A German adaptation of the scale, with discussion of results and suggestions for improvement.)

9.—CHOTZEN, F.—" Die Intelligenzprüfungsmethode von Binet-Simon bei Schwachsinnigen Kindern." *Zeitschrift für Angewandte Psychologie,* 1912, vi., pp. 411–494.

    (Application of tests to children in German special schools.)

10.—SAFFIOTTI, F. U.—*La Misura dell' Intelligenza nei Fanciulli.* Roma : Tipografia dell' Unione Editrice, 1916. pp. 286.

    (One of the most thorough and critical discussions of the Binet-Simon scale. Contains an ingenious substitute for the mental-age method of grading the results [" Treves-Saffiotti Method "] ; also a bibliography of 603 numbers. A detailed summary will be found in the *Eugenics Review,* 1917, viii., pp. 365–373.)

Mental Deficiency.

11.—BINET, A., and SIMON, TH.—*The Intelligence of the Feebleminded.* Translated by Elizabeth S. Kite. Publications of the Vineland Training School, New Jersey, 1916. pp. 328.

    (Many of the Binet-Simon tests are used, but the scale itself is not systematically applied.)

12.—HUEY, E. B.—*Backward and Feebleminded Children.*—Warwick and York, 1912. pp. 221.

    (Detailed descriptions of typical borderline cases variously treated.)

13.—WALLIN, J. E. W.—*Problems of Subnormality.* The World Book Co., 1917. pp. 485.

    (A systematic discussion of practical problems relating to mental deficiency.)

14.—BRONNER, AUGUSTA F.—*The Psychology of Special Abilities and Disabilities.* Kegan Paul, Trench, Trübner and Co., 1919. pp. 269.

    (A discussion of special disabilities in reading, arithmetic, handwork and self-control among normals, and of special abilities among defectives, illustrated by cases, mostly delinquent, variously tested.)

15.—BINET, A., and SIMON, TH.—*Mentally Defective Children.* Translated by W. B. Drummond. Edward Arnold, 1914. pp. 180.

16.—GODDARD, H. H.—*Feeblemindedness : Its Causes and Consequences.* The Macmillan Co., 1913. pp. 599.

17.—TREDGOLD, A. F.—*Mental Deficiency.* Ballière, Tindall and Cox. 3rd edition. 1920. pp. 525.

(The last three are textbooks of a more general nature dealing with mental deficiency.)

Deficiency and Delinquency.

18.—HEALY, WILLIAM.—*The Individual Delinquent.* William Heinemann, 1915. pp. 830.

(Systematic discussion of the causes of juvenile delinquency in the light of 1000 cases.)

19.—GODDARD, H. H.—*The Criminal Imbecile: An Analysis of Three Murder Cases.* Macmillan Co., 1915. pp. 157.

(Describes the first court cases in which the Binet-Simon scale was used in evidence. Strongly emphasises the importance of mental deficiency in the production of crime.)

20.—MINER, J. BURT.—*Deficiency and Delinquency: An Interpretation of Mental Testing.* Warwick and York, 1918. pp. xiv. +355.

(Excellent statistical discussion. Urges a percentage definition of deficiency.)

21.—WALLIN, J. E. W. (*loc. cit. sup.*, No. 13, pp. 123–155).

(Contains an excellent résumé of examinations of delinquents by the Binet-Simon scale.)

Periodical Literature.

22.—JOHNSTON, KATHERINE L.—"Binet's Method for the Measurement of Intelligence." *Journal of Experimental Pedagogy*, i., 1911, pp. 24–31.

(The first investigation carried out in England by means of this scale.)

23.—DUMVILLE, B.—"A Trial of Binet's Tests on Five-Year-Olds." *Ibid.*, ii., 1913, pp. 113–118.

24.—TAYLOR, N. G.—"Further Data Towards the Study of the Binet-Simon Scale." *Ibid.*, iii., 1916, pp. 256–266.

25.—MOORE, R. C.—"The Application of the Binet-Simon Scale to Normal English Children." *Ibid.*, iv., 1917, pp. 113–128.

26.—LEWIS, E. O.—"The Binet and Point-Scale Methods of Testing Intelligence." *Ibid.*, iv., 1918, pp. 198–202.

27.—BURT, C.—"Experimental Tests of Higher Mental Processes." *Ibid.*, i., 1911, pp. 93–112.

28.—*Id.* and MOORE, R. C.—"The Mental Differences between the Sexes." *Ibid.*, i., 1912, pp. 273–284, 233–388.

29.—*Id.*—"The Development of Reasoning in School Children." *Ibid.*, v., 1919, pp. 68–77, 121–127.

30.—*Id.*—"The Measurement of Intelligence by the Binet Tests." *Eugenics Review*, vi., 1914, pp. 36–50, 140–152.

(A critical discussion of the theoretical principles underlying the scale.)

31.—SIMON, TH.—"The Measurement of Intelligence." *Ibid.*, vi., 1915, pp. 290–370.

32.—WINCH, W. H.—" Binet's Mental Tests : What they are, and what we can do with them." *Child Study*, vi.-viii., 1913–15.

> (A free but excellent revision of the tests as far as age VIII., based upon experiments with London school children.)

33.—ROGERS, AGNES L., and McINTYRE, J. L.—" The Measurement of Intelligence in Children by the Binet-Simon Scale." *British Journal of Psychology*, vii., 1914, pp. 265–300.

34.—GODDARD, H. H.—" The Binet and Simon Tests of Intellectual Capacity." *Training School Bulletin*, v., 1908, pp. 3–9. (" Revised," *ibid.*, viii., 1911, pp. 56–62. " Standard Method," *ibid.*, x., 1913, pp. 22–30.)

35.—KOHS, SAMUEL C.—" The Binet-Simon Measuring Scale for Intelligence." *Journal of Educational Psychology*, v., 1914, pp. 215–224, 279–290, 335–346. (An annotated bibliography containing 457 numbers, practically complete to date of publication.)

> Other references will be found above, pp. 136 and 214–16.

Other Mental Tests.[1]

36.—WHIPPLE, G. M.—*Manual of Mental and Physical Tests*. Warwick and York. 2nd edition, 1914–15. pp. 366 + 336.

37.—PINTNER, R., and PATERSON, D. G.—*A Scale of Performance Tests.* Appleton and Co., 1917. pp. 218.

38.—STERN, W.—*The Psychological Methods of Measuring Intelligence*. Translated by G. M. Whipple. Warwick and York, 1913. pp. 160.

> (And references under Periodical Literature.)

Educational Tests.

39.—STARCH, D.—*Educational Measurements*. The Macmillan Co., 1916. pp. 202. (Contains a useful bibliography of American literature upon the subject.)

40.—MONRO, W. S., DE VOSS, J. C., and KELLY, F. S.—*Educationa Tests and Measurements*. Houghton Mifflin Co., 1917. pp. 309.

41.—BALLARD, P. B.—" Norms of Performances in the Fundamental Processes of Arithmetic." *Journal of Experimental Pedagogy*, iv., 1914, pp. 396–405.

42.—*Id.*—" Norms of Performances in Reading." *Ibid.*, v., 1915, pp. 153–161.

The literature on the subject of mental and scholastic tests is now so vast, and so many bibliographies are available, that it is neither possible or necessary to include an adequate and up-to-date survey in the present volume. The beginner will find useful sets of references appended to the several chapters of R. Pintner's *Intelligence Testing* (University of London Press, 1924). References to more recent British work will be found in my book on *The Backward Child* (University of London Press, 3rd impression, 1946). On measurement generally the references appended at the end of my *Factors of the Mind* (University of London Press, 1940) will be found sufficiently complete for the ordinary student.

---

[1] See note added on p. 235.

INDEX OF SUBJECTS

Ability,
  arithmetical, 294, 326, 328, 331, 364
  artistic, 353, 354
    See Drawing
  attainments, compared with, 187-194
  distribution of,
    among normal children, 159-161
    among special school children, 162
    normality of, 174
  general (*see also* General Factor,
    Intelligence)
    defined, 129-134, 211
    hypothesis of, 129-134, 219
    dominant in early years, 294
  graphical, *see* Drawing
  intellectual, *see* Intelligence
  linguistic, *see* Verbal Ability ; Read-
    ing ; Spelling ; Composition
  literary, *see* Literary ; Composition
  manual, *see* Manual Skill
  musical, 294, 353
  range of, at each age, 169, 170
  scholarship, 190
  special, 4, 135-139, 277, 294, 314,
    315, 449-456
    See Disabilities, Group factors
  verbal, *see* Verbal Ability
Abstract processes, failure of defectives in, 364
Abstraction, power of children in,
  332, 359
Absurdities in children's responses, 12
Absurdities (tests), 56, 248, 249
Accuracy,
  pubertal decline in, 330
  tests of,
    in Mental Arithmetic, 324
    in Written Arithmetic, 326
    in Reading, 305
Adding,
  pence and halfpence (test), 44
  written test of, 326-330, 394
Adults, Terman's tests for, 70
Age,
  influence on intelligence, 159, 160
  influence on promotion, 193, 194
Age-assignments of Binet-Simon tests,
  222
  Binet's original, 5, 224
  changes in, table of, 141, 142
  comparison of, 224
  compilations of, 150, 222
  correlations of, 222, 224
  criterion for, 152
  different investigators', 224, 225

Age basis in scholastic tests, 286
Age basis of Binet-Simon tests, 4, 142,
  150
Age, " chronological " defined, 143, 152
  " educational," 249, 363
  finding number of tests to be passed
    at a given, 19
  -groups, overlapping of, 171
  " mental," *see* Mental age
  -norms, *see* Norms, 7
  relation between, and school-stand-
    ing, tests, and intelligence, 194,
    278-284
  -scales in composition, drawing, and
    writing tests, 435-438
American adult level, 71
  army tests, 71, 256, 442
  averages, 71, 286
  colloquialisms and phraseology, 71
Analogies test, 72, 248
Analyses of backward cases, *see* Cases
Analysis,
  mathematical and statistical, 142
    See Factor analysis
  testing the power of, 332
Antonyms and synonyms (test), 240
Arithmetic,
  backwardness in : three cases ana-
    lysed and treated, 333-335
  backwardness of girls and defectives
    in problem type, 328
Arithmetic Tests,
  Fundamental Rules, *see infra* Written
  Mental, 324
  Oral, graded, 384-388
  Written,
    graded mechanical, 326, 389-391
    graded problems, 391-393
    uniform, fundamental rules, 394-
    397
Arithmetical ability, *see* Ability
Arranging weights (test), 35, 51
Articulation, 297, 298, 314, 320
Artistic ability, *see* Ability ; Drawing
Association,
  articulatory, 313, 332
  auditory, 332
  controlled, free or uncontrolled, 240
  graphic, ideational, visual, 313
  logical, rhyme, verbal, 60
  statistical, method of, 209
    See Coefficient of Association
Associative reaction of words, 60
Auditory perception, case of poor, 314
Assuage test, 62

Backward children,
    defined, 188
    See Mental defectives, and Special
        school children
Backwardness,
    analysis of,
        in Arithmetic, 332, 333
        in Reading, 311
        in non-scholastic abilities, 295,296
        in Spelling, 322
    cases of,
        in Arithmetic, 333-335
        in Handwork, 357
        in Reading, 314
        in Spelling, 315
    correlation of, with delinquency, 195,
        196
    See also Retardation
Binet-Simon Tests, 1-228
Birth-rate, iv, 203
Bow-knot test, 68, 71
Boxes test, 70
Boys and girls,
    artistic differences in, 354
    average mental age, 205
    inferiority of, see Girls (superiority
        of)
    left-handedness commoner among,
        339
    superiority of,
        in Arithmetic : problems, sub-
            traction, division, 219, 328, 330
        in Drawing, 354
        in Manual Work, 356
        in memory and perceptual sub-
            jects, 208
Bright Children, see Central School ;
        Scholarship ; and Supernormal
        Children ; also Genius, 2, 13, 60,
        165-170, 191, 250, 298
Bucket and fish test, 70

Cannon-ball test, 70
Capacities, see Ability, Disabilities
Card system of records, 11
Cases, illustrative, 314, 315, 323, 333,
        334, 357
Central school children, 2, 3, 14, 186,
        250, 288
Change of school, effect of, 324
Change test, 49
Changes in level of ability, 167-169
    See Mental Ratio
Chorea, 344, 345
Clinics, 166
Clock-hands test, 70, 71
Code diagram test, 70
Coefficient,
    of Association, definition and calcu-
        lation of, 209, 214, 228, 231
        fourfold table for, 229
    of Colligation, 209, 215, 217, 232
    Partial, 149, 193, 194
    of Regression, 74, 162, 186, 193, 270,
        278-284, 306-312
    Reliability, 213
Coins' tests, 39, 44, 49
Colligation, see Coefficient of
Colour blindness, 34

Coloured forms' tests, 234
Colours' test, 34, 97
Combinations-methode, 245
Completion tests,
    (argument), 245
    (story), 245
    norms for, 234
    pictorial form of, 234, 304
Complex, 60
    See also Psycho-analysis
Composition, 359-364, 423-426
Comprehension (reading) test, 303, 305
Construction puzzle test, 70
Correlation,
    of Binet-Simon tests and specific
        subjects, 196
    of chronological and mental ages of
        defectives, 167
    of educational and mental ratios, 189
    of order of difficulty of various in-
        vestigators, 149
    of persons, v, 148, 205
    of teachers' estimates and tests, 212
    partial, 136, 149, 193, 278-284, 453
    partial and observed of age, attain-
        ments, Binet-Simon tests, and
        intelligence, 194
    tetrachoric, 232
Correlations : method of calculating,
        148
Crime and mental deficiency, 202
    See Delinquency
Criterion for age assignments, 152
Criterion for mental deficiency, 180
Cumulative reproduction, 307, 308
Curve of mental growth, 256

Disabilities, see Abilities, special, 293,
        294, 296, 312, 314, 315
Discriminating forms test, 68
Displaced triangle test, 66, 69
Divided card test, position illustrated,
        39, 41
Division, written test of, 328, 397
Drawing, 347-353
Dream analysis, 307

Easy questions test, 47, 68
Educational ability, 169, 177, 192, 295,
        358
Educational age, 363
Educational attainments, 192-201, 295
    See Scholastic tests
Emotions,
    abnormal, of delinquents, 201
    and left-handedness : relation of, 339
    confusion produced by, 310
    effect of, on tests, 16, 43, 59, 60, 62,
        187, 220, 306, 307
    See also Instability ; Psycho-
        analysis ; Temperament
Epilepsy, 166
Equality of the intervals of the tests,
        150
Error, normal curve of, 174
Errors, see under Arithmetic ; Reading ;
        Spelling

Fables test, 70
Factor analysis, v, 135-139, 270 *et seq.*,
451
Factor, general, *see* Ability, general ;
General Factor
Factors, multiple, 136, 139
Factors, special, *see* Group Factors
Faculties, 130, 139
Family, size of, 203
Fatigue, 11, 15, 327
Feeble-mindedness, *see* Mental defec-
tives and Mental deficiency
Fingers test, 35
Fish and bucket test, 70
Fluency in reading, measurement of,
305
Folded paper test, 64, 65, 70
Fox and the goose test, 70

General Factor, 129-134, 269, 452
See also Intelligence
Genius, 13, 361
Geometrical tests, 72, 234
Girls,
æsthetic development of adolescent,
350
average mental age of, 205
conversational powers of, 208
greater effect of general mental
factor on, 353
inferiority of, *see* Boys, superiority of
specific talent for drawing small, 354
superiority of,
in addition and multiplication, 330
in composition (speed), 358
in colour sense, 208
in handwriting, 339
in literary and linguistic subjects,
208
in reading, 208, 300
in rote memory, 208, 330
Graded tests, 243, 298, 303, 315, 324,
326, 427, 432
Greek key pattern test, 53, 55
Group factors, 136, 137, 273, 449-456 ;
see Special Abilities
Group tests, 234, 325, 327
Growth, mental,
curve of, *see* Curve
upper limit of, *see* Limit

Handwork, *see* Manual tests
Hierarchy, 138, 148, 273
Home conditions, 203, 284

Imaginative type, 307
Imbeciles and idiots, borderlines for,
185
Industrial schools, 143, 197, 201
Ingenuity test, 70
Inheritance, mental, 141, 202, 284, 311
Instability, 166, 178, 191, 201
Instructions test, 243
Intelligence,
See also Ability
and educational ability compared,
170

Intelligence, (*contd.*)—
and educational attainments : relation of, 187
and educational attainments : contrasted, 189, 190
and sex, 205-210
and social status, 202-206
correlation of,
with age, schoolwork, and Binet-
Simon tests, 194
with drawing, 346-353
with composition and geometrical
drawing, 346-358
definition of, 129-134, 211
distribution of, 159-167
measurement,
in terms of mental age, 4, 439-447
in terms of standard deviation, 172
quotient (*see also* Mental ratio), 163
range of variability in, 170
Interpretation of pictures, 27
Intersection of distribution curves, 177
Inverted writing ; illustrations, 340-
343
Ionic a minore rhythm, 362
Item analysis, v, 214, 215, 217, 231

Judgment and intelligence, 52, 74
Juvenile courts, 7, 197

King and President test, 67

Labourers : mental ratios of dock- and
farm-, 183
Left-handedness, 339-345
Limit (average upper) of development,
256
Linear scale of tests, 72, 150, 151
Linguistic ability, *see* Verbal Ability
Literary ability (*see also* Composition),
195, 196, 266, 331
Look-and-say method, 292, 299, 311

Manual ability, 74, 137, 196, 294, 345,
356, 394, 436, 437
Marks, computation of, 13, 329
Maze tests, 254-265
Memory, 74, 137, 313-323, 330
Memory tests, 25, 28, 30, 32, 34, 35,
46, 50, 59, 60, 63, 64, 70
Mental age, 4, 18, 19, 150, 153, 156-
162, 181, 439-447
See also Educational Age
Mental arithmetic, 325, 326, 431
Mental clinics, need of, 154
Mental defectives, 43, 155, 164-186,
196, 215, 216, 318, 331, 340, 364
Mental growth : curve and limit of, 256
Mental growth : irregularity of, 165
Mental quotient, *see* Mental ratio
Mental ratio, 13, 163
and educational ratio : correspond-
ence of, 188, 189, 190
and power of self-support, 183
borderline for defectives, 180

Mental ratio, (contd.)—
  cases of very high, 13, 191, 361
  constancy of, 13, 167, 170
  approximate of defectives, 167
  different for different mental functions, 169, 185
  of genius, 13
  of Liverpool dock labourers, 183
  of special school children, 167
  of Warwickshire rural parish, 183
Mental year, 4, 258, 259
  See also Mental age
Mirror script, 340-343
Missing words test, 245, 256, 310
Missing features test, 43, 102-109
Mixed sentences test, 61
Mixed instructions test, 242
Mixed schools, 326
Moral imbecility, 178
Morals of fables test, 70
Morning and afternoon test, 34
Multiple factors, see Factor analysis
Multiplication, written test of, 329, 396
Musical ability, 294, 353

Nellie Dale method, 292
Neuropathic cases, 166
Neurotics, left-handedness in, 339
Norms, age,
  based on averages of normal children, 7, 160, 181
  for English children, 14, 288
  for Scholastic tests, 427 et seq.
  for Supplementary tests, 250

Occupation of parents, 202
Opposites test, 235-238
Order of difficulty of the tests, 143, 146, 147, 206, 207
Order of giving tests, 9

Partial correlation, see Correlation
Partial correlation of Binet-Simon tests with age, intelligence, and schoolwork, 194
Pedagogical tests, see Scholastic tests
Percentiles, method of, 160
Percentiles, table of, 163
Perseveration, 25, 320
Personality, iv, 362, 456
  See Temperament
Phonic method, 292, 315, 323
Phonic words, 299, 311
Phrenology, 139
Physical relations test, 70
Pictorial form, 234, 305
Picture test, 10, 30, 43, 61, 81-85, 89-93, 103-109, 235
Pint vessels test, 70
Point Scale method, 9, 24, 72
Pointing test, 24
Porteus maze tests, 74, 254-268
President and King test, 67
Probit method, 446-448
Problem tests, 62
Profile drawing, 349, 351, 355

Prose rhythm, 362
Psycho-analysis of a backward boy, 334
Psycho-analytic mechanisms, 202, 306, 307, 321, 334, 345, 350
Psychogram, 294
Psychopathic cases, 166
Psycho-physical methods, 440 et seq.
Puberty, 204, 330
Puzzle test, Healy's, 70

Qualitative characteristics, method of testing, 336-337

Ratio, see Educational ratio ; Mental ratio
Reading, 50, 70, 292, 297-311, 370-378
Reasoning, 249, 250, 299, 327, 332, 334, 364
Reasoning tests, 249-253
Record card, 4, 5, 11, 19-21
Regression, 74, 162, 186, 193, 195, 270, 278-284, 306-312
Reliability coefficients, 213
Repeating numbers tests, 25, 28, 34, 43, 50, 60
Repeating syllables tests, 28, 32, 43, 63
Representative sampling, v, 143
Reproduction test, 307, 309, 310
Retardation, 4, 163, 169-171, 180, 188, 197
Revenge test, 245, 246
Rhymes test, 60
Rhythm in prose, 362
Right and left test, 43

Sampling, representative, v, 143
Scholarship ability, 2, 14, 186, 250, 288
  See Supernormal Children
Scholastic tests, 285-429
Selection, correction for, vi, 207, 284
Sentence building test, 52, 60
Sentences: length of, 360
Seven-pint test, 70
Sewing, test of, 357
Sex differences,
  See Boys, Girls, Social status and intelligence, 205-207
  chiefly acquired, 205, 208
  general influence of, 74, 208, 325, 328, 358
  in drawing, 353, 354
  in linguistic and literary subjects, 208
  in manual and perceptual subjects, 208
  in mixed schools, 326
  in reading, 300
Sex (naming own) test, 25
Similarities test, 68
Simple summation formula, 272-273, 276
Sixty words test, 59
Social status, 202 et seq.
  association between the tests and differences in, 203
  classification of schools according to, 143, 203
  influence of, 74, 200 et seq.

Social status, (contd.)—
　on individual tests, 205
　on Binet-Simon measurement, 209, 210
　on reading, 300
Solving problems test, 62
Special abilities, see Abilities
Special classes, 191, 200, 290, 292
Special school children, see Mental defectives
Specific capacities, see Abilities
Specific disabilities, see Disabilities
Speed tests, 235, 301, 305, 358
Spelling, 315 et seq., 383
Square copying test, see Tests; Drawing
Stammering, 329, 330
Standard deviation, 150, 151, 157, 169-174
Standardization of tests, 142 et seq., 235, 286
Stanford Revision, 71, 185, 225-227
Stuttering, see Stammering
Style, 361, 362
Subtraction, 328, 330, 433
Suggestibility, 26, 62
Suggestion test, 62, 72, 116, 219
Summary test, 67
Summation, simple; see Simple summation formula
Superior adult, tests for, 70
Supernormal children, see Bright children
Supplementary tests, 235, 269-277
Surname test, 26
Surveys, iii, 143, 202, 203
Syllabus, 290, 297
Syllogism tests, see Reasoning
Synonyms test, 240

Teachers' estimates, 190,211, 212, 216, 217, 285, 289
Teaching, 278 et seq., 297, 312, 323, 324
Temperament, 220
Test materials for Binet-Simon tests, 75 et seq.
Testimony test, 62
Tetrachoric correlation, 232
Three- and five-pint tests, 70

Three words (sentence building) test, 52, 60
Treves-Saffiotti method, 73
Triangle test, 66, 69
Triple order test, 30
Truncated cone test, 53, 113
Two matches test, 245
Two- and three-letter words test, 301
Types, psychological, 307, 455, see Group factors

Unit, 150, 172, 287 337, 439-447
Unstable children, see Instability
Upper limit of development of intelligence, see Limit

Variability, 170, 171, 337
Verbal ability, v, 137, 421
　and attainments, 207, 294, 295
　bias,
　　of Binet-Simon tests, 196, 311
　　of Stanford revision, 71
　　of Supplementary Intelligence tests, 234
　influence of, on Binet-Simon tests, 196, 205, 220
　measurement of, 207
　processes, 312
　subjects, 209, 210, 294 295, 315, 364
　tests, see Composition; Reading; Spelling; and Supplementary tests
Visualization, 313
Vocabulary test, 68, 71, 242, 298, 315, 368
Vocational diagnosis, 297

War, effect of, 324
Weber's law, 51, see Psycho-physical methods
Weighting, 72, 74, 143, 159, 215, 271, 288, 451
Weights tests, 35, 51
Word blindness, 293, 312
Words: definition of, 60, 242
Writing, 335-345, 399-409, 435

INDEX OF NAMES

Abelson, A. R., 71
Auden, G. A., 165
Ayres, L. P., 175

Bacon, F., 245
Ballard, P. B., 288, 302, 309, 329, 330, 345, 460
Bartlett, F., 307
Bell, J. C., 222, 225, 228
Binet, A., 1-228, 248, 269, 307, 362, 439
Bleuler, E., 307
Bobertag, O., 26, 32, 40, 43, 48, 136, 223-227, 458
Bonser, F. G., 237
Booth, C., 202
Bridges, J. W., 457
Bridie, Marion, 8
Bronner, Augusta, F., 458
Brown, W., 130

Chotzen, F., 224-227, 458
Chesterton, G. K., 362
Childs, S. M., 148, 149, 152
Corkhill, F., 235
Cornell, W. S., 175
Courtis, S. A., 309, 330

Dale, Nellie, 292
Decroly, O., 223-226
Degand, J., 223-226
Devoss, J. C., 460
Doll, E. A., 166
Drummond, W. B., 40, 175

Ebbinghaus, H., 245, 309
Eltes, M., 225, 227, 228

Fernald, Grace M., 56, 70
Fisher, R. A., 446-447, 451
Flugel, J. C., 307, 321
Freud, S., 59, 307

Galton, F., 13, 130, 142, 161
Garnett, M., 455
Goddard, H. H., 32, 44, 48, 50, 56, 61, 66, 70, 75, 148, 149, 152, 153, 166, 183, 196, 224, 226, 458, 459, 460
Gordon, H., 345
Goring, C., 197

Hardwick, Rose S., 457
Healy, W., 56, 70, 459
Hervieu, P. E., 67
Heron, D., 232
Hinckley, Alice C., 148, 149
Hollingworth, Miss, 322
Holzinger, K. J., 279-283
Hood, C., 227
Huey, E. B., 66, 72

Jaederholm, G. A., 152, 176
James, W., 307
Jeffrey, F., 360
Johnstone, Katherine L., 68, 89, 223, 224, 226, 227, 459
Jones, E., 321, 345
Jung, C. G., 307

Kelley, E. L., 284
Kerr, J., 345
Kimmins, C. W., 359

Levistre, T., 226
Lewis, E. O., 8, 43, 73, 459
Lionardo da Vinci, see Vinci

Macaulay, T. B., 360
McDougall, W., 133
McIntyre, J. L., 6, 8, 40, 225, 227, 228, 460
Masefield, J., 244
Mason-Thompson, E. R., 241
Mateer, Florence, 166
Melville, N. J., 26, 29, 40, 43, 45, 50, 53, 57, 67, 68, 457
Meumann, E., 52
Miner, J. Burt, 459
Monro, W. S., 460
Moore, R. C., 6, 8, 142, 146, 148, 149, 222, 225, 227, 228, 235, 238, 270, 459
Morlé, M., 226
Müller, G., 307
Murdock, Katherine, 357
Muscio, B., 397

Ostwald, E., 307

466

Pater, W., 362
Paterson, D., 460
Pearson, K., 130, 152, 175, 176, 232, 271
Pelling, Violet G., 17, 459
Pfeiffer, O., 307
Pintner, R., 460
Porteus, S. D., 71, 254, 255

Rackstraw, A. F., 202
Reiss, Mlle. E., 8
Rice, J. N., 285
Rogers, Agnes L., 41, 68, 225, 227, 228, 460
Roget, P. M., 240
Ruskin, J., 305

Saffiotti, F. U., 26, 39, 41, 43, 72, 79, 148, 149, 223, 225, 227, 228, 458
Saintsbury, G., 362
Schiller, J. C. F., von, 307
Schmitt, Clara, 148
Scott, W., 333
Sheppard, W. F., 274
Shrubsall, F. C., 225, 227
Simon, Th., 3, 4, 7, 9, 15, 17, 24-29, 35-38, 40, 41, 43-46, 48-52, 56-58, 60-64, 66, 67, 79, 183, 223, 224, 226, 285, 457, 458, 459
Simpson, B. R., 237
Smith, May, 241
Spearman, C., 131-133, 136, 232, 269-273, 449
Starch, D., 336, 460
Stern, W., 146, 163, 176, 182, 185, 275, 309, 460
Stevenson, R. S., 245
Stout, G. F., 132
Strong, Alice C., 225, 227, 228
Swift, E. T., 307

Taylor, Nina G., 8, 148, 149, 223, 225, 227, 228, 459
Terman, L. M., 24-29, 32, 34, 39, 43-45, 48, 50, 52, 55, 56, 57, 59, 60-64, 66, 68, 71, 74, 148, 149, 152, 225, 227, 457
Thomson, G., 130, 284, 449
Thorndike, E. L., 130, 232, 236, 237, 269
Thurstone, L. L., 440-445
Town, Clara M., 7, 39, 49
Tredgold, A. F., 459
Treves, Z., see Saffiotti

Vaney, V., 285
Van Sickle, J. H., 175
Vinci, Lionardo da, 340, 342, 362

Wallin, J. E. W., 148, 149, 224, 226
Watts, G. F., 361
Weber, H., 51
Wells, F. L., 236, 237
Whipple, G. M., 45, 56, 232, 234, 235, 460
Whitley, Mary T., 237
Winch, W. H., 8, 26, 28, 38, 39, 41, 75, 79, 225, 228, 460
Wissler, C., 130
Witmer, L., 175
Woodworth, R. S., 236, 237, 447
Woursell, Pearl, C., 17

Yerkes, R. M., 24, 34, 35, 40, 41, 45, 48, 50, 51, 52, 53, 61, 62, 64, 72, 79, 457, 460
Yoakum, C. S., 460
Yule, G. U., 215, 230, 232, 276, 279, 282, 445, 453